THE BIOGRAPHY OF MUḤAMMAD

ISLAMIC HISTORY AND CIVILIZATION

STUDIES AND TEXTS

EDITED BY

WADAD KADI

VOLUME 32

THE BIOGRAPHY OF MUḤAMMAD

The Issue of the Sources

EDITED BY

HARALD MOTZKI

BRILL
LEIDEN · BOSTON · KÖLN
2000

This book is printed on acid-free paper.

Library of Congress Cataloging-in-Publication Data

The Biography of Muḥammad : the issue of the sources / edited by
Harald Motzki.
p. cm. — (Islamic history and civilization. Studies and
texts, ISSN 0929-2403 ; v. 32)
ISBN 9004115137 (cloth : alk. paper)
1. Muḥammad, Prophet, d. 632 Biography. 2. Muḥammad, Prophet, d.
632 Biography Sources. I. Motzki, Harald. II. Series.
BP75.B477 2000
297.6'3—dc21 99-41850
[B] CIP

Die Deutsche Bibliothek – CIP-Einheitsaufnahme

The biography of Muḥammad : the issue of the sources / ed. by
Harald Motzki. - Leiden ; Boston ; Köln : Brill, 2000
(Islamic history and civilization ; Vol. 32)
ISBN 90-04-11513-7

ISSN 0929-2403
ISBN 90 04 11513 7

PRINTED IN THE NETHERLANDS

In memory of
Albrecht Noth (1937-1999)

CONTENTS

PREFACE AND ACKNOWLEDGMENTS

Founders of religions have always fascinated human beings. They cast their spell not only on their followers, but also on people who are impressed by their diversity in human, cultural and religious appearances and who search for explanations of their peculiarities and similarities. During the nineteenth century, the academic study of religions from a humanist, non-partisan point of view arose and within this framework the founders of religions became the object of lively research. The life of Muḥammad, the prophet of Islam, became a central issue in the study of Islam. Since then, many books and articles have been written on this topic, but even so, it seems that at the end of the twentieth century Muḥammad's life is as opaque and controversial as it was a century earlier—a situation which has a parallel in the study of the life of Jesus and other founders of great religions. The most disputed issue was and is the historical reliability of the sources: What do they reflect? The salvation history as conceived by the Muslims of the first two centuries of Islam, or also historical reality?

In October 1997, on the occasion of the fiftieth anniversary of the Department of Languages and Cultures of the Middle East of the University of Nijmegen, the Netherlands, a colloquium was organized in order to take stock of the state of the art in this field and open up new horizons in the study of the Prophet's biography. The idea was to bring together a group of scholars using different methodological approaches and acquainted with varying types of sources, in order to examine the issue of the sources anew. Ten papers were presented and discussed during the conference. The present volume contains all of them in a revised form.

It is my pleasure as organizer of the colloquium and editor of the papers to express thanks to the Board of Governors of the University of Nijmegen, the Faculty of Humanities, the Department of Languages and Cultures of the Middle East, the Nijmegen Institute of Comparative Culture and Development Studies (NICCOS), the Nijmegen University Fund (SNUF), the Center for Non-Western Studies (Leiden), the International Institute of Social History (Amsterdam) and the publishing houses of Brill and Benjamins for their financial support in the organization of the anniversary celebrations.

The volume has been divided into two parts. The articles written by Rubin, Schöller, Leites, Schoeler and Jarrar, which focus on the development of the *sīra* tradition have been placed in part one. The articles by Lecker, Motzki, Görke, Hoyland and Rippin, in which the issue of historical reliability of the sources is prominent, have been brought together in part two. A uniform system of transliteration has been implemented. Since the authors used different editions of the same sources, each article is followed by its own bibliography in order to make the identification of the sources easier. The system of quoting the primary sources has been harmonized throughout the volume, but not to the extent of obliterating every trace of individuality. In the bibliographies, the first names of authors of books and of editors of sources are given in full (if they are known), authors of articles only with their initials. The book closes with a general index to the text of the articles but not the notes and the appendices in Arabic.

I am very grateful to Peri Bearman who assisted me in editing and proofreading the papers, checked the style and made many suggestions to improve the texts. Chantal Willems, a graduate student of our institute, showed much dedication in entering the changes on a word processor. I wish to thank Wadad al-Qadi for accepting the volume in her series; the book has benefited from her careful reading and her suggestions. My colleagues at the Institute gave me every support I needed.

This volume is dedicated to the memory of Albrecht Noth, who was a friend and teacher to most of the contributors. We missed him already at the colloquium at which he had wished to participate but was prevented by an insidious disease. Now, we will miss him forever. His example as a scholar, teacher and person shall always live with us.

Nijmegen, June 1999
H.M.

INTRODUCTION

Harald Motzki

The academic study of the life of Muḥammad, the founder of Islam, began in the West during the first half of the nineteenth century. The first scholarly biography to be published, in 1843 by Gustav Weil, was based, in addition to the Qur'ān, on late Islamic sources dating from the sixteenth century onwards.[1] In the course of the nineteenth century, manuscripts of earlier sources were discovered and edited so that at the beginning of the twentieth century a corpus of four major biographical sources compiled between the end of the second and the end of the third Islamic centuries had become available: al-Wāqidī's *Maghāzī*, Ibn Hishām's *Sīra*, Ibn Saʿd's *Ṭabaqāt* and al-Ṭabarī's *Taʾrīkh*. Together with the Qur'ān and al-Bukhārī's *ḥadīth* collection, these compilations have remained the standard sources for the biographies of the Prophet Muḥammad up to the present day.

The fact that these sources had been compiled two or three centuries after the death of Muḥammad did not disturb the first Western biographers of the Prophet very much because the sources consisted of traditions which purported to go back to earlier times, often even to eyewitnesses of the event itself. The biographers realized, of course, that there were contradictions in the sources, traces of legends, exaggerations, and many kinds of biases, but they were nonetheless convinced that a critical mind would be able to reconstruct what really happened.

This optimistic stance received its first blow when in 1890 Ignaz Goldziher published the second part of his *Muhammedanische Studien*.[2] He argued that most of the *ḥadīth*-material reflects later developments of Islam and therefore cannot be used as a historical source for the time of Muḥammad himself. Goldziher's conclusions affected the biographical traditions relating to the Prophet even though his studies were not based on them but mostly on legal *ḥadīth*. At the beginning of the twentieth century, Goldziher's skepticism was adopted by several scholars concerned with the biography of Muḥammad. Leone

---

[1] G. Weil, *Muḥammad der Prophet, sein Leben und seine Lehre*, n.p., 1843.
[2] I. Goldziher, *Muhammedanische Studien*, Halle, 1889-90.

Caetani and Henri Lammens held the opinion that almost all the traditions about the Prophet's life were apocryphal.[3]

Without the elementary chronological and topographical framework provided by the Muslim tradition, even the Qur'ān lost much of its usefulness for the historian. Consequently, the idea that it might be possible to write a historical biography of Muḥammad would have to be abandoned. This radical skepticism, however, was only adopted by a few scholars working in the field. During the first half of the twentieth century, several biographies of the Prophet Muḥammad were published which, in introductions or postscripts, pointed out the precarious or doubtful value of the *sīra* and *maghāzī* material, but nevertheless heavily relied on it. The most cautious and reserved among these books on Muḥammad is Régis Blachère's *Le problème de Mahomet*, published in 1952, with the significant subtitle *Essai de biographie critique.*[4]

Around the same time, the reliability of the *ḥadīth* as source for the first Islamic century was again fiercely attacked by Joseph Schacht in his study *The Origins of Muhammadan Jurisprudence.*[5] Traditions alleged to go back to the Prophet or to his Companions are, according to him, the product of legal, theological and political developments of the second Islamic century and lack any historical value for the time of the Prophet. Although this verdict resulted—like that of Goldziher—from a study of legal *ḥadīth*s, Schacht claimed that it held true for the early Muslim tradition in general; he even tried to prove it for some *maghāzī* material.[6] The specialists of *sīra* and *maghāzī*, however, were not very impressed by Schacht's arguments. A few years after the appearance of his book, the most exhaustive biographical study on the Prophet Muḥammad written in this century by a non-Muslim scholar was published. Its author, William Montgomery Watt, disputed that Schacht's findings were applicable to the *sīra* material. He admitted a "tendentious shaping" of the traditions, but was convinced that with a critical mind it is possible to find out what really had

---

[3] L. Caetani, *Annali dell'Islam*, I, Milan, 1905, 28-58, 121-43, 192-215 and passim; H. Lammens, "Qoran et tradition. Comment fut composée la vie de Mahomet", in *Recherches de Science Religieuse*, 1 (1910), 27-51.

[4] R. Blachère, *Le problème de Mahomet*, Paris, 1952.

[5] J. Schacht, *The Origins of Muhammadan Jurisprudence*, Oxford, 1950.

[6] Cf. his "A Revaluation of Islamic Tradition", in *Journal of the Royal Asiatic Society*, 49 (1949), 143-54 and "On Mūsā b. ʿUqba's Kitāb al-Maghāzī", in *Acta Orientalia*, 21 (1953), 288-300.

happened.[7] His confident standpoint found favor with Rudi Paret and Maxime Rodinson.[8] The introduction of the latter to his book *Mahomet*, however, reveals the paradoxical situation to which the study of the Prophet's biography had been brought by Goldziher's and Schacht's criticism of the *ḥadīth*. Rodinson wrote: "Une biographie de Mahomet, qui ne mentionnerait que de faits indubitables, d'une certitude mathématique, serait réduite à quelques pages et d'une affreuse sécheresse. Il est pourtant possible de donner de cette vie une image vraisemblable, parfois très vraisemblable. Mais il faut, pour cela, utiliser des données tirées de sources sur lesquelles nous n'avons que peu de garanties de véracité."[9] That a reconstruction of the Prophet's life could claim historical probability although it was based on sources considered as "hardly reliable", "doubtful" and "rather far away from the facts"[10] is not so easy to accept and, indeed, not everyone did.

In the seventies and eighties, several studies on Muḥammad and early Islamic history were published whose authors accepted Goldziher's and Schacht's views in a more consistent manner. They refused to use *ḥadīth* material as a source for a historical reconstruction of the time of the Prophet and the first Islamic century. Some of them, like John Wansbrough in his *The Sectarian Milieu*, were content with a literary analysis of *ḥadīths* and *ḥadīth* literature, abandoning every claim to reconstruction of historical facts.[11] Others, like Patricia Crone and Michael Cook in *Hagarism*, tried to base such a reconstruction exclusively on non-Muslim sources.[12] Following Wansbrough's ideas expounded in his *Quranic Studies*, they even doubted the authenticity of the Qur'ān as a document of Muḥammad's preaching. With this, the last and until then nearly undisputed source for the history of the Prophet had been swept away. Consequently, the idea that a historical biography of Muḥammad could be written had to be definitely

---

[7] W. Montgomery Watt, *Muhammad at Mecca*, Oxford, 1953, esp. pp. xiii-xvi; *Muhammad at Medina*, Oxford, 1956; "The Reliability of Ibn Isḥāq's Sources", in *La Vie du prophète Mahomet*. Colloque de Strasbourg (octobre 1980), Paris, 1983, 31-43.

[8] R. Paret, *Muḥammad und der Koran*, Stuttgart, 1957; M. Rodinson, *Mahomet*, Paris, 1961.

[9] Ibid., 12.

[10] Other attributes used by Rodinson in his introduction.

[11] J. Wansbrough, *The Sectarian Milieu. Content and Composition of Islamic Salvation History*, Oxford, 1978.

[12] P. Crone and M. Cook, *Hagarism. The Making of the Islamic World*, Cambridge, 1977.

abandoned. This is perfectly illustrated in Michael Cook's book *Muhammad*, published in 1983, which is limited to an account based on the Qur'ān and the customary sources for the life of the Prophet, explicitly without trying to "assess its reliability".[13] It simply retells what the Muslim sources say. Afterwards, Cook explains to the reader that the sources of this account are not only dubious but in important aspects misleading and, actually, historically unreliable.

At present, the study of Muḥammad, the founder of the Muslim community, is obviously caught in a dilemma. On the one hand, it is not possible to write a historical biography of the Prophet without being accused of using the sources uncritically, while on the other hand, when using the sources critically, it is simply not possible to write such a biography.[14]

Are we faced here with a hopeless situation? There are reasons to assume that a solution is possible. This optimism is nurtured by the observation that the dispute on the reliability of the source material is blurred by several serious shortcomings: 1) Systematic source-critical studies of the biographical traditions concerning Muḥammad's life are almost lacking; the authors of historical biographies have been allowed to choose from the sources the information which they personally liked best. Source-critical studies which compare the different accounts available and attempt to date them are a prerequisite for the use of these traditions as historical sources. 2) Until now, reflection on the methods which have been used or could be used in assessing the reliability of the biographical *ḥadīth*s has been in very short supply. There are almost no criteria for the comparison of the texts (*matn*s) of the traditions, and the methodology of *isnād* analysis has made progress only recently and has been applied to the *sīra* material only in exceptional instances. 3) As a consequence of these shortcomings, the dispute on the reliability of the sources took place on a rather abstract

[13] M. Cook, *Muhammad*, Oxford, 1983, 12.

[14] For a more detailed and thoughtful introduction into the source problems with which Western scholars are confronted when studying Muḥammad's biography, see F.E. Peters, "The Quest of the Historical Muhammad", in *The International Journal of Middle East Studies*, 23 (1991), 291-315. The impossibility of a historical biography was also recently maintained by J. Chabbi, "Histoire et Tradition Sacrée—la biographie impossible de Mahomet", in *Arabica*, 43 (1996), 189-205 and W. Raven, "Sīra", in C.E. Bosworth et al. (eds.), *The Encyclopaedia of Islam. New Edition*, IX, Leiden 1997, 660-63, esp. 662-63; more cautious is M.J. Kister in "The *Sirah* literature", in A.F.L. Beeston et al. (eds.), *Arabic Literature to the End of the Umayyad Period*, Cambridge, 1983, 352-67, esp. 367.

level, and mostly not on the basis of the biographical traditions themselves. The skepticism about their reliability evolved from studies on legal *ḥadīth*s. That the findings in this field can be transferred to the *sīra* traditions was claimed by some and rejected by others without studying the question in detail on the basis of the sources themselves. 4) The discussion of the possible relationship between the Qur'ān as source and exegetical, biographical and legal traditions is blurred by general assertions which are based on the study of a few individual cases. The general validity of these assertions remains doubtful. 5) The biographies written on the Prophet's life up till now are based on a limited range of sources, almost exclusively the large compilations of *sīra* traditions dating from the third Islamic century (al-Wāqidī, Ibn Saʿd, Ibn Hishām, al-Ṭabarī). The material contained in later sources has not yet been studied systematically and compared to earlier material. Besides, a number of new sources, early and later ones, has become available in the last three decades. These sources, which were virtually unknown or only known by title, improve the material basis for the study of Muḥammad's life considerably and may throw new light on several aspects of the debate concerning the reliability of the sources.

The ten essays of this book are all attempts to tackle the abovementioned shortcomings and to find a way out of the impasse in which the study of Muḥammad's biography is. The articles offer insight into various approaches which the scholars are using today when studying the issue of the sources of Muḥammad's biography. The main approaches to be found in the articles can be identified as follows:

1) *Textual history*. This approach investigates the development of a tradition or complex of traditions over a period of time, comparing the versions found in earlier sources with those in later ones. The goal is not only to learn how traditions changed but also why. Rubin, Leites and Schöller travel along this path in their articles.

2) *Transmission history*. This approach differs from the previous one in that its primary aim is to find out what the original text looked like and when, where and by whom it was circulated. In the process, the textual developments of a tradition are revealed also, though not their motives, motives being mostly considered as an issue of its own. The contributions of Görke, Schoeler and Motzki are examples of this type of source analysis.

3) *Reconstruction of sources*. This approach tries to recover fragments

of lost sources from later compilations and study them in order to find out whether or not they are rightly ascribed to a certain transmitter, compiler or author. This aim is present in the essays written by Schoeler, Jarrar, Görke, Motzki and Schöller.

4) *Unearthing unorthodox traditions.* This approach examines reports which differ from mainstream biographical traditions and which are often disregarded, either through suppression, so that they are only rarely found in the sources or only reappear in late ones, or because they belong to another religious group, such as Shīʿites or Christians, and there lead a life of their own. Unearthing them can shed some light on the diversity of the traditions concerning the Prophet's life before the standard collections, which became authoritative, were compiled. Other possible motives for their being disregarded by the majority might come to light also. This goal is pursued by Lecker, Schöller, Jarrar, Leites and Hoyland.

5) *Determining the historical value of traditions.* Some of the articles are concerned with the crucial question whether and to what extent, various sources for Muḥammad's life reflect what really happened. This issue is dealt with by Rippin, Hoyland, Görke, Motzki and Lecker.

Finally, it is worth pointing out that the articles in this volume vary also in their methods. Some authors rely exclusively or for the most part on the texts of the sources while others try to complement the analysis of the form and content of the texts by examining their chains of transmitters.

Taken together, the essays in this volume indicate that the study of the Prophet's biography is about to set off to new horizons. They also reveal that the question of the historical reality which the sources reflect is an issue which has been scarcely studied in depth and is indeed far from being settled. Much remains to be done. A variety of useful approaches are provided by the articles in this volume; it is to be hoped that they will stimulate further research into the sources so that the mystery of the origin and development of the Prophet Muḥammad's *sīra* will eventually become explained.

PART I

THE DEVELOPMENT OF THE *SĪRA* TRADITION

THE LIFE OF MUḤAMMAD AND THE ISLAMIC SELF-IMAGE

A Comparative Analysis of an Episode in the Campaigns of Badr and al-Ḥudaybiya[1]

Uri Rubin

This article does not deal with the question of the authenticity of the texts describing the life of Muḥammad, but rather with their textual history. In what follows, a single episode in Muḥammad's *sīra* will be examined, and it will be demonstrated that, by comparing its various versions, insight can be gained into the manner in which the story of Muḥammad's life developed and was transmitted through the ages. In particular it will be shown how the self-image of the Muslims of the first Islamic century, as well as tensions within the Islamic *umma* of that era, imprinted their mark on the manner in which Muḥammad's period was remembered. On the literary level, aspects of the process in which the Qurʾān became part of the *sīra* will be elucidated.

The basic methodology of this article is not different from that adopted in my *The Eye of the Beholder,*[2] the only difference is that now an episode from the Medinan period of Muḥammad's *vita* is analyzed. This period is usually taken by Islamicists to be much more "historical" than the Meccan one, to which my book was dedicated, but in what follows it will become clear that a textual analysis of the Medinan period is no less rewarding.

The episode selected for the present discussion is a council of war which Muḥammad holds with his Companions. There are various versions describing it, each providing different and contradicting details about its time and place, as well as about its proceedings. While some versions tell it within the story of al-Ḥudaybiya (6/627-8), other versions present it as part of the events that took place at Badr (2/623-24). Let us begin with al-Ḥudaybiya.

---

[1] I am grateful to Michael Lecker and Harald Motzki for their comments on an earlier version of this article.

[2] U. Rubin, *The Eye of the Beholder: The Life of Muḥammad as Viewed by the Early Muslims*, Princeton, 1995.

I. Al-Ḥudaybiya

The general outline of the story of al-Ḥudaybiya is well known: In 6/627-8, the Prophet has a vision in which he receives a divine command to set out to Mecca and perform the lesser pilgrimage—*ʿumra*—at the Kaʿba. The sanctuary is still dominated by the unbelievers of the Quraysh, and as he and his followers approach the Meccan territory, the Meccans send forth forces to stop them, and the Muslims halt near al-Ḥudaybiya, where negotiations take place between the Meccans and the Muslims. The talks conclude with the well-known treaty of al-Ḥudaybiya.

The affair of al-Ḥudaybiya is treated in the sources as a crucial turning point in the history of Islam, and the commentators of the Qurʾān identify it with the term *fatḥ* (opening, and hence conquest) of Q 48:1; they explain that the final agreement concluded at al-Ḥudaybiya enabled the Prophet to achieve his goal and perform the rites at the Kaʿba, and this in turn opened the final stage in a process culminating in the fall of Mecca.[3]

Our interest in the present context focuses on the manner in which the Muslims react as soon as they are forced to halt while on their way to the Kaʿba. As in other cases in the *sīra*, the description of the reaction is available in two types of narrative: Qurʾānic and non-Qurʾānic.

The non-Qurʾānic level is revealed in two parallel versions of ʿUrwa b. al-Zubayr (Medinan, d. 94/712-3) which he quotes from Miswar b. Makhrama (Medinan Companion, d. 64/683-4) and Marwān b. al-Ḥakam (the caliph; Medinan, d. 65/684-5). Both versions describe a scene in which the Prophet meets on his way to Mecca some members of the tribe of Khuzāʿa who used to spy for him in Mecca, and they break to him the news that the road to Mecca has been cut off. The first version is quoted from ʿUrwa by al-Zuhrī (Medinan, d. 124/742), and is included in Ibn Isḥāq's *Sīra*.[4] In this version one of the Khuzāʿa (of the sub-tribe of Kaʿb) tells Muḥammad that the Quraysh have left Mecca in two parties that are camped in two different places. One group comprises men wearing leopard

---

[3] See for example Ibn Saʿd, *Ṭabaqāt*, II, 104-05, and the commentaries on 48:1. On *fatḥ*, al-Ḥudaybiya and Mecca, see more in G.R. Hawting, "Al-Ḥudaybiyya and the Conquest of Mecca: A Reconsideration of the Tradition about the Muslim Takeover of the Sanctuary", in *JSAI*, 8 (1986), 1-24.

[4] Ibn Hishām, *Sīra*, III, 322-24. The same is quoted from Ibn Isḥāq in Ibn Ḥanbal, *Musnad*, IV, 323; Ṭabarānī, *Kabīr*, XX, no. 14.

skins [probably to signify their elevated rank as members of a holy tribe, and as guardians of the sanctuary who should not be attacked],[5] and includes women and children. They are camped in Dhū Ṭuwā. The second party is a cavalry unit under the command of Khālid b. al-Walīd; it is camped ahead of the former group, at Kurāʿ al-Ghamīm. Upon hearing this, the Prophet declares that the Quraysh had better leave him alone, because they have already been exhausted by the previous battles that they had with him. They should now let him deal freely with the rest of the polytheists, and wait and see who has the upper hand. If the polytheists should overcome him, that is what the Quraysh desire, and if he should defeat the polytheists, the Quraysh can then choose between joining him as Muslims or fighting him after having regained their military power. Then the Prophet declares:

> ...by God, I will go on fighting (*ujāhidu*) for the mission with which God has entrusted me till God makes it prevail....

In attributing such an utterance to the Prophet, the tradition elevates the notion of holy war (*jihād*) to the rank of a divine duty that should be carried out at all costs. However, the tradition goes on to relate that the Prophet gave orders to find an alternative road to Mecca, which eventually brought him to al-Ḥudaybiya, where negotiations finally prevented full-scale war.

The second version of ʿUrwa (again on the authority of Miswar and Marwān) is quoted from him by Maʿmar b. Rāshid (Baṣran/Yemeni, d. 154/771) through al-Zuhrī. In this version a certain change has occurred: The Prophet's heroic devotion to God's mission is not solely his own, but is shared by one of his Companions, and thus a typical phenomenon in the *sīra* traditions is revealed: Scenes that revolve solely around Muḥammad's own image may be expanded to include his Companions. In the latter case, political pressures seem to have left their mark on the shaping of the story, which is adapted to elaborate on the virtues (*faḍāʾil*) of certain Companions.[6]

In the present version of Maʿmar, the Prophet sends out a spy from

---

[5] Wearing and riding on leopard skins are considered in Islam as signifying wealth and luxury, and are therefore forbidden. See ʿAbd al-Razzāq, *Muṣannaf*, I, nos. 217, 218, 220; Ibn Ḥanbal, *Musnad*, IV, 95, 96, 99, 132, 135; Nasāʾī, *Kubrā*, VII, 176 (41:7); Abū Dāwūd, *Sunan*, II, 388 (31:40); Ṭaḥāwī, *Mushkil*, IV, 263-64. In other traditions, however, leopard skins are permitted. See ʿAbd al-Razzāq, *Muṣannaf*, I, nos. 229, 231, 232, 233, 234, 235; Ṭaḥāwī, *Mushkil*, IV, 264-65.

[6] For more such instances of the political impact on the shaping of *sīra* traditions, see Rubin, *The Eye of the Beholder*, 44-53, 171-75.

the Khuzāʿa who comes back with the news that the Quraysh have gathered their armed forces, and that they are determined not to let the Muslims enter Mecca. The Prophet says to his Companions: "Advise me (*ashīrū ʿalayya*)." Before hearing the advice of his Companions, the Prophet himself formulates an option. He says that they might consider taking a different route and attacking the camp of the unarmed families. Abū Bakr says that they had better resume their original journey to the Kaʿba and attack no one, but with determination to fight whoever tries to stop them. The Prophet follows his advice and commands his men to go on.

This version in which the Prophet holds a council of war was preserved by Aḥmad b. Ḥanbal (d. 241/855-6),[7] and was the one preferred by several authors of canonical *ḥadīth* collections, including al-Bukhārī (d. 256/870).[8] The actual course of the discussion during the consultation is focused on the virtues of Abū Bakr, the first caliph, who is actually the sole speaker. He features as a resolute believer who encourages the Prophet to adhere to his original mission and approach the Meccan sanctuary, fighting only if necessary.

The interpolation of the scene of consultation (*mashūra*) reflects the role of the life of Muḥammad as a precedent for all kinds of practices. Consultation is indeed an important issue treated in many traditions about the Prophet and his Companions, the latter figuring as Muḥammad's worthy advisers.[9] These traditions can be found in the commentaries on a verse in Sūrat Āl ʿImrān (3:159). This verse requests the Prophet to consult the believers. In some versions of our particular tradition, al-Zuhrī adds a gloss to the effect that the Companion Abū Hurayra (d. 57/677) said that he had seen no one consulting his Companions as frequently as the Prophet had done.[10] There were, however, attempts at reducing the scope of recommended consultation to specific matters only, such as military schemes. After all, thanks to divine inspiration, the Prophet did not need to rely heavily on human advice. Therefore, Abū Hurayra's statement was sometimes expanded to include a remark to the effect that the

[7] Ibn Ḥanbal, *Musnad*, IV, 328. See also Tabarānī, *Kabīr*, XX, no. 13; Bayhaqī, *Dalāʾil*, IV, 99-101.

[8] Bukhārī, *Ṣaḥīḥ*, V, 161 (64:35); Nasāʾī, *Kubrā*, V, nos. 8581-82 (78:1); Bayhaqī, *Sunan*, IX, 218, X, 109; Ibn Hibbān, *Ṣaḥīḥ*, XI, no. 4872. And see also ʿAbd al-Razzāq, *Muṣannaf*, V, 330-31 (no. 9720) [Abū Bakr's name does not occur].

[9] For more general aspects of the theme of councils as a topos, see A. Noth and L. I. Conrad, *The Early Islamic Historical Tradition: A Source Critical Study*, Princeton, 1994, 138-42.

[10] For the tradition of Abū Hurayra, see also Ibn Wahb, *Jāmiʿ*, I, no. 288.

Prophet only consulted his Companions concerning military actions.[11] A variant reading of Q 3:159 was also circulated, turning it into a request for consultation on certain matters only.[12] At any rate, a scene of council of war reappears frequently in various *futūḥ* stories, for example the one about the take-over of Jerusalem, where Abū ʿUbayda consults the local commanders whether to take Jerusalem first or Caesarea.[13]

In the third version of ʿUrwa, which is this time quoted on his authority by his own son, Hishām b. ʿUrwa (Meccan, d. 146/763-4), a Qur'ānic verse emerges. The *isnād* of this version does not contain a Companion, which makes it *mursal*.[14] Here one more Companion joins Abū Bakr in the consultation. The Prophet suggests two options: either to approach the main armed force of the Quraysh, or to raid the unarmed families at the rear of the hostile tribes assisting the Quraysh. Abū Bakr again prefers the first option, and then another Companion voices a similar view. He is al-Miqdād b. al-Aswad (= Ibn ʿAmr), who says:

> By God, we shall not tell you what the Children of Israel told their prophet: "Go forth, you and your Lord, and do battle; we will be sitting here." Nay, we say: "Go forth, you and your Lord, and do battle; we will be fighting with you."

Al-Miqdād's speech contains an allusion to Sūrat al-Mā'ida (5:24):

> They said: "Moses, we will never enter it so long as they are in it. Go forth, you and your Lord, and do battle; we will be sitting here."

In the Qur'ān, this passage forms part of a story about the insubordination of the Children of Israel, who refuse to comply with the command of Moses to wage war on the inhabitants of the Promised Land. The story is based on the well-known biblical affair of the spies.[15] As soon as the spies sent forth by Moses return with the report about the mighty inhabitants possessing the land of Canaan, the Children of Israel lose heart and refuse to raid the land, and express their wish to return to Egypt. Their punishment for this is that they perish in the wilderness while wandering there for 40 years. Only a

---

[11] Wāqidī, *Maghāzī*, II, 580.

[12] *Wa-shāwirhum fī baʿḍi l-amri.* See Bukhārī, *Adab*, I, 350 (Ibn ʿAbbās).

[13] Al-Wāqidī (pseud.), *Futūḥ al-Shām*, 143-44. See also H. Busse, "ʿOmar's Image as the Conqueror of Jerusalem", in *JSAI*, 8 (1986), 151.

[14] Ibn Abī Shayba, *Muṣannaf*, XIV, 429-30 (no. 18686). See also *Kanz*, X, no. 30153.

[15] Numbers, 13-14.

few of Moses's generation (mainly Joshua and Caleb) enter the Promised Land with the new Israelite generation. The Qur'ān has reproduced the same story in Sūrat al-Mā'ida (5:21-26). Here Moses commands the Children of Israel to enter the holy land which God has prescribed for them, but they refuse, saying (v. 24):

> Moses, we will never enter it so long as they are in it. Go forth, you and your Lord, and do battle; we will be sitting here.

The interpolation of the allusion to this verse into al-Miqdād's speech is designed to contrast Israelites and Arabs. The Arab believer, namely, al-Miqdād, changes the Israelite refusal of Q 5:24 ("...We will be sitting here"), and turns it into a positive Islamic version ("...We will be fighting with you"). Implicit in this tradition is the idea that the Islamic war waged by the Arab believers represents a renewal of an ancient command of God that has already been enjoined upon the Children of Israel, and the Arab believers are those who carry it out. This link of the Arabian battles to the ancient Israelite exodus serves the initial historiographical aim of Muḥammad's biographers, i.e., to elevate the Ḥijāzī stage of Islam to the rank of a divine scheme and a sacred history.

The selection of al-Miqdād for the role of the spokesman of Muḥammad's Arab believers is not accidental. He features in *awā'il* traditions as the first to have engaged in war with infidels,[16] and he is also said to have been entrusted with the duty of a *qāri'*, i.e., one who recites [militant] Qur'ānic passages during battle to encourage the Muslim warriors.[17] Moreover, a Qur'ānic reading (*qirā'a*) bearing his name was also in existence, and the people of Ḥimṣ reportedly used to follow it.[18] In our tradition al-Miqdād acts as a *qāri'* already in Muḥammad's lifetime, but here he does not merely repeat a Qur'ānic passage, but also edits it, and turns it into a statement of distinctive non-Israelite self-definition.

Al-Miqdād belongs to the Muhājirūn (Emigrants), and in saying his lines he actually speaks for his comrades, as does Abū Bakr who belongs to the same group. The *faḍā'il* (virtues) of the Muhājirūn as warriors encouraging the entire community of believers on their renewed exodus are brought out here most clearly. However, al-Miqdād is also remembered as a supporter of ʿAlī and as having

---

[16] Ibn ʿAsākir (*Mukhtaṣar*), XXV, 213.
[17] See ibid., 209 (on the battle of Yarmūk).
[18] G.H.A. Juynboll, "al-Miḳdād b. ʿAmr", in *EI*², VII, 32.

refrained from pledging allegiance to Abū Bakr,[19] and therefore his role in the story seems also to have been inspired by a Shīʿī bias.

There are versions reflecting various degrees of attempts at shifting to—or at least sharing with—other Arab groups the honor of expressing the communal devotion to the idea of holy war. This is the case in al-Wāqidī's report of the Prophet's expedition to al-Ḥudaybiya. Here a third Companion speaks after Abū Bakr and al-Miqdād. He is Usayd b. Ḥuḍayr, a Medinan leader (*naqīb*) of the Anṣār (of the tribe of Aws), who took part in the holy war in Palestine. The occurrence of his name in the scene at al-Ḥudaybiya projects his valor back to Arabia and is designed to let the Anṣār share the glory with the Muhājirūn. After al-Miqdād utters his revised version of the cowardly reaction of the Children of Israel, Usayd says to the Prophet: "We think that we should stick to what we have set out for, and if anyone defies us, we shall fight him."[20]

Generally speaking, traditions with Qurʾānic allusions in them could be used for exegetical purposes. The commentaries on Q 5:24 indeed contain traditions describing the events at al-Ḥudaybiya. Thus, al-Ṭabarī has recorded a tradition of Qatāda b. Diʿāma (Baṣran, d. 117/735) which is focused just on the person uttering the revised Qurʾānic verse, namely, al-Miqdād. No council of war is mentioned here, and al-Miqdād is the only Companion speaking.[21] The tradition concludes with the statement that when al-Miqdād spoke, all the Muslims joined in collectively with a similar response.

II. Badr

The Islamic tradition linked the scene of the council of war not only to al-Ḥudaybiya, but to Badr as well, which took place in 2/623-4. This event marked a great victory over the infidels, and therefore the exegetes of the Qurʾān identified this battle with the "day of the *furqān*", which is mentioned in Q 8:41.[22] The term *furqān* means

---

[19] E.g. Yaʿqūbī, *Taʾrīkh*, II, 124.
[20] Wāqidī, *Maghāzī*, II, 580-81.
[21] Ṭabarī, *Tafsīr*, VI, 115-16. The *isnād*: Yazīd b. Zurayʿ (Baṣran, d. 182)—Saʿīd b. Abī ʿArūba (Baṣran, d. 156/773)—Qatāda.
[22] E.g. Ṭabarī, *Tafsīr*, X, 7.

"deliverance", and in other Qur'ānic verses it appears as something bestowed by God on Moses and Aaron.[23]

The council is said to have been held in the mosque of ʿIrq al-Ẓabya.[24] The descriptions of this council contain again the same allusion to the Qur'ānic refusal of the Children of Israel to go to war, which is again designed to mark the contrast between the sinful Israelites and the devoted Muslims.

In the story of Badr as recorded by Ibn Isḥāq[25] and al-Wāqidī,[26] the Prophet sets out from Medina on his way to attack a Meccan caravan coming from Syria, but due to news he receives [from his spies] about armed forces having come from Mecca to defend the caravan, he halts on his way, and asks his men to advise him. Abū Bakr speaks first, then ʿUmar, and it is stated that they spoke well, which seems to mean that they have supported the idea to go to battle.

At al-Ḥudaybiya, ʿUmar is not mentioned as taking part in the war council, and his absence accords with his militant disposition and with his alleged opposition to the final agreement. In the present context, however, his name is coupled with that of Abū Bakr, and both act as Muḥammad's senior Companions, with whose advice the Prophet is perfectly pleased. There are, in fact, numerous other traditions in which both Abū Bakr and ʿUmar are praised as Muḥammad's best advisers.[27] Most noteworthy are the traditions stating that Q 3:59, which requests the Prophet to consult the believers, refers to this pair of Companions.[28]

However, Abū Bakr and ʿUmar are not alone here. As in the story of al-Ḥudaybiya, another Companion speaks, and he is again the Muhājir al-Miqdād b. ʿAmr. To make his point, he repeats the Qur'ānic response of the Children of Israel in the same revised manner as he does in the story of al-Ḥudaybiya. The Prophet is extremely pleased with his words and prays for him. Thus the campaign of Badr, too, has gained a link to the Israelite exodus, and

---

[23] Q 2:53; 21:48. On the Qur'ānic derivatives of *f.r.q.*, see further S. Bashear, "The Title *Fārūq* and its Association with ʿUmar I", in *Studia Islamica*, 72 (1990), 49-50.

[24] Samhūdī, *Wafā'*, III, 1009.

[25] Ibn Hishām, *Sīra*, II, 266-67. See also Ṭabarī, *Ta'rīkh*, II, 434 (I, 1300).

[26] Wāqidī, *Maghāzī*, I, 48-49. And see also Balādhurī, *Ansāb*, I, 293-94 (no. 659).

[27] E.g. Ibn Ḥanbal, *Musnad*, IV, 227; Ibn Kathīr, *Tafsīr*, I, 420 (Ibn Ḥanbal).

[28] See the tradition of al-Kalbī (Muḥammad b. al-Sā'ib, Kūfan, d. 146/763-4)—Abū Ṣāliḥ (Bādhām, a *mawlā* of Umm Hāni'), in Ibn Kathīr, *Tafsīr*, I, 420; Suyūṭī, *Durr*, II, 90 (*Mustadrak*). And see also the tradition of ʿAmr b. Dīnār (Meccan, d. 126/743-4)—Ibn ʿAbbās, in Bayhaqī, *Sunan*, X, 109; Ibn Kathīr, *Tafsīr*, I, 420 (*Mustadrak*); Suyūṭī, *Durr*, II, 90 (*Mustadrak* and Bayhaqī, *Sunan*).

this link is based again on a contrast between sinful—and hence inferior—Israelites, and devoted—and hence superior—Arabs.

However, this is not the end of the version. After al-Miqdād, the Anṣār are asked to clarify their standpoint, which is most essential because they gave Muḥammad shelter in their own town and therefore might refuse to join him in battles outside Medinan territory. Their leader, however, expresses his utter support, and is willing to join the Prophet in his war at any place, even far away from their own abode. The name of the Anṣārī leader is this time not Usayd, as at al-Ḥudaybiya, but rather his fellow tribesman, Saʿd b. Muʿādh. The latter is remembered as a martyr who was mortally wounded during the battle of the Khandaq, which explains why the role of expressing unlimited devotion to the Islamic holy war on behalf of the Anṣār was assigned to him as well. The Prophet is pleased with the Anṣār's reaction.

There are more versions of the episode at Badr, in which the honor of revising the Qurʾānic response of the disobeying Israelites remains with al-Miqdād, but the role of the Muhājirūn, for whom he speaks, is magnified at the expense of the Anṣār. One of the traditions of this kind is traced back to the Anṣārī Companion Abū Ayyūb, a well-known warrior who died in the attack on Constantinople. He is made to tell the story in the first person, in a manner that puts the Anṣār in an unflattering light. The tradition was preserved by al-Ṭabarānī (d. 360/971).[29] Abū Ayyūb relates that the Prophet summoned the Anṣār to join him in the raid on the Meccan caravan, and that they came along. However, they found out that the Meccans had discovered their plans, and when the Prophet asked for their advice, the Anṣār said: "By God, we have no power to do battle with the foe, we have only set out for the [unarmed] caravan." The Prophet asked them again, and they repeated their refusal to fight. Then al-Miqdād spoke, saying: "We will not tell you what the People of Moses told him: 'Go forth, you and your Lord, and do battle; we will be sitting here.'" Upon hearing this, the Anṣār became ashamed of themselves, and wished they had spoken the words of al-Miqdād.

In this specific setting of the episode, a contrast is implied not only between faithful Arabs and insubordinate Israelites, but also between

[29] The *isnād*: Ibn Lahīʿa, ʿAbd Allāh (Egyptian, d. 174/790-1)—Yazīd b. Abī Ḥabīb (Egyptian, d. 128/745-6)—Aslam b. Yazīd Abū ʿImrān al-Tujībī (Egyptian)—Abū Ayyūb. See Ṭabarānī, *Kabīr*, IV, no. 4056. See also Ibn Kathīr, *Tafsīr*, II, 287 (on Q 8:5); idem, *Bidāya*, III, 263-64 (from the *Tafsīr* of Ibn Mardawayhi).

Muhājirūn and Anṣār. While the Muhājirūn agree to fight, the Anṣār refuse, which puts them on a par with the Israelites, and excludes them for the moment from the chosen community.

The tradition of Abū Ayyūb appears already in the *Tafsīr* of Ibn Abī Ḥātim (d. 327/939), in his commentary on Q 8:5-7.[30] This passage says that some of the believers showed reluctance when God brought the Prophet out of his home, and disputed with him concerning the truth, wishing that the share with no "sting" (*shawka*) should be theirs. The commentators have linked this passage to the dilemma of Badr, and Ibn Abī Ḥātim has adduced the tradition of Abū Ayyūb to explain which party of the faithful Arabs was the reluctant one. In the present case they are the Anṣār.

There are more traditions in which the contrast between Arabs and Israelites applies to the Muhājirūn alone, to the exclusion of the disobedient Anṣār. Thus the following tradition zooms in on al-Miqdād, leaving aside all other Companions. Al-Miqdād's lines are elevated here to the highest rank of devotion and faithfulness to the value of *jihād*. The tradition has an *isnād* reaching back to the Companion ʿAbd Allāh b. Masʿūd (Medinan/Kūfan, d. 32/652-3),[31] who declares:

> I have witnessed a valiant performance (*mashhad*) of al-Miqdād, and to have the same deed to my own credit would be dearer to me than anything else equal to it. He approached the Prophet when the latter was asking God to defeat the polytheists, and said: "O Prophet of God, by God, we shall not tell you what the Children of Israel told their prophet: 'Go forth, you and your Lord, and do battle; we will be sitting here.' Nay, we will fight in front of you, and behind you, and on your right and on your left." I saw the Prophet's face brighten with joy.

This version gained wide circulation; it was recorded by Ibn Abī ʿĀṣim (d. 287/900) in a chapter entitled: "About the Perseverance of the People with their Leader under any State of Trial."[32] The tradition recurs in various historiographical and biographical compilations,[33] and was included by al-Bukhārī in a chapter about Badr.[34] In

---

[30] Ibn Abī Ḥātim, *Tafsīr*, V, no. 8805. Quoted from Ibn Abī Ḥātim in *Fatḥ al-bārī*, VII, 224.

[31] The *isnād*: Mukhāriq b. ʿAbd Allāh [Khalīfa] b. Jābir (Kūfan)—Ṭāriq b. Shihāb (Kūfan, d. 82/701-2)—Ibn Masʿūd. There is also a less current *isnād*: ʿImrān b. Ẓabyān (Kūfan, d. 157/773-4)—Abū Yaḥyā Ḥakīm b. Saʿd (Kūfan)—Ibn Masʿūd. For the tradition with the latter *isnād*, see Ṭabarānī, *Kabīr*, X, no. 10502.

[32] Ibn Abī ʿĀṣim, *Jihād*, II, no. 221.

[33] Ṭabarī, *Taʾrīkh*, II, 434 (I, 1300); Ibn Ḥanbal, *Musnad*, I, 389-90, 428; Bayhaqī, *Dalāʾil*, III, 45-46.

another version with the same *isnād*, the name of Badr is mentioned explicitly, but the admiring comment of Ibn Masʿūd is missing.[35] There is also a version in which the name of Ibn Masʿūd is missing from the *isnād* as well (*mursal*).[36] These two versions recur in the commentaries on Q 5:24.[37]

In contrast to the traditions surveyed thus far, there are traditions pertaining to the council of war at Badr, in which the honor of the Anṣār is restored at the expense of the Muhājirūn. These traditions clearly reflect Anṣārī apologetics, as they try hard to highlight the role of the Anṣār in the collective Islamic warlike efforts. It is maintained here that the Anṣār not only provided Muḥammad with shelter in Medina, but were also ready to support him anywhere outside Medinan territory, in contrast to the Muhājirūn who were reluctant to join him in battle. This is achieved chiefly by changing the order of the speakers in the council of war.

Some of these pro-Anṣār versions appear in the commentaries on the above-mentioned passage of Q 8:5-7. In some of them, the Anṣār are those supporting the military option. This is the case in the version of al-Suddī (Ismāʿīl b. ʿAbd al-Raḥmān, Kūfan, d. 128/745-6), in which the Anṣārī leader Saʿd b. Muʿādh is the first to express complete support for the military option, whereas Abū Bakr who spoke before him only recommended raiding the caravan, not the armed troops. Al-Miqdād, too, endorses the military option, and again repeats the revised Qurʾānic response of the Children of Israel. However, he makes his statement after Saʿd b. Muʿādh, which diminishes the significance of his contribution. The Prophet is, of course, more pleased with the militant advice than he is with that of Abū Bakr.[38]

In the commentary of Muqātil b. Sulaymān (d. 150/767-8) on the same passage,[39] the Prophet consults the Muslims concerning "one of the two parties" promised by God, and the Muslims suggest that they deal with the caravan and not fight the armed forces. The Prophet then repeats the same question and the same plan is suggested by the

[34] Bukhārī, *Ṣaḥīḥ*, V, 93 (64:4). And see *Mustadrak*, III, 349 (*Maʿrifat al-ṣaḥāba*).
[35] Ibn Abī ʿĀṣim, *Jihād*, II, no. 220; Bukhārī, *Ṣaḥīḥ*, VI, 64-65 (65, *sūra* 5); Nasāʾī, *Kubrā*, VI, no. 11140 (82:114).
[36] Ibn Ḥanbal, *Musnad*, IV, 314.
[37] Ṭabarī, *Tafsīr*, VI, 115; Wāḥidī, *Wasīṭ*, II, 174; Ibn Kathīr, *Tafsīr*, II, 39.
[38] Ṭabarī, *Tafsīr*, IX, 124-25 (on Q 8:5). The *isnād*: Asbāṭ (Kūfan, d. 200/815-6)—al-Suddī.
[39] Muqātil, *Tafsīr*, II, 100-01.

Muslims, but then Saʿd b. ʿUbāda, a leader of the Anṣār, speaks and expresses the Anṣār's utter readiness to do whatever the Prophet sees fit, even to follow him as far as to Aden. The Prophet is happy with this response. The last to speak is the Muhājir al-Miqdād who confirms that he will join the Prophet. The allusion to the Qurʾānic Israelite verse is missing from his words, which renders al-Miqdād's belated response somewhat insignificant.

In this specific version of Muqātil, the name of the Anṣārī leader is slightly different: Saʿd b. ʿUbāda rather than Saʿd b. Muʿādh. The former belonged to the Khazraj, not to the Aws, as did the latter, and after the death of the Prophet, he settled in Damascus, where he died. The occurrence of his name in our story is significant, because some authorities have claimed that he never witnessed the battle of Badr.[40] However, since he is remembered as having taken part in all other battles of the Prophet, during which he was the bearer of the standard of the Anṣār,[41] his name could easily replace that of Saʿd b. Muʿādh at Badr. In fact, these two persons were known as al-Saʿdān (the two Saʿds), which means that their names were interchangeable.

In another tradition of this pro-Anṣārī group, the name of al-Miqdād is entirely omitted from the council of war, and so also is the allusion to the Israelite cowardly reaction of Q 5:24. Moreover, the rest of the Muhājirūn, namely, Abū Bakr and ʿUmar, are told by the Prophet to be seated, which means that he is either uninterested in, or not satisfied with, their advice. Only the advice of the Anṣārī leader, Saʿd b. ʿUbāda, is quoted verbatim by the narrator. Saʿd expresses his readiness to follow the Prophet in his battle to the most remote place. This version, which was recorded by ʿAbd al-Razzāq, is traced back to ʿIkrima (*mawlā* of Ibn ʿAbbās, Medinan, d. 105/723-4).[42] A similar setting of the events is provided in a tradition traced back to the Baṣran Companion Anas b. Mālik (d. between 91/710 and 95/713-4),[43] which was recorded by some authors of *muṣannaf* compilations.[44]

In more versions the allusion to the Qurʾānic Children of Israel

---

[40] See Ibn ʿAsākir (*Mukhtaṣar*), IX, 236.

[41] Ibid., 238.

[42] The *isnād*: Maʿmar b. Rāshid (Baṣran/Yemeni, d. 154/771)—Ayyūb al-Sakhtiyānī (Baṣran, d. 131)—ʿIkrima. See ʿAbd al-Razzāq, *Muṣannaf*, V, 350 (no. 9727).

[43] The *isnād*: Ḥammād b. Salama (Baṣran, d. 167/783-4)—Thābit al-Bunānī (Baṣran, d. 123/740-1)—Anas.

[44] Ibn Abī Shayba, *Muṣannaf*, XIV, 377-78 (no. 18555); Muslim, *Ṣaḥīḥ*, V, 170 (32, *Bāb ghazwat Badr*); Ibn Ḥibbān, *Ṣaḥīḥ*, XI, no. 4722. And see also Ibn Ḥanbal, *Musnad*, III, 257-58; Bayhaqī, *Dalāʾil*, III, 47.

reappears, but al-Miqdād remains absent,[45] and the role of repeating its revised version has been transferred to the Anṣār. With this change the process of shifting the glory from the Muhājirūn to the Anṣār has been completed. The most explicit tradition of this kind is the one with the *isnād*: Muḥammad b. ʿAmr b. ʿAlqama (Medinan, d. 144/761-2)—his father ʿAlqama b. Waqqāṣ al-Laythī (Medinan). It was recorded by Ibn Abī Shayba.[46] Abū Bakr and ʿUmar again offer an insignificant piece of advice, in which they merely refer to the location of the Meccans, whereas the Anṣārī leader, who this time is Saʿd b. Muʿādh, explicitly recommends a military clash. He says: "We are not like the Children of Israel who said to Moses: 'Go you and your Lord and do battle... [etc.].'"

There is one more tradition with a similar gist, which is again traced back to Anas b. Mālik.[47] Here, however, the Anṣār speak collectively, and no individual spokesman is mentioned by name. The advice of Abū Bakr and ʿUmar, who speak first, remains unspecified. The tradition was recorded by Ibn Abī ʿĀṣim, and recurs in some *muṣannaf* compilations, as well as in commentaries on Q 5:24.[48]

Finally, there is a version rising beyond inner Islamic conflicts, in which the contrast between the Qurʾānic Children of Israel and the faithful Arabs is expressed collectively on behalf of the entire community of the believers. The Companion ʿUtba b. ʿAbd al-Sulamī (Ḥimṣī Companion, d. 87/706), who is renowned as an outstanding warrior, is reported to have related that when the Prophet ordered the Muslims to wage war on the infidels, they said:

> O Prophet of God, in that case we shall not tell you what the Children of Israel said: "Go forth, you and your Lord, and do battle; we will be sitting here." Nay [we say]: "Go forth, you and your Lord, and do battle. We will be fighting with you."[49]

---

[45] But see Ibn Ḥanbal, *Musnad*, III, 219, where Saʿd's name is replaced by that of al-Miqdād as the Anṣār's [!] spokesman, in the tradition of Anas.

[46] Ibn Abī Shayba, XIV, 355 (no. 18507). And see also Ibn Kathīr, *Bidāya*, III, 264 (from Ibn Mardawayhi); idem, *Tafsīr*, II, 287 (on Q 8:5-7).

[47] The *isnād*: Ḥumayd al-Ṭawīl (Baṣran, d. 142/759-60)—Anas.

[48] Ibn Abī ʿĀṣim, *Jihād*, no. 222; Nasāʾī, *Kubrā*, V, no. 8580 (78:1), VI, no. 11141 (82:114); Ibn Ḥibbān, *Ṣaḥīḥ*, XI, no. 4721; Bayhaqī, *Sunan*, X, 109; Wāḥidī, *Wasīṭ*, II, 174-75 (on Q 5:24); Ibn Kathīr, *Tafsīr*, II, 39 (on Q 5:24). See also Ibn Ḥanbal, *Musnad*, III, 105, 188; Abū Yaʿlā, *Musnad*, VI, nos. 3766, 3803.

[49] The *isnād*: al-Ḥasan b. Ayyūb al-Ḥaḍramī—ʿAbd Allāh b. Nāsij al-Ḥaḍramī—ʿUtba b. ʿAbd. See Ibn Ḥanbal, *Musnad*, IV, 183; Ṭabarānī, *Kabīr*, XVII, no. 306; Ibn Kathīr, *Tafsīr*, II, 39 (on Q 5:24).

The entire Arabian *umma* as one collective group constitutes here the new chosen community that replaces the Children of Israel.

Bibliography

ʿAbd al-Razzāq, Abū Bakr b. Hammām al-Ṣanʿānī, *al-Muṣannaf*, ed. Ḥabīb al-Raḥmān al-Aʿẓamī, 11 vols., Beirut, 1970.
Abū Dāwūd, *al-Sunan*, 2 vols., Cairo, 1952.
Abū Yaʿlā, Aḥmad b. ʿAlī al-Mawṣilī, *al-Musnad*, ed. Ḥusayn Salīm Asad, 13 vols., Damascus, Beirut, 1984-90.
al-Balādhurī, Aḥmad b. Yaḥyā, *Ansāb al-ashrāf*, Vol. I., ed. Muḥammad Ḥamīdullāh, Cairo, 1959.
Bashear, S., "The Title *Fārūq* and its Association with ʿUmar I", in *Studia Islamica*, 72 (1990), 47-70.
al-Bayhaqī, Aḥmad b. al-Ḥusayn, *Dalāʾil al-nubuwwa*, ed. ʿAbd al-Muʿṭī Qalʿajī, 7 vols., Beirut, 1988.
———, *al-Sunan al-kubrā*, 10 vols., Hyderabad, 1355/1936, repr. Beirut, n.d.
Bukhārī, Adab = Faḍlullāh al-Jaylānī, *Faḍlullāh al-ṣamad fī tawḍīḥ al-adab al-mufrad li-l-Bukhārī*, Hims, 1969.
al-Bukhārī, Muḥammad b. Ismāʿīl, *al-Ṣaḥīḥ*, 9 vols., Cairo, 1958.
Busse, H., "ʿOmar's Image as the Conqueror of Jerusalem", in *Jerusalem Studies in Arabic and Islam*, 8 (1986), 73-119.
Fatḥ al-bārī = Shihāb al-Dīn Aḥmad b. Ḥajar al-ʿAsqalānī, *Fatḥ al-bārī sharḥ Ṣaḥīḥ al-Bukhārī*, 13 vols., Bulaq, 1310/1892, repr. Beirut, n.d.
Hawting, G.R., "Al-Ḥudaybiyya and the Conquest of Mecca: A Reconsideration of the Tradition about the Muslim Takeover of the Sanctuary", in *Jerusalem Studies in Arabic and Islam*, 8 (1986), 1-24.
Ibn Abī ʿĀṣim al-Shaybānī, *Kitāb al-Jihād*, ed. Abū ʿAbd al-Raḥmān al-Ḥamīd, 2 vols., Medina, 1989.
Ibn Abī Ḥātim, ʿAbd al-Raḥmān b. Muḥammad, *Tafsīr al-Qurʾān al-ʿaẓīm*, ed. Asʿad Muḥammad al-Ṭayyib, 10 vols., Riyad, 1997.
Ibn Abī Shayba, ʿAbd Allāh b. Muḥammad, *Kitāb al-Muṣannaf fī l-aḥādīth wa-l-āthār*, ed. ʿAbd al-Khāliq al-Afghānī, 15 vols., Bombay, 1979-83.
Ibn ʿAsākir (*Mukhtaṣar*) = Ibn Manẓūr Muḥammad b. Mukarram, *Mukhtaṣar Taʾrīkh Dimashq li-Ibn ʿAsākir*, 29 vols., Damascus, 1984-88.
Ibn Ḥanbal, Aḥmad, *al-Musnad*, 6 vols., Cairo, 1313/1895, repr. Beirut, n.d.
Ibn Ḥibbān, Muḥammad b. Aḥmad al-Bustī, *al-Iḥsān fī taqrīb Ṣaḥīḥ Ibn Ḥibbān, tartīb ʿAlāʾ al-Dīn al-Fārisī*, ed. Shuʿayb al-Arnaʾūṭ, 16 vols., Beirut, 1988.
Ibn Hishām, ʿAbd al-Malik, *al-Sīra al-nabawiyya*, ed. Muṣṭafā al-Saqqā et al., 4 vols., repr. Beirut, 1971.
Ibn Kathīr, Ismāʿīl b. ʿUmar, *al-Bidāya wa-l-nihāya*, 14 vols., repr. Beirut, 1974.
———, *Tafsīr al-Qurʾān al-ʿaẓīm*, 4 vols., Cairo, n.d.
Ibn Saʿd, Muḥammad, *Kitāb al-Ṭabaqāt*, 8 vols., Beirut, 1960.
Ibn Wahb, ʿAbd Allāh, *al-Jāmiʿ fī l-ḥadīth*, ed. Muṣṭafā Ḥasan Ḥusayn Muḥammad, 2 vols., Riyad, 1996.
Kanz = ʿAlāʾ al-Dīn al-Muttaqī b. Ḥusām al-Dīn al-Hindī, *Kanz al-ʿummāl fī sunan al-aqwāl wa-l-afʿāl*, ed. Ṣafwat al-Saqqā and Bakrī Ḥayyānī, 16 vols., Beirut, 1979.
Muqātil b. Sulaymān, *Tafsīr al-Qurʾān*, ed. ʿAbd Allāh Maḥmūd Shiḥāta, 5 vols., Cairo, 1979.
Muslim b. al-Ḥajjāj, *al-Ṣaḥīḥ*, 8 vols., Cairo, 1915, repr. Cairo, n.d.

Mustadrak = al-Ḥākim Muḥammad b. ʿAbd Allāh al-Nīsābūrī, *al-Mustadrak ʿalā l-Ṣaḥīḥayn*, 4 vols., Hyderabad, 1342/1923.
al-Nasāʾī, Aḥmad b. Shuʿayb, *al-Sunan al-kubrā*, ed. ʿAbd al-Ghaffār al-Bandārī and Sayyid Ḥasan, 6 vols., Beirut, 1991.
Noth, Albrecht, and Lawrence I. Conrad, *The Early Islamic Historical Tradition: A Source Critical Study*, Princeton, 1994.
Rubin, Uri, *The Eye of the Beholder: The Life of Muḥammad as Viewed by the Early Muslims*, Princeton, 1995.
al-Samhūdī, Nūr al-Dīn ʿAlī b. Aḥmad, *Wafāʾ al-wafā bi-akhbār dār al-Muṣṭafā*, ed. Muḥammad Muḥyī al-Dīn ʿAbd al-Ḥamīd, Beirut, 1984.
al-Suyūṭī, Jalāl al-Dīn, *al-Durr al-manthūr fī l-tafsīr bi-l-maʾthūr*, 6 vols., Cairo, 1314/1869, repr. Beirut, n.d.
al-Ṭabarānī, Sulaymān b. Aḥmad, *al-Muʿjam al-kabīr*, ed. Ḥamdī ʿAbd al-Majīd al-Salafī, 25 vols., Baghdad, 1980-85.
al-Ṭabarī, Muḥammad b. Jarīr, *Jāmiʿ al-bayān fī tafsīr al-Qurʾān*, 30 vols., Bulaq, 1323/1905, repr. Beirut, 1972.
———, *Taʾrīkh al-rusul wa-l-mulūk*, ed. Michael Johan de Goeje et al., 15 vols., Leiden, 1879-1901 (also ed. Muḥammad Abū l-Faḍl Ibrāhīm, 10 vols. repr. Cairo, 1987).
al-Ṭaḥāwī, Abū Jaʿfar Aḥmad b. Muḥammad, *Mushkil al-āthār*, 4 vols., Hyderabad, 1333/1914, repr. Beirut, n.d.
al-Wāḥidī, ʿAlī b. Aḥmad, *al-Wasīṭ fī tafsīr al-Qurʾān al-majīd*, ed. ʿĀdil Aḥmad ʿAbd al-Mawjūd et al., Beirut, 1994.
al-Wāqidī, Muḥammad b. ʿUmar, *Kitāb al-Maghāzī*, ed. Marsden Jones, 3 vols., London, 1966.
(pseudo-) al-Wāqidī, *Futūḥ al-Shām*, Cairo, 1949, repr. Beirut, n.d.
al-Yaʿqūbī, Aḥmad b. Isḥāq, *al-Taʾrīkh*, Beirut, 1960.

SĪRA AND *TAFSĪR*: MUḤAMMAD AL-KALBĪ ON THE JEWS OF MEDINA

Marco Schöller

Both the history of the Prophet Muḥammad's conflict with the Jews of Medina as well as the content and significance of the transmission from al-Kalbī have been much discussed in recent scholarship, although at the moment there is little hope of solving once and for all the problems involved. I nevertheless propose further discussion of some salient points, because the advantage offered by confronting the traditions concerning the Medinan Jews and al-Kalbī's account of it lies in the fact that these traditions are part of the source material itself, whereas al-Kalbī's account is one of the many forms in which this material is available. Thus, by confronting substance and form, we might learn something about both.

I. Muḥammad al-Kalbī and His Position in Islamic Scholarship

Abū l-Naḍr Muḥammad b. al-Sā'ib b. Bishr al-Kalbī was born in 66/685 and died in Kūfa in 146/763, and is thus a contemporary of the *maghāzī* authority Ibn Isḥāq and the *mufassir* Muqātil b. Sulaymān (both d. 150/767). The little we know about his life is hardly worth mentioning. His scholarly fame rests almost exclusively on his interpretation of the Qur'ān, as becomes clear from the frequent characterization of Muḥammad al-Kalbī as "*ṣāḥib al-tafsīr*".[1] Quite often he is also remembered as an important authority on poetry, genealogy, and tribal lore (*ayyām al-ʿArab*), a field in which his son Hishām (d. 204/819), "*ṣāḥib al-ansāb*", was to excel later in the second/eighth century. His scholarly fame, however, is not so much due to his pro-

---

[1] For Muḥammad al-Kalbī, see Ibn Saʿd, *Ṭabaqāt,* VI, 358 f.; Ibn Qutayba, *Maʿārif,* 535; al-Nadīm, *Fihrist,* 107 f.; Ibn Khallikān, *Wafayāt,* IV, 309-11; Yaghmūrī, *Nūr al-qabas,* 256-62 (the most detailed entry with much information not found elsewhere); Ibn al-Athīr, *Lubāb,* III, 47; Samʿānī, *Ansāb,* V, 86; Yāfiʿī, *Mir'āt,* I, 236; Ṣafadī, *Wāfī,* III, 83; Dhahabī, *Siyar,* VI, 248 f.; Dā'ūdī, *Ṭabaqāt,* II, 149.

fessional achievement as to the notoriety he achieved in the eyes of later generations that took him to be a cheat and an unreliable transmitter, showing extremist Shīʿī leanings.[2] Muḥammad al-Kalbī's connection with Kūfa, a Shīʿī stronghold from the early days of Islam onwards, and the close relation of his informant Abū Ṣāliḥ (d. 101/719) with the ʿAlid family[3] seem to corroborate this. Yet al-Kalbī's Shīʿī tendencies are not particularly evident from what we find in the traditions attributed to him.[4]

In later sources al-Kalbī is commonly, with few exceptions, judged as *matrūk*, that is, a deceptive and untrustworthy transmitter.[5] This term ranks among the worst labels that could possibly be applied to a traditionist or, for that matter, to every scholar.[6] Therefore traditions in the name of al-Kalbī were in general considered worthless, with the

---

[2] He is said to have believed in the immortality of ʿAlī and his return on the Last Day, see Ibn al-Athīr, *Lubāb,* III, 47; Sibṭ Ibn al-ʿAjamī, *Kashf,* 373; Ibn Khallikān, *Wafayāt,* IV, 310; Ṣafadī, *Wāfī,* III, 83 (in a report from al-Kalbī, ʿAlī is said to have received pieces of revelation at times when the Prophet was unavailable). Cf. below, note 86.

[3] Abū Ṣāliḥ Bādhām (or Bādhān) from Kūfa, the intermediate transmitter between Ibn ʿAbbās and al-Kalbī, was the *mawlā* of Umm Hāniʾ, ʿAlī's sister, see Ibn Saʿd, *Ṭabaqāt,* VI, 296; Ibn Ḥabīb, *Muḥabbar,* 475; Dhahabī, *Siyar,* V, 37. See also below, note 17.

[4] Cf. J. van Ess, *Ungenützte Texte zur Karrāmīya. Eine Materialsammlung,* Heidelberg, 1980, 47 f.

[5] Bukhārī, *Ḍuʿafāʾ,* 105 f., and idem, *Taʾrīkh,* I, 101 (the transmission al-Kalbī—Abū Ṣāliḥ is said to consist only of lies); Nasāʾī, *Ḍuʿafāʾ,* 231 ("*matrūk al-ḥadīth*"); ʿIyāḍ, *Shifāʾ,* II, 112 ("it is not allowed to transmit from al-Kalbī or to mention him, because of the distinct weakness [of his traditions] and his being a liar", cited also in Qasṭallānī, *Mawāhib,* I, 130); Ibn al-Jawzī, *Ḍuʿafāʾ,* III, 62; Mughulṭāy, *Ishāra,* 125 f.; Ibn Sayyid al-Nās, *ʿUyūn,* I, 308 ("al-Kalbī is considered weak, especially when he transmits from Ibn ʿAbbās via Abū Ṣāliḥ"); Dhahabī, *Siyar,* VI, 248; Ibn Kathīr, *Tafsīr,* II, 71 *ad* Q 5:56 ("*matrūk al-ḥadīth*"); Qasṭallānī, *Mawāhib,* I, 129 (with a remark very similar to Ibn Ḥajar's in *Fatḥ,* VIII, 561). The entry in Ṣafadī, *Wāfī,* III, 83 reads slightly different and tries to put al-Kalbī in a more positive light: "He has been accused of being both a liar and a Shīʿī, and yet he was a prodigious interpreter of the Qurʾān possessing a vast knowledge, notwithstanding the weakness of what he transmitted. ... Ibn ʿAdī [d. 365/976] said: 'It is for the fame he enjoys among the weak transmitters that his traditions are still handed on.'" In Zarkashī, *Burhān,* II, 159, we find another quotation taken from Ibn ʿAdī's *al-Kāmil fī maʿrifat ḍuʿafāʾ al-muḥaddithīn*: "Some of al-Kalbī's traditions are sound (*ṣāliḥa*), especially those he transmitted from Abū Ṣāliḥ. He is a famous *tafsīr* authority ... Next to him ranges Muqātil b. Sulaymān, but al-Kalbī has to be preferred to him" (also cited in Suyūṭī, *Itqān,* II, 416).

[6] See Ibn Rajab, *Sharḥ ʿIlal,* 231. The criteria for someone's being *matrūk* were normally neither bad learning nor weak memory, but deliberate deception or manipulation of traditions.

further implication that they must not be used in legal argumentation (*iḥtijāj*).[7] But still, traditions bearing the stamp of al-Kalbī were not regularly suppressed in the first centuries and thus gained certain currency, although mentioning him or citing his traditions could arouse harsh criticism. Some scholars decided that it was better not to quote al-Kalbī in their writings or allegedly covered up their transmission on his authority.[8] It so happens that traditions from al-Kalbī found their way into only a limited number of commentaries of the Qur'ān and related works: they are cited quite frequently in the *Tafsīr* of al-Thaʿlabī, its shorter version by al-Baghawī, the *Tafsīr* of al-Qurṭubī, the *Asbāb al-nuzūl* by al-Wāḥidī and his *Tafsīr* called *al-Wasīṭ*,[9] but less frequently or rarely in the *tafsīr* works of ʿAbd al-Razzāq, Abū al-Layth al-Samarqandī, Fakhr al-Dīn al-Rāzī, Ibn Kathīr and Abū Ḥayyān. On the other hand, we have evidence that over the centuries the *Tafsīr al-Kalbī* was always studied and transmitted, especially in the eastern part of the Islamic world.[10]

---

[7] Sibṭ Ibn al-ʿAjamī, *Kashf*, 373; Ibn al-Jawzī, *Ḍuʿafāʾ*, II, 62 quoting from Ibn Ḥibbān al-Bustī (d. 354/965): "His [sc. al-Kalbī's] being a liar is so evident that it needs no proof... It is not permitted to use his reports in legal reasoning."

[8] Thus al-Kalbī is not mentioned in the greater *Ṣaḥīḥ* works. Ibn Isḥāq was criticized for having covered up al-Kalbī's name by using the unknown *kunya* "Abū l-Naḍr", a device called *tadlīs*, "fibbing", that is, deliberately disguising or omitting the name of one's immediate informant, see Bukhārī, *Ḍuʿafāʾ*, 106; Ibn Khallikān, *Wafayāt*, IV, 310; Ibn al-Athīr, *Lubāb*, III, 47; Ibn Ḥajar, *Taʿrīf*, 25 ff.; J. Burton, *An Introduction to the Ḥadīth*, Edinburgh, 1994, 112. Yet no Ibn Isḥāq—Abū l-Naḍr transmission is known to me, except in Bayhaqī, *Dalāʾil*, IV, 308 which, however, refers to Abū l-Naḍr Sālim b. ʿAbd Allāh, the grandson of ʿUmar. On the contrary, sometimes one encounters the overt *isnād* Ibn Isḥāq—al-Kalbī, for instance in Ibn Kathīr, *Bidāya*, I, 189, and Suyūṭī, *Khaṣāʾiṣ*, I, 292. The same applies to Sufyān al-Thawrī: He is also said to have concealed al-Kalbī's name (Ibn Khallikān, *loc. cit.*; Dhahabī, *Siyar*, VI, 249), although the overt *isnād* al-Thawrī (Sufyān b. Saʿīd)—al-Kalbī is cited in Wāqidī, *Maghāzī*, II, 864, and quotations from al-Kalbī—Abū Ṣāliḥ—Ibn ʿAbbās appear in Thawrī, *Tafsīr*, 73 (*ad* Q 2:281), 115 (*ad* Q 8:1), and 160 (*ad* Q 15:47); the *riwāya* from al-Kalbī is acknowledged by al-Thawrī himself in Tirmidhī, *Sunan*, V, 398. Finally, another scholar allegedly referred to al-Kalbī using the *kunya* "Abū Saʿīd", see Ibn Ḥanbal, *ʿIlal*, III, 118 and Samʿānī, *Ansāb*, V, 86. Possibly, the *isnād* (M. b. Marwān) al-Suddī—Abū Mālik—Abū Ṣāliḥ—Ibn ʿAbbās (Bayhaqī, *Dalāʾil*, II, 536) offers an example of *tadlīs*, because it corresponds to that of al-Suddī—al-Kalbī—Abū Ṣāliḥ—Ibn ʿAbbās (idem, II, 196), ill-famed among scholars as "the liars' chain", cf. Suyūṭī, *Itqān*, II, 416 (ch. 80).

[9] Frequent quotations from al-Kalbī are presumably one of the reasons why Ibn Taymiyya, *Muqaddima*, 69 f. severely criticizes the *tafsīr* works of Wāḥidī, Thaʿlabī, and Baghawī for their "unorthodoxy". Besides the *tafsīr* works named above, al-Kalbī appears also in writings on *ʿilm al-tafsīr*, e.g. Ibn Qutayba, *Mushkil*, 160, 269 and, much later, Zarkashī, *Burhān*, I, 220, 283, II, 80.

[10] In the *riwāya* from al-Kalbī's son Hishām, the *Tafsīr* was transmitted by Abū

Outside *tafsīr* literature, al-Kalbī is quoted more regularly, not only in writings of historiographical or administrative nature that date from the third/ninth century,[11] but also in *sīra* and *dalāʾil* literature.[12] In this respect, al-Kalbī's impact on Islamic scholarship is comparable to that of Muḥammad b. ʿUmar al-Wāqidī, who was equally ill-reputed, but whose traditions in the field of *maghāzī* and *sīra* seem to have been equally indispensable to Muslim scholars.[13] The important

Bakr M. b. Ibr. al-Karkhī who died in 381/991 (Rāfiʿī, *Tadwīn,* I, 148), *Tafsīr Ibn al-Kalbī* becoming thus synonymous with *Tafsīr al-Kalbī,* see also Ibn Ḥajar, *Fatḥ,* VIII, 538. Some decades earlier, Abū M. al-Dīnawarī (d. 308/920) compiled *al-Wāḍiḥ fī tafsīr al-Qurʾān,* the content of which is identical to the *Tafsīr al-Kalbī,* see A. Rippin, "Al-Zuhrī, *Naskh al-Qurʾān* and the Problem of Early *Tafsīr* Texts", in *BSOAS,* 47 (1984), 23, and idem, "*Tafsīr Ibn ʿAbbās* and Criteria for Dating Early *Tafsīr* Texts", in *JSAI,* 18 (1994), 47 ff.; cf. also van Ess, *Ungenützte Texte,* 44 and 51 ff. In another *riwāya,* Abū ʿAmr ʿUthmān b. M. al-Balkhī (d. 537/1143) heard the *Kitāb al-Tafsīr li-l-Kalbī* (al-Samʿānī, *Taḥbīr,* I, 554); the *isnād* given does not include any of the scholars that make up the *isnād* of the *Tafsīr Ibn ʿAbbās/al-Kalbī* as reconstructed in Rippin, "*Tafsīr Ibn ʿAbbās*", 77. The lines of transmission of the *Tafsīr al-Kalbī,* quoted by Thaʿlabī and Baghawī at the beginning of their respective *tafsīr* works, point equally to the East, particularly to the region of Khurāsān, see I. Goldfeld, "The *Tafsīr* of ʿAbdallāh b. ʿAbbās", in *Der Islam,* 58 (1981), 132 ff. Finally, an (incomplete) copy of the *Tafsīr al-Kalbī* was among the books of the Shīʿī scholar Ibn Ṭāwūs, see E. Kohlberg, *A Medieval Muslim Scholar at Work,* Leiden, 1992, 343.

[11] Transmissions from al-Kalbī (often via Abū Ṣāliḥ—Ibn ʿAbbās) are contained in Abū Yūsuf, *Kharāj*; Yaḥyā, *Kharāj*; Ibn Saʿd, *Ṭabaqāt*; Ibn Shabba, *Taʾrīkh*; Ibn Ḥabīb, *Muḥabbar*; Balādhurī, *Futūḥ*. Further in Fazārī, *Siyar,* and Ṣūlī, *Adab,* regularly also in Balādhurī's *Ansāb al-ashrāf* as well as in the first volumes of Ṭabarī's *Taʾrīkh al-rusul wa-l-mulūk.*

[12] In *sīra* works proper, al-Kalbī is cited in Kalāʿī, *Iktifāʾ,* I, 178; Mughulṭāy, *Ishāra,* 125 f.; Ibn Sayyid al-Nās, *ʿUyūn,* I, 30, 48, 308, II, 183, 356; Qasṭallānī, *Mawāhib,* I, 45, 135, 324, II, 410, 440, 447; Ḥalabī, *Insān al-ʿuyūn,* I, 40. Early *maghāzī* authorities were divided over al-Kalbī's reputation: Yaḥyā b. Saʿīd al-Umawī (d. 194/809) accepted his transmissions (Ibn Kathīr, *Bidāya,* III, 138), when in fact, Sulaymān al-Taymī (d. 143/760) called him a liar (Ibn al-Jawzī, *Ḍuʿafāʾ,* III, 62); Ibn Sayyid al-Nās, ibid., 308, finally, has the *isnād* Ibn ʿĀʾidh—al-Walīd b. Muslim, from al-Kalbī. As to *dalāʾil* literature, al-Kalbī is quoted in Abū l-Shaykh, *Akhlāq,* 202; Khayḍarī, *al-Lafẓ al-mukarram,* 40; reportedly also by Ibn Mandeh (Ibn Ḥajar, *Fatḥ,* VIII, 454) and Abū Nuʿaym (quoted in Ibn Kathīr, ibid., 312; Suyūṭī, *Khaṣāʾiṣ,* I, 189, 239, II, 494). In Bayhaqī, *Dalāʾil,* al-Kalbī is repeatedly cited, in different transmissions (II, 196, III, 459, IV, 166, VI, 274), but most quotations, about 20, are in Suyūṭī, *Khaṣāʾiṣ,* five of them taken over from Bayhaqī (I, 214, 318 f., 323, II, 169). Hence it is not the case that Suyūṭī either did not know or did not consider citing the traditions of al-Kalbī, as suggested by Rippin, "*Tafsīr Ibn ʿAbbās*", 54 f.

[13] Cf. Nīsābūrī, *Mustadrak,* III, 64, but also Ibn Taymiyya, *Ṣārim,* 132 and Sibṭ Ibn al-ʿAjamī, *Kashf,* 396 for the interesting arguments these authors put forward in order to justify quoting Wāqidī's material in the field of *maghāzī*; see also my study *Exegetisches Denken und Prophetenbiographie,* Wiesbaden, 1998, 62 ff.

Shāfiʿī authority al-Bayhaqī therefore points to the fact that al-Kalbī may be quoted in matters of *tafsīr* or *maghāzī*, but not in the field of *ḥadīth* proper.[14] However, by citing al-Kalbī's traditions exclusively in the name of his main authority Ibn ʿAbbās or attaching another *isnād* to them, Muḥammad al-Kalbī is present in the Islamic tradition on a much larger scale than becomes apparent at first sight.[15]

In this paper, I am not only concerned with the *Tafsīr al-Kalbī.*[16] Every tradition regarding Muḥammad's conflict with the Jews, which in other sources is transmitted in the name of al-Kalbī, will be taken into consideration. Formally speaking, the *Tafsīr al-Kalbī* is not al-Kalbī's *Tafsīr* in the sense in which, for instance, the *Tafsīr Mujāhid* claims to be the interpretation of Mujāhid (d. 104/722), because al-Kalbī appears only as a transmitter of Ibn ʿAbbās's commentary, with the intermediate link between the two of them being Abū Ṣāliḥ.[17] The *isnād* Ibn ʿAbbās—Abū Ṣāliḥ—al-Kalbī was, of course, known to later

[14] Bayhaqī, *Dalāʾil,* I, 35 f. Muslim scholars were in general less critical concerning the fields of *tafsīr* and *maghāzī*, as long as no legal rulings ("*al-ḥalāl wa-l-ḥarām*") were involved, see Bayhaqī, ibid., 34 and Ibn Taymiyya, *Ḥadīth,* 151. According to Ibn Ḥanbal, *tafsīr* and *maghāzī* traditions belong to "material without *aṣl*" (or "without *isnād*"), that is, material of uncertain origin and poorly authenticated: Ibn Taymiyya, *Muqaddima,* 52 f.; Suyūṭī, *Itqān,* II, 391, 393 (ch. 78), also quoted by I. Goldziher, *Die Richtungen der islamischen Koranauslegung,* Leiden, 1920, 57. Nevertheless, al-Kalbī was "edited" (*akhraja*) by important *ḥadīth* scholars like Ibn Mardawayh (cited in Suyūṭī, *Lubāb,* 111 *ad* Q 4:58) and Ibn ʿAsākir (cited in Suyūṭī, *Khaṣāʾiṣ,* I, 64, 140, 383). Ibn Ḥajar in his *Fatḥ* likewise quotes al-Kalbī (VI, 655, VII, 430, VIII, 558, 639, 700, 807) or refers to the *Tafsīr (Ibn) al-Kalbī,* e.g. *Fatḥ,* VIII, 537 f.

[15] Some traditions that are known via al-Kalbī—... Ibn ʿAbbās have been, for example, incorporated in the *Tafsīr* of Ṭabarī with the *isnād* Ibn ʿAbbās—Saʿīd/ʿIkrima—M. b. Abī M.—Ibn Isḥāq—Salama/Ibn Bukayr, see also H. Horst, "Zur Überlieferung im Korankommentar aṭ-Ṭabarīs", in *ZDMG,* 28 (1953), 303.

[16] We still lack a critical edition of the *Tafsīr al-Kalbī* based on the various manuscripts. For the present paper, I have used the ms. *Ar.* 4224 of the Chester Beatty Library, Dublin (following C. Versteegh, *Arabic Grammar and Qurʾānic Exegesis in Early Islam,* Leiden, 1993, and Rippin, "*Tafsīr Ibn ʿAbbās*". Another ms., *Ayasofya* 118, was used by J. Wansbrough, *Quranic Studies,* London-Oxford, 1977) as well as the *Tanwīr al-miqbās min tafsīr Ibn ʿAbbās,* printed in the margin of Suyūṭī's *al-Durr al-manthūr,* cf. Rippin, ibid., 39 ff. Although most manuscripts are entitled *Tafsīr Ibn ʿAbbās,* it is no "Orientalist notion" (Rippin, ibid., 52) to call it *Tafsīr al-Kalbī,* because such was the usual practice among the Muslim scholars; see notes 10 and 14 above.

[17] Cf. above, note 3. His transmission from Ibn ʿAbbās was by some said to be faulty, because Abū Ṣāliḥ never met Ibn ʿAbbās (Ibn al-Jawzī, *Ḍuʿafāʾ,* I, 135; cf. also Ibn Ḥanbal, *ʿIlal,* II, 502), while others, like Ibn Maʿīn (d. 233/847), found nothing wrong with it, except when quoted by al-Kalbī (Dhahabī, *Siyar,* V, 37; Mizzī, *Tahdhīb,* IV, 7; cf. also the comment of Bukhārī, cited above in note 5).

scholars, but, owing to the negative judgment about al-Kalbī's competence and reliability, this transmission was considered the weakest of all.[18] In view of this situation, two questions come to mind: How are we to decide whether the content of al-Kalbī's transmission does indeed go back to Ibn ʿAbbās? If it does not, does the *Tafsīr al-Kalbī* then at least include traditions that date from al-Kalbī's lifetime, or is it merely a redaction of some spurious traditions attributed to al-Kalbī? In the following I will try to answer these questions by analyzing the account al-Kalbī offers of the Prophet's conflict with the Jews.

II. Muḥammad al-Kalbī's Account of the Prophet's Conflict With the Jews

It is no easy task to reconstruct the account of al-Kalbī concerning the Prophet's conflict with the Arabian Jews in a straightforward and fairly systematic way. His traditions are less frequently cited in later sources than those of other early authorities—for the reasons mentioned above—and for some points we are left mainly with his *Tafsīr*, which exhibits the typical piecemeal-approach of exegesis that offers unconnected bits of information, lacking any outspoken statements as to chronological and causal sequences. Also, the *Tafsīr* as we have it seems to be everything but complete. Much of al-Kalbī's material found elsewhere does not appear in it, or, when it does, it does so in a different form. Yet bringing together the traditions found in his *Tafsīr* and those quoted in later writings, the following picture emerges at first sight.

As the Jews of Medina are famous for their religious learning, they are approached by Meccan leaders who doubt the prophethood of Muḥammad.[19] After the *hijra*, when Muḥammad himself had come to Medina, he entered into long and futile discussions with the Jewish rabbis.[20] These discussions centered around the basic tenets of Mu-

[18] Suyūṭī, *Itqān,* II, 416 (ch. 80); Ṭāshköprüzādeh, *Miftāḥ,* I, 401 f.

[19] Ibn Saʿd, *Ṭabaqāt,* I, 165; Baghawī, *Tafsīr,* III, 449 (*ad* Q 28:48); Suyūṭī, *Khaṣāʾiṣ,* I, 30.

[20] For example, Kalbī, *Tafsīr,* 23a (*ad* Q 3:7); Baghawī, *Tafsīr,* I, 289 (*ad* Q 3:23: an enlarged version of what we find in Kalbī, ibid., 24b, and *Tanwīr,* I, 162); Kalbī, ibid., 27a (*ad* Q 3:69, 72); Wāḥidī, *Asbāb,* 115 (*ad* Q 3:77); Qurṭubī, *Tafsīr,* IV, 127 (*ad*

ḥammad's new faith and often end in mutual misunderstanding or even physical attacks, the most famous among them being the slap the Jewish scholar Finḥāṣ received from Abū Bakr.[21] Nonetheless, some Jews do convert to Islam.[22] When the Prophet nearly falls victim to a Jewish attempt on his life,[23] the period of polemics and discussion comes to an end—according to the *Tafsīr al-Kalbī* after the battle of Uḥud—with Muḥammad's siege and defeat of one of the Jewish tribes, the Banū l-Naḍīr.[24] They are expelled from Medina and reach finally the Syrian towns of Jericho and Adhriʿāt (modern Darʿā);[25] their conquered land, consisting mainly of seven gardens, is distributed among the poor Muhājirūn, those Muslims who had recently emigrated from Mecca to Medina (see below). The Prophet also turns on the second major Jewish tribe, the Banū Qurayẓa. He forces them to surrender, their fate being, as is well known, death (for the combatants) and slavery (for the wives and children).[26] The Muslim conquest of Khaybar, following the treaty of al-Ḥudaybiya,[27] puts an end to Jewish resistance in the Ḥijāz, the land being again distributed among the Muhājirūn. Less severe is the Muslim treatment of the little oasis of Fadak, hometown of the rabbi Ibn Ṣūrīyā,[28] where the inhabitants are allowed to remain on the condition of crop-sharing (see below).

As given in this outline, al-Kalbī's account seems straightforward enough. It matches in many aspects the "orthodox" account of his contemporary Ibn Isḥāq. But this is not the whole truth, for we still have to study carefully some points which have not been taken into

---

Q 3:83); Wāḥidī, ibid., 138 (*ad* Q 3:183); Baghawī, ibid., I, 440 (*ad* Q 4:49; a similar story in Farrā', *Maʿānī*, I, 272); Wāḥidī, ibid., 202 (*ad* Q 5:57).

[21] Baghawī, *Tafsīr*, I, 381 (*ad* Q 3:186).

[22] See Baghawī, *Tafsīr*, I, 285 f. (*ad* Q 3:18); Wāḥidī, *Asbāb*, 188, and Baghawī, ibid., 489 (*ad* Q 4:136). Together with Muqātil and al-Ḍaḥḥāk—Ibn ʿAbbās, al-Kalbī has more details concerning converted Jews than found in the "orthodox" *sīra* literature, a trait certainly due to the homiletic and hortative character of these *tafsīr* works, cf. Rippin, "*Tafsīr Ibn ʿAbbās*", 70.

[23] Wāḥidī, *Asbāb*, 196, and Baghawī, *Tafsīr*, II, 19 (*ad* Q 5:11); with a short version that stresses ʿAlī's presence: Furāt, *Tafsīr*, I, 122. In *Tanwīr*, I, 325, reference is made to the B. Qurayẓa.

[24] Kalbī, *Tafsīr*, 226a (*ad* Q 59:2); *Tanwīr*, VI, 27.

[25] Kalbī, *Tafsīr*, 226a (*ad* Q 59:2: read *Adhriʿāt* instead of *idhā jāʾat*); *Tanwīr*, VI, 27. *Adhriʿāt* is also mentioned in Muqātil, *Tafsīr*, I, 379 (*ad* Q 4:51), and IV, 275 (*ad* Q 59:2).

[26] Kalbī, *Tafsīr*, 174a (*ad* Q 33:27); *Tanwīr*, IV, 244; cf. also Kalbī, ibid., 80a (*ad* Q 8:56-62).

[27] Kalbī, *Tafsīr*, 174a (*ad* Q 33:28), 209b-210b (*ad* Q 48:15, 18-20, 27).

[28] Baghawī, *Tafsīr*, I, 289 (*ad* Q 3:23).

consideration so far. Having done this, we will see that substantial parts of al-Kalbī's account turn out to be rather different from the "orthodox" *sīra* version.

III. Chronological Considerations

First of all, there is almost no chronological information in the material transmitted by al-Kalbī. As mentioned above, this is due to the characteristic method of exegesis which precludes any chronological or sequential arrangement of traditions. Moreover, al-Kalbī's account was not rewritten by himself or by anyone else in the form of a continuous *maghāzī* compilation. Interest in chronology had priority among the *maghāzī* authorities and jurists, such as al-Zuhrī (d. 124/742), who tried to establish a sequence of events in order to formulate a continuous account of the Prophet Muḥammad's life.[29] Similarly, chronology was important for assessing the validity of the *aḥkām*, especially when applying the principle of what comes last has the best claim to validity, that is, the principle of abrogation (*naskh*). As far as can be seen, al-Kalbī, like most *mufassirūn*, was not particularly keen on tackling problems of *fiqh*, even if his transmission betrays more concern with legal problems than do other *tafsīr* works from the second/eighth century (see below).

The reconstruction of al-Kalbī's account as summarized above therefore avoids, with few exceptions, clear chronological statements. The rough order of events runs: (a) Muḥammad's discussion with the Jewish rabbis, (b) the expulsion of the B. al-Naḍīr and the defeat of the B. Qurayẓa, and (c) the conquest of Khaybar and Fadak. The first thing one notices about this order is the absence of any tradition concerning the conflict with the Jewish tribe Qaynuqāʾ. This episode of conflict has been an integral part of the "orthodox" *sīra* tradition since (at least) the account of Ibn Isḥāq. Secondly, we are still dealing with a relative chronology based on about two or three events only. If we now compare this chronology with that found in the "orthodox" *sīra* tradition, numerous difficulties begin to arise.

---

[29] For the importance of chronological features in the *maghāzī* material, see Wansbrough, *Quranic Studies*, 180; M. Lecker, "The Death of the Prophet Muḥammad's Father: Did Wāqidī Invent Some of the Evidence?", in *ZDMG*, 145 (1995), 9-27; M. Schöller, "Die Palmen (*līna*) der Banū n-Naḍīr und die Interpretation von Koran 59:5", in *ZDMG*, 146 (1996), 362 ff.

It will be remembered that, according to the "orthodox" tradition in the wake of Ibn Isḥāq, the B. Qaynuqāʾ episode took place after Badr, the B. al-Naḍīr episode after Uḥud, the B. Qurayẓa episode after the "battle of the trench" (*yawm al-khandaq, yawm al-aḥzāb*), and the Khaybar episode after the treaty of al-Ḥudaybiya. Yet in al-Kalbī's account there is no mention of the Qaynuqāʾ episode, and this corresponds to the following tradition in the name of al-Kalbī—Abū Ṣāliḥ—Ibn ʿAbbās (*ad* Q 3:12):

> After the Messenger of God had defeated the heathen on the day of Badr, the Jews of Medina said: "He truly is the Prophet we have been told of ...", and they were about to become his followers. Then one of them proposed: "Let us not hasten, but wait for the result of another battle!" When the Messenger of God and his Companions were routed in the battle of Uḥud, the Jews doubted [Muḥammad's prophethood], were won over by obstinacy and did not convert to Islam. As there had been stipulated a treaty [30] between them and the Messenger of God, the Jews now broke that treaty and Kaʿb b. al-Ashraf went to Mecca, accompanied by sixty horsemen, in order to incite the Meccan leaders until they agreed to join their forces to fight the Messenger of God.[31]

This tradition is important in many ways for assessing al-Kalbī's account. For the moment, it is enough to emphasize that obviously no conflict with the Jews took place prior to the battle of Uḥud, nor was a treaty broken by the Jews before that. Moreover, al-Kalbī states that

[30] The text has *ʿahd ilā muddatin*. This could mean "for a (limited) period", similar to *ilā ajalin*. In the context above, however, this is unlikely, because, to my knowledge, the limitation of the treaty between Muḥammad and the Medinan Jews is not mentioned elsewhere in the sources. (Only the treaty with the Jews of Khaybar was said to last "until further notice".) So probably, *mudda* is used here in the sense of "truce" or "suspension of hostilities" (cf. Dozy, *Supplément*, II, 573). *ʿAhd ilā muddatin* then conveys the meaning of "a treaty on non-aggression/non-belligerency", with *ilā* being synonymous with either *li-* or *ʿalā*, as stated in various Arabic dictionaries. This would fit the widespread tradition that the treaty between the Prophet and the Jews was concluded on the basis of neutrality, see Farrāʾ, *Maʿānī*, III, 143; Ibn Ḥajar, *Fatḥ*, VII, 419; Diyārbakrī, *Taʾrīkh al-khamīs*, I, 460.

[31] The translation follows Baghawī, *Tafsīr*, I, 282 (*ad* Q 3:12). It is also cited in Wāḥidī, *Asbāb*, 100 (with some variation in the wording and more details towards the end), and Qurṭubī, *Tafsīr*, IV, 24; a similar report is to be found, yet without mentioning al-Kalbī, in Farrāʾ, *Maʿānī*, I, 191. Cf. U. Rubin, "The Assassination of Kaʿb b. al-Ashraf", in *Oriens*, 32 (1990), 67, and M. Schöller, "In welchem Jahr wurden die Banū n-Naḍīr aus Medina vertrieben?", in *Der Islam*, 73 (1996), 21. Kaʿb's journey to Mecca after Uḥud likewise appears in Muqātil, *Tafsīr*, I, 378 f. (*ad* Q 4:51). Finally, both the *Tafsīr al-Kalbī* (23b) and the *Tanwīr* (I, 156 f.) give a different report *ad* Q 3:12, according to which Muḥammad two years before Badr (!) announced to the Jews the future defeat of the al-Naḍīr and Qurayẓa. This notice, however, is quite unheard of, and here indeed the text seems corrupt.

the B. al-Naḍīr were the first *ahl al-kitāb* to be expelled from the Arabian peninsula,[32] which means that again he seems to be ignorant of the B. Qaynuqāʾ episode and its consequences. Thus, no conflict took place between Muḥammad and the Jews immediately after Badr, the earliest date for such a conflict being some time after Uḥud. This is indeed what we find in the *Tafsīr al-Kalbī*, *ad* Q 59:2: "*baʿd mā naqaḍū ʿuhūdahum maʿa l-nabī baʿd waqʿat Uḥud.*" The expression "*min ḥaythu lam yaḥtasibū*" of the same verse, he glosses with the words: "when the murder of Kaʿb b. al-Ashraf befell them",[33] and the Jewish poet Kaʿb was generally said to have been a member of the B. al-Naḍīr. But apart from being incompatible with the "orthodox" *sīra* version, according to which Kaʿb was killed a considerable time before the B. al-Naḍīr episode, al-Kalbī's mention of Kaʿb in the context of verse Q 59:2 is problematic for still other reasons.

To start with, in reports transmitted by al-Kalbī, Kaʿb b. al-Ashraf, together with Ḥuyayy b. Akhṭab, figures as the most prominent leader of the Jewish opposition who is involved in all major episodes of conflict.[34] He must have been present on the Medinan scene not only up to the B. al-Naḍīr episode, as al-Kalbī states *ad* Q 59:2, but also during and after the B. Qurayẓa episode. Therefore in the *Tafsīr al-Kalbī*, Kaʿb b. al-Ashraf is mentioned alongside the B. Qurayẓa and Ḥuyayy b. Akhṭab in a passage which obviously relates to the B. Qurayẓa episode and its aftermath.[35] (According to the "orthodox" version, Kaʿb was killed before Uḥud and did not take part in any

---

[32] Kalbī, *Tafsīr*, 226a (*ad* Q 59:2), also quoted in Balādhurī, *Futūḥ*, 20; Baghawī, *Tafsīr*, II, 315; Schöller, *In welchem Jahr*, 20 and 24. Cf. Farrāʾ, *Maʿānī*, III, 143: "They were the first to be expelled from the *jazīrat al-ʿArab*, that is, the Ḥijāz."

[33] Kalbī, *Tafsīr*, 226a. Reports that establish a connection between the murder of Kaʿb and the B. al-Naḍīr episode are widely quoted in *tafsīr* literature, see Rubin, *Assassination*, and Schöller, *In welchem Jahr*, 17 ff.

[34] Kaʿb b. al-Ashraf is mentioned in traditions from al-Kalbī *ad* Q 2:6 (Qurṭubī, *Tafsīr*, I, 184), *ad* Q 3:72 (Baghawī, *Tafsīr*, I, 315), *ad* Q 3:77 (Wāḥidī, *Asbāb*, 115), *ad* Q 3:83 (Qurṭubī, ibid., IV, 127), *ad* Q 3:183 (Baghawī, ibid., 380), *ad* Q 4:51 (ʿAbd al-Razzāq, *Tafsīr*, I, 160), *ad* Q 4:60 (Wāḥidī, ibid., 166), *ad* Q 5:11 f. (Furāt, *Tafsīr*, I, 122; Wāḥidī, ibid., 196), *ad* Q 8:55 f. (Baghawī, ibid., II, 257), *ad* Q 33:26 (see the following note) and *ad* Q 59:2 (see note 33).

[35] Kalbī, *Tafsīr*, 174a (*ad* Q 33:26): "*wa-harabū Qurayẓa [wa-]Kaʿb b. al-Ashraf wa-Ḥuyayy b. Akhṭab wa-aṣḥābuhumā min*, etc." Instead, in *Tanwīr*, IV, 243 we find: "*wa-hum Banū Qurayẓa wa-l-Naḍīr Kaʿb b. al-Ashraf wa-Ḥuyayy b. Akhṭab wa-aṣḥābuhumā.*" The variant *harabū/hum Banū* may be due to a scribal error, but the mention of the B. al-Naḍīr in *Tanwīr* gives the wording a slightly more "orthodox" coloring, with Kaʿb being thus not uniquely associated with the B. Qurayẓa and Ḥuyayy.

episode, whereas Ḥuyayy fled to Khaybar after the B. al-Naḍīr episode, came back later and was executed together with the Qurayẓa.) In the same vein, Kaʿb is named among the Jews of Qurayẓa who furnished the Meccan allies with weapons on *yawm al-aḥzāb*,[36] and *ad* Q 3:12 (cited above) we are told that Kaʿb went to Mecca after Uḥud to stir up the Meccan allies. But did not al-Kalbī mention *ad* Q 59:2 that Kaʿb was murdered before (or during) the B. al-Naḍīr episode? So we are left with two possibilities: either one of these traditions (namely, Kaʿb being murdered or being still alive later) is simply false, and al-Kalbī (or, in this case, the redactor of the *Tafsīr*) got it wrong, for whatever reasons, or both the B. al-Naḍīr and the B. Qurayẓa were involved, according to some accounts, in one bigger episode, that is, a single event or episode of conflict. Such an event could be called "Naḍīr-*cum*-Qurayẓa episode".[37]

I would suggest that the second possibility is more likely. The episode in question, the so-called "Naḍīr-*cum*-Qurayẓa episode", could have happened during or after the "battle of the trench", the siege of Medina by the allied Meccan forces (*aḥzāb*) that are supported by the Jewish tribes. This would not only fit the tradition that Kaʿb b. al-Ashraf and Ḥuyayy instigated the heathen *aḥzāb* before the *yawm al-aḥzāb* to attack the Prophet, but it would explain several other "unorthodox" elements in the reports that are transmitted from al-Kalbī. It is to these "unorthodox" elements that we must turn now.

IV. How Many Episodes?

The above quoted tradition *ad* Q 3:12 does seem to imply that there was neither a B. Qaynuqāʾ nor a B. al-Naḍīr episode as we know it from the "orthodox" *sīra* version. On the contrary, al-Kalbī's tradition

[36] Baghawī, *Tafsīr,* II, 257 (*ad* Q 8:55 f.), from al-Kalbī and Muqātil (cf. Muqātil, *Tafsīr,* III, 484 f. *ad* Q 33:26). Less detailed is Mujāhid, *Tafsīr*, 357, also cited in Ṭabarī, *Tafsīr,* X, 25. In Kalbī's *Tafsīr,* (80a, *ad* Q 8:55 ff.), the B. Qurayẓa are mentioned, but nothing else is said of the events that occurred during or after *yawm al-aḥzāb*.

[37] This does not necessarily mean that a "Naḍīr-*cum*-Qurayẓa episode" really happened—and it does not matter at the moment, because we are trying to reconstruct sources, not historical realities—but it means that there were traditions concerning a *single* episode of conflict between the Jews and Muḥammad, in the context of which some scholars made reference to the B. al-Naḍīr and some to the B. Qurayẓa, while others held that both Jewish tribes were involved.

does not distinguish between the various tribes, but speaks only of "the Medinan Jews" (*yahūd ahl al-Madīna*). We further learn that the breaking of the treaty on the part of the Jews was due to Kaʿb's mission to Mecca after Uḥud, whereas no episode of conflict in Medina itself is mentioned. To be sure, to maintain that therefore no separate episodes were said to have taken place would be an argument *e silentio*, yet it remains at least possible that Kaʿb's mission constituted the decisive Jewish break with Muḥammad, in consequence of which a single episode of conflict between them and the Prophet occurred.[38]

There exist some "unorthodox" traditions in the name of other authorities to support this interpretation. One of these "unorthodox" reports is introduced by al-Baghawī, *Tafsīr*, I, 348 (*ad* Q 3:124 f.) with the following explanation:

> God promised the Muslims on the day of Badr that He would assist them in all their warfare, provided they persevered in being obedient towards Him and in avoiding what He forbade. But they persevered only on *yawm al-aḥzāb*, and so He assisted them when they were besieging Qurayẓa and al-Naḍīr.[39]

This not only implies, but explicitly states that a sort of Naḍīr-*cum*-Qurayẓa episode took place during (or shortly after) *yawm al-aḥzāb*. The tradition to support that view is quoted by al-Baghawī (*loc. cit.*) in the name of ʿAbd Allāh b. Abī Awfā:[40]

> We were besieging Qurayẓa and al-Naḍīr, as it pleased God, but He did not have us defeat them, and so we retreated .... Suddenly Gabriel appeared and said: "You put away your weapons, although the angels did not lay down their arms yet?" So the Messenger of God ... summoned us and we set out, until we came to Qurayẓa and al-Naḍīr. On

---

[38] One tradition in the *Tafsīr al-Kalbī*, however, draws a neat distinction between the B. al-Naḍīr and the B. Qurayẓa episode, for *ad* Q 59:15 (227b) we read: "*min qabla B. Qurayẓa* {*qarīban*} *bi-sanatayn ... wa-hum B. al-Naḍīr*." Although this does not accord with the "orthodox" chronology that has less than two years between both episodes, it nevertheless states that two separate episodes took place; also Qatāda is said to have understood *qarīban* in that way, see Qurṭubī, *Tafsīr,* XVIII, 36.

[39] Ṭabarī, *Tafsīr,* IV, 78 f. has the same passage, but leaves out the mention of the B. al-Naḍīr!

[40] Interestingly, ʿAbd Allāh b. Abī Awfā, who was a Companion of the Prophet from around the year 6 AH onwards, later in life went to Kūfa, the hometown of al-Kalbī, where he died in the late eighties of the first century AH (Ibn Ḥajar, *Iṣāba,* IV, 19).

> that day, God helped us by sending 3,000 angels, and He made our victory an easy one.[41]

This report mentions both al-Naḍīr and Qurayẓa in the context of a single episode. No episode is explicitly referred to, but there is one detail that clearly points to the time of the "orthodox" B. Qurayẓa episode after *yawm al-aḥzāb*, namely, the appearance of Gabriel and his admonition.[42]

A second tradition mentioning a Naḍīr-*cum*-Qurayẓa episode is cited by al-Khayḍarī. It says that "on the day of Qurayẓa and al-Naḍīr" (*yawm Qurayẓa wa-l-Naḍīr*), Ṣafiyya, the daughter of the Jewish leader Ḥuyayy b. Akhṭab and Muḥammad's later wife, was taken prisoner.[43] According to the "orthodox" *sīra* version, Ṣafiyya was captured during the siege of Khaybar. Thus, here *yawm Qurayẓa wa-l-Naḍīr* quite possibly refers to that episode, for there is another report that seems to use the term "day of Qurayẓa and al-Naḍīr" in that sense.[44] Yet this leads us away from al-Kalbī and cannot be resolved here.[45] It is, however, worth remembering that there are at least three traditions which explicitly mention a Naḍīr-*cum*-Qurayẓa episode that took place during or after *yawm al-aḥzāb*, either in Medina or, maybe, in Khaybar.

---

[41] The translation follows Baghawī, *Tafsīr*, I, 348 (*ad* Q 3:124 f.). It is also found, almost verbally, in Ṭabarī, *Tafsīr*, IV, 78 f., and Suyūṭī, *Khaṣā'iṣ*, I, 386. Muqātil, *Tafsīr*, II, 171 (*ad* Q 9:40) states that the Muslims were aided by the angels at Badr, during the *yawm al-khandaq*, and Khaybar. Most scholars, however, held that verse Q 3:125 refers only to the Badr episode, see Mujāhid, *Tafsīr*, 259, and Qurṭubī, *Tafsīr*, IV, 195. Cf. also Ṭabarī, ibid., XXVIII, 36 (*ad* Q 59:6) where we find a report transmitted from Ibn ʿAbbās saying that God ordered the Prophet to attack both the B. Qurayẓa and the B. al-Naḍīr.

[42] The appearance of Gabriel after the "battle of the trench" is generally viewed as the prelude to the B. Qurayẓa episode, see the traditions from Mujāhid (*Tafsīr*, 357, *ad* Q 8:58, also cited in Ṭabarī, *Tafsīr*, X, 72), Muqātil (*Tafsīr*, III, 484, *ad* Q 33:26), and al-Zuhrī (ʿAbd al-Razzāq, *Tafsīr*, I, 100 f. *ad* Q 2:214; Suyūṭī, *Lubāb*, 172 f.).

[43] Khayḍarī, *al-Lafẓ al-mukarram*, 222 (he quotes it from Bayhaqī).

[44] M. Lecker, *The Banū Sulaym. A Contribution to the Study of Early Islam*, Jerusalem, 1989, 97 f. It is worth mentioning that in lexicographical literature the B. al-Naḍīr and Qurayẓa are described as being from among the Jews of Khaybar, see Ibn Durayd, *Jamhara*, II, 367 and 378; cf. also Ibn Manẓūr, *Lisān*, V, 214 (s.v. *nḍr*). Furthermore, there is an interesting passage in Kalbī, *Tafsīr*, 24b (*ad* Q 3:23) which points in a similar direction, because it has "*B. Qurayẓa wa-l-Naḍīr min ahl Khaybar*"; this is changed in *Tanwīr*, I, 162 into: "*B. Qurayẓa wa-ahl Khaybar*", which suggests that here again (cf. above, note 34) someone tried to emend the original wording in order to make the text less "unorthodox".

[45] Cf. my study *Exegetisches Denken und Prophetenbiographie*, 289 ff.

But there is more to it, for *ad* Q 8:56 we read in the name of al-Kalbī:

> [This verse refers] to the Jews of Qurayẓa who broke the treaty between themselves and the Messenger of God by furnishing the heathen with weapons in order to help them in fighting the Prophet. But afterwards they said: "We forgot, and we did wrong." Therefore the Prophet concluded a second treaty with them, until they broke it by inciting the unbelievers against the Messenger of God on *yawm al-aḥzāb*. Kaʿb b. al-Ashraf went to Mecca and established an alliance, directed against the Prophet, between them.[46]

This tradition, which in a less detailed form is also transmitted by Mujāhid and Muqātil,[47] is "orthodox" insofar as it puts the B. Qurayẓa episode in the context of *yawm al-aḥzāb*, but it is still quite "unorthodox" in mentioning Kaʿb as their agent, in claiming that a treaty was concluded twice, and in asserting that the Qurayẓa gave weapons to the Meccans some time before *yawm al-khandaq*. Even more astonishing is the fact that the B. al-Naḍīr are not referred to at all. As this report does not mention any episode of conflict, it leaves unresolved whether there occurred one or more (separate) episodes, though a single Naḍīr-*cum*-Qurayẓa episode would fit the context better. I presume that this tradition combines the idea of more than one episode of conflict with traditions that mention only a single episode. Therefore, the hostility of the Jews is "doubled", as is the conclusion of the treaty. But as the fate of the Jews, according to the Qurʾān, consisted of death and slavery,[48] there was only one B. Qurayẓa episode to be conceived of, and this is why the first conflict is said to have been settled by peaceful means. On the whole, this tradition seems like a compromise between those which explicitly do not mention more than one episode, and those "orthodox", which interpret the first Jewish hostility to be the B. al-Naḍīr episode, drop the talk of a renewed treaty, and eliminate the person of Kaʿb b. al-Ashraf from the context of the B. Qurayẓa episode.[49]

---

[46] Baghawī, *Tafsīr*, II, 257 (*ad* Q 8:56).

[47] Mujāhid, *Tafsīr*, 357 (a very short notice); Ṭabarī, *Tafsīr*, X, 25; Qurṭubī, *Tafsīr*, VIII, 30 (where both the B. al-Naḍīr and the B. Qurayẓa are mentioned!). From Muqātil: Muqātil, *Tafsīr*, II, 177 (*ad* Q 8:56).

[48] Cf. Kalbī, *Tafsīr*, 174 (*ad* Q 33:26).

[49] In the "orthodox" version, it is Kaʿb b. Asad who dominates the B. Qurayẓa episode, whereas the mission to Mecca is assigned to Ḥuyayy b. Akhṭab and some other members of the B. al-Naḍīr, see Ibn Isḥāq, *Sīra*, III, 231 and 240 ff.

The element of a treaty concluded twice (or renewed) is echoed in traditions that belong more closely to the field of *maghāzī*. One of these traditions is transmitted from Mūsā b. ʿUqba—Nāfiʿ—Ibn ʿUmar:

> The Jews of B. al-Naḍīr and Qurayẓa attacked the Messenger of God. So the Messenger of God expelled the B. al-Naḍīr, but warranted the security of the Qurayẓa and made an agreement with them. [This lasted] until the Qurayẓa took to military action after that.[50]

This tradition from Mūsā reflects a tradition from al-Zuhrī, which, however, is longer and exhibits some more details.[51] At the same time, it is similar to that quoted above from al-Kalbī (*ad* Q 8:56), but it differs in that it interprets the first hostility as the B. al-Naḍīr episode, while only the second time the Prophet is said to clash with Qurayẓa. What is more, we know of another tradition via Mūsā b. ʿUqba (and Ibn Lahīʿa) that shows parallels with the tradition from al-Kalbī. Regarding the cause that made the Prophet attack the B. al-Naḍīr, we read:

> They [sc. the Muslims] believed that the B. al-Naḍīr had secretly collaborated with the Quraysh when they encamped at Uḥud in order to fight the Messenger of God. So they incited them [sc. the Quraysh] to fight and gave them information about the weak spots [in the Muslim defense].[52]

---

[50] ʿAbd al-Razzāq, *Muṣannaf*, VI, 54; Ibn Ḥanbal, *Musnad*, IX, 181; Bukhārī, *Ṣaḥīḥ*, III, 15; Bayhaqī, *Dalāʾil*, III, 183; Ibn Kathīr, *Tafsīr*, IV, 333.

[51] ʿAbd al-Razzāq, *Muṣannaf*, V, 360; Bayhaqī, *Dalāʾil*, III, 179; Samhūdī, *Wafāʾ*, I, 298 (an abridged version); M.J. Kister, "The Massacre of the Banū Qurayẓa—A Reexamination of a Tradition", in *JSAI*, 8 (1986), 83. For other reports from al-Zuhrī mentioning an agreement between Muḥammad and the Jews, see ʿAbd al-Razzāq, *Tafsīr*, I, 144 *ad* Q 3:186 (concluding a *ṣulḥ* after the assassination of Kaʿb); idem, *Muṣannaf*, V, 203 f.; Ibn Shabba, *Taʾrīkh*, I, 253 (writing down a *ṣaḥīfa*).

[52] Bayhaqī, *Dalāʾil*, III, 180; Abū Nuʿaym, *Dalāʾil*, 423; Ibn Sayyid al-Nās, *ʿUyūn*, II, 70; Ibn Ḥajar, *Fatḥ*, VII, 421; M. Kister, "Notes on the Papyrus Text about Muḥammad's Campaign against the Banū al-Naḍīr", in *Archiv Orientální*, 32 (1964), 233-36. It is worth noting, however, that "pointing out the weak spots" (*al-dalāla ʿalā l-ʿawra* or *al-ʿawrāt*) makes little sense when referring to a battle like that of Uḥud, but it would be appropriate when referring to a siege. (We find one such instance in Ibn Saʿd, *Ṭabaqāt*, V, 225, where we are told that during the siege of Medina in the year 63/682, the forces of Yazīd were "shown the weak spots"). Therefore, the context of *yawm al-aḥzāb*, the siege of Medina by the Meccan allies, seems to be more suited to the report about the Jews pointing out the weak spots in the Muslim defense. More crucially, the wording of Q 33:13 ("*innā buyūtanā ʿawratun*", "our houses lie open", that is, unprotected from the enemy) was generally said to have been revealed on *yawm al-aḥzāb*.

This obviously means that the Jews supported the Meccans on at least one occasion before the *yawm al-aḥzāb*. This tradition is thus again quite close to al-Kalbī's tradition cited above, though no weapons are mentioned in Mūsā's report. Yet the similarity is noteworthy, because in the "orthodox" account of the B. al-Naḍīr episode, for instance in Ibn Isḥāq's *Maghāzī*, there is no trace left of the Jews assisting the Meccans, the only cause for the attack being the planned murder of the Prophet when he came to the Jewish quarter. Nor is there any evidence that, as according to Ibn Isḥāq, the Prophet was ever to fight the al-Naḍīr and Qurayẓa together, only to expel the former and to establish an agreement with the latter.

At this point, two preliminary conclusions may be drawn. First, al-Kalbī's "unorthodox" traditions seem less strange now, for when compared to reports that are ascribed to early authorities in the fields of *tafsīr* and *sīra*, some similarities and common tendencies appear. Second, Ibn Isḥāq's "orthodox" account is the one least similar to the reports known from al-Kalbī. It also goes a step further in separating the B. al-Naḍīr episode from the B. Qurayẓa episode than do the accounts known from al-Zuhrī and Mūsā b. ʿUqba. In the latter, some traces are left which possibly reflect traditions concerning a Naḍīr-*cum*-Qurayẓa episode: the joint fighting during the first conflict, the renewed agreement with Qurayẓa, and the Jewish support of the Meccans on more than one occasion (that is, the topos of supporting the enemy has been "doubled", as has the treaty with the Jews).

On the basis of these preliminary conclusions, we should see what else we can find in al-Kalbī's account of the Prophet's conflict with the Medinan Jews. For one thing, together with Muqātil b. Sulaymān, al-Kalbī is one of the few scholars to maintain, as we read in his *Tafsīr*, that Q 59:11 ff. do not refer to the B. al-Naḍīr episode, but rather to the B. Qurayẓa and the contacts they had established with the *munāfiqūn*.[53] In general, these verses were understood to refer to the same episode as Q 59:2 ff., which are said to have been revealed on the occasion of the B. al-Naḍīr episode.[54] In view of what has been

---

[53] Kalbī, *Tafsīr*, 227a-b; Muqātil, *Tafsīr*, IV, 280 f. From al-Ḍaḥḥāk: Qurṭubī, *Tafsīr*, XVIII, 36.

[54] It is, however, known that al-Ḥasan al-Baṣrī connected 59:2 ff. to the B. Qurayẓa episode (Abū Ḥayyān, *Tafsīr*, VIII, 242; Qurṭubī, *Tafsīr*, XVIII, 3); Muqātil (b. Ḥayyān) and Qatāda referred to that episode when commenting on Q 59:5 (Ibn Kathīr, *Tafsīr*, IV, 333).

said so far, and considering the possibility that Q 59:2-16 (with the probable addition of Q 59:7?)[55] could indeed refer to a single event, I take al-Kalbī's (and Muqātil's) mention of the Qurayẓa as evidence that here again we have come across some trace of a Naḍīr-*cum*-Qurayẓa episode. But when compared to what al-Kalbī has to say about the legal rulings that are tied to the conflict between the Jews and the Prophet, the interpretation of Q 59:11 ff. is a point of minor importance.

V. Legal Rulings and "Meta-Exegesis"

In the *Tafsīr al-Kalbī*, we learn that the booty taken from both the B. al-Naḍīr and the B. Qurayẓa was given to the poor among the Muhājirūn: "*wa-qasama l-nabī ghanīmat Qurayẓa wa-l-Naḍīr ʿalā fuqarāʾ al-muhājirīn.*"[56] This makes sense if one considers the actual wording of Q 59:7 and the following one (*li-l-fuqarāʾ al-muhājirīn*), but it obviously does not differentiate between the rulings applied after the episode (or each of the episodes, if seen as separate). Additionally, the *Tafsīr al-Kalbī* mentions seven gardens from the possessions of the B. al-Naḍīr, which the Prophet kept for himself.[57] The *Sīra* version of how the Prophet distributed the booty differs from al-Kalbī's account: The land of the B. al-Naḍīr is said by some scholars to have remained in the hands of Muḥammad (al-Zuhrī's claim),[58] while the booty from

[55] Cf. R. Bell, "Sūrat al-Ḥashr: A Study of its Composition", in *Muslim World*, 38 (1948), 31 f.

[56] Kalbī, *Tafsīr*, 226b (*ad* Q 59:7). In the transmission Abū Bakr b. ʿAyyāsh—al-Kalbī, a similar report, concerning the B. al-Naḍīr episode, is cited in Yaḥyā, *Kharāj*, 34 f., and Ibn Shabba, *Taʾrīkh*, I, 265. Concerning the B. Qurayẓa episode, see (via Abū Bakr) Yaḥyā, ibid., 41, and Balādhurī, *Futūḥ*, 22; cf. also Farrāʾ, *Maʿānī*, III, 145, and Ibn Sayyid al-Nās, *ʿUyūn*, II, 105. As quoted in Ṭabarī, *Tafsīr*, XXVIII, 36, Mujāhid was of the opinion that the *amwāl* of Qurayẓa were given to the Muhājirūn of Quraysh.

[57] Al-Kalbī, *Tafsīr*, 226b-227a. This is cited via Abū Bakr from al-Kalbī in Yaḥyā, *Kharāj*, 38, and Balādhurī, *Futūḥ*, 20. From al-Zuhrī: Ibn Shabba, *Taʾrīkh*, I, 122, and Samhūdī, *Wafāʾ*, III, 989. Cf. also M. Lecker, "Muḥammad at Medina: A Geographical Approach", in *JSAI*, 6 (1985), 33 f.

[58] Ibn Isḥāq, *Sīra*, III, 203. It is widely reported from Maʿmar—al-Zuhrī, see Ibn Shabba, *Taʾrīkh*, I, 129 f.; Shāfiʿī, *Musnad*, 493 f.; Ibn Ḥanbal, *Musnad*, I, 228; Yaḥyā, *Kharāj*, 35; Ibn Zanjawayh, *Amwāl*, I, 91. Yet al-Zuhrī's transmission concerning that question is exceedingly confusing, since in other sources Maʿmar—al-Zuhrī states that the Prophet distributed the land among the Muhājirūn, see Wāqidī, *Maghāzī*, I, 378 f.; Ṭabarī, *Tafsīr*, XXVIII, 35 f.; Bayhaqī, *Dalāʾil*, III, 178 f.; Ibn Sayyid al-Nās,

the B. Qurayẓa was distributed among the Muslims, that is to say, not only among the poor of the Muhājirūn, but among all Muslims (or, at least, among all the combatants present, according to the *ghanīma* ruling).[59]

Another "unorthodox" legal ruling is offered by al-Kalbī's statement that the booty—that is, the land or its revenue—taken from the Jews of Khaybar was assigned to the persons who had been present at al-Ḥudaybiya as well as to the Muslims returning from Ethiopia during the siege of Khaybar.[60] (In this case, however, al-Kalbī's transmission according to different sources is far from consistent; also in the *Tafsīr al-Kalbī* a different report is given.)[61] This tradition clearly reflects the wording of Q 59:8 ("*li-l-fuqarāʾ al-muhājirīn*"), with the wording of Q 59:10 ("*wa-lladhīna jāʾū min baʿdihim*") restricting the Muhājirūn mentioned in Q 59:8 to the so-called "first emigrants" (*al-muhājirūn al-awwalūn*; cf. also Q 9:100). As there are some traditions saying that either the emigrants to Ethiopia[62] or the Muslims converted up to the time of al-Ḥudaybiya[63] should be labeled "the first emigrants", there is little doubt that this account of the distribution of the booty in Khaybar is based on the wording of Q 59:8-10 and its interpretation.[64] Of course, it does not amount to a general legal

---

ʿUyūn, II, 73 f. The Zuhrī-transmission adopted in Bukhārī, *Ṣaḥīḥ,* III, 16, and Muslim, *Ṣaḥīḥ,* XII, 75 seems to be a compromise, as it speaks of the distribution as well as of Muḥammad's keeping the *amwāl* for himself. The distribution among the Muhājirūn is also mentioned in Muqātil, *Tafsīr,* IV, 279; Ibn Isḥāq, *Sīra,* III, 201 f.; from Mūsā b. ʿUqba: Bayhaqī, ibid., 182 f.

[59] Ibn Isḥāq, *Sīra,* III, 256. From Mūsā b. ʿUqba: ʿAbd al-Razzāq, *Muṣannaf,* VI, 54 f.; Ibn Ḥanbal, *Musnad,* IX, 181; Bayhaqī, *Dalāʾil,* III, 183, IV, 19; Ibn Ḥajar, *Fatḥ,* VII, 418.

[60] From al-Kalbī quoted in Yaḥyā, *Kharāj,* 42; via Abū Bakr—al-Kalbī—Abū Ṣāliḥ—Ibn ʿAbbās in Ibn Shabba, *Taʾrīkh,* I, 118; Balādhurī, *Futūḥ,* 28; Ibn Sayyid al-Nās, *ʿUyūn,* II, 183.

[61] Kalbī, *Tafsīr,* 226b: Khaybar was made a *waqf* for the benefit of poor Muslims (*al-masākīn*) and therefore not distributed. This is contrasted by a report via Abū Bakr—al-Kalbī in Balādhurī, *Futūḥ,* 22, saying that the *amwāl* Khaybar were given to the Muslims, and another report in Abū Yūsuf, *Kharāj,* 50 f., and Ibn Shabba, *Taʾrīkh,* I, 115, stating that the land was left to the Jews (on the condition of crop-sharing).

[62] From al-Suddī: Ṭabarī, *Tafsīr,* V, 204 (*ad* Q 4:92); cf. also Ibn Ḥajar, *Fatḥ,* VII, 618 f.

[63] From al-Shaʿbī: Ibn Shabba, *Taʾrīkh,* I, 266; Ibn Qutayba, *Maʿārif,* 572; Baghawī, *Tafsīr,* II, 321.

[64] In Ibn Isḥāq, *Sīra,* III, 201, the *muhājirūn al-awwalūn* are explicitly mentioned as the group to receive the *amwāl* from the B. al-Naḍīr (this is paralleled in Wāqidī, *Maghāzī,* I, 382; Farrāʾ, *Maʿānī,* III, 145; Bayhaqī, *Dalāʾil,* III, 182: from Mūsā b. ʿUqba).

ruling for it is applicable only in the specific context of Khaybar and with many Muhājirūn around. Later jurists may have asked: To whom should a booty like that taken at Khaybar be assigned on the day when the last of the Muhājirūn has died? So the "orthodox" version, influenced by legal reasoning, was to interpret Q 59:8-10 in a completely different way; equally different were the legal rulings that were said to be involved in the Khaybar episode.[65]

In order to lay down generally applicable legal rules, the jurists from the second/eighth century onwards had to use traditions concerning events during the Prophet's life—if they were interested in these traditions at all, that is—which were of such a nature as to allow the generalization of the rulings stated or implied in them. Finding those traditions and applying them to the Qur'ānic wording is part of what I would like to call "meta-exegesis", insofar as it transcends other forms of interpreting the Qur'ān by combining it with interest in legal reasoning.[66] As was mentioned above, al-Kalbī's account of what happened to the booty at Medina and Khaybar would therefore not have been very useful in the eyes of the jurists, because it mentions the class of the Muhājirūn that was already extinct in the time of, for instance, al-Zuhrī. Hence it did not allow for generalization. Nevertheless, if compared to the Qur'ānic wording, al-Kalbī's account seems to be a valid interpretation. It only falls short as a legal argument because it is too specific and tied to certain circumstances. In other words, al-Kalbī's account is "haggadic" which I take here to mean "exegesis that bears no trace of legal reasoning and exhibits details connected with specific circumstances".[67]

---

[65] The land conquered in Khaybar was said (a) to have been distributed to the Muslims in its entirety or partially, according to several versions, or (b) to have been left to the inhabitants on the condition of crop-sharing and the payment of revenues. Version (a) is reflected in the later Shāfiʿī position (cf. Shāfiʿī, *Umm,* IV, 256, and idem, *Aḥkām,* II, 157), whereas (b) probably comes near to Mālik's view, see Mālik, *Muwaṭṭaʾ,* II, 703; Ibn Zanjawayh, *Amwāl,* II, 1068). In the *sīra* tradition, all versions are almost equally present, leading more often than not to hopelessly confused and inconsistent accounts of the events at Khaybar. However, account (a) is given in Ibn Isḥāq, *Sīra,* III, 371 (from al-Zuhrī), while (b) is quoted from Mūsā b. ʿUqba in Ibn Ḥanbal, *Musnad,* IX, 182 f.

[66] That is, by combining it with traditions of "juridical value" (Wansbrough, *Quranic Studies*, 186).

[67] The term is used differently by Wansbrough, *Quranic Studies*, 122 ff., and Rippin, *"Tafsīr Ibn ʿAbbās"*, 66, for both stress the narrative continuity that is involved in the haggadic method when interpreting the Qur'ānic wording as if it were a continuous story.

Most of al-Kalbī's traditions are of that kind. This is true not only of his report concerning the booty of Khaybar, but it applies also to what he tells us about the booty taken from al-Naḍīr and Qurayẓa. Another good example of a legal ruling put in terms of a haggadic interpretation is al-Kalbī's statement, contained in his *Tafsīr*, that Q 59:6 refers to the booty taken from the B. al-Naḍīr, because they were settled at only a short distance from Medina[68] so that the Muslims could reach their boroughs on foot, without the need of horses or camels.[69] Although this is a verbatim paraphrase of what is said in Q 59:6, it cannot claim to be a legal ruling which is generally applicable. Jurists like al-Zuhrī, not satisfied with the interpretation of Q 59:6 as a legal ruling that applies only in the case of booty taken near Medina or by assault on foot, took the meaning of "*mā awjaftum ʿalayhi* ..." (Q 59:6) not to be "you did not attack them riding on horses or camels", but as "you took the booty without having to fight for it", that is, the concept of *ghayr ījāf* is interpreted to mean *bi-ghayr qitāl*.[70] This is equally backed by the Qur'ānic wording, the crucial question being to which part of Q 59:6 the negation refers: al-Kalbī and other *tafsīr* authorities stress the fact that no riding animals were used, whereas al-Zuhrī and most jurists stressed the fact that no attack was made. At the same time, al-Zuhrī's interpretation is another example of "meta-exegesis", because with his interpretation he construes the binary opposition "attack/no attack" or "fighting/no fighting" which evolved in Islamic *fiqh* into the important concept of *ʿanwatan/ṣulḥan*.[71] Compared to that, the circumstantial detail that they

---

[68] The B. al-Naḍīr were settled, according to Islamic tradition, two miles outside Medina, see ʿAbd al-Razzāq, *Muṣannaf*, V, 357; Farrā', *Maʿānī*, III, 144 (*ad* Q 59:6); Ibn Saʿd, *Ṭabaqāt*, II, 57; cf. also M. Lecker, *Muslims, Jews and Pagans. Studies on Early Islamic Medina*, Leiden, 1995, 14 f.

[69] Kalbī, *Tafsīr*, 226b. The same is said in Mujāhid, *Tafsīr*, 652, and Farrā', *Maʿānī*, III, 144. In Ṭabarī, *Tafsīr*, XXVIII, 35 f. we find this report attributed to Ibn ʿAbbās and Qatāda. Cf. also Rāzī, *Tafsīr*, XXIX, 285 (*ad* Q 59:6): "It was not a long journey, and as the Muslims these days did not possess many horses and camels, they walked the two miles from Medina."

[70] The traditions from al-Zuhrī, however, do not mention the expression *bi-ghayr qitāl*, but have *bi-ghayr ījāf*, see Shāfiʿī, *Umm*, IV, 178; Yaḥyā, *Kharāj*, 33; Ibn Shabba, *Ta'rīkh*, I, 128; Ibn Ḥanbal, *Musnad*, I, 301. But it becomes clear by implication that here *bi-ghayr ījāf* means "without fighting" or *ṣulḥan* (cf. the following note). Later scholars understood it likewise in that sense, for example Qarāfī, *Dhakhīra*, III, 427 (from Mālik:): "*al-ījāf innamā huwa maqṣūd al-qitāl*."

[71] It is reported from Maʿmar—al-Zuhrī that the *amwāl* of al-Naḍīr were taken by *ṣulḥ*, not *ʿanwatan*, see ʿAbd al-Razzāq, *Tafsīr (Ms.)*, 278; Ṭabarī, *Tafsīr*, XXVIII, 35 f.; Bayhaqī, *Dalā'il*, III, 178 f.

did not attack on horses, but were on foot, would not lead very far under the constraints of legal reasoning.

The reports from al-Kalbī concerning the booty taken from the Jews are variously paralleled or quoted in other *tafsīr* and early *fiqh* sources (the latter mostly of ʿIrāqī origin). One of them also appears in the "orthodox" *sīra* version of Ibn Isḥāq, for he maintains that the *amwāl* of the B. al-Naḍīr were given to the Muhājirūn;[72] the same is reported by Mūsā b. ʿUqba[73] and in some, though not all, of the transmissions from al-Zuhrī.[74] The appearance of this element does not contradict the fact that most of al-Zuhrī's traditions and those in the "orthodox" *sīra* version are influenced by legal "meta-exegesis". It merely shows that the element of the Muhājirūn receiving the booty "survived" in the context of the B. al-Naḍīr episode because the *fayʾ* ruling was treated much more extensively in the context of the Khaybar episode and the conquest of the Sawād. Having occurred later, both the events at Khaybar and in southern ʿIrāq could be considered to supersede the ruling as practiced during the B. al-Naḍīr episode. Accordingly, the element of the emigrants returning from Ethiopia does not turn up in the "orthodox" Khaybar episode of Ibn Isḥāq[75] (yet it is present in that of Mūsā b. ʿUqba),[76] while the participants in al-Ḥudaybiya are mentioned only *en passant*.[77] Instead, two different claims dominate the "orthodox" Khaybar episode: Either the Prophet left the land to the Jews on the condition of crop-sharing,

---

[72] Ibn Isḥāq, *Sīra*, III, 201 f. (from ʿAl. b. Abī Bakr), cited in Yaḥyā, *Kharāj*, 34; Ibn Shabba, *Taʾrīkh*, I, 266; Balādhurī, *Futūḥ*, 18 f. (cf. above, note 64).

[73] Bayhaqī, *Dalāʾil*, III, 182 f.

[74] See above, note 58. Additionally, in some works of the third/ninth century, al-Zuhrī is quoted with the opinion that Khaybar was one of Muḥammad's *ṣafāyā* ("lion's shares", but later sometimes understood as a synonym of *ṣawāfī*, the land property belonging to the ruler and his entourage). He divided it into three parts, allotting two of them to the Muslims and keeping the third for his own expenses, but gave a part of his share to the poor of the Muhājirūn, see Yaḥyā, *Kharāj*, 36; Ibn Shabba, *Taʾrīkh*, I, 122; Balādhurī, *Futūḥ*, 20; Khaṣṣāf, *Awqāf*, 3. From ʿUmar, Wāqidī, *Maghāzī*, I, 378 has a similar report, but al-Wāqidī mixes up the components by mentioning the Muhājirūn twice.

[75] Ibn Isḥāq, *Sīra*, IV, 3 ff. lists the emigrants returned from Ethiopia, but nothing is said of them sharing in the booty of Khaybar. It is even doubtful whether this lengthy chapter on the emigrants was collocated by Ibn Isḥāq in this context, because it is only Ibn Hishām's citation from al-Shaʿbī at the beginning of the chapter which establishes the connection between these emigrants and the Khaybar episode.

[76] From al-Shaʿbī and Mūsā b. ʿUqba: Kalāʿī, *Iktifāʾ*, II, 198 f.; Diyārbakrī, *Taʾrīkh al-khamīs*, II, 55 f.

[77] Ibn Isḥāq, *Sīra*, III, 364. From Mūsā b. ʿUqba—al-Zuhrī: Ibn Shabba, *Taʾrīkh*, I, 116. Cf. also Wāqidī, *Maghāzī*, II, 684; Suyūṭī, *Khaṣāʾiṣ*, I, 410.

or he took some of the land for himself and distributed the remainder among the combatants.[78] Both versions are much closer to the pressing needs of legal reasoning.

The third interpretation mentioned by al-Kalbī—the Muslims walking to the B. al-Naḍīr in order to attack them—is known from *tafsīr* authorities,[79] but it does not appear in the "orthodox" *sīra* versions, since al-Zuhrī had interpreted *ghayr ījāf* to mean "without fighting" or *ṣulḥan*, at least in the context of the B. al-Naḍīr episode. In the Fadak episode, conversely, al-Zuhrī retained the more literal meaning of *ghayr ījāf*, now understood as "without a military expedition" (*bi-lā ʿudda, sayr*), that is, no Muslim force had, literally, to move to Fadak, because the surrender of the town was accomplished by emissaries who went to and fro between the Prophet and the Jews.[80] Therefore, Fadak fell to Muḥammad alone, but he left the land to the inhabitants on the condition of crop-sharing. Ibn Isḥāq incorporated this version in his account.[81] In other sources, the same report, including the very same details, is cited in the name of al-Kalbī.[82]

What we find in the *Tafsīr al-Kalbī*, however, reads slightly differently.[83] It contains a remarkable statement:

---

[78] See above, note 65. The report according to which the land was allotted to the Muslims obviously implies that the Jews of Khaybar had been expelled by Muḥammad. This, however, contradicts the widespread tradition that the Jews were not forced to leave Khaybar during the lifetime of the Prophet. Moreover, many traditions from Nāfiʿ state that the land was distributed among the Muslims only by ʿUmar, see Yaḥyā, *Kharāj,* 39; Abū Yūsuf, *Kharāj,* 50; Ibn Shabba, *Taʾrīkh,* I, 117 f.; Ibn Zanjawayh, *Amwāl,* II, 1067 f. This is also cited from Nāfiʿ in Ibn Isḥāq, *Sīra,* III, 372.

[79] Mujāhid, *Tafsīr,* 652; Muqātil, *Tafsīr,* IV, 278 (*ad* Q 59:6).

[80] Cf. Ibn Isḥāq, *Sīra,* III, 352 and 363 f.; Abū Yūsuf, *Kharāj,* 51 from al-Kalbī (Muḥayyiṣa b. Masʿūd as emissary).

[81] From al-Zuhrī: Ibn Isḥāq, *Sīra,* III, 352 and 368; Ibn Ḥajar, *Fatḥ,* VI, 249. In the *riwāya* al-Bakkāʾī—Ibn Isḥāq—Ibn Abī Bakr in Yaḥyā, *Kharāj,* 43; Balādhurī, *Futūḥ,* 30; in the *riwāya* Ibn Abī Zāʾida—Ibn Isḥāq in Yaḥyā, ibid., 37; Ibn Shabba, *Taʾrīkh,* I, 120 f.; Balādhurī, ibid., 29 f.

[82] Abū Yūsuf, *Kharāj,* 50 f. (al-Kalbī—Abū Ṣāliḥ—Ibn ʿAbbās); cf. also Yaḥyā, *Kharāj,* 41, and Ibn Kathīr, *Bidāya,* IV, 204.

[83] Kalbī, *Tafsīr,* 226b: Fadak was made a *waqf* for the benefit of the poor (cf. also above, note 61). This seems, however, to come near to a tradition from al-Zuhrī according to which Fadak, being one of the Prophet's *ṣafāyā,* was reserved for the needs of travelers (or *jihād* fighters?), which possibly implies *waqf* status, see Yaḥyā, *Kharāj,* 36; Ibn Shabba, *Taʾrīkh,* I, 112; Khaṣṣāf, *Awqāf,* 3.

> Fadak and Khaybar were made a *waqf* by the Prophet for the benefit of the poor, so they remained in his hands during his life. After the Prophet's death, they were left in the hands of Abū Bakr, then likewise in the hands of ʿUmar, ʿUthmān and ʿAlī b. Abī Ṭālib, always remaining in the same condition, and they have remained this way until today.[84]

This is a strong Sunnī claim, because traditions concerning the land at Fadak had become a cornerstone in the polemics between Sunnites and Shīʿites, the latter maintaining that the Prophet (or Abū Bakr, ʿUmar or later caliphs) had assigned the *arḍ* of Fadak as a *ṣadaqa*, unalienable property, to Fāṭima and her family.[85] Thus, the report in the *Tafsīr al-Kalbī* clearly favors the Sunnī view. As it is not attributed to him in other sources, I am inclined to interpret this passage as an interpolation made by the compiler. In the context of one of the most sensitive topics, he deliberately and not without cleverness inserts this Sunnī claim, presumably in order to safeguard al-Kalbī from the criticism of having harbored Shīʿī opinions.[86]

With the exception of the reports concerning Fadak, we find the account of Ibn Isḥāq again to be the least similar to al-Kalbī's. As mentioned above, the "orthodox" *sīra* version offers in regard to the B. Qurayẓa episode a different legal ruling compared to al-Kalbī's statement that the booty from both al-Naḍīr and Qurayẓa was distributed among the poor Muhājirūn. Some of the details, such as walking to the B. al-Naḍīr or giving shares of Khaybar to the emigrants returning from Ethiopia, do not appear in Ibn Isḥāq's *Maghāzī*, although they are mentioned by Mūsā b. ʿUqba and al-Zuhrī. Other haggadic elements are mentioned by Ibn Isḥāq, but their importance is usually dwarfed by different, much longer reports that show the influence of legal reasoning.

---

[84] Kalbī, *Tafsīr*, 226b; *Tanwīr*, VI, 31 f.

[85] For the whole complex of traditions concerning the *ṣadaqāt* allegedly allotted to Fāṭima and her family, see Ibn Shabba, *Taʾrīkh*, I, 122-35; Samhūdī, *Wafāʾ*, III, 995 ff.; cf. also M.J. Kister, "Land Property and *Jihād*. A Discussion of Some Early Traditions", in *JESHO*, 34 (1991), 270-311. The Shīʿī *tafsīr* of Furāt (I, 322, *ad* Q 30:38; see also Ibn Saʿd, *Ṭabaqāt*, II, 315 f.; Khayḍarī, *al-Lafẓ al-mukarram*, 167) explicitly states that Fadak was handed over to Fāṭima and her family.

[86] See above under I. Al-Kalbī is quoted in Furāt, *Tafsīr* (see above, note 23). U. Rubin, *The Eye of the Beholder: The Life of Muḥammad as Viewed by the Early Muslims*, Princeton, 1995, 91 and 94 quotes traditions from al-Kalbī that recur in Shīʿī commentaries; cf. above, note 2.

VI. Conclusion 1.: Al-Kalbī and the *Sīra* Tradition

The reports from al-Kalbī concerning Muḥammad's conflict with the Arabian Jews contain more information on legal topics than other *tafsīr* material of the second/eighth century. Yet most of those reports are couched in the form of interpretations that lack the generality demanded by the jurists, and stick to specific events or circumstances. In this, they are similar to many traditions that are known from Mujāhid, Muqātil, and al-Shaʿbī, to mention only a few. Most of what we find in al-Kalbī's transmission is quite "unorthodox", and does not fit the standard *sīra* account.[87] Whereas the major part of these "unorthodox" elements are paralleled or echoed in reports transmitted from al-Zuhrī and Mūsā b. ʿUqba, it is largely absent from Ibn Isḥāq's *Maghāzī* and the later "orthodox" tradition.

Concerning legal rules, the exegetes and jurists came up with different interpretations that more often than not were incompatible with each other. Various verses could be invoked to support certain interpretations. This led to the result that one verse became tied to numerous interpretations, a difficult situation especially in view of Qurʾānic redundancy—the best example in our case being the much debated question whether Q 8:1 (the *anfāl* verse), Q 8:41 (the *ghanīma* verse), and Q 59:7 (the second *fayʾ* verse) contain the same legal ruling or not. Different interpretations, however, often meant different stories or episodes which were intended to prove the point made. Finally, and perhaps most importantly, the more episodes, the better the chances to illustrate or strengthen one's own interpretation by them. This is due to the technique of *naskh*, because what happened in a later episode would have superseded or invalidated the practice of an earlier episode. Thus episodes offering information on topics as vital as practices of warfare, sharing the booty, and assigning tracts of

---

[87] The most "unorthodox" tradition which I was able to find in the name of al-Kalbī, has not been mentioned yet. It is preserved in Baghawī's *Tafsīr*, *ad* Q 9:29, and says: "[This verse] was revealed when the Prophet concluded a treaty (*ṣulḥ*) with the Qurayẓa and al-Naḍīr. This was the first *jizya* the Muslims (*ahl al-Islām*) received, and the first humiliation of the *ahl al-kitāb* ...." This tradition could refer to the Khaybar episode, for there are some reports mentioning that the Jews of Khaybar were effectively paying the *jizya* tribute; cf. also H. Busse, "The Destruction of the Temple and its Reconstruction in the Light of Muslim Exegesis of *Sūra* 17:2-8", in *JSAI*, 20 (1996), 7 (for the interpretation of Q 17:8; the quoted texts, however, hardly sustain Busse's view that the Jews of al-Naḍīr and Qurayẓa actually paid the *jizya*). But the implications of this tradition merit another study.

land—as all the episodes of conflict between the Prophet and the Jews—multiplied, as did the respective interpretations in legal dispute, in order to find the reported practice/legal interpretation that could be considered most valid.[88] The "orthodox" *sīra* account, as it developed in the Medinan milieu, is strongly influenced by this kind of legal reasoning, yet it was of little interest to *tafsīr* scholars. Therefore, up to the third/ninth century, *tafsīr* is the field where one encounters many traditions that are decidedly "unorthodox".

The fact that these "unorthodox" elements have been preserved in works of *tafsīr* as well as in some early *maghāzī* traditions, but are no longer present in the pivotal accounts of Ibn Isḥāq and al-Wāqidī, shows to my mind that we are dealing here with an evolutionary process that is rooted in exegesis. Accordingly, we find many (implicit and explicit) traces of the *tafsīr* material in traditions ascribed to *sīra* authorities from the period before Ibn Isḥāq. Thus it seems that the exegetical material and the traditions in early *tafsīr* literature are not abstracted from or adapted to the accounts as we find them in *maghāzī* traditions, but, on the contrary, precede them.[89] Due to the lack of interest in solving legal problems, these traditions have been preserved in works of *tafsīr*, whereas they were often pushed aside in the *sīra* and *maghāzī* tradition.

VII. Conclusion 2.: Al-Kalbī and His *Tafsīr*

The *Tafsīr al-Kalbī* is a confusing document.[90] It has been noted that even when the *isnād* al-Kalbī—Abū Ṣāliḥ—Ibn ʿAbbās is used, much

[88] It is very interesting to observe that the later an episode occurred in Muḥammad's lifetime, the less undisputed are the legal rulings involved in it, and, even more striking, the more similar to what was usually put forward by the jurists of the second/eighth century. Cf. also J. Schacht, "A Revaluation of Islamic Tradition", in *JRAS*, 49 (1949), 151: "[The] transformation of legal propositions into pseudo-historical information is one aspect. ... We find new traditions at every successive stage of doctrine."

[89] It has recently been argued to the contrary by Uri Rubin. He considers the Qur'ānic wording as a secondary, intrusive element in the *sīra* tradition, which is seen as a "basically non-Quranic framework" (*Eye of the Beholder,* 224). The *asbāb al-nuzūl*, an important part of the *maghāzī* tradition, are likewise said to consist of "independent non-Quranic *sīra* material which gained its Quranic links at a secondary stage"; therefore, the "Quran does not belong to the literary hard core of *sīra* material" (ibid., 227).

[90] For the following, cf. Rippin, "*Tafsīr Ibn ʿAbbās*".

of it is not transmitted in other sources, while many traditions are missing from the *Tafsīr* that we may reasonably assume to be part of al-Kalbī's transmission. Moreover, the *Tafsīr* is very concise and does not exhibit the style of many reports from al-Kalbī that we find elsewhere. "Unorthodox" traditions intermingle with those more "orthodox". No consistent account can be reconstructed that is based exclusively on the *Tafsīr* and at the same time gives equal weight to all the reports contained in it; we also came across some cases of later interpolation. Therefore, it probably is correct to assign the actual compilation of the *Tafsīr*, as we have it today, to the late third or early fourth/tenth century.[91]

On the other hand, the *Tafsīr al-Kalbī* is not wholly invaluable as a source for the *tafsīr* of the second/eighth century and, for that matter, source reconstruction. The "unorthodox" elements it contains show in many cases striking similarities or connections to interpretations that in other sources are attributed either to al-Kalbī himself or to other *tafsīr* and *maghāzī* authorities of the second/eighth century. Many of these interpretations are quoted in sources earlier than the late third/ninth century. For example, with regard to the passage *ad* Q 59:2-15, verbatim or almost verbatim quotations of most of the wording in the name of al-Kalbī can easily be found in al-Farrā', *Ma'ānī*, and al-Balādhurī, *Futūḥ*.[92] So much can be said on the basis of intrinsic criteria. What cannot be said, however, is whether anything of what we find in al-Kalbī's name goes further back to Ibn ʿAbbās. The case of Ibn ʿAbbās is of unparalleled complexity and many undoubtedly late and secondary traditions are connected with his name. As one of the most important *tafsīr* authorities in the Islamic tradition, almost every tradition was sooner or later attributed to him. It seems impossible to make out the historical core, if there is any.[93] This was already recognized by al-Shāfiʿī to whom the sentence is

[91] Rippin, "Al-Zuhrī", 23 , and idem, "*Tafsīr Ibn ʿAbbās*", 71.

[92] For the resemblance between the grammatical terminology employed in Farrā', *Maʿānī*, and that used in the *Tafsīr al-Kalbī*, see Versteegh, *Grammar and Qur'ānic Exegesis*, 197 f.

[93] See C. Gilliot, "Portrait «mythique» d'Ibn ʿAbbās", in *Arabica*, 32 (1985), 179 ff., and Rippin, "*Tafsīr Ibn ʿAbbās*", 73 ff. Western scholars largely agree that the *Tafsīr al-Kalbī* in the present form does not go back to the teaching of Ibn ʿAbbās, cf. F. Leemhuis, "Origins and Early Development of the *tafsīr* Tradition", in A. Rippin (ed.), *Approaches to the History of the Interpretation of the Qur'ān*, Oxford, 1988, 25. It has been argued to the contrary, however, by Versteegh, *Grammar and Qur'ānic Exegesis*, 59 f.

ascribed: "Of all the reports from Ibn ʿAbbās, only about a hundred are truly reliable."[94]

Therefore I suggest that the *Tafsīr al-Kalbī*, notwithstanding its late redaction or literary form, indeed contains a core of old material that might be attributed to al-Kalbī or, at least, to his generation. The bulk of this material would consist of the "unorthodox" traditions that can be cross-checked with quotations in other sources; this material must have been current in the East where the transmission from al-Kalbī was fairly known. These "unorthodox" elements should not be discarded or invalidated for external reasons only. To reject al-Kalbī and other early *mufassirūn* was the prerogative of al-Jāḥiẓ;[95] as to ourselves, we maybe should adopt the pragmatism of Sufyān al-Thawrī.[96] He said: "Beware of al-Kalbī!" and some people objected: "But you yourself are transmitting from him!" "Right," he answered, "but I know which of his traditions are correct and which are faulty."

Bibliography

ʿAbd al-Razzāq, Abū Bakr al-Ṣanʿānī, *al-Muṣannaf*, ed. Ḥabīb al-Raḥmān al-Aʿẓamī, 12 vols., ²Beirut, 1403/1983.
———, *al-Tafsīr*, ed. ʿAbd al-Muʿṭī Aḥmad Qalʿajī, 2 vols., Beirut, 1411/1991.
———, *al-Tafsīr*, ms. *tafsīr* 242, Dār al-kutub, Cairo.
Abū Ḥayyān, Muḥammad b. Yūsuf, *al-Tafsīr al-kabīr* (*al-Baḥr al-muḥīṭ*), 8 vols., repr. Riyad, n.d. [1911].
Abū Nuʿaym, Aḥmad b.ʿAbd Allāh, *Dalāʾil al-nubuwwa*, ²Hyderabad, 1369/1950.
Abū l-Shaykh, ʿAbd Allāh b. Muḥammad, *Akhlāq al-nabī*, ed. ʿIṣām al-Dīn al-Ṣabābaṭī, ²Cairo, 1413/1993.
Abū Yūsuf, Yaʿqūb b. Ibrāhīm, *Kitāb al-Kharāj*, repr. Beirut, n.d. [Cairo, 1352/1933].
al-Baghawī, al-Ḥusayn b. Masʿūd, *al-Tafsīr* (*Maʿālim al-tanzīl*), ed. Khālid al-ʿAkk and Marwān Sawār, 4 vols., Beirut, 1413/1992.
al-Balādhurī, Aḥmad b. Yaḥyā, *Kitāb Futūḥ al-buldān*, ed. M.J. de Goeje, Leiden, 1866.
al-Bayhaqī, Aḥmad b. al-Ḥusayn, *Dalāʾil al-nubuwwa wa-maʿrifat aḥwāl ṣāḥib al-sharīʿa*, ed. ʿAbd al-Muʿṭī Qalʿajī, 7 vols., Beirut, 1408/1988.
Bell, R., "Sūrat al-Ḥashr: A Study of its Composition", in *Muslim World*, 38 (1948), 29-42.
al-Bukhārī, Muḥammad b. Ismāʿīl, *al-Jāmiʿ al-ṣaḥīḥ (matn mashkūl bi-ḥāshiyat al-Sindī)*, 4 vols., Cairo, n.d.
———, *Kitāb al-Ḍuʿafāʾ al-ṣaghīr*, ed. Maḥmūd I. Zāhid, Beirut, 1406/1986.
———, *al-Taʾrīkh al-kabīr*, 8 vols., Beirut, n.d.
Burton, John, *Introduction to the Ḥadīth*, Edinburgh, 1994.
Busse, H., "The Destruction of the Temple and its Reconstruction in the Light of

[94] Quoted in Subkī, *Ṭabaqāt*, II, 71. Further cited in Rippin, "*Tafsīr Ibn ʿAbbās*", 52, and Leemhuis, "Origins", 25, both from Suyūṭī, *Itqān*, II, 417.
[95] Cf. Jāḥiẓ, *Ḥayawān*, I, 343.
[96] As quoted in Tirmidhī, *Sunan*, V, 398.

Muslim Exegesis of *Sūra* 17:2-8", in *Jerusalem Studies in Arabic and Islam*, 20 (1996), 1-17.
al-Dāʾūdī, Shams al-Dīn Muḥammad, *Ṭabaqāt al-mufassirīn*, 2 vols., Beirut, n.d.
al-Dhahabī, Shams al-Dīn Muḥammad b. Aḥmad, *Siyar aʿlām al-nubalāʾ*, ed. Shuʿayb al-Arnāʾūṭ and Ḥusayn al-Asad, vols. V-VI, ²Beirut, 1402/1982.
al-Diyārbakrī, al-Ḥusayn, *Taʾrīkh al-khamīs fī aḥwāl anfas nafīs*, 2 vols., repr. Beirut, n.d. [Cairo, 1283/1866].
Dozy, Reinhart, *Supplément aux dictionnaires arabes*, 2 vols., Leiden, 1881.
van Ess, Josef, *Ungenützte Texte zur Karrāmīya. Eine Materialsammlung*, Heidelberg, 1980.
al-Farrāʾ, Yaḥyā b. Ziyād, *Maʿānī al-Qurʾān*, ed. Muḥammad al-Najjār et al., 3 vols., Cairo, 1955 f. (I-II), 1973 (III).
al-Fazārī, Abū Isḥāq, *Kitāb al-Siyar*, ed. Fārūq Ḥammāda, Beirut, 1408/1987.
Furāt, Abū l-Qāsim b. Ibrāhīm, *al-Tafsīr*, ed. Muḥammad al-Kāẓim, 2 vols., Beirut, 1412/1992.
Gilliot, C., "Portrait «mythique» d'Ibn ʿAbbās", in *Arabica*, 32 (1985), 127-84.
Goldfeld, I., "The *Tafsīr* of Abdallah b. ʿAbbās", in *Der Islam*, 58 (1981), 125-35.
Goldziher, Ignaz, *Die Richtungen der islamischen Koranauslegung*, Leiden, 1920.
al-Ḥalabī, Nūr al-Dīn ʿAlī, *Insān al-ʿuyūn fī sīrat al-amīn al-maʾmūn*, 3 vols., repr. Beirut, n.d. [Cairo, 1320/1902].
Horst, H., "Zur Überlieferung im Korankommentar aṭ-Ṭabarīs", in *Zeitschrift der Deutschen Morgenländischen Gesellschaft*, 28 (1953), 290-307.
Ibn al-Athīr, ʿAlī b. Muḥammad ʿIzz al-Dīn, *al-Lubāb fī tahdhīb al-ansāb*, ed. Ḥusām al-Dīn al-Qudsī, 3 vols., Cairo, 1356 ff./1938 ff.
Ibn Durayd, Muḥammad Abū Bakr, *Kitāb Jamharat al-lugha*, 4 vols., Hyderabad, 1345.
Ibn Ḥabīb, Muḥammad Abū Jaʿfar, *Kitāb al-Muḥabbar*, ed. Ilse Lichtenstaedter, Hyderabad, 1361/1942.
Ibn Ḥajar al-ʿAsqalānī, Aḥmad b. ʿAlī, *Fatḥ al-bārī bi-sharḥ Ṣaḥīḥ al-Bukhārī*, ed. ʿAbd al-ʿAzīz b. Bāz and Muḥammad Fuʾād ʿAbd al-Bāqī, 15 vols., Beirut, 1410/ 1989.
———, *al-Iṣāba fī tamyīz al-ṣaḥāba*, ed. ʿAlī al-Bajāwī, 8 vols., Cairo, 1971 f.
———, *Taʿrīf ahl al-taqdīs bi-marātib al-mawṣūfīn bi-l-tadlīs*, ed. ʿAbd al-Ghaffār al-Bandārī and Muḥammad Aḥmad ʿAbd al-ʿAzīz, ²Beirut, 1407/1987.
Ibn Ḥanbal, Aḥmad (*ʿanhu*), *Kitāb al-ʿIlal wa-maʿrifat al-rijāl*, ed. Waṣiyy Allāh b. Muḥammad ʿAbbās, 4 vols., Beirut, Riyad, 1408/1988.
———, *al-Musnad*, ed. Aḥmad Muḥammad Shākir, vols. I-IX, Cairo, 1368 ff./1949 ff.
Ibn Isḥāq, Muḥammad (—al-Bakkāʾī—Ibn Hishām), *al-Sīra al-nabawiyya*, ed. Muṣṭafā al-Saqqā et al., 4 vols., repr. Beirut, n.d.
Ibn al-Jawzī, ʿAbd al-Raḥmān b. ʿAlī, *Kitāb al-Ḍuʿafāʾ wa-l-matrūkīn*, ed. Abū l-Fidāʾ ʿAlī al-Qāḍī, 3 vols. in 2, Beirut, 1406/1986.
Ibn Kathīr, Ismāʿīl b. ʿUmar, *al-Bidāya wa-l-nihāya*, ed. Aḥmad Abū Mulḥim et al., 15 vols., Beirut, n.d.
———, *Tafsīr al-Qurʾān*, 4 vols., Cairo, n.d.
Ibn Khallikān, Aḥmad b. Muḥammad, *Wafayāt al-aʿyān wa-anbāʾ abnāʾ al-zamān*, ed. Iḥsān ʿAbbās, 7 vols., Beirut, n.d.
Ibn Manẓūr, Muḥammad b. Mukarram, *Lisān al-ʿArab*, 15 vols., Beirut, 1374-76/ 1955 f.
Ibn Qutayba, ʿAbd Allāh b. Muslim, *Kitāb al-Maʿārif*, ed. Tharwat ʿAkāshah, Cairo, 1960.
———, *Taʾwīl mushkil al-Qurʾān*, ed. Aḥmad Ṣaqr, Cairo, n.d.
Ibn Rajab, ʿAbd al-Raḥmān Zayn al-Dīn, *Sharḥ ʿIlal al-Tirmidhī*, ed. Ṣubḥī al-Samarrāʾī, ²Beirut, 1405/1985.

Ibn Saʿd, Muḥammad, *al-Ṭabaqāt al-kubrā*, 8 vols., Beirut, 1376 ff./1957 ff.

Ibn Sayyid al-Nās, Fatḥ al-Dīn Muḥammad, *ʿUyūn al-athar fī funūn al-maghāzī wa-l-shamāʾil wa-l-siyar*, ed. Ibrāhīm Muḥammad Ramaḍān, 2 vols., Beirut, 1414/1993.

Ibn Shabba, ʿUmar, *Taʾrīkh (Akhbār) al-Madīna*, ed. ʿAlī Muḥammad Dandal and Yāsīn Bayān, 2 vols., Beirut, 1417/1996.

Ibn Taymiyya, Aḥmad b.ʿAbd al-Ḥalīm, *ʿIlm al-ḥadīth*, ed. Mūsā Muḥammad ʿAlī, Beirut, 1405/1985.

———, *al-Muqaddima fī uṣūl al-tafsīr*, ed. F. Aḥmad Zamarlī, Beirut, 1414/1994.

———, *al-Ṣārim al-maslūl ʿalā shātim al-rasūl*, ed. Khālid al-ʿAlamī, Beirut, 1416/1996.

Ibn Zanjawayh, Ḥumayd, *Kitāb al-Amwāl*, ed. Shākir Fayyāḍ, 3 vols., Riyad, 1406/1986.

ʿIyāḍ, al-Qāḍī, *Kitāb al-Shifāʾ bi-taʿrīf ḥuqūq al-muṣṭafā*, ed. Kamāl Basyūnī Zaghlūl al-Miṣrī, 2 vols. in 1, Beirut, 1416/1995.

al-Jāḥiẓ, *Kitāb al-Ḥayawān*, ed. ʿAbd al-Salām Muḥammad Hārūn, 7 vols., Cairo, 1378/1958.

al-Kalāʿī, Sulaymān Abū l-Rabīʿ, *al-Iktifāʾ bi-mā taḍammanahū min maghāzī rasūlillāh*, ed. Muḥammad Kamāl al-Dīn, 4 vols., Beirut, 1417/1997.

al-Kalbī, Muḥammad b. al-Sāʾib, *al-Tafsīr (ʿan Ibn ʿAbbās)*, Ms. *Ar.* 4224, Chester Beatty Library, Dublin.

al-Khaṣṣāf, Aḥmad b. ʿAmr, *Kitāb Aḥkām al-awqāf*, repr. Cairo, n.d. [Cairo, 1322/1904].

al-Khayḍarī, Quṭb al-Dīn Muḥammad, *al-Lafẓ al-mukarram bi-khaṣāʾiṣ al-nabī al-muʿaẓẓam*, ed. Muṣṭafā Ḥamīda, Beirut, 1417/1997.

Kister, M.J., "Notes on the Papyrus Text about Muḥammad's Campaign against the Banū al-Naḍīr", in *Archiv Orientální*, 32 (1964), 233-36.

———, "The Massacre of the Banū Qurayẓa—A Reexamination of a Tradition", in *Jerusalem Studies in Arabic and Islam*, 8 (1986), 61-96.

———, "Land Property and *Jihād*. A Discussion of Some Early Traditions", in *Journal of the Economic and Social History of the Orient*, 34 (1991), 270-311.

Kohlberg, Etan, *A Medieval Muslim Scholar at Work. Ibn Ṭāwūs and his Library*, Leiden, 1992.

Lecker, Michael, "Muḥammad at Medina: A Geographical Approach", in *Jerusalem Studies in Arabic and Islam*, 6 (1985), 29-62.

———, *The Banū Sulaym. A Contribution to the Study of Early Islam*, Jerusalem, 1989.

———, *Muslims, Jews and Pagans. Studies on Early Islamic Medina*, Leiden, 1995.

———, "The Death of the Prophet Muḥammad's Father: Did Wāqidī Invent Some of the Evidence?", in *Zeitschrift der Deutschen Morgenländischen Gesellschaft*, 145 (1995), 9-27.

Leemhuis, F., "Origin and Early Development of the *tafsīr* Tradition", in A. Rippin, *Approaches*, 13-30.

Mālik b. Anas, *al-Muwaṭṭaʾ* (*ʿan* Yaḥyā b. Yaḥyā), ed. Muḥammad Fuʾād ʿAbd al-Bāqī, 2 vols., repr. Beirut, 1406/1985.

al-Mizzī, Yūsuf, *Tahdhīb al-kamāl fī asmāʾ al-rijāl*, ed. Shuʿayb al-Arnāʾūṭ and B. ʿAlī Maʿrūf, 15 vols., ^{3}Beirut, 1408/1988.

Mughulṭāy b. Qulayj, *al-Ishāra ilā sīrat al-muṣṭafā*, ed. Muḥammad al-Futayḥ, Damascus-Beirut, 1416/1996.

Mujāhid b. Jabr al-Makkī, *al-Tafsīr*, ed. Muḥammad ʿAbd al-Salām Abū l-Nīl, Cairo, 1410/1989.

Muqātil b. Sulaymān, *al-Tafsīr*, ed. ʿAbd Allāh Maḥmūd Shiḥāta, 4 vols., Cairo, 1979-88.

Muslim b. al-Ḥajjāj, *Kitāb al-Ṣaḥīḥ (bi-sharḥ al-Nawawī)*, ed. Muḥammad ʿAbd al-Laṭīf, 18 vols., ²Beirut, 1392/1972.
al-Nadīm, Muḥammad b. Isḥāq, *Kitāb al-Fihrist*, ed. Riẓā Tajaddud b. ʿAlī al-Māzandarānī, ³Beirut, 1408/1988.
al-Nasāʾī, Aḥmad b. ʿAlī, *Kitāb al-Ḍuʿafāʾ wa-l-matrūkīn*, printed in al-Bukhārī, *Ḍuʿafāʾ*.
al-Nīsābūrī, al-Ḥākim, *al-Mustadrak ʿalā l-Ṣaḥīḥayn*, ed. Muṣṭafā ʿAbd al-Qādir ʿAṭāʾ, 4 vols., Beirut, 1411/1990.
al-Qarāfī, Aḥmad Shihāb al-Dīn, *al-Dhakhīra*, ed. Muḥammad Ḥajjī, 14 vols., Beirut, 1414/1994.
al-Qasṭallānī, Shihāb al-Dīn Aḥmad, *al-Mawāhib al-ladunīya bi-l-minaḥ al-muḥammadīya*, ed. Maʾmūn al-Jannān, 3 vols., Beirut, 1416/1996.
al-Qurṭubī, Muḥammad b. Aḥmad, *al-Tafsīr (al-Jāmiʿ li-aḥkām al-Qurʾān)*, ed. Aḥmad al-Bardūnī, 20 vols., Beirut, 1385/1966 f.
al-Rāfiʿī, ʿAbd al-Karīm al-Qazwīnī, *al-Tadwīn fī akhbār Qazwīn*, ed. ʿAzīzullāh al-ʿUṭāridī, 4 vols., Hyderabad, 1404/1984.
al-Rāzī, Fakhr al-Dīn Muḥammad, *al-Tafsīr (Mafātīḥ al-ghayb...)*, 30 vols., Beirut, n.d.
Rippin, Andrew, "Al-Zuhrī, *Naskh al-Qurʾān* and the Problem of Early *Tafsīr* Texts", in *Bulletin of the School of Oriental and African Studies*, 47 (1984), 22-43.
———, "*Tafsīr Ibn ʿAbbās* and Criteria for Dating Early *Tafsīr* Texts", in *Jerusalem Studies in Arabic and Islam*, 18 (1994), 38-83.
———, (ed.), *Approaches to the History of the Interpretation of the Qurʾān*, Oxford, 1988.
Rubin, Uri, *The Eye of the Beholder: The Life of Muḥammad as Viewed by the Early Muslims*, Princeton, 1995.
al-Ṣafadī, Ṣalāḥ al-Dīn Khalīl b. Aybak, *al-Wāfī bi-l-wafayāt*, vol. III, ed. Sven Dedering, Damascus, 1953.
al-Samʿānī, Abū Saʿd ʿAbd al-Karīm, *Kitāb al-Ansāb*, ed. ʿAbd Allāh al-Bārūdī, 5 vols., Beirut, 1408/1988.
———, *al-Taḥbīr fī l-muʿjam al-kabīr*, ed. Munīra Sālim, 2 vols., Baghdad, 1395/1975.
al-Samhūdī, Nūr al-Dīn ʿAlī, *Wafāʾ al-wafā bi-akhbār dār al-muṣṭafā*, ed. Muḥammad ʿAbd al-Ḥamīd, 4 vols. in 3, repr. Beirut, 1404/1984 [Cairo, 1374/1955].
Schacht, J., "A Revaluation of Islamic Tradition", in *Journal of the Royal Asiatic Society*, 3-4 (1949), 143-54.
Schöller, Marco, "In welchem Jahr wurden die Banū n-Naḍīr aus Medina vertrieben? Eine Untersuchung zur 'kanonischen' *Sīra*-Chronologie", in *Der Islam*, 73 (1996), 1-39.
———, "Die Palmen (*līna*) der Banū n-Naḍīr und die Interpretation von Koran 59:5. Eine Untersuchung zur Bedeutung des koranischen Wortlauts in den ersten Jahrhunderten islamischer Gelehrsamkeit", in *Zeitschrift der Deutschen Morgenländischen Gesellschaft*, 146 (1996), 317-80.
———, *Exegetisches Denken und Prophetenbiographie. Eine quellenkritische Analyse der* Sīra-*Überlieferung zu Muḥammads Konflikt mit den Juden*, Wiesbaden, 1998.
al-Shāfiʿī, Muḥammad b. Idrīs, *Aḥkām al-Qurʾān (compiled by al-Bayhaqī)*, ed. Muḥammad al-Kawtharī and Qāsim al-Rifāʿī, 2 vols. in 1, Beirut, n.d.
———, *Kitāb al-Umm*, ed. Maḥmūd Maṭarjī, 9 vols. in 8, Beirut, 1413/1993.
———, *al-Musnad*, printed in *Kitāb al-Umm*, vol. IX, 353-520.
Sibṭ Ibn al-ʿAjamī, al-Burhān al-Ḥalabī, *al-Kashf al-khathīth ʿamman rumiya bi-waḍʿ al-ḥadīth*, ed. Ṣubḥī al-Samarrāʾī, Baghdad, 1984.
al-Subkī, ʿAbd al-Wahhāb Tāj al-Dīn, *Ṭabaqāt al-Shāfiʿīya al-kubrā*, ed. Maḥmūd al-Ṭunāḥī and ʿAbd al-Fattāḥ Muḥammad al-Ḥilw, 10 vols., repr. Beirut, n.d. [Cairo, 1969-76].
al-Ṣūlī, Muḥammad b. Yaḥyā, *Adab al-kuttāb*, ed. Muḥammad al-Atharī, repr. Beirut, n.d.

al-Suyūṭī, Jalāl al-Dīn, *al-Itqān fī ʿulūm al-Qurʾān*, 2 vols., Beirut, 1407/1987.
———, *al-Khaṣāʾiṣ al-kubrā*, 2 vols., Beirut, 1405/1985.
———, *Lubāb al-nuqūl fī asbāb al-nuzūl*, printed in the margin of *Tafsīr al-Jalālayn*, ed. Marwān Sawār, Damascus, 1407/1987.
al-Ṭabarī, Muḥammad b. Jarīr, *al-Tafsīr (Jāmiʿ al-bayān)*, 30 vols., ³Cairo, 1388/ 1968.
Tanwīr al-miqbās min tafsīr Ibn ʿAbbās, printed in the margin of al-Suyūṭī, *al-Durr al-manthūr fī l-tafsīr bi-l-maʾthūr*, 6 vols., repr. Beirut, n.d. [Cairo, 1314].
Ṭāshköprüzādeh, Aḥmad b. Muṣṭafā, *Miftāḥ al-saʿāda wa-miṣbāḥ al-siyāda*, 3 vols., Hyderabad, 1328 ff.
al-Thawrī, Sufyān b. Saʿīd, *al-Tafsīr*, ed. Ibrāhīm ʿAlī ʿArshī et al., Beirut, 1403/ 1983.
al-Tirmidhī, Muḥammad b. ʿĪsā, *Kitāb al-Sunan (al-Jāmiʿ al-ṣaḥīḥ)*, ed. ʿAbd al-Raḥmān Muḥammad ʿUthmān, 5 vols., Medina, n.d.
Versteegh, Cornelius H.M., *Arabic Grammar and Qurʾānic Exegesis in Early Islam*, Leiden, 1993.
al-Wāḥidī, ʿAlī b. Aḥmad, *Asbāb nuzūl al-Qurʾān*, ed. Kamāl Basyūnī Zaghlūl, Beirut, 1411/1991.
Wansbrough, John, *Quranic Studies: Sources and Methods of Scriptural Interpretation*, Oxford, 1977.
al-Wāqidī, Muḥammad b. ʿUmar, *Kitāb al-Maghāzī*, ed. Marsden Jones, 3 vols., repr. Beirut, 1409/1989 [London, Oxford, 1966].
al-Yāfiʿī, ʿAbd Allāh b. Asʿad, *Mirʾāt al-jinān fī maʿrifat mā yuʿtabir min ḥawādith al-zamān*, ed. Khalīl al-Manṣūr, 4 vols., Beirut, 1417/1997.
al-Yaghmūrī, Yūsuf b. Aḥmad, *Nūr al-qabas al-mukhtaṣar min al-Muqtabas fī akhbār (li-l-Marzubānī)*, ed. Rudolf Sellheim, Wiesbaden, 1384/1964.
Yaḥyā b. Ādam, *Kitāb al-Kharāj*, ed. Aḥmad Muḥammad Shākir, repr. Beirut, n.d. [Cairo, 1347].
al-Zarkashī, Badr al-Dīn Muḥammad, *al-Burhān fī ʿulūm al-Qurʾān*, ed. Muḥammad Abū l-Faḍl Ibrāhīm, 4 vols., Cairo, 1376 f./1957 f.

SĪRA AND THE QUESTION OF TRADITION

Adrien Leites

Works devoted, either wholly or in part, to the life of the Prophet Muḥammad were produced by Muslim scholars—Sunnī as well as Shīʿī—from the eighth century up to the nineteenth AD. The *Sīra* of Muḥammad b. Isḥāq (d. 150/767) and the *Jawāhir al-biḥār fī faḍāʾil al-nabī al-mukhtār* of Yūsuf b. Ismāʿīl al-Nabhānī (d. 1930 AD) may be taken as representing the first and the last point respectively in this range of works. Such works are composed of individual accounts separated by chains of transmission or mentions of source, and arranged chronologically, thematically, or partly in chronological order and partly according to theme. Such accounts are generally subsumed under the term *sīra*, or "conduct" (of the Prophet). These two facts, namely, a range of works extending over a long time span and covering a vast area of scholarship divided by confessional boundaries on the one hand, and their fragmentation into discrete units on the other hand, suggest the existence of a *sīra* Tradition. By "Tradition", I mean a process whereby objects of the past are handed down over time in a certain group, and thus are brought forward as worthy of consideration in the present.[1]

Once we have acknowledged the fact that Tradition is concerned not with the preservation of inherited objects but with their actualization, to what extent can we actually reconstruct the development of *sīra* Tradition? My central argument here will be that any attempt to answer this question should involve an inquiry into the structure of *sīra* Tradition, as well as an effort to discern its significance. Before presenting my method and my interpretation, I would like to review briefly the Western treatments of *sīra* relevant to the issue addressed here.

[1] This definition, as well as the general approach to Tradition adopted here, is inspired by the work of E. Shils, *Tradition*, Chicago, 1981.

I. Western Treatments

The first kind of treatment which we should consider is commonly known as source criticism; it aims at eliciting developments from the material included in available works. The basic tool of source criticism is comparison. By comparing divergent accounts of the same event, we are able to identify an original version, and to detect the changes it underwent in the course of transmission. Such a reconstruction can be achieved on the basis of the periods in which works were produced, or on the basis of the chains of transmission. These two kinds of evidence are used exclusively of one another by two distinct kinds of source criticism, which themselves reach different results.

The use of the periods in which works were produced as evidence of developments is governed by a general principle, which may be stated as follows: when an account found in a work W departs from the accounts found in previous works, we should conclude that the departure came about during the period separating W from the last of its predecessors. This principle can be applied at any point in the range of works delineated above, and thus is potentially relevant to the reconstruction of the development of *sīra* Tradition. However, the results achieved by this kind of source criticism, in addition to being questionable, seldom go beyond the detection of material changes, to the exclusion of structural ones. A convenient, though not unambiguous, designation of such changes is "the introduction of new elements". On the other hand, the comparison is generally restricted to two or a few early Sunnī works, both because the introduction of new elements over a long time span is unlikely to have taken place and because the practitioners of this kind of source criticism are primarily interested in the formative period of the Islamic Tradition.[2]

The use of *isnād*s as evidence of developments implies, on the one

[2] The first scholar to use the periods in which works were produced as evidence of the introduction of new elements was J. Horovitz (see "Salmān al-Fārisī", in *Der Islam*, 12 (1922), 178-80). More recently, this kind of source criticism was practiced by M. Cook (see *Muhammad*, Oxford, 1983, 63-7) and P. Crone (see *Meccan Trade and the Rise of Islam*, Princeton, 1987, 223-25). The results of Horovitz, as well as those of Cook and Crone, are attained through comparison of Ibn Isḥāq (d. 150/767) and al-Wāqidī (d. 207/823). It is likewise through comparison of Ibn Isḥāq, al-Wāqidī and al-Bukhārī (d. 256/870) that the gradual shift from *narratio* to *exemplum* is reconstructed by J. Wansbrough (see *The Sectarian Milieu. Content and Composition of Islamic Salvation History*, Oxford, 1978, 76-9).

hand, that early works constitute by far the majority of sources. Indeed, accounts provided with a chain of transmission, which are the norm in early works, gradually disappear over time to the advantage of quotations from previous works. Late works are taken into consideration only when they preserve channels of transmission unattested in early ones. On the other hand, Shīʿī works are disregarded, or not fully used, because the existence of distinctively Shīʿī chains of transmission precludes the establishment of a relation between Sunnī accounts and Shīʿī ones.

Considerable progress in this kind of source criticism was recently achieved by a method combining the investigation of *isnād*s with literary analysis, and involving the use of an exhaustive corpus of sources.[3] The general results attained through the application of this method may be summarized as follows: after a brief period of fluidity, textual transmission became the norm until nearly total stability was achieved at a later stage. Two specific results should be mentioned here. On the one hand, it was demonstrated that we are able to trace the earliest works to their ultimate sources, and thus to reconstruct the processes which led to the constitution of the material included in these works. In particular, it was shown that individual accounts of Ibn Shihāb al-Zuhrī (d. 124/742) and of ʿUrwa b. al-Zubayr (d. 94/712) can be largely retrieved, and that the processes of derivation from such accounts can be reconstructed. On the other hand, the use of the periods in which works were produced as evidence of developments was proven to be entirely misleading.[4] However, it should be stated that this method, in addition to exhibiting the limits of *isnād* analysis mentioned above, is applicable only to accounts whose chains of transmission have common links.

---

[3] This method was elaborated by G. Schoeler, and is applied in the two case studies of his *Charakter und Authentie der muslimischen Überlieferung über das Leben Mohammeds*, Berlin, 1996. For further refinements, see, in this volume, H. Motzki, "The Murder of Ibn Abī l-Ḥuqayq: On the Origin and Reliability of Some *Maghāzī*-Reports".

[4] See Schoeler, *Charakter*, 142-3, where Wansbrough's hypothesis of a gradual shift from *narratio* to *exemplum* is undermined. The application of Schoeler's method leads to the conclusion that the inverse process, in fact, took place. See also M. Lecker, "The Death of the Prophet Muḥammad's Father: Did Wāqidī Invent Some of the Evidence?", in *ZDMG*, 145 (1995), 9-27, where the results reached by Cook and Crone through comparing Ibn Isḥāq and al-Wāqidī are contested. Lecker convincingly argues that an extensive comparison will lead to the conclusion that the variation among scholars derives from their reliance upon distinct sources which originated in the seventh century.

The treatment of M.J. Kister should be distinguished from both kinds of source criticism. In his extensive corpus of articles, Kister does not aim at reconstructing developments, either on the basis of the periods in which works were produced or on the basis of the chains of transmission; rather, he aims at providing surveys of the material pertaining to specific topics and issues. Such surveys involve the use of a wide range of works, including late as well as Shīʿī ones. Late works are used merely as additional attestations of material included in early works, or as late attestations of early material. In the last case, the implicit view that large parts of early Arabic literature have been lost to us, and hence that a late attestation should automatically be taken as an instance of preservation, does not seem to be fully satisfactory.[5] The use of Shīʿī works enables Kister to give the other side's position on each issue or, conversely, to show the uniformity of views between Sunnīs and Shīʿīs. In both cases, the establishment of a relation between Sunnī and Shīʿī material is seldom attempted.[6] It should be obvious from my brief description that Kister's treatment exhibits a strong sense of the extension of *sīra* Tradition, but no distinct conception of its structure and development.

A common feature of Western treatments is the avoidance of interpretation. Two views may underlie this avoidance. On the one hand, the texts of which *sīra* is composed are mostly of a narrative character and, as such, have a plain meaning. The tendencies of these texts are immediately discernible, and thus, no significance is to be found beyond the text. On the other hand, the fact that *sīra* is composed of texts implies that the validity of any argument depends upon its textual foundation. Thus, no significance, however complex the meaning

---

[5] See, for instance, M.J. Kister, "Rajab is the Month of God...", in *IOS*, 1 (1971), 197, where attestations of the view that Muḥammad was conceived in Rajab are provided by the works of Ibn Ḥajar al-Haytamī (d. 974/1567) and al-Shāṭibī (fl. mid-9th/15th century) [note 43]. It may indeed be, in this case, that late works preserve early material, but the fact that the material is not found in earlier works needs some explanation.

[6] See, for instance, M.J. Kister, "'... And He Was Born Circumcised...' Some Notes on Circumcision in *Ḥadīth*", in *Oriens*, 34 (1994), 12-13, where attestations of the view that Muḥammad was born circumcised are provided by the work of Abū Nuʿaym (d. 430/1038) and later Sunnī works, as well as by the Shīʿī works of Ibn Bābawayh (d. 381/991) and al-Majlisī (d. 1111/1700). This parallel, however, receives no further attention.

of *sīra* may be, should be sought beyond the text.[7] It is clear from my remarks that the practice of interpretation will involve a marked departure from two characteristics of Western scholarship: the focus on narrative features, and the exclusive reliance upon textual evidence.

II. Method and Interpretation

My method is based on the distinction between two kinds of transmitted objects: reports and traditions. The term "report" designates the verbal unit, which is handed over among individual scholars. The term "tradition" designates the unit of meaning, which is handed down over time in the group of Muslim scholars, and which can be discerned in verbal units.

This distinction is particularly significant in the case of narrative reports. Indeed, if we are able to discern units of meaning in verbal units, the narrative features of reports can be regarded as contingencies. The structural relation between two (or among several) units of meaning in a verbal unit is termed "association". By "association", I indicate that the two (or several) units are parts of a cohesive whole.

My method consists of two steps. In the first step, which is exclusively concerned with the structure of *sīra* Tradition, I examine the occurrences of a tradition in reports, in order to determine its different associations and to identify groups of reports exhibiting these associations. In the second step, which is concerned with the development of *sīra* Tradition, I examine the occurrences of these reports in works, in order to determine the various fates of each association.

---

[7] See, for instance, Schoeler, *Charakter*, chap. 2, where the author identifies three "recensions" of the "story" of the earliest revelation. The al-Zuhrī recension is characterized by the description of the earliest revelation as an "eerie encounter" with Gabriel experienced by Muḥammad in the cave of Ḥirāʾ; its narrative features exhibit the "tendency to restrict oneself to the essential" (62-79). The Ibn Lahīʿa recension emphasizes the intimacy between Muḥammad and Gabriel at their first encounter; its narrative features are seen as "embellishments" and "fantastic expansions" undergone by the original story in its further transmission (81-85). The Ibn Isḥāq recension is characterized by the placing of the eerie encounter in a dream; its narrative features are "pictorial detail", "narrative trimmings", "repetition of motifs" (89-98). It would seem that the different significances of the story in the three recensions may reflect doctrinal concerns (as opposed to narrative ones). The existence of such concerns, however, is nowhere considered by Schoeler.

This last step involves the distinction between "Tradition" and "memory". The former term refers to the process of transmission, which is itself composed of individual acts. The latter term refers to the operation of selection involved in each individual act of transmission, and which may itself conform to collective patterns.[8] More specifically, "memory" refers to the selection among associations uniformly operated by either Sunnī or Shīʿī scholars during a certain period. The discernment of distinctively Sunnī and Shīʿī patterns of selection is possible when reports exhibiting a certain association regularly appear in either Sunnī or Shīʿī works over a long period of time, while reports exhibiting a different association are absent from the works in question. The existence of such patterns is expressed through the use of the phrases "Sunnī memory" and "Shīʿī memory".

My interpretation ultimately derives from the distinction which lies at the basis of my method: if we are able to discern units of meaning in verbal units, and thus to regard the narrative features of reports as contingencies, we may assume that such units serve to articulate specific conceptions, rather than mere tendencies.

It was one of Tor Andrae's achievements to show that the figure of Muḥammad gave rise to two rival conceptions of his prophethood. According to the first conception, Muḥammad is a mere man invested with the function of prophethood at a certain point of his life. According to the second conception, Muḥammad is a superhuman being invested with the attribute of prophethood through an election preceding his terrestrial existence. It appears from Andrae's study that the first conception, which is indeed exhibited in the Qurʾān, was favored by Sunnī scholars. The second conception was originally the product of Shīʿī and Ṣūfī speculations, but permeated, from an early period on, Sunnī tradition, too.[9]

The distinction manifested by Andrae between two conceptions of Muḥammad's prophethood, which I refer to as the functional and the

[8] The term "memory" is borrowed from the works of the sociologist M. Halbwachs (*Les cadres sociaux de la mémoire*, Paris, 1925; *La topographie légendaire des évangiles en terre sainte. Etude de mémoire collective*, Paris, 1941; *La mémoire collective*, Paris, 1950) and of contemporary historians (for instance, Y.H. Yerushalmi, *Zakhor. Jewish History and Jewish Memory*, Seattle, 1982). It expresses there the idea that the past is remembered by groups, and that collective remembrance involves selection of events and their interpretation according to distinctive patterns.

[9] *Die Person Muḥammeds in Lehre und Glauben seiner Gemeinde*, Uppsala, 1917, 290-390.

ontological prophet, provides the basis of my interpretation. It must be noted, however, that these conceptions were discerned by Andrae through a study of dogmatic material, and of traditional material directly related to dogmatic issues. The relevance of Andrae's distinction to *sīra*, whose content is indeed not reducible to dogma, lies in the marks of salvation history exhibited there. By "salvation history" I mean the perception of history as animated by the salvatory will of God, itself manifested by the carrying out of an elaborate design as to the guidance of man. Whereas this perception does not involve speculation on the nature of Muḥammad's prophethood, it does involve a concern with the historical realization of his prophethood. In view of this specific concern, Andrae's distinction has to be somewhat reconsidered. Thus, it is not a distinct view as to the nature of Muḥammad's prophethood, but it is its distinct historical implication that will be taken as constituting the core of each of the two conceptions when sought in *sīra*. That these conceptions as articulated in *sīra* knew of parallel dogmatic formulations will not be suggested anywhere in my argument. My method, as well as my interpretation, will be illustrated in the following example.

III. The Shooting Stars Tradition

The shooting stars tradition belongs to the group of the "new order traditions", where the occurrence of a supernatural phenomenon indicates the collapse of the old order and the emergence of a new one.[10] In the present case, the new order is experienced in the neutralization of demonic powers.

In Sunnī Tradition, with one exception, the shooting stars tradition is associated with the beginning of the prophetic mission. Let us first consider the reports exhibiting this association. In a report transmitted by Yūnus b. Bukayr (d. 199/814-15) and Ziyād b. ʿAbd Allāh al-Bakkāʾī (d. 183/799) from Muḥammad b. Isḥāq (d. 150/767), we read:

> When the Messenger of God was about to receive his call and when his mission was about to start (*lammā taqāraba amr rasūli llāh wa-ḥaḍara*

[10] Among the phenomena indicating this shift of order, and constituting the object of distinct traditions, the following may be mentioned here: the disintegration of Kisrā's palace, the rupture between women soothsayers and genies, the collapse of idols, Gabriel's protection of Muḥammad against Iblīs.

> *mab'athuhu*), the devils were debarred from hearing [words uttered in the heavens], the sitting places which they habitually used in order to listen by stealth were rendered inaccessible to them, and they were pelted with stars. Thus, the genies knew that a divine decree concerning human creatures was being carried out.[11]

The following report is adduced by Ibn Sa'd (d. 230/844):

> When the mission of Muḥammad was initiated (*lammā bu'itha*), the genies were driven away and pelted with stars. Previously, they used to listen [to words uttered in the heavens], and each class of genies had a sitting-place for that purpose...[12]

The access of genies to celestial information, ending with the beginning of the prophetic mission, is described at length in a variant report adduced by Abū Nu'aym (d. 430/1038), with a chain having as intermediate link Muḥammad b. 'Uthmān b. Abī Shayba (d. 297/909).[13]

The following report is adduced by Abū Nu'aym, with a chain having as intermediate link Muḥammad b. 'Umar al-Wāqidī (d. 207/823):

> When the day came on which the Messenger of God started to prophesy (*lammā kāna l-yawmu lladhī tanabba'a fīhi*), the devils were denied access to the heavens, and they were pelted with shooting stars...[14]

---

[11] 'Uṭāridī, *Maghāzī*, 90-91; Ibn Hishām, *Sīra*, I, 217.

[12] Ibn Sa'd, *Ṭabaqāt*, I, 132.

[13] Abū Nu'aym, *Dalā'il*, I, 293-94. The link of Muḥammad b. 'Uthmān is likely to represent the source of Abū Nu'aym, which may in turn be identified as the former's *Ta'rīkh* (see Sezgin, I, 164).

[14] Abū Nu'aym, *Dalā'il*, I, 295. This report, as well as other reports of al-Wāqidī, reached Abū Nu'aym through the following channel: al-Ḥusayn b. al-Faraj [Ibn al-Khayyāṭ al-Baghdādī]—al-Ḥasan b. al-Jahm [al-Wādhārī] (d. 290/903)—Abū 'Umar Muḥammad b. Aḥmad b. al-Ḥasan b. Muḥammad b. Ḥamza [al-Haysānī] (d. 358/969). Abū Nu'aym informs us that al-Ḥusayn b. al-Faraj "came to Isfahan and *ḥaddatha bihā 'ani l-Wāqidī bi-l-mubtada' wa-l-maghāzī*" (*Ta'rīkh*, I, 329), and that al-Ḥasan b. al-Jahm "heard the *Kitāb al-Maghāzī* from al-Ḥusayn b. al-Faraj" (ibid., 312). The wording used by Abū Nu'aym suggests that, unlike the *maghāzī*, the *mubtada'* transmitted by al-Ḥusayn b. al-Faraj from al-Wāqidī (and then, presumably, by al-Ḥasan b. al-Jahm from al-Ḥusayn b. al-Faraj) was not a distinct work, but rather isolated material. It is not unreasonable to assume, however, that a work of al-Wāqidī's had a part entitled *al-Mubtada'*, which comprised the material pertaining to the period preceding the prophetic mission (unlike his *Maghāzī*), and that al-Ḥusayn b. al-Faraj transmitted this material. The best candidate seems to be Wāqidī's *Kitāb al-Ta'rīkh al-kabīr* (mentioned by Ibn al-Nadīm), proposed by M. Jones as the source used by Ibn Sa'd in his account of events preceding the prophetic mission (introduction to the edition of Wāqidī's *Kitāb al-Maghāzī*, Oxford, 1966, I, 13-14).

In a report adduced by Abū Nuʿaym with the same chain, we read:

> The devils used to listen to revelation. When God initiated the mission of Muḥammad (*fa-lammā baʿatha llāh Muḥammadan*), they were debarred from doing so.[15]

This report is adduced by Ibn Kathīr (d. 774/1372), quoting al-Wāqidī,[16] and by al-Suyūṭī (d. 911/1505), quoting al-Wāqidī and Abū Nuʿaym.[17]

Let us now consider the single Sunnī report evidencing the association of the shooting stars tradition with the birth of Muḥammad. In a report adduced by Ibn ʿAsākir (d. 571/1176) with a chain going back to the *mawlā* of ʿUthmān Maʿrūf b. Kharrabūdh, and having as intermediate link al-Zubayr b. Bakkār (d. 256/870), we read:

> Iblīs used to travel across the seven heavens. When Jesus was born, he was debarred from [entering] the three [upper] heavens but still had access to the four [lower] heavens. When the Messenger of God was born, he was debarred from [entering] the seven heavens, and the devils were pelted with stars.[18]

The report as adduced by al-Suyūṭī and al-Ṣāliḥī (d. 942/1535), both quoting Ibn Bakkār and Ibn ʿAsākir, ends with "he was debarred from [entering] the seven heavens".[19]

---

[15] Abū Nuʿaym, *Dalāʾil*, I, 296.

[16] Ibn Kathīr, *Sīra*, I, 420.

[17] Suyūṭī, *Khaṣāʾiṣ*, I, 278.

[18] Ibn ʿAsākir, *Taʾrīkh*, I, 57. It seems reasonable to assume that the link of Ibn Bakkār represents the source of Ibn ʿAsākir. In the case of a report pertaining to the death of ʿAbd Allāh b. ʿAbd al-Muṭṭalib, Lecker has proposed Ibn Bakkār's *Akhbār al-Madīna* as the source of Ibn ʿAsākir (M. Lecker, "The Death", 19, note 26). This suggestion, which has obvious relevance to the report treated by Lecker (ʿAbd Allāh died in Medina), may be extended to the present report, if we suppose that the two reports were adduced together by Ibn Bakkār. Indeed, the death of ʿAbd Allāh and the birth of Muḥammad stand close to each other in the chronological framework of the latter's life. This hypothesis itself presupposes that thematic consistency can be disrupted by association of contents, something which the reader familiar with Arabic literature will easily concede. Ibn Bakkār transmits here from his teacher Muḥammad b. al-Ḥasan b. Zabāla (d. towards the end of the 2nd century AH), who is likewise credited with a work dealing with the history of Medina (see Sezgin, I, 343-44). It may well be that the two reports were adduced together—if my hypothesis is correct—already by Ibn Zabāla, and that their contiguity was simply inherited by Ibn Bakkār as a feature of his teacher's work.

[19] Suyūṭī, *Khaṣāʾiṣ*, I, 127; Ṣāliḥī, *Subul*, I, 350.

The following paraphrase is adduced by Ibn Ḥajar al-Haytamī (d. 974/1567):

> That night [i. e., the night Muḥammad was born], the devils who used to listen by stealth were pelted from the heavens with shooting stars.[20]

The pelting of devils at the birth of Muḥammad appears in the paraphrase of Tradition provided by Jaʿfar b. Ḥasan al-Barzanjī (d. 1179/1621).[21]

In Shīʿī Tradition, the shooting stars tradition is always associated with the birth of Muḥammad. Let us finally consider the Shīʿī reports. In a report adduced by Ibn Bābawayh (d. 381/991) with a chain going back to Jaʿfar al-Ṣādiq, and having as intermediate link Aḥmad b. Abī ʿAbd Allāh [Muḥammad] al-Barqī (d. 274/887-88 or 280/893-94), we read:

> Iblīs used to travel across the seven heavens. When Jesus was born, he was debarred from [entering] the three [upper] heavens but could still travel across the four [lower] heavens. When the Messenger of God was born, he was debarred from [entering] the seven heavens altogether, and the devils were pelted with stars.[22]

This passage is excerpted from the report by Ibn Shahrāshūb (d. 588/1192).[23] The same passage appears in the paraphrase of Tradition provided by Rāwandī (d. 573/1177-78).[24]

In a report adduced by Ibn Bābawayh with a chain going back to Abān b. ʿUthmān (a disciple of Jaʿfar al-Ṣādiq and Mūsā al-Kāẓim), and having as intermediate link ʿAlī b. Ibrāhīm [b. Hāshim al-Qummī] (alive in 307/919), Āmina tells about her delivery of Muḥammad:

> When he fell onto the earth, he protected himself against [its impurities] with his hands and knees, and he raised his head toward the sky. A light came out of me which illuminated what is between the heavens

[20] Ibn Ḥajar's *Mawlid*, *apud* Nabhānī, *Jawāhir*, 1118.

[21] Barzanjī, *ʿIqd*, 13.

[22] Ibn Bābawayh, *Amālī*, 253. It seems reasonable to assume that the link of al-Barqī represents the source of Ibn Bābawayh. The identification of the work from which the report was transmitted, however, is made difficult by the uncertainty as to whether the works of Aḥmad b. Muḥammad mentioned by Muslim scholars existed independently or as parts of the *Kitāb al-Maḥāsin*, and as to whether he or his father Muḥammad b. Khālid compiled this work (and each of its parts). A possible candidate is the *Kitāb al-Tibyān* mentioned by Masʿūdī (see C. Pellat, "al-Barḳī", in *EI*², Supplement 1-2, s.v., and E. Kohlberg, *A Medieval Muslim Scholar at Work. Ibn Ṭāwūs and his Library*, Leiden, 1992, 273 and 308-09).

[23] Ibn Shahrāshūb, *Manāqib*, I, 31.

[24] Rāwandī, *Kharāʾij*, I, 21.

> and the earth. The devils were pelted with stars, and they were debarred from [entering] the heavens...[25]

In a report adduced by Abū Manṣūr al-Ṭabrisī (fl. early 6th/12th century) on the authority of Mūsā al-Kāẓim, ʿAlī informs a Jewish contradictor of the miracles concomitant with the birth of Muḥammad:

> The wonders which Iblīs had seen that night prompted him to travel in the heavens. He had a sitting-place in the third heaven, [where] the devils used to listen by stealth. When the devils saw the wonders, they tried to listen by stealth. They found themselves debarred from [entering] the heavens altogether, and they were pelted with shooting stars. That was a sign of Muḥammad's prophethood (*dalālatan li-nubuwwatihi*).[26]

The examination of the occurrences of the shooting stars tradition leads us to identify two groups of reports. The Sunnī reports vary as to the nature of the creatures in question (devils or genies), and as to the character of the celestial words heard by them (information or revelation), but they uniformly state, except for the Ibn Kharrabūdh report, that the creatures were debarred from hearing the celestial words at the beginning of the prophetic mission. The phenomenon is implicitly associated with the revelation of the Qurʾān, and signifies that this process, unlike previous descents of celestial words, was concealed to all creatures until the words reached their human recipient. Indeed, those words were of unprecedentedly important content, and their communication to Muḥammad was an unprecedented event, which God's design did not allow to be shared by intrusive ears. On the other hand, the Ibn Kharrabūdh report and the Shīʿī reports associate the phenomenon with the birth of Muḥammad. This association, which seems at first sight less consistent,

---

[25] Ibn Bābawayh, *Kamāl*, 196-97. Abān is credited with a *kitāb yajmaʿu l-mubtadaʾ wa-l-maghāzī wa-l-wafāt wa-l-ridda* (see Najāshī, 11). On the problems posed by references to a *kitāb* of Abān, see, in this volume, M. Jarrar, "*Sīrat Ahl al-Kisāʾ*. Early Shīʿī Sources on the Biography of the Prophet". As shown by Jarrar, the composition of a distinct work can hardly be ascribed to Abān, while we should acknowledge his role in the diffusion of a distinctively Shīʿī corpus. It seems reasonable to assume, however, that the link of Qummī represents the source of Ibn Bābawayh. The work from which the report was transmitted may be identified as Qummī's *Kitāb al-Mabʿath*. This work (quoted by Ibn Ṭāwūs) has been proposed by Kohlberg, alternatively to Qummī's *Tafsīr*, as the source used by Ṭabrisī in the *Iʿlām* (Kohlberg, *Scholar*, 239).

[26] Abū Manṣūr, *Iḥtijāj*, I, 331-32.

implies that the birth of Muḥammad, rather than the revelation of the Qur'ān, is an unprecedented event.

The first step of my method is exclusively concerned with the structure of *sīra* Tradition, as I stated above, and does not aim at reconstructing the transmission of reports prior to their inclusion in works. Such a reconstruction, however, must be attempted in the case of the Ibn Kharrabūdh report, both because its content is paralleled only in the Shīʿī reports and because its ascription hardly conforms to a Sunnī pattern. The ascription to Ibn Kharrabūdh in itself suggests some marginal origin, but does not lead us to more specific conclusions. Such conclusions, however, can be reached on the basis of biographical evidence. In Sunnī *rijāl* literature, Ibn Kharrabūdh appears as a rather controversial figure, although it is his mere reliability as a transmitter that seems to have been questioned.[27] It is Shīʿī *rijāl* literature that provides us with a decisive piece of information, namely, that Ibn Kharrabūdh was a disciple of Muḥammad al-Bāqir and Jaʿfar al-Ṣādiq, and that he played an important role in the transmission of their teaching.[28] On the basis of this evidence, and in view of the ascription of al-Barqī's report, we may conclude that the present report was originally transmitted by Shīʿī scholars on the authority of Jaʿfar al-Ṣādiq, perhaps ultimately from him, and through a channel starting with Ibn Kharrabūdh. Two further conclusions may be drawn here. First, the report was deprived of the ascription to Jaʿfar al-Ṣādiq at an initial stage of its transmission among Sunnī scholars, and thus reached Ibn Bakkār with the mere ascription to Ibn Kharrabūdh.[29] Second, the report was combined at some stage with other reports likewise transmitted by Shīʿī scholars, through various channels, on the authority of Jaʿfar al-Ṣādiq. This composite report, whose chain preserved the name of only one disciple of Jaʿfar al-Ṣādiq, was

---

[27] See Ibn Ḥajar, *Tahdhīb*, X, 230-31.

[28] See Kashshī, *Rijāl*, 184-85 and Māmaqānī, *Tanqīḥ*, III, 227-28. The information that Ibn Kharrabūdh transmitted from Muḥammad al-Bāqir also appears, though less conspicuously, in Sunnī *rijāl* literature (see Ibn Ḥajar, ibid.). I owe my knowledge of the Shīʿī allegiance of Ibn Kharrabūdh, as well as the substance of my conclusions, to Professor Wilferd Madelung (written communication of 9/27/97).

[29] That Ibn Zabāla was responsible for this suppression is suggested by the obscurity of the link between him and Ibn Kharrabūdh, a certain ʿAbd al-Salām b. ʿAbd Allāh. This ʿAbd al-Salām does not seem to be much more than a name, which is itself likely to conceal the identity of a Shīʿī informant. Note that the reliability of Ibn Zabāla as a transmitter was seriously questioned by *rijāl* scholars (see Ibn Ḥajar, *Tahdhīb*, IX, 115-17).

eventually adduced by al-Barqī.[30] In view of the processes just reconstructed, the fact that the report as adduced by Ibn Bakkār and the passage of al-Barqī's report are nearly identical in form provides a remarkable instance of textual transmission.

The second step of my method may now be carried out. The combined evidence of Ibn Isḥāq's report, al-Wāqidī's two reports, Ibn Saʿd's report and that of Ibn Abī Shayba shows that the association of the shooting stars tradition with the beginning of the prophetic mission existed at an early stage of Sunnī Tradition. On the other hand, the occurrence of the Ibn Kharrabūdh report in Ibn Bakkār shows, in view of the reconstruction just indicated, that the association of the shooting stars tradition with the birth of Muḥammad was integrated into Sunnī Tradition by the turn of the second/eighth century. The occurrence of Ibn Abī Shayba's report and of al-Wāqidī's two reports in Abū Nuʿaym, as well as the occurrence of al-Wāqidī's second report in Ibn Kathīr and al-Suyūṭī on the one hand, and the disappearance of the Ibn Kharrabūdh report after Ibn Bakkār (except in Ibn ʿAsākir), as well as its appearance in amputated form (in al-Suyūṭī and al-Ṣāliḥī), on the other hand, suggest that the shooting stars tradition was associated in Sunnī memory with the beginning of the prophetic mission. However, the reappearance of the Ibn Kharrabūdh report in a paraphrastic form (in Ibn Ḥajar) and its persistent appearance in such a form (in al-Barzanjī) suggest that the association of the shooting stars tradition with the birth of Muḥammad was eventually integrated into Sunnī memory.

The combined evidence of the Ibn Kharrabūdh report (whose

[30] For an analogous instance of parallel transmissions, see Lecker, "The Death", 24. Lecker produces two reports placing the death of ʿAbd Allāh b. ʿAbd al-Muṭṭalib two months after the birth of Muḥammad: one adduced by Ibn Bakkār with the chain Ibn Zabāla—ʿAbd al-Salām b. ʿAbd Allāh—Ibn Kharrabūdh, and one adduced by Yaʿqūbī on the authority of Jaʿfar al-Ṣādiq. "Shīʿite provenance" is correctly inferred by Lecker, but without the support of biographical evidence. Incidentally, the information provided by Lecker may confirm my hypothesis that the report on the death of ʿAbd Allāh and the report on the birth of Muḥammad were adduced together by Ibn Bakkār, perhaps already by Ibn Zabāla, in a work dealing with the history of Medina (see above, note 18). Indeed, the fact that the two reports have the same chain, and perhaps were heard during the same session, could be a further reason to adduce them together. The reader will concede that association of transmissions, in addition to association of contents, can disrupt the thematic consistency of Arabic works.

form is preserved in al-Barqī's report), al-Qummī's report and that of Abū Manṣūr shows that the association of the shooting stars tradition with the birth of Muḥammad came about in Shīʿī Tradition. It could even be argued, on the basis of the ascription to a disciple of Jaʿfar al-Ṣādiq shared by the first two reports, that this association was part of the teaching of the Imam as transmitted in the generation following him. The absence of specific narrative features in the relevant passage of al-Qummī's report, however, may suggest that the association of the shooting stars tradition with the birth of Muḥammad did not originally take the form of an independent account. Whereas such an account exists in the Ibn Kharrabūdh report and in that of Abū Manṣūr, al-Qummī's report exhibits the mere combination of the shooting stars tradition with accounts pertaining to the birth of Muḥammad. The occurrence of al-Barqī's report and that of al-Qummī in Ibn Bābawayh, as well as the occurrence of the passage of al-Barqī's report in Ibn Shahrāshūb and in Rāwandī, shows that the shooting stars tradition was associated in Shīʿī memory with the birth of Muḥammad.

My interpretation presupposes the comprehensive analysis of the new order traditions undertaken elsewhere,[31] and cannot be fully illustrated in the present article. The reconstruction proposed below originally belongs to this wider framework, and is not intended to convince the reader on the sole basis of the results reached in the preceding pages.

My interpretation starts with the argument that the two conceptions of Muḥammad's prophethood referred to above bear different implications as to the respective roles played by the beginning of his mission and by his birth in salvation history. It suffices here to mention that, in a larger context, this argument would prove not to be entirely valid. According to the conception of the functional prophet, then, the beginning of Muḥammad's mission represents the accession of a mere man to the prophetic office. The birth of Muḥammad deserves attention in so far as it initiates the life of the prophet-to-be, but plays otherwise no role in salvation history. It is the beginning of the prophetic mission that initiates the carrying out

[31] A. Leites, The Time of Birth of Muḥammad. A Study in Islamic Tradition, Ph.D. dissertation (under the supervision of Michael Cook), Princeton University, June 1997, 92-124.

of God's design. According to the conception of the ontological prophet, however, the birth of Muḥammad represents the emergence to personal existence of a being pre-existently invested with the attribute of prophethood. The beginning of the prophetic mission deserves attention in so far as it initiates Scriptural revelation, but plays no determining role in salvation history. It is the birth of Muḥammad that initiates the carrying out of God's design.

I further argue that, through their different associations, the new order traditions serve to articulate the conception of the functional prophet and that of the ontological prophet, in the sense defined above. The former conception is seen to be articulated by the association of the new order traditions with the beginning of the prophetic mission, and the latter conception by their association with the birth of Muḥammad. In the first case, it is with the appearance of Muḥammad in the capacity of prophet that the old order collapses and a new one emerges. The establishment of a new order represents a corollary of Scriptural revelation which, as the utmost manifestation of the salvatory will of God, has a deleterious impact on the forces leading man to damnation. In the second case, it is with the actualization of Muḥammad's prophethood that the old order collapses and a new one emerges. The establishment of a new order represents an independent manifestation of the salvatory will of God, whereby man is enduringly protected from the forces leading him to damnation.

On the basis of the preceding argument, and in consideration of the parallel results attained in my analysis of the new order traditions, a conceptual development may now be reconstructed. The combined evidence of Ibn Isḥāq's report, al-Wāqidī's two reports, Ibn Saʿd's report and that of Ibn Abī Shayba shows that the functional prophet was indeed the original conception among Sunnī scholars. On the other hand, the occurrence of the Ibn Kharrabūdh report in Ibn Bakkār shows that the conception of the ontological prophet had appeared among Sunnī scholars by the turn of the second/eighth century. The reasons for this evolution must, in the absence of historical evidence, remain undetermined. The occurrence of Ibn Abī Shayba's report and of al-Wāqidī's two reports in later works on the one hand, and the disappearance of the Ibn Kharrabūdh report after Ibn Bakkār on the other hand, suggest that the functional prophet came to be the dominant conception among Sunnī scholars. However, the reappearance of the Ibn Kharrabūdh report in Ibn Ḥajar and in al-Barzanjī suggests that later Sunnī scholars were gradually won over by the conception of the ontological prophet. That this evolution reflects increased receptiveness to Ṣūfī doctrine, where the latter conception was indeed an all-pervasive one,[32] seems to be a historically viable assumption.

The combined evidence of the Ibn Kharrabūdh report, al-Qummī's report and that of Abū Manṣūr shows that the conception of the ontological prophet was originally articulated by Shīʿī scholars. The occurrence of the passage of al-Barqī's report, and of al-Qummī's report, in later works shows that the ontological prophet was the only conception that ever existed among Shīʿī scholars.

It should be obvious from the preceding example that the acknowledgement of the existence of a *sīra* Tradition, as defined at the beginning of this article, implies a dynamic approach to works. Such an approach is implicitly suggested by Kister who, for the first time in Western scholarship, devoted equal attention to early and late works, as well as to Sunnī and Shīʿī ones. The use of a wide range of works, however, makes a substantial difference when each work is taken as representing a stage of development, rather than a mere point in the extension of Tradition as in Kister's treatment. My original contribution essentially lies in the argument that, once we adopt a dynamic approach to works, the development of *sīra* Tradition can be actually reconstructed if we are able to discern units of meaning in verbal units, and thus to regard the narrative features of reports as contingencies. Indeed, it is the discernment of "traditions", and the determination of their different "associations", that lead me to discern collective patterns of selection and, also, to detect in *sīra* the articulation of specific conceptions.

The question remains whether my method is applicable, and my interpretation relevant, to *sīra* as a whole. The kind of material treated in this article consists of accounts concerned with a supernatural phenomenon. The kind of material predominant in *sīra*, however, consists of complex information, such as information on persons and places. Can such information be reduced to simple units? On the other hand, accounts concerned with a supernatural phenomenon convey the central theme of rupture in the course of events. The extensive accounts of the military campaigns of Muḥammad, to take

[32] See Leites, The Time, 135-38.

a characteristic example of the complex information predominant in *sīra*, exhibit by contrast the attempt to define the causal link among events. Can we go beyond the historical narrative, with its intrinsic tendentiousness, and discern there the marks of salvation history? A positive answer to both questions would require considerable progress in the elaboration of methods, and in the contrivance of interpretative tools.

Bibliography

Abū Manṣūr, Aḥmad b. ʿAlī al-Ṭabrisī, *al-Iḥtijāj ʿalā ahl al-lijāj*, ed. Muḥammad Bāqir al-Kharsān, Najaf, 1965-66.

Abū Nuʿaym, Aḥmad b. ʿAbd Allāh al-Iṣbahānī, *Dalāʾil al-nubuwwa*, ed. ʿAbd al-Barr ʿAbbās and Muḥammad Rawwās Qalʿajī, Aleppo, 1970.

———, *Taʾrīkh Iṣbahān*, ed. Sayyid Kasrawī Ḥasan, Beirut, 1990.

Andrae, Tor, *Die Person Muḥammeds in Lehre und Glauben seiner Gemeinde*, Uppsala, 1917.

al-Barzanjī, Jaʿfar b. Ḥasan, *ʿIqd al-jawhar fī mawlid al-nabī al-azhar*, Bombay, 1897.

Cook, Michael, *Muhammad*, Oxford, 1983.

Crone, Patricia, *Meccan Trade and the Rise of Islam*, Princeton, 1987.

Halbwachs, Maurice, *Les cadres sociaux de la mémoire*, Paris, 1925.

———, *La topographie légendaire des évangiles en terre sainte. Etude de mémoire collective*, Paris, 1941.

———, *La mémoire collective*, Paris, 1950.

Horovitz, J., "Salmān al-Fārisī", in *Der Islam*, 12 (1922), 178-80.

Ibn ʿAsākir, ʿAlī b. al-Ḥasan al-Dimashqī, *Taʾrīkh madīnat Dimashq*, ed. Nashāṭ Ghazzāwī et al., Damascus, 1984-.

Ibn Bābawayh, Muḥammad b. ʿAlī al-Qummī, *al-Amālī*, Najaf, 1970.

———, *Kamāl al-dīn wa-tamām al-niʿma*, ed. ʿAlī Akbar al-Ghaffārī, Tehran, 1970.

Ibn Ḥajar al-ʿAsqalānī, Aḥmad b. ʿAlī b. Muḥammad, *Tahdhīb al-tahdhīb*, 12 vols., Hyderabad, 1325-27 AH.

Ibn Hishām, ʿAbd al-Malik al-Ḥimyarī, *al-Sīra al-nabawiyya*, ed. Muṣṭafā al-Saqqā et al., 4 vols., Cairo, 1936.

Ibn Kathīr, Ismāʿīl b. ʿUmar, *al-Sīra al-nabawiyya*, ed. Muṣṭafā ʿAbd al-Wāḥid, Cairo, 1964-66.

Ibn Saʿd, Muḥammad al-Baṣrī, *al-Ṭabaqāt al-kubrā*, ed. Muḥammad ʿAbd al-Qādir ʿAṭāʾ, Beirut, 1990.

Ibn Shahrāshūb, Muḥammad b. ʿAlī al-Sarawī, *Manāqib āl Abī Ṭālib*, ed. Muḥammad Ḥusayn al-Dānish and Hāshim al-Rasūlī al-Maḥallātī, 4 vols., Qum, 1980.

Jarrar, M., "'*Sīrat Ahl al-Kisāʾ*'. Early Shīʿī Sources on the Biography of the Prophet", article 5 of this volume.

Jones, Marsden (ed.), *al-Wāqidī's Kitāb al-Maghāzī*, 3 vols., Oxford, 1966.

al-Kashshī, Muḥammad b. ʿUmar, *al-Rijāl*, ed. Aḥmad al-Ḥusaynī, Karbala, n.d.

Kister, M.J., "Rajab is the Month of God...", in *Israel Oriental Studies*, 1 (1971), 197.

———,"'... And He Was Born Circumcised...' Some Notes on Circumcision in Ḥadīth", in *Oriens*, 34 (1994), 12-13.

Kohlberg, Etan, *A Medieval Muslim Scholar at Work. Ibn Ṭāwūs and his Library*, Leiden, 1992

Lecker, M., "The Death of the Prophet Muḥammad's Father: Did Wāqidī Invent Some of the Evidence?", in *Zeitschrift der Deutschen Morgenländischen Gesellschaft*, 145 (1995), 9-27.

Leites, Adrien, The Time of Birth of Muḥammad. A Study in Islamic Tradition, Ph.D. dissertation (under the supervision of Michael Cook), Princeton University, June 1997.
al-Māmaqānī, ʿAbd Allāh al-Jarawī, *Tanqīḥ al-maqāl fī ʿilm al-rijāl*, Najaf, 1930-33.
Motzki, H., "The Murder of Ibn Abī l-Ḥuqayq: On the Origin and Reliability of Some *Maghāzī*-Reports", article 7 of this volume.
al-Nabhānī, Yūsuf b. Ismāʿīl, *Jawāhir al-biḥār fī faḍāʾil al-nabī al-mukhtār*, Beirut, 1907 or 1908-09 or 1910.
al-Najāshī, Aḥmad b. ʿAlī, *al-Rijāl*, Tehran, n.d.
Pellat, C., "al-Barḳī", in *EI²*, Supplement 1-2, s.v.
Rāwandī, Saʿīd b. Hibatallāh, *al-Kharāʾij wa-l-jarāʾiḥ*, Qum, 1989.
al-Ṣāliḥī, Muḥammad b. Yūsuf, *Subul al-hudā wa-l-rashād fī sīrat khayr al-ʿibād*, ed. ʿĀdil Aḥmad ʿAbd al-Mawjūd and ʿAlī Muḥammad Muʿawwaḍ, Beirut, 1993.
Schoeler, Gregor, *Charakter und Authentie der muslimischen Überlieferung über das Leben Mohammeds*, Berlin, 1996.
Sezgin, Fuat, *Geschichte der arabischen Schrifttums*, Leiden, 1967-.
Shils, Edward, *Tradition*, Chicago, 1981.
al-Suyūṭī, ʿAbd al-Raḥmān b. Abī Bakr, *al-Khaṣāʾiṣ al-kubrā*, ed. Muḥammad Khalīl Harrās, 2 vols., Cairo, 1967.
al-ʿUṭāridī, Aḥmad b. ʿAbd al-Jabbār (putative editor of) *al-Maghāzī li-Ibn Isḥāq* (in the recension of Yūnus b. Bukayr), ed. Muḥammad Ḥamīd Allāh, Konya, 1981.
Wansbrough, John, *The Sectarian Milieu. Content and Composition of Islamic Salvation History*, Oxford, 1978.
Yerushalmi, Yosef Hayim, *Zakhor. Jewish History and Jewish Memory*, Seattle, 1982.

MŪSĀ B. ʿUQBAS *MAGHĀZĪ*[*]

GREGOR SCHOELER

I

Unter "Mūsā b. ʿUqbas *Maghāzī*" [1] wird im Folgenden das kurze Berliner "Fragment" Ahlwardt Nr. 1554 verstanden, das Eduard Sachau im Jahre 1904 zum ersten Male herausgegeben, mit einer Einleitung versehen, ins Deutsche übersetzt und kommentiert hat.[2]

Das sogenannte Fragment—man sollte es besser als *Muntakhab*, Epitome, bezeichnen[3]—ist enthalten in einer Sammelhandschrift aus dem 8./14. Jahrhundert. Es besteht aus neunzehn dem Mūsā b. ʿUqba (st. 141/758)[4] zugeschriebenen Traditionen und einer weiteren Tradition. Sie werden vom Epitomator ausdrücklich als "aus den

---

[*] A summary in English of this paper follows below, pp. 90 ff.

[1] Der Begriff *al-maghāzī*, Kriegszüge, meint im engeren Sinn die Kriegszüge Muḥammads (die ausschliesslich in die medinensische Epoche seines Wirkens fallen), dann auch das gesamte Wirken Muḥammads in der medinensischen Zeit, und schliesslich im weitesten Sinne das gesamte Leben und Wirken Muḥammads. In letzterem Fall ist *maghāzī* identisch mit *sīra* (Verhalten, Lebensweise, Biographie). Die berühmteste Biographie Muḥammads, die von Ibn Isḥāq, wird zumeist *Kitāb al-Maghāzī* genannt (vgl. aber M. Jarrar, *Die Prophetenbiographie im islamischen Spanien. Ein Beitrag zur Überlieferungs- und Redaktionsgeschichte*, Frankfurt/Bern, 1989, 1 ff. und 32 ff.; gegen M. Hinds, "al-Maghāzī" in *EI*[2], s.v.).—Mūsā b. ʿUqbas Werk, das ebenfalls das ganze Leben des Propheten abdeckte, wird einhellig als *(Kitāb) al-Maghāzī* zitiert.—Siehe unten unter Abschnitt II.

[2] E. Sachau, " Das Berliner Fragment des Mūsā Ibn ʿUḳba", in *SPAW*, 1904, 445-70. Eine neue Ausgabe hat Mashhūr Ḥasan Salmān unter dem Titel *Aḥādīth muntakhaba min Maghāzī Mūsā b. ʿUqba* 1991 in Beirut erscheinen lassen.—Ich danke Herrn Avraham Hakim, Tel Aviv, dafür, dass er mich beim Nimwegener Kolloquium auf diese Ausgabe aufmerksam gemacht und mir eine Kopie davon besorgt hat.—Diese Neuausgabe des Berliner Unicums bietet sehr oft einen besseren Text als die Sachausche. Ausserdem besticht sie durch die gehaltvolle Einleitung sowie durch den systematischen Nachweis von Paralleltraditionen in den Fussnoten.—Ich zitiere im Folgenden nach dieser Ausgabe.—Eine z. T. gekürzte Übersetzung des "Fragments" ins Englische bietet A. Guillaume in der Einleitung zu seiner Ibn Isḥāq-Übersetzung *The Life of Muhammad. A Translation of Ibn Isḥāq's* Sīrat Rasūl Allāh, Oxford, 1955, xliii-xlvii.

[3] Der Titel in der Handschrift lautet *Aḥādīth muntakhaba*; siehe Sachau, "Fragment", 470; Salmān, *Aḥādīth*, 55.

[4] Zu ihm s. *GAS* I, 286 f.; J. Horovitz, "The Earliest Biographies of the Prophet and Their Authors", III, in *Islamic Culture*, 2 (1928), 164-167; Salmān, *Aḥādīth*, 7 ff.; Abū Mālik, *al-Maghāzī li-Mūsā b. ʿUqba* (*al-Qism al-dirāsī*), Agadir, 1994, 15 f.

Maghāzī (sc. Mūsās) ausgewählt" bezeichnet und sind jeweils einem Teil eines zehnteiligen Grundwerks zugeordnet. Dem kleinen Werk geht eine *riwāya* (Überliefererkette) voraus, die von einem Gelehrten des 8./14. Jahrhunderts bis zum Urheber des Werkes (*ṣāḥib al-maghāzī*), Mūsā b. ʿUqba, führt.[5] Wir brauchen hier nur Mūsās unmittelbaren Tradenten (*rāwī*) sowie dessen Tradenten und den Epitomator zu erwähnen: Es sind Mūsās Neffe Ismāʿīl b. Ibrāhīm b. ʿUqba (st. 158/774—*GAS,* I, 286), dessen Schüler Ismāʿīl b. Abī Uways ʿAbd Allāh (st. 226/840-41) und Muḥammad b. ʿAbd Allāh Ibn ʿAttāb (st. 344/955-6).[6]

Die Mehrzahl der neunzehn Traditionen enthält Äusserungen des Propheten oder berichtet—seltener ausführlicher (III, VII, XVIII, XIX)—über Ereignisse aus seinem Leben. Zwei Traditionen beziehen sich auf die Zeit nach seinem Tode: Sie betreffen eine Ansprache Abū Bakrs (XIX) und eine Massnahme ʿUmars (XIV) aus der Zeit ihrer Kalifate. Tradition XI setzt X fort, XV und XVI gehören zusammen, wahrscheinlich auch XIII und XIV; VIII und IX bilden sogar ursprünglich *eine einzige* Tradition (siehe unten, S. 73 ff.); unter XIII laufen dagegen wahrscheinlich *zwei* Traditionen, wobei der *isnād* der zweiten offenbar durch eine Lücke in der Handschrift verloren ist.[7]

Die Intention einer chronologischen Ordnung der Traditionen ist erkennbar, eine solche Ordnung ist aber nicht ganz konsequent durchgeführt:[8] Tradition II spielt vor der Hijra, III und IV während derselben, V und VI während oder kurz nach der Schlacht von Badr (2/624), VII bezieht sich auf die Ereignisse bei Biʾr Maʿūna (4/625), X f. auf ein Ereignis während der Razzia gegen die Banū l-Muṣṭaliq (nach Mūsās Datierung 5/626-7), XII und XIII auf Geschehnisse während und nach der Eroberung von Khaybar (7/628), XV f. auf die Verteilung der Beute von Ḥunayn (8/630), XVII berichtet über die Abschiedswallfahrt (10/632), XVIII handelt von einem Ereignis im Jahr der Gesandtschaften (9/630-1) und XIX schließlich von einem solchen kurz nach dem Regierungsantritt Abū Bakrs. Ganz aus der chronologischen Folge fallen VIII f., die sich auf eine Entschei-

---

[5] Sachau, "Fragment", 470; Salmān, *Aḥādīth,* 57 f.

[6] Zu ihnen siehe Sachau, "Fragment", 449; J. Schacht, "On Mūsā b. ʿUqba's *Kitāb al-Maghāzī*", in *Acta Orientalia,* 21 (1953), 289; und Salmān, *Aḥādīth,* 47 ff.

[7] Siehe Sachau, "Fragment", 457 und Salmān, *Aḥādīth,* 84, Anm.

[8] Dieselbe Feststellung macht man bei Maʿmars *K. al-Maghāzī*; vgl. hierzu G. Schoeler, *Charakter und Authentie der muslimischen Überlieferung über das Leben Mohammeds,* Berlin/New York, 1996, 40 f.

dung Muḥammads kurz vor seinem Tode beziehen, und XIV, die über eine Anordnung ʿUmars zur Zeit seines Kalifates berichtet. Diese Tradition (XIV) ist allerdings durch ihr Thema (die Frage, ob und wielange die *ahl al-kitāb* sich auf der arabischen Halbinsel aufhalten dürfen) mit der vorausgehenden (XIII) verknüpft.

Sieht man einmal von Tradition XVII ab, die hier eine gewisse Ausnahme bildet (siehe sogleich unten), so sind sämtliche Traditionen ausser im *Muntakhab* auch in anderen Werken überliefert und werden auch anderweitig Mūsā zugeschrieben. Zwölf finden sich—jeweils zitiert mit demselben *isnād* von Mūsā "abwärts" und derselben Überliefererkette (*riwāya*) bis zum fünften Glied von Mūsā "aufwärts"[9]—in al-Bayhaqīs *Dalāʾil al-nubuwwa,* elf davon mit identischem oder fast identischem Wortlaut.[10] Allerdings sind sie hier oft etwas länger als im *Muntakhab,* nur die Entsprechung von XIII ist geringfügig kürzer;[11] in einem Fall (der Entsprechung von XVII = *Dalāʾil,*V, 448) wird die Tradition nicht im Wortlaut angeführt, vielmehr wird nur auf ihren Inhalt hingewiesen. Diese Tradition scheint sich sonst in der Traditionsliteratur nirgends zu finden.—Andere auf Mūsā zurückgeführte Paralleltraditionen[12] finden sich bei al-Bukhārī und in den übrigen kanonischen Traditionssammlungen, bei al-Ṭayālisī, Ibn Saʿd, ʿAbd al-Razzāq, ʿUmar b. Shabba und in vielen anderen Werken.

E. Sachau hat in seinen Kommentaren zu den einzelnen Traditionen bereits die ihm bekannt gewordenen Paralleltraditionen sowie weiteres Vergleichsmaterial angeführt; M. Ḥ. Salmān ist ihm hierin in seiner Neuausgabe gefolgt und hat in den Fussnoten zum Text eine beeindruckend grosse Menge weiterer Belege beigebracht. Vor wenigen Jahren hat ein marokkanischer Gelehrter, Muḥammad Bāqshīsh Abū Mālik, den Versuch unternommen, die auf Mūsā zurückgeführten Traditionen zusammenzustellen.[13] Derselbe Versuch soll auch im Rahmen einer unveröffentlichten ʿAmmāner Magisterarbeit un-

---

[9] Unter "aufwärts" wird hier und im Folgenden "in der chronologischen Abfolge später", unter "abwärts" "in der chronologischen Abfolge früher" verstanden.

[10] II = *Dalāʾil,* II, 433 und 441; III = *Dalāʾil,* II, 487 f.; V = *Dalāʾil,* III, 117; VI = *Dalāʾil,* III, 141; VII = *Dalāʾil,* III, 343; X = *Dalāʾil,* IV, 57; XI = *Dalāʾil,* IV, 57; XIII = *Dalāʾil,* IV, 234; XV = *Dalāʾil,* V, 192 unten; XVI = *Dalāʾil,* V, 193 oben; XVIII = *Dalāʾil,* VI, 319.

[11] Es fehlt nur der letzte Satz.

[12] Unter "Paralleltraditionen" verstehe ich Traditionen gleichen oder ähnlichen Inhalts, die in anderen Werken mit identischem *isnād* (mindestens von Mūsā "abwärts") auf Mūsā zurückgeführt werden.

[13] *Al-Maghāzī li-Mūsā b. ʿUqba.*

ternommen worden sein.[14] Abū Māliks Sammlung, die übrigens einiges zu wünschen übrig lässt—ein Desiderat wäre z. B. gewesen, die einzelnen in verschiedenen Überlieferungen vorliegenden Mūsā-Traditionen einer Synopse zu unterziehen—hat immerhin doch das Verdienst, die in der Literatur auf Mūsā zurückgeführten Texte einigermassen vollständig zusammengestellt und in den Fussnoten auf Paralleltraditionen hingewiesen zu haben.—Salmāns Edition des Berliner Unicums (mit sehr viel mehr Nachweisen von Parallelen) ist Abū Mālik unbekannt geblieben.

Die wissenschaftliche Beschäftigung mit dem *Muntakhab*, die mit E. Sachau begonnen hatte, wurde von J. Schacht in seinem Aufsatz "On Musā b. ʿUqba's *Kitāb al-Maghāzī*" fortgesetzt.[15] Schacht geht es in diesem Aufsatz darum, seine wohlbekannte, an der rechtlichen islamischen Überlieferung entwickelte Theorie nun auch am Beispiel der historischen Überlieferung zu demonstrieren.[16] Diese Theorie besagt, dass ein erheblicher Teil der gesamten islamischen Überlieferung, wie sie uns in der zweiten Hälfte des zweiten Jahrhunderts entgegentritt, ganz rezenten Ursprungs und somit historisch wertlos ist. Die einzelnen historischen Traditionen, so wie sie jetzt vorliegen, erklären sich nach Schacht durch Formalisierung, Systematisierung und Ausschmückung einer vagen kollektiven Erinnerung der Gemeinde; die mit den Traditionen verknüpften Herkunftsbezeichnungen (*isnāde*) haben—so Schacht—durchweg als spätere Hinzufügungen (nicht vor dem 2. Jahrhundert H.) und als fiktiv zu gelten.

Nachdem nun in den letzten Jahren so viele neuen Quellenwerke mit Mūsā b. ʿUqba-Material zutage getreten und zugänglich gemacht worden sind und nachdem in der neueren Forschung die Schachtschen Thesen stark angefochten oder sogar regelrecht widerlegt worden sind,[17] ist eine erneute systematische Untersuchung des *Muntakhab* an der Zeit.

Ansätze zu einer Auseinandersetzung mit Schachts Auffassungen bezüglich des *Muntakhab* finden sich in zwei Werken Muḥammad M. al-Aʿẓamīs.[18] Etwas mehr in die Tiefe gehend und in der Sache

[14] Der Kompilator ist Walīd Qaysīya; vgl. Salmān, *Aḥādīth*, 24, Anm. 1.

[15] Siehe Anm. 6.

[16] Schacht, "On Mūsā", 288.

[17] Siehe vor allem H. Motzki, *Die Anfänge der islamischen Jurisprudenz. Ihre Entwicklung in Mekka bis zur Mitte des 2./8. Jahrhunderts*, Stuttgart, 1991 und ders., "Der Fiqh des -Zuhrī: die Quellenproblematik", in *Der Islam*, 68 (1991), 1-44.—Eine Auseinandersetzung mit Schacht aus muslimischer Perspektive ist M.M. Azamis Buch *On Schacht's Origins of Muhammadan Jurisprudence*, Riyad, 1985.

[18] In der Einleitung zu seiner Edition von Muslims *K. al-Tamyīz*, 89 ff. und in

durchweg berechtigt, wegen ihres polemischen Tons aber unerfreulich, ist die Kritik Salmāns in der Einleitung zu seiner Neuedition des *Muntakhab*.[19] Was bislang fehlt, ist eine umfassende und systematische "Revaluation" der Thesen Schachts. Eine solche soll im Folgenden unternommen werden.[20]

II

Bevor wir in die Auseinandersetzung mit Schacht eintreten, soll aber das Nötige über das hypothetische Grundwerk Mūsās und die Überlieferungen (Rezensionen), in denen es umlief, gesagt werden. Dazu ist ein Blick in die biographische Literatur erforderlich. Dass es "die *Maghāzī* Mūsās" gegeben hat, ist schon für eine frühe Zeit bezeugt; Mālik b. Anas soll gesagt haben: *ʿalaykum bi-Maghāzī Mūsā b. ʿUqba*.[21] Mālik und Yaḥyā b. Maʿīn sprechen auch von einem *kitāb Mūsā* bzw. von einem *kitāb Mūsā ʿan al-Zuhrī*.[22] Wie man sich das *kitāb* Mūsā zu dieser frühen Zeit vorzustellen hat, ist nicht genau auszumachen.[23] Sicher ist aber, dass es das gesamte Leben des Propheten—die Zeit vor[24] und nach der Hijra—sowie die Epoche der rechtgeleiteten Kalifen abdeckte, und möglicherweise behandelte es darüber hinaus auch die Zeit der ersten Umayyaden.[25] Nach al-Dhahabī war es das erste systematisch geordnete Werk (*taṣnīf*) über die *Maghāzī* überhaupt.

seinen *Dirāsāt fī l-ḥadīth al-nabawī*, II, 386 ff.—Die Werke liegen mir nicht vor; ich zitiere nach Salmān, *Aḥādīth*, 34, Anm. 2.

[19] S. 33 f. und 37 ff. Salmān, *Aḥādīth* referiert S. 34 f. auch die Argumente al-Aʿẓamīs und setzt sich damit auseinander.

[20] Hingewiesen sei hier noch auf die Untersuchung M. Jarrars über die Verbreitung von Mūsās *Maghāzī* in al-Andalus; siehe dessen *Die Prophetenbiographie*, 71-76.

[21] Dhahabī, *Siyar*, VI, 115; mehrfach.

[22] Ebd., VI, 116 f.; siehe auch Ibn Saʿd, *Ṭabaqāt*, III b, 120.

[23] Mit dem "*kitāb Mūsā ʿan al-Zuhrī*" sind wohl Mūsās Nachschriften seiner Vorlesungen bei al-Zuhrī gemeint.

[24] Siehe etwa Bayhaqī, *Dalāʾil*, II, 285, wo eine lange Tradition Mūsās über die erste Auswanderung nach Abessinien ausdrücklich nach seinem *kitāb* überliefert wird.

[25] Dass das Werk auch Ereignisse *nach* dem Tod des Propheten behandelte, wie schon Horovitz richtig festgestellt hat ("The Earliest Biographies", III, 165, 166), ist von Schacht ("On Mūsā", 292) zu Unrecht bestritten worden. Unser *Muntakhab* enthält zwei Traditionen (XIV und XIX), die in der Zeit der Kalifate Abū Bakrs und ʿUmars spielen. Die chronologisch spätesten unter Mūsās Namen überlieferten Traditionen handeln von der Schlacht auf der Ḥarra (63/863) und von einem Ereignis während der Statthalterschaft Khālid al-Qasrīs (91/710); siehe Abū Mālik, *Maghāzī*, 351 ff.—Es ist allerdings sehr wohl möglich, dass Mūsā solche Traditionen ausserhalb des *Kitāb al-Maghāzī* überliefert hat.

Mūsās Ordnungsprinzip war sehr wahrscheinlich die Chronologie, denn von ihm sind zahlreiche—oft von Ibn Isḥāq abweichende—Datierungen von Ereignissen überliefert.[26] Ausser Traditionen enthielt das Werk zahlreiche Listen von Teilnehmern an Schlachten und anderen wichtigen Ereignissen des Frühislams, Listen, von denen viele erhalten sind.[27]

Sicher ist, dass Mūsās *K. al-Maghāzī* nicht in einer vom Verfasser authentisch redigierten und für ein breiteres Publikum von Lesern bestimmten Form (*syngramma*; *ekdosis*) vorlag, sondern dass es nur in Kollegnachschriften (Weiterüberlieferungen, Rezensionen) von Schülern und Schülersschülern umlief (Mālik wird in dem oben zitierten Bericht gefragt: "Wessen *maghāzī* sollen wir (nach)schreiben?").—Wir gehen vielleicht nicht fehl, wenn wir uns Mūsās Werk, wie es in dieser Zeit umlief, etwa so vorstellen wie den erhaltenen *Taʾrīkh al-Madīna* von ʿUmar b. Shabba (st. 264/877). Dieses Werk ist eine von einem Schüler nachgeschriebene Sammlung historischer Traditionen nach Ibn Shabba,[28] die wenn möglich in chronologischer Ordnung, aber ohne verbindende Bemerkungen und Kommentare des Verfassers oder Überlieferers dargeboten werden.

Der wichtigste Tradent von Mūsās *kitāb* war sein Neffe Ismāʿīl b. Ibrāhīm.[29] Er scheint das Werk seines Onkels als Ganzes weiterüberliefert zu haben. Auf dieser *riwāya* beruhen sowohl unser *Muntakhab* als auch die damit z. T. identischen Auszüge al-Bayhaqīs in seinen *Dalāʾil.* Es ist wichtig festzuhalten, dass neben der Weiterüberlieferung des gesamten Werkes (oder grösserer Teile hiervon) auch eine Menge einzelner Traditionen nach Mūsā fortgepflanzt worden ist, solche aus dem *K. al-Maghāzī*, wahrscheinlich aber auch solche, die Mūsā ausserhalb dieses Werkes überliefert hat.

Weitere Tradenten Mūsās waren Muḥammad b. Fulayḥ (st. 197/812-3, *GAS,* I, 287)[30] und al-Fuḍayl b. Sulaymān (st. 185/801).[31] Letzterer (sowie ein anderer Gelehrter) soll einmal zu Mūsā gegangen

---

[26] Siehe J.M.B. Jones, "The Chronology of the *Maghāzī*—A Textual Survey", in *BSOAS,* 19 (1957), 245-80.

[27] Siehe z. B. die Liste der Auswanderer nach Abessinien, in Abū Mālik, *Maghāzī,* 74 ff., die Liste der Gefallenen und der Teilnehmer an der Schlacht von Badr, ebd., 143 ff. bzw. 147 ff., die Liste der in der Schlacht von Uḥud Gefallenen, ebd., 195 ff., die Liste der im Grabenkrieg Gefallenen, ebd., 222 f.—Mūsā überliefert die genannten Listen nach al-Zuhrī.

[28] Siehe *Taʾrīkh al-Madīna,* I, 133.

[29] Vgl. Ibn Saʿd, *Ṭabaqāt,* V, 310.

[30] Ibn Ḥajar, *Tahdhīb,* IX, 360 f.

[31] Ibn Ḥajar, *Tahdhīb,* VIII, 262.

sein, sich von ihm "ein Buch" (das *K. al-Maghāzī*?) geliehen haben, es ihm aber nicht zurückgegeben haben.[32] Aus diesem Bericht geht u. a. hervor, dass Mūsā sein Wissen nicht nur in Vorlesungen weitergab, sondern dass er seinen Schülern—wie übrigens auch schon sein Lehrer al-Zuhrī und seine Zeitgenossen Mālik b. Anas und Ibn Isḥāq[33]—gelegentlich seine privaten Aufzeichnungen zur Abschrift überliess. (Es handelt sich also um die wenig anerkannte Überlieferungsweise der *munāwala*).

Al-Dhahabī charakterisiert das *K. al-Maghāzī* Mūsās, das er selbst "gehört" und in seiner Prophetenbiographie (den ersten beiden Teilen seines *K. al-Taʾrīkh al-kabīr*) exzerpiert hat, als "einen nicht grossen Band", der zwar zum grössten Teil "authentisch" (*ṣaḥīḥ*), aber so kurz sei, dass er erklärungs- und ergänzungsbedürftig sei.[34]

III

Im Folgenden sei zunächst an einem Beispiel demonstriert, wie sehr sich die Beurteilung einer bzw. zweier Einzeltraditionen aus dem *Muntakhab* allein dadurch ändern kann, dass heute—durch das Vorliegen eines (einigermassen) vollständigen Korpus der Mūsā-Überlieferungen—so viel mehr Vergleichsmaterial vorliegt als zu Sachaus und Schachts Zeit.[35] Es geht um die beiden Traditionen VIII und IX.

VIII hat den *isnād*: Ismāʿīl b. Ibrāhīm b. ʿUqba (das Glied Mūsā b. ʿUqba fehlt im *Muntakhab*)—Sālim b. ʿAbd Allāh—ʿAbd Allāh b. ʿUmar.

Im Text heisst es, dass einige Leute unzufrieden damit waren, dass der Prophet dem erst neunzehnjährigen Usāma b. Zayd das Oberkommando gegen die Byzantiner übertragen hatte. Der Prophet entgegnete darauf:

> Wenn ihr jetzt die Führerschaft Usāmas anfechtet, so habt ihr vorher auch die Führerschaft seines Vaters (Zayd b. Ḥāritha) angefochten. Er (Zayd) war aber, bei Gott, sehr wohl geeignet für das Kommando, und er war mir einer der liebsten von allen Menschen. Und dieser hier nun (Usāma) ist mir einer der liebsten Menschen nach ihm. So seid ihm

[32] Ebd.

[33] Siehe Schoeler, *Charakter*, 6, Anm. 4, und 34 f. und 39.

[34] Dhahabī, *Siyar*, VI, 116.

[35] Vgl. zum Folgenden Salmān, *Aḥādīth*, 38 ff., der zu denselben Ergebnissen kommt.

nach meinem Tode wohlwollend gesinnt, denn er gehört zu den Edelsten von euch.

Die sehr kurze Tradition IX hat den *isnād* Mūsā—Sālim b. ʿAbd Allāh—ʿAbd Allāh b. ʿUmar. Der Text lautet:

> *mā kāna rasūl Allāh yastathnī Fāṭima.* Der Gesandte Gottes pflegte (seine Tochter) Fāṭima nicht auszunehmen.

Zu VIII hatte bereits Sachau einige Parallelen aus al-Bukhārī und Ibn Isḥāq zusammengestellt.[36] Darunter findet sich eine Tradition, die ebenfalls nach Mūsā b. ʿUqba—Sālim—ʿAbd Allāh überliefert wird.[37] Allerdings ist der Tradent Mūsās hier nicht sein Neffe Ismāʿīl, sondern al-Fuḍayl b. Sulaymān. Es handelt sich also um eine andere Weiterüberlieferung (Rezension) der Tradition. Sinngemäss entspricht diese Version der Tradition des *Muntakhab* genau, jedoch ist sie bei al-Bukhārī gekürzt. Sie lautet hier:

> *istaʿmala al-nabī Usāma fa-qālū fīhi. fa-qāla al-nabī: qad balaghanī annakum qultum fī Usāma wa-innahū aḥabb al-nās ilayya.* Der Prophet machte Usāma zum Heerführer. Da redeten sie über ihn [Nachteiliges]. Der Prophet sagte darauf: "Es ist mir zu Ohren gekommen, dass ihr [Nachteiliges] über Usāma geredet habt, dabei ist er mir der liebste der Menschen."

Von IX hatte Sachau angenommen, dass damit ein Ausspruch Muḥammads gemeint sei, der sonst wie folgt überliefert wird: "Und wenn es Fāṭima selbst wäre, die gestohlen hätte, so würde ich ihr die Hand abschlagen."[38]

Schacht will VIII gar nicht als Teil des *K. al-Maghāzī* von Mūsā b. ʿUqba anerkennen. Grund dafür ist zum einen seine Annahme, dass das ursprüngliche *K. al-Maghāzī* Mūsās ausschliesslich nach al-Zuhrī überlieferte Traditionen enthalten habe (siehe dazu unten, S. 76 ff.) und zum anderen der Umstand, dass im *isnād* der Berliner Handschrift des *Muntakhab* das Glied Ibn ʿUqba fehlt.[39] Wenn dieses Glied im entsprechenden *isnād* der Paralleltradition bei al-Bukhārī[40] dennoch auftrete, so handle es sich hier eben um eine "relatively late, improved form of the isnād".—Dass das Fehlen des Gliedes Ibn ʿUqba im *isnād* der (späten und schlechten) Handschrift des *Muntakhab*

---

[36] Siehe jetzt zahlreiche weitere Nachweise bei Salmān, *Aḥādīth*, 75 f., Anm. 8, und 77, Anm. 9, sowie bei Abū Mālik, *Maghāzī*, 327, Anm. 654-56.

[37] Bukhārī, *Ṣaḥīḥ*, IV, 1620, Nr. 4198 = Ibn Ḥajar, *Fatḥ*, XVI, 287, Nr. 4468.

[38] Sachau, "Fragment", 456; siehe die Belege dort.

[39] Schacht, "On Mūsā", 291.

[40] Siehe Anm. 37.

auch ein Flüchtigkeitsfehler des Schreibers sein könnte, zumal im Glied davor—Ismāʿīl b. Ibrāhīm b. ʿUqba—das Element "b. ʿUqba" gerade vorgekommen war, an diese Möglichkeit scheint Schacht nicht einmal gedacht zu haben.[41]

Tradition IX, die Schacht ebenfalls für eine spätere Hinzufügung zu Mūsās *K. al-Maghāzī* hält (weil Mūsās Gewährsmann nicht al-Zuhrī ist; siehe unten), deutet er als "anti-ʿalidisch"—das heisst bei ihm: als eine Zweckfälschung mit anti-ʿalidischer Tendenz. Der Grund für diese Deutung ist, dass diese Tradition "denies privileges in penal law to the descendants of the Prophet".[42]

Nun gibt es eine ganze Reihe von Parallelen zu der Tradition VIII f., die Sachau und Schacht noch unbekannt waren.[43] Hätten die beiden Gelehrten sie gekannt, so wäre ihre Einschätzung der in Rede stehenden Tradition mit Sicherheit anders ausgefallen. Eine dieser Paralleltraditionen findet sich in al-Ṭayālisīs *Musnad*.[44] Ihr *isnād* lautet: Abū Dāwūd (al-Ṭayālisī)—Ḥammād b. Salama—Mūsā b. ʿUqba—Sālim b. ʿAbd Allāh—ʿAbd Allāh b. ʿUmar; der Text:

> *samiʿtu rasūl Allāh yaqūlu: Usāma aḥabb al-nās ilayya wa-lam yastathni Fāṭima wa-lā ghayrahā.* Ich hörte den Gesandten Gottes sagen: "Usāma ist mir der liebste aller Menschen." Er nahm dabei auch Fāṭima nicht aus, und auch niemand anderen.

Eine fast gleichlautende Parallele mit demselben *isnād* bis Ḥammād b. Salama "aufwärts" bringt unter anderen auch Aḥmad b. Ḥanbal in seinem *Musnad*:

> *inna rasūl Allāh qāla: Usāma aḥabb al-nās ilayya mā ḥāshā Fāṭima wa-lā ghayrahā.*[45]

Wir haben es hier also mit einer dritten Weiterüberlieferung (Rezension) der Tradition Mūsās zu tun, nämlich der nach dem Mūsā-Tradenten Ḥammād b. Salama. Aus ihrem Text ergibt sich mit Sicherheit: 1) dass die Traditionen VIII und IX ursprünglich eine einzige Überlieferung bildeten, die in der Rezension Ismāʿīl b. Ibrāhīms im *Muntakhab* durch einen Überlieferungsfehler auseinandergerissen ist, die in der gekürzten Rezension al-Fuḍayls bei al-Bukhārī den Tradition IX entsprechenden Teil verloren hat, aber in der Rezension

[41] Dies ist auch ein Kritikpunkt Salmāns (*Aḥādīth*, 38 f.).
[42] Schacht, "On Mūsā", 290.
[43] Siehe Anm. 36.
[44] Ṭayālisī, *Musnad*, Nr. 1812.
[45] Ibn Ḥanbal, *Musnad*, II, 96.

Ḥammād b. Salamas vollständig erhalten ist, 2) dass VIII ursprünglich denselben *isnād* wie IX hatte und dass mithin von einer "Ausbesserung" des *isnād*es von VIII bei al-Bukhārī keine Rede sein kann; 3) dass die Feststellung, Muḥammad habe Fāṭima "nicht ausgenommen", sich nicht auf eventuelle Strafmassnahmen, sondern auf seine erklärte Vorliebe für Usāma bezieht; 4) dass die Tradition VIII f. in Mūsās Überlieferungsschatz war oder zumindest auf Autorität Mūsās weiterüberliefert wurde, denn auch al-Ṭayālisī und Aḥmad b. Ḥanbal führen sie auf Mūsā zurück, und zwar in einer von unserem *Muntakhab* und von al-Bukhārī unabhängigen Überlieferung. Damit fällt Schachts gesamte Deutung in sich zusammen.

IV

Wie schon erwähnt, möchte Schacht—zumindest in der Regel—nur jene Traditionen im *Muntakhab* dem ursprünglichen Bestand von Mūsās Buch zurechnen, 1) in deren *isnād* Mūsā selbst genannt ist und 2) in denen Mūsā als seinen Gewährsmann *al-Zuhrī* angibt.[46] Von dieser Regel macht er allerdings Ausnahmen.[47] Die restlichen Überlieferungen hält er für spätere Hinzufügungen.[48] Dabei ist zu beachten, dass ihm Mūsās Herkunftsangabe (ursprünglich angeblich immer *ʿan* al-Zuhrī) durchweg als fiktiv gilt: "it is impossible to regard the original stock of the *Kitāb al-Maghāzī*, consisting of traditions related by Mūsā on the authority of Zuhrī, as authentic statements made by the latter."[49] Übrigens scheint Schacht zunächst sogar gezögert zu haben, überhaupt einen echten, d. h. wirklich auf Mūsā zurückgehenden, Kernbestand des *Muntakhab* anzuerkennen;[50] er hat sich schliesslich aber dann doch dazu entschlossen.

Im folgenden Abschnitt sei Schachts Behauptung, alle nicht auf al-Zuhrī zurückgeführten Traditionen im *Muntakhab* seien "spätere Hinzufügungen" noch an einem weiteren Beispiel nachgeprüft.[51] Wir wenden uns den beiden (zusammengehörigen) Traditionen X und XI zu. Nach Schacht soll Tradition X f. irgendwann während der 100 Jahre

[46] Schacht, "On Mūsā", 293 f.
[47] Siehe nächsten Abschnitt.
[48] Schacht, "On Mūsā", 290 f.
[49] Ebd., 292.
[50] Ebd., 290.
[51] Dass Tradition VIII f. zu Mūsās ursprünglichem Überlieferungsschatz gehörte, ist bereits im vorigen Abschnitt wahrscheinlich gemacht worden.

zwischen Mūsā und al-Bukhārī dem *K. al-Maghāzī* einverleibt worden sein.[52] Für uns stellt sich—nach dem in Abschnitt II über Mūsās "Buch" Ausgeführten—die Frage etwas anders: Es soll nicht darum gehen, ob und wann Überlieferung X f. in Mūsās *K. al-Maghāzī* eingefügt wurde, sondern ob die beiden Traditionen dem ursprünglichen Überlieferungsschatz Mūsās angehört haben oder nicht.

Die Traditionen finden sich mit demselben *isnād* (von Mūsā "abwärts") auch bei al-Bukhārī und in al-Bayhaqīs *Dalāʾil al-nubuwwa*.[53] Der *isnād* lautet: Mūsā—ʿAbd Allāh b. al-Faḍl—Anas b. Mālik. Der Tradent Mūsās ist in allen drei Fällen Ismāʿīl b. Ibrāhīm b. ʿUqba. Der Text besagt kurz zusammengefasst das folgende:

X: Anas b. Mālik erzählt, er habe getrauert wegen seiner in der Schlacht auf der Ḥarra (63/683) gefallenen Stammesangehörigen. Da habe ihm Zayd b. Arqam zum Trost geschrieben, er habe den Propheten sagen hören: "O Gott, verzeih den Anṣār und ihren Nachkommen!"

XI: ʿAbd Allāh b. al-Faḍl bemerkt dazu: Jemand habe Anas b. Mālik nach Zayd b. Arqam gefragt. Darauf habe dieser gesagt: "Das ist derjenige, zu dem der Gesandte Gottes sprach: "Dieser ist es, den Gott begnadet hat durch sein *Ohr*" (nämlich weil er dem Propheten als Spion gedient hat).

Damit endet der Text im *Muntakhab* und bei al-Bukhārī. Aus Ibn Ḥajars Kommentar zu al-Bukhārī[54] sowie aus einer entsprechenden Bemerkung (samt Zitat) al-Bayhaqīs[55] geht aber hervor, dass diese Tradition noch über einen anderen Weg auf Mūsā zurückgeführt wird, nämlich über Muḥammad b. Fulayḥ. Ibn Ḥajar und al-Bayhaqī sagen, in dieser anderen Rezension (*riwāya*) habe die Tradition noch eine Ergänzung. Diese bestehe aus einer Tradition Mūsās nach al-Zuhrī. Sowohl Ibn Ḥajar als auch al-Bayhaqī führen die ergänzende Tradition im Wortlaut an. Sie berichtet über jenes Ereignis, bei dem Zayd b. Arqam dem Propheten den angesprochenen Spionage-Dienst erwiesen hat. Zum Schluss wird noch ein Koranvers erwähnt, der zur Bestätigung von Zayds Behauptung geoffenbart wurde (Sure 9:74).

---

[52] Schacht, "On Mūsā", 292.

[53] Bukhārī, *Ṣaḥīḥ*, IV, 1862, Nr. 4623 = Ibn Ḥajar, *Fatḥ*, XVIII, 291, Nr. 4906; Bayhaqī, *Dalāʾil*, IV, 57. Belege für zahlreiche weitere Paralleltraditionen bringen Salmān, *Aḥādīth*, 78 f., Anm. 10-11 und Abū Mālik, *Maghāzī*, 351 f., Anm. 808, und 233, Anm. 90.

[54] Ibn Ḥajar, *Fatḥ*, XVIII, 292.

[55] Bayhaqī, *Dalāʾil*, IV, 57, 58.

Glücklicherweise ist die zur Rede stehende Tradition—zumindest deren *Muntakhab* Nr. XI entsprechender Teil—in der Rezension Ibn Fulayḥ—Mūsā auch sonst erhalten, nämlich in ʿUmar b. Shabbas (st. 264/877) *Taʾrīkh al-Madīna*.[56] Der Text setzt mit Worten ein, die dem Beginn von Überlieferung XI ähnlich sind, ihm aber nicht wörtlich entsprechen.

XI (Rezension Ismāʿīl—Mūsā):

> *qāla Ibn al-Faḍl: fa-saʾala nās baʿḍ man kāna ʿindahū ʿan Zayd b. Arqam; fa-qāla...*
> *huwa alladhī yaqūlu lahū rasūl Allāh: hādhā alladhī awfā Allāh bi-udhnih.*

Ibn Shabba (Rezension Ibn Fulayḥ—Mūsā):

> ... *ḥaddathanā ʿAbd Allāh b. al-Faḍl annahū samiʿa Anas b. Mālik—wa-qad suʾila ʿan Zayd b. Arqam—fa-qāla:*
> *huwa alladhī yaqūlu l-nabī: huwa alladhī awfā Allāh bi-udhnih.*

Im Anschluss daran bringt ʿUmar b. Shabba tatsächlich jene Ergänzung, die auch Ibn Ḥajar und al-Bayhaqī nach Ibn Fulayḥ zitieren, und zwar fast wörtlich gleich wie bei diesen. Allerdings sagt er nicht, dass es sich um eine neue Tradition nach al-Zuhrī handelt,[57] vielmehr schliesst der Text unmittelbar an den anderen an:

> *samiʿa rajulan min al-munāfiqīn yaqūlu—wa-l-nabī yakhṭubu—laʾin kāna hādhā ṣādiqan la-naḥnu sharr min al-ḥamīr. fa-qāla Zayd b. Arqam:* ...

Wir haben hier also offensichtlich zwei unterschiedliche Weiterüberlieferungen oder Rezensionen (*riwāyāt*) einer (kombinierten) Tradition vor uns. Die eine *riwāya* (die über Ismāʿīl auf Mūsā zurückgeführt wird) hat der anderen den Anfang (das Nr. X entsprechende Stück) voraus, dafür fehlt ihr aber die Ergänzung (die angehängte Tradition nach al-Zuhrī). In der anderen *riwāya* (die über Ibn Fulayḥ auf Mūsā zurückgeführt wird) fehlt dagegen der Anfang,[58] dafür ist aber die Ergänzung vorhanden. Die Rezensionen haben also je ihren spezifischen Textbestand und Wortlaut. Der gemeinsame Archetypus kann aus ihnen sinngemäss rekonstruiert werden. Da dieser in beiden voneinander unabhängigen Rezensionen auf Mūsā zurückgeführt wird, ist nicht zu bezweifeln, dass sich die Tradition in Mūsās Überlieferungsschatz befunden hat. Wegen der Einhelligkeit der Überliefe-

---

[56] Ibn Shabba, *Taʾrīkh*, I, 354 f.

[57] Möglicherweise liegt das an einer Lücke in der Handschrift des *Taʾrīkh al-Madīna*.

[58] Dies gilt jedenfalls für die Version dieser Rezension, wie sie bei ʿUmar b. Shabba vorliegt. Es kann natürlich auch sein, dass erst ʿUmar (oder sein Gewährsmann Ibrāhīm b. al-Mundhir) den Text am Anfang gekürzt hat.

rung ist auch nicht zu bezweifeln, dass Mūsā den *Anfang* der kombinierten Tradition auf Autorität von ʿAbd Allāh b. al-Faḍl—Anas b. Mālik, und nicht nach al-Zuhrī, überliefert hat.

Mūsā weiss noch sehr viel mehr über jene Begebenheit zu berichten, während derer auch die hier zur Rede stehende Episode sich ereignet hat, nämlich die Razzia gegen die Banū l-Muṣṭaliq.[59] Den Grossteil überliefert er hier nach al-Zuhrī; auch die oben besprochene Ergänzung zu XI hat er ja von al-Zuhrī empfangen. Dass er Überlieferungen nach *einer* Autorität durch solche nach *anderen* Autoritäten ergänzt, ist ein zu seiner Zeit in seiner Zunft absolut übliches Verfahren. Kein einziger *Maghāzī*-Autor hat ausschliesslich nach *einem* Gewährsmann überliefert, man denke an Mūsās jüngere Zeitgenossen Ibn Isḥāq und Maʿmar b. Rāshid, die zwar einen grossen Teil, aber keineswegs ihr gesamtes *Maghāzī*-Material auf al-Zuhrī zurückführen. Selbst Ibn Hishām, der im Wesentlichen nur eine Bearbeitung von Ibn Isḥāqs Werk angefertigt hat, ergänzt die Berichte seiner Hauptquelle Ibn Isḥāq gelegentlich durch Traditionen, die auf andere Autoritäten zurückgehen. Warum sollte Mūsā das nicht auch getan haben? Es ist also völlig abwegig, aus dem (oben S. 71 angeführten) Ibn Maʿīn-Zitat ("*kitāb Mūsā ʿan al-Zuhrī*");[60] sowie aus einer ähnlichen Formulierung bei al-Bukhārī[61] zu schliessen, dass Mūsās *K. al-Maghāzī* in seiner ursprünglichen Form ausnahmslos Traditionen nach al-Zuhrī enthielt—wie Schacht es tut.

V

Nun gibt es für Schacht aber doch mindestens eine Ausnahme zu der von ihm aufgestellten Regel, dass Traditionen im *Muntakhab*, die *nicht* nach al-Zuhrī überliefert werden, "spätere Hinzufügungen zu Mūsās Buch" sind: Tradition XIII soll in Mūsās Buch gestanden haben, obwohl der *isnād* im *Muntakhab* Mūsā—Nāfiʿ—Ibn ʿUmar lautet.[62] Je-

---

[59] Siehe die lange Tradition bei Ibn Shabba, *Taʾrīkh*, I, 349 ff.

[60] Siehe Dhahabī, *Siyar*, VI, 116 f.

[61] *ḥaddathanā* Ibrāhīm b. Mundhir *ḥaddathanā* Muḥammad b. Fulayḥ *ʿan* Mūsā b. ʿUqba *ʿan* Ibn Shihāb al-Zuhrī, *qāla: hādhihī Maghāzī rasūl Allāh fa-dhakara al-ḥadīth* (Bukhārī, *Ṣaḥīḥ*, IV, 1476, Nr. 3802 = Ibn Ḥajar, *Fatḥ*, XV, 196, Nr. 4026).—Schacht meint hierzu "Bukhārī quotes [here] what appears to be the first words of Mūsā's work, the whole of which is presented as being derived from Zuhrī" ("On Mūsā", 291).

[62] Ebd., bes. Anm. 1 und 298.

doch zeigten—so Schacht—Parallelen in Mālik b. Anas' *Muwaṭṭa'*[63] und Ibn Isḥāq—Ibn Hishāms *Sīra*,[64] dass auch diese Tradition ursprünglich nach al-Zuhrī überliefert wurde. In solchen Fällen sei der ursprüngliche (fiktive) Überlieferer (al-Zuhrī) in einem späteren Stadium der Überlieferung eliminiert worden. Schacht stellt sich die Entwicklung also wie folgt vor: Der ursprüngliche *isnād* war Mūsā—al-Zuhrī (so in Mūsās "Buch", aber von diesem fingiert); in einer späteren Phase wurde der *isnād* zu Mūsā—al-Zuhrī—Nāfiʿ—Ibn ʿUmar; schliesslich wurde das Glied al-Zuhrī eliminiert und es entstand Mūsā—Nāfiʿ—Ibn ʿUmar (so im *Muntakhab*). Dies beweist nach Schacht wieder einmal, dass der *isnād* ein "künstliches Mittel" sei. Für ihn fällt diese Erscheinung unter jenes Phänomen, das er als "spreading out of *isnād*s" bezeichnet.

Für uns stellt sich hier die Frage, ob sich irgendwelche Anhaltspunkte dafür finden, dass Mūsā Tradition XIII ursprünglich wirklich nach al-Zuhrī überliefert hat. Wir wenden uns im Folgenden dieser Tradition zu. Ihr Inhalt ist: Nach der Eroberung von Khaybar erlaubt der Prophet den Juden, "so lange wie wir es wollen" in Khaybar zu bleiben, und zwar unter der Bedingung, dass sie den Muslimen die Hälfte ihrer Ernte abliefern. So blieb es, heisst es dann, bis ʿUmar die Juden aus Khaybar vertrieb. Eine Durchsicht der zahlreich vorhandenen Traditionen dieses Inhalts[65] ergibt, dass sich diese in zwei Gruppen aufteilen lassen: Die eine Gruppe überliefert das Ereignis nach Nāfiʿ—Ibn ʿUmar (so unter anderen Mūsā), die andere nach al-Zuhrī—Saʿīd b. al-Musayyab (so unter anderen Mālik b. Anas). In ʿAbd al-Razzāqs *Muṣannaf* finden sich beide "Varianten" nebeneinander.[66]

Eine Gegenüberstellung erweist sofort, dass es sich sich in Wirklichkeit um zwei verschiedene Traditionen handelt. Beide haben freilich ein ähnliches Kernstück, in welchem dasselbe Ereignis berichtet wird: nämlich dass Muḥammad nach der Eroberung Khaybars mit den Juden verhandelte und ihnen die Oasenstadt unter bestimmten Bedingungen beliess.—Bei genauerem Hinsehen zeigen sich aber

[63] Mālik, *Muwaṭṭa'*, *kitāb* 45, *bāb* 18. Eine genauere Parallele findet sich in *kitāb* 33, *bāb* 1, 1; siehe sogleich unten.

[64] Ibn Hishām, *Sīra*, ed. Wüstenfeld, 776; ed. al-Saqqā, II (3-4), 256.

[65] Belege für die Tradition nach Nāfiʿ—Ibn ʿUmar bei Salmān, *Aḥādīth*, 82 ff., Anm. 13 und Abū Mālik, *Maghāzī*, 252, Anm. 208.

[66] In V, 372 f., Nr. 9738 [84], VI, 56, Nr. 9990 und X, 360, Nr. 19369 überliefert er das Ereignis nach Maʿmar nach al-Zuhrī nach Ibn al-Musayyab; in VI, 55, Nr. 9989 und in X, 359, Nr. 19366 nach Ibn Jurayj nach Mūsā nach Nāfiʿ von Ibn ʿUmar.

auch in diesem Kernstück charakteristische Unterschiede zwischen den beiden Traditionen. Am deutlichsten wird dies am Wortlaut der Rede des Propheten. Während diese—wo immer sie wörtlich angeführt wird—in der al-Zuhrī-Überlieferung wie folgt lautet: *uqirrukum fīhā mā aqarrakum* [*Allāh*], heisst es in der Nāfiʿ-Überlieferung: *nuqirrukum fīhā ʿalā dhālika mā shiʾnā.*

Dies ist ausnahmslos in der gesamten Nāfiʿ—Ibn ʿUmar-Überlieferung so.[67] Mālik b. Anas überliefert im *Muwaṭṭaʾ* diesen rechtlich so relevanten Ausspruch Muḥammads über al-Zuhrī nach Ibn al-Musayyab;[68] erwartungsgemäss zitiert er den Propheten ganz entsprechend der übrigen al-Zuhrī-Überlieferung (*uqirrukum fīhā mā aqarrakum Allāh*). Auch Ibn Isḥāq folgt in seinem Bericht über Khaybar für das in Rede stehende Ereignis der al-Zuhrī-Überlieferung.[69] Seine Version steht der Maʿmars—al-Zuhrī sehr nahe, ohne freilich immer mit ihr wörtlich übereinzustimmen. Der Prophet sagt erwartungsgemäss auch hier: *uqirrukum fīhā mā aqarrakum Allāh.* Daran schliesst sich bei Ibn Isḥāq eine Tradition nach Nāfiʿ—Ibn ʿUmar an, aber *nicht* die inhaltlich entsprechende Tradition, die Mūsā nach Nāfiʿ überliefert. In ihr paraphrasiert der Kalif ʿUmar in einer Ansprache den fraglichen Ausspruch des Propheten in Khaybar; selbst hier ist der Wortlaut der in Rede stehenden Nāfiʿ—Ibn ʿUmar-Überlieferung noch erkennbar: ... *idhā shiʾnā*!

Die Berichte nach Mūsā—Nāfiʿ—Ibn ʿUmar und nach al-Zuhrī—Ibn al-Musayyab über die Behandlung der Juden von Khaybar sind also trotz ihrer inhaltlichen Überschneidung *zwei verschiedene Traditionen.* Sie wurden schon in der ersten Hälfte des 2./8. Jahrhunderts als unterschiedlich angesehen. So ist nicht nur sicher, dass Tradition XIII f. in Mūsās Überlieferungsschatz war (was ja auch Schacht annimmt). Es ist genau so sicher, dass schon Mūsā—wie z. B. auch Ibn Jurayj—sie mit dem *isnād* Nāfiʿ—Ibn ʿUmar weitergab; ebenso wie Mālik, Maʿmar und Ibn Isḥāq in ihrem Repertoire die auf den ersten Blick ähnliche, aber nicht identische Tradition nach al-Zuhrī—Ibn al-Musayyab hatten und diese Tradition mit eben diesem *isnād* weitergaben. Sollten beide Traditionen letztlich auf dieselbe Quelle

---

[67] Beispiele bei Bukhārī, *Ṣaḥīḥ*, II, 824, Nr. 2213 = Ibn Ḥajar, *Fatḥ*, X, 88, Nr. 2338; Bukhārī, *Ṣaḥīḥ*, III, 1149, Nr. 2983 = Ibn Ḥajar, *Fatḥ*, XII, 239 f., Nr. 3152; weitere Belege bei Salmān, *Aḥādīth*, 83, Anm.

[68] Mālik, *Muwaṭṭaʾ*, *kitāb* 33, *bāb* 1, 1.

[69] Ibn Hishām, *Sīra*, ed. Wüstenfeld, 776; ed. al-Saqqā, II (3-4), 356 f.

zurückgehen, so muss diese Quelle sehr früh angesetzt werden: nicht weniger als *zwei* Generationen vor den *muṣannifūn* Mūsā, Ibn Isḥāq, Mālik und Ibn Jurayj.

Anhangsweise sei hier noch Tradition XIV behandelt; sie steht mit XIII thematisch in engem Zusammenhang. Ihr *isnād* lautet—wie bei XIII—Mūsā—Nāfiʿ—ʿAbd Allāh b. ʿUmar. Inhaltlich besagt sie: ʿUmar b. al-Khaṭṭāb liess Handeltreibende von den *ahl al-kitāb* nicht länger als drei Tage in Medina weilen. Paralleltraditionen[70] hierzu nach anderen Tradenten Mūsās finden sich in ʿAbd al-Razzāqs *Muṣannaf*[71] (*isnād*: ʿAbd al-Razzāq—Ibn Jurayj—Mūsā—Nāfiʿ—ʿAbd Allāh b. ʿUmar) und in al-Bayhaqīs *Sunan*[72] (*isnād*: Ḥafṣ b. Maysara—Mūsā usw.). Alle drei Rezensionen haben ein "eigenes Gesicht". Ibn Jurayj und Ḥafṣ fügen am Schluss noch den Satz hinzu: "Ich weiss nicht, ob ihnen das schon vorher (sc. vor ʿUmars Kalifat) auferlegt wurde oder nicht." In der Ḥafṣ-Rezension ist der Bericht Schlussteil einer längeren Tradition, in der es zu Beginn um die Vertreibung der Juden aus Medina geht. Bei ʿAbd al-Razzāq wiederum bildet Ḥafṣ' Anfangsteil eine selbständige Tradition nach Ibn Jurayj—Mūsā—Nāfiʿ—Ibn ʿUmar.[73] Fast unnötig zu sagen: Es steht fest, dass auch Tradition XIV schon von Mūsā mit dem *isnād*—Nāfiʿ—Ibn ʿUmar weitergegeben wurde[74].

Möglicherweise sind alle in diesem Abschnitt behandelten Traditionen nach Mūsā—Nāfiʿ Teil eines längeren Berichtes gewesen, in dem systematisch das Schicksal der Juden in und um Medina (einschliesslich Khaybar) dargelegt wurde und der erst von den Tradenten Mūsās in Einzelteile (einzelne z. T. rechtsrelevante *ḥadīthe*) zerlegt wurde.

---

[70] Belege für Paralleltraditionen bei Salmān, *Aḥādīth*, 86 f., Anm. 14 und Abū Mālik, *Maghāzī*, 347, Anm. 773.

[71] VI, 52, Nr. 9979 und X, 358, Nr. 19362.

[72] IX, 208.

[73] ʿAbd al-Razzāq, *Muṣannaf*, VI, 54, Nr. 9988, X, 358, Nr. 19364.

[74] ʿAbd al-Razzāq bringt die Tradition noch in einer *riwāya*, die *nicht* über Mūsā zu Nāfiʿ führt (ʿAbd al-Razzāq, *Muṣannaf*, VI, 51, Nr. 9977 und X, 357, Nr. 19360). Sie hat den *isnād* Maʿmar—Ayyūb—Nāfiʿ und enthält eine zusätzliche Information (eine Stellungnahme ʿUmars zu der in Rede stehenden Rechtsfrage, nachdem er von seinem Mörder getroffen wurde). Eine weitere nicht über Mūsa, sondern über Mālik b. Anas auf Nāfiʿ zurückgeführte Version der Tradition bringt Bayhaqī in *Sunan*, IX, 209. Auch in ihr hat der Text ein "eigenes Gesicht".—Es sei hier dahingestellt, ob man aus allen diesen Belegen schliessen kann, dass schon Nāfiʿ den Bericht verbreitet hat (*common link* ist).

VI

Wie wir bereits sahen, hält Schacht die Herkunftsangaben Mūsās, die sich nach ihm ursprünglich ausschliesslich auf al-Zuhrī bezogen haben sollen, grundsätzlich für *fiktiv*. Diese seine Auffassung erklärt sich aus seiner Theorie vom "Rückwärts-Wachsen" (*growing backwards*) der *isnād*e. In einem ersten Schritt sollen die ursprünglich anonymen (noch nicht "formalisierten" und "systematisierten") Berichte auf Prophetennachfolger (*tābiʿūn*), in einem zweiten dann weiter auf Prophetengenossen (*ṣaḥāba*) und evtl. schliesslich in einem dritten Schritt noch auf den Propheten zurückprojiziert worden sein. Dass Mūsā den Zuhrī als seinen Gewährsmann angibt, entspricht genau dem "ersten Schritt" in Schachts Modell.

Für uns stellt sich hier die Frage, ob Mūsās Zurückführung seiner Überlieferungen auf al-Zuhrī tatsächlich fiktiv ist. Diese Auffassung Schachts wäre dann zu widerlegen, wenn sich eine frühe, von Mūsā nachweislich unabhängige Überlieferung dieser al-Zuhrī-Materialien aufzeigen liesse. Nun finden sich in ʿAbd al-Razzāqs *Muṣannaf* Parallelen zu einer ganzen Reihe von al-Zuhrī-Traditionen des *Muntakhab*.[75] Alle Traditionen überliefert ʿAbd al-Razzāq über Maʿmar b. Rāshid (also *nicht* über Mūsā!) nach al-Zuhrī. Die *isnād*e der Paralleltraditionen sind von al-Zuhrī an "abwärts" jeweils identisch. Die parallelen Texte sind alle sinngemäss gleich, aber im Wortlaut und manchmal auch in der Länge und in der Textanordnung recht verschieden.—Wir betrachten im Folgenden die Tradition *Muntakhab* III[76] und ihre Parallele im *Muṣannaf*.[77]

Ihr *isnād* lautet: al-Zuhrī—ʿAbd al-Raḥmān b. Mālik b. Juʿshum—dessen Vater—dessen Bruder Surāqa b. Juʿshum. In der Überlieferung nach Mūsā gibt die al-Zuhrī-Tradition einen zweiteiligen Bericht. Inhalt des ersten Teiles ist: Unmittelbar nachdem der Prophet bei der Hijra Mekka verlassen hat, setzen die Quraysh für denjenigen, der ihn zurückbrächte, einen hohen Preis aus. Surāqa b. Juʿshum, der sich den Preis verdienen will, bewaffnet sich und verfolgt Muḥam-

---

[75] Es sind dies: *Muntakhab* III = ʿAbd al-Razzāq, *Muṣannaf*, V, 392 ff. [101 f.]; IV = ʿAbd al-Razzāq, V, 395 [103]; VII = ʿAbd al-Razzāq, V, 382 [94 f.]; XV = ʿAbd al-Razzāq, V, 382 oben [93 f.]; XVI = ʿAbd al-Razzāq, V, 381, 382 Mitte [93, 94].

[76] = Bayhaqī, *Dalāʾil*, II, 487 f.—Weitere Paralleltraditionen bei Salmān, *Aḥādīth*, 64, Anm. 3 und Abū Mālik, *Maghāzī*, 108 f., Anm. 356.

[77] ʿAbd al-Razzāq, *Muṣannaf*, V, 392 ff. [101 f.] = Ibn Ḥanbal, *Musnad*, IV, 175 f. = al-Ḥākim al-Nīsābūrī, *Mustadrak*, III, 6 = Ṭabarānī, *Muʿjam*, VII, 132, Nr. 6601.

mad. Sein Orakel durch Lospfeile sagt ihm aber zweimal, dasss er kein Glück haben werde. Auch stolpert sein Pferd zweimal. Trotzdem setzt er die Verfolgung fort. Er bemerkt schliesslich Muḥammad und dessen Gefährten in einer Rauchwolke und schliesst daraus, dass der Prophet vor ihm gefeit sei. Er ruft die Flüchtigen an und versichert ihnen, dass er ihnen nichts zuleide tun werde. Darauf bittet er sie um einen Brief, in dem ihm Sicherheit (*amān*) verbürgt wird. Abū Bakr schreibt ihm diesen Brief auf Geheiss Muḥammads. Der zweite Teil spielt acht Jahre später, als Muḥammad Mekka erobert hat. Surāqa gerät in eine Kriegsschar von Medinensern, die nach ihm mit ihren Lanzen zu stechen beginnen. Er begibt sich zu Muḥammad und zeigt ihm den Brief. Der Prophet erkennt diesen an, Surāqa nimmt den Islam an usw.

Vergleichen wir nun diese al-Zuhrī-Tradition nach Mūsā mit derselben al-Zuhrī-Tradition nach Maʿmar, so zeigt sich, dass hier der ganze zweite Teil fehlt. Auch andere Unterschiede gibt es: Während es in der ersteren Rezension Abū Bakr ist, der auf Anordnung Muḥammads ein Schreiben ausstellt, so tut dies in der anderen Rezension Abū Bakrs *mawlā* ʿĀmir b. Fuhayra usw. Diese und weitere Entsprechungen sowie Unterschiede der beiden Rezensionen können am besten in einer Synopse dargestellt werden. Hier nur als Probe ein kleines sich entsprechendes Stück:

Al-Zuhrī in der Überlieferung nach Mūsā (im *Muntakhab*):

> *fa-baynamā anā jālis fī nādī qawmī idh jāʾā rajul minnā fa-qāla:*
> *wa-llāh, la-qad raʾaytu thalāthatan marrū ʿalayya ānifan. innī la-aẓunnuhū Muḥammadan.*
> *qāla: fa-awmaʾtu lahū bi-ʿaynī an uskut fa-qultu: innamā hum banū fulān yabghūna ḍāllatan lahum. qāla laʿallahū. thumma sakata.*
> *qāla: fa-makathtu qalīlan thumma qumtu fa-dakhaltu baytī fa-amartu bi-farasī.*

Al-Zuhrī in der Überlieferung nach Maʿmar (in ʿAbd al-Razzāqs *Muṣannaf*):

> *fa-baynā anā jālis fī majlis min majālis qawmī min banī Mudlij aqbala rajul minhum ḥattā qāma ʿalaynā fa-qāla:*
> *yā Surāqa, innī raʾaytu ānifan aswidatan bi-l-sāḥil arāhā Muḥammadan wa-aṣḥābahū.*
> *qāla Surāqa: fa-ʿaraftu annahum hum. fa-qultu: innahum laysū bihim, wa-lākinnaka raʾayta fulānan wa-fulānan inṭalaqū bughātan.*
> *qāla: thumma mā labithtu fī l-majlis illā sāʿatan ḥattā qumtu fa-dakhaltu baytī fa-amartu jāriyatī an tukhrija lī farasī.*

Weitere Rezensionen dieser al-Zuhrī-Tradition sind: eine nach Ibn Isḥāq[78] und eine nach Ṣāliḥ b. Kaysān.[79] Beide Rezensionen geben den vollständigen zweiteiligen Bericht und stehen auch sonst der Rezension Mūsās näher (Abū Bakr ist der Schreiber usw.).—Eine andere Rezension, die al-Bukhārī mit *qāla al-Zuhrī* einführt, ohne den Tradenten al-Zuhrīs zu nennen, die al-Bayhaqī indes auf al-Layth—ʿUqayl zurückführt, steht dagegen der Maʿmar-Rezension so nahe, dass man bezweifeln kann, ob es sich tatsächlich um eine unabhängige Rezension handelt.[80]

VII

Ich stelle im Folgenden noch den gesamten (kurzen) Text von Tradition IV,[81] die übrigens in der Maʿmar-Rezension sowie bei al-Bukhārī (siehe oben) auf die Entsprechung des ersten Teiles von Tradition III folgt, in den Überlieferungen nach Mūsā und Maʿmar, diesmal in Übersetzung, gegenüber:

> Er (Mūsā) sagte: Ibn Shihāb (al-Zuhrī) berichtete, dass ʿUrwa b. al-Zubayr gesagt habe, dass al-Zubayr dem Gesandten Gottes mit einer Karawane von Muslimen begegnet sei, die als Kaufleute in Syrien (*tujjāran bi-l-Shām*) waren und nach Mekka zurückkehrten. Diese tauschten mit ihm [ihre Waren] aus (*fa-ʿāraḍū rasūl Allāh)*. Dabei bekleidete al-Zubayr den Gesandten Gottes und Abū Bakr mit weissen Gewändern.[82]

> Maʿmar sagte: al-Zuhrī sagte: ʿUrwa b. al-Zubayr teilte mir mit, dass er (der Prophet) al-Zubayr mit einer Karawane von Muslimen begegnete, die medinensische Kaufleute (?) (*tujjār al-Madina* [oder *tujjāran li-l-Madīna* (?)]) in Syrien waren und nach Mekka zurückkehrten. Da gaben sie (*fa-ʿarraḍū)* dem Propheten und Abū Bakr weisse Gewänder.[83]

Die Unterschiede zwischen den beiden Versionen sind in dieser kurzen Tradition erwartungsgemäss geringer als in der langen Tradition *Muntakhab* III, deren Varianten wir im vorigen Paragraph verglichen haben, aber es gibt auch hier Differenzen im Wortlaut.

---

[78] Ibn Hishām, *Sīra*, ed. Wüstenfeld 331 f.; ed. al-Saqqā, I (1-2), 489 f.
[79] Ṭabarānī, *Muʿjam*, VII, 134 f., Nr. 6603.
[80] Bukhārī, *Ṣaḥīḥ*, III, 1420, Nr. 3693; Ibn Ḥajar, *Fatḥ*, XV, 93 ff., Nr. 3906; Bayhaqī, *Dalāʾil*, II, 485.
[81] Paralleltraditionen bei Salmān, *Aḥādīth*, 68, Anm. 4 und Abū Mālik, *Maghāzī*, 110, Anm. 360.
[82] *Muntakhab* IV.
[83] ʿAbd al-Razzāq, *Muṣannaf*, V, 395 [103].

Die Untersuchung der verbleibenden Parallelen ergäbe dasselbe Bild: Wegen des unterschiedlichen Charakters der beiden Überlieferungen nach al-Zuhrī, des "eigenen Gesichts", das die al-Zuhrī-Texte in den beiden Traditionssträngen haben, ist unwahrscheinlich, dass etwa ʿAbd al-Razzāq oder schon Maʿmar Mūsās Text imitiert hat (oder umgekehrt). Vielmehr müssen ʿAbd al-Razzāq—Maʿmars und Mūsās Versionen des Textes auf eine gemeinsame Quelle zurückgehen: al-Zuhrī. Es ist auch nicht möglich, im Sinne Schachts zu argumentieren, sowohl Mūsā wie Maʿmar hätten dieselben anonymen Traditionen unabhängig voneinander aufgegriffen und ihnen dieselbe fiktive Herkunftsbezeichnung, nämlich al-Zuhrī, angehängt, da al-Zuhrī damals als fiktive Quelle *en vogue* gewesen sei. Denn zum einen wären die Paralleltexte dann noch unterschiedlicher, als sie tatsächlich sind, und zum anderen macht al-Zuhrī ebenfalls Herkunftsangaben, und zwar solche, die sich von Mal zu Mal unterscheiden, aber bei Mūsā und ʿAbd al-Razzāq—Maʿmar dieselben sind.[84] Es ist aber undenkbar, dass ʿAbd al-Razzāq—Maʿmar und Mūsā unabhängig voneinander auch diese weiteren Namen hier und dort gleichlautend mitgefälscht haben könnten.

VIII

Wie steht es nun aber mit al-Zuhrīs Quellen? Hat al-Zuhrī fiktive Autoritäten angegeben? Sollte es sich so verhalten, so behielte Schacht immerhin ein Stück weit recht. Der Fälschungsvorgang, den er postuliert, wäre dann lediglich eine Generation früher geschehen.

Es lässt sich heute mit Sicherheit sagen, dass zumindest ein erheblicher Teil von al-Zuhrīs Herkunftsangaben authentisch ist. Dies trifft jedenfalls für eine grosse Anzahl von Traditionen zu, die al-Zuhrī nach seinem Lehrer ʿUrwa überliefert. Denn wir besitzen die meisten dieser Traditionen nach ʿUrwa ausser in der Überlieferung al-Zuhrīs auch in der (davon unabhängigen) Überlieferung Hishām b. ʿUrwas, eines Sohnes ʿUrwas.[85]

Zu den Traditionen nach al-Zuhrī—ʿUrwa, die im *Muntakhab* stehen, lässt sich mindestens in einem Fall eine Paralleltradition nach

---

[84] Zum Beispiel in VII = ʿAbd al-Razzāq, *Muṣannaf*, V, 382 f. [94 f.]: ʿAbd al-Raḥmān b. ʿAbd Allāh b. Kaʿb b. Mālik; in XV = ʿAbd al-Razzāq, V, 381 [93 f.]: ʿUrwa; in XVI = ʿAbd al-Razzāq, V, 381, 382 Mitte [93, 94]: Saʿīd b. al-Musayyab (zusammen mit ʿUrwa im *Muntakhab*).

[85] Siehe hierzu Schoeler, *Charakter*, 20 f., 144 ff., 150 ff.

Hishām b. ʿUrwa—ʿUrwa nachweisen. Es handelt sich um ein Gegenstück zu der oben behandelten Tradition IV.[86] Sie findet sich in Ibn Abī Shaybas *Muṣannaf*.[87] Der *isnād* lautet Yazīd b. Hārūn—Ḥammād b. Salama—Hishām b. ʿUrwa—ʿUrwa—sein Vater (al-Zubayr); der Text:

> Als der Gesandte Gottes mit Abū Bakr und ʿĀmir b. Fuhayra nach Medina auswanderte, kam ihnen auf dem Weg das Geschenk Ṭalḥas für Abū Bakr entgegen, in dem weisse Kleider waren. So betraten der Gesandte Gottes und Abū Bakr in ihnen [in weissen Kleidern] Medina.

(Nach Ibn Ḥajar[88] soll es noch eine dritte Weiterüberlieferung dieser ʿUrwa-Tradition geben, nämlich nach Ibn Lahīʿa—Abū l-Aswad Yatīm ʿUrwa –ʿUrwa.)

Dass diese Weiterüberlieferung von jener nach al-Zuhrī unabhängig ist, dass also keine Imitation vorliegt, steht wegen der erheblichen Unterschiede ausser Frage. Diese Unterschiede sind, wie zu erwarten, grösser als die zwischen den beiden al-Zuhrī-Versionen. Am erstaunlichsten ist, dass ʿUrwa hier (und laut Ibn Ḥajar ebenfalls in der Überlieferung Abū l-Aswad—ʿUrwa) nicht seinen Vater al-Zubayr, sondern dessen Freund und späteren Verbündeten Ṭalḥa dem Propheten begegnen lässt. Da diese Episode auch in einer nicht von ʿUrwa stammenden Überlieferung über Ṭalḥa, also nicht über al-Zubayr, berichtet wird,[89] könnte man—in Unkenntnis der Hishām-Version—allzu leicht annehmen, ʿUrwa habe einen ursprünglich *nicht* seinen Vater betreffenden Bericht auf seinen Vater übertragen. Dies ist aber wohl kaum der Fall, wie die Hishām- (und Abū l-Aswad-) Versionen zeigen. Vielmehr handelt es sich bei der Ersetzung Ṭalḥas durch al-Zubayr sehr wahrscheinlich um einen Überlieferungsfehler, der erst al-Zuhrī unterlaufen ist. Vergleicht man die *isnād*e in beiden Überlieferungen, so zeigt sich nämlich, dass Hishām b. ʿUrwa darin als letztes Glied al-Zubayr nennt, während al-Zuhrī dies nicht tut. Bei al-Zuhrī ist also—sicher durch ein Versehen—der von ʿUrwa angeführte ursprüngliche Gewährsmann des Berichtes, ʿUrwas Vater al-Zubayr, zum Akteur des Berichtes geworden.

---

[86] Siehe Abschnitt VII.
[87] XIV, 335, Nr. 18470.
[88] *Fatḥ*, XV, 97.
[89] Ibn Saʿd, *Ṭabaqāt*, III a, 153, Zeile 19.

Wie dem auch sei, Tradition IV ist mit Sicherheit weder von Mūsā noch in der Generation davor, etwa von al-Zuhrī, erfunden worden, sondern bereits von ʿUrwa gegen Ende des 1. Jahrhunderts H. sinngemäss so verbreitet worden, wie wir es aus der Weiterüberlieferung erschliessen können. Dass der Bericht deshalb den historischen Tatsachen genau entspricht, kann freilich nicht mit Sicherheit behauptet werden; doch hat ʿUrwa hier offensichtlich den Bericht eines Zeitgenossen des Ereignisses (seines Vaters) festgehalten und weitergegeben (*oral history*).—Dies ist jedenfalls sehr viel wahrscheinlicher, als dass es sich bei der Tradition um eine anti-ʿalidische Zweckfälschung handelt, wie Schacht—auch hier wieder—annimmt ("no. 4 extols ʿAlī's adversary Zubayr").[90]

IX

Im Vorangegangenen haben wir uns mit folgenden Thesen Schachts zum *Muntakhab* explizit auseinandergesetzt:

1) Die im *Muntakhab* nicht auf al-Zuhrī zurückgeführten Traditionen Mūsās sind spätere Hinzufügungen.—Demgegenüber war in mehreren Fällen zu zeigen, dass die betreffenden Traditionen mit Sicherheit Bestandteil des Überlieferungsschatzes Mūsās waren.

2) Mūsās Berufung auf al-Zuhrī als Gewährsmann ist in jedem Fall fiktiv. Mūsās Quelle ist vielmehr eine "vage kollektive Erinnerung der Gemeinde" (falls er die betreffende Tradition nicht gar selbst erfunden hat).—Demgegenüber war mehrfach zu zeigen, dass es sich um tatsächlich auf al-Zuhrī zurückgehende Traditionen handelt. In einem Fall konnte sogar nachgewiesen werden, dass der von al-Zuhrī genannte Gewährsmann, ʿUrwa, die betreffende Tradition tatsächlich verbreitet hat, was uns ins 1. Jahrhundert der Hijra zurückführt.

3) Der *Muntakhab* zeigt eine starke anti-ʿalidische Tendenz; viele Traditionen sind anti-ʿalidische Zweckfälschungen.—Diese These Schachts konnte in zwei Fällen (Traditionen IV, VIII und IX) als auf falschen Voraussetzungen beruhend oder als unwahrscheinlich nachgewiesen werden. Lediglich in einem (von uns bisher nicht behandelten) Fall, Tradition XIX (Inhalt: Abū Bakr bringt in einer Ansprache zum Ausdruck, dass er niemals Gier nach der Herrschaft verspürt

---

[90] Schacht, "On Mūsā", 289.

habe; ʿAlī und al-Zubayr gestehen ihm zu, am meisten Anrecht auf die Herrschaft zu haben), könnte eine anti-ʿalidische Einstellung die Tradition beeinflusst haben.

Abschliessend sei noch zu einer vierten, bisher nicht behandelten These Schachts Stellung genommen:

4) Im *Muntakhab* sind "ʿabbāsidische Spuren unverkennbar" (*Abbasid traces are unmistakable*); die betreffenden Traditionen weisen deshalb "in eine Periode etwas später als die ersten Jahre der ʿabbāsidischen Regierung" (*point to a period somewhat later than the very first years of Abbasid rule*).[91] Die These impliziert, dass ein erheblicher Teil der Traditionen des *Muntakhab* nicht vor ca. 132/750 entstanden ist, also—zumindest in der Form, wie er jetzt vorliegt—von Mūsā selbst fingiert wurde. *Ein* Argument für diese These, die sich übrigens gegen eine anders lautende Feststellung Sachaus[92] richtet, gewinnt Schacht aus der, wie er nachgewiesen zu haben glaubt, manifesten anti-ʿalidischen Tendenz vieler Traditionen. Dazu ist unter Punkt 3) das Wesentliche gesagt. Hinzuzufügen bleibt, dass anti-ʿalidisch nicht einfach mit pro-ʿabbāsidisch gleichgesetzt werden kann und dass anti-ʿalidische Tendenzen schon in einer sehr frühen Periode wirksam gewesen sein können.—Im vorliegenden Fall schliesst sich Schachts These aber regelrecht aus.[93] Denn in der einzigen von ʿAbbās, dem Vorfahren der ʿAbbāsiden, handelnden Tradition im *Muntakhab,* VI[94] (Inhalt: der Prophet ordnet an, seinem bei Badr gefangengenommenen Oheim ʿAbbās das Lösegeld *nicht* zu erlassen), wird Muḥammad eindeutig in einer unfreundlichen Haltung gegen ʿAbbās gezeigt.[95] Wenn es sich bei dieser Tradition also um eine Zweckfälschung handelt, so um eine mit *anti-ʿabbāsidischer* Tendenz. Dabei gibt es anderswo—wie man seit einem wichtigen Aufsatz Th. Nöldekes[96] weiss—in der Tat ʿAbbās-freundliche Traditionen, die nun wirklich von einer pro-ʿabbāsidischen Tendenz beeinflusst sein könnten.

---

[91] Schacht, "On Mūsā", 290.

[92] Sachau, "Fragment", 446.

[93] Zum Folgenden vgl. die ähnliche Beweisführung Salmāns (*Aḥādīth,* 37 f.).

[94] = Ibn Saʿd, *Ṭabaqāt,* IVa, 8 = Bukhārī, *Ṣaḥīḥ,* II, 896, Nr. 2400 = Ibn Ḥajar, *Fatḥ,* X, 261, Nr. 2537; weitere Belege bei Abū Mālik, *Maghāzī,* 146, Anm. 571.

[95] Dies hat schon Guillaume, *The Life,* xlvii, festgestellt, und auch Salmān, *Aḥādīth,* 37 f., weist im Zusammenhang seiner Widerlegung von Schachts Thesen darauf ausdrücklich hin.

[96] Th. Nöldeke, "Zur tendenziösen Gestaltung der Urgeschichte des Islām's", in *ZDMG,* 52 (1898), 21 f.

Wenn Schacht seinerzeit eine "revaluation" der islamischen Tradition durchführen wollte,[97] so ist es heute an der Zeit, *seine* Theorien einer "revaluation" zu unterziehen. Es war unsere Absicht in diesem Beitrag, einen möglichen Weg hierzu aufzuzeigen.

ENGLISH SUMMARY

I

I shall be taking Mūsā b. ʿUqba's *Maghāzī* to refer to the short Berlin "fragment" Ahlwardt No. 1554, first edited, annotated and translated into German in 1904 by Eduard Sachau.[98] This so-called fragment, or rather *muntakhab* "selection"—the exact title in the manuscript is *Aḥādīth muntakhaba* (selected traditions)—, is contained in a collection of the 8th/14th century. It consists of nineteen traditions attributed to Mūsā b. ʿUqba (d. 141/758; *GAS*, I, 286 f.). All these traditions have also been transmitted in other works besides the *Muntakhab* and are attributed there also to Mūsā.

Scholarly work on the *Muntakhab,* which began with Sachau, was continued by Joseph Schacht in his article "On Mūsā b. ʿUqba's *Kitāb al-Maghāzī*".[99] Schacht's aim there was to show that his well-known theory with regard to the Islamic legal tradition can be applied also to the historical tradition. Since many new sources with Mūsā material have come to light and have been made accessible in recent years, and since recent research has strongly challenged or even wholly refuted Schacht's theories,[100] the time seems to be ripe for a renewed examination of the *Muntakhab.*

---

[97] Vgl. Schacht's Aufsatz mit dem Titel "A Revaluation of Islamic Traditions", in *JRAS,* 49 (1949), 143-54.

[98] E. Sachau, " Das Berliner Fragment des Mūsā Ibn ʿUḳba", in *SPAW,* 1904, 445-70. A new edition by Mashhūr Ḥasan Salmān was published in Beirut several years ago; see Bibliography.

[99] In *Acta Orientalia,* 21 (1953), 288-300.

[100] Cf. Motzki, *Die Anfänge*; idem, "Der Fiqh des -Zuhrī"; Salmān in the Introduction of his new edition of the work, 33 f., 37 ff.

II

I would like to start by giving an example of how much the appraisal of a tradition can change by virtue of the fact that today so many more parallel traditions are known than in Sachau's or Schacht's time. I refer to traditions VIII and IX in the *Muntakhab*.

VIII has the *isnād*: Ismāʿīl b. Ibrāhīm b. ʿUqba (the link Mūsā b. ʿUqba is missing in the *Muntakhab* manuscript)—Sālim b. ʿAbd Allāh—ʿAbd Allāh b. ʿUmar. The text concludes with the Prophet saying:

> He (Zayd b. Ḥāritha) was one of the dearest to me of all men. And this person here (his son Usāma) is one of the dearest after him. So be kindly disposed to him after my death, for he belongs to the noblest among you.

The very short tradition IX has the *isnād*: Ismāʿīl b. Ibrāhīm b. ʿUqba—Mūsā b. ʿUqba—Sālim b. ʿAbd Allāh—ʿAbd Allāh b. ʿUmar. The text reads:

> *mā kāna rasūl Allāh yastathnī Fāṭima.* The Messenger of God used not to make an exception of (his daughter) Fāṭima.

Sachau assumed that the latter tradition referred to the alleged saying of Muḥammad: "And if it were Fāṭima herself who had stolen, I would cut off her hand."[101] For his part, Schacht was unwilling to recognize both traditions as part of the original *Kitāb al-Maghāzī* by Mūsā b. ʿUqba. His reasons for this are twofold, namely, that Mūsā is not mentioned in the *isnād* of VIII, and that in both traditions Mūsā's source is not al-Zuhrī. According to Schacht, only those traditions that Mūsā relates on the authority of al-Zuhrī formed part of Mūsā's original *Kitāb al-Maghāzī*. Moreover, he considers IX to be a tendentious falsification with anti-ʿAlid bias ("9 ...denies privileges in penal law to the descendants of the Prophet").[102]

Now there are a number of parallels to tradition VIII f., one of which is in al-Ṭayālisī's *Musnad*.[103] Its *isnād* runs as follows: Abū Dāwūd (al-Ṭayālisī)—Ḥammād b. Salama—Mūsā b. ʿUqba—Sālim b. ʿAbd Allāh—ʿAbd Allāh b. ʿUmar; the text reads:

---

[101] Sachau, "Fragment", 456.
[102] Schacht, "On Mūsā", 290.
[103] No. 1812.

> *samiʿtu rasūl Allāh yaqūlu: Usāma aḥabb al-nās ilayya wa-lam yastathni Fāṭima wa-lā ghayrahā.* I heard the Messenger of God saying: 'Usāma is the dearest to me of all people.' He did not (even) make an exception of Fāṭima nor of anyone else.

From this parallel tradition (which belongs to another strand of transmission: Ḥammād b. Salama—Mūsā b. ʿUqba; as against Ismāʿīl b. Ibrāhīm b. ʿUqba—Mūsā b. ʿUqba) it follows that 1) traditions VIII and IX originally formed one tradition which was severed in the *Muntakhab* by a transmission error, 2) the observation that Muḥammad had not made an exception of Fāṭima refers not to potential punishments but to his declared preference for Usāma; and 3) tradition VIII f.—with an *isnād* that does not go back to al-Zuhrī—did form part of Mūsā's original book or was at least transmitted on Mūsā's authority, for al-Ṭayālisī, too, traces it back to Mūsā in a strand of transmission independent of our *Muntakhab*.[104] Thus Schacht's entire interpretation collapses.

III

Schacht considers Mūsā's source indications—allegedly always originally al-Zuhrī—to be basically fictitious.[105] This can be explained by his theory of the "growing backward" of the *isnād*s. But are Mūsā's ascriptions to al-Zuhrī really always fictitious? In ʿAbd al-Razzāq's *Muṣannaf* we find parallels to a whole range of al-Zuhrī traditions of the *Muntakhab*,[106] and ʿAbd al-Razzāq transmits them on the authority of Maʿmar b. Rāshid from al-Zuhrī. In one case (III and its parallel), the al-Zuhrī tradition as transmitted by Mūsā provides a two-part account; the second part takes place eight years later. In the same al-Zuhrī tradition reported by Maʿmar (in ʿAbd al-Razzāq's *Muṣannaf*), however, the second part is missing. There are other differences, too. Here is a part of the text in the two corresponding versions:

Al-Zuhrī as transmitted by Mūsā (in the *Muntakhab*):

> *fa-baynamā anā jālis fī nādī qawmī idh jāʾā rajul minnā fa-qāla:*
> *wa-llāh, la-qad raʾaytu thalāthatan marrū ʿalayya ānifan. innī la-aẓunnuhū Muḥammadan.*

---

[104] Salmān, *Aḥādīth*, 38 ff., reaches the same conclusions.

[105] Schacht, "On Mūsā", 292.

[106] III = ʿAbd al-Razzāq, *Muṣannaf*, V, 392 ff. [101 f.]; IV = ʿAbd al-Razzāq, V, 395 [103]); VII = ʿAbd al-Razzāq, V, 382 [94 f.]; XV = ʿAbd al-Razzāq, V, 382 [93 f.]; XVI = ʿAbd al-Razzāq, V, 382 [94].

> *qāla: fa-awmaʾtu lahū bi-ʿaynī an uskut fa-qultu: innamā hum banū fulān yabghūna ḍāllatan lahum. qāla laʿallahū. thumma sakata.*
> *qāla: fa-makathtu qalīlan thumma qumtu fa-dakhaltu baytī fa-amartu bi-farasī.*

Al-Zuhrī as transmitted by Maʿmar (in ʿAbd al-Razzāq's *Muṣannaf*):

> *fa-baynā anā jālis fī majlis min majālis qawmī min banī Mudlij aqbala rajul minhum ḥattā qāma ʿalaynā fa-qāla:*
> *yā Surāqa, innī raʾaytu ānifan aswidatan bi-l-sāḥil arāhā Muḥammadan wa-aṣḥābahū.*
> *qāla Surāqa: fa-ʿaraftu annahum hum. fa-qultu: innahum laysū bihim, wa-lākinnaka raʾayta fulānan wa-fulānan inṭalaqū bughātan.*
> *qāla: thumma mā labithtu fī l-majlis illā sāʿatan ḥattā qumtu fa-dakhaltu baytī fa-amartu jāriyatī an tukhrija lī farasī.*

Here is—as another example—the complete text of tradition IV in the transmissions of Mūsā and Maʿmar, this time in translation, set side-by-side for comparison:

> He (Mūsā) said: Ibn Shihāb (al-Zuhrī) said that ʿUrwa b. al-Zubayr had said that [his father] al-Zubayr met the Messenger of God with a caravan of Muslims who were merchants in Syria (*tujjāran bi-l-Shām*) and were returning to Mecca. They exchanged with the Messenger of God [their wares for other wares] (*fa-ʿāraḍū rasūl Allāh*). Al-Zubayr clothed him and Abū Bakr in white robes.[107]
>
> Maʿmar said that al-Zuhrī said: ʿUrwa b. al-Zubayr told me that al-Zubayr met a caravan with Muslims who were Medinan merchants (?) (*tujjār al-Madīna* [or *tujjāran li-l-Madīna* (?)]) in Syria and were returning to Mecca. They gave (*fa-ʿarraḍū*) the Prophet and Abū Bakr white robes.[108]

It is not surprising that the differences between the two versions are fewer in this short tradition than in the long tradition III and its parallel; nonetheless, there are differences here, too, mainly in the wording of the text. Because of the different characteristics of the two transmissions reported by al-Zuhrī—the distinctive quality that al-Zuhrī's texts have in both strands of the tradition—it is improbable that ʿAbd al-Razzāq or Maʿmar before him have imitated Mūsā's text (or vice versa). On the contrary, ʿAbd al-Razzāq—Maʿmar's and Mūsā's versions of the text must go back to a common source: al-Zuhrī.

---

[107] *Muntakhab*, IV.
[108] ʿAbd al-Razzāq, *Muṣannaf*, V, 395 [103].

IV

But what about al-Zuhrī's sources? Today we can safely say that a considerable part of al-Zuhrī's source indications are authentic. This is true at any rate for a large number of traditions that al-Zuhrī transmitted from his teacher ʿUrwa b. al-Zubayr, for we possess most of these traditions going back to ʿUrwa not only in the al-Zuhrī transmission but also in the independent transmission of Hishām, a son of ʿUrwa.[109] In at least one case it is possible to demonstrate that a tradition reported by al-Zuhrī from ʿUrwa which is found in the *Muntakhab* has a parallel transmitted on the authority of Hishām b. ʿUrwa from his father. It is the counterpart of tradition IV discussed above. It is to be found in Ibn Abī Shayba's *Muṣannaf*.[110] The *isnād* is: Yazīd b. Hārūn—Ḥammād b. Salama—Hishām b. ʿUrwa—ʿUrwa b. al-Zubayr—his father (al-Zubayr); the text reads:

> When the Messenger of God emigrated to Medina with Abū Bakr and ʿĀmir b. Fuhayra, there came towards them on their way [a caravan with] Ṭalḥa's gift for Abū Bakr which contained white garments. So the Messenger of God and Abū Bakr entered Medina in them [i.e., in white garments].

Because of the considerable differences between this text and the two versions transmitted on the authority of al-Zuhrī, there can be no doubt that this transmission is independent of that by al-Zuhrī and is not an imitation. What surprises us most of all is that ʿUrwa—in this version—has his father's friend and later ally Ṭalḥa, and not his father al-Zubayr, meet the Prophet. Since this is also reported of Ṭalḥa (not of al-Zubayr) in a tradition deriving neither from al-Zuhrī nor from ʿUrwa,[111] the substitution of Ṭalḥa by al-Zubayr is probably a transmission error on al-Zuhrī's part.

We can be certain that tradition IV was not invented by Mūsā nor a generation previously by al-Zuhrī, but had already been circulated by ʿUrwa towards the end of the 1st century AH in roughly the form we can reconstruct from later transmission. We cannot, however, claim with certainty that this report accurately corresponds to historical fact; but what we can assert is that in this case ʿUrwa obviously

---

[109] Cf. Schoeler, *Charakter und Authentie*, 20 f., 144 ff., 150 ff.
[110] XIV, 335, no. 18470.
[111] Ibn Saʿd, *Ṭabaqāt*, IIIa, 153.

recorded and transmitted the report of a contemporary of the event, namely, his father.

V

Let us finally consider one further claim of Schacht: "In the *Muntakhab* Abbasid traces are unmistakable"; the traditions in question therefore "point to a period somewhat later than the very first years of Abbasid rule".[112] This claim by Schacht is quite untenable,[113] because in the tradition most relevant here—the only one in the *Muntakhab* which is about ʿAbbās, the ancestor of the ʿAbbāsids and the Prophet's uncle[114]—Muḥammad is shown to have an unfriendly attitude towards ʿAbbās. The gist of this tradition is: The Prophet ordered that the ransom should not be waived for his uncle captured at Badr.

If Schacht originally meant to carry out "a *revaluation* of Islamic traditions" (cf. his article bearing this title), it is now time to subject his theories to a revaluation. My aim in this paper was to show one possible way in which this might be achieved.

Bibliography

ʿAbd al-Razzāq b. Hammām al-Ṣanʿānī, *al-Muṣannaf*, ed. Ḥabīb al-Raḥmān al-Aʿẓamī, 11 vols., Beirut, 1970-72.

———, [*al-Muṣannaf. K. al-Maghāzī*] = al-Zuhrī, Muḥammad b. Muslim, *al-Maghāzī al-nabawiyya*, ed. Suhayl Zakkār, Damascus, 1980.

Abū Mālik, see Mūsā b. ʿUqba, *al-Maghāzī* (*al-Qism al-dirāsī*).

Aḥādīth muntakhaba min Maghāzī Mūsā b. ʿUqba, ed. Mashhūr Ḥasan Salmān, Beirut, 1991.

Azami, Muhammad Mustafa, *On Schacht's Origins of Muhammadan Jurisprudence*. Riyad, 1985.

al-Bayhaqī, Abū Bakr Aḥmad b. al-Ḥusayn, *Dalāʾil al-nubuwwa wa-maʿrifat aḥwāl ṣāḥib al-sharīʿa*, ed. ʿAbd al-Muʿṭī Qalʿajī, 7 vols., Beirut, 1985.

———, *al-Sunan al-kubrā*, 10 vols., Hyderabad, 1344-55 AH.

al-Bukhārī, Abū ʿAbd Allāh Muḥammad b. Ismāʿīl, *al-Ṣaḥīḥ*, ed. Muṣṭafā Dīb al-Bughā, 6 vols., [4]Beirut, 1990.

---

[112] Schacht, "On Mūsā", 290.

[113] Cf. Salmān, *Aḥādīth*, 37 f.

[114] *Muntakhab*, VI = Ibn Saʿd, *Ṭabaqāt*, IVa, 8 = Bukhārī, *Ṣaḥīḥ*, II, 896, no. 2400 = Ibn Ḥajar, *Fatḥ*, X, 261, no. 2537.

al-Dhahabī, Muḥammad b. Aḥmad, *Siyar aʿlām al-nubalāʾ*, ed. Shuʿayb al-Arnāʾūṭ et al., 23 vols., 3Beirut, 1985.

———, *Taʾrīkh al-islām wa-wafayāt al-mashāhīr wa-l-aʿlām*, I, *al-Sīra al-nabawiyya*. II, *al-Maghāzī*, ed. ʿUmar ʿAbd al-Salām Tadmurī, Beirut, 1987.

EI^2 = *The Encyclopaedia of Islam*. New edition, 10 vols. to date, Leiden 1960 –.

GAS = Fuat Sezgin, *Geschichte des arabischen Schrifttums*, I, Leiden, 1967.

Guillaume, Alfred, *The Life of Muhammad. A Translation of Ibn Isḥāq's Sīrat Rasūl Allāh*, with introduction and notes, Oxford, 1955.

al-Ḥākim al-Nīsabūrī, Abū ʿAbd Allāh Muḥammad b. ʿAbd Allāh, *al-Mustadrak ʿalā l-Ṣaḥīḥayn fī l-ḥadīth*, 4 vols., Hyderabad, 1334-42 AH.

Horovitz, J., "The Earliest Biographies of the Prophet and Their Authors", I-IV, in *Islamic Culture*, 1 (1927), 535-59, 2 (1928), 22-50, 164-82 and 495-526.

Ibn Abī Shayba, ʿAbd Allāh b. Muḥammad, *al-Kitāb al-Muṣannaf*, ed. ʿAbd al-Khāliq al-Afghānī et al., 15 vols., Hyderabad, Bombay, 1966-83.

Ibn Ḥajar al-ʿAsqalānī, Shihāb al-Dīn Aḥmad b. ʿAlī, *Fatḥ al-bārī bi-sharḥ Ṣaḥīḥ al-Bukhārī*, eds. Ṭāhā ʿAbd al-Raʾūf Saʿd and Muṣṭafā Muḥammad al-Hawārī, 28 vols., Cairo, 1978.

———, *Tahdhīb al-tahdhīb*, 14 vols., Beirut, 1984-85.

Ibn Ḥanbal, Aḥmad, *Musnad*, 6 vols., Cairo, 1313 AH.

Ibn Hishām, ʿAbd al-Malik, *Sīrat sayyidinā Muḥammad rasūl Allāh. Das Leben Muhammed's nach M. Ibn Isḥāq*, ed. Ferdinand Wüstenfeld, 2 vols., Göttingen, 1858-60.

———, *al-Sīra al-nabawiyya*, ed. Muṣṭafā al-Saqqā et al., I-II (1-4), 2Cairo, 1955.

Ibn Isḥāq, see Ibn Hishām and Guillaume.

Ibn Saʿd, Muḥammad, *Kitāb al-Ṭabaqāt al-kabīr. Biographien Muhammeds, seiner Gefährten und der späteren Träger des Islams bis zum Jahre 230*, 9 vols., ed. Eduard Sachau et al., Leiden, 1905-40.

Ibn Shabba, ʿUmar, *Taʾrīkh al-Madīna al-munawwara* (*Akhbār al-Madīna al-nabawiyya*), 4 vols., ed. Fahīm Maḥmūd Shaltūt, Qum 1368/1991.

Jarrar, Maher, *Die Prophetenbiographie im islamischen Spanien. Ein Beitrag zur Überlieferungs- und Redaktionsgeschichte*, Frankfurt/Bern, 1989.

Jones, J.M.B., "The Chronology of the *Maghāzī*—A Textual Survey", in *Bulletin of the School of Oriental and African Studies*, 19 (1957), 245-280.

al-Khaṭīb al-Baghdādī, Abū Bakr Aḥmad b. ʿAlī, *Taʾrīkh Baghdād*, 14 vols., Cairo, 1931.

Mālik b. Anas, *al-Muwaṭṭaʾ*, [*riwāyat* Yaḥyā b. Yaḥyā] ed. Muḥammad Fuʾād ʿAbd al-Bāqī, 2 vols., Cairo, 1951.

Motzki, Harald, *Die Anfänge der islamischen Jurisprudenz. Ihre Entwicklung in Mekka bis zur Mitte des 2./8. Jahrhunderts*, Stuttgart, 1991.

———, "Der Fiqh des -Zuhrī: Die Quellenproblematik", in *Der Islam*, 68 (1991), 1-44.

Mūsā b. ʿUqba, *al-Maghāzī*, ed. Muḥammad Bāqshīsh Abū Mālik, Agadir, 1994.

———, see also *Aḥādīth Muntakhaba*.

———, see also Sachau, Eduard.

Nöldeke, Th., "Zur tendenziösen Gestaltung der Urgeschichte des Islām's", in *Zeitschrift der Deutschen Morgenländischen Gesellschaft*, 52 (1898), 16-33.

Sachau, E., "Das Berliner Fragment des Mūsā Ibn ʿUḳba", in *Sitzungsberichte der Preussischen Akademie der Wissenschaften*, [Berlin] 1904, 445-70.

Salmān, see *Aḥādīth Muntakhaba*.

Schacht, J., "On Mūsā b. ʿUqba's *Kitāb al-Maghāzī*", in *Acta Orientalia*, 21 (1953), 288-300.

———, "A Revaluation of Islamic Traditions", in *Journal of the Royal Asiatic Society*, 49 (1949), 143-54.
Schoeler, Gregor, *Charakter und Authentie der muslimischen Überlieferung über das Leben Mohammeds*, Berlin/New York, 1996.
al-Ṭabarānī, Abū l-Qāsim Sulaymān b. Aḥmad, *al-Muʿjam al-kabīr fī asmāʾ al-ṣaḥāba*, ed. Ḥamdī ʿAbd al-Majīd al-Salafī, 26 vols., Beirut, 1984 ff.
al-Ṭayālisī, Abū Dāwūd Sulaymān b. Dāwūd, *Musnad*, Hyderabad, 1321 AH.

"*SĪRAT AHL AL-KISĀ'*"
EARLY SHĪʿĪ SOURCES ON THE BIOGRAPHY OF THE PROPHET[1]

Maher Jarrar

I. The Nature of the Sources

While much thorough and competent work has been carried out since the turn of the century on the early sources of Muḥammad's biography, no such efforts have been made to study the Shīʿī *sīra-maghāzī*-tradition *per se*, whether Zaydī, Ismāʿīlī or Imāmī.[2] Apart from a brief and cursory mention of the Shīʿī inclination of this author or that compiler, there exists no special study of value. This is partly due to the fact that no early Shīʿī work has reached us and that later compilations which did survive do not deal with *sīra-maghāzī* in the strict sense. Moreover, part of these compilations is still in manuscript form. Here I confine my examination to Imāmī sources and will leave the study of other Shīʿī sources to another occasion.

It should first be stated that contrary to the Sunnī tradition which was in the process of being recorded and handed down in written form as early as the middle of the second/eighth century (e.g., Ibn Isḥāq and Mālik b. Anas, to name only two prominent works),[3] the Shīʿī tradition had to wait more than a century, although the first attempts go back to the time of the fifth Imam Muḥammad al-Bāqir and his pupils.[4] The earliest preserved Imāmī works do not contain

---

[1] I would like to thank Harald Motzki for his valuable comments.

[2] I am using the word Imāmī throughout this study to denote both the Twelver Shīʿa, i.e., those who believe in the *naṣṣ* and *nasaq*, and such Shīʿī scholars, disciples of the fifth and sixth Imams, who were adopted later by the Twelver Shīʿa although they might have had other sectarian dogmatic tendencies (which are difficult to prove), as in the case of Abān b. ʿUthmān al-Aḥmar. Cf. H.M. Hodgson, "How Did the Early Shīʿa Become Sectarian", in *JAOS*, 75 (1955), 1-13; H. Modarressi, *Crisis and Consolidation in the Formative Period of Shīʿite Islam*, Princeton, 1993, 1-53.

[3] Cf. on the writing down of early traditions, H. Motzki, *Die Anfänge der islamischen Jurisprudenz. Ihre Entwicklung in Mekka bis zur Mitte des 2./8. Jahrhunderts*, Stuttgart, 1991, 217-61.

[4] Cf. A. Falaturi, "Die Zwölfer-Schia aus der Sicht eines Schiiten: Probleme ihrer Untersuchung", in *Festschrift Werner Caskel*, ed. E. Gräf, Leiden, 1968, 64-65; E. Kohlberg, "Al-uṣūl al-arbaʿumi'a", in *JSAI*, 10 (1987), 128-66.

any material of value regarding the life of the Prophet.[5] Only with al-Kulīnī (d. 329/941) does one find a systematic compilation of *ḥadīth* arranged according to *fiqh* chapters (after the example of the Sunnī *muṣannafāt* of the early third/ninth century), but unlike the Sunnī *muṣannafāt*, Shīʿī compilations do not dedicate a special section to *ta'rīkh* or *maghāzī*;[6] they nevertheless do assemble separate traditions derived from early works which cover some aspects of the Prophet's life. This convention was taken over by Ibn Bābawayh al-Qummī (d. 381/991) and reached its culmination with al-Shaykh al-Mufīd (d. 413/1022) before it was carried further by both an *akhbārī* and an *uṣūlī* trend. It is thanks to these three compilers that the main bulk of the *sīra-maghāzī*-tradition was primarily preserved. Exegetical works form a second group of sources; here the *tafsīr* of ʿAlī b. Ibrāhīm al-Qummī (d. after 307/919) is of paramount importance. The third group of sources is represented by works dealing with the lives of the twelve Imams; these are works of a hagiographic nature (can one not say this of the Prophet's biography as well?); but they preserve a considerable amount of material derived from the *sīra-maghāzī*-genre. Al-Majlisī's (d. 1111/1699) encyclopaedic work *Biḥār al-anwār*[7] is an indispensable source for the study of the Shīʿī tradition. He represents the *akhbārī* school and has preserved a wealth of early traditions and material from extinct works; seven volumes of his book are dedicated to the life of the Prophet,[8] while some extra material is to be found as well in the volumes dedicated to Fāṭima, her sons and the subsequent Imams.

These books exhibit the main armamentarium for the study of the *sīra-maghāzī*-genre by the Imāmīs. However, one should be cautious in using them as a means to study the nature and form of the primary sources from which they derived their materials, for the following reasons: 1) They never (or only rarely) mention the title of the source they are using; 2) the chain of transmitters—even when sound and complete—does not necessarily mean that the author has derived his

---

[5] I am thinking here of *al-Maḥāsin* of al-Barqī (d. ca. 280/894), who is also an author of a *maghāzī*-work (cf. below) and *al-Baṣā'ir* of al-Ṣaffār (d. 290/902).

[6] Although the first volume of *al-Kāfī* and the last volume of its *furūʿ* do contain quite a number of *akhbār* that depict the history of the earliest Islamic community, in addition to apocalyptic and *faḍā'il*-traditions; *al-Kāfī (furūʿ: rawḍat al-Kāfī)*, vol. 8.

[7] Cf. K.H. Pampus, *Die theologische Enzyklopädie Biḥār al-anwār des Muḥammad Bāqir al-Majlisī,* University of Bonn, Ph.D. thesis, 1970.

[8] Vols. 15-21 (covering *al-mabʿath* and *al-maghāzī*); vols. 11-14 are dedicated to the *mubtada'* part.

material from the primary source in question or even that this material is identical to that source; 3) the early sources themselves have undergone a development of their own owing to the long process of transmission before taking on tentative final form in one or more versions; 4) the material they are using relates separate traditions and/or *akhbār* (stories) which have been taken from their original setting to be used in a new form within a new genre. These are some of the problems (and not the only ones) with which we are confronted when trying to "reconstruct" early sources which are only available in later compilations. These problems have been the subject of several studies in the last two decades. I would like to tackle them with regard to the Imāmī sources in three steps: First I will try to trace from the available data in the sources and the biographical (*rijāl*) collections the beginnings of this genre among the Imāmīs. Next, I will try to isolate the quotations attributed to one of the earliest compilers, Abān b. ʿUthmān al-Aḥmar, attempting thus to approach his *akhbār* critically, study his sources and compare this material with that of well-known early compilers such as Ibn Isḥāq and al-Wāqidī. And, finally, I will focus on the materials used by the Imāmī exegete ʿAlī b. Ibrāhīm al-Qummī.

II. The Imam as Source

According to the Shīʿī tradition, the systematic study of the different Islamic sciences started with the fifth and sixth Imams Muḥammad al-Bāqir (d. between 114/732 and 117/735)[9] and his son Jaʿfar al-Ṣādiq (d. 148/765). The Imāmī sources believe that the Imams narrated (*rawā*) the stories of the Genesis (*mubtadaʾ* or *mabdaʾ*) and of the biblical prophets, and it was from them that the *maghāzī* were transmitted, along with other disciplines such as jurisprudence, pilgrimage rituals, Qurʾānic exegesis and theology. This is perceived as a sign of their Imamate, for it is not known that they acquired their knowledge from other scholars; they thus consider this knowledge as being inherited from their fathers through a chain that leads directly back to the Prophet.[10] The words of the Imams and their knowledge are believed to be of a sacred nature and they are recognized as the source

[9] Regarding the dates, see M. Jarrar, "Tafsīr Abī l-Jārūd ʿan al-Imām al-Bāqir", in *Festschrift Sami N. Makarem* (forthcoming), note 48.

[10] Al-Shaykh al-Mufīd, *al-Irshād*, 264; Ibn Bābawayh al-Qummī, *Kamāl al-dīn*, 91.

of all sciences;[11] hence a considerable number of the Shīʿī traditions on *sīra* and *maghāzī* will show chains of transmission which have either of these two Imams as their first narrator. The Imams, who resided in Medina, were surely among the first masters in the various fields of Islamic learning and their students should have participated actively in the activities of learning which were taking place at the time. Historically, it is the disciples of the fourth, fifth and sixth Imams who began to record systematically the different branches of Islamic sciences. One of the first compilers in the field of *maghāzī*, the famous Ibn Shihāb al-Zuhrī (d. 124/742), was a disciple of the fourth Imam ʿAlī b. al-Ḥusayn Zayn al-ʿĀbidīn (33-95/653-713) and al-Zuhrī held him in high esteem.[12] Ibn Abī Shayba (d. 235/849) considers his transmission from Zayn al-ʿĀbidīn as the most trustworthy (*aṣaḥḥ al-asānīd kullihā*).[13] However, it seems that he transmitted from him mainly *raqāʾiq* and questions of jurisprudence,[14] and only a few reports concerning *sīra-maghāzī*-material.[15] Nevertheless, al-Zuhrī is known for his pro-Umayyad sympathies and his antipathy for ʿAlī b. Abī Ṭālib.[16]

---

[11] Cf. H.-J. Kornrumpf, "Untersuchungen zum Bild ʿAlīs und des frühen Islams bei den Schiiten", in *Der Islam*, 45 (1969), 276-85; M.A. Amir-Moezzi, *The Divine Guide in Early Shiʿism. The Source of Esotericism in Islam*, trans. D. Streight, Albany, 1994, 24 ff., 69 ff.; H. Corbin, *En Islam iranien: Aspects spirituels et philosophiques, I, Le Shīʿisme duodécimain,* Paris, 1971, 212 ff.

[12] Ibn Saʿd, *Ṭabaqāt*, V, 214, 215; Abū Zurʿa, *Taʾrīkh*, I, 413, 536; Ibn ʿAsākir, *Taʾrīkh*, XLI, 366, ll. 14-19; 371 f., 374, l. 1; 375, l. 1; 376, ll. 4-6.

[13] Ibn ʿAsākir, *Taʾrīkh*, XLI, 376, ll.1-2; idem, *Tarjamat al-Zuhrī*, 101.

[14] Cf. e.g. Ibn Bābawayh al-Qummī, *al-Khiṣāl*, 64, 111, 119, 240, 534; Ibn ʿAsākir, *Taʾrīkh*, XLI, 360, ll.16 ff.; 376, ll.4-7; 376, ll.7-12; 387, ll.13-15; 398, ll.1-12; 403 ff. (poetry); Qummī, Abū l-Qāsim, *Kifāyat al-athar*, 241: Maʿmar—al-Zuhrī—ʿAlī b. al-Ḥusayn, a strange report which starts with *faḍl al-hundubāʾ* and continues with the designation of al-Bāqir as the fifth Imam (?); cf. as well Ardabīlī, *Jāmiʿ al-ruwāt*, II, 201; Khūʾī, *Muʿjam rijāl al-ḥadīth*, XXIII, 345-56.

[15] Ibn Hishām, *Sīra*, I, 220; Ibn Saʿd, *Ṭabaqāt*, I, 124, 368, II, 284, 297; Balādhurī, *Ansāb*, I, 572, 578; Ṭabarī, *Taʾrīkh*, III, 212; the tradition by Abū Zurʿa, *Taʾrīkh*, I, 417 might be a *maghāzī*-tradition.

[16] Cf. Ibn Abī l-Ḥadīd, *Sharḥ*, IV, 63 f., 102; and M. Jarrar, *Die Prophetenbiographie im islamischen Spanien*, Frankfurt/Bern, 1989, 23-28; cf. now, idem, "*Sīra*, *Mashāhid* and *Maghāzī*: The Genesis and Development of the Biography of Muḥammad", in *Studies in Late Antiquity and Early Islam*, III, ed. L.I. Conrad and A. Cameron, Princeton, (in press), 21-27. I have shown there that ʿAbd al-Razzāq al-Ṣanʿānī (d. 211/826) relies in the *maghāzī*-section of his *Muṣannaf* (vol. 5) mainly on al-Zuhrī's material and that he adds to it extra material to emphasize ʿAlī's role whenever al-Zuhrī's reports fail to do so or when they reveal pro-Umayyad tendencies; ʿAbd al-Razzāq was accused by Sunnī scholars of having Shīʿī tendencies (cf. Motzki, *Die Anfänge der islamischen Jurisprudenz*, 63 ff.; and, accordingly, the Imāmīs regard him as Shīʿī, Ḥāʾirī al-

The Shīʿī tradition considers Ibn Isḥāq (d. 151/768) among al-Bāqir's disciples (*min aṣḥābih*) and claims that his grandfather Yasār was also a disciple of both al-Sajjād and al-Bāqir.[17] Still, he is regarded as a Sunnī (*ʿāmmī*) who has sympathy for the Imams (or *ahl al-Bayt*) and harbors immense love for them.[18] On their part, the Sunnī scholars accuse him of having Shīʿī sympathies;[19] in Ibn Hishām's version of Ibn Isḥāq's *Sīra* there appears only one story which is related from Muḥammad al-Bāqir.[20] By the same token, al-Wāqidī (d. 207/822) is accused of having "pirated" the books of the Medinan scholar Ibrāhīm b. Abī Yaḥyā (d. 184/800),[21] a follower and propagandist (*dāʿī*) of the Zaydī Imam Yaḥyā b. ʿAbd Allāh; Ibn Abī Yaḥyā was held by the Imāmī scholars in high esteem, for he was a disciple of both al-Bāqir and al-Ṣādiq. This accusation seems totally unfounded and, moreover, Zaydī sources make neither mention of it nor of Ibn Abī YaḥĀ yā's having compiled a *sīra* or a *maghāzī* book.[22]

III. Abān b. ʿUthmān al-Aḥmar[23]

The only name among these disciples which can be regarded seriously and which appears as a compiler of *sīra* and *maghāzī* is that of Abān b. ʿUthmān al-Aḥmar, a client of the South Arabian clan Bajīla which resided in Kūfa during the Islamic conquests.[24] Whereas al-Kashshī mentions that Abān was a Baṣran but used to dwell in Kūfa[25]—which

Māzandarānī, *Muntahā al-maqāl*, IV, 121-22); nevertheless Ibn ʿAsākir gives a report from al-Zuhrī—ʿUbayd Allāh b. ʿAbd Allāh b. ʿUtba—Ibn ʿAbbās (*Taʾrīkh*, XII, 267 f.) which shows the Prophet's love for ʿAlī and warns whoever hates him.

[17] M. b. ʿAlī al-Ardabīlī, *Jāmiʿ al-ruwāt*, II, 65, 66, 67; Āghā Buzurg al-Ṭihrānī, *al-Dharīʿa ilā taṣānīf al-Shīʿa*, XXI, 290.

[18] Kashshī, *Ikhtiyār maʿrifat al-rijāl*, 390 (no. 733); Ardabīlī, *Jāmiʿ al-ruwāt*, II, 66.

[19] Cf. al-Khaṭīb al-Baghdādī, *Taʾrīkh Baghdād*, I, 224; Yāqūt, *Muʿjam al-udabāʾ*, VI, 2419.

[20] Ibn Hishām, *al-Sīra al-nabawiyya*, I, 340.

[21] Ṭūsī, *Fihrist*, 16; Najāshī, *Rijāl*, I, 85; Ardabīlī, *Jāmiʿ al-ruwāt*, I, 33 f.; M. Jarrar, "Some Lights on an Early Zaydite Manuscript",in *Asiatische Studien*, 47/2 (1993), 285-86; idem, "Arbaʿ rasāʾil Zaydiyya mubakkira", in *Fī miḥrāb al-maʿrifa: Festschrift for Iḥsān ʿAbbās*, ed. I. al-Saʿāfīn, Beirut, 1997, 270-71.

[22] Cf. e.g. Ibn Abī l-Rijāl, *Maṭlaʿ al-budūr*, I, 68 ff.

[23] See detailed biographical data on him, and a list of his teachers and sources in Appendix 2, below.

[24] Cf. F. Donner, *The Early Islamic Conquests*, Princeton, 1981, 78, 175, 196 f., 221-23 (and see index, 473).

[25] Kashshī, *Ikhtiyār maʿrifat al-rijāl*, 352 (no. 660); Ibn Dāwūd al-Ḥillī, *Rijāl*, 26 (*kūfī*

seems unlikely because Bajīla didn't reside in Baṣra[26]—al-Najāshī and al-Ṭūsī affirm his Kūfan origin but mention that he used to frequent both cities[27] and it was in Baṣra that the renowned authors of genealogy and *akhbār*, Abū ʿUbayda Maʿmar b. al-Muthannā (110-209/728-824) and Muḥammad b. Sallām al-Jumaḥī (150-232/767-846) studied with him. Not much is known about his life and career except that he was a disciple of both al-Ṣādiq (83-148/702-65) and al-Kāẓim (128-83/745-99), although I did not come across any transmission of his from the latter.[28] His chain of transmission (*riwāya*) from al-Bāqir runs always through a transmitter. All this leads to the conclusion that he died sometime during the last quarter of the second century AH/ca. 790-815 AD.[29] Al-Kashshī mentions that Abān was a Nāwūsī,[30] i.e., an adherent of a certain Baṣran named Ibn Nāwūs (or al-Nāwūs), who believed that Jaʿfar al-Ṣādiq was the awaited *Mahdī* (Messiah) and preached his return as savior (*rajʿa*) after his death;[31] but this claim had not been mentioned by either al-Najāshī or al-Ṭūsī and became controversial among later Shīʿī authors, who claimed that the word *al-nāwūsiyya* was a distortion of *al-Qādisiyya*, a place near Kūfa.[32] Nevertheless, Abān was considered among the six most trustworthy disciples of Jaʿfar al-Ṣādiq in jurisprudence (*fiqh*),[33] and I have not found any evidence in the material delivered from him which recalls

---

al-maskin baṣrī al-aṣl); Ḥāʾirī al-Māzandarānī, *Muntahā al-maqāl*, I, 189-93; ʿUqaylī, *K. al-Ḍuʿafāʾ*, I, 37 gives him the *nisba* "al-kūfī"; cf. Ibn Ḥajar, *Lisān*, I, 24; J. van Ess in his *Theologie und Gesellschaft*, Berlin/New York, 1993, II, 425 counts him among the Baṣran Shīʿa. It is clear from the sources that most of his teachers were Kūfans (cf. Appendix 2).

[26] Donner, *The Early Islamic Conquests*, 215 (except for Shibl b. Maʿbad and his son).

[27] Najāshī, *Rijāl*, I, 80; Ṭūsī, *Fihrist*, 18.

[28] Cf. as well A. Bāktačī, in *Dāʾirat al-maʿārif al-islāmiyya al-kubrā*, ed. K.M. al-Bujnūrdī, Tehran, 1995, II, 44.

[29] One notices as well that a number of his teachers died in 150/767 (cf. Appendix 2), whereas his students were disciples of the seventh and eighth Imams.

[30] Kashshī, *Ikhtiyār maʿrifat al-rijāl*, 352 (no. 660); and after him Ibn Dāwūd al-Ḥillī, *Rijāl*, 226 (among the untrustworthy scholars, though he mentioned him the first time as trustworthy, 30); Ardabīlī, *Jāmiʿ al-ruwāt*, I, 12.

[31] Nawbakhtī, *Firaq al-Shīʿa*, 67; (pseudo-) Nāshiʾ, *Masāʾil al-imāma*, 46; Ashʿarī, *Maqālāt al-islāmiyyīn*, 25; Shahrastānī, *al-Milal wa-l-niḥal*, 71; van Ess, *Theologie und Gesellschaft*, II, 424; Modarressi, *Crisis and Consolidation*, 55-57.

[32] Tustarī, *Qāmūs al-rijāl*, I, 114, 116; Ḥāʾirī al-Māzandarānī, *Muntahā al-maqāl*, I, 138-40; Bāktačī, in *Dāʾirat al-maʿārif al-islāmiyya al-kubrā*, II, 45; Modarressi, *Crisis and Consolidation*, 55 note.

[33] Kashshī, *Ikhtiyār maʿrifat al-rijāl*, 375 (no. 705).

"unorthodox" Imāmī ideas he might have had, although one has to be aware that such material in all likelihood underwent falsification by later scholars,[34] especially if we keep in mind that he enjoyed high esteem among the Imāmīs.[35]

Abān's maghāzī

Both al-Najāshī and al-Ṭūsī attribute to Abān a work of history comprising material about the Genesis and the biblical prophets (*mabdaʾ*), Muḥammad's birth and vocation (*mabʿath*), his military campaigns (*maghāzī*), his death (*wafāt*), the *saqīfa*-meeting, and the tribal wars that broke out after his death (*ridda*),[36] a book that had not been referred to by the Shīʿī Ibn al-Nadīm (d. after 385/995) or by other early sources before the beginning of the fourth/tenth century; even the famous Imāmī scholar and bibliophile ʿAlī b. Mūsā Ibn Ṭāwūs (d. 664/1265) did not mention it in his works.[37] Many quotations probably from this book, however, are to be found in the sources without mentioning it by name; moreover, the Shīʿī historian al-Yaʿqūbī (d. after 292/904) names Abān among his sources regarding the life of the Prophet (*aṣḥāb al-siyar wa-l-maghāzī wa-l-tawārīkh*),[38] and al-Ṭabrisī (d. 548/1154) states that he is copying from "Abān's book".[39] Al-Najāshī and al-Ṭūsī give the *isnād*s of this book, all of which meet at a common link who reports directly from Abān,[40] namely, Aḥmad b. Muḥammad b. Abī Naṣr al-Bizanṭī (d. 221/835), a Kūfan scholar who enjoyed a high status among the eighth Imam al-Riḍā's entourage.[41]

---

[34] Cf. Modarressi, *Crisis and Consolidation*, 43, 47.

[35] His "dogmatic credo" which I summed up from the sources resembles that which was current during the second and third centuries AH among the Imāmiyya although one can say that it more likely tends to the *mufawwiḍa* faction (Modarressi, *Crisis and Consolidation*, 21 ff.); cf. Kashshī, *Ikhtiyār maʿrifat al-rijāl*, 94 (no. 148), 107 (172), 235 (425); Majlisī, *Biḥār al-anwār*, XXIII, 119, XXIV, 76, XXVI, 46, 48, 227, XXVII, 264, XXVIII, 41, 70, XXXII, 210, XXXVI, 226, 272, 392, XXXVII, 311, 336, XXXVIII, 102, XXXIX, 247, XL, 3, XLII, 103, XLIII, 98.

[36] Najāshī, *Rijāl*, I, 80-81; Ṭūsī, *Fihrist*, 18-19.

[37] At least it is not mentioned by E. Kohlberg in his *A Medieval Muslim Scholar at Work*, Leiden, 1992.

[38] Yaʿqūbī, *Taʾrīkh*, II, 6.

[39] Ṭabrisī, *Iʿlām al-warā*, 82-130, 137-38.

[40] Cf. for a detailed diagram, Appendix 3.

[41] Kashshī, *Ikhtiyār maʿrifat al-rijāl*, index, 37; Najāshī, *Rijāl*, I, 202-04; Ṭūsī, *Fihrist*, 19-20; Ardabīlī, *Jāmiʿ al-ruwāt*, I, 59-61; Ḥāʾirī al-Māzandarānī, *Muntahā al-maqāl*, I, 307-11; Kohlberg, *A Medieval Muslim Scholar*, 222; van Ess (*Theologie und Gesellschaft*, I,

Besides these chains of al-Najāshī and al-Ṭūsī, there is another well-attested chain, that of Ibn Bābawayh which runs through ʿAlī b. Ibrāhīm al-Qummī and ends with Muḥammad b. Ziyād, known as Ibn Abī ʿUmayr (d. 217/832), who transmits directly from Abān. Ibn Abī ʿUmayr is a Baghdādī client of al-Muhallab b. Abī Ṣufra's family.[42] He was a very prominent Shīʿī scholar and served as a deputy (*wakīl*) to the seventh Imam Mūsā al-Kāẓim (d. 183/799), transmitting directly from Imam al-Riḍā (d. 203/818). He was beaten up and imprisoned under the ʿAbbāsid caliph al-Rashīd and a second time after the death of al-Riḍā. Like al-Bizanṭī, he was also a direct disciple of the theologian Hishām al-Jawālīqī, and al-Jāḥiẓ (d. 255/868) considers him one of the heads of the *Rāfiḍa*,[43] which probably means the Imāmiyya.[44] Ibn Abī ʿUmayr is said to have written a number of books, among them a *Kitāb al-Maghāzī*. Alongside these Kūfan lines of transmission (*riwāyāt*), al-Ṭūsī mentions still a second Qummī *riwāya* which he describes as incomplete (*anqaṣ*). It runs through Jaʿfar b. Bashīr Abū Muḥammad (d. 208/823), an ascetic who, like Abān, was a Kūfan client of Bajīla and had his mosque within its quarter. He is said to have been among the entourage of the caliph al-Maʾmūn after the death of Imam al-Riḍā.[45]

Form and Structure

I have examined the historical material attributed to Abān in the sources relaying mainly on al-Kulīnī, Ibn Bābawayh al-Qummī, al-Ṭabrisī and al-Majlisī's *Biḥār al-anwār* and have concentrated mainly on the transmission chains of both Ibn Abī Naṣr al-Bizanṭī and Ibn Abī ʿUmayr. Bearing in mind the reservations I mentioned at the beginning, I will try to approach this material as a Shīʿī corpus.

---

384) says he was a disciple of the theologian Hishām al-Jawālīqī.

[42] Kashshī, *Ikhtiyār maʿrifat al-rijāl*, index, 231, 250 (Muḥammad b. Ziyād); Najāshī, *Rijāl*, II, 204-08; Ṭūsī, *Fihrist*, 138; Ardabīlī, *Jāmiʿ al-ruwāt*, II, 50-57; Ḥāʾirī al-Māzandarānī, *Muntahā al-maqāl*, V, 302-08; Aḥmad Bādkūba Hazāwa, in *Dāʾirat al-maʿārif al-islāmiyya al-kubrā*, I, 342-43; van Ess, *Theologie und Gesellschaft*, I, 384-86.

[43] Ḥāʾirī al-Māzandarānī, *Muntahā al-maqāl*, V, 303 quoting *al-Bayān wa-l-tabyīn*, I, 88, although the name there is Muḥammad b. ʿUmayr.

[44] Cf. hereto, Jarrar, "Arbaʿ rasāʾil", 272.

[45] Kashshī, *Ikhtiyār maʿrifat al-rijāl*, index, 65; Najāshī, *Rijāl*, I, 297-98; Ibn Dāwūd al-Ḥillī, *Rijāl*, 62; Ardabīlī, *Jāmiʿ al-ruwāt*, I, 150-51; Ḥāʾirī al-Māzandarānī, *Muntahā al-maqāl*, II, 234-36.

The first remark to be made here is that Abān is one generation younger than Ibn Isḥāq, so that he should have known his work which was already in wide circulation at the time as well as, possibly, other works in this genre such as that of the Medinan Mūsā b. ʿUqba (d. 141/758) and the Baṣran Sulaymān b. Ṭarkhān al-Taymī (d. 143/761), the renowned scholar and author of a *sīra*-work, who might have had some Shīʿī leanings.[46] We have seen that Abān used to reside in Baṣra for long intervals of time, so that he most probably knew al-Taymī's work although I have not found any mention of it in Abān's transmission.

Now, the division of these early historical works into three parts: Genesis (*mubtadaʾ*), Muḥammad's birth and vocation (*mabʿath*), and his military campaigns (*maghāzī*), has been regarded as canonical since (or actually with) Ibn Isḥāq.[47] One can thus conclude that the title of Abān's book as it appears in both al-Najāshī and al-Ṭūsī is original and indeed describes the order in which Abān arranged his material. Nevertheless, this does not mean that this was the title of Abān's book (one did not give a title to his book at that early stage), and even the material might not have already taken the form of a book; it would rather have been a kind of *hypomnēmata* as G. Schoeler has shown regarding the development of early works.[48]

I have restricted the scope of my study to only these three parts although Abān's book should have comprised, in addition, materials on the *al-saqīfa*-meeting and *al-ridda*.[49] The material I have gathered amounts to one hundred and thirty-three reports (*khabar*),[50] sixty-one of which deal with the Genesis and seventy-two with *mabʿath* and

[46] Cf. Jarrar, *Die Prophetenbiographie*, 76-81. Ibn Saʿd says that he had a liking (*kāna māʾilan ilā*) for ʿAlī b. Abī Ṭālib (*Ṭabaqāt*, VII, 353); whereas Ibn Qutayba counts him among the Shīʿa (*al-Maʿārif*, 624). One should pause for a moment before taking Ibn Qutayba's label at face value. Baṣra was known for its support for ʿUthmān's cause and any preference for ʿAlī would be regarded by an "intemperate" Sunnī traditionalist and theologian such as Ibn Qutayba as a *tashayyuʿ*. I think that Ibn Saʿd's comment is more trustworthy and I regard it as denoting only Sulaymān's political stand or preference, a stand which was taken over by Aḥmad b. Ḥanbal later on, when he counted ʿAlī as the fourth righteous Caliph.

[47] Cf. R. Sellheim, "Prophet, Caliph und Geschichte. Die Muḥammad-Biographie des Ibn Isḥāq", in *Oriens*, 18-19 (1967), 38-42; Jarrar, *Die Prophetenbiographie*, 31 f.

[48] See his studies in *Der Islam*, 62 (1985), 201-30, 66 (1989), 38-67, 69 (1992), 1-43.

[49] Cf. as well a report on Ṣiffīn in Majlisī, *Biḥār al-anwār*, XXXII, 601 f.

[50] The material attributed to Abān in the sources is much more numerous, but I have limited my choice to a narrower sense of the *sīra-maghāzī*-genre and have left out some traditions which do not directly serve this study.

maghāzī. Of the reports on the Genesis, twenty-six have al-Bizanṭī as their main transmitter and twenty one have Ibn Abī ʿUmayr, whereas fifteen from the *mabʿath* and *maghāzī* reports have al-Bizanṭī as their main transmitter, eleven have Ibn Abī ʿUmayr, four have both of them and forty-two have various other transmitters. This ascription to a wide range of transmitters (beside a few central ones) might be seen as a criterion for the authenticity of the material in general.[51] In these one-hundred and thirty-three reports, Abān transmits twenty times directly from Jaʿfar al-Ṣādiq (6 Genesis and 14 *mabʿath* and *maghāzī*), and thirty-six times indirectly via different "authorities" (*ruwāt*).[52] He transmits twenty-four times from al-Bāqir through a link (14 *mubtadaʾ* and 10 *sīra*), thirty-nine times from Jaʿfar al-Ṣādiq (14 *mubtadaʾ* and 25 *sīra*), two times indirectly from both Imams (unidentified), and once from ʿAlī b. al-Ḥusayn al-Sajjād. This amounts to eighty-four traditions (*akhbār*), or 64.1%, which go back to the Imams either directly or through a link (at times through two links). This does not mean that all these stories and reports, whether claimed to be heard directly from the Imams or through a transmission link, actually stem from them because several of them reveal later Shīʿī doctrines. The Imams often present only a point of reference, authenticity and legitimacy and the attribution of the material to them should not bother us here, except if we meet a family-*isnād* conveying a family story or other material that does not reveal a particularly Shīʿī tenet or ascribe superhuman qualities to the Prophet, ʿAlī or Fāṭima. In fact, the sequence of Abān's narration, its language and style resemble in many ways that of his contemporary al-Wāqidī and at times that of Yūnus b. Bukayr's (d. 199/814) version of Ibn Isḥāq's *Sīra*, but it is difficult—at this stage of the research—to say with certainty which of these texts originated first, even though al-Wāqidī seems to have known the transmission of Abān—not necessarily through a book—as a report on the battle of Badr by Ibn Saʿd suggests.[53] I am suggesting that during the first half of the second century AH/ca. 720-67 AD, a significant corpus of materials, narrations with quite an elaborate

[51] Cf. the arguments of Motzki concerning the authenticity of ʿAṭāʾs material in the *Muṣannaf* of ʿAbd al-Razzāq, in *Die Anfänge der islamischen Jurisprudenz*, 71-89.
[52] Cf. Appendix 4.
[53] *Ṭabaqāt*, IV, 43; I could not find it in Wāqidī's *Maghāzī*. The transmission chain reads: [al-Wāqidī]—ʿAlī b. ʿĪsā al-Nawfalī—Abān b. ʿUthmān—Muʿāwiya b. ʿAmmār al-Duhnī (instead of the erroneous "al-Dhahabī").

form, topoi and schemata,[54] was already circulating in the various centers of study in al-Ḥijāz, Iraq and Syria. I have shown in a study on the *faḍāʾil al-jihād*-genre that both the *fabula* and the narrative discourse were well elaborated—as I am suggesting here—already at the beginning of the second/eighth century and entailed both transformation and self-regulation. Now in the process of their development, these narratives grasped new motifs and underwent a process of "habitualization";[55] they needed only to be loaded with codes and to be habitualized to serve the worldview of a specific group or sect, or be adjusted to the somewhat vague diction of the Qurʾān and its uncertain chronology—one should keep in mind here the problem of abrogation—to be used for legal purposes. Accordingly, one should emphasize the relationship between these narrations and their historical and social contexts, and their interaction with the pragmatic aspects of dogma and ideology. This is a well-attested phenomenon in the development of narrative genres and could inspire our approach here. No study has as yet dealt exclusively with the structural elements of both the *fabula* and the *sujet* of these narratives and the style specifications of the different authors/redactors of the *sīra-maghāzī*-literature.[56] Before I take this step I will restrict my scope in this essay to delineating the main features of this Shīʿī material.

One chain of transmission from among the remaining 35.9% is particularly interesting: Abān transmits ten times, i.e., 7.63%, from Abū Saʿīd Abān b. Taghlib al-Bakrī (6 *mubtadaʾ* and 4 *sīra*). Abān b. Taghlib (d. 141/758), is a well-known Imāmī, Kūfan linguist, Qurʾān reciter (*qāriʾ*) and exegete, who is praised and recognized by both Sunnī and Shīʿī authorities and is an author of a book on Qurʾānic readings.[57] Ibn Taghlib transmits five times via ʿIkrima from Ibn ʿAbbās; in addition to Ibn Taghlib, two other main authorities of Abān b. ʿUthmān transmit reports through this chain, each once;[58]

---

[54] Cf. A. Noth in collaboration with L.I. Conrad, *The Early Arabic Historical Tradition*, Princeton, 1994.

[55] Cf. R. Fowler, *Linguistic Criticism*, ²Oxford, 1996, 44-56.

[56] See, however, J. Wansbrough, *The Sectarian Milieu. Content and Composition of Islamic Salvation History*, Oxford, 1978, and N. Abū Zayd, "al-Sīra al-nabawiyya sīra shaʿbiyya", in *Majallat al-Funūn al-Shaʿbiyya*, 32-33 (June-December 1991), 17-36.

[57] Cf. Najāshī, *Rijāl*, I, 73-79; Ardabīlī, *Jāmiʿ al-ruwāt*, I, 9-11; Ḥāʾirī al-Māzandarānī, *Muntahā al-maqāl*, I, 132-35; Ṣafadī, *al-Wāfī*, V, 300; Suyūṭī, *Bughyat al-wuʿāt*, I, 404; ʿAlī Akbar Diyāʾī, in *Dāʾirat al-maʿārif al-islāmiyya al-kubrā*, 2 (1995), 46-47; van Ess, *Theologie und Gesellschaft*, I, 334, II, 344 ff.

[58] These are Abū Baṣīr al-Kūfī and Abū Ḥamza al-Thumālī, cf. Appendix 2.

this brings the number of reports attributed to ʿIkrima—Ibn ʿAbbās to seven, i.e., 5.34% of the material: four of these reports deal with the Genesis and Prophets and three with *maghāzī* (see Appendix 1.A., nos. 9, 10; 1.B., no. 1). ʿIkrima (d. 105/723) is a celebrated exegete and is regarded as an authority on *sīra* as well (*kāna aʿlamahum bi-sīrat al-nabī*),[59] two twin fields of scrutiny. Most of his *maghāzī*-material, which is scattered in the early sources,[60] is built around Qurʾānic verses and its *narratio* deals mainly with occasions of revelation.[61] I could not find in the sources any of the reports attributed here to him, although none of them reveals any kind of Shīʿī tenets or any preference to ʿAlī. Nevertheless, such tenets are transmitted from ʿIkrima through the same chain we are discussing here, in Ibn Bābawayh's *Amālī*.[62] This is quite bizarre since ʿIkrima is accused by Sunnī scholars to have had Khārijī tendencies,[63] and even Imāmī sources regard him as a non-Imāmī (*laysa ʿalā ṭarīqatinā wa-lā min aṣḥābinā*) and untrustworthy (*ḍaʿīf*).[64] This leads us anew to the problem of the originality of the early chains of transmission and their authenticity, albeit the tradition of ʿIkrima needs a more detailed study.

Genesis (al-mabdaʾ wa-l-anbiyāʾ)

The material discussed in this section is of the *isrāʾīliyyāt*-genre typical of Muslim exegetical works, even the early ones, and common to both the Sunnī and Shīʿī traditions. This material not only serves as a historical worldview of the community of believers, confirming that Muḥammad was the last Prophet, his community the last community,

---

[59] Fasawī, *al-Maʿrifa wa-l-taʾrīkh*, II, 16.

[60] I have counted 15 reports which are attributed to him by Ibn Hishām, 55 by Ṭabarī (*sīra*-section), 18 by Wāqidī, 13 by ʿAbd al-Razzāq in his *maghāzī*-section and 5 in his *jihād*-section, and 31 by Balādhurī; for his *riwāyāt* in the Sunnī canonical compendia, cf. Mizzī, *Tuḥfat al-ashrāf*, V, 107-82.

[61] On *asbāb al-nuzūl* in the *sīra-maghāzī*-tradition, cf. J. Wansbrough, *The Sectarian Milieu*, 7, 11, 29.

[62] Cf. e.g. Majlisī, *Biḥār al-anwār*, XXIII, 119, XXVIII, 41, XXXII, 601, XXXVIII, 102, XXXIX, 247, XLIII, 98.

[63] Ibn Saʿd, *Ṭabaqāt*, V, 292; Ibn Qutayba, *al-Maʿārif*, 457; Ashʿarī, *Maqālāt al-islāmiyyīn*, 109, 120; Dhahabī, *Mīzān*, III, 93-97, on p. 95, l.1 it is specified that he was an *ibāḍī*; Ibn ʿAbd al-Barr defends him against this claim, cf. *Tamhīd*, II, 26-35.

[64] Kashshī, *Ikhtiyār maʿrifat al-rijāl*, 216 (no. 387); Ḥāʾirī al-Māzandarānī, *Muntahā al-maqāl*, I, 4, 313-14.

and that God has promised them dominion over the lands and nations;[65] but it also shows Islamic history to be a continuation of the salvation history of the Jews and Christians, placing Muḥammad at the center of this history, its starting and end point, as R. Sellheim has shown.[66] It serves, moreover, polemic ends as the stories were used to prove the falsifications of the holy Scriptures (Torah, Psalms, Old and New Testaments) which, according to the Islamic understanding, were undertaken by Jews and Christians. Nevertheless, these stories serve in the Imāmī exegesis still another purpose in that they are a sign of the supremacy of the Imams, whose essence and light stem directly from the light of Muḥammad and ʿAlī which was created by God thousands of years before the creation of the world, an idea which constitutes perhaps the most important element of the capital idea of *waṣiyya*.[67] As Amir-Moezzi puts it, "[T]his is why, throughout the Imamite tradition, the imams are constantly compared to the prophets and saints of Israel, although they [i.e. the Imams] are superior to them, since through the light of the imams, they [i.e., the Prophets] have acquired their sacred status."[68] Even the number of Imams—twelve—had served in biblical tradition as the number of election.[69] This is a very crucial point in approaching the Imāmī understanding of the ideational role of the *sīra-maghāzī* literature and might explain why no such work has survived, as I will be arguing later on. Apart from that, these stories are often used as a means to justify and legitimize some Shīʿī tenets or to serve polemic, theological or juridical ends.[70] Thus, Noah's son who refused to enter the Ark was not his own son, but actually his wife's son, since a son of a prophet who carries in himself the divine light cannot be an unbeliever;[71] the milt was prohibited because it was Satan's share from Abraham's sacrifice; Jacob asked God in his prayer through the intervention of *ahl al-kisāʾ* to bring him back Joseph and Benjamin; statues that the

---

[65] Cf. M. Jarrar, "The *Sīra*. Its Formative Elements and Its Transmission", in *BUC Public Lecture Series*, April 1993, 1.

[66] Cf. Sellheim, "Prophet", 38 ff.

[67] Amir-Moezzi, *The Divine Guide in Early Shiʿism*, 31 ff., 42.

[68] Amir-Moezzi, *The Divine Guide in Early Shiʿism*, 42; cf. as well U. Rubin, "Pre-Existence and Light. Aspects of the Concept of Nūr Muḥammad," in *IOS*, 5 (1975), 62-118; idem, "Prophets and Progenitors in the Early Shīʿa Tradition", in *JSAI*, 1 (1979), 51 ff.

[69] Amir-Moezzi, *The Divine Guide in Early Shiʿism*, 107.

[70] Cf. Wansbrough, *The Sectarian Milieu*, 2-3.

[71] See Appendix 1.A. for details and comparison.

jinn made for Solomon were trees and not human figures; if Asph ben Berechiah, the *waṣī* of Solomon, made miracles, then ʿAlī, the *waṣī al-awṣiyāʾ*, is even more suitable for miracles; Jesus was born on *ʿāshūrāʾ*; Jesus praised God the Almighty when Satan told him that the day will come when Jesus will govern over the heavens and earth; the mercifulness of God regarding the punishment of children (*ʿadhāb al-aṭfāl*) was proven to Ezra through a parable.

Birth, vocation and career (al-mabʿath wa-l-maghāzī)

Whereas the main preoccupation of the Imāmī tradition in the *mubtadaʾ* part exhibits a dominant concern with the notion of the ubiquitous divine light of the Prophet and Imams, around which the entire salvation history of humankind rotates, a different but related approach dominates the portrayal of events in the *maghāzī* section. The narration here centers on the fulfillment of this light as it articulates itself through the pair of divine light, Muḥammad and ʿAlī, during the last stage of this salvation history. As early as 1930, Rudi Paret pointed out the importance given to ʿAlī b. Abī Ṭālib in the popular versions of the *sīra*, especially in that of Abū l-Ḥasan al-Bakrī;[72] and in the early sixties, Henri Laoust cited examples denoting the special role of ʿAlī in the events of the *sīra* from two sources which do not belong to the *sīra-maghāzī*-genre, namely, al-*Irshād* of al-Shaykh al-Mufīd (d. 413/1022) and *Minhāj al-karāma* of al-ʿAllāma al-Ḥillī (d. 726/1325).[73] As I have argued before,[74] the narrative body here resembles that of the well-known *maghāzī* of its time, although it assembles new elements which aim at a more vivid presentation of ʿAlī and are plainly meant to give a paradigmatic illustration of his charisma and ministry which he shares with Muḥammad, his partner in the pair of light, so that the Imāmī traditions concerning *mabʿath* and *maghāzī* appear to belong not only to the *faḍāʾil*-genre but also, and more precisely, to the *dalāʾil al-nubuwwa*-genre, which is usually restricted to the Prophet.[75] Moreover, the role assumed by both Abū Bakr and

---

[72] *Die legendäre maghāzī-Literatur*, Tübingen, 1930, 190-211; for ʿAlī's portrayal in the Sunnī sources, cf. W. Sarasin, *Das Bild ʿAlīs bei der Historikern der Sunna*, Basel, 1907 (cited after Kornrumpf, "Untersuchungen", 262).

[73] H. Laoust, "Le role de ʿAlī dans la *sīra* Chiite", in *Revue des Etudes islamiques*, 30 (1963), 7-26.

[74] See above p. 107 f.

[75] See Appendix 1.B. 5, 6, 7.

ʿUmar in the Sunnī sources (one can even speak of ʿUmar's charisma) is either completely omitted or, especially in the case of ʿUmar, given a negative significance. There is as well a tendency to produce new deeds and sayings attributed to ʿAlī, in part as a contribution or a revision of deeds and sayings which already exist in other works of the genre. Precedence in crucial events is given to those companions (*ṣaḥāba*) who either were friendly towards ʿAlī or fought on his side during the first civil war. We find thus, for example, a different list from that of the other sources for those who attended the first ʿAqaba-meeting,[76] while during the battle of Uḥud *only* the name of Abū Dujāna appears beside that of ʿAlī.[77] When dealing with the material attributed to Abān, one should keep in mind some reservations: 1) that this material consists of citations drawn from later compilations which do not belong to the genre; 2) that even these quotations cited by al-Majlisī in the volumes dedicated to the life of the Prophet are often partial quotations which are used at times only to clarify a point or as extra textual narrative; these quotations are scattered over a number of chapters whose division has become canonical, a division which reflects neither Abān's original plan nor his chronological order of the sequence of the events. For example, Abān dates the killing of al-ʿAṣmāʾ during the battle of Ḥamrāʾ al-Asad, directly after Uḥud, whereas al-Wāqidī and al-Balādhurī date it after Badr;[78] and he dates ʿĀmir b. al-Ṭufayl's and Arbad b. Qays's delegation to Medina directly after the event with the Banū l-Naḍīr, whereas both Ibn Isḥāq and al-Wāqidī do not date it at all and al-Bukhārī mentions it before the Banū l-Naḍīr.[79]

I will now end my discussion of Abān's book and will turn my attention to other issues concerning the Imāmī *sīra-maghāzī*-genre in general.[80]

---

[76] See Appendix 1.B. 8.

[77] See Appendix 1.B. 11.

[78] Compare Ṭabrisī, *Iʿlām al-warā*, 54-55; Majlisī, *Biḥār al-anwār*, XX, 95 ff. With Wāqidī, *Maghāzī*, I, 172-74; Ibn Saʿd, *Ṭabaqāt*, II, 27-28; Balādhurī, *Ansāb*, I, 373; Bayhaqī, *Dalāʾil*, III, 312, and cf. hereto, M. Lecker, *Muslims, Jews and Pagans. Studies in Early Islamic Medina*, Leiden, 1995, 38-41.

[79] See Appendix 1.B.15.

[80] For a discussion of those reports of Abān which diverge from other *sīra*-works or which either are not mentioned in them or reveal a particularly Shīʿī tradition, cf. Appendix 1.B. and see Appendix 4 for the remaining tradition.

IV. The *Maghāzī* of ʿAlī b. Ibrāhīm al-Qummī

Imāmī sources mention a number of works dedicated to the *sīra-maghāzī* genre, none of which is extant.[81] Of special importance, it would seem, is the work of Ibn Abī ʿUmayr (d. 217/832), one of the chief transmitters of Abān's work.[82] He is also a main source of ʿAlī b. Ibrāhīm al-Qummī in his *Tafsīr* and many of his reports are quoted by al-Majlisī in his *Biḥār*. Ostensibly, his work is a kind of redaction with additions to and variations on his mentor's *hypomnēmata*. The name of Aḥmad b. Muḥammad b. Khālid al-Barqī,[83] the author of *K. al-Maḥāsin*, appears twice, once as an author of a book on *mubtadaʾ* (Genesis and Prophets) and again as an author of a book on *maghāzī*.[84] Another important work which seems to have consisted of more than one part as well is that of Ibrāhīm b. Muḥammad al-Thaqafī (d. 283/896),[85] a renowned Imāmī historian who seems to have known Abān's work. Only very few quotations of his *maghāzī*-work have survived and can be traced in al-Majlisī's *Biḥār al-anwār*. A work of special interest in this regard is the *maghāzī* of ʿAlī b. Ibrāhīm al-Qummī (d. after 307/919).[86] Al-Qummī is one of the earliest Qurʾān exegetes among the Imāmiyya, whose *Tafsīr* has reached us through the transmission of his student Abū l-Faḍl al-ʿAbbās b. Muḥammad.[87] The role of this student is that of a redactor, for he added new material from other sources to the *Tafsīr* of his teacher, mainly from a *Tafsīr* attributed to Abū l-Jārūd Ziyād b. al-Mundhir (d. between 150 and 160/767 and 776),[88] the head of the Jārūdiyya sect of the Zaydiyya. Al-

[81] See Āghā Buzurg al-Ṭihrānī, *al-Dharīʿa*, XIX, 47-48 and XXI, 289-91.
[82] See p. 105 above.
[83] Ṭūsī, *Fihrist*, 20-22; Ḥāʾirī al-Māzandarānī, *Muntahā al-maqāl*, I, 319-21; Āghā Buzurg al-Ṭihrānī, *al-Dharīʿa*, XXI, 289.
[84] See about the division of books and their transmission, Jarrar, *Die Prophetenbiographie*, 29-43. Ṭūsī counts among al-Barqī's books: *K. al-Taʾrīkh, K. Khalq al-samāwāt wa-l-arḍ, K. Badʾ khalq iblīs wa-l-jinn, K. Maghāzī al-nabī* and *K. Banāt al-nabī wa-azwājih*. His father Muḥammad is an author of a *K. al-Mubtadaʾ*, cf. Kohlberg, *A Medieval Muslim Scholar*, 273 (no. 411); many of his reports are to be found in *Biḥār al-anwār*.
[85] Ṭūsī, *Fihrist*, 4-6 (*K. al-Sīra*); Ḥāʾirī al-Māzandarānī, *Muntahā al-maqāl*, I, 194-96; Āghā Buzurg al-Ṭihrānī, *al-Dharīʿa*, XXI, 289; For his *maghāzī*, cf. Kohlberg, *A Medieval Muslim Scholar*, 362 (no. 611); and see Appendix 1.B. 6.
[86] Ṭūsī, *Fihrist*, 89; Najāshī, *Rijāl*, II, 86 f.; Ḥāʾirī al-Māzandarānī, *Muntahā al-maqāl*, IV, 324-25.
[87] Āghā Buzurg al-Ṭihrānī, *al-Dharīʿa*, IV, 303-05.
[88] Cf. Jarrar, "Tafsīr Abī l-Jārūd".

Qummī is the author of a number of other books as well, among which a *K. al-Maghāzī*, or *al-Mabʿath wa-ghazawāt al-nabī* as Ibn Ṭāwūs, who used a copy of it which goes back to the year 400/1009-10, calls it.[89] This book did not reach us, but numerous reports on *maghāzī* are found in the Imāmī sources with a transmission chain that goes back to ʿAlī b. Ibrāhīm al-Qummī; but it is still difficult to determine whether these reports belong to his *K. al-Maghāzī* or to his *Tafsīr*. Al-Ṭabrisī, for example, reproduces in his *Iʿlām al-warā* six reports from al-Qummī,[90] four of which are found in the *Tafsīr* in different or much longer versions, and the other two are not found in the *Tafsīr* because they are not of an exegetical nature nor do they reveal the occasion of the revealed verses (*asbāb al-nuzūl*). In his *Tafsīr*, al-Qummī gives some thirty-one reports dealing with the events of the *mabʿath* and the *maghāzī*, mostly without mentioning his sources and without giving an *isnād* (but it is noteworthy that Ibn Abī ʿUmayr, a student of Abān b. ʿUthmān and an author of a *maghāzī*-work himself,[91] appears as a main source of al-Qummī throughout the book). These reports cover approximately some ninety pages. In only nine short reports does he give material which goes back to Abān through either one of the attested *isnād*s of his work. This material requires more thorough study; nevertheless, I can for the moment conclude that again, like that of Abān, it is directly related to a larger corpus which was in circulation around the beginning of the second/eighth century, but has undergone a process of *habitualization* which is revealed through changes in names and through the accentuation of ʿAlī's role, and as such comes nearer to the popular folk motifs than the material portrayed by Abān. One report could help us in approaching the chronology of al-Qummī (or his source; the exegetes are usually interested in the chronology of the events of the *maghāzī*, in particular to justify abrogation cases, although it is worth mentioning that al-Qummī's *Tafsīr* offers a Shīʿī esoteric interpretation);[92] al-Qummī mentions it as a cause of revelation (*sabab nuzūl*) for Q 4:90:[93] On his way to al-Ḥudaybiya in

[89] Kohlberg, *A Medieval Muslim Scholar*, 239 (no. 330).

[90] Ṭabrisī, *Iʿlām*, 12 (= *Tafsīr al-Qummī*, I, 375), 36 f. (not in the *Tafsīr*), 39 f. (= *Tafsīr al-Qummī*, I, 381 f.), 48 (not in the *Tafsīr*), 56-60 (= *Tafsīr al-Qummī*, I, 371 f.), 69-72.

[91] See p. 105 above.

[92] Cf. Jarrar, "Tafsīr Abī l-Jārūd", 23 f.

[93] Qummī, *Tafsīr*, I, 153-54; it is not mentioned by Ṭabarī, *Tafsīr*, V, 124 ff.

Rabīʿ I of the year 6 AH, the Prophet sent Usayd b. Ḥuḍayr to meet the Banū Ashjaʿ under the leadership of Masʿūd b. Rukhayla and the Banū Ḍamra in Shiʿb Salʿ; the Prophet then came to an arrangement (*muwādaʿa*) with them. Masʿūd b. Rukhayla and a part of the Ashjaʿ are mentioned by Ibn Hishām and al-Wāqidī to have been among the clans who joined forces against the Prophet during *ghazwat al-aḥzāb* in the year 5 AH.[94] The dating seems to have been controversial even in Sunnī sources as Ibn Saʿd, who makes a cursory mention of this event during the listing of the delegations (*wufūd*), notes when he says that Masʿūd b. Rukhayla along with one hundred men from the Banū Ashjaʿ came to meet the Prophet in the year of al-Khandaq (i.e., 5 AH), "but it is said that [the delegation of] Ashjaʿ arrived after the battle of Banū Qurayẓa (again in the year 5 AH) and that they counted seven hundred men".[95] In al-Qummī's narration, the whole event is not reported as a delegation, but rather as a flight of the Banū Ashjaʿ into Shiʿb Salʿ due to a drought, a fact which made the Prophet cautious of their move and hence he sent Usayd to check the news for him. Ibn Saʿd does not mention Usayd in connection with this delegation and we should keep in mind that Usayd was a controversial figure in the Imāmī sources.[96]

Another report, named by al-Qummī as *ghazwat wādī yābis*,[97] is found only in Imāmī sources (I have not been able to locate it yet in the Sunnī *maghāzī* literature); M. Kister sees in it a "Shīʿī" version of the *ghazwat dhāt al-salāsil*,[98] which seems unlikely to me because, first, the two narrations are totally different, and, second, the Shīʿī narration aims clearly at giving a cause of revelation of Q 100:1 related directly to ʿAlī's bravery, whereas the Sunnī tradition does not mention this cause of revelation at all.[99] It seems that Kister came to this conclusion on account of al-Mufīd's remark: "It is said (*yuqāl*) that *ghazwat wādī al-raml* used to be called *ghazwat dhāt al-salāsil*."[100]

---

[94] Ibn Hishām, *Sīra*, II, 215; Wāqidī, *Maghāzī*, 443, 467, 470, 484, 490.
[95] Ibn Saʿd, *Ṭabaqāt*, I, 306.
[96] Cf. Appendix 1.B. 8.
[97] Qummī, *Tafsīr*, II, 435-39.
[98] M.J. Kister, "On the Papyrus of Wahb b. Munabbih," in *BSOAS*, 37 (1974), 560-64.
[99] Cf. Ṭabarī, *Tafsīr*, XXX, 175 ff.
[100] Al-Shaykh al-Mufīd, *Irshād*, 60, 86; and cf. Laoust, "Le role de ʿAlī", 18.

V. Conclusion

In this preliminary examination, I have tried to pave the way for a more detailed and thorough study of the early Imāmī *sīra-maghāzī*-literature, concentrating my observations mainly on the *Kitāb* of Abān b. ʿUthmān al-Aḥmar al-Bajalī since it is regarded as the first Imāmī book of this genre. There remains a crucial unanswered question: Why are all these Imāmī works on *sīra-maghāzī*-literature no longer extant or more precisely, why does one not hear of them after the sixth and seventh/twelfth and thirteenth centuries? Did the Imāmīs not have any special interest in this literature or did they adopt the more current books such as those of Ibn Isḥāq and al-Wāqidī after they claimed that both scholars had studied with Jaʿfar al-Ṣādiq (indirectly in the case of the latter),[101] or should one seek other explanations?

In our quest for an explanation it is important to answer the following question: What does the *sīra-maghāzī*-literature stand for? As J. Wansbrough rightly argues, a central issue in this "salvation history" literature is the formation of the *umma*, its origin, its function and its destiny. It is there that the earliest Islamic eschatology is located; it served, moreover, as a source of legitimation and redemption.[102] It is through the *sīra-maghāzī*-literature, which describes the events of a trans-historical time, i.e., the era of the direct interference of the theophany within the mundane time, that the *umma* sought to find its new identity and its new self-consciousness. Although this may be true for the Sunnī understanding, it is not necessarily valid for the formation of the Shīʿī self-consciousness.[103] The point of departure lies in the messianic understanding of the Imāmīs and in the manner they perceived their Imam and his role in the salvation history; the "holy family", the *ahl al-kisāʾ* and their descendants, the nine Imams, and the offspring of Fāṭima (*majmaʿ al-nūrayn*), play an outstanding role in this history.[104] All the Prophets acquired their status through the light that sprang forth before God created the world.[105] The Imams are superior to the angels, they are infallible and *muḥaddathūn* (veracious),

[101] See p. 101-02 above.
[102] Cf. Wansbrough, *The Sectarian Milieu*, 1 ff., 46, 85-90, and chapter 4 "Epistemology".
[103] Cf. Jarrar, "The *Sīra*", 2-3.
[104] Cf. Amir-Moezzi, *The Divine Guide in Early Shiʿism*, 29 ff.
[105] Cf. p. 110 and note 68 above.

and they are the sole interpreters of the esoteric meaning of the Qurʾān; they can see into the future and know the death dates of people, and they master the languages of all the nations, ancient and new, and the language of animals.[106] With this Imamology, there remains no place to seek legitimacy, self-identity or eschatology in the events of the *sīra*, for it is the *living* Imam—and starting with the fourth/tenth century, the hidden Imam—who offers light, guidance and redemption. Hence, guidance, self-consciousness and identity should be sought in the lives of these exemplary Imams. This is the reason why the crucial stories around which this Imāmī *kerygma* has been developed were filtered out of the *sīra-maghāzī*-literature, elaborated and habitualized with new motifs, to be scattered over the different chapters designated for the lives of the "fourteen proofs", as we find in the Imāmī books since the end of the third/ninth and the beginning of the fourth/tenth centuries. In place of "ʿAlī of the *sīra*", appears now in the *kerygma* not only the mythical ʿAlī, the beam of divine light, but even a mythical, cosmic "Holy Family". In fact, the bulk of the *sīra-maghāzī*-literature *per se* (i.e., *mabʿath* and *maghāzī*) became an arena to show off the "legendary" heroic role of ʿAlī and to belittle his enemies, and that in order to boast of the *faḍāʾil* of those Companions who fought later on his side, on the one hand, and, on the other hand, to serve as a polemic against the Sunnīs and other sects.

APPENDIX 1

A. Genesis (*al-mubtadaʾ*):

1)[107] ... al-Bizanṭī—Abān—Mūsā b. Akīl—al-ʿAlāʾ b. Sayyāba—Jaʿfar al-Ṣādiq:[108] Commenting on Q 11:42: "And Noah cried unto his son, come ride with us and be not with the unbelievers,"[109] Abān cites Jaʿfar al-Ṣādiq, who explains that by his son, actually his wife's son is meant, according to the dialect (*lugha*) of Ṭayʾ. According to Shīʿī tradition, a son of a Prophet who carries in himself the eternal divine

[106] Amir-Moezzi, *The Divine Guide in Early Shīʿism*, Chap. 3.
[107] For biographical data about the names of the *ruwāt*, see Appendix 2 above.
[108] ʿAlī b. Ibrāhīm al-Qummī, *Tafsīr*, I, 329; Majlisī, *Biḥār al-anwār*, XI, 337.
[109] *The Meaning of the Glorious Koran*, trans. M.M. Pickthall, New York/Ontario, 168.

light of the Imams, could not have been an unbeliever, and thus one of the solutions was to replace him by Noah's stepson. The Sunnī scholar al-Qāsim b. Sallām (d. 224/838) gives the same explanation, without mentioning his source,[110] and al-Ṭabarī attributes it in his *Tafsīr* to al-Bāqir.[111] In Salama b. al-Faḍl's version of Ibn Isḥāq's *Sīra,* he gives a tradition from Ibn ʿAbbās saying that this son was *shaqī* (wretched; predestined for Hell)[112] and that he had concealed disbelief.[113] These verses have actually caused a lot of trouble for both Sunnī, Shīʿī and other sectarian exegetes, and a variety of explanations has been suggested which I am not going to go into here.[114]

2) ... al-Bizanṭī—Abān—Abū Baṣīr—al-Bāqir or al-Ṣādiq:[115] Isaac, and not Ishmael, was the one to be sacrificed. This has always been controversial among Muslim scholars, whether Shīʿī or Sunnī, although the majority later agreed by *consensus doctorum* that the boy was Isaac.[116] In the controversy between Arabs and Persians of the early Islamic centuries, some Persian scholars claimed that the Persians were descendants of Isaac.[117]

3) ... al-Bizanṭī—Abān:[118] In this connection Abān cites a juridical opinion from Jaʿfar al-Ṣādiq (*qultu li-Abī ʿAbd Allāh*), regarding the prohibition of eating the milt (*ṭiḥāl*) and the testicles (*khiṣyatān*), where this taboo is explained as being Satan's share of the sacrificed lamb.

4) ... ʿAbd Allāh b. al-Mufaḍḍal—Abān—Abān b. Taghlib—Ibn Jubayr—Ibn ʿAbbās:[119] In a long *narratio* about Joseph, Gabriel appears to Jacob and teaches him to say a certain prayer (*duʿāʾ*), directly after which the herald brings the good news about Joseph and Benjamin and throws Joseph's shirt on his face so that Jacob recovers his sight. In this prayer Jacob asks God through the intervention of the *ahl al-kisāʾ* to bring him back both Joseph and Benjamin.

---

[110] Ibn Sallām, *Lughāt al-qabāʾil al-wārida fī l-Qurʾān*, 134.

[111] Ṭabarī, *Jāmiʿ al-bayān*, XII, 31, ll. 1-4.

[112] *Shaqī* should not be directly understood as predestined to Hell: in early Islam it used to be understood, especially in anti-predestinarian circles as "unlucky" or "wretched", cf. J. van Ess, *Zwischen Ḥadīṯ und Theologie*, Berlin, 1975, 26 ff.; one should keep in mind that Ibn Isḥāq was accused of being a defender of free will (*qadarī*).

[113] Ṭabarī, *Taʾrīkh*, I, 184.

[114] Cf. Ṭabarī, *Jāmiʿ al-bayān*, XII, 30-33; Ṭabrisī, *Majmaʿ al-bayān*, XI, 158, 164-65.

[115] Majlisī, *Biḥār al-anwār*, XII, 128.

[116] Ṭabarī, *Taʾrīkh*, I, 272-74; Ṭabarī, *Jāmiʿ al-bayān*, XXIII, 51-57, mainly 54 f.

[117] Cf. W.M. Watt, "Isḥāḳ," in *EI*², IV, 109-10.

[118] Majlisī, *Biḥār al-anwār*, XII, 130.

[119] Majlisī, *Biḥār al-anwār*, XII, 256-61, particularly 260.

5) ... Aḥmad b. al-Ḥasan al-Mīthamī—Abān—Mūsā al-Numayrī:[120] A report about al-Bāqir who was heard reciting Elijah's prayer in Hebrew. This report serves as a confirmation of the Imam's knowledge of human languages.[121]

6) ... ʿAlī b. al-Ḥakam—Abān—Abū l-ʿAbbās—Jaʿfar al-Ṣādiq:[122] Commenting on Q 34:13: "They made for him what he willed: synagogues and statues...,"[123] al-Ṣādiq explains that by statues not human figures are meant, but rather figures of trees. This is an allusion to the controversy regarding the prohibition of plastic arts in early Islam.[124]

7) ... Ibn Abī ʿUmayr—Abān—Jaʿfar al-Ṣādiq:[125] A report confirming the supernatural powers of ʿAlī, the best *waṣī* of the best Prophet, by comparing him to Āṣaf,[126] the *waṣī* of Solomon.

8) ... al-Bizanṭī—Abān—Kathīr al-Nawwāʾ—al-Bāqir:[127] *ʿĀshūrāʾ* is the day on which Jesus was born, a kind of circular time which makes al-Ḥusayn a counterpart of Jesus.

9) ... Ibn Abī ʿUmayr—Abān—Abān b. Taghlib—ʿIkrima—Ibn ʿAbbās:[128] In a polemic against the Christians, Jesus should have replied to Satan when the latter told him that the day will come when he [Jesus] will be governing over the heavens and the earth, by saying in refutation to that claim: "God be praised, [etc.]..."

10) ... Ibn Abī ʿUmayr—Abān—Abān b. Taghlib—ʿIkrima—Ibn ʿAbbās:[129] A report about Ezra (ʿUzayr) in which the dogma about the *ʿadhāb al-aṭfāl* and the mercifulness of God are defended. This was an issue of topical interest at the end of the second/eighth century and was actively debated.[130]

---

[120] Majlisī, *Biḥār al-anwār*, XIII, 400.

[121] Cf. Ṣaffār al-Qummī, *Baṣāʾir al-darjāt*, 335-54; Kulīnī, *al-Kāfī*, I, 227-28.

[122] Majlisī, *Biḥār al-anwār*, XIV, 74.

[123] *The Meaning of the Glorious Koran*, 308.

[124] For the Shīʿī point of view, cf. R. Paret, "Das islamische Bilderverbot und die Schia", in *Rudi Paret. Schriften zum Islam*, ed. J. van Ess, Stuttgart, 1981, 226-37.

[125] Majlisī, *Biḥār al-anwār*, XIV, 115-16.

[126] Asaph b. Berechiah, cf. *The Jewish Encyclopedia*, New York/London, 1902, I, 162.

[127] Majlisī, *Biḥār al-anwār*, XIV, 214.

[128] Majlisī, *Biḥār al-anwār*, XIV, 270.

[129] Majlisī, *Biḥār al-anwār*, XIV, 371.

[130] Cf. Ashʿarī, *Maqālāt al-islāmiyyīn*, 200-01, 555-56; Khayyāṭ, *Kitāb al-Intiṣār*, 65.

b. Birth, Vocation and Career (*al-mabʿath wa-l-maghāzī*)

1) ... Ibn Abī ʿUmayr and al-Bizanṭī—Abān—Abān b. Taghlib—ʿIkrima—Ibn ʿAbbās:[131] When the Jewish notable Kaʿb b. Asad was brought in front of the Prophet after the defeat of the Banū Qurayẓa, the Prophet reminded him of the prophecy of Ibn Ḥiwwāsh (or Khirāsh), a Jewish Rabbi who came from Syria [i.e., Palestine?], concerning the expected appearance of an Arab Prophet[132] and Ibn Ḥiwwāsh's request that the Jews believe in him. Kaʿb affirmed the incident, but said that he would rather die as a Jew lest his kinsmen say he changed his religion out of fear of death. Although Kaʿb b. Asad is mentioned by the different *sīra* authors, this particular incident appears only in al-Wāqidī[133] with a transmission chain that leads to Ayyūb b. Bashīr al-Muʿāwī. A few pages earlier, al-Wāqidī gives another report going back to Muḥammad b. Maslama[134] which clarifies this incident;[135] according to this account, Kaʿb himself tried at the beginning of the battle to convince the Banū Qurayẓa to believe in Muḥammad, reminded them of Ibn Khirāsh's [so the reading in al-Wāqidī] prophecy, but they refused.[136] This report appears as one of the signs of prophecy by both al-Kulīnī and al-Majlisī; keeping in mind that we are dealing only with extracts attributed to Abān, it is difficult to judge whether the original report in the *maghāzī* circulating under Abān's name was longer. Nevertheless, Abān's report seems to be a summarized version of the two reports mentioned by al-Wāqidī. Abān's chain of transmission leads him back to Ibn ʿAbbās through Abān b. Taghlib—ʿIkrima, which I have discussed earlier.

2) ... Three long reports, transmitted from Ibn Abī ʿUmayr and al-Bizanṭī—Abān with an incomplete chain of transmission, all covering

---

[131] Ibn Bābawayh al-Qummī, *Kamāl al-dīn*, 198; Majlisī, *Biḥār al-anwār*, XV, 206, XX, 247; Ṭabrisī, *Iʿlām al-warā*, 69; Qummī mentions this report in his *Tafsīr* (II, 166) within a longer narration about Banū Qurayẓa without mentioning his chain of transmission.

[132] Some of the words mentioned in the prophecy as given by both Abān and al-Wāqidī appear in the prophecy of Ibn al-Hayyabān, another Jew from Syria who settled some years before Islam among the B. Qurayẓa, cf. e.g. Ibn Bukayr in Bayhaqī, *Dalāʾil al-nubuwwa*, II, 80-81; Ibn Hishām, *Sīra*, I, 213 f.; Ibn Saʿd, *Ṭabaqāt*, I, 160 f.

[133] *Kitāb al-Maghāzī*, II, 516.

[134] Ibn Saʿd, *Ṭabaqāt*, III, 443-45.

[135] *Kitāb al-Maghāzī*, II, 501-02.

[136] In the other sources as well, Kaʿb is said to have tried in vain to convince the B. Qurayẓa to believe in Muḥammad.

the birth of the Prophet and the subsequent events; the reports a and b can best be described as a synthesis of the different reports known to us from the sources about the sudden change that occurred both in the cosmic and earthly worlds upon his birth;[137] one thing is of interest here, namely, al-Ṣādiq's remark in the first report that the term *āl Allāh,* which appears in the text to refer to the Quraysh, has been given them only because they dwell in the sanctuary, differentiating it thus from the term *āl al-bayt* which is restricted to the *ahl al-kisāʾ* and the Imams; report c deals with the actual moment of Āmina's delivery, the accompanying light and the extraterrestrial beings that descended upon her.[138] Not only is the description here more complicated and fantastic than in other reports of the genre, an act of purification (which nonetheless does not entail an opening of the breast)[139] takes place directly upon delivery and the infant is sealed with the seal of prophethood.

3) ... al-Bizanṭī—Abān—Kathīr al-Nawwāʾ—Jaʿfar al-Ṣādiq:[140] "on the 27th of Rajab prophethood [sic!] descended on the Prophet." This is a unique tradition regarding both the dating and the use of the expression "prophethood had been descended upon him" instead of *waḥy* or Qurʾān.

4) ... al-Bizanṭī—Abān—al-Ḥasan al-Ṣayqal—Jaʿfar al-Ṣādiq:[141] "The *ummī* Prophet" means that the Prophet could neither write nor read. This is a controversial dogmatic issue among the various Islamic sects. It seems that the early Imāmiyya propagated this meaning, whereas later *uṣūlī* scholars did not approve of it. To the eighth Imam al-Riḍā is attributed that the Prophet could read and write in seventy-two (or seventy-three) languages.[142] A widespread opinion was that the Prophet was taught all languages at the moment that Gabriel descended upon him for the first time; he could not have been illiterate

---

[137] a) Majlisī, *Biḥār al-anwār,* XV, 257-59; b) Ibn Bābawayh al-Qummī, *Kamāl al-dīn,* 196-98; Majlisī, *Biḥār al-anwār,* XV, 269-70.

[138] c) Ibn Shahrāshūb, *Manāqib Āl Abī Ṭālib,* I, 28-29; Majlisī, *Biḥār al-anwār,* XV, 272-73.

[139] Cf. H. Birkeland, *The Legend of the Opening of Muhammed's Breast,* Uppsala, 1955; Jarrar, *Die Prophetenbiographie,* 188-95; cf. now U. Rubin, *The Eye of the Beholder: The Life of Muḥammad as Viewed by the Early Muslims,* Princeton, 1995, 59-75.

[140] Majlisī, *Biḥār al-anwār,* XVIII, 189.

[141] Majlisī, *Biḥār al-anwār,* XVI, 132.

[142] Cf. Ibn Shahrāshūb, *Manāqib Āl Abī Ṭālib,* I, 231-32.

after that moment because he taught ʿAlī the different scripts of the previous prophets.[143]

5) ... al-Washshāʾ—Abān—Abū Baṣīr—Jaʿfar al-Ṣādiq:[144] When the Banū Quraysh (*al-nās*) accused the Prophet of being a liar, God was about to destroy the inhabitants of the world except for ʿAlī, etc. A similar tradition is found in the *Tafsīr* of al-Qummī (Q 51:54-55),[145] but without the clause "except for ʿAlī"; in quite a contradictory report, al-Ṭabarī quotes Mujāhid's (d. 104/722) saying that when this verse was revealed ʿAlī was sad and said: "The Prophet has been ordered to desert us."[146]

6) Ibrāhīm b. Muḥammad al-Thaqafī (d. 283/896),[147] the author of a book on *maghāzī*, relates from Abān—Abū Dāwūd—Abū Burayda al-Aslamī:[148] "The Prophet told ʿAlī: 'God has made you attend with me seven occasions.'" Three of these incidents took place in Heaven during the two nocturnal journeys,[149] one during the *laylat al-qadr*,[150] one when the Prophet met the *jinn*, one when prophethood[151] descended upon him, and the last during the battle of al-Aḥzāb. This tradition aims at confirming the outstanding and privileged rank of ʿAlī.

7) ... al-Bizanṭī—Abān—Zurāra and Ismāʿīl b. ʿAbbād—Sulaymān al-Juʿfī—Jaʿfar al-Ṣādiq:[152] God chose ʿAlī as Muḥammad's successor in the fourth heaven during the nocturnal journey.

8) ... Ibn Abī ʿUmayr and al-Bizanṭī—Abān—his sources (*jamāʿat mashyakha*):[153] The Prophet chose twelve *naqīb*s from among his community (*umma*), whom Gabriel had alluded to, following the example of Moses,[154] nine Khazrajīs and three Anṣārīs.[155] All the sources agree

---

[143] Cf. Majlisī, *Biḥār al-anwār*, XVIII, 266, 278-82.

[144] Majlisī, *Biḥār al-anwār*, XVIII, 213.

[145] Qummī, *Tafsīr*, II, 306 (he cites the two verses as proof for *badāʾ*).

[146] Ṭabarī, *Tafsīr*, XXVII, 7-8.

[147] Cf. p. 113 in the main text above.

[148] Majlisī, *Biḥār al-anwār*, XVIII, 405.

[149] I could not find out when the second nocturnal journey took place.

[150] On the special importance of *laylat al-qadr* for the Shīʿa, cf. Kulīnī, *al-Kāfī (al-uṣūl)*, I, 250-52.

[151] Cf. no. 3) above.

[152] Majlisī, *Biḥār al-anwār*, XVIII, 341.

[153] Ibn Bābawayh al-Qummī, *al-Khiṣāl*, 491-92; Majlisī, *Biḥār al-anwār*, XXII, 102 (read in both sources: *al-qawāqil*, instead of: *al-qawāfil*).

[154] *Ka-ʿiddati nuqabāʾ Mūsā.*

[155] On various Shīʿī traditions concerning the first ʿAqaba-meeting, cf. as well Qummī, ʿAlī b. Ibrāhīm, *Tafsīr*, I, 271-73; Ṭabrisī, *Iʿlām al-warā*, 59-60; Majlisī, *Biḥār al-anwār*, XIX, 8-16.

on the same names, ten Khazrajīs and two Anṣārīs who took part in this meeting known as *al-ʿaqaba al-ūlā*.[156] None of them mentions the interference of Gabriel. The list given in Abān's report coincides partially with the one mentioned in the other sources: only four names are common between the two lists. One immediately assumes that Shīʿī traditionists would have dropped the names of those men who might have felt some kind of enmity towards ʿAlī b. Abī Ṭālib, or had lived to fight against him; or would have added names of those who were known to have supported him. But strangely enough the name of Usayd b. Ḥuḍayr appears on this list, although the Imāmīs include him among those who tried to set Fāṭima's house on fire.[157] These names deserve a thorough investigation.

9) ... Ibn Abī ʿUmayr—Abān—Fuḍayl al-Barājimī:[158] Fuḍayl relates a conversation he heard in Mecca between Khālid al-Qasrī (d. 126/743-44),[159] who was then the governor of Mecca, and the Baṣran exegete Qatāda b. Diʿāma al-Sadūsī (d. 118/736).[160] The report is interesting in more than one respect. First, it gives information about the battles of Badr and Uḥud; second, it shows the importance of the *maghāzī* battles in the tribal polemic and boasting during the formative period; and, third, it reveals the well-known enmity of Khālid al-Qasrī towards both the clan of Muḍar and ʿAlī b. Abī Ṭālib.[161]

10) ... Ibn Abī ʿUmayr—Abān—Abān b. Taghlib—Jaʿfar al-Ṣādiq:[162] When al-Qāʾim al-Mahdī appears, he will be supported by 13,013 angels; these are the angels who were with Noah in the ark, with Abraham when he was thrown into the fire, with Jesus when he ascended to Heaven, those who attended Badr and the 4,000 who wanted to fight with al-Ḥusayn but were not allowed to. This tradition is of a dogmatic nature; Ibn Bābawayh cites a number of tradi-

---

[156] Ibn Hishām, *Sīra*, I, 431-33; Ibn Saʿd, *Ṭabaqāt*, I, 219-20; Balādhurī, *Ansāb al-ashrāf*, I, 239; Bayhaqī, *Dalāʾil al-nubuwwa*, II, 430-41.

[157] Cf. Ḥāʾirī al-Māzandarānī, *Muntahā al-maqāl*, II, 100.

[158] Majlisī, *Biḥār al-anwār*, XIX, 298-300.

[159] See on him, S. Leder, *Das Korpus al-Haiṯam ibn ʿAdī*, Frankfurt a.M., 1991, 141-96; idem, "Features of the Novel in Early Historiography", in *Oriens*, 32 (1990), 72-104.

[160] *GAS*, I, 31 f.

[161] Cf. Jarrar, *Die Prophetenbiographie*, 24-27; see now idem, "*Sīra, Mashāhid* and *Maghāzī*", 23-27.

[162] Ibn Bābawayh al-Qummī, *Kamāl al-dīn*, 671-72; Majlisī, *Biḥār al-anwār*, XIX, 305.

tions with the same *isnād* which deal with al-Qāʾim, but only this one is of direct interest regarding *maghāzī* material, although it need not have been mentioned in Abān's *Maghāzī* during the story of Badr.

11) ... al-Bizanṭī and Ibn Abī ʿUmayr—Abān—Jaʿfar al-Ṣādiq:[163] When the Muslims retreated from the Prophet during the battle of Uḥud, only ʿAlī and Abū Dujāna remained defending him.[164] The Prophet asked Abū Dujāna to leave and join his people, but the latter refused. ʿAlī went on fighting one crowd after another slaughtering them until his sword broke. Thereupon the Prophet gave him his sword *dhū l-faqār*, Gabriel descended upon the Prophet and told him: "Verily, this is the consolation [from ʿAlī towards you]," whereupon the Prophet said: "He is part of me, and I of him." Gabriel responded: "And I [am a part] of both of you." A voice was heard from heaven saying: "There is no sword but *dhū l-faqār*, and there is no hero but ʿAlī."

This incident is famous and well attested in the historical tradition; Abū Dujāna's role and bravery meet consensus in the sources as well. Nevertheless, other men were mentioned in this regard[165] and it is clear that such an incident was a point used by later generations in political and tribal debates and in claiming eminence (*faḍl*) and priority (*sābiqa*). Al-Wāqidī says that fourteen men remained with the Prophet, seven Anṣārīs and seven Qurashīs (the golden mean!), and he names Abū Bakr. Another tradition from Jābir b. ʿAbd Allāh (d. 78/697, an Anṣārī known for his love for ʿAlī and who took active part on his side during his wars),[166] says that eleven Anṣārīs remained to defend the Prophet, among them the Qurashī Ṭalḥa b. ʿUbayd Allāh, ʿAlī's rival during the battle of the Camel.[167] Ṭalḥa's name appears in different sources alongside Saʿd b. Abī Waqqāṣ. Sulaymān al-Taymī, who harbors love for ʿAlī,[168] mentions only Ṭalḥa and Saʿd b. Abī Waqqāṣ.[169]

---

[163] Majlisī, *Biḥār al-anwār*, XX, 70-71; cf. with another *isnād* leading to Abān—Nuʿmān al-Rāzī—Jaʿfar al-Ṣādiq, in Majlisī, *Biḥār al-anwār*, XX, 107.

[164] Cf. Laoust, "Le role de ʿAlī,", 11.

[165] Cf. e.g. Ibn Hishām, *Sīra*, II, 82; Ibn Saʿd, *Ṭabaqāt*, II, 42; Bayhaqī, *Dalāʾil al-nubuwwa*, III, 258-66.

[166] Ibn Saʿd, *Ṭabaqāt*, III, 574; Ibn Qutayba, *al-Maʿārif*, 307; Ḥāʾirī al-Māzandarānī, *Muntahā al-maqāl*, II, 209-12.

[167] Bayhaqī, *Dalāʾil al-nubuwwa*, III, 236-37.

[168] Cf. main text above, p. 106, and note 46.

[169] Bayhaqī, *Dalāʾil al-nubuwwa*, III, 235.

12) al-Ṭabrisī:[170] Abān—Zurāra b. Aʿyan—al-Bāqir:[171] After ʿAlī had opened al-Qamūṣ, the fortress (*ḥiṣn*) at Khaybar, the Prophet told him that both he and God are glad and satisfied with him (*raḍiya*).

13) Ibn Shahrāshūb: Before the Prophet entered Mecca, Abū Sufyān paid him a visit in Medina pledging not to break the peace treaty although the Quraysh[172] had attacked the Khuzāʿa, who were Muḥammad's allies. Whereas all the sources assert that Abū Sufyān came from Mecca, this tradition says that he came from Syria.[173]

14) ... Ibn Abī ʿUmayr—Abān—ʿAjlān b. Ṣāliḥ—Jaʿfar al-Ṣādiq:[174] ʿAlī killed forty men with his bare hands during the battle of Ḥunayn.

15) al-Ṭabrisī (from Abān's book):[175] The story of the visit by ʿĀmir b. al-Ṭufayl and Arbad b. Qays to the Prophet. This story is usually mentioned at the end of the *maghāzī*-narration, when counting the delegations that came to pay alliance in Medina.[176] This tradition is interesting because it is dated as having taken place after the event of the Banū al-Naḍīr. This report might help shed light on the dating system used by Abān. Ibn Isḥāq and al-Wāqidī do not date this delegation;[177] al-Ṭabarī mentions it according to the *riwāya* of Salama—Ibn Isḥāq,[178] and he puts it under the events of the year 10 AH. Al-Bukhārī mentions it with the events of Biʾr Maʿūna which should have occurred before al-Khandaq according to him, and he does not speak of a delegation.[179] In fact, Ibn Isḥāq and al-Wāqidī mention that ʿĀmir b. al-Ṭufayl came to Medina before the event of the Banū l-Naḍīr but left without embracing Islam, and that he killed Ḥarām b. Milḥān whom the Prophet sent with a delegation to teach the people of Najd the principles of Islam and this caused the events of Biʾr

---

[170] Ṭabrisī states usually that he is copying from "Abān's book" and does not give his chain of transmission.

[171] Ṭabrisī, *Iʿlām al-warā*, 100-01; Majlisī, *Biḥār al-anwār*, XXI, 22.

[172] Some sources say it was B. Bakr, Quraysh allies, who launched the attack.

[173] Ibn Shahrāshūb, *Manāqib Āl Abī Ṭālib*, I, 206 ff.; Majlisī, *Biḥār al-anwār*, XXI, 126.

[174] Majlisī, *Biḥār al-anwār*, XXI, 176.

[175] Ṭabrisī, *Iʿlām al-warā*, 365-66; Majlisī, *Biḥār al-anwār*, XXI, 365.

[176] Cf. e.g. Ibn Hishām, *Sīra*, II, 567-68; Ibn Saʿd, *Ṭabaqāt*, I, 310-11; Yaʿqūbī, *Taʾrīkh*, II, 79.

[177] Ibn Hishām, *Sīra*, II, 568 f.; Ibn Saʿd, *Ṭabaqāt*, I, 310-12; Bayhaqī, *Dalāʾil al-nubuwwa*, V, 318 ff.

[178] Ṭabarī, *Taʾrīkh*, III, 144.

[179] Ibn Ḥajar, *Fatḥ al-Bārī*, VIII, 390; Bayhaqī, *Dalāʾil al-nubuwwa*, V, 320.

Maʿūna.[180] Thus, whereas al-Bukhārī does not mention any delegation and treats both events as one, Ibn Isḥāq and al-Wāqidī give three events: a first delegation, the events of Biʾr Maʿūna, and a second, undated delegation during the year of the delegations. Abān b. ʿUthmān dates this last delegation after the event of the Banū l-Naḍīr, although we do not know whether he had mentioned a first delegation.

Bibliography

Abū Zayd, N.Ḥ., "Al-Sīra al-nabawiyya sīra shaʿbiyya", in *Majallat al-funūn al-shaʿbiyya*, 32-33 (June-December, 1991), 17-36.

Abū Zurʿa, ʿAbd al-Raḥmān b. ʿAmr, *Taʾrīkh*, ed. Shukr Allāh b. Niʿmat Allāh al-Qūjānī, 2 vols., Damascus, 1980.

Āghā Buzurg al-Ṭihrānī, *al-Dharīʿa ilā taṣānīf al-Shīʿa*, 24 vols., Tehran, 1360.

Amir-Moezzi, Muḥammad ʿAlī, *The Divine Guide in Early Shiʿism. The Source of Esotericism in Islam*, trans. D. Streight, Albany, 1994.

al-Ardabīlī, Muḥammad b. ʿAlī, *Jāmiʿ al-ruwāt wa-izāḥat al-ishtibāhāt ʿan al-ṭuruq wa-l-isnād*, 2 vols., Tehran, 1334.

al-Ashʿarī, ʿAlī b. Ismāʿīl, *Maqālāt al-islāmiyyīn wa-khtilāf al-muṣallīn*, ed. Hellmut Ritter, ²Wiesbaden, 1963.

al-Balādhurī, Aḥmad b. Yaḥyā, *Ansāb al-ashrāf*, vol. I, ed. Muḥammad Ḥamīd Allāh, Cairo, 1959.

al-Bayhaqī, Aḥmad b. al-Ḥusayn, *Dalāʾil al-nubuwwa wa-maʿrifat aḥwāl ṣāḥib al-sharīʿa*, ed. ʿAbd al-Muʿṭī Qalʿajī, 7 vols, Beirut, 1405/1985.

Birkeland, Harris, *The Legend of the Opening of Muhammed's Breast*, Uppsala, 1955.

Dāʾirat al-maʿārif buzurg islāmī, 5 vols., ed. Kāẓim Mūsawī al-Bujnūrdī, Tehran, 1367/1988-1372/1993; Arabic edition, *Dāʾirat al-maʿārif al-islāmiyya al-kubrā*, 2 vols., ed. Kāẓim Mūsawī al-Bujnūrdī, Tehran, 1370/1991-1374/1995.

al-Dhahabī, Muḥammad b. Aḥmad, *Mīzān al-iʿtidāl fī naqd al-rijāl*, ed. ʿAlī Muḥammad al-Bijāwī, 4 vols., Cairo, 1965.

Donner, Fred McGraw, *The Early Islamic Conquests*, Princeton, 1981.

van Ess, Josef, *Theologie und Gesellschaft im 2. und 3. Jahrhundert Hidschra. Eine Geschichte des religiösen Denkens im frühen Islam*, vols. I and II, Berlin/New York, 1991-96.

———, *Zwischen Ḥadīṯ und Theologie. Studien zur Entstehung prädestinatianischer Überlieferungen*, Berlin, 1975.

Falaturi, A., "Die Zwölfer-Schia aus der Sicht eines Schiiten: Probleme ihrer Untersuchung", in *Festschrift Werner Caskel*, ed. Erwin Gräf, Leiden, 1968, 63-95.

al-Fasawī, Yaʿqūb b. Sufyān, *al-Maʿrifa wa-l-taʾrīkh*, ed. Akram Ḍiyāʾ al-ʿUmarī, 3 vols., Baghdad, 1974-76.

Fowler, Roger, *Linguistic Criticism*, ²Oxford, 1996.

Günther, Sebastian, *Quellenuntersuchungen zu den "Maqātil aṭ-Ṭālibiyyīn" des Abū l-Faraj al-Iṣfahānī (gest. 356/967)*, Hildesheim, 1991.

al-Ḥāʾirī al-Māzandarānī, Muḥammad b. Ismāʿīl, *Muntahā al-maqāl fī aḥwāl al-rijāl*, 7 vols., Qum, 1995.

[180] Ibn Hishām, *Sīra*, II, 184 ff.; Wāqidī, *Maghāzī*, I, 346 ff.; Ibn Saʿd, *Ṭabaqāt*, II, 51 ff.; Bayhaqī, *Dalāʾil al-nubuwwa*, III, 338 ff.

Hodgson, H.M., "How did the Early Shīʿa Become Sectarian", in *Journal of the American Oriental Society*, 75 (1955), 1-13.
Ibn ʿAbd al-Barr, Yūsuf b. ʿAbd Allāh, *al-Tamhīd li-mā fī l-Muwaṭṭaʾ min al-maʿānī wa-l-asānīd*, vol. II, Rabat, 1970.
Ibn Abī l-Ḥadīd, ʿAbd al-Ḥamīd b. Hibat Allāh, *Sharḥ Nahj al-balāgha*, ed. Muḥammad Abū l-Faḍl Ibrāhīm, vol. IV, Cairo, 1965.
Ibn Abī l-Rijāl, Aḥmad b. Ṣāliḥ, *Maṭlaʿ al-budūr wa-majmaʿ al-buḥūr*, Ms. Cairo, Dār al-Kutub, no. 4322.
Ibn ʿAsākir, ʿAlī b. al-Ḥasan, *Taʾrīkh madīnat Dimashq*, ed. Muḥibb al-Dīn ʿUmar al-Amrawī, vol. XLI, Damascus, 1417/1996; *Tarjamat al-Zuhrī*, ed. Shukr Allāh b. Niʿmat Allāh al-Qūjānī, Beirut, 1402/1982.
Ibn Bābawayh al-Qummī, Muḥammad b. ʿAlī, *ʿIlal al-sharāʾiʿ*, ed. Muḥammad Ṣādiq Āl Baḥr al-ʿUlūm, Najaf, 1963.
———, *Kamāl al-dīn wa-itmām al-niʿma*, ed. ʿAlī Akbar Ghifārī, [2]Qum, 1405/1984.
———, *al-Khiṣāl*, ed. ʿAlī Akbar Ghifārī, Qum, 1403.
Ibn Dāwūd al-Ḥillī, Ḥasan b. ʿAlī, *Rijāl*, Tehran, 1342.
Ibn Ḥajar al-ʿAsqalānī, Aḥmad b. ʿAlī, *Fatḥ al-bārī bi-sharḥ al-Bukhārī*, vols. VIII-X, Cairo, 1378/1959.
———, *Lisān al-Mīzān*, 6 vols., Ḥyderabad, 1911/1329-1913/1331.
Ibn Hishām, ʿAbd al-Malik, *al-Sīra al-nabawiyya*, ed. Muṣṭafā al-Saqqā, Ibrāhīm al-Abyārī and ʿAbd al-Ḥāfiẓ Shalabī, 4 vols., reprint, Beirut, n.d.
Ibn Qutayba, al-Dīnawarī, ʿAbd Allāh b. Muslim, *al-Maʿārif*, ed. Tharwat ʿUkāsha, Cairo, 1992.
Ibn Saʿd, Muḥammad, *K. al-Ṭabaqāt al-kubrā [al-kabīr]*, 9 vols., Beirut, 1956-57.
Ibn Sallām, Abū ʿUbayd al-Qāsim, *Lughāt al-qabāʾil al-wārida fī l-Qurʾān*, ed. ʿAbd al-Ḥamīd al-Sayyid Ṭalab, Kuwait, 1985.
Ibn Shahrāshūb, Muḥammad b. ʿAlī, *Manāqib Āl Abī Ṭālib*, 4 vols., Qum, 1379.
al-Jāḥiẓ, ʿAmr b. Baḥr, *al-Bayān wa-l-tabyīn*, ed. ʿAbd al-Salām Muḥammad Hārūn, 4 vols., [3]Cairo, 1388/1968.
Jarrar, Maher, *Die Prophetenbiographie im islamischen Spanien. Ein Beitrag zur Überlieferungs- und Redaktionsgeschichte*, Frankfurt /Bern, 1989.
———, "Some Lights on an Early Zaydite Manuscript", in *Asiatische Studien*, 47/2 (1993), 279-97.
———, "Arbaʿ rasāʾil Zaydiyya mubakkira", in *Fī miḥrāb al-maʿrifa: Festschrift for Iḥsān ʿAbbās*, ed. I. al-Saʿāfīn, Beirut, 1997, 267-304.
———, "The *Sīra*. Its Formative Elements and Its Transmission", in *BUC Public Lecture Series*, April 1993, in press.
———, "*Sīra, Mashāhid* and *Maghāzī*: The Genesis and Development of the Biography of Muḥammad", in *Studies in Late Antiquity and Early Islam*, vol. III, ed. Lawrence I. Conrad and Averil Cameron, Princeton, N.J., 1-44, in press.
———, "Tafsīr Abī l-Jārūd ʿan al-Imām al-Bāqir. Musāhama fī dirāsat al-ʿaqāʾid al-Zaydiyya al-mubakkira", in *Festschrift Sami N. Makarem*, forthcoming.
al-Jazāʾirī, Niʿmat Allāh b. ʿAbd Allāh, *al-Nūr al-mubīn fī qaṣaṣ al-anbiyāʾ*, [8]Beirut, 1978.
The Jewish Encyclopedia, vol. I, New York/London, 1902.
al-Kashshī, Muḥammad b. ʿUmar, *Ikhtiyār maʿrifat al-rijāl*, transmitted by Abū Jaʿfar Muḥammad b. al-Ḥasan al-Ṭūsī, ed. Ḥasan al-Muṣṭafāwī, Mashhad, 1348.
al-Khaṭīb al-Baghdādī, Aḥmad b. ʿAlī, *Taʾrīkh Baghdād*, 14 vols., Cairo, 1349/1931.
al-Khayyāṭ al-Muʿtazilī, ʿAbd al-Raḥīm b. Muḥammad, *K. al-Intiṣār wa-l-radd ʿalā Ibn al-Rāwandī al-mulḥid*, ed. Henrik Samuel Nyberg, Cairo, 1344/1925.
Khoury, Raif Georges, *Wahb b. Munabbih, Der Heidelberger Papyrus PSR Heid Arab 23. Leben und Werk des Dichters*, Wiesbaden, 1972.

al-Khūʾī, Abū l-Qāsim al-Mūsawī, *Muʿjam rijāl al-ḥadīth wa-tafṣīl ṭabaqāt al-ruwāt*, 23 vols., [3]Beirut, 1403/1983.
Kister, M.J., "On the Papyrus of Wahb b. Munabbih", in *Bulletin of the School of Oriental and African Studies*, 37 (1974), 560-64.
Kohlberg, Etan, *A Medieval Muslim Scholar at Work: Ibn Ṭāwūs and His Library*, Leiden, 1992.
———, "Al-uṣūl al-arbaʿumiʾa", in *Jerusalem Studies in Arabic and Islam*, 10 (1987), 128-66.
Kornrumpf, H.-J., "Untersuchungen zum Bild ʿAlīs und des frühen Islams bei den Schiiten (nach dem *Nahǧ al-Balāġa* des Šarīf ar-Raḍī)", in *Der Islam*, 45 (1969), 1-63, 262-98.
al-Kulīnī, Muḥammad b. Yaʿqūb, *al-Kāfī*, ed. ʿAlī Akbar Ghifārī, 8 vols., [2]Beirut, 1405/1985.
Laoust, H., "Le role de ʿAlī dans la *sīra* chiite," in *Revue des Etudes Islamiques*, 30 (1963), 7-26.
Lecker, Michael, *Muslims, Jews and Pagans. Studies in Early Islamic Medina*, Leiden, 1995.
Leder, Stefan, *Das Korpus al-Haiṯam ibn ʿAdī*, Frankfurt a.M., 1991.
———, "Features of the Novel in Early Historiograpy", in *Oriens*, 32 (1990), 72-104.
al-Majlisī, Muḥammad Bāqir, *Biḥār al-anwār al-jāmiʿa li-durar akhbār al-aʾimma al-aṭhār*, 104 vols. on CD-ROM, Qum, 1995.
The Meaning of the Glorious Koran, trans. M.M. Pickthall, New York/Ontario, n.d.
Modarressi, Hossein, *Crisis and Consolidation in the Formative Period of Shīʿite Islam*, Princeton, 1993.
Motzki, Harald, *Die Anfänge der islamischen Jurisprudenz. Ihre Entwicklung in Mekka bis zur Mitte des 2./8. Jahrhunderts*, Stuttgart, 1991.
al-Najāshī, Aḥmad b. ʿAlī, *Rijāl*, ed. Muḥammad Jawād al-Nāʾīnī, 2 vols., Beirut, 1408/1988.
(pseudo-) al-Nāshiʾ, ʿAbd Allāh b. Muḥammad, *Masāʾil al-imāma*, ed. Josef van Ess, Beirut, 1971.
al-Nawbakhtī, al-Ḥasan b. Mūsā, *Firaq al-Shīʿa*, ed. Hellmut Ritter, [2]Beirut, 1984.
Noth, Albrecht, in collaboration with Lawrence I. Conrad, *The Early Arabic Historical Tradition*, trans. M. Bonner, Princeton, 1994.
Pampus, Karl-Heinz, *Die theologische Enzyklopädie Biḥār al-anwār des Muḥammad Bāqir al-Maǧlisī*, Ph.D. thesis, University of Bonn, 1970.
Paret, Rudi, "Das islamische Bilderverbot und die Schia", in *Rudi Paret. Schriften zum Islam*, ed. Josef van Ess, Stuttgart, 1981.
———, *Die legendäre maghāzī-Literatur*, Tübingen, 1930.
al-Qummī, Abū l-Qāsim ʿAlī b. Muḥammad, *Kifāyat al-athar fī l-naṣṣ ʿalā al-aʾimma al-ithnay ʿashar*, ed. ʿAbd al-Laṭīf al-Ḥusaynī al-Kūh-kumrī, Qum, 1981.
al-Qummī, ʿAlī b. Ibrāhīm, *Tafsīr*, ed. al-Sayyid Ṭayyib Mūsawī al-Jazāʾirī, 2 vols., Beirut, 1411/1991.
Rubin, Uri, "Pre-Existence and Light. Aspects of the Concept of Nūr Muḥammad", in *Israel Oriental Studies*, 5 (1975), 62-118.
———, "Prophets and Progenitors in the Early Shīʿa Tradition", in *Jerusalem Studies in Arabic and Islam*, 1 (1979), 41-65.
———, *The Eye of the Beholder: The Life of Muḥammad as Viewed by the Early Muslims*, Princeton, 1995.
al-Ṣaffār al-Qummī, Muḥammad b. al-Ḥasan, *Baṣāʾir al-darjāt al-kubrā fī faḍāʾil Āl-Muḥammad*, ed. Mirzā Muḥsin Kūča-bāghī, Tabriz, 1961.
Schoeler, G., "Die Frage der schriftlichen oder mündlichen Überlieferungen der Wissenschaften im frühen Islam", in *Der Islam*, 62 (1985), 201-30.
———, "Mündliche Tora und Ḥadīṯ", in *Der Islam*, 66 (1989), 38-67.
———, "Schreiben und Veröffentlichen", in *Der Islam*, 69 (1992), 1-43.

Sellheim, R., "Prophet, Caliph und Geschichte. Die Muḥammad-Biographie des Ibn Isḥāq", in *Oriens*, 18-19 (1967), 33-91.
Sezgin, Fuat, *Geschichte des arabischen Schrifttums*, vol. I, Leiden, 1967.
al-Shahrastānī, Muḥammad b. ʿAbd al-Karīm, *al-Milal wa-l-niḥal*, Beirut, 1981.
al-Shaykh al-Mufīd, Muḥammad b. Muḥammad, *al-Irshād*, Beirut, 1399/1979.
al-Suyūṭī, Jalāl al-Dīn ʿAbd al-Raḥmān, *Bughyat al-wuʿāt fī ṭabaqāt al-lughawiyyīn wa-l-nuḥāt*, ed. Muḥammad Abū l-Faḍl Ibrāhīm, 2 vols., Cairo, 1384/1964-1385/1965.
al-Ṭabarī, Muḥammad b. Jarīr, *Taʾrīkh al-rusul wa-l-mulūk*, ed. Muḥammad Abū l-Faḍl Ibrāhīm, 11 vols., Cairo, 1968-69.
al-Ṭabrisī, al-Faḍl b. al-Ḥasan, *Iʿlām al-warā fī aʿlām al-hudā*, ^{3}Najaf, 1970.
———, *Majmaʿ al-bayān fī tafsīr al-Qurʾān*, 1-30, in 6 vols., Beirut, 1961.
al-Ṭūsī, Abū Jaʿfar Muḥammad b. al-Ḥasan, *al-Fihrist*, ed. Muḥammad Ṣādiq Āl Baḥr al-ʿUlūm, Najaf, 1937.
al-Tustarī, Muḥammad Taqī, *Qāmūṣ al-rijāl*, 8 vols., Tehran, 1379.
al-ʿUqaylī, Abū Jaʿfar Muḥammad b. ʿAmr, *K. al-Ḍuʿafāʾ al-kabīr*, ed. ʿAbd al-Muʿṭī Qalʿajī, vol. I, Beirut, 1404/1984.
al-Yaʿqūbī, Aḥmad b. Abī Yaʿqūb, *Taʾrīkh*, 2 vols., Beirut, 1960.
Wansbrough, John, *The Sectarian Milieu. Content and Composition of Islamic Salvation History*, Oxford, 1978.
al-Wāqidī, Muḥammad b. ʿUmar, *K. al-Maghāzī*, ed. Marsden Jones, 3 vols., London, 1966.
Yāqūt b. ʿAbd Allāh al-Rūmī, *Muʿjam al-buldān*, 5 vols., Beirut, 1399/1979.
———, *Muʿjam al-udabāʾ = Irshād al-arīb ilā maʿrifat al-adīb*, ed. Iḥsān ʿAbbās, 7 vols., Beirut, 1993.

APPENDIX 2

a: biographical data

أبان بن عثمان بن يحيى بن زكريّاء البَجَلي الؤلؤي الأحمر الكوفي

مولى بجيلة من بطون كِندة، تفرّقت بعد حرب الفِجار مع كلب بن وبرة في بطون العرب، كانت تنزل الكوفة (جمهرة ابن حزم 387-88؛ مقاتل الطالبين 102)؛ أصله من الكوفة وكان يسكنها تارة وفي البصرة أُخرى؛ أكثر عنه من البصريّين أبو عبيدة معمر بن المُثنّى (-824/209) وأبو محمّد ابن سلاّم الجُمَحي (-846/232)، كما روى عنه الجاحظ (-868/255) في مؤلّفاته.

له كتاب يجمع **المبدأ والمغازي والوفاة والسّقيفة والرّدّة**

نقل عنه اليعقوبي (ح 904/292) وعدّه فيمن روى عنهم في كتابه من أصحاب السير والمغازي والتواريخ (تاريخ اليعقوبي 6/2)؛

و لم يترجم ابن النّديم (بعد 995/385) لأبان و لم يذكر بالتّالي كتابه؛

وذكره النّجاشي (-1058/450) في رجاله 80/1-81؛

والطوسي (-1067/460) في الفهرست 18-19؛

و لم يذكره علي بن موسى بن طاووس (-1265/664) في سعد السعود ولا في غيره من كتبه (cf. Kohlberg, *Ibn Ṭāwūs*).

نقل عنه دون ذكر الكتاب بالاسم:

ابن بابويه (-991/381) في الخصال 50/1-51؛ والعلل 29/1، 35، 37؛

الشيخ المفيد (-1022/413) في الأمالي 53، 212؛ والاختصاص 299؛

الرّاوندي، سعيد بن هبة الله (-1177/573) في الدّعوات 41، 42، 48، 53؛

الطَّبْرِسي (-1154/548) في إعلام الورى 82-130، 137-138 "في كتاب أبان بن عثمان"؛ وغيرهم.

مصادر ترجمته:

الّثقات لابن حِبّان، أبو حاتم محمّد البُسْتي (-965/354) 131/8 "أبان بـــن عثمـــان الأحمر، كوفي يروي عن أبان ابن تغلب، روى عنه أهل الكوفة، يُخطـــئ ويَـــهِم"؛ الضُّعفاء للعُقَيْلي، محمّد بن عمرو (-934/322) 1/37-38؛ اختيار معرفـــة الرّجـــال للكشي 352 (659-660)، 375 (705)، 411 (773)، رجال النّجاشي 1/80-81 (7)؛ فهرست الطّوسي 18-19 (52)؛ معجم الأدباء لياقوت (-1229/626) 1/39 (3) نقلاً عن الطّوسي؛ رجال ابن داود الحِلّي (بعد -1307/707) 30 (6)، 226 (3) في قسم المجروحين والمجهولين:"كوفي المسكن بصري الأصل كان ناووسيّاً"؛ ميزان الاعتـــدال للذهبي، محمدّ ابن أحمد (-1348/748) 10/1 (13): "أبان بن عثمان الأحمر عن أبان بن تغلب تُكُلِّم فيه و لم يُتْرك بالكلّية، وأمّا العُقيلي فاتّهمه"؛ الوافي للصّفـــدي 302/5 (2364) نقلاً عن الطّوسي؛ لسان الميزان لابن حجر العَسْقلاني (-1448/852) 1/24؛ جـــامع الـــرّواة للأردبيلـــي 1/12-15؛ الذّريعـــة لآغـــا بـــزرك 47/19 (248)، 289/21 (5106) أعيان الشّيعة لمحسن الأمين 2/100-02؛ معجم رجال الحديـــث للخوئي 1/139، 157-70؛ أحمد باكتجي، في: دائرة المعارف الاســـلاميّة الكـــبرى 1 (1367)، ص 44-45؛ J. van Ess, *Theologie*, 2/425.

b. direct sources and teachers

أبان بن تغلب (-758/141): 10 = 4 سيرة، 6 مبتدأ (المبتدأ: 2 عن السيفان، 3 عن عكرمة، 1 عن ابن جبير؛ السيرة: 1 عن الصادق، 1 عن ابن ظريف، 2 عن عكرمة)؛ أبو سعيد البكري، مولى بني جرير، قارىء، فقيه، لغوي، روى عن زيـــن العـــابدين والباقر والصادق، ثقة جليل القدر صنّف كتاب غريب القـــرآن (رجـــال النجاشـــي 1/73-79؛ طبقات ابن الجزري 14؛ جامع الرواة 1/9-11؛ منتهى المقـــال 1/132-35؛ علي أكبر ضيائي في: دائرة المعارف 2/46-47؛ رجال الخوئـــي 1/133-53؛ (van Ess, *Theologie*, 1/334.

إسماعيل الجعفي (مات في حياة الصّادق): 1 مبتدأ (أو لو العزم من الرسل، 5 أسطر)؛ هو إسماعيل بن عبد الرحمن الجعفي الكوفي تابعي مات في حياة أبي عبد الله (جامع الرواة 94/1،98؛ منتهى المقال 2/71-72)؛ وثمّة إسماعيل بن جابر الجعفي كان يقول بالاستطاعة من حلقة زرارة و لم يرد في جامع الرواة 1/93-94 أنّ أبان روى عنه، انظر فيه (van Ess, *Theologie*, 1/332-33).

الأعمش (-765/148): 1 سيرة (أسماء النفر الذين أرادوا الايقاع بالرسول بعد تبوك)؛ قال الأردبيلي 383/1 "ترك المصنفون من أصحابنا ذكره وقد كان حريا لاستقامته".

بُرَيْد (مات في حياة الصادق؛ وقيل -767/150): 1 سيرة؛ هو بريد بن معاوية العجلي الكوفي، عربي، روى عن الباقر والصادق؛ ثقة فقيه له محلّ عند الأئمة؛ عن الصادق: "بشّر المخبتين بالجنّة بريد بن معاوية العجلي وأبو بصير ليث بن البختري المرادي ومحمد بن مسلم وزرارة، أربعة نجباء أمناء الله على حلاله وحرامه، لولا هؤلاء لانقطعت آثار النبوّة واندرست" (جامع الرواة 1/117-19؛ منتهى المقال 2/133-36؛ van Ess, *Theologie*, 1/331).

بشير النبّال: 1 مبتدأ (خبر خالد بن سنان العبسي)؛ توقّف في روايته وفي مدحه، جامع الرواة 1/124-25؛ وفي منتهى المقال 2/157-58 أنّه من أصحاب الصّادق وأنّه ممدوح.

أبو بصير: 15 = 8 سيرة، 7 مبتدأ؛ الأرجح أنّه ليث بن البختري المرادي الكوفي، روى عن الباقر والصادق، وروى عنه أبان بن عثمان (جامع الرواة 34/2)؛ وثمّة أبو بصير يحيى بن القاسم الأسدي الكوفي الأعمى -767/150؛ وقد اتّهم بالغلوّ والوقف، وروى عنه أبان الأحمر وقد اختلط أمرهما على مؤلفي الشيعة (جامع الرواة 2/334-48؛ منتهى المقال 5/263-69؛ van Ess, *Theologie*, 1/331-32).

الثمالي = أبو حمزة

أبو الجارود (بين 767/150 و776/160): 1 سيرة؛ زياد بن المنذر الهمداني الكوفي، رأس الجاروديّة من الزيدية، روى عن الباقر وزيد بن على (رجال النجاشي 1/387-

88؛ فهرست الطوسي 72-73؛ جامع الرواة 339/1-40؛ علي بهرميان، في: دائـــرة المعارف 5 (1372)، 289-91، ماهر جرّار، في: الكتاب التكريمي لسامي مكارم).

جعفر الصّادق (أبو عبد الله): 19 = 6 مبتدأ، 13 سيرة

الحارث بن يعلى بن مرّة: 1 سيرة (موت الرسول)

حُجْر: 1 مبتدأ: هو حُجر بن زائدة الحضرمي الكوفي روى عن الباقر والصادق، ثقـــة صحيح المذهب صالح (جامع الرواة 180/1؛ منتهى المقال 335/2-37).

الحسن الصيقل: 1 سيرة؛ هو الحسن بن زياد الصيقل الكوفي (جامع الـــرواة 199/1-200؛ منتهى المقال 383/2-84).

الحسين بن دينار > الحسن البصري: 1 سيرة (المباهلة).

أبو حمزة = الثُمالي -765/148 (أو 767/150): 6 مبتدأ، (واحد منها مكـــرّر)، 1 سيرة (سيرة علي في أهل الشرك)؛ هو أبو حمزة ثابت بن دينار الثُمالي الكـــوفي الأزدي من خيار أصحاب الباقر والصادق والكاظم، ثقة وله كتب؛ وكتابٌ في التفسير؛ لـــه ميول زيديّة وقتل أبناؤه الثلاثة في صفوف زيد بن علي؛ كان يقول بالرجعة، وبانّ الله شيء لا كالأشياء (جامع الرواة 134/1-38؛ منتهى المقال 191/2-97؛ 1/302-304 .(van Ess, *Theologie*,

أبو داود: 1 سيرة (قول الرسول لعليّ كنت معي في سبعة مواطن).

زرارة (-767/150): 7 = 5 سيرة، 2 مبتدأ؛ ابن أعين الشبياني مولاهم، اسمه عبد ربّه وزرارة لقب؛ له كتاب في الاستطاعة والجبر رواه عن بعض أصحابه عنـــه ابـــن أبي عمير، (جامع الرواة 324/1-29؛ منتهى المقال 250/3-56؛ *Theologie*, 1/321-30 . (van Ess,

زيد الشحام: 2 = 1 مبتدأ، 1 سيرة؛ هو زيد بن يونس الكوفي روى عن الصـــادق والكاظم (جامع الرواة 344/1-46؛ منتهى المقال 295/3-97).

سعيد الأعرج: 1 سيرة (حجّ النساء)؛ سعيد بن عبد الرحمن التيمي مولاهم الكـــوفي، روى عن الصادق وله كتاب، يروي عنه أبان بن عثمان بواسطة سعيد السمّان (جامع

الرواة 1/360-61؛ منتهى المقال 3/340).

ابن سيابة: 2 مبتدأ؛ هو صباح بن سيابة الكوفي (جامع الرواة 1/409-10؛ منتهى المقال 4/21).

عبد الله بن عطاء: 1 سيرة (وصف البُراق)؛ ثمّة أكثر من واحد بهذا الاسم، ويبدو أنّ أبان يروي عن الهاشمي مولاهم المكّي يروي عن الباقر (جامع الرواة 1/497).

عجلان بن صالح: 1 سيرة (قتل علي بيديه يوم حنين 40)؛ الأرجح أنّه عجلان أبو صالح المدائني وهو الذي يروي عنه أبان (جامع الرواة 1/536-37؛ منتهى المقال 4/303: عجلان أبو صالح).

عقبة: 1 مبتدأ؛ عقبة بن بشير الأسدي الكوفي (جامع الرواة 1/539).

عمرو بن صهبان: 1 سيرة (بعير شكي بعد غزوة ذات الرّقاع).

عيسى بن عبد الله: 1 سيرة (قال لفاطمة اعملي)؛ ابن سعد الأشعري، روى عن الصادق والكاظم وله مسائل للرضا (جامع الرواة 1/652؛ منتهى المقال 5/166-68).

الفضل أبو العبّاس: 1 سيرة (آية نزلت في بني مدلج)؛ يبدو أنّه الفضل بن عبد الملك، أبو العبّاس البقباق الكوفي، روى عن الصّادق، وروى عنه أبان بن عثمان (جامع الرواة 2/6-7؛ منتهى المقال 5/201-02).

كثير النوّاء: 3 = 2 مبتدأ، 1 سيرة؛ هو كثير بن إسماعيل، زيدي بتري (جامع الرواة 2/28؛ منتهى المقال 5/250-52).

محمد بن الحسن بن زياد: 1 سيرة (حنين والطائف)؛ الأرجح أنّه العطّار الكوفي (منتهى المقال 6/14).

محمد الحلبي: 5 مبتدأ؛ هو محمّد بن علي بن أبي شعبة الحلبي، "وجه أصحابنا وفقيههم والثقة الذي لا يعطن عليه" (جامع الرواة 2/151-52؛ منتهى المقال 6/114-15).

محمد بن مسلم (-150/767): 4 = 3 مبتدأ (1 مكرّر)، أبو جعفر الأوقص الطحّان الثقفي، طائفي انتقل إلى الكوفة ومات بها وله نحو من 70 سنة، من أصحاب الباقر

والصادق، طُعن عليه قوله بالاستطاعة مع زرارة وبريد وإسماعيل الجُعْفي، وكلّهم يروي عنهم أبان الأحمر (جامع الرواة 2/193-200؛ منتهى المقال 6/197-202؛ van Ess, *Theologie*, 1/330-31).

أبو مريم: 1 سيرة؛ هو عبد الغفار بن قاسم الأنصاري الكوفي روى عن الباقر والصادق، ثقة (جامع الرواة 1/461-62 ؛ منتهى المقال 4/143).

معاوية بن عمّار الدُّهني (-175/791): 1 سيرة (نقلاً عن ابن سعد وفيه خطأ: الذهبي)؛ ودُهن من بَجيلة، مولاهم الكوفي، "عظيم المحل في أصحابنا ثقة، وهو ثقة في العامّة" (منتهى المقال 6/280-84).

موسى بن أكيل: 1 مبتدأ؛ النميري كوفي ثقة، روى عن الصادق (جامع الرواة 2/271-72؛ منتهى المقال 6/343).

ابن ميمون القدّاح: 1 سيرة؛ = ميمون القدّاح، صحّح اسمه في جامع الرواة، مولى بني مخزوم المكّي، روى عن الباقر (جامع الرواة 2/286-87).

نعمان الرّازي: 2 سيرة (منها 1 شمائل)؛ روى عنه محمد بن سنان في مشيخته (جامع الرواة 2/295؛ منتهى المقال 6/385).

يحيى بن أبي العلاء: 1 سيرة؛ الرازي، له كتاب (منتهى المقال 7/8-9).

يعقوب بن شعيب: 1 مبتدأ (اخلع نعليك..) ؛ ابن مِيثَم الأسدي الكوفي، ثقة روى عن الصادق، له كتاب، وعنه محمد بن أبي عمير والحسن بن سماعة (جامع الرواة 2/347-49؛ منتهى المقال 7/67).

APPENDIX 3

أبان بن عثمان (رواية القُمِّيين وهي ناقصة)

جعفر بن بشير[1]

محمّد بن الحسين بن أبي الخطّاب[2]   محمّد بن جمهور العَمِّي[3]

أحمد بن إدريس[4]   المُعلّى بن محمّد البصري[5]

أحمد بن جعفر بن سيفان[6]   محمّد بن الحسن بن الوليد[7]

الحسين بن عبيد الله[8]   أبو الحسين بن أبي جيد القُمِّي[9]

أبو جعفر الطّوسي

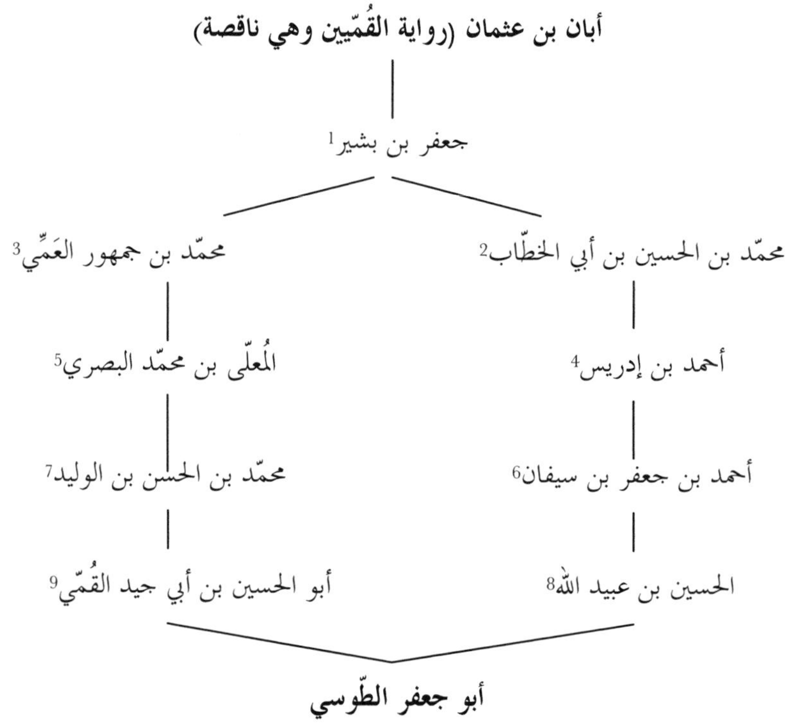

[1] أبو محمّد البَجَلي الوشّاء، من زُهّاد أصحابنا وعُبّادهم، له مسجد بالكوفة في بَجيلة، ثقـــة مـــات بالأبواء 208/823 (اختيار معرفة الرّجال، فهارسه 65؛ رجال ابن داود الحِلِّي 62 (303)؛ جـــامع الرّواة 1/150-51).

[2] كوفي زيّات، روى عنه الصفّار، همداني ثقة جليل -262/875 (اختيار معرفة الرّجال، فهارســـه 245؛ جامع الرّواة 2/96-99).

[3] عربي بصري غال، ضعيف فاسد المذهب لا يُلتفت إلى ما يرويه (اختيار معرفة الرّجال، فهارســـه 241؛ رجال ابن دَاود الحِلِّي 271 (439) ''رأيت له شعراً يحلل فيه محرّمات الله تعالى''؛ جامع الرّواة 2/87).

[4] أبو علي الأشعري القُمِّي، ثقة صحيح الرواية والحديث -306/918 (اختيار معرفـــة الرّجـــال، فهارسه 32؛ رجال ابن داود الحِلِّي 36 (57)؛ جامع الرّواة 2/87).

[5] أبو الحسن البصري، مضطرب الحديث والمذهب (رجال ابن داود الحِلِّي 190 (1580) بصري لـــه كتاب، ثمّ ذكره مع الضعفاء والمجروحين 279 (507) مضطرب الحديث والمذهـــب ويـــروي عـــن الضّعفاء؛ جامع الرّواة 2/251).

[6] البَزَوفَري (قرية كبيرة قرب واسط وبغداد على النّهر المُوفّقي غربيّ دجلة معجم البلـــدان 412/1)، روى عنه التَلْعُكْبري (هارون بن موسى الشيباني -995/385) ســـــنة 975/365 (جـــامع الـــرّواة 43/1، 440/2).

[7] قمّي، جليل عارف بالرّجال موثوق به (جامع الرّواة 96/2).

[8] الغضائري -1020/411 (جامع الرّواة 246/1)

[9] علي بن أحمد الكوفي، شيخ النّجاشي (جامع الرّواة 554/1، 428/2).

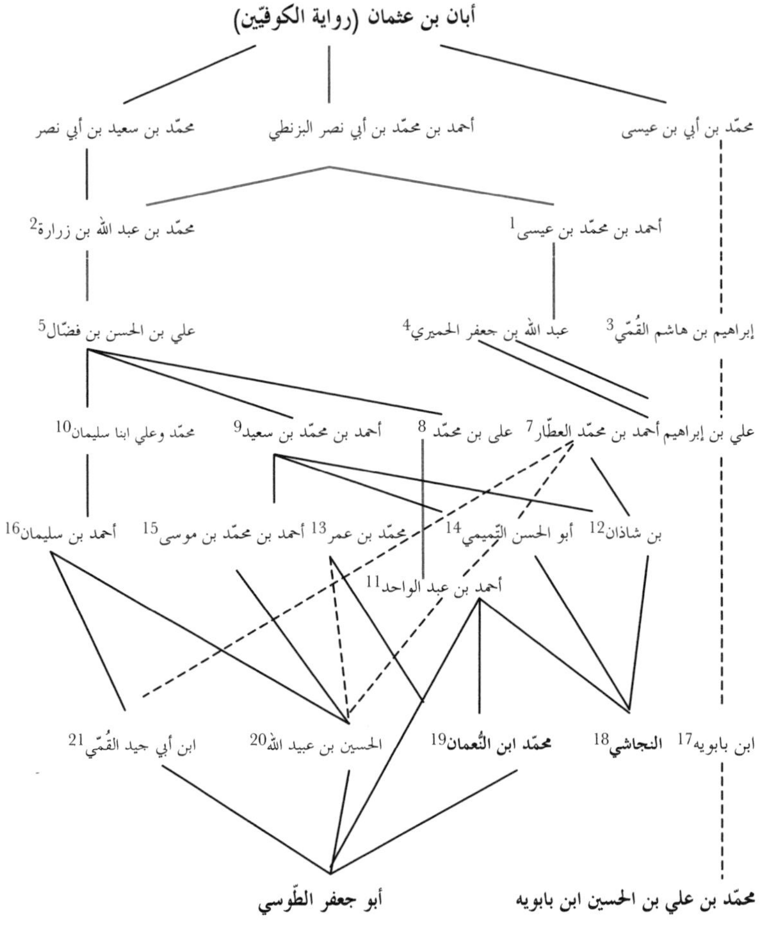

[1] أبو جعفر القُمّي، شيخ قُمّ ووجهها وفقيهها غير مُدافع؛ لقي الرّضا (818/203-765/148) والجواد (835/220-810/195) والهادي (868/254-827/212)، ثقة (اختيار معرفة الرّجال، فهارسه 40-38؛ رجال ابن داود الحلّي 44 (131)؛ جامع الرّواة 1/69-70؛ منتهى المقال 1/337-41).

[2] حفيد زرارة بن أَعْيَن، رجل فاضل دَيِّن مجهول الحال (اختيار معرفة الرّجال، فهارسه 256؛ جامع الرّواة 141/2؛ منتهى المقال 6/97-98).

[3] أبو إسحاق، أصله كوفي انتقل إلى قُمّ وهو أوّل من نشر حديث الكوفيّين بقُمّ؛ روى عن الجواد 835/220-810/195 (اختيار معرفة الرّجال، فهارسه 12؛ رجال ابن داود الحلّي 34 (43)؛ جامع الرّواة 38/1؛ منتهى المقال 1/213-18).

[4] أبو العبّاس القُمّي، شيخ القُمّيين ووجههم، قدم الكوفة بعد سنة 902/290 فسمع منه أهلُها، ثقة صنّف

كُتُباً كثيرة (اختيار معرفة الرّجال، فهارسه 161؛ رجال ابن داود الحلّـــي 117 (845)؛ جـــامع الـــرّواة 478/1-79؛ منتهى المقال 168/4).

5 أبو الحسن الكوفي، فقيه أصحابنا بالكوفة ووجههم وثقتهم وعارفهم بالحديث؛ كان فطحيّاً [يعني يقـــول بإمامة عبد الله بن جعفر الصّادق المعروف بالأفطح الذي عاش 70 يوماً فقط بعد أبيه، ثمّ بإمامـــة موســـى الكاظم] (اختيار معرفة الرّجال، فهارسه 188-190؛ رجال ابن داود الحلّي 261 (340) قسم المجروحـــين و289 (7) في عداد الفطحيّة؛ جامع الرّواة 569/1-72؛ منتهى المقال 379/4-82).

6 القُمّي، ابن الذي قبله، ثقة في الحديث، ثبت معتمد، أكثر عنه الكليني، سمع وأكثر وصنّف كتباً وأضـــرّ في وسط عمره (اختيار معرفة الرّجال، فهارسه 179؛ رجال ابن داود الحلّي 130 (1018)؛ جامع الـــرّواة 545/1-46؛ منتهى المقال 324/3-25).

7 القمّي، سمع عنه ابن أبي جيد القُمّي (رقم 21) سنة 356/966 (رجال ابن داود الحلّي 45 (136) مهمل؛ جامع الرّواة 71/1-72؛ منتهى المقال 348/1-50).

8 ابن الزبير القُرشي الكوفي -348/959 وقد ناهض المائة؛ روى عن ابن فضّال جميع كتبه (جـــامع الـــرّواة 598/1؛ منتهى المقال 55/5-57) .

9 أبو العبّاس ابن عقدة، الزيدي الجارودي، ثقة جليل عظيم الحفظ 249/863-330/941 (رجال النّجاشي 240/1-42؛ جامع الرّواة 65/1-67؛ منتهى المقال 323/1-25؛ أحمد باكتجي في : دائـــرة المعـــارف الإسلامية الكبرى 318/4-20؛ *GAS*, 1/182؛ Günther, *Quellenuntersuchungen*, 127-31 S.).

10 أبو الحسن علي بن سليمان الزراري، ''كان له اتّصال بصاحب الأمر عليه السّلام، وخرجت إليه توقيعات، ورع ثقة لا يُطعن عليه في شيء'' (رجال ابن داود الحلّي 138 (1054)؛ جامع الرّواة 583/1-84؛ منتهى المقال 18/5-19)؛ وأخوه محمّد -301/913 (رجال ابن داود الحلّـــي 173 (1392)؛ جـــامع الـــرّواة 120/2؛ منتهى المقال 60/6-61).

11 أبو عبد الله ابن عُبْدون من شيوخ الأدب، لقي علي بن محمّد بن الزبير القرشي -423/1031 (رجـــال النّجاشي 288/1 (209)؛ رجال ابن داود الحلّـــي 39 (87)؛ جـــامع الـــرّواة 53/1؛ منتـــهى المقـــال 280/1-82).

12 محمّد بن علي بن شاذان القزويني شيخ النّجاشي (منتهى المقال 123/6؛ مشيخة النّجاشي 178).

13 لم أقع على ترجمة له.

14 لم أقع على ترجمة له.

15 ابن أبي الصّلت الأهوازي، روى عنه الطوسي جميع رواية ابن عقدة وكتبه (جامع الرّواة 71/1؛ منتـــهى المقال 344/1).

16 الزراري.

[17] أبو الحسن علي بن الحسين شيخ القُمّيين في عصره، ثقة جليل له كتب كثيرة، عاصر السّفراء وأخذ عنـهم 329/940- (جامع الرّواة 574/1-75؛ منتهى المقال 396/4-97).

[18] 372/982-450/1058.

[19] الشيخ المفيد 333/944-413/1022.

[20] الغضائري 411/1020 (جامع الرّواة 246/1؛ منتهى المقال 47/3-49).

[21] علي بن أحمد الكوفي، شيخ النّجاشي (جامع الرّواة 554/1، 428/2؛ مشيخة النّجاشي 156-57).

APPENDIX 4

سندا البزنطي وابن أبي عمير عن أبان في قسم المبتدأ من بحار الأنوار

* البزنطي هو أحمد بن محمد بن أبي نصر (-835/221)، كوفي لقي الرّضا وكان عظيم المنزلة عنده، **فهرست الطوسي** 19-20؛ **رجال النّجاشي** 1/202-204 (رقم 178)؛ **جامع الرّواة** 1/59-61؛ Kohlberg, *Ibn Ṭāwūs*, 222; van Ess, *Theologie*, 1/348.

** ابن أبي عمير هو محمد بن أبي عمير زياد بن عيسى (-832/217)، بيّاع السابري مولى الأزد من موالي المهلّب بن أبي صفرة بغدادي الأصل والمقام ووجه من وجوه الرّافضة حُبِس زمن الرّشيد، كان وكيل موسى الكاظم، **فهرست الطوسي** 138؛ **جامع الرّواة** 2/50-57؛ **دائرة المعارف** 1/342-43؛ van Ess, *Theologie*, 1/348-86.

*- 11/33 الخصال:..محمد بن علي الكوفي > البزنطي > **أبان** > إسماعيل الجعفي > أبو جعفر [أولو العزم من الرسل، 5 أسطر]؛

- 11/36 الخصال:..ابن أبي عمير > **أبان بن عثمان > أبان بن تغلب > سيفان بن أبي ليلى > الحسن ابن علي [سأله ملك الروم عن خمسة أشياء خلقها الله لم تخرج من رحم..، 3 أسطر]؛

*- 11/100 علل الشرائع:..ابن عيسى > البزنطي > **أبان** > محمد الحلبي > أبو عبد الله [تسمية آدم، سطران]؛

*- 11/103 علل الشرائع:..ابن عيسى > البزنطي > **أبان** > محمد الحلبي > أبو عبد الله [خلق آدم، 8 أسطر]؛

- 11/113 قصص الأنبياء:..ابن أبي عمير > **أبان > محمد الحلبي > [مثل 11/103]؛

*- 11/175: معاني الأخبار: ماجيلويه > عمّه > البرقي > البزنطي > **أبان** > ابن سيابة > أبو عبد الله [طاف آدم بالبيت مائة عام، 8 أسطر]

- 178/11 تفسير القُمّي: أبوه > ابن أبي عمير > **أبان > أبو عبد الله [بقي آدم ساجداً أربعين صباحاً، 32 سطراً]

*- 181/11 قصص الأنبياء:..ابن عيسى > البزنطي > **أبان** > محمد بن مسلم > أبو جعفر [الكلمات التي تلقّى بهنّ آدم ربّه، 5 أسطر]؛

*- 210/11 قصص الأنبياء: ماجيلويه > عمّه > البرقي > البزنطي > **أبان** > ابن سيابة > أبو عبد الله [مثل 175/11]؛

*- 291/11 علل الشرائع:..ابن عيسى > البزنطي > **أبان** > محمد بن مسلم > أبو جعفر [سمّي نوح عبداً شكوراً، 4 أسطر]؛

- 293/11 الكافي:..علي بن إبراهيم > ابوه > ابن أبي نصر [عمير؟] > **أبان > زرارة > أبو جعفر [لمّا هبط نوح من السفينة، 13 سطراً].

*- 318/11 الخصال:..ابن عيسى > البزنطي > **أبان** > كثير النوّاء > أبو عبد الله [ركب نوح السفينة في أوّل يوم من رجب، سطران]؛

*- 324/11 قصص الأنبياء:..ابن عيسى > البزنطي > **أبان** > أبو حمزة > أبو رزين الأسدي > علي [لمّا فرغ نوح من السفينة، 6 أسطر]؛

*- 337/11 تفسير القمّي:..أحمد بن إدريس > البزنطي > **أبان** > موسى بن أكيل > العلاء بن سيابة > أبو عبد الله [{ونادى نوح ابنه} ابن زوجته، 3 أسطر]، والخبر في التفسير 329/1؛

- 385/11 علل الشرائع:..محمد بن زياد الأزدي > **أبان > أبان بن تغلب > سفيان بن [أبي] ليلى [مثل 36/11]؛ [سأله ملك الروم عن خمسة أشياء خلقها الله لم تخرج من رحم..، 3 أسطر]؛

- 5-4/12 علل الشرائع:..ابن يزيد > ابن أبي عمير > **أبان > محمد بن مروان > عمن رواه > أبو جعفر [لما اتخذ الله إبراهيم خليلا أرسل له ملك الموت..، 10 أسطر].

- 39/12 قصص الأنبياء:..ابن أبي عمير > **أبان > أبو عبد الله ... النبي [النمـــرود وإبراهيم والنّار، 8 أسطر]؛

- 44/12 الكافي:..علي بن إبراهيم > أبوه > البزنطي > **أبان > حجر > أبـــو عبد الله [إبراهيم، 15 سطراً] ؛

- 77/12 علل الشّرائع:..علي بن الحكم > **أبان** > محمد الواسطي > أبو عبـــد الله [أوحى الله إلى إبراهيم أنّ الأرض قد شكت من عورتك، 4 أسطر]؛

*- 79/12 علل الشرائع:..ابن عيسى > البزنطي > **أبان** > أبو بصير > أبو جعفر أو أبو عبد الله [لمّا قضى إبراهيم مناسكه أتاه ملك الموت، 12 سطراً]؛

- 85/12 تفسير القمّي: علي بن إبراهيم > أبوه > ابن أبي عمـــير > **أبـــان > الصادق [إبراهيم وزوجة إسماعيل، 7 أسطر]؛

*- 104/12 علل الشرائع: ماجيلويه > عمّه > البزنطي > **أبان** > عمّن ذكره > مجاهد > ابن عبّاس [الخيل العراب إسماعيل، 8 أسطر]؛

- 111/12 قصص الأنبياء:..ابن أبي عمير > **أبان > عقبة > أبو عبد الله [تزوّج إسماعيل من العماليق، 27 سطراً]؛

*- 116-115/12 الكافي: علي بن إبراهيم..البزنطي > **أبان** > أبو العبّاس> أبـــو عبد الله [لما ولد إسماعيل حمله إبراهيم وأمّه على حمار وأقبل معه جبريل..، 11 سطراً، خبران]؛

- 116/12 الكافي:..علي بن الحكم > **أبان** > محمد الواسطي > أبـــو عبـــد الله [شكوى إبراهيم من سوء خلق سارة، 4 أسطر].

*- 117/12 الكافي:..علي بن الحكم > **أبان** > محمد الواسطي > أبـــو عبـــد الله [سأل إبراهيم ربّه ابنة تبكيه بعد موته، 3 أسطر].

*- 128/12 الكافي:..البزنطي > **أبان** > أبو بصير > أبو جعفر أو أبـــو عبـــد الله [إبراهيم والذّبيح إسحاق خبر طويل]؛

*- 130/12 علل الشرائع:..البرقي > البزنطي > **أبان** [قلت لأبي عبد الله: كيف أصبح الطحال حراماً (الذبيح)، 7 أسطر]؛

*- 160/12 علل الشرائع:..ابن عيسى > البزنطي > **أبان** > أبو بصير [هلاك قوم لوط، 23 سطراً]؛

*- 161/12 علل الشرائع:..البزنطي > **أبان** > أبو بصير [لوط، 6 أسطر]؛

*- 162/12 علل الشرائع:..محمد بن الحسين > البزنطي > **أبان** > أبو بصير > أحدهما [لوط، 6 أسطر]؛

- 260-256/12 أمالي الصّدوق: جعفر بن سليمان > عبد الله بن المفضل > **أبان بن عثمان** > أبان بن تغلب > ابن جُبَيْر > ابن عبّاس [يعقوب ويوسف]؛

- 303/12 تفسير العيّاشي: عن **أبان** > محمد بن مسلم عنهما [إنّ رسول الله قال لو كنت بمنزلة يوسف حين أرسل إليه الملك يسأله عن رؤياه، 3 أسطر]؛

- 341/12 و192/14 الكافي:..أحمد بن الحسن الميثمي > **أبان** > عبد الأعلى مولى آل سام > الصادق [يؤتى بالمرأة الحسناء يوم القيامة ..الفتنة..فيضرب المثل بمريم وبيوسف، 8 أسطر]؛

- 10/13 علل الشرائع:..علي بن مهزيار حماد بن عيسى > **أبان** > عمن أخبره > الباقر [التلبية سميت كذلك لأن موسى أجاب ربّه، 3 أسطر]؛

*- 11/13 الكافي:..أحمد بن محمد > البزنطي > **أبان** > زيد الشحّام > عمن رواه > أبو جعفر [حجّ موسى ومعه سبعون نبيّاً، 4 أسطر]؛

*- 42-38/13 إكمال الدين:..جماعة > ابن عيسى > البزنطي > **أبان بن عثمان** > بسندين وخبرين بعد أبان [موسى]؛

- 64/13 علل الشرائع:..ابن يزيد > ابن أبي عمير > **أبان بن عثمان > يعقوب بن شعيب > أبو عبد الله [إخلع نعليك، جلد حمار ميّت، 3 أسطر]؛

- 123-120/13 تفسير علي بن إبراهيم: أبوه > ابن فضّال > **أبان بن عثمان** > أبو عبد الله [موسى وهارون]؛

*- 176/13 الاختصاص:..ابن عيسى > البزنطي > **أبان** > أبو حمزة > أبو جعفر [تيه بني إسرائيل، 16 سطراً]؛

- 177/13 قصص الأنبياء:..ابن هاشم > ابن أبي عمير > **أبان بن عثمان > أبو حمزة > أبو جعفر [نفس الذي قبله، 10 أسطر]؛

- 243-242/13 رجال الكشّي:..الحسن بن فضال > العباس بن عامر > **أبان** > الحارث بن مغيرة > الصادق (و)..ابن أبي عمير > يحيى الحلبي > أيوب الحرّ > بشير > الصادق [موت عبد الله بن عجلان ومثل موسى والسبعين من قومه، 8 أسطر]؛

*- 265/13 قصص الأنبياء:..سعد > ابن عيسى > البزنطي > **أبان بن عثمان** > أبو حمزة > عكرمة > ابن عبّاس [قصّة ذبح البقرة، 18 سطراً]؛

- 400/13 بصائر الدرجات:..أحمد بن الحسين الميثمي > **أبان** > موسى النميري، جئت إلى باب أبي جعفر [معرفة اللغات ومناجاة إيليا، 9 أسطر]؛

- 11-10/14 الكافي:..فضالة بن أيّوب > **أبان** > عمن أخبره > أبو عبد الله [داود والقضاء، 11 سطراً]؛

- 39-38/14 قصص الأنبياء: سند الصّدوق..ابن عيسى > ابن أبي عمير > **أبان بن عثمان > الحلبي > أبو عبد الله [داود، 13 سطراً]؛

- 72/14 تفسير القمّي: أبوه > ابن أبي نصر [عمير؟] > **أبان > أبو حمزة [سليمان بن داود، 8 أسطر]؛

- 116-115/14 الاختصاص:..ابن أبي عمير > **أبان > الصادق [آصف والوصيّة وعليّ، 6 أسطر]؛

- 138-137/14 علل الشرائع: أبوه > ابن أبي عمير > **أبان > أبو بصير > أبو جعفر [سليمان والجن وموته]؛

*- 139/14 علل الشرائع:..البزنطي > **أبان** > أبو بصير > أبو جعفر [سليمان، سطران]؛

- 180/14 قصص الأنبياء: الصّدوق > أبوه > عليّ > أبوه > ابن أبي عمير > **أبان > أبو حمزة > أبو جعفر [يحيى ونُوره، غُذي بأنهار الجنّة حتى فطم، 3 أسطر]؛

*- 214/14 التهذيب:..محمد بن عبد الله بن زرارة > البزنطي > **أبان بن عثمان** > كثير النّواء > أبو جعفر [ولد عيسى يوم عاشوراء، 3 أسطر]؛

- 219/14 الكافي:..عليّ بن الحسن الطاطري > محمد بن زياد بيّاع السّابري (= ابن أبي عمير) > **أبان > رجل > أبو عبد الله [مريم حملت بعيسى تسع ساعات كل ساعة شهر]؛

*- 252-251/14 قصص الأنبياء: الصدّوق..ابن عيسى > البزنطي > **أبان بن عثمان** > محمد الحلبي > أبو عبد الله [رسالة عيسى]؛

- 270/14 أمالي الصّدوق: ابن شاذويه > محمد الحميري > أبوه > ابن يزيد > ابن أبي عمير > **أبان بن عثمان > أبان بن تغلب > عكرمة > ابن عبّاس [عيسى، 24 سطراً]؛

- 371/14 قصص الأنبياء: الصدوق > جعفر بن محمد بن شاذان > أبوه > الفضل > محمد بن زياد > **أبان بن عثمان > أبان بن تغلب > عكرمة > ابن عبّاس [عزير (عذاب الأطفال)، 8 أسطر]؛

- 427/14 قصص الأنبياء:..إبراهيم بن مهزيار > أخوه > **أبان** > أبو جميلة > عبد الله بن حارث البرادي > ابن أبي أوفى > رسول الله [3 نفر والكهف والعمل الصّالح، مثل، 20 سطراً]؛

- 447-445/14 قصص الأنبياء: الصّدوق > جعفر بن محمد بن شاذان > أبوه > الفضل > محمد بن زياد > **أبان بن عثمان > أبان بن تغلب > عكرمة > ابن عبّاس [جرجيس، 50 سطراً]؛

- 450/14 الكافي:..محمد بن الوليد الخزاز والسندي بن محمد معاً > ابن أبي عمير > **أبان بن عثمان الأحمر > بشير النبّال > الباقر والصّادق [خالد بن سنان

العبسي، 6 أسطر]؛ (له متابعة أطول من حديث آخر بسند آخر عن أبـــان: 448/14 الكافي:..محسن بن أحمد بن معاذ > **أبان** > بشير النبّال > الصادق، 15 سطراً)؛

= 60 خبراً منها 2 وردت بسندين؛ 26 عن البزنطي؛ 21 عن ابن أبي عمـــير؛ 3 عن علي بن الحكم؛ 10 عن عدد غير هؤلاء.

*

النّقول عن أبان بن عثمان الأحمر البجلي في قسم السيرة من بحار الأنوار

- 127/15 الخصال للصّدوق:..علي > ابن أبي عمير > **أبان الأحمر > جعفر بن محمّد [ولد عبد المطّلب عشرة]؛

*- 171-170/15 الكافي:..أحمد بن محمد بن أبي نصر > **أبان** > أبو بصير > أبـــو جعفر (ع) [عدنان ابن أدد وجرهم]؛

- 201-200/15 إكمال الدين 187-188:..علي > أبوه > ابن أبي عمير > **أبان بن عثمان يرفعه [خروج أبي طالب إلى الشّام]؛

***- 206/15 إكمال الدين:..علي > أبوه > ابن أبي عمير والبزنطي معاً > **أبان بن عثمان** > أبان بن تغلب > عكرمة > ابن عبّاس [ضرب عنق كعب بن أسد من بني قُرَيظة ونبوءة ابن حواش؟ الحبر]، والخبر في الواقدي 503/2، 512 (وفيـــه ابـــن خراش)؛ وتفسير القمّي 166/2 (وفيه ابن الحواس)؛ وإعلام الورى 69؛

*- 258-257/15 أمالي الصّدوق:..ابن البرقي > أبوه > جدّه > البزنطي > **أبان بن عثمان** > أبو عبد الله الصّادق [علامات ولادة الرسول..إيوان كسرى إلخ]؛

- 271-269/15 إكمال الدين:..علي > أبوه > ابن أبي عمير > **أبان بن عثمان يرفعه بإسناده [تزويج عبد المطّلب لعبد الله من آمنة وحملها برسول الله، وليس فيه خبر النور المعروف]؛

- 273-272/15 مناقب ابن شهراشوب:..**أبان بن عثمان** رفعه بإسناده [رؤيا آمنة عند الولادة]؛

*- 295-297/15 الكافي:..علي > أبوه > البزنطي > **أبان بن عثمان** > أبو بصير > أبو جعفر (ع) [ولادة الرسول وذهاب النبوّة من بني إسرائيل]؛

- 1/16 أمالي الطّوسي:..العبّاس بن عامر > **أبان** > الصّادق [موت خديجة وفزع فاطمة]؛

- 124/16 الكافي:..الطاطري > محمد بن زياد > **أبان > يحيى بن أبي العلاء > أبو عبد الله [درع لرسول الله..لبسها علي يوم الجمل]؛

- 125-124/16 الكافي:..الطاطري > محمد بن زياد > **أبان > أبو بصير [القصواء ناقة رسول الله]؛

*- 132/16 علل الشرائع:..أبوه > ابن عيسى > البزنطي > **أبان** > الحسن الصيقل > أبو عبد الله [أُمّي لا يكتب ولا يقرأ الكتاب]؛

- 172/16 بصائر الدراجات:..الحسن بن علي بن النعمان > يحيى بن عمر > **أبان الأحمر** > زرارة > أبو جعفر [معشر الأنبياء تنام عيوننا ولا..]؛

- 193/16 الكافي:..أحمد بن الحسن الميثمي > **أبان بن عثمان** > نعمان الرازي > أبو عبد الله [أُحد، انحدر على جبينه مثل اللؤلؤ]؛

- 214/16 الخصال والأمالي للصّدوق:..علي > أبوه > ابن أبي عمير > **أبان الأحمر > الصّادق [كرم الرسول]؛

- 258/16 الكافي:..المعلى > الوشاء > **أبان** > ابن ميمون القدّاح > أبو جعفر [الرسول كيف لا أشيب إذا قرأت القرآن]؛

- 261/16 الكافي:..المعلى > الوشاء > **أبان بن عثمان** > زيد الشحام > أبو عبد الله [أكله]؛

- 274/16 الكافي:..علي بن الحكم > أبو الفرج: سأل **أبان** أبا عبد الله [طواف الرسول]؛

- 282/16 كتابا الحسين بن سعيد: فضالة > **أبان** > عبد الله بن طلحة > أبو عبد الله [رجل ضرب عبداً]؛

- 282/16 كتابا الحسين بن سعيد: فضالة > **أبان** > سلمة بن أبي حفص > أبو عبد الله > أبوه > جابر [مثل]؛

- 331-330/16 المحاسن: أبو إسحاق الثقفي > محمد بن مروان > **أبان بن عثمان** > عمّن ذكره > أبو عبد الله [شرائع محمد]؛

*- 330/16 الكافي: علي > أبوه > البزنطي > **أبان** > [مثل الذي سبقه]؛

- 340/16 تفسير العيّاشي: **أبان** > أبو عبد الله [لمّا نزلت النساء 84/4]؛

- 402-401/17 بصائر الدرجات: السندي بن محمد > **أبان بن عثمان** > عمرو بن صهبان > عبد الله ابن الفضل الهاشمي > جابر بن عبد الله [بعيرٌ شكى، بعد غزوة ذات الرّقاع]؛

- 404/17 الكافي: ..سهل بن زياد > محمد بن الوليد شباب الصيرفي > **أبان بن عثمان** > أبو عبد الله [حمار الرسول ووفاته]؛

- 55/18 تفسير العيّاشي: عن **أبان الأحمر** رفعه [أسماء المستهزئين الخمسة من قريش]؛

*- 189/18 أمالي الطّوسي: ..الأشعري > البزنطي > **أبان بن عثمان** > كثير النّواء > أبو عبد الله [27 رجب نزلت النبوّة]؛

- 213/18 الكافي: الحسين بن محمد > المعلى > الوشاء > **أبان بن عثمان** > أبو بصير > أبو عبد الله [لما كذّب الناس الرسول همّ الله بهلاك أهل الأرض إلاّ علياً.. آيتين]؛

*- 309/18 الكافي: علي بن إبراهيم > أبوه > أحمد بن محمد بن أبي نصر > **أبان بن عثمان** > أبو عبد الله [لمّا أُسري برسول الله قعد فحدّثهم]؛

- 311/18 الكافي: ..أحمد بن الحسن الميثمي > **أبان** > عبد الله بن عطاء > أبو جعفر [وصف البُراق]؛

- 337-336/18 أمالي الصّدوق: أبوه > علي > أبوه > ابن أبي عمير > **أبان بن عثمان > أبو عبد الله جعفر [خبر بيت المقدس]؛

*- 341/18 أمالي الصّدوق:..أحمد بن هلال > البزنطي > **أبان** > زرارة وإسماعيل بن عبّاد القصري > سليمان الجعفي > الصّادق [نودي في السماء أثناء المعراج عليّ الخليفة بعده]؛

- 406-405/18 تفسير علي بن إبراهيم: أبوه > إبراهيم بن محمد الثقفي > **أبان بن عثمان** > أبو داود > أبو بريدة الأسلمي [لعليّ كنت معي في سبع مواطن، أكثرها فيه جبريل]؛

*- 173/19 الكافي: علي > أبوه > البزنطي > **أبان** > الفضل أبو العبّاس > أبو عبد الله [آية نزلت في بني مدلج]؛

*- 176/19 الكافي: علي > أبوه > البزنطي > **أبان بن عثمان** > زرارة > أبو جعفر [ثمامة بن أثال]؛

- 270-269/19 تفسير علي بن إبراهيم:..فضالة بن أيوب > **أبان بن عثمان** > إسحاق بن عمّار > أبو عبد الله [تقسيم الأنفال]؛

- طبقات ابن سعد 43/4 [و لم أجده في مغازي الواقدي]: [الواقدي] > علي بن عيسى النوفلي > **أبان بن عثمان** > معاوية بن عمّار الدُهني [في الطبقات: الذّهبي وهو خطأ] > جعفر بن محمّد [عقيل يوم بدر، 9 أسطر]؛

- 300-298/19 الكافي:..الطاطري > محمد بن زياد بن عيسى > **أبان بن عثمان > فضيل البراجمي [خالد القسري وقتادة، بدر وأُحُد]؛

- 305-304/19 الكافي: محمد بن يحيى > ابن عيسى > ابن أبي عمير > **أبان > زرارة > أبو جعفر [بدر، إبليس وجبريل]؛

- 305/19 الكافي:..ابن يزيد > ابن أبي عمير > **أبان بن عثمان > ابن تغلب > أبو عبد الله [كأنّي أنظر إلى القائم]؛

*- 19/313-315 سعد السّعود نقلاً عن تفسير محمد بن العبّاس بن علي بن مروان: ..أحمد بن محمد ابن أبي نصر > **أبان بن عثمان الأحمر** > أبو بصير > عكرمة > ابن عبّاس [بدر، عتبة وشيبة والوليد]؛

***- 20/70-71 علل الشرائع: الهمداني > علي > أبوه > البزنطي وابن أبي عمير > **أبان بن عثمان** > أبو عبد الله [أُحُد، لا سيف..]؛

- 20/95-101 وفي **كتاب أبان بن عثمان** [أُحد وحمراء الأسد، وقتل العصماء (قارن ب: Lecker, 38-41)]؛

- 20/107 الكافي: ..أحمد بن الحسن الميثمي > **أبان بن عثمان** > نعمان الرازي > أبو عبد الله [أُحُد، لا سيف..]؛

- 20/212 معاني الأخبار: ..ابن أبي الخطّاب وغيره > ابن أبي عمير > **أبان بن عثمان > الصّادق [لا سيف..]؛

- 20/170-171 تفسير علي بن إبراهيم: ..الحسن بن علي بن أبي حمزة > **أبان بن عثمان** > أبو بصير [غزوة بني النّضير]؛

***- 20/247 الكافي: أبوه > ابن أبي عمير والبزنطي > **أبان بن عثمان** > أبان بن تغلب > عكرمة > ابن عبّاس [كعب بن أسد، بنو قُرَيظَة]؛

*- 20/268-296 الكافي: علي > أبوه > البزنطي > هشام بن سالم > **أبان بن عثمان** > من حدّثه > أبو عبد الله [الأحزاب]؛

*- 20/270 الكافي: ..سهل > البزنطي > **أبان بن عثمان** > بعض رجاله > أبو عبد الله [الخندق، كنوز كسرى]؛

- 20/288 تفسير علي بن إبراهيم: ..الحسن بن علي بن أبي حمزة > **أبان بن عثمان** [قتل عبد الله بن أُبَيّ، قتله ابنه]؛

- 21/22-23 إعلام الورى (ص 100-101): قال **أبان** > زرارة > الباقر [خيبر وفدك، دور عليّ وجبريل يأمر فدك لفاطمة]؛

- 21/55-57 إعلام الورى (ص 102-103): **وفي كتاب أبان بن عثمان** [مؤتة]؛

- 133-126/21 إعلام الورى (ص 105-106): **وفي كتاب أبان بن عثمان** [فتح مكّة، عليّ أوّل من أجار]؛

- 139/21 الكافي: الحسين بن محمد > المعلى > الوشاء > **أبان** > الثمالي > علي بن الحسين [سيرة علي في أهل الشرك]؛

- 142/21 أمالي الصّدوق:..ابن مهزيار > فضالة > **أبان** > محمد بن مسلم > الباقر [خالد بن الوليد في بني المصطلق، وقسمة عليّ فيهم، أنت مني بمنزلة هارون]؛

- 168/21 إعلام الورى (ص 116): قال **أبان** > محمد بن الحسن بن زياد > أبو عبد الله [حُنَيْن والطّائف]؛

- 176/21 الكافي:..الطاطري > محمد بن زياد > **أبان > عجلان بن صالح > أبو عبد الله [قتل علي بيديه يوم حنين أربعين].

- 248/21 إعلام الورى (ص 124): **وفي كتاب أبان بن عثمان** > الأعمش [أسماء النفر الذين أرادوا الإيقاع بالرسول بعد تبوك]؛

- 338/21 إعلام الورى (ص 129-30): قال **أبان** > الحسين بن دينار > الحسن البصري [المباهلة]؛

- 366-365/21 إعلام الورى (ص 126-27): **وفي كتاب أبان بن عثمان** [الوفود]؛

- 394/21 الكافي:..المعلى > الوشاء > **أبان** > سعيد الأعرج > أبو عبد الله [حجّ النّساء]؛

- 401/21 الكافي: علي بن الحكم وجماعة > **أبان** > أبو عبد الله [عمرة الحديبية]؛

***- 102/22 الخصال: الهمداني > علي > أبوه > ابن أبي عمير والبزنطي > **أبان الأحمر** > جماعة مشيخة [جبريل أشار إلى النقباء]؛

- 164/22 الكافي: الحسن بن محمد بن سماعة > غير واحد > **أبان** > أبو بصير [موت رُقيّة ابنة الرسول]؛

- 209/22 الكافي:..المعلى > الحسن بن علي > **أبان بن عثمان** > أبو الجارود > أبو عبد الله [العنكبوت 8، { ووصّينا بوالديه إحسانا} رسول الله وعليّ]؛

– 347-346/22 الاختصاص:..أبو أحمد الأزدي > **أبان الأحمر** > أبان بن تغلب > ابن ظريف > ابن نباتة [مدحُ عليّ في سلمان]؛

*– 403-402/22 الكافي:..علي > أبوه > البزنطي > **أبان بن عثمان** > أبو بصير > أبو عبد الله [أبو ذرّ]؛

– 530-529/22 إعلام الورى (ص 137): قال **أبان** > أبو مريم > أبو جعفر [وفاة الرّسول ودفنه]؛

– 457-456/22 الكافي وعلل الشرائع:..سهل > محمد بن الوليد الصيرفي > **أبان بن عثمان** > أبو عبد الله [وصية الرسول لعلي عند وفاته وميراثه]؛

*– 465-464/22 بصائر الدرجات: البزنطي > **أبان بن عثمان** > عيسى بن عبد الله وثابت > حنظلة > أبو عبد الله [قال لفاطمة اعملي]؛

– 539/22 الكافي: حميد بن زياد > الحسن بن محمد > غير واحد > **أبان** > بعض أصحابنا > أبو عبد الله [قبر رسول الله محصّب حصباء حمراء]؛

– 542-541/22 التهذيب: أحمد بن محمد > علي بن الحكم > **أبان بن عثمان** > الحارث بن يعلى بن مرّة > أبوه > جدّه [موت الرسول].

= 71 خبراً؛ منها 15 عن البزنطي؛ 11عن ابن أبي عُمير؛ 4 مشتركة عن كليهما؛ 41 عن غيرهما.

PART II

THE HISTORICAL RELIABILITY OF BIOGRAPHICAL SOURCE MATERIAL

DID THE QURAYSH CONCLUDE A TREATY WITH THE ANṢĀR PRIOR TO THE HIJRA?[1]

MICHAEL LECKER

Our knowledge of Islamic literature is far from complete, hence the study of the Prophet's biography in general, and his diplomatic history in particular, has not yet gone beyond the initial stages. The following article deals with some unusual reports on the aftermath of the great (or second, or third,[2] or last[3]) ʿAqaba meeting between Muḥammad and the Anṣār which took place several months before the Hijra. These reports mention or allude to a treaty between the Quraysh and the Anṣār which prevented bloodshed and allowed the Prophet's Companions, and in due course the Prophet himself, to travel from Mecca to Medina.

I

Let us start with a passage from William M. Watt's biography of the Prophet which represents what he correctly calls the "standard traditional account":

> For the pilgrimage of 622 a party of Muslims, seventy-three men and two women, went to Mecca, met Muḥammad secretly by night at al-ʿAqabah and took an oath not merely to obey Muḥammad but to fight for him—the Pledge of War, *bayʿat al-ḥarb*. Muḥammad's uncle ʿAbbās was present[4] to see that the responsibilities of Hāshim to Muḥammad

[1] I am indebted to Harald Motzki and Kees Versteegh for the invitation to participate in the workshop. Also to Harald Motzki and several other participants for their comments on the draft. The final version of this article includes several improvements suggested by Michael Cook.

[2] Samhūdī, *Wafāʾ al-wafā*, I, 228; Ṣāliḥī, *Subul* (*Sīra Shāmiyya*), III, 277.

[3] Ibn Saʿd, *Ṭabaqāt*, I, 226.

[4] Cf. Th. Nöldeke's skepticism at this point, in his "Die Tradition über das Leben Muhammeds", in *Der Islam*, 5 (1914), 160-70, at 165. At an earlier period Nöldeke ascribed to this report more credibility; see his "Zur tendenziösen Gestaltung der Urgeschichte des Islām's", in *ZDMG*, 52 (1898), 16-33, at 23; also F. Buhl, *Das Leben Muhammeds*, trans. Hans Heinrich Schaeder, [2]Leipzig, 1930, repr. Heidelberg, 1955, 187 (originally written shortly after Nöldeke's earlier article). See on this matter M.J.

> were genuinely shouldered by the Aws and the Khazraj. Muḥammad asked for twelve representatives (*nuqabā'*) to be appointed, and that was done. The Quraysh got word of the negotiations, which appeared to them hostile, and questioned some of the pagan Medinans, who answered in good faith that there was no truth in the report. Muḥammad now began encouraging his followers to go to Medina—Abū Salamah is even said to have gone *before* the Pledge of al-ʿAqabah—and eventually there were about seventy of them there, including Muḥammad himself.[5]

But why was the Hijra of Muḥammad and his Companions postponed for several months? After all, he could have gone to Medina together with the Anṣār during the sacred month of Dhū l-Ḥijja in which all forms of warfare were forbidden.

According to the dominant Ibn Isḥāq/Ibn Hishām version of the ʿAqaba meeting, immediately after the Anṣār's pledge of allegiance the devil (*al-shayṭān*) or the enemy of God divulged the secret of the treaty between the Prophet and the Anṣār. The Prophet threatened to deal with him later and ordered the Anṣār to disperse quietly and return to their temporary dwellings. At this point one of the Anṣār, al-ʿAbbās b. ʿUbāda b. Naḍla (of ʿAwf b. al-Khazraj)[6] offered to launch a morning attack on the people of Minā[7] (i.e., the pilgrims from different tribes who were preparing to leave the holy precincts and return to their territories). The Prophet turned the offer down, saying: "We were not ordered [by God] to do it" (*lam nu'mar bi-dhālika*). Then the Prophet repeated his order that the Anṣār return to their dwelling places.[8] A version of this report found in a Shīʿite source makes the Prophet's nonbelligerent approach even more pronounced: upon hearing the news from the invisible informant, the Quraysh were mobilized.[9]

Kister, "Notes on the Papyrus Account of the ʿAqaba Meeting", in *Le Muséon*, 76 (1963), 403-17, at 406-11.

[5] W.M. Watt, *Muhammad at Mecca*, Oxford, 1953, 145.

[6] More precisely, of Sālim b. ʿAwf b. ʿAmr b. ʿAwf b. al-Khazraj; Ibn Ḥajar, *Iṣāba*, III, 630-31; Ibn Qudāma, *Istibṣār*, 196 (who omits his father's name, calling him al-ʿAbbās b. Naḍla).

[7] The ʿAqaba in which the meeting took place was ʿAqabat Minā; see my "*Yahūd/ʿUhūd*: A Variant Reading in the Story of the ʿAqaba Meeting", in *Le Muséon*, 109 (1996), 169-84, at 169.

[8] Ibn Hishām, *Sīra*, II, 90; Ṭabarī, *Ta'rīkh*, II, 365.

[9] ... *Wa-hājat Quraysh fa-aqbalū bi-l-silāḥ*; Majlisī, *Biḥār*, XIX, 48. The mobilization motive is further developed in the *Biḥār* which gives Ḥamza and ʿAlī a role in repel-

Some versions of this report include the following significant exchange between the Anṣār and the Prophet:

> Then they said to the Messenger of God: "Would you leave with us?" He said: "I was not ordered to do so" (*mā umirtu bihi*).[10]

This conversation which is not found in Ibn Hishām and al-Ṭabarī appears immediately after ʿAbd Allāh b. Ubayy's questioning by the Quraysh regarding the alliance between Muḥammad and the Anṣār. (It is reported that Ibn Ubayy knew nothing since he was not part of it.)

II

Two sources place after this approach by the Anṣār a passage which is far more at variance with the traditional story of the ʿAqaba meeting and its aftermath. We begin with the text (Appendix I) found in the biography of the Prophet compiled in the 10th/16th century by al-Ḥusayn b. Muḥammad al-Diyārbakrī (d. 990/1582).[11] The compiler is quoting from a monograph written some four and a half centuries before his time by the Andalusian Razīn b. Muʿāwiya (d. 524/1129, or 535/1140).[12] The passage is probably from Razīn's history of Medina entitled *Akhbār dār al-hijra*.[13] It explains Muḥammad's stay in Mecca after the ʿAqaba meeting in mundane rather than theological terms, taking us from the domain of divine providence to that of politics:

> Razīn reported: And it was said that there was a dispute between the Quraysh and the Anṣār because of the Prophet's [imminent] departure with them [i.e., with the latter]. Then the Quraysh took fright [literally: fear was cast by God into the hearts of the Quraysh,[14] i.e., they backed

ling the Quraysh. In Ibn Isḥāq/Ibn Hishām's version the Quraysh only come in the morning to enquire about the goings-on.

[10] Diyārbakrī, *Khamīs*, I, 319, l. 16; Marāghī (d. 816/1413; *GAL*, II, 172), *Taḥqīq al-nuṣra*, 14a.

[11] Diyārbakrī, *Khamīs*, I, 319, l. 16 (the biography is followed by a general history).

[12] See *EI*², s.v. (Maribel Fierro).

[13] Ḥamad al-Jāsir, "Mu'allafāt fī ta'rīkh al-Madīna", no. 4, in *al-ʿArab*, IV/v (1970), 385-8, 465-8, at 388, mentions that Razīn's history of Medina is often quoted by the later historian of Medina, al-Marāghī. The same is true of Samhūdī's *Wafāʾ al-wafā* which quotes many passages taken from Razīn's monograph.

[14] Cf. the *ḥadīth*: *nuṣirtu bi-l-ruʿb masīrata shahr*, e.g. in Ibn al-Athīr, *Nihāya*, s.v. *r-ʿ-b*, II, 233.

> off because they feared the consequences of a military confrontation with the Anṣār], and said: "[We agree to his departure, on condition that] he would only leave with you[15] during a [normal] month [i.e., not during a sacred month], or the Bedouin would say that you gained ascendancy over us."[16]
> The Anṣār said: "The authority regarding this matter is in the hands of the Messenger of God and we shall obey his command." And God brought down to His Messenger [the following verse]: "And if they want to trick you, then God is sufficient for you,"[17] i.e., if the pagans of Quraysh want to deceive you, then God will cause His trials to befall them. And the Anṣār left for Medina.[18]

Although the text is rather elusive at this point, it seems that the heavenly protection from the perfidious Quraysh implies permission to enter into a potentially dangerous accord with them.

It is not impossible to discern suspected *topoi* in the text, such as the fear cast into the hearts of the pagan Quraysh (implying that they agreed to terms more favorable to the Muslims than to themselves), and their concern about their political and military prestige among the Bedouin. But I believe that they all belong to the literary garb of this report rather than to its historical core.

III

The second fragment (Appendix II) is taken from the *Sīra Shāmiyya*, a biography of the Prophet compiled in the 10th/16th century by al-Ṣāliḥī (d. 942/1535-36). The compiler interrupts the common story of the ʿAqaba meeting in order to incorporate a new text. In it we are told that the Quraysh proposed to give the Prophet and his followers safe conduct three months later. Again we realize that beside the

---

15 The preposition *maʿakum* is noteworthy. It is as if the Anṣār were expected to stay in Mecca until the Prophet's departure. Cf. below, p. 164.

16 One expects here the preposition *ʿalā*: *bi-annakum ghalabtumūnā ʿalayhi*. See Appendix II, ll. 5-6.

17 Q 8:62. The context is given in the preceding verse: "And if they incline to peace, do also incline to it, and put your confidence in God, for He hears and knows."

18 See also Marāghī, *Taḥqīq al-nuṣra*, 14a, who omits Razīn's name and adds that the Anṣār (or rather the Medinans, not all of whom could be called Anṣār at that stage) who took part in the pilgrimage that year numbered 500. See also Ibn Saʿd, *Ṭabaqāt*, I, 221. Interestingly, some 500 of the Anṣār are said to have received the Prophet upon his arrival at Medina; Bukhārī, *al-Taʾrīkh al-awsaṭ*, I, 78. For Razīn's text, see also Samhūdī, *Wafāʾ al-wafā*, I, 233-34.

dominant and almost ubiquitous version of the ʿAqaba meeting, a substantially different account was circulating in Islamic historiography:

> Sulaymān b. Ṭarkhān mentioned in his *Kitāb al-Siyar* that upon the conversion to Islam of those of the Anṣār who converted, Iblīs[19]—may God's curse be upon him—shrieked, making him [= the Prophet] distinct[20] among the pilgrims: "If you have an interest in Muḥammad, then come to him at such-and-such place, since those who live in Yathrib concluded an alliance with him." He [= the compiler] said: "And Gabriel descended but none of the people saw him." The assembly of the Quraysh gathered upon Iblīs's shriek. Matters between the [Qurashī] pagans and the Anṣār became grave to the point that fighting between them nearly broke out. Abū Jahl regarded fighting in those [sacred] days with aversion. He said: "O company of the Aws and Khazraj, you are our brothers[21] and you have entered into a weighty matter—you want to forcibly take away one of us." Ḥāritha b. al-Nuʿmān told him: "Yes, and in spite of your objection, too. By God, had we known that it was the Messenger of God's command that we take you with us as well, we would do so." Abū Jahl said: "We propose that after three months we shall allow any of Muḥammad's Companions wishing to join you to do so, and we shall give you a compact that will satisfy both you and Muḥammad, prescribing that we shall not withhold him after that." The Anṣār said: "Yes, if the Messenger of God is satisfied [with this]." And he [= the compiler] mentioned the [rest of the] story.[22]

Al-Ṣāliḥī copied this report from the biography of the Prophet compiled eight centuries before his own time by Abū l-Muʿtamir Sulaymān b. Ṭarkhān al-Taymī (d. 143/761). Al-Taymī was the Baṣran *mawlā*[23] and ascetic[24] who for forty years officiated as the *imām* of the Great Mosque of Baṣra.[25] The biography was quoted by Ibn Rajab al-

[19] See *EI*², s.v. (A.J. Wensinck-L. Gardet).

[20] Instead of *bi-banīhi*, I propose to read: *yubīnuhu* or *yubayyinuhu*. However, the text is not smooth.

[21] One expects here *akhwālunā* instead of *ikhwānunā*. Cf. my "The Death of the Prophet Muḥammad's Father: Did Wāqidī Invent Some of the Evidence?", in *ZDMG*, 145 (1995), 9-27, at 14 and passim.

[22] Ṣāliḥī, *Subul* (*Sīra Shāmiyya*), III, 284-85. See also the more recent edition by ʿĀdil Aḥmad ʿAbd al-Mawjūd and ʿAlī Muḥammad Muʿawwaḍ, Beirut, 1414/1993, III, 206.

[23] The *nisba* al-Taymī goes back to the fact that he lived among the B. Taym; Mizzī, *Tahdhīb al-kamāl*, XII, 5.

[24] Abū Nuʿaym, *Ḥilya*, III, 27-37.

[25] See, for example, Dhahabī, *Nubalāʾ*, VI, 200.

Ḥanbalī (d. 795/1392)[26] and was still available to al-Ṣāliḥī more than a century later.[27]

For some reason al-Ṣāliḥī chose to discontinue his quotation from Ibn Ṭarkhān's biography of the Prophet. Since no fighting broke out between the Quraysh and the Anṣār, and since the Prophet stayed in Mecca and did not depart with his new allies, we can assume that the Prophet's reply was positive.

Obviously, this is not a colorless account of the event but a literary piece meant to entertain both listeners and readers. This is above all evident in the dialogue between the defiant Ḥāritha and the cool-headed Abū Jahl. But the literary garb adorns a framework of a presumed historical fact, namely, the negotiations and treaty immediately after the ʿAqaba meeting.

IV

The third text (Appendix III) is found in a small monograph compiled by the historian of the Yemenite town Zabīd, Ibn al-Daybaʿ (d.

[26] See his *Fatḥ al-bārī*, II, 212 (*wa-fī kitābi l-sīra li-Sulaymān al-Taymī*).

[27] In other words, it was extant at least five centuries after al-Khaṭīb al-Baghdādī (d. 463/1071) received its *ijāza* in Damascus; cf. J. van Ess, *Theologie und Gesellschaft im 2. und 3. Jahrhundert Hidschra: Eine Geschichte des religiösen Denkens im frühen Islam*, Berlin and New York, 1991-95, II, 368; *GAS*, I, 285; M. Jarrar, *Die Prophetenbiographie im islamischen Spanien*, Frankfurt a.M., 1989, 77-81. For Sulaymān's Shīʿite sympathies see also Mizzī, *Tahdhīb al-kamāl*, XII, 9 (*wa-kāna Sulaymān māʾilan ilā ʿAlī b. Abī Ṭālib r.*); Ibn ʿAsākir, *Taʾrīkh madīnat Dimashq*, XLII, 531 = Ibn Manẓūr, *Mukhtaṣar taʾrīkh Dimashq*, XVIII, 81 (the text is not smooth). These sympathies are confirmed by the fragment preserved in Mughalṭay, *al-Zahr al-bāsim*, II, 188a, regarding the respective roles of Abū Bakr and ʿAlī in Muḥammad's Hijra; see M.J. Kister, "On the Papyrus of Wahb b. Munabbih", in *BSOAS*, 37 (1974), 545-71, at 565-66 (*wa-fī Siyar Abī l-Muʿtamir Sulaymān al-Taymī: aqbala Abū Bakr ḥattā saʾala ʿAliyyan ʿani l-nabiyyi ṣ fa-qāla: in kānat laka bihi ḥāja fa-lqahu bi-ghār Thawr*). The *Siyar* of Sulaymān b. Ṭarkhān is presumably identical to his *Maghāzī*, mentioned in *GAS*, I, 285-86. Sulaymān's son, al-Muʿtamir (d. 187/803), transmitted the whole *sīra* compiled by his father to Muḥammad b. ʿAbd al-Aʿlā (d. in Baṣra in 245/859); see M. Muranyi, "Ibn Isḥāq's *Kitāb al-Maghāzī* in der *Riwāya* von Yūnus b. Bukair: Bemerkungen zur frühen Überlieferungsgeschichte", in *JSAI*, 14 (1991), 214-75, at 225. For entries on al-Muʿtamir and Muḥammad b. ʿAbd al-Aʿlā, see Mizzī, *Tahdhīb al-kamāl*, XXVIII, 250-56 and XXV, 581-83, respectively. (Jarrar, *Die Prophetenbiographie*, 79, suspects that the creator of the book ascribed to Sulaymān was either al-Muʿtamir or Muḥammad b. ʿAbd al-Aʿlā.) For two reports going back to Sulaymān (through his son al-Muʿtamir), probably taken from his biography of the Prophet, see Abū Nuʿaym, *Dalāʾil*, 176-77, 199.

944/1537)[28] who was a contemporary of al-Ṣāliḥī (they both preceded al-Diyārbakrī by half a century). In Ibn al-Daybaʿ's book we read the following:

> ... When the Quraysh found out about what the Aws and Khazraj had done, his [= the Prophet's] closest cousins[29] came to them [= to the Aws and Khazraj]. Among them [i.e., among the former] were Abū Jahl,[30] ʿUtba [b. Rabīʿa al-Umawī], Abū Sufyān, Shayba [b. Rabīʿa al-Umawī, ʿUtba's brother], Ubayy [b. Khalaf al-Jumaḥī], Umayya [b. Khalaf al-Jumaḥī, Ubayy's brother], Suhayl [b. ʿAmr al-ʿĀmirī], Nubayh [b. al-Ḥajjāj al-Sahmī], Munabbih [b. al-Ḥajjāj al-Sahmī, Nubayh's brother], al-Naḍr b. al-Ḥārith [al-ʿAbdarī] and ʿAmr b. al-ʿĀṣ [al-Sahmī]. They told them: "O people of Yathrib, we have a better claim to him[31] than you, since we are his kin and flesh." The Aws and Khazraj told them: "Not at all, our claim to him is better than yours, because we both worship one god." When the Quraysh realized that their zeal was sincere and their resolution firm, they feared the outbreak of violence and put them off with that which is best[32] [i.e., peacefully]. They said: "Leave him to us [for a while], and we undertake to grant him security and protection. We shall treat him and those who follow him favorably, and those of them [i.e., of his followers] who want to join you we shall not prevent from doing so"—they meant the Muhājirūn. The Aws and Khazraj disliked it, [but] the Messenger of God said: "Accept their request, O people of the Aws and Khazraj, since God attains his purpose[33] and fulfills his promise." They said: "Will you be satisfied if we do so, O Messenger of God?" He said: "Yes." They said: "Then we hear and obey." And they concluded a nonbelligerency treaty for four months, then they returned to Yathrib. And when they dispersed, the Quraysh intended treachery. But God, may He be exalted, protected His prophet from their evil and he [= the Prophet] left Mecca with the revelation which was sent down to him, in a state of fear and on his guard until he arrived at Medina, because of God's decree to him to do so.[34]

---

[28] On whom see *EI*², s.v. (C. van Arendonk-G. Rentz).
[29] One expects here: his fellow tribesmen.
[30] Whom we have already met in Appendix II.
[31] The preposition *bihi* is from Ālūsī, *Bulūgh al-arab*, I, 190 (quoting the *Nashr al-maḥāsin*).
[32] Cf., for example, Q 41:34.
[33] Q 65:3.
[34] Ibn al-Daybaʿ, *Nashr al-maḥāsin*, 173-76.

V

There are obvious differences among the reports under discussion, none of which is a verbatim reflection of the episode it purports to describe. By far the crucial matter is the treaty. Now while the first report alludes to an understanding with regard to the postponement of the Prophet's departure, the second mentions a three month period after which the Companions, followed by the Prophet himself, will be allowed to emigrate. The third report speaks of a delayed departure of the Prophet and his Companions and refers to a four month truce. Differences in Islamic historiography come as no surprise, given its nature and emergence.[35] Yet there is a significant common denominator: at the initiative of the pragmatic Quraysh, the departure of the Prophet and his Companions was postponed for several months. The delay prevented a military confrontation between the Quraysh and the Anṣār, while at the same time safeguarding the unhindered emigration of the Prophet and his Companions.

Assuming that there was a treaty between the Quraysh and the Anṣār, how are we to interpret the reported attempt to harm the Anṣār on their way back from the pilgrimage? Did the Quraysh act treacherously?[36] Were the alleged perpetrators Qurashīs who were opposed to the treaty?[37] Was the report invented in order to glorify the two Anṣār involved?[38]

In the context of the said treaty a special category of Muhājirūn should be mentioned, namely, Anṣār who were also entitled to be called Muhājirūn. They may have served as a small armed escort which either came from Medina to Mecca on the eve of the Hijra, or stayed in Mecca after the ʿAqaba meeting in order to see to the fulfillment of the Qurashī undertaking. Ibn Saʿd lists four men belonging to this category: Dhakwān b. ʿAbd Qays (of the Zurayq—Khazraj), ʿUqba b. Wahb b. Kalada (a Ghaṭafānī *ḥalīf* of the ʿAwf b.

---

[35] Cf. M. Lecker, "The Death".

[36] Appendix III, l. 3 from bottom; also Samhūdī, *Wafāʾ al-wafā*, I, 234: *wa-qīla inna Qurayshan badā lahum fa-kharajū fī āthārihim fa-adrakū minhum rajulayni kānā takhallafā fī amr*, etc.

[37] But the chief aggressor, Suhayl b. ʿAmr (Ibn Hishām, *Sīra*, II, 93), is listed in Appendix III among the Qurashīs who approached the Anṣār.

[38] It is noteworthy that both Saʿd b. ʿUbāda and al-Mundhir b. ʿAmr were of the Sāʿida (Khazraj), albeit of different subdivisions; Ibn Qudāma, *Istibṣār*, 93 and 101, respectively. In one source Saʿd is replaced by al-ʿAbbās b. ʿUbāda; Samhūdī, *Wafāʾ al-wafā*, I, 234, which does suggest a *faḍāʾil* contest.

al-Khazraj, more precisely of the Banū l-Ḥublā[39]), the above-mentioned al-ʿAbbās b. ʿUbāda b. Naḍla of the ʿAwf b. al-Khazraj[40] and Ziyād b. Labīd (of the Bayāḍa—Khazraj). After the ʿAqaba meeting they are said to have returned to Medina with the rest of the Anṣār. When the first Muhājirūn arrived at Qubāʾ, they set out to the Prophet in Mecca and participated in the Hijra of his Companions.[41] A fifth Anṣārī reportedly entitled to the same status was Rifāʿa b. ʿAmr b. Zayd (of the ʿAwf b. al-Khazraj, more precisely of the Banū l-Ḥublā[42]) who set out to join the Prophet and returned to Medina as a Muhājir.[43]

According to other reports which refer to three of the five men mentioned above, they stayed in Mecca between the ʿAqaba meeting and the Hijra. It is mentioned that ʿUqba b. Wahb came to the Prophet and stayed with him in Mecca until the Hijra,[44] and there are similar reports regarding Ziyād b. Labīd[45] and al-ʿAbbās b. ʿUbāda.[46]

The reports on a treaty between the Quraysh and the Anṣār which preceded the Hijra seem to be rare. This impression could, however, be misleading, since it is only based on the small part of Islamic historiography which has survived to our time.[47] In any case, assuming that they are indeed rare, we have to deduce that the Prophet's biographers gave precedence to reports portraying a persecuted prophet. Their motivation was probably pious: the humbler the Prophet's starting point, the greater God's grace and deliverance.[48] Besides,

---

[39] Ibn Ḥajar, *Iṣāba*, IV, 528; Ibn Qudāma, *Istibṣār*, 187; mentioned in Buhl, *Leben*, 188, note 155.

[40] Above, note 6.

[41] Ibn Saʿd, *Ṭabaqāt*, I, 226. Dhakwān participated in the first and second ʿAqaba meetings. Then (i.e., having returned to Medina) he travelled from Medina to Mecca and was with the Prophet until the Hijra; Ibn Qudāma, *Istibṣār*, 171.

[42] Ibn Ḥajar, *Iṣāba*, II, 493; Ibn Qudāma, *Istibṣār*, 186 (where his pedigree is abridged).

[43] Fākihī, *Akhbār Makka*, IV, 245 (who only mentions in this category Rifāʿa and al-ʿAbbās b. ʿUbāda).

[44] Ibn Qudāma, *Istibṣār*, 187; Ibn Ḥajar, *Iṣāba*, IV, 528.

[45] Ibn Qudāma, *Istibṣār*, 176.

[46] Ibn Ḥajar, *Iṣāba*, III, 631; Ibn Qudāma, *Istibṣār*, 196.

[47] Most of the works mentioned in Ibn al-Nadīm's *Fihrist* and Ḥājjī Khalīfa's *Kashf al-ẓunūn* were lost; G. Makdisī, "Hanbalite Islam", in M.L. Swartz (trans. and ed.), *Studies on Islam*, New York-Oxford, 1981, 216-64, at 217.

[48] The circumstances of the Hijra are closely related to the interpretation of the term Hijra. Buhl, *Leben*, 196 correctly remarks that Hijra does not mean "Flucht" but "Bruch, Auflösung einer früheren Verbindung". See also C.H. Becker, *Islamstudien. Vom Werden und Wesen der islamischen Welt*, I, Leipzig, 1924, 340 ("eine innerlich

stories of humiliation and danger are more effective than ones of political expediency.

The reports quoted above demonstrate the importance of late biographies of the Prophet which are outside what is now widely considered as the mainstream of the *sīra* literature.[49] A voluntary limitation of the scope of sources used in Islamic research deprives one of rich and at times crucial source material. Several centuries ago scholars in Damascus, Cairo and elsewhere in the Muslim world were still copying into their own compilations extracts from old books, some of them dating back to the dawn of Islamic historiography. (Needless to say, we must not equate "early" with "historical" or "true".)

To conclude, the study deals with the aftermath of the ʿAqaba meeting which took place several months before the Hijra. Three biographies of the Prophet compiled in the 10th/16th century include reports, no doubt copied from earlier biographies, which mention or allude to a treaty between the Quraysh and the Anṣār. These reports

---

bedingte, freiwillige Auswanderung"). Becker adds that the reports on the suffering and dangers to which the Prophet was exposed before and during the Hijra are exaggerated, "um dem Propheten den Ruhm eines Märtyrers für Gottes Sache zu verschaffen".

[49] In the words of M.J. Kister, the late compilations "contain a great number of early Traditions derived from lost or hitherto unpublished compilations". He continues: "Some Traditions, including early ones, were apparently omitted in the generally accepted *Sīrah* compilations, faded into oblivion, but reappeared in these late compilations"; see his "The *Sīrah* Literature", in A.F.L. Beeston et al. (eds.), *Arabic Literature to the End of the Umayyad Period*, Cambridge, 1983, 352-67, at 366, 367. A somewhat updated version will appear in L.I. Conrad (ed.), *History and Historiography in Early Islamic Times: Studies and Perspectives*. For the importance of late compilations (Ibn Kathīr, Ibn Sayyid al-Nās) as a source of primary materials from historians earlier than Ibn Isḥāq, see A.A. Duri, *The Rise of Historical Writing among the Arabs*, ed. and trans. L.I. Conrad, Princeton, 1983, 8. Rudi Paret reported (*Arabistik und Islamkunde an deutschen Universitäten*, Wiesbaden, 1966, 10) that Gustav Weil (1808-89) used for his biography of Muḥammad "alle ihm irgendwie erreichbaren Quellen", and that Weil made a special trip to Gotha in order to look for relevant manuscripts at the Herzoglichen Bibliothek. There he found al-Diyārbakrī's *Khamīs* (quoted earlier in this article) and the *Sīra Ḥalabiyya* which, although they were only compiled in the 16th or 17th century, included rich and old source material. Buhl (*Leben*, 371) was suspicious of the later biographies of the Prophet (he listed authors who lived in the 14th, 16th and 17th centuries) and was confident that the early sources contained the most important reports which were in existence at their time. Watt was of the same opinion. Having mentioned Ibn Hishām, al-Ṭabarī, al-Wāqidī and Ibn Saʿd, he said: "There are later Muslim biographers of Muḥammad but none appears to have had access to any important primary sources other than those used by the above-mentioned writers"; see his *Muhammad at Mecca*, xii.

may have been suppressed in the mainstream *sīra* literature which preferred a persecuted and humiliated prophet to one whose road to Medina was paved by political compromise.

Bibliography

Abū Nuʿaym, Aḥmad b. ʿAbdallāh al-Iṣfahānī, *Dalāʾil al-nubuwwa*, ed. Muḥammad Rawwās Qalʿajī and ʿAbd al-Barr ʿAbbās, ²Beirut, 1406/1986.

———, *Ḥilyat al-awliyāʾ*, 10 vols., Cairo, n.d., repr. Beirut 1387/1967.

al-Ālūsī, Maḥmūd Shukrī, *Bulūgh al-arab fī maʿrifat aḥwāl al-ʿarab*, 3 vols., Cairo, 1342-43/1924-25, repr. Beirut, n.d.

Becker, Carl Heinrich, *Islamstudien. Vom Werden und Wesen der islamischen Welt*, 2 vols., Leipzig, 1924, 1932.

Buhl, Frants, *Das Leben Muhammeds*, trans. H.H. Schaeder, ²Leipzig, 1930, repr. Heidelberg, 1955.

al-Bukhārī, Muḥammad b. Ismāʿīl, *al-Taʾrīkh al-awsaṭ*, ed. Muḥammad b. Ibrāhīm al-Luḥaydān, 2 vols., Riyad, 1418/1998.

Conrad, Lawrence I. (ed.), *History and Historiography in Early Islamic Times: Studies and Perspectives*, forthcoming.

al-Dhahabī, Muḥammad b. ʿUthmān, *Siyar aʿlām al-nubalāʾ*, ed. Shuʿayb al-Arnāwūṭ et al., 25 vols., Beirut, 1401-09/1981-88.

al-Diyārbakrī, Ḥusayn b. Muḥammad, *Taʾrīkh al-khamīs*, Cairo, 1283/1866, repr. Beirut, n.d.

al-Duri, ʿAbd al-ʿAzīz, *The Rise of Historical Writing Among the Arabs*, ed. and trans. L.I. Conrad, Princeton, 1983.

van Ess, Josef, *Theologie und Gesellschaft im 2. und 3. Jahrhundert Hidschra: Eine Geschichte des religiösen Denkens im frühen Islam*, Berlin and New York, 1991-95.

al-Fākihī, Muḥammad b. Isḥāq, *Akhbār Makka*, ed. ʿAbd al-Malik b. ʿAbd Allāh b. Duhaysh, 6 vols., Mecca, 1407/1987.

Ibn ʿAsākir, ʿAlī b. al-Ḥasan, *Taʾrīkh madīnat Dimashq*, ed. ʿUmar b. Gharāma al-ʿAmrawī, Beirut, 1415/1995 ff.

Ibn al-Athīr, al-Mubārak b. Muḥammad, *al-Nihāya fī gharīb al-ḥadīth wa-l-athar*, ed. Ṭāhir Aḥmad al-Zāwī and Maḥmūd Muḥammad al-Ṭanāḥī, 5 vols., Cairo, 1385/1965.

Ibn al-Daybaʿ, ʿAbd al-Raḥmān b. ʿAlī, *Nashr al-maḥāsin al-yamaniyya fī khaṣāʾiṣ al-Yaman wa-nasab al-Qaḥṭāniyya*, ed. Aḥmad Rātib Ḥamūsh, Damascus, 1413/1992.

Ibn Ḥajar, Aḥmad b. ʿAlī al-ʿAsqalānī, *al-Iṣāba fī tamyīz al-ṣaḥāba*, ed. ʿAlī Muḥammad al-Bijāwī, 8 vols., Cairo, 1392/1972.

Ibn Hishām, ʿAbd al-Malik, *al-Sīra al-nabawiyya*, ed. Muṣṭafā al-Saqqā et al., 4 vols., repr. Beirut, 1391/1971.

Ibn Manẓūr, Muḥammad, *Mukhtaṣar taʾrīkh Dimashq li-Ibn ʿAsākir*, ed. Rūḥiyya al-Naḥḥās et al., 29 vols., Damascus, 1404-09/1984-89.

Ibn al-Nadīm, *Fihrist*, Cairo, 1347 AH, repr. Beirut, 1398/1978.

Ibn Qudāma, ʿAbd Allāh al-Maqdisī, *al-Istibṣār fī nasab al-ṣaḥāba min al-anṣār*, ed. ʿAlī Nuwayhiḍ, Beirut, 1392/1972.

Ibn Rajab al-Ḥanbalī, Abū l-Faraj, *Fatḥ al-bārī sharḥ ṣaḥīḥ al-Bukhārī*, ed. Maḥmūd b. Shaʿbān b. ʿAbd al-Maqṣūd et al., 10 vols., Medina, 1417/1996.

Ibn Saʿd, Muḥammad, *al-Ṭabaqāt al-kubrā*, 8 vols., Beirut, 1380-88/1960-68.
Jarrar, Maher, *Die Prophetenbiographie im islamischen Spanien*, Frankfurt a.M., 1989.
al-Jāsir, Ḥamad, "Muʾallafāt fī taʾrīkh al-Madīna", no. 4, in *al-ʿArab*, IV/v (1970), 385-8, 465-8.
Kister, M.J., "Notes on the Papyrus Account of the ʿAqaba Meeting", in *Le Muséon*, 76 (1963), 403-17.
———, "On the Papyrus of Wahb b. Munabbih", in *Bulletin of the School of Oriental and African Studies*, 37 (1974), 545-71.
———, "The *Sīrah* Literature", in Alfred F.L. Beeston et al. (eds.), *Arabic Literature to the End of the Umayyad Period*, Cambridge, 1983, 352-67.
Lecker, M., "The Death of the Prophet Muḥammad's Father: Did Wāqidī Invent Some of the Evidence?", in *Zeitschrift der Deutschen Morgenländischen Gesellschaft*, 145 (1995), 9-27.
———, "*Yahūd/ʿUhūd*: A Variant Reading in the Story of the ʿAqaba Meeting", in *Le Muséon*, 109 (1996), 169-84.
al-Majlisī, Muḥammad Bāqir, *Biḥār al-anwār*, 110 vols., Tehran, 1376-94/1956-74.
Makdisī, G., "Hanbalite Islam", in Merlin L. Swartz (trans. and ed.), *Studies on Islam*, New York-Oxford, 1981, 216-64.
al-Marāghī, Zayn al-Dīn Abū Bakr b. al-Ḥusayn, *Taḥqīq al-nuṣra bi-talkhīṣ maʿālim dār al-hijra*, ms Br. Lib. Or. 3615.
al-Mizzī, Yūsuf, *Tahdhīb al-kamāl fī asmāʾ al-rijāl*, ed. Bashshār ʿAwwād Maʿrūf, 35 vols., Beirut, 1405-13/1985-92.
Mughalṭay b. Qilij, *al-Zahr al-bāsim fī sīrati Abī l-Qāsim*, ms Leiden Or. 370.
Muranyi, M., "Ibn Isḥāq's *Kitāb al-Maghāzī* in der *Riwāya* von Yūnus b. Bukair: Bemerkungen zur frühen Überlieferungsgeschichte", in *Jerusalem Studies in Arabic and Islam*, 14 (1991), 214-75.
Nöldeke, Th., "Zur tendenziösen Gestaltung der Urgeschichte des Islām's", in *Zeitschrift der Deutschen Morgenländischen Gesellschaft*, 52 (1898), 16-33.
———, "Die Tradition über das Leben Muhammeds", in *Der Islam*, 5 (1914), 160-70.
Paret, Rudi, *Arabistik und Islamkunde an deutschen Universitäten*, Wiesbaden, 1966.
al-Ṣāliḥī al-Shāmī, Muḥammad b. Yūsuf, *Subul al-hudā wa-l-rashād fī sīrat khayr al-ʿibād. Sīra Shāmiyya*, III, ed. ʿAbd al-ʿAzīz ʿAbd al-Ḥaqq Ḥilmī, Cairo, 1395/1975.
al-Samhūdī, ʿAlī b. Aḥmad, *Wafāʾ al-wafā bi-akhbār dār al-muṣṭafā*, ed. Muḥammad Muḥyī al-Dīn ʿAbd al-Ḥamīd, 2 vols., Cairo, 1374/1955, repr. Beirut, 1401/1981.
al-Ṭabarī, Abū Jaʿfar Muḥammad b. Jarīr, *Taʾrīkh al-rusul wa-l-mulūk*, ed. Muḥammad Abū l-Faḍl Ibrāhīm, 10 vols., Cairo, 1380-87/1960-67.
Watt, William Montgomery, *Muhammad at Mecca*, Oxford, 1953.

APPENDIX I

قال رزين: وقد قيل وقع بين قريش والانصار كلام في سبب خروج النبي ص معهم ثم القي الرعب في قلوب قريش فقالوا: ليس يخرج معكم إلا في بعض اشهر السنة ولا تتحدث العرب بانكم غلبتمونا. فقالت الانصار: الامر في ذلك لرسول الله ص ونحن سامعون لامره فانزل الله على رسوله: وان يريدوا ان يخدعوك فان حسبك الله اي ان كان كفار قريش يريدون المكر بك فسيمكر الله بهم، فانصرفت الانصار الى المدينة.

APPENDIX II

وذكر سُليمان بن طَرْخان التيْميُّ في كتاب السير له ان إبليس لعنه الله لما اسلم من اسلم من الانصار صاح ببنيه [sic] بين الحجاج: ان كان لكم بمحمد حاجة فأْتوه بمكان كذا وكذا فقد حالفه الذين يسكنون يثرب. قال: ونزل جبريل فلم يبصره من القوم احد واجتمع الملأ من قريش عند صرخة إبليس فعظم الامر بين المشركين والانصار حتى كاد ان يكون بينهم قتال ثم ان ابا جهل كره القتال في تلك الايام فقال: يا معشر الاوس والخزرج انتم اخواننا وقد اتيتم امرا عظيما تريدون ان تغلبونا على صاحبنا فقال له حارثة بن النُعمان: نعم وانفك راغم والله لو نعلم انه من امر رسول الله ص ان نخرجك ايضا لاخرجناك فقال ابو جهل: نعرض عليكم ان نلحق بكم من اصحاب محمد من شاء بعد ثلاثة اشهر ونعطيكم ميثاقا ترضون به انتم ومحمد لا نحبسه بعد ذلك فقالت الانصار: نعم إذا رضي رسول الله ص، فذكر الحديث.

APPENDIX III

فلما رأت قريش ما كان من فعل الاوس والخزرج جاءت اليهم بنو عمه الاقربين [sic] منهم ابو جهل وعتبة وابو سفيان وشيبة وأُبَيّ وامية وسهيل ونُبيْه ومنبَّه والنضر بن الحارث وعمرو بن العلص فقالوا لهم: يا اهل يثرب إنا اولى منكم [به] لانا صلته ولحمته فقال [sic] لهم الاوس والخزرج: بل نحن اولى به منكم لانا واياه نعبد ربا واحدا. فلما رات قريش منهم صدق الهمة وقوة العزم خافوا حدوث الشر فدافعوهم بالتي هي احسن وقالوا: خَلّوا بيننا وبينه على ان له الامان والذمام فلا يعرض له الا الخير [sic] ولا لمن تبعه ومن احب منهم ان يلحق بكم لم نمنعه، يريدون بذلك المهاجرين. فكرهت الاوس والخزرج. فقال رسول الله ص: اجيبوهم يا معشر الاوس والخزرج فان الله بالغُ أمرِهِ ومُنْجزُ وعْدِهِ فقالوا تَطيب عن نفْسك [sic] يا رسولَ الله أن نفعل ذلك؟ قال: نعم قالوا: فالسمْعُ والطاعة وضربوا بيْنهم أجلا اربعة اشهر ثم رجعوا إلى يثرب. فلما افترقوا همت قريش بالغدر فكفى الله تعلى نبيه شرهم وخرج من مكة بالوحي الذي انزل عليه خائفا يترقب حتى ورد المدينة عن امر الله له بذلك.

THE MURDER OF IBN ABĪ L-ḤUQAYQ: ON THE ORIGIN AND RELIABILITY OF SOME *MAGHĀZĪ*-REPORTS

Harald Motzki

I. Introduction[1]

From the viewpoint of historical source criticism, our sources for a biography of the Prophet Muḥammad must be classified as traditions. They contain information that has been consciously produced in order to inform later generations on what happened. This is a truism for scholars of Islam. This feature of the sources, however, permits different approaches when using them. On the one hand, this kind of sources can serve to write a history of ideas which are reflected in the description of the past; on the other hand, they may be considered as pieces of a broken mirror which reflect what really happened and therefore can be used to reconstruct historical reality. Both approaches have a validity of their own which can only be assessed on philosophical grounds. I leave such a discussion to those who are better qualified for these matters. Convinced that it is possible to reconstruct historical reality—whatever that may mean—I have chosen to deal with the second approach, and in the following source analysis, I venture to explore what the historical reality that could be reconstructed from the available sources looks like, and to test the methods which can be used for such a reconstruction. This approach necessitates, however, some preliminary remarks which outline my views concerning the possibility of using the sources in this manner.

As every historian knows, the informative value of the kind of sources termed traditions is blurred by several limitations. Traditions are subjective due to their choice of what they mention and what not; they put facts into a certain perspective, sequence and connection; and they use topoi or even create facts which have never existed or not in the manner that they describe them. As far as these limitations are concerned, the situation is not any different in the case of

[1] I am grateful to the participants of the colloquium, especially Michael Lecker, and to Kees Versteegh, John Nawas and Peri Bearman for their useful comments on the first draft of this article.

Muḥammad from that which the historian encounters for many other historical persons with regard to whom sources classified as remnants are not available to any substantial extent. The fact that the traditions concerning the founder of Islam originated primarily in the circle of the followers of this religion certainly increases the danger that the information could be biased, but this is the case as well with many other historical personalities and should—in my view—not lead to the *a priori* assumption that *all* the pieces of information are necessarily biased or that among those that are biased, the unbiased ones cannot be detected and, therefore, the sources on the whole are useless for a historical biography.

The special biases which Muslim sources of the life of Muḥammad can have have often been dealt with in Western scholarship. The most important biases can be summarized as follows: 1) The material which constitutes the biography of Muḥammad has a *tafsīr* character and owes its existence to the efforts of the Muslims of the first two Islamic centuries to understand and explain the Qurʾān.[2] 2) The background is theological, in that the traditions tried to create a specific theology of history, or in that the Muslims simply tended to put a halo around the founder of their religion.[3] 3) Actions of the Prophet were invented or trimmed to fit a specific form in order to serve as legal precedents which could supplement or even abrogate the legislation of the Qurʾān.[4]

All these biases and many others[5] are certainly found in the sources which form the customary basis for the biography of Muḥammad. It should not immediately be concluded, however, that all reports are the result of one or more of those motives, or that the historical reality of the Prophet's time is generally so badly distorted that there is no hope of recovering even parts of it. In order to reduce the risk of bias, I did not choose one of the highly sensitive issues which constitute the

---

[2] A thesis put forward for the first time by H. Lammens, "Qoran et tradition. Comment fut composée la Vie de Mahomet", in *Recherches de science religieuse*, 1 (1910), 27-51 and recently favored again, amongst others, by J. Burton, *An Introduction to the Ḥadīth*, Edinburgh, 1994.

[3] As has been argued among others by J. Wansbrough, *The Sectarian Milieu. Content and Composition of Islamic Salvation History*, Oxford, 1978 and recently by U. Rubin, *The Eye of the Beholder: The Life of Muḥammad as Viewed by the Early Muslims*, Princeton, 1995.

[4] A theory advanced, among others, by J. Schacht, "A Revaluation of Islamic Traditions", in *JRAS*, 49 (1949), 143-54.

[5] See the extensive list of possible biases in W. Muir's Introduction to his *The Life of Mahomet and the History of Islam to the Era of the Hegira*, London, 1861.

Meccan part of the *sīra* for investigation, nor did I choose one of the central events of the Medinan period. Instead I chose an episode which is rather marginal in the *sīra*: The expedition of a group of Anṣār to kill Abū Rāfiʿ Sallām b. Abī l-Ḥuqayq, a Jew living (according to some of the sources) at Khaybar. The Prophet himself does not even play a central role in this event, which seems not to be religiously problematic, at least not from the Muslim point of view. That does not mean that I expect the reports to be completely free of any tendentiousness. A second advantage of this episode is that there are varying accounts of it preserved in different sources.

This episode is mentioned in most biographies of Muḥammad written by Western scholars; however, the sources which they used to present what happened vary. Some authors used Ibn Saʿd (Sprenger, Muir), others Ibn Hishām (Grimme, Margoliouth), a third group even mixed the reports of these two and other sources such as al-Wāqidī, al-Bukhārī or al-Ṭabarī (Dermenghem, Gaudefroy-Demombynes, Watt).[6] None justified their choice of sources nor did they give a reason why they mixed a new cocktail from varying reports. The much criticized A. Sprenger, writing around the middle of the last century, was the only one who pointed out that there were reports on the event which were not compatible; he even tried to use this insight for a source-critical argument.

An overview of the manner in which the expedition against Ibn Abī l-Ḥuqayq has been depicted in Western biographies on Muḥammad and of what sources they used reveals a fundamental weakness of all of these books: They lack a sound source-critical foundation. The reports of different sources are treated as equal, and no attempts are made to date them or to explore their *Sitz im Leben*.

Some of the reports on the murder of Ibn Abī l-Ḥuqayq as contained in Muslim sources have been discussed in two articles, both of which were published in 1986. In one of them, G.D. Newby mentions that there are different accounts of the event preserved in Ibn Hishām's *Sīra*, al-Ṭabarī's *Taʾrīkh*, Ibn Saʿd's *Ṭabaqāt* and al-Wāqidī's

[6] A. Sprenger, *Das Leben und die Lehre des Moḥammad*, Berlin, 1861-65, III, 235-36; W. Muir, *The Life*, 348-49; H. Grimme, *Mohammed, I, Das Leben*, Münster, 1892, 94; D.S. Margoliouth, *Moḥammed and the Rise of Islam*, New York/London, 1905, 336; E. Dermenghem, *The Life of Mahomet*, London, 1930, 216-18; M. Gaudefroy-Demombynes, *Mahomet*, [2]Paris, 1969, 143; W.M. Watt, *Muhammad at Medina*, Oxford, 1956, 213.

Maghāzī and lists a few differences.[7] He then expounds the thesis that some details, which are only narrated in al-Wāqidī's version, indicate "that the raid took place during one of the Seder nights of Pesaḥ"[8] and that with this account "we glimpse the ways that the Jews of Khaybar, and probably the rest of the Ḥijāz, practised Passover".[9] According to Newby, the narrative preserved by al-Wāqidī has to be regarded as a trustworthy tradition because "the material makes reasonable internal sense in light of the network of information we already have",[10] i.e., about Jewish ritual practices of the time.

In the other article, J.N. Mattock translates four narratives on the event preserved by al-Ṭabarī, Ibn Hishām and al-Wāqidī and studies them as literary texts, discussing the points which he considers to be inconsistent or implausible or which may seem to be obscure.[11] His approach is much more sophisticated than Newby's superficial comparison of the variants. As a result, he qualifies the different versions as "perfunctory", "more coherent", "the most sophisticated", "something of a black comedy" or the like. He eventually touches upon the question of authenticity. His conclusion, based on a comparison of all four reports, is that "none of these accounts is authentic" and that "it is practically impossible to judge which may approximate most closely to the truth".[12] As far as the version of al-Wāqidī is concerned, Mattock comes to the opposite conclusion of Newby. He regards the details which al-Wāqidī's version alone displays as "explanatory matter", added "with an eye to obtaining the most dramatic effect possible" or "simply because it was needed".[13] The presence of common elements in several and even in all versions speaks, according to his view, in favor of an archetype of the story which must have existed and "from which the extant versions derive, at various removes".[14]

The research which has been done so far on the stories relating the

---

[7] G.D. Newby, "The *Sīrah* as a Source for Arabian Jewish History: Problems and Perspectives", in *JSAI*, 7 (1986), 131-32.

[8] Newby, "The *Sīrah*", 133. This date is based, however, on a questionable reading of the expression *fī khamar al-nās* as *fī khamr al-nās*. See below, p. 209.

[9] Newby, "The *Sīrah*", 135.

[10] Newby, "The *Sīrah*", 138.

[11] J.N. Mattock, "History and Fiction", in *OPSAS*, 1 (1986), 80-97.

[12] Mattock, "History and Fiction", 95.

[13] Mattock, "History and Fiction", 95, 96.

[14] Mattock, "History and Fiction", 96.

murder of Ibn Abī l-Ḥuqayq can be described as perfunctory at best. In the biographies of Muḥammad written by Western scholars, one or all of the narrations are accepted as reports of historical facts, without bothering about the differences between them. Among the few attempts to analyze them, Newby neglects most of the versions in favor of one, without giving his reasons for this, whereas Mattock does not wonder about the fact that some versions resemble each other more than others, and he does not ask where the supposed archetype may have come from. The *isnād*s of the traditions in question have been completely neglected. To fill this gap, a thorough *isnād-cum-matn* analysis of them will be presented.

The aim of the *isnād-cum-matn* analysis is to trace the transmission history of a tradition by comparing their variants contained in the different compilations of traditions available. The method makes use of both the text (*matn*) and the chain of transmitters (*isnād*). It is thus a prerequisite of the method that there be variants of the tradition in question and that they be equipped with *isnād*s. The method proceeds from several premises: 1) Variants of a tradition are (at least partially) the result of a process of transmission. 2) The *isnād*s of the variants reflect (at least partially) the actual paths of transmission. The first premise is based on the observation that textual variants of a *ḥadīth* often reveal more or less clearly an original text from which they derive. In the case of traditions with many variants it is even possible to arrange them into stemmas. The second premise follows from the experience that the different chains of transmission belonging to one and the same tradition more often than not have common links above the level of the authority to whom the tradition allegedly goes back. 3) A further premise of the *isnād-cum-matn* analysis is that cases in which the textual affinity correlates with the common links in the *isnād*s are most probably instances of real transmission. If the *isnād*s, however, give the impression of a relationship between variants but the respective texts do not show it, it is to be concluded that either the *isnād*s and/or the texts of the traditions are faulty, either from the carelessness of transmitters or because of intentional changes.

The method of *isnād-cum-matn* analysis which I used in the following investigation consisted of several steps. 1) As many variants as possible equipped with an *isnād* (or fragments of it) were collected. 2) The lines of transmission were compiled in order to detect their common links in the different generations of transmitters. On the basis of the results, first hypotheses on the transmission history were formulated. 3) The texts of the variants were compared in order to establish relationships and differences between them concerning structure and wording. This also allowed the formulation of statements about their transmission history. 4) The results of *isnād* and *matn* analyses were compared. At this point conclusions with regard to the transmission history of the tradition in question could be drawn: an approximate date from when the tradition in question must have been in circulation, who were the earliest transmitters, how did the text change in the course of transmission and who was responsible for it, etc.[15]

Such a detailed analysis of *isnād*s and *matn*s runs the risk of being boring for the reader. The alternative, however, would be to maintain that a *ḥadīth* goes back to a certain time, region or persons, or that some variants are unreliable, without presenting sufficient proof for it.

II. *Isnād* Analysis

When looking at the *isnād*s of the different traditions dealing with the murder of Ibn Abī l-Ḥuqayq, it becomes clear that there are four different groups of transmission. One goes back to the Companion of the Prophet al-Barāʾ b. ʿĀzib, another stops at a son (or grandson) of the Companion Kaʿb b. Mālik, a third has the Companion ʿAbd Allāh b. Unays as the original transmitter of the story, and a fourth has a common link in the Egyptian scholar Ibn Lahīʿa (d. 174/790-1) but purports to go back to the Successor ʿUrwa b. al-Zubayr. Let us deal with them one by one.

The tradition of al-Barāʾ

Variants of this version equipped with an *isnād* are to be found in five sources: al-Bukhārī's *al-Jāmiʿ al-ṣaḥīḥ*, al-Ṭabarī's *Taʾrīkh al-rusul wa-l-mulūk*, al-Rūyānī's *Musnad*, al-Bayhaqī's *al-Sunan al-kubrā* and his *Da-*

---

[15] The functioning and methodological implications of this type of *ḥadīth* analysis are described in more detail in two of my recent articles: "*Quo vadis Ḥadīṯ*-Forschung? Eine kritische Untersuchung von G.H.A. Juynboll: 'Nāfiʿ the *mawlā* of Ibn ʿUmar, and His Position in Muslim *Ḥadīth* Literature'", in *Der Islam*, 73 (1996), 40-80; and "The Prophet and the Cat. On Dating Mālik's *Muwaṭṭaʾ* and Legal Traditions", in *JSAI*, 22 (1998), 18-83; and by G. Schoeler in his *Charakter und Authentie der muslimischen Überlieferung über das Leben Mohammeds*, Berlin/New York, 1996.

lā'il al-nubuwwa (see diagram 1 on p. 237).[16] Al-Bukhārī gives five variants, three detailed and two short ones. The three long traditions go back to three different transmitters, Yūsuf [b. Isḥāq], Isrā'īl [b. Yūnus] and Zakariyyā' b. Abī Zā'ida,[17] who all have Abū Isḥāq [al-Sabīʿī] as their informant. The latter allegedly transmits the story from al-Barā'. Abū Isḥāq is the common link in this *isnād* bundle.[18] Isrā'īl, one of the three transmitters from Abū Isḥāq, is what G.H.A. Juynboll terms "a partial common link". He is a grandson of Abū Isḥāq and known for his expertise concerning the traditions of his grandfather. Three transmission lines go via him: that of Muṣʿab b. al-Miqdām contained in al-Ṭabarī's *Ta'rīkh*, that of Muḥammad b. Sābiq preserved in al-Bayhaqī's *Sunan* and that of ʿUbayd Allāh b. Mūsā[19] which is not only to be found in al-Bukhārī's *Jāmiʿ* but also in al-Bayhaqī's *Dalā'il*. The latter gives in his *Sunan* an additional transmission line and notes the most important differences between ʿUbayd Allāh's tradition and that of Muḥammad b. Sābiq.

The short versions display a peculiarity. They have a partial common link in Yaḥyā b. Ādam with the following *isnād*: Yaḥyā b. Abī Zā'ida *ʿan abīhi ʿan* Abī Isḥāq, etc.[20] This Yaḥyā b. Abī Zā'ida is, however, no one other than Yaḥyā b. Zakariyyā' b. Abī Zā'ida and his father is not Abū Zā'ida, but the same Zakariyyā' from whom al-Bukhārī has also a complete tradition. This suggests that Yaḥyā b. Ādam (d. 203/818-9) is the one who is to be held responsible for the shortened version of the al-Barā' tradition.

The different transmission lines display, in addition, several family connections: Isrā'īl [b. Yūnus] and Yūsuf [b. Isḥāq] transmit from their grandfather Abū Isḥāq, Yūsuf's version continues via his son Ibrāhīm and that of Zakariyyā' via his son Yaḥyā. A transmission line

---

[16] Bukhārī, *Jāmiʿ*, 56:155 (3022, 3023); 64:16 (4038-40); Ṭabarī, *Ta'rīkh*, prima series, III, 1375-77; Rūyānī, *Musnad*, I, 215-16; Bayhaqī, *Sunan*, IX, 80, 81; *Dalā'il*, IV, 34-38.

[17] Yūsuf b. Isḥāq (d. 157/774) was the grandson of Abū Isḥāq al-Sabīʿī: Ibn Ḥajar, *Tahdhīb*, XI, 408-09; Isrā'īl b. Yūnus (d. 160/776-7, 161/777-8 or 162/778-9) was another grandson of Abū Isḥāq: Ibn Ḥajar, *Tahdhīb*, I, 261-63; Zakariyyā' b. Abī Zā'ida (d. 147/764-5, 148/765-6 or 149/766-7): Ibn Ḥajar, *Tahdhīb*, III, 329-30. All three were Kūfans.

[18] Abū Isḥāq ʿAmr b. ʿAbd Allāh al-Sabīʿī (d. 126/743-4 or 127/744-5), Kūfan: Ibn Ḥajar, *Tahdhīb*, VIII, 63-67; Dhahabī, *Tadhkira*, I, 114-16.

[19] ʿUbayd Allāh b. Mūsā al-ʿAbsī (d. 213/828-9), Kūfan: Dhahabī, *Tadhkira*, I, 353-54.

[20] Bayhaqī, *Dalā'il*, IV, 34 has only "Ibn Abī Zā'ida".

not recorded by al-Bukhārī is that of Sharīk contained in al-Rūyānī's *Musnad*.[21]

From the fact that Abū Isḥāq is the common link in the *isnād* bundle we can provisionally conclude that the tradition about the murder of Ibn Abī l-Ḥuqayq which is connected with the name of the Companion al-Barāʾ as original transmitter, spread in Kūfa in the first quarter of the second century by Abū Isḥāq al-Sabīʿī (d. 126/743-4 of 127/744-5).

The tradition of Ibn Kaʿb

Variants of the tradition which report the attack on Ibn Abī l-Ḥuqayq on the authority of a son (or grandson) of the Companion Kaʿb b. Mālik and which are provided with an *isnād* are found in a number of sources: Mālik's *Muwaṭṭaʾ*, al-Shāfiʿī's *Umm*, ʿAbd al-Razzāq's *Muṣannaf*, al-Ḥumaydī's *Musnad*, Saʿīd b. Manṣūr's *Sunan*, Ibn Hishām's *Sīra*, Ibn Shabba's *Taʾrīkh al-Madīna*, al-Ṭabarī's *Taʾrīkh al-rusul wa-l-mulūk*, al-Ṭabarānī's *al-Muʿjam al-kabīr* and al-Bayhaqī's *al-Sunan al-kubrā* and *Dalāʾil al-nubuwwa*.[22]

As in the case of the al-Barāʾ tradition, there are versions with a short *matn* and others with a detailed one. In compiling an *isnād* bundle from all the variants (see diagram 2 on p. 238),[23] a common link appears on the level above the alleged original transmitter Ibn Kaʿb. This common link is the well-known Medinan scholar Ibn Shihāb al-Zuhrī (d. 124/742). As many as seven transmitters allege to have the story from him: Mālik b. Anas, Sufyān b. ʿUyayna, Maʿmar b. Rāshid, Ibn Jurayj, Ibn Isḥāq, Mūsā b. ʿUqba[24] and Ibrāhīm b.

---

[21] Sharīk b. ʿAbd Allāh (d. 177/786-7), Kūfan: Dhahabī, *Tadhkira*, I, 232-33.

[22] Mālik, *Muwaṭṭaʾ* (Yaḥyā), 21:8; Shāfiʿī, *Umm*, IV, 239 (*K. al-Ḥukm fī qitāl al-mushrikīn wa-masʾalat māl al-ḥarbī*); ʿAbd al-Razzāq, *Muṣannaf*, V, 407-10 (9747), 202 (9385); Ibn Hishām, *Sīra*, 714-16; Saʿīd b. Manṣūr, *Sunan*, III/2, 281 (2627); Ḥumaydī, *Musnad*, II, 385 (874); Ibn Shabba, *Taʾrīkh*, II, 467; Ṭabarī, *Taʾrīkh*, prima series, III, 1378-80; Ṭabarānī, *al-Muʿjam al-kabīr*, XIX, 75 (150); Bayhaqī, *Sunan*, IX, 77, 78; idem, *Dalāʾil*, IV, 33-4, 38-9.

[23] Several variants of this tradition have already been studied by N. van der Voort in her unpublished M.A. thesis "Zoektocht naar de waarheid met behulp van het *Kitāb al-Maghāzī* in de *Muṣannaf* van ʿAbd ar-Razzāq b. Hammām aṣ-Ṣanʿānī (gest. 211/827)", Nijmegen/TCMO 1996, 67-100. I shall use some of her findings.

[24] Al-Zuhrī's name is lacking in the *isnād* given in Bayhaqī's *Dalāʾil*, but this seems to be due to the carelessness of a transmitter, because later in the text, Ibn Shihāb al-Zuhrī's name is mentioned.

Saʿd, all of them scholars connected with Medina or Mecca. Among these transmitters from al-Zuhrī, four are partial common links: Ibn Isḥāq by virtue of three transmitters (al-Bakkāʾī, Salama [b. al-Faḍl], Muḥammad[25] b. Salama), Maʿmar by virtue of two (ʿAbd al-Razzāq, ʿAbd Allāh b. al-Mubārak), Mūsā b. ʿUqba by virtue of two (Muḥammad b. Fulayḥ, Ismāʿīl b. Ibrāhīm b. ʿUqba) and Sufyān [b. ʿUyayna] by virtue of five (al-Shāfiʿī, al-Ḥumaydī, Saʿīd b. Manṣūr, ʿAlī b. al-Madīnī, al-Ḥasan b. Muḥammad al-Zaʿfarānī).

It should be pointed out that there are unusual differences with regard to the original informant of the story, from whom al-Zuhrī allegedly heard it. According to one of the transmissions of ʿAbd al-Razzāq from Maʿmar as well as that of Muḥammad b. Salama from Ibn Isḥāq, the name of al-Zuhrī's informant was ʿAbd al-Raḥmān b. Kaʿb b. Mālik; according to al-Bakkāʾī's, Ibn Bukayr's and Salama's versions from Ibn Isḥāq, however, it was ʿAbd Allāh b. Kaʿb b. Mālik, i.e., his brother. Muḥammad b. Sulaymān's transmission from Ibrāhīm b. Saʿd, that of ʿAbd Allāh b. al-Mubārak from Maʿmar and that of ʿAbd al-Razzāq from Ibn Jurayj give ʿAbd al-Raḥmān b. ʿAbd Allāh b. Kaʿb b. Mālik. All transmissions from Sufyān b. ʿUyayna and Mūsā b. ʿUqba, and a second transmission of ʿAbd al-Razzāq from Maʿmar, give only Ibn Kaʿb b. Mālik, as does Mālik b. Anas according to most of his pupils. The latter add, however, that Mālik hesitated over the name of this Ibn Kaʿb given by al-Zuhrī. According to the majority of Mālik's pupils, Mālik thought that al-Zuhrī called him ʿAbd al-Raḥmān; al-Qaʿnabī reports that Mālik had hesitated between ʿAbd Allāh and ʿAbd al-Raḥmān; Mālik's pupil al-Walīd b. Muslim has only ʿAbd al-Raḥmān, and another of Mālik's pupils, ʿAbd Allāh b. Wahb, has only "a son (or descendant: *ibn*) of Kaʿb b. Mālik" without mentioning any doubt on Mālik's part.[26] Only three of the transmissions provide an additional earlier person as the original informant: The versions from Sufyān have "his [Ibn Kaʿb b. Mālik's] paternal uncle",[27] that of Ibn Jurayj gives the *isnād* "from his

[25] In the edition of Ibn Shabba's *Taʾrīkh al-Madīna*, the name Ḥammād b. Salama is given. This must be an error by a transmitter. See the biographies of Ḥammād b. Salama, Muḥammad b. Salama and Muḥammad b. Isḥāq in Ibn Ḥajar's *Tahdhīb*.

[26] For the different *isnāds* of Mālik's pupils, see Ibn ʿAbd al-Barr, *Istidhkār*, XIV, 56.

[27] That the sons of Kaʿb b. Mālik transmitted from their paternal uncle is not attested anywhere else—as far as I know. Probably, with "Ibn Kaʿb" Sufyān meant ʿAbd al-Raḥmān b. ʿAbd Allāh b. Kaʿb, who transmitted from his uncle ʿAbd al-Raḥmān b. Kaʿb b. Mālik. In this case, the *isnād* remains *mursal*.

[ʿAbd al-Raḥmān b. ʿAbd Allāh b. Kaʿb's] father from his paternal uncle [ʿAbd al-Raḥmān b. Kaʿb] from Kaʿb [b. Mālik], and al-Walīd b. Muslim, one of Mālik's pupils, mentions Kaʿb b. Mālik as well. In view of the majority of the transmissions from al-Zuhrī, these singular ones have to be considered as attempts of Sufyān, Ibn Jurayj and al-Walīd to improve al-Zuhrī's *isnād* which stops at the Successor's level, i.e., it is *mursal* according to the terminology of *ḥadīth* experts.

The same confusion is also found in al-Zuhrī's transmission from the Kaʿb family in general. There are traditions which are ascribed to each of the three members of the Kaʿb b. Mālik family, to ʿAbd al-Raḥmān, ʿAbd Allāh and ʿAbd al-Raḥmān b. ʿAbd Allāh.[28] In addition, ʿAbd al-Raḥmān b. Kaʿb is said to have transmitted from his brother ʿAbd Allāh,[29] so that ʿAbd al-Raḥmān *ibn* ʿAbd Allāh can sometimes also be a distortion of ʿAbd al-Raḥmān *ʿan* ʿAbd Allāh. Some critical *ḥadīth* scholars contested, however, that al-Zuhrī heard ʿAbd al-Raḥmān b. Kaʿb and claimed that he had the traditions of the Kaʿb family from ʿAbd al-Raḥman's nephew ʿAbd al-Raḥmān b. ʿAbd Allāh.[30] In the case of the story about the murder of Ibn Abī l-Ḥuqayq, the confusion among the transmitters from al-Zuhrī and their pupils about the identity of the person from whom he actually had it, speaks in favor of the conclusion that al-Zuhrī himself was not always clear on this point and may have sometimes called his informant ʿAbd al-Raḥmān, and at other times ʿAbd Allāh or even only Ibn Kaʿb b. Mālik. Later, the transmitters had to guess and tried to give an answer themselves. The issue of which member of the Kaʿb b. Mālik family the informant actually was, is, in the end, not so important because the *isnād* does not go back to an eyewitness anyway. What matters is that, according to al-Zuhrī, the information originates from the Kaʿb b. Mālik family. I shall return to this issue at the end of the *matn* analysis. For the moment, it suffices to single out al-Zuhrī (d. 124/742) as the undeniable common link of this *isnād* bundle; al-Zuhrī was a key figure in spreading the story connected with the name of a grandson or son of the Companion Kaʿb b. Mālik at Medina and Mecca.

---

[28] See e.g. the transmissions from them in Ibn Hishām's *Sīra*.

[29] Ibn Ḥajar, *Tahdhīb*, VI, 259.

[30] Ibn Ḥajar, *Tahdhīb*, VI, 259. See also M. Lecker, "Wāqidī's Account on the Status of the Jews of Medina: A Study of a Combined Report", in *JNES*, 54 (1995), 16-18.

The tradition of ʿAbd Allāh b. Unays

From this version there are only a few variants left. A detailed text and a fragment is to be found in al-Wāqidī's *Maghāzī*, another version in al-Ṭabarī's *Ta'rīkh*[31] and a third in al-Ḥākim al-Nīsābūrī's *Iklīl* from which only a few quotations are available.[32] We have thus only two variants and a fragment at our disposal. Al-Wāqidī gives the following *isnāds*:[33]

Abū Ayyūb b. al-Nuʿmān—his father—ʿAṭiyya b. ʿAbd Allāh b. Unays—his father.

The fragment which al-Wāqidī adds at the end of this version has the *isnād*:

Ayyūb b. al-Nuʿmān—Khārija b. ʿAbd Allāh [b. Unays].

These *isnāds* for two variants of the same tradition seem odd. Ayyūb b. al-Nuʿmān is often quoted by al-Wāqidī as the informant of transmissions from his father. His full name is Ayyūb b. al-Nuʿmān b. ʿAbd Allāh b. Kaʿb b. Mālik.[34] The name Abū Ayyūb b. al-Nuʿmān, on the contrary, is only found twice in al-Wāqidī's *Maghāzī*, every time as a transmitter from his father. I assume that "Abū Ayyūb" is a transmission error. The first name of the first *isnād* has probably to be emended to Ayyūb b. al-Nuʿmān and the second *isnād* has to be added to: Ayyūb b. al-Nuʿmān—his father—Khārija b. ʿAbd Allāh—his father.[35]

Al-Ṭabarī gives the *isnād*:[36]

Mūsā b. ʿAbd al-Raḥmān al-Masrūqī and ʿAbbās b. ʿAbd al-ʿAẓīm al-ʿAnbarī—Jaʿfar b. ʿAwn—Ibrāhīm b. Ismāʿīl—Ibrāhīm b. ʿAbd al-Raḥmān[37] b. Kaʿb b. Mālik—his father—his mother, the daughter of ʿAbd Allāh b. Unays—ʿAbd Allāh b. Unays.[38]

---

[31] In addition, there is an allusion to it in Bayhaqī's *Dalā'il*, IV, 34.

[32] See Ibn Ḥajar, *Fatḥ al-bārī*, VII, 434-36.

[33] Wāqidī, *Maghāzī*, I, 391-95.

[34] See for instance Wāqidī, *Maghāzī*, II, 441.

[35] ʿAṭiyya is mentioned in biographical sources as a son of ʿAbd Allāh b. Unays, but Khārija is not. The latter name is perhaps a corruption and should be read Ḍamra. See Ibn Ḥajar, *Tahdhīb*, V, 149-51; Ibn Ḥibbān, *Thiqāt*, V, 262.

[36] Ṭabarī, *Ta'rīkh*, prima series, III, 1381-83.

[37] One of the manuscripts of al-Ṭabarī's *Ta'rīkh* adds "b. ʿAbd Allāh" (see note i of the editor on p. 1381). But it is more probable that a daughter of Ibn Unays was the mother of ʿAbd al-Raḥmān b. Kaʿb than of ʿAbd al-Raḥmān b. ʿAbd Allāh b. Kaʿb.

[38] Jaʿfar b. ʿAwn (d. 197/812-3, 206/821-2 or 207/822-3), Kūfan: Ibn Ḥajar, *Tahdhīb*, II, 101; Ibrāhīm b. Ismāʿīl is to be identified as Ibn Mujammiʿ b. Yazīd, a Medinan student of among others al-Zuhrī, who is considered unreliable: Ibn Ḥajar,

In the transmission complex constituted by the versions of al-Wāqidī and al-Ṭabarī (see diagram 3 on p. 239), the common link seems to be the Companion ʿAbd Allāh b. Unays (d. 54/674).[39] The transmitters from him are three of his children. The *isnād*s are in the lower part Medinan, and in the upper part Kūfan and Baṣran (at least that of al-Ṭabarī, and perhaps that of al-Wāqidī, too). Moreover, members of the Kaʿb b. Mālik family are to be found as transmitters in both *isnād*s.

The tradition of ʿUrwa

This account on the expedition against Ibn Abī l-Ḥuqayq is not well documented in the sources. There is only a single transmission line available. The common link is Ibn Lahīʿa (d. 174/790-1).

Ibn Lahīʿa—Abū l-Aswad—ʿUrwa b. al-Zubayr.[40]

III. *Matn* Analysis

Analyzing the *isnād*s of all the variants which report, in some form or another, the murder of Ibn Abī l-Ḥuqayq, has given us a clue how to classify the different versions. With the identification of common links and partial common links, a first step towards dating the transmission groups has been made, but certainty of their origin and development cannot be gained from the transmission lines alone. The dating can be improved and made safer by a thorough analysis of the texts, and by combining those results with that of the *isnād* scrutiny. Several

---

Tahdhīb, I, 105-06. A son with the name of Ibrāhīm is not quoted as a transmitter from his father ʿAbd al-Raḥmān b. Kaʿb, only a son named Kaʿb (see Ibn Ḥajar, *Tahdhīb,* VI, 259. According to W. Caskel, *Ǧamharat an-nasab. Das genealogische Werk des Hišām ibn Muḥammad al-Kalbī,* Leiden, 1966, I, 190, ʿAbd al-Raḥmān had a son called Bashīr), nor a son called Ibrāhīm as transmitter of ʿAbd al-Raḥmān b. ʿAbd Allāh b. Kaʿb b. Mālik (see Ibn Ḥajar, *Tahdhīb,* VI, 214-15) who is often confused with his uncle. This does not necessarily mean that they had no sons of that name. A daughter of ʿAbd Allāh b. Unays named Khalda is mentioned in an *isnād* of another tradition going back to her father (see Ibn Ḥajar, *Iṣāba,* IV, 37-38 (4041), but not as transmitter from him in the biographical entry of her father in Ibn Ḥajar, *Tahdhīb,* V, 149-51.

[39] According to others, but less probable, in the year 80. Ibn Ḥajar, *Tahdhīb,* V, 150.

[40] ʿUrwa's tradition is preserved in Bayhaqī, *Dalāʾil,* IV, 38 and fragments of it in Dhahabī, *Taʾrīkh,* I, 345 and Ibn Ḥajar, *Fatḥ,* VII, 435. The latter mentions this tradition only *min ṭarīq* al-Aswad [*sic*] *ʿan* ʿUrwa.

recent studies[41] have shown that *isnād*s are not always arbitrary, as has often been assumed due to the misinterpretation of the ideas of J. Schacht, but may reflect the transmission history of the texts with which they are connected. These studies have illustrated that the *matn* variants of an *isnād* bundle have recognizable common elements which appear in all its different versions. This typical kernel goes back, at least, to the person who forms the common link in the *isnād* bundle. The question as to whether some of these textual elements are older than the common link can only be answered by a comparison of versions going back to different common links reporting on the same event. This is the case here. Consequently, we can use the texts about the murder of Ibn Abī l-Ḥuqayq as a test to see what results a neat textual analysis of *maghāzī* traditions can produce and whether historical conclusions can be deduced from it. The first step of textual analysis must be the comparison of the variants which belong to one and the same *isnād* bundle; the second step will be a comparison of the *matn*s belonging to the different *isnād* bundles.

The tradition of al-Barāʾ

The oldest collection known to me containing reports about the murder of Ibn Abī l-Ḥuqayq transmitted on the authority of al-Barāʾ b. ʿĀzib is al-Bukhārī's *al-Jāmiʿ al-ṣaḥīḥ*. Of the three detailed versions he presents, the one transmitted by Isrāʾīl from Abū Isḥāq is the most suitable as a starting point for textual analysis since it has variants in other sources. The tradition reads:

> Yūsuf b. Mūsā—ʿUbayd Allāh b. Mūsā—Isrāʾīl—Abū Isḥāq—al-Barāʾ b. ʿĀzib. He said:
>
> The Messenger of God sent people of the Anṣār to the Jew Abū Rāfiʿ. He gave the command to ʿAbd Allāh b. ʿAtīk. Abū Rāfiʿ had hurt (*yuʾdhī*) the Prophet and had assisted [his enemies] against him (*yuʿīnu ʿalayhi*). He lived in one of his fortresses in the Ḥijāz. When they came near it—the sun was setting and people were returning (going) with their pasturing cattle (*sarḥ*)—ʿAbd Allāh said to his companions: "Sit down here. I will go and talk friendly with the gatekeeper, so that perhaps I can enter." He went on until he came near the gate. Then he concealed his face as if he was going about his business. People entered and the gatekeeper called out to him: "Servant of God! If you wish to enter, do it [now], because I wish to close the door!" I entered and hid.

[41] Cf. note 15.

After the people had entered, he closed the gate and then he hung the keys (*aghālīq*) on a pin (*watid/wadd*[42]). I reached for the keys (*aqālīd*), took them and opened the gate. An evening party was taking place (*yusmaru ʿindahu*) at [the place of] Abū Rāfiʿ on the upper floor of his [house]. After the people of his party had left, I climbed up to him. Every time I opened a door, I locked it behind me from inside. I said [to myself]: "If people have been alarmed by me they cannot touch me until after I have killed him." Finally, I found him. He was, however, in a dark room (*bayt*) in the midst of his family. I did not know where in the room he was. I said: "Abū Rāfiʿ!" He answered: "Who is there?" I rushed (*ahwaytu*) towards the direction of the voice and gave him a stroke with the sword. I was [too] perplexed/excited (*dahish*) and so could not finish him off. He cried out and I ran out of the room and waited not far away. Then I entered anew and said: "What was the reason for this noise, Abū Rāfiʿ?" He answered: "Damn you! (*li-ummika al-wayl*, literally: Woe unto your mother!). A man in the house just struck me with a sword." When he said it, I gave him a heavy stroke without killing him. Then I plunged the blade (*ẓuba/ḍubayb*)[43] of the sword into his belly until it forced its way right to his back. Now I knew I had killed him. I began to open door after door until I finally arrived at a stair (*daraja*) of his [house]. When I thought that I had reached the ground, I took my feet [off the stair] and fell, although the night was moonlit, breaking my leg. I tied it with my turban and then left. I sat down at the gate and said [to myself]: "I shall not leave this night until I know that I have [really] killed him." When the cock crowed and the announcer of the death (*al-nāʿī*) appeared on the wall and cried: "I announce the death of Abū Rāfiʿ, the merchant of the people of the Ḥijāz," I left, went to my companions and said: "Escape! God has killed Abū Rāfiʿ!" I then went to the Prophet and reported it to him. He said to me: "Show me your foot [*sic*]." I did and he touched it with his hand. Then it was as if I had never had pain in it.[44]

A variant of ʿUbayd Allāh's transmission is preserved in al-Bayhaqī's *Dalāʾil*. It has a combined *isnād*, i.e., it goes back to two different transmitters from ʿUbayd Allāh, namely Isḥāq b. Ibrāhīm and Abū Bakr b. Abī Shayba. The fact that al-Bayhaqī gives only one *matn* means that the versions of both transmitters are almost identical. A comparison of al-Bukhārī's and al-Bayhaqī's versions leads to a simi-

[42] Some manuscripts have *watid*, others *wadd*, see the edition of Ḥassūna al-Nawāwī first published in 1313 (repr. Beirut, n.d.) V, 117. The printed editions which I consulted had *watid*, Ibn Ḥajar's commentary *Fatḥ al-bārī*, V, 432 gives, however, *wadd*.

[43] The manuscripts differ as to the word, see the previous note.

[44] Bukhārī, *Jāmiʿ*, 64:16 (4039).

lar conclusion. The differences are typical copyist errors with one exception: the omission of the words *tājir ahl al-Ḥijāz,* which may have been left out on purpose. ʿUbayd Allāh b. Mūsā allegedly received the tradition from Isrāʾīl. A comparison with another version which is contained in al-Ṭabarī's *Taʾrīkh* and is also said to have come from Isrāʾīl but is transmitted by Muṣʿab b. al-Miqdām, reveals such a correspondence that both texts must derive from a common source by way of written transmission. There are, however, some differences which exclude the possibility that al-Ṭabarī or his informant copied al-Bukhārī's *matn* and provided it with a fabricated *isnād.* There are several additions and omissions in comparison with ʿUbayd Allāh b. Mūsā's text which go beyond normal copyist errors, and even the differences of the latter type are more frequent than in the manuscript tradition of al-Bukhārī's *matn.* Among the most significant additions are: *wa-kāna bi-arḍ al-Ḥijāz, taḥta āriyy ḥimār* and the insertion of *ʿAbd Allāh b. ʿUqba aw* before the name of ʿAbd Allāh b. ʿAtīk in two places.[45] Among the differences are: *yabghī* instead of *yuʿīn, akhrajtuhu min* instead of *akhadha fī* and *rabbāḥ* (or *rubbāḥ*?) in place of *tājir.* The peculiarities of both texts show that they are independent transmissions which go back to a common source which, according to the *isnād,* is the *matn* transmitted by Isrāʾīl.

This conclusion is corroborated by comparison with a third variant which is also said to derive from the latter and is contained in al-Bayhaqī's *al-Sunan al-kubrā.*[46] The transmitter from Isrāʾīl is Muḥammad b. Sābiq. This version corresponds largely to the two preceding ones except for some details. It differs from ʿUbayd Allāh's text, among others, by the additions *wa-kāna yaskunu arḍ al-Ḥijāz* and by *lahum* instead of *li-aṣḥābihi* and several minor differences in which it corresponds to the text of al-Ṭabarī. Additionally, we find variations from both of them such as *fa-nadaba lahu sarāyā* in place of *rijāl, mutaṭalliʿ al-abwāb* instead of *mutalaṭṭif li-l-bawwāb, nazala* in place of *dhahaba, ghayr ṭāʾil* instead of *bi-sayf, jiʾtu* in place of *dakhaltu, thāniyat* instead of *athkhanathu, ḍabāba* in place of *ẓuba* or *ḍabīb,* the insertion of *thumma ntakaytu ʿalayhi...samiʿtuhu* and *ataʿajjal,* and the word *rijlī* in place

[45] Some other additions, such as the frequent insertion of *qāla,* might be of the editorial kind for which al-Ṭabarī himself or one of his informants could be responsible.

[46] Bayhaqī, *Sunan,* IX, 80.

of *sāqī.*[47] In a few details al-Bayhaqī's version corresponds to ʿUbayd Allāh's text against that of al-Ṭabarī, notably in the lack of the name ʿAbd Allāh b. ʿUqba. The insertion of this name seems to derive from al-Ṭabarī or his informant doubting whether the *nasab* of the murderer was ʿAtīk or ʿUqba, their doubt possibly encouraged by bad handwriting. From the substantial correspondences among the three versions, combined with only few differences in wording, we have to conclude that al-Bayhaqī's text is not copied from al-Bukhārī nor al-Ṭabarī. This is corroborated by the fact that al-Bayhaqī also quotes al-Bukhārī's version of ʿUbayd Allāh b. Mūsā in an abridged form[48] noting only the major differences from the version transmitted by Muḥammad b. Sābiq. The three texts are therefore to be regarded as independent transmissions from a common source which, according to the *isnād,* is the transmission of Isrāʾīl from Abū Isḥāq.

There remain three other detailed versions of the tradition in question to be studied: those of Yūsuf b. Isḥāq, Zakariyyāʾ b. Abī Zā'ida and Sharīk. After a mere glance, it is apparent that they differ much more from each other and from Isrāʾīl's *matn* than the variants of the latter.

The version of Yūsuf b. Isḥāq[49] names next to ʿAbd Allāh b. ʿAtīk a certain ʿAbd Allāh b. ʿUtba among the members of the expedition who played, however, no further role. The murderer and actual narrator of what happened is—as in the version of Isrāʾīl—ʿAbd Allāh b. ʿAtīk. In addition, it is reported that the inhabitants of the fortress missed a donkey and that the search for it made it easy for Ibn ʿAtīk to slip into the fortress. He hid in a donkey stable. According to this version, the gatekeeper put the key in a niche (*kuwwa*) whereas in the version of Isrāʾīl he put the keys on a pin (*wadd/watid*). An explanation is given why Ibn ʿAtīk opened the gate of the fortress before looking for Abū Rāfiʿ. The assassin locked the doors of the rooms from outside without giving a reason for this measure, in contrast to the story of Isrāʾīl where he locked the doors through

[47] Some differences displayed in al-Bayhaqī's text in relation to the two others, such as *aqtuluhu* instead of *aqbala,* are clearly "edition" or printing errors.

[48] He knew two versions, one of which was transmitted by Abū Bakr b. Abī Shayba, but is not contained in his *Muṣannaf.*

[49] Bukhārī, *Jāmiʿ,* 64:16 (4040); Bayhaqī, *Dalāʾil,* IV, 35-36. Both versions are almost identical. The variations are typical copying errors with sometimes the addition of the word *qāla.*

which he passed behind him in order to hinder his being pursued before he had attained his goal. The detail that Ibn ʿAtīk left the room after his first unsuccessful attack is not mentioned. An addition is that he changed his voice when starting on the second and third attack and that Abū Rāfiʿ's family got up after the second attack (without further consequences). The description of the assassin's state of mind as *dahish* is placed after the murder was completed, not as an explanation why the first attack failed. He then fell from a ladder (*sullam*), not from a stair (*daraja*),[50] and instead of breaking his lower leg (*inkasarat sāqī*), his foot became dislocated (*inkhalaʿat rijlī*).[51] After the murder, he did not wait by the gate of the fortress until dawn in order to hear the announcement of Abū Rāfiʿ's death, but sent first his companions away to report the success to the Prophet. Later he caught up with them before they had reached the Prophet. There is no mention of the Prophet's healing of the injured foot.

In addition to these major differences between the versions of Isrāʾīl and Yūsuf, there are several variations in wording. The differences, however, cannot blur the fact that the structure of the narration and a substantial portion of the text are identical. From this we can conclude that the two versions are not copied one from the other but must independently derive from a common source.

In Zakariyyāʾ b. Abī Zāʾida's version[52] the name of the assassin and actual narrator of the story is missing. This seems, however, to be due to al-Bukhārī's informant, ʿAlī b. Muslim, because the two abbreviated versions which also go back to Zakariyyāʾ contain the name ʿAbd Allāh b. ʿAtīk.[53] Besides, it is reported that he managed to enter a stable obviously situated inside the fortress and then its gate was locked. Only afterwards did the inhabitants miss a donkey and went out looking for it, and ʿAbd Allāh mingled among them, feigning to be one of them, and later re-entered together with the people. Most of the remainder is similar in structure and choice of words to the version of Yūsuf b. Isḥāq. In some places, however, Zakariyyāʾ's story is shorter or uses other words. The differences between the two versions are such that any dependence on each other is not probable.

[50] *Sullam* and *daraja* may be synonyms.
[51] But the difference is perhaps not all that significant because it already exists in the version of Isrāʾīl in which later the injured "foot" is mentioned.
[52] Bukhārī, *Jāmiʿ*, 56:155 (3022).
[53] Bukhārī, *Jāmiʿ*, 56:155 (3023), 64:16 (4038).

What they have in common must therefore go back to a common source.

Sharīk's version[54] is more like the one by Isrāʾīl but is much shorter. The name of the leader of the expedition is given in the manuscript as ʿAbd Allāh b. Ghaniyya which the editor correctly emended to ʿAbd Allāh b. ʿAtīk. The name of the victim is not given; he is only called "a Jew". There is no change from the third to the first person in the course of the narration as in the other versions. Several little textual variations from Isrāʾīl's version can be observed. Some are simply copyist errors by later transmitters such as *kāna ... yusammī ʿabdahu* instead of *kāna yusmaru ʿindahu,* while others derive from the use of synonyms such as *ʿataba* in place of *daraja*, *ṣulb* instead of *ẓahr*. The differences between the two versions are so many and sometimes so substantial, that it is not conceivable that al-Rūyānī's text is based on that of al-Bukhārī or vice versa. Sharīk's version seems to be another independent transmission from Abū Isḥāq.

Our comparison of *matns*, ascribed to different transmitters who all relate on the authority of Abū Isḥāq, has brought to light that all of them are independent from each other and must go back to a common source which, according to the *isnāds*, must be Abū Isḥāq. Stated differently: The conclusion reached by the analysis of the *isnād* bundle that there is a common link is corroborated by the *matn* analysis; additionally, the *isnād* analysis shows that this common link is Abū Isḥāq. The common link is not artificially created by the so-called "spread of *isnāds*".[55] There is a contrast between the variants deriving from the second generation of transmitters after Abū Isḥāq (e.g. ʿUbayd Allāh b. Mūsā, Muḥammad b. Sābiq and Muṣʿab b. al-Miqdām) in which the differences are small, and those from the first generation (Yūsuf b. Isḥāq, Zakariyyāʾ b. Abī Zāʾida, Isrāʾīl and

---

[54] Rūyānī, *Musnad,* I, 215-16 (300).

[55] "Spread of *isnāds*" means that only one of the transmitters really heard the text from the supposed common link or allegedly did so, and that all others heard it from this one transmitter or from someone who had it taken over from him, concealing, however, their real source and pretending that they had it directly from the informant of the person from whom the text really came. J. Schacht was the first to assert that this had been a usual device by *muḥaddithūn* in order to make a tradition look more trustworthy. See his *The Origins of Muhammadan Jurisprudence,* Oxford, 1950, 166-69 and "On Mūsā b. ʿUqba's *Kitāb al-Maghāzī*", in *Acta Orientalia,* 21 (1953), 295-99. M. Cook has argued in favor of Schacht's assumption in his *Early Muslim Dogma,* Cambridge, 1981, 107-16.

Sharīk) in which the differences among the texts are much more substantial. The reason seems to be that in the generation of Abū Isḥāq's pupils, who received their texts from him in the first quarter of the second Islamic century, the methods of preserving them were not yet as sophisticated as they had become a generation later.

A striking phenomenon is that, on the one hand, the versions of Isrāʾīl and Sharīk resemble each other and, on the other hand, the same is true of the versions of Yūsuf b. Isḥāq and Zakariyyāʾ b. Abī Zāʾida. If my conclusion is correct that the four versions must go back, independently from each other, to a common source, then the difference between the two types of stories (or the correspondence between two of each) must be explained by supposing that Abū Isḥāq related the story in at least two different ways. One version might be his older version (possibly that of Yūsuf and Zakariyyāʾ, both of whom died a little earlier than the other two).

The two short versions transmitted by Yaḥyā b. Ādam via Yaḥyā b. Zakariyyāʾ b. Abī Zāʾida from his father are clearly abbreviations of the latter's detailed *matn*. The text of one of the variants is as follows:

> The Messenger of God sent a group to Abū Rāfiʿ. ʿAbd Allāh b. ʿAtīk entered his house during the night when he was asleep and killed him.[56]

Following the theory of J. Schacht, the shorter versions of a tradition are usually older, the more elaborate ones, younger. Such a generalization is, however, not acceptable. It is unlikely that the whole story was invented on the basis of such a short piece of information. Moreover, the analysis of the *matn*s and the *isnād*s suggests that the short versions are younger.[57] They are summaries serving as arguments for the legal question whether it is allowed to kill an enemy[58] when he is asleep. This is a good example of a legal argument derived relatively late from *maghāzī* traditions.

The gist of the two different types of the story which Abū Isḥāq related on the authority of the Companion al-Barāʾ b. ʿĀzib is the

---

[56] Bukhārī, *Jāmiʿ*, 64:16 (4038). The other variant, *op. cit.*, 56:155 (3023), differs only slightly.

[57] See above p. 176.

[58] Al-Bukhārī gives one of the versions (56:155) under the heading "The killing of a polytheist (*mushrik*) who is asleep". The example is not very convincing since Abū Rāfiʿ was Jewish, a fact not mentioned, however, in the versions collected in the chapter.

following (the versions of Isrāʾīl and Sharīk are labelled A, those of Yūsuf and Zakariyyāʾ are labelled B): The Prophet sent a group of Anṣār under the command of ʿAbd Allāh b. ʿAtīk to Abū Rāfiʿ (his full name is not mentioned), who only in version A is labelled a Jew. The second person, mentioned in two of the variants and called either ʿAbd Allāh b. ʿUqba or ʿAbd Allāh b. ʿUtba, is probably due to a later gloss which reflects uncertainty as to the correct reading of the *nasab* of the murderer.[59] The reason why the expedition was sent against Abū Rāfiʿ and the fact that he lived in one of his fortresses in the Ḥijāz is only given in version A. Ibn ʿAtīk left his companions close by the fortress and managed to enter with the people returning in the evening with their cattle. At this point the narration changes from the third person (narrator: al-Barāʾ) to the first person (narrator: Ibn ʿAtīk) until the end. In version B the theme of how he managed to enter the fortress is more elaborate in reporting that the inhabitants of the fortress missed a donkey and left in the night to search for it. After having entered the fortress, Ibn ʿAtīk first hid and when the party or dinner in Abū Rāfiʿ's house was over and the people had left, he took the key and opened the central gate. Then he went to Abū Rāfiʿ's house or apartment, locking on his way the doors which he went through, according to version A, or the doors of the houses he passed, according to version B. The apartment was on the upper floor and dark inside so that the assassin could not see where his target was. He called him and attacked him with his sword without killing him, left the room and returned soon to attack him again. Eventually, he was able to wound him mortally. On the way back, he missed a step and broke his lower leg (version A) or fell from a ladder and dislocated his foot (version B). After having bandaged it, he left the fortress, waiting close by until the morning when the death of Abū Rāfiʿ was publicly announced (according to version B: after having informed his com-

[59] This is corroborated by the erroneous writing of the name in the manuscript of al-Rūyānī's *Musnad* and by the fact that an Anṣārī Companion with the *ism* ʿAbd Allāh and the *nasab* ibn ʿUqba is unknown and one with the *nasab* ibn ʿUtba seems to be known only from the tradition of al-Bukhārī on the murder of Abū Rāfiʿ, see Ibn Ḥajar, *al-Iṣāba,* IV, 100-01 (4803-05). Probably, Yūsuf b. Isḥāq's transmission (al-Bukhārī, al-Bayhaqī) had originally *aw ʿAbd Allāh b. ʿUtba* instead of *wa-ʿAbd Allāh b. ʿUtba* like Muṣʿab b. al-Miqdām's version from Isrāʾīl, retained by al-Ṭabarī, with the name ʿAbd Allāh b. ʿUqba. Ibn Ḥajar's guess (*Fatḥ,* VII, 434) that by ʿAbd Allāh b. ʿUtba actually ʿAbd Allāh b. Unays, who is mentioned in the tradition of Ibn Kaʿb, is meant, is less convincing.

panions and ordering them to return to the Prophet). Upon reaching Medina, he reported to the Prophet what had happened and (according to version A) the latter healed his injured leg by rubbing it.

According to Abū Isḥāq (d. 126/743-4 or 127/744-5), to whom the different versions of the story go back, he received the story from the Companion al-Barāʾ b. ʿĀzib (d. 72/691-2), a Medinan of the tribe of Aws, on the authority of whom he spread many traditions. This Companion[60] obviously did not participate in the expedition himself but is supposed to have heard a report about it from its leader ʿAbd Allāh b. ʿAtīk who had already died in the battle of al-Yamāma in the year 12/633-4.[61] At that time al-Barāʾ was approximately 24 years old. The veracity of this ascription cannot be substantiated on the basis of this tradition alone. The only thing that can be said at this stage of our analysis is that, assuming the ascription to be true, there are long periods of time between the supposed date when al-Barāʾ heard the story (before the year 10/631-2), the possible reception of it by Abū Isḥāq from al-Barāʾ (between 50/670-1 and 72/691-2)[62] and the transmission of it to Abū Isḥāq's pupils (around 125/742). During these periods the story was probably only preserved by memory and its form changed—even if only slightly—every time it was retold as the two different versions which go back to Abū Isḥāq illustrate.

The tradition of Ibn Kaʿb

For the study of the variants of this tradition I proceed not from the version of Ibn Isḥāq, which is preserved in three different transmissions and is the one best known,[63] but from that of his contemporary Maʿmar b. Rāshid (d. 153/770) as transmitted in ʿAbd al-Razzāq's *Muṣannaf*.[64]

---

[60] On him, see Ibn Ḥajar, *Iṣāba,* I, 147 (615).

[61] On him, see Ibn Ḥajar, *Iṣāba,* IV, 101 (4807).

[62] If the tradition on Abū Isḥāq's birth around the year 33/653-4 can be trusted (which makes him 93 or 94 at the time of his death), he was 39 years old at the time of al-Barāʾ's death.

[63] Translations are available in A. Guillaume, *The Life of Muhammad. A Translation of Ibn Isḥāq's* Sīrat Rasūl Allāh, Oxford, 1955, 482-83; M. McDonald/W. Montgomery Watt, *The Foundation of the Community,* Albany, 1987, 101-03; J.N. Mattock, "History and Fiction", 84-85.

[64] ʿAbd al-Razzāq, *Muṣannaf,* V, 407-10 (9747). The numbers and insertions in brackets are introduced to facilitate comparison with other versions provided below.

ʿAbd al-Razzāq—Maʿmar—al-Zuhrī—ʿAbd al-Raḥmān b. Kaʿb b. Mālik:

{1} Among the things which God did for his Prophet was that these two tribes of the Anṣār, Aws and Khazraj, competed one with the other for (*fī*) Islam like two stallions. Every time the Aws did something, the Khazraj said: "By God, they shall never surpass us with it in merit for Islam!" and when the Khazraj did something, the Aws said the same. {2} When the Aws had killed Kaʿb b. al-Ashraf, the Khazraj said: "By God, we shall not rest until we satisfy the Messenger of God as they did." They conferred over the most important person among the Jews and asked the Prophet for permission to kill him—he was Sallām b. Abī l-Ḥuqayq al-Aʿwar Abū Rāfiʿ [who lived] in Khaybar. He [the Prophet] gave them permission to kill him. {3m, 6i} He said [however]: "Don't kill any child or woman!" {4} Among the group (*rahṭ*) which left were: ʿAbd Allāh b. ʿAtīk {5i} who was the leader of the group (*qawm*), {4} one of the Banū Salima, ʿAbd Allāh b. Unays, Masʿūd b. Sinān, Abū Qatāda, Khuzāʿī b. Aswad, a man of Aslam, their confederate, and another man named so-and-so b. Salama. {7} They rode until they arrived at Khaybar. [8i]{9m} When they entered the place (*balad*) they went to each house and locked it from the outside [locking] the inhabitants [in]. [9i]{10} By way of the trunk of a palm in which steps had been cut (*ʿajla*), they then went to him, [who was] in one of his high rooms (*mashraba*). {11} They mounted it [the ladder] and finally knocked at his door. {12} His wife came out and said: "Where do you come from?" {13} They answered: "[We are] a group of Arabs in want of provisions." She said: "This man [shall help you], please come in!" {14} When they entered they locked the door on both [Ibn Abī l-Ḥuqayq and his wife] and on themselves, [15i] {16} then they rushed unto him with their swords. {17} One of them said: "By God, the only thing that guided me towards him in the darkness of the night was his whiteness on the bed, like a cast-off Egyptian garment (*qubṭiyya*)." {18} His wife shouted at us. He said: One of us lifted his sword to hit her with it. At this moment, he remembered the prohibition of the Prophet. (He said:) Otherwise we would have finished her off that night. [19i]{20}He continued: ʿAbd Allāh b. Unays attacked his [Abū Rāfiʿ's] belly with his sword and ran it through it. {21} [...[65] had] poor sight, {22} fell from the ladder and sprained his foot seriously. {23} (He continued:) We descended and carried him with us {24} until we reached one of those water-channels (*manhar ʿayn*)[66] where we stayed. {25} (He continued:) People made fires, lit palm-branches (*saʿaf*) and began to search for us intensively, but God hid our place

[65] The comparison with other versions suggests that several words are missing here, among others the name of ʿAbd Allāh b. ʿAtīk. See below, p. 193.

[66] A subterranean water-channel which was out of use?

> from them. {26} (He continued:) They finally returned. {27} (He continued:) One of our companions said: "Should we leave without knowing whether the enemy of God is dead or not?" (He continued:) One of us went out, mingled with the people and entered with them. {28} He found his [Abū Rāfiʿ's] wife bent [over him] with a lamp in her hand {29m} and the Jews around him. One of them said: "By God, I certainly heard the voice of Ibn ʿAtīk; but then I convinced myself of the contrary saying to myself: 'How [can] Ibn ʿAtīk be in this country!'" {30} She said something and then lifted her head, saying: "By the God of the Jews [i.e., the God of Israel], he passed away (*fāẓa*)—she meant he had died. {31} He [the Muslim present] said: "I never heard a word sweeter to me than that. (He continued:) I then went out and reported to my companions that he had died." {32} [The original narrator said:] We carried our companion, went to the Messenger of God and reported to him. {33m} He [Ibn Kaʿb] said: They came to him on Friday when the Prophet stood on the *minbar* preaching. When he saw them he said: "May they [or: you?] be happy" [33i, 34i, 34mʿu].[67]

This text resembles the structure and wording of the version of Ibn Isḥāq which is known from Ibn Hishām's *Sīra*[68] and al-Ṭabarī's *Taʾrīkh*.[69] But whereas these two variants—one transmitted by al-Bakkāʾī (d. 182/798-9 or 183/799-800), the other by Salama b. al-Faḍl (d. 190/805 or 191/806) from Ibn Isḥāq—differ only in minor points which are mostly due to either copyist errors or to some slight editing by the transmitters,[70] a comparison of Maʿmar's version with that of Ibn Isḥāq brings more differences to light. We have here a similar phenomenon as in the case of the al-Barāʾ tradition. The versions going back to the first generation of transmitters after the common link vary more than the variants originating from a partial common link which belongs to that first generation of transmitters. Put another way, we can say that there is a characteristic version of

[67] The comparison with other versions shows that the *matn* is incomplete at the end. See below, pp. 194, 200-01.

[68] Ibn Hishām, *Sīra*, 714-15.

[69] Ṭabarī, *Taʾrīkh*, prima series, III, 1378-80.

[70] See the list of variations in N. van der Voort, "Zoektocht", pp. 86-88. Even the few differences which seem to be of a more substantial type can be explained as copying errors, such as *al-bayt* in place of *al-layl*, *yaduhu* instead of *rijluhu*, *al-ʿiẓām* in place of *al-ṭaʿām* and *thamāniya* instead of *khamsa*. In the latter case, the argument of de Goeje, the editor of al-Ṭabarī's *Taʾrīkh*, against the correction to *khamsa* is not convincing. Ibn Khaldūn, or a transmitter between al-Ṭabarī and him, could have inserted *minhum* in order to remove the contradiction between the numeral eight and the five names of the participants actually given.

Ibn Isḥāq which differs to a certain degree from that of Maʿmar. In what follows, I shall sum up the most notable differences between both texts.

Maʿmar's introduction to the story in which the antecedents of the expedition are related is somewhat shorter and more concise than that of Ibn Isḥāq and there is no repetition of narrative elements such as *wa-llāhi lā tadhhabūna bi-hā/dhihi*[71] *abadan faḍlan ʿalaynā*. Additionally, some narrative elements appear in other places of the text. The prohibition to kill children and women is mentioned in the introduction, whereas Ibn Isḥāq introduces it at the beginning of the narrative of the expedition itself.[72] Two of the names of the participants are mentioned in another sequence, one name is shortened in Maʿmar's *matn* and, most oddly, one is added in the vague form "*fulān* b. Salama", though in Ibn Isḥāq's version it is explicitly stated that they had been five in number.[73]

As in the introductory part, Maʿmar's account of the expedition is more concise; there is, for example, no repetition of elements such as mentioning twice that the wife of Abū Rāfiʿ cried. In Ibn Isḥāq's version the narrative changes suddenly from the third to the first person when the assassins enter Abū Rāfiʿ's house. In Maʿmar's version the change is introduced by the direct speech of one of the assassins which makes this change smoother. As already indicated in the translation, there seems to be a gap in Maʿmar's text which the reader only perceives after comparison with other versions. The text of ʿAbd al-Razzāq's *Muṣannaf* reads: "ʿAbd Allāh b. Unays ran his sword through Abū Rāfiʿ's belly, had poor sight and fell from the ladder." According to Ibn Isḥāq's *matn*, however, it was ʿAbd Allāh b. ʿAtīk who had the poor sight and who fell from the ladder when the assassins left the flat. Since Maʿmar's text in its actual form is grammatically defective and also the tradition of al-Barāʾ relates that Ibn ʿAtīk injured his foot, Ibn Isḥāq's version is to be preferred. The missing text, which represents roughly one line, was in all probability overlooked by a copyist.

---

[71] A variation in Ibn Hishām's and al-Ṭabarī's text.

[72] In many details Maʿmar's version corresponds with the text contained (without *isnād*) in Ibn Ḥibbān, *Thiqāt*, I, 246-48.

[73] The mystery of this additional name will be unveiled below.

According to al-Bakkāʾī's transmission from Ibn Isḥāq, preserved in Ibn Hishām's *Sīra*, Ibn ʿAtīk sprained his hand (*wuthiʾat yaduhu wathʾan shadīdan*).[74] Salama b. al-Faḍl's variant contained in al-Ṭabarī's *Taʾrīkh*, however, has *rijluhu*, his foot, instead, and this is also Maʿmar's text.[75] The correspondence between Maʿmar's *matn* and Salama's transmission from Ibn Isḥāq in the word *rijl* suggests that this is the original text and that *yad* is an error by al-Bakkāʾī. This is corroborated by the context of the story as well, since it is reported that Ibn ʿAtīk's companions carried him away—which makes no sense if he had sprained his hand.

After the inhabitants of Khaybar had become aware of the attack on Abū Rāfiʿ, they started to look for the assassins, the story continues. In this context Maʿmar's *matn* displays some additional elements in comparison with that of Ibn Isḥāq in stating that "they lit palm-branches" and that "God hid their place from them". In the episode of the man who returned to Khaybar to assure himself that Abū Rāfiʿ was really dead, Maʿmar's version changes from the third to the first person some lines later than Ibn Isḥāq's text. The latter puts the statement "I heard the voice of Ibn ʿAtīk, etc." into the mouth of Abū Rāfiʿ's wife, which seems more logical than Maʿmar's version in which one of the Jews who surround her speak these words.

At the end of the story there is one more noticeable difference between the two texts. Ibn Isḥāq has the following *matn*:

> "We disputed before him [the Prophet] as to who had killed him, each of us laying claim to it. The Messenger of God said: "Give [me] your swords." He [the original narrator] said: We brought them to him. He looked at them and said: "It is the sword of ʿAbd Allāh b. Unays that killed him; I see the trace of food on it."[76]

In Maʿmar's text as preserved in ʿAbd al-Razzāq's *Muṣannaf*, however, there is no mention of a dispute. It is only narrated in the third person that the assassins reached Medina when Muḥammad stood on the *minbar* preaching and that he welcomed them. Aside from these

[74] This is also said in Ibn Ḥibbān's version. Cf. note 72.

[75] Ibn Hishām pointed out this difference already. See his gloss in Ibn Hishām, *Sīra*, 715.

[76] Ibn Hishām, *Sīra*, 715; Ṭabarī, *Taʾrīkh*, prima series, III, 1380.

major differences, synonyms are used in several places throughout the text.[77]

From a study of all the variations in Maʿmar's and Ibn Isḥāq's texts we can conclude, on the one hand, that one text was not the *Vorlage* of the other. Both texts are, on the other hand, in structure, and for a great part in wording as well, identical. They must therefore derive from a common source which is, according to their *isnād*, al-Zuhrī's narration, the common link of both transmissions. Those parts of the two texts which are identical are obviously al-Zuhrī's *matn*. The differences, insofar as they are not errors by later copyists, originate either from al-Zuhrī's pupils—their power of memory or ability to write down after dictation may not have been the same, or they might have used different means to preserve the texts—or from al-Zuhrī himself, since it is possible that he did not always repeat the text in exactly the same wording.

One may wonder whether the differences could be due to al-Zuhrī's different informants who, in turn, had received the story from the same person. Such an idea could find support in the *isnāds*. As mentioned earlier, Maʿmar's transmission names al-Zuhrī's informant ʿAbd al-Raḥmān b. Kaʿb b. Mālik, while Ibn Isḥāq, on the contrary, names ʿAbd Allāh b. Kaʿb b. Mālik. There are arguments, however, that speak against such an assumption. Both texts correspond to such an extent that they must have been preserved in written form. This can be attributed to al-Zuhrī and his pupils, but hardly to his informants who would have had to have written down the text after having heard it from one of the participants in the expedition or from someone else whose name is not mentioned. Although some information may have been written down in the first century AH, this seems to have been more the exception than the rule. As a rule, it was preserved by memory. I will come back to this issue after the discussion of the remaining versions.

For the comparison between Maʿmar's and Ibn Isḥāq's versions, only the two most complete variants preserved from Ibn Isḥāq have been used. There are, in addition, two shorter ones: that of Yūnus b. Bukayr (d. 199/814-5) preserved in al-Bayhaqī's *Dalāʾil*[78] and that of

[77] A complete list of differences is to be found in N. van der Voort, "Zoektocht", 76-81.

[78] Bayhaqī, *Dalāʾil,* IV, 33-34.

Muḥammad b. Salama (d. 167/783-4) contained in Ibn Shabba's *Taʾrīkh.*[79] Both versions are paraphrases which in several places summarize the original *matn* of Ibn Isḥāq. Ibn Bukayr's text stops with the murder of Ibn Abī l-Ḥuqayq; Muḥammad b. Salama's version narrates the story until the point when the wife of Ibn Abī l-Ḥuqayq says that she recognized the "speech" of one of the assassins. The end of the story is lacking in both texts.

In addition to shortening and paraphrasing, there are other noteworthy differences compared with Ibn Isḥāq's detailed version. In Ibn Salama's text, only four participants in the expedition are mentioned. One of them is called Abyaḍ b. al-Aswad, which seems to be a corruption of Khuzāʿī b. al-Aswad.[80] More interesting than Ibn Salama's defective list of participants is that of Ibn Bukayr, which contains all five names known from Ibn Hishām's and al-Ṭabarī's transmission,[81] albeit in a shortened way, resembling thus the version of Maʿmar, and with the difference that Khuzāʿī b. (al-)Aswad is called al-Aswad b. Khuzāʿī. One could be tempted to conclude that the latter name must be an error made by Ibn Bukayr or a transmitter after him, because two transmitters from Ibn Isḥāq (al-Bakkāʾī, Salama b. al-Faḍl) and one transmitter from al-Zuhrī (Maʿmar) agree that the name was Khuzāʿī b. (al-)Aswad.[82] We shall see below, however, that such a conclusion would be premature. Additionally, Ibn Bukayr states that Ibn Isḥāq thought that "among them" there was a "*fulān* b. Salama". This remark is not to be found in the other transmissions from Ibn Isḥāq, but in Maʿmar's *matn* we came across a similar terminology. We can conclude from this correspondence that this "*fulān* b. Salama" must have already been part of (one of) al-Zuhrī's version(s) and that two transmitters from Ibn Isḥāq left out the incomplete name, or that Ibn Isḥāq only sometimes mentioned that al-Zuhrī had also given this name. In both cases, there remains the contradiction that—according to al-Bakkāʾī's transmission from him, and probably

[79] Ibn Shabba, *Taʾrīkh,* II, 462-63 (the edition erroneously has Ḥammād b. Salama).

[80] See Ibn Isḥāq's text in Ṭabarī, *Taʾrīkh,* III, 1379. Maʿmar's version and that of Ibn Isḥāq in Ibn Hishām's *Sīra* have Khuzāʿī b. Aswad. I wonder whether the edition reproduces the manuscript correctly, since according to Ibn Ḥajar's *Iṣāba,* I, 39 (145), Ḥammād [sic] b. Salama transmitted the name as al-Aswad b. Abyaḍ.

[81] "ʿAbd Allāh b. Anas" in place of "ʿAbd Allāh b. Unays" seems to be a printing error.

[82] Only al-Ṭabarī has "al-Aswad".

originally also according to that of Salama[83]—Ibn Isḥāq clearly stated that there had been five participants in the expedition. As we shall see below, however, this contradiction is only superficial and can be explained.

There are, in addition, some other deviations from Ibn Isḥāq's *matn* as transmitted by al-Bakkāʾī and Salama. In the version of Muḥammad b. Salama, the name of the man who sprained his foot is not given. The man who returned to the place after the attack in order to verify that Abū Rāfiʿ was in fact dead is called ʿAbd Allāh b. Unays, and there is a statement put into the mouth of Abū Rāfiʿ's wife that she heard the voice of ʿAbd Allāh b. Unays, whereas in the text as presented by Maʿmar and Ibn Isḥāq, it is said that she heard the voice of ʿAbd Allāh b. ʿAtīk. "Ibn Unays" seems to be due to a transmission or copyist error. In Ibn Bukayr's variant, the prohibition of the Prophet is expressed by the words "*kāna qad nahāhum rasūl Allāh (ṣ) ḥīna baʿathahum ʿan qatl al-nisāʾ wa-l-wildān*" whereas the other variants, that of Ibn Isḥāq and that of Maʿmar, have "*lā taqtulū walīdan*[84] *aw/wa-lā mraʾatan*". Ibn Bukayr's wording is in this case obviously not a true reproduction of Ibn Isḥāq's *matn*, but, as we shall see below, it is a *matn* of al-Zuhrī though not that of the *maghāzī* account.

In Muḥammad b. Salama's *isnād*, al-Zuhrī's informant is not called ʿAbd Allāh b. Kaʿb as in Ibn Isḥāq's original version, but ʿAbd al-Raḥmān b. Kaʿb, as is the case in Maʿmar's transmission (long version) preserved by ʿAbd al-Razzāq. This must be a transmission error, too, because three transmitters from Ibn Isḥāq (al-Bakkāʾī, Salama b. al-Faḍl and Ibn Bukayr) agree on the name ʿAbd Allāh.

Who is responsible for the shortening and (at least partial) distortion of Ibn Isḥāq's transmission from al-Zuhrī? Yūnus b. Bukayr and Muḥammad b. Salama or later transmitters? This question cannot be answered as long as other transmissions going back to them are not available. Be that as it may, these paraphrasing versions show that even at a time when literal transmission became customary, not all transmitters followed the trend to transmit religiously what they had received, at least not stories of the *maghāzī* type.

---

[83] See note 69.

[84] Only the version of Muḥammad b. Salama has *ṣabiyyan*.

In addition to the two long versions of Maʿmar and Ibn Isḥāq and the abbreviated ones transmitted in the name of the latter discussed above, there are several shorter ones as well. According to their *isnād*, they go back to al-Zuhrī and are, without any doubt, abbreviated transmissions of al-Zuhrī's originally more detailed story. As in the case of the tradition complex connected with the name of al-Barāʾ b. ʿĀzib, the shorter versions are not the older ones on the basis of which the more detailed ones have been elaborated. This will be demonstrated in what follows. For the sake of clarity, I distinguish between "short stories" and "legal deductions". The usefulness of this distinction shall become obvious very shortly.

In Ibn Shabba's *Taʾrīkh al-Madīna* and al-Bayhaqī's *Dalāʾil* two "short stories" of the event have been preserved which go back to other pupils of al-Zuhrī, namely, Mūsā b. ʿUqba (d. 141/758-9) and Ibrāhīm b. Saʿd (d. 182/798-9 or 183/799-800). In the *isnād* of Mūsā's version[85] the name of al-Zuhrī's informant, one Ibn Kaʿb according to most of the other versions, is missing. This seems to be due to carelessness by Mūsā because later, when relating the return of the expedition to Medina, Ibn Kaʿb is named as al-Zuhrī's informant after all.[86] The names of the participants are given in the same sequence as in Maʿmar's text, some of them with additions in the *nasab*, but instead of Khuzāʿī b. Aswad, as he is called by Maʿmar and Ibn Isḥāq, the fifth name is Aswad b. Khuzāʿī. The same name occurs in Ibrāhīm b. Saʿd's transmission, and the name Aswad al-Khuzāʿī is found in the version of ʿUrwa b. al-Zubayr, as we shall see below.[87] Here, again, we come across the phenomenon that textual variations are corroborated by two or more scholars so that the conclusion

---

[85] Ibn Shabba, *Taʾrīkh,* II, 464-66 (this version is reproduced in M. Bāqshīsh Abū Mālik (ed.), *al-Maghāzī li-Mūsā b. ʿUqba*, Agadir, 1994, 228-29; I am grateful to Gregor Schoeler for making this book available to me); al-Bayhaqī, *Dalāʾil,* IV, 38-39.

[86] The editor of Ibn Shabba's *Taʾrīkh* added the name Ubayy to the *nasab* "Ibn Kaʿb" following a variant of the text found in Ibn al-Kathīr's *Bidāya,* IV, 139. This is, however, an erroneous insertion. The question who was responsible for it, Ibn Kathīr or his sources, cannot be answered because he does not mention where he has the text from.

[87] Bayhaqī, *Dalāʾil,* IV, 38. The uncertainty regarding this name continues in later sources. Ibn Ḥabīb, *Muḥabbar,* 283 has Khuzāʿī b. al-Aswad. Later biographical dictionaries, on the contrary, prefer Aswad b. Khuzāʿī. See Ibn al-Athīr, *Usd,* I, 83; Ibn Ḥajar, *Iṣāba,* I, 41 (153). Even the reproduction of al-Bakkāʾī's version by al-Dhahabī displays the latter form. See his *Taʾrīkh,* I, 342.

suggests itself that the difference has been caused by the common link, here al-Zuhrī, himself.

Mūsā b. ʿUqba's version contains—like Maʿmar's text and Ibn Bukayr's transmission from Ibn Isḥāq—a further name: in this case Asʿad b. Ḥarām. This man is further characterized as *aḥad al-turk* (Ibn Shabba) or *aḥad al-burak* (al-Bayhaqī) *ḥalīf li-Banī Sawād*. In front of this name, the following remark is inserted: "It is said: We found him only in this notebook (*ṣaḥīfa/kitāb*)"[88], i.e., in that of Mūsā, not in that of other pupils of al-Zuhrī. Later biographers like Ibn Ḥajar tried to read the name as al-Aswad b. Ḥuzām and equated it with al-Aswad b. Khuzāʿī or al-Aswad b. al-Abyaḍ.[89] This does not correspond, however, with the additional information given on him in Mūsā's *matn* ("*aḥad al-turk/burak*", etc.) which seems very odd indeed. I found the solution of this problem when checking the name Asʿad b. Ḥarām. He turns out to be the grandfather of ʿAbd Allāh b. Unays who was one of the participants in the expedition, and belonged to the Wuld al-Bark (neither Turk nor Burak!) b. Wabara of the Quḍāʿa tribe. His grandson ʿAbd Allāh b. Unays b. Asʿad b. Ḥarām was a *ḥalīf* of the Banū Sawād from the Banū Salima.[90] In view of this evidence and the fact that in no other variant transmitted from al-Zuhrī is the grandfather of ʿAbd Allāh b. Unays mentioned as participant in the

[88] In the edition of al-Bayhaqī's *Dalāʾil*, "*najdatan*" should be corrected to "*wa-lam najidhu*" following Ibn Shabba's text. This remark is odd for two reasons. It should actually have its place after the name Asʿad b. Ḥarām, not before it. As it stands now, one would relate it to the preceding name Aswad b. Khuzāʿī. An explanation could be that the insertion was made between the lines of the manuscript above the names. A copyist of the manuscript might have considered it as a remark concerning Aswad b. Khuzāʿī and inserted it after his name. It is also curious that both transmissions from Mūsā b. ʿUqba contain this additional remark although, according to their *isnād* and in light of a few differences between them, they seem to be independent transmissions from Mūsā. An explanation for this strange fact could be that this remark was added in the copy made by one of Mūsā's pupils (possibly Mūsā's nephew Ismāʿīl b. Ibrāhīm, d. 169/785-6) which was used by other pupils (e.g. Muḥammad b. Fulayḥ, d. 197/812-3) as model for the text. Another, but to my mind less convincing explanation could be that there has been a "spread of *isnāds*", i.e., that parts of the *isnād* have been fabricated; see above note 55. The singularity of this name has also been mentioned by Ibn Sayyid al-Nās, *ʿUyūn*, II, 66. Ibn Ḥajar, however, remarks in his *Fatḥ*, VII, 435 that in a version going back to ʿAbd Allāh b. Unays, an Aswad b. Ḥarām is mentioned instead of Aswad b. Khuzāʿī.

[89] See Ibn Ḥajar, *Iṣāba*, I, 39 (145); 41 (152) and the preceding note.

[90] See Ibn Ḥabīb, *al-Muḥabbar*, 282-83; Ibn Ḥajar, *Iṣāba*, IV, 37 (4541); Caskel, *Ǧamhara*, I, 279.

expedition, the sixth name of Mūsā's text appears to be a corruption of the *nasab* of ʿAbd Allāh b. Unays.

One of the variants of Mūsā b. ʿUqba's *matn*[91] also provides a clue for the strange "*fulān* b. Salama" whom we came across in Maʿmar's transmission from al-Zuhrī and in that of Ibn Bukayr from Ibn Isḥāq. It contains after the first four names the addition "*min Banī Salima*", which addition is also found in al-Bakkāʾī's and Salama's transmission from Ibn Isḥāq before the list of the names, and in Maʿmar's version after the name ʿAbd Allāh b. ʿAtīk. Some of al-Zuhrī's pupils must have misunderstood these words as the name of a sixth participant (Maʿmar) or as an element of one of the five participants' names (Ibn Isḥāq).[92] A comparative study of the different variants thus allows us to establish that the original story transmitted by al-Zuhrī contained the names of five participants and what these names were. We shall see below that another variant corroborates this conclusion. This is an example which illustrates that contradictions appearing in different variants of a tradition are not necessarily the result of deliberate and arbitrary inventions or embellishments of texts by the transmitters, as is often assumed, but may have been and often are caused by transmission errors.

In Mūsā b. ʿUqba's text, the whole story of the expedition itself is summarized in only one phrase: "They went to Abū Rāfiʿ b. Abī l-Ḥuqayq at Khaybar and killed him in his house." What happened when the assassins returned to Medina is, however, reported in detail. This allows us to compare the text with the versions of Ibn Isḥāq[93] and Maʿmar[94] which also relate this episode. Mūsā's text reads as follows:

> Ibn Shihāb—Ibn Kaʿb:
>
> They came to the Messenger of God when he stood on the *minbar*. He said: "May you be happy (*aflaḥat al-wujūh*)!" They answered: "May you

---

[91] The version of Ismāʿīl b. Ibrāhīm b. Mūsā b. ʿUqba preserved in Bayhaqī, *Dalāʾil*, IV, 38-39.

[92] Maʿmar's *matn* clearly states that "*fulān* b. Salama" was another participant. According to Ibn Bukayr, Ibn Isḥāq thought that a man with this name had been "among them". He could have meant: among the five. This would fit the statement in the other versions deriving from Ibn Isḥāq that the number of participants had been five.

[93] See above, p. 194.

[94] See above, p. 192.

> be happy (*aflaḥa wajhuka*), O Messenger of God!" He said: "Have you killed him?" They answered: "Yes!" He said: "Give me the sword!" He pulled it out (*sallahu*). [Then the Prophet] said: "This is his [Abū Rāfiʿ's] food on the tip of the sword!"[95]

This text differs clearly from that of Ibn Isḥāq which narrates that the participants argued among themselves about who had killed Abū Rāfiʿ, and that the Prophet settled the dispute by checking their swords. In Mūsā's version, there is no mention of a dispute, but the Prophet checked the sword of the man who had actually killed him, obviously in order to verify whether their report was true. This shows that both versions are independent of each other. The epilogue of Mūsā's transmission corresponds, however, to that of Maʿmar's text, at least in the part preserved. The comparison of both versions suggests, in addition, that the end of Maʿmar's long version contained in ʿAbd al-Razzāq's *Muṣannaf* is incomplete. The content of the lost piece can be recovered from Mūsā's transmission. The correspondence between Mūsā b. ʿUqba's version and that of Maʿmar, however, does not mean that the former had the latter as *Vorlage*. Even if Mūsā's text is short, it is nonetheless long enough to reveal slight differences between both texts. One of them is the phrase mentioned after the list of the participants: "The Messenger of God gave the command over them to ʿAbd Allāh b. ʿAtīk (*wa-ammara ʿalayhim rasūl Allāh (ṣ) ʿAbd Allāh b. ʿAtīk*)." This statement is to be found in Ibn Isḥāq's *matn* in the same place, but not in that of Maʿmar. In his text, we find the following notice after Ibn ʿAtīk's name in the list of participants: "He was the leader of the group (*wa-kāna amīr al-qawm*)."

The second "short story" contained in Ibn Shabba's *Taʾrīkh* goes back to Ibrāhīm b. Saʿd, another well-known pupil of al-Zuhrī. He names as al-Zuhrī's informant ʿAbd al-Raḥman b. ʿAbd Allāh b. Kaʿb b. Mālik. Recall that Maʿmar has the name ʿAbd al-Raḥmān b. Kaʿb b. Mālik (i.e., his uncle), Ibn Isḥāq has ʿAbd Allāh b. Kaʿb b. Mālik (his father) and Mūsā b. ʿUqba has only Ibn Kaʿb b. Mālik. As in Mūsā's version, the story is reduced to a list of the participants,

[95] Ibn Shabba, *Taʾrīkh,* II, 465-66; Bayhaqī, *Dalāʾil,* IV, 39. This fragment is quoted in Ibn Kathīr, *Bidāya,* IV, 139 with an almost identical text, but without information on who the transmitter from al-Zuhrī was. On the *isnād* of this fragment, see above, p. 198.

here placed at the end, and to what happened when the expedition returned. The expedition itself is only briefly told: "The group (*rahṭ*)[96] which the Messenger of God sent in order to kill Ibn Abī l-Ḥuqayq, killed him." The account of the episode after the return is similar to that transmitted by Mūsā b. ʿUqba and Maʿmar, without being wholly identical with either of them. From the fact that two versions (three if we include Maʿmar's) correspond against one (Ibn Isḥāq) in that they do not report a dispute among the participants in the expedition as to who really killed Abū Rāfiʿ, we have to conclude that Ibn Isḥāq, not al-Zuhrī himself, is responsible for this detail. However, as we shall see later, there are indications that both versions may originate from al-Zuhrī himself.[97]

Ibrāhīm b. Saʿd's list of participants contains only four names, but he explicitly states that he forgot the fifth. This corroborates our conclusion that the original number had been five. Like Mūsā b. ʿUqba he has Aswad b. Khuzāʿī instead of Khuzāʿī b. (al-) Aswad. The addition "*ḥalīf lahum*" (a confederate of theirs) is also found in the other versions, but here—as in the version of Mūsā b. ʿUqba preserved by Ibn Shabba—the *lahum* makes no sense because the name of the tribe to which this expression refers is missing. In Ibn Isḥāq's text and most clearly in Mūsā b. ʿUqba's version preserved by al-Bayhaqī, the reference is to the Banū Salima whereas Maʿmar's *matn* suggests the Aslam as reference. Since Maʿmar's list shows some corruption, it seems more acceptable to follow Ibn Isḥāq and Mūsā b. ʿUqba in that—according to al-Zuhrī—the group consisted exclusively of members of the Banū Salima and their confederates. Little inconsistencies such as this *lahum* corroborate our conclusion that the "short stories" are indeed abbreviations of longer versions. It is, however, not always clear who is responsible for this shortening. Had al-Zuhrī's pupils already done it or were it the transmitters after them, or perhaps the compiler Ibn Shabba (it is indeed remarkable that all four of his versions are shortened ones), or even the transmitters of Ibn Shabba's material?

Alongside the abbreviated versions which I call "short stories", there are brief texts which do not function as summaries of the major

[96] This word is also used in Maʿmar's *matn*, whereas the variants of Ibn Isḥāq's text have *nās* or *nafar*.

[97] See below, pp. 205, 220.

events but are concerned with details which could be used as legal arguments. We have already come across this phenomenon in our analysis of the tradition of al-Barāʾ. In that case, it was a later transmitter, Yaḥyā b. Ādam (d. 203/818-9), who could be identified as the author of the "legal deduction". As we shall see in the following, the "legal deductions" of al-Zuhrī's tradition are much older.

The best known versions are those of Mālik b. Anas (d. 179/795-6) and al-Shāfiʿī (d. 204/819-20). In Yaḥyā b. Yaḥyā's recension of Mālik's *Muwaṭṭaʾ* we find the following tradition:

> Yaḥyā—Mālik—Ibn Shihāb—a son of Kaʿb b. Mālik; [Mālik] said: I guess that he [Ibn Shihāb al-Zuhrī] said "ʿAbd al-Raḥmān b. Kaʿb":
>
> The Messenger of God forbade those who killed Ibn Abī l-Ḥuqayq to kill women and children (*nahā rasūl Allāh alladhīna qatalū Ibn Abī l-Ḥuqayq ʿan qatl al-nisāʾ wa-l-wildān*). He [al-Zuhrī] said: One of them reported: The wife of Ibn Abī l-Ḥuqayq worried us by [her] crying. I raised my sword against her, then remembered the Prophet's prohibition and abstained [from killing her]. Without that [prohibition] we would have gotten rid of her.[98]

This text is also known from a number of Mālik's pupils who differed only about the name of al-Zuhrī's informant.[99]

Al-Shāfiʿī's version is shorter:

> Sufyān [b. ʿUyayna]—al-Zuhrī—Ibn Kaʿb b. Mālik—his paternal uncle:
>
> The Messenger of God forbade those whom he sent to Ibn Abī l-Ḥuqayq to kill women and children (*anna rasūl Allāh nahā lladhīna baʿatha ilā Ibn Abī l-Ḥuqayq ʿan qatl al-nisāʾ wa-l-wildān*).[100]

Sufyān's version is transmitted in slightly different wording by others as well: al-Ḥumaydī (d. 219/834),[101] Saʿīd b. Manṣūr (d. 227/841-2),[102] ʿAlī b. al-Madīnī (d. 234/848-9) and al-Ḥasan b. Muḥammad al-

---

[98] Mālik, *Muwaṭṭaʾ* (Yaḥyā), 21:8.

[99] See above pp. 178. It is not mentioned, however, in Shaybānī's recension of the *Muwaṭṭaʾ*.

[100] Shāfiʿī, *Umm*, IV, 239 (*K. al-Ḥukm fī qitāl al-mushrikīn wa-masʾalat māl al-ḥarbī); Bayhaqī, *Sunan*, IX, 78; Majdī b. Muḥammad al-Miṣrī, *Shifāʾ al-ʿiyy*, II, 239 (394).

[101] Ḥumaydī, *Musnad*, II, 385 (874).

[102] Saʿīd b. Manṣūr, *Sunan*, III/2, 281 (2627).

Zaʿfarānī (d. 260/873-4).[103] All transmissions from Sufyān b. ʿUyayna have in common the addition *ʿan ʿammihi* in the *isnād*, which shows that this detail really goes back to him. Almost the same *matn* is, finally, transmitted by ʿAbd Allāh b. al-Mubārak and ʿAbd al-Razzāq from Maʿmar[104] and by ʿAbd al-Razzāq from Ibn Jurayj.[105] It is, however, notable that they call al-Zuhrī's informant either ʿAbd al-Raḥmān b. ʿAbd Allāh b. Kaʿb (Ibn al-Mubārak *ʿan* Maʿmar and ʿAbd al-Razzāq *ʿan* Ibn Jurayj) or only Ibn Kaʿb b. Mālik (ʿAbd al-Razzāq *ʿan* Maʿmar).

These four short versions are only interested in the prohibition of the Prophet to kill women and children. The fact that this prohibition is not simply produced as one of the many *ḥadīth*s of the Prophet, but is explicitly linked to the expedition against Ibn Abī l-Ḥuqayq,[106] shows that this short tradition is extracted from the more detailed *maghāzī*-story of this event. This is most clear in Mālik's version which preserved an additional fragment of it. A comparison of this fragment with the appropriate texts of Maʿmar and Ibn Isḥāq shows that the *maghāzī*-tradition on which Mālik relied was not identical to any of them. This means that Mālik had not received his version from them, but from another of al-Zuhrī's pupils, or—why not?—from al-Zuhrī himself. This corroborates our conclusion that al-Zuhrī must have retold the story in slightly varying versions or that his pupils did not always reproduce his text or words religiously.

The "legal deduction" from the *maghāzī*-report is transmitted with a similar but not identical text by four different people, who all say that they transmitted it from al-Zuhrī. He is, therefore, the common link of the "legal deduction". This means that he himself had already used this shortened version in legal discussion and education, in addition to transmitting the detailed *maghāzī*-tradition. It is noteworthy that the wording of the "legal deduction" is not identical to the appropriate phrase in the *maghāzī*-tradition. According to Ibn Isḥāq's and

---

[103] Bayhaqī, *Sunan,* IX, 77, 78. An abbreviated version without *isnād* is also to be found in Abū Dāwūd, *Sunan,* III, 54 (*Bāb fī qatl al-nisāʾ,* 2672).

[104] Ibn Shabba, *Taʾrīkh,* II, 467 ("*ilā Banī l-Ḥuqayq*" is a transmission error and should be emended to "*ilā Ibn Abī l-Ḥuqayq*"); ʿAbd al-Razzāq, *Muṣannaf,* V, 202 (9385).

[105] Transmitted via Ibrāhīm b. Suwayd al-Shibāmī; Ṭabarānī, *al-Muʿjam al-kabīr,* XIX, 75 (150). It is not found in ʿAbd al-Razzāq's *Muṣannaf.*

[106] Only in Ibn Jurayj's version is this not the case.

Maʿmar's version of it, the Prophet used the words *walīd aw/wa-mraʾa*;[107] in the three versions of the "legal deduction", however, he spoke of *al-nisāʾ wa-l-wildān* (Mālik, Sufyān) or *al-nisāʾ wa-l-ṣibyān* (Maʿmar) in the plural form and in a reversed order. This change seems to reflect the priorities and the generalizing tendency of legal thinking. Most remarkable is that both versions were spread by one and the same scholar, Ibn Shihāb al-Zuhrī. This explains why the wording of the "legal deduction" was able to intrude in transmissions of the *maghāzī*-tradition, as we have seen above.[108]

Our comparison of different variants of the tradition which allegedly go back to Ibn Kaʿb b. Mālik and which contain an *isnād*, has produced the following findings: The conclusion drawn from the *isnād* analysis that there is a common link in the transmission of the tradition and that he, therefore, must have spread the tradition, is supported by a study of the different *matns*. It became clear that all the versions are independent transmissions from that common source which, according to the *isnāds*, is al-Zuhrī. It is most unlikely that his status as common link in the *isnād* is the result of a "spread of *isnāds*". This conclusion is based in the first place on a comparison of the long versions which are written transmissions, but I am assuming that it can be transferred in this case to the short versions as well. It has become obvious that al-Zuhrī must have related the story at different times with a slightly varying *isnād* and *matn*. Additionally, he used one element of it as a legal argument which later was transmitted on his authority as a separate *ḥadīth*.

The gist of al-Zuhrī's story on the murder of Ibn Abī l-Ḥuqayq (the form of the name preferred in his version, not Abū Rāfiʿ as in the tradition of al-Barāʾ) can be summarized as follows. As antecedents which lead to it, the competition of Aws and Khazraj and the wish of the latter to accomplish a similar deed as the Aws in their murder of Kaʿb b. al-Ashraf is highlighted. The reason why the Prophet approved of their plan to kill this particular Jew living in Khaybar is not given, only that he forbade the killing of any child or woman—which probably meant originally: of Ibn Abī l-Ḥuqayq's family. Five men of the Banū Salima and their confederates were chosen for the

---

[107] Only Muḥammad b. Salama's short version from Ibn Isḥāq has *ṣabiyy wa-mraʾa*.
[108] See p. 197.

detachment and ʿAbd Allāh b. ʿAtīk was nominated as their leader. Al-Zuhrī also mentioned the names of the other four, but for one of them he sometimes confused *ism* and *nasab*. A sixth participant mentioned in three variants is due to transmission errors. The whole group entered Khaybar without problems. Only Ibn Isḥāq's version says explicitly that it happened at night, but this must be assumed from the context anyway. They locked all the houses from the outside and went to the flat of Ibn Abī l-Ḥuqayq. There they were let in by his wife who cried or shouted at them when they locked the door and pulled out their swords, but her life was spared because of the Prophet's prohibition to kill children and women. What they did to silence her is not mentioned. Ibn Abī l-Ḥuqayq was attacked by ʿAbd Allāh b. Unays who slew him with his sword. When descending, ʿAbd Allāh b. ʿAtīk, who had bad eyesight, fell from the ladder and sprained his foot so seriously that his companions had to carry him away. They hid in a water-channel since the people of Khaybar had begun to search immediately for the assassins, but without success. Then one of the group, who was neither Ibn ʿAtīk nor Ibn Unays nor the original narrator of the story, returned to the house of Ibn Abī l-Ḥuqayq to verify whether he was really dead. He witnessed that the wife of Ibn Abī l-Ḥuqayq had recognized Ibn ʿAtīk by his voice (background information on this memorable fact is not given, however) and that Ibn Abī l-Ḥuqayq had passed away. When the whole detachment returned to the Prophet, he checked the sword of the man who had attacked Ibn Abī l-Ḥuqayq, according to several transmitters. According only to Ibn Isḥāq, the Prophet checked the swords of all because they disputed who had actually killed him, and declared Ibn Unays the killer. This variation does not really fit the context because no other person had been mentioned attacking Ibn Abī l-Ḥuqayq. It may have been motivated by the question as to why the Prophet checked the sword.

The analysis of the *matn*s has produced no further evidence which could be used to decide who al-Zuhrī's informant actually was. It is only certain that he said he had it from the Kaʿb b. Mālik family. The fact that the *isnād* is defective and does not name Kaʿb b. Mālik himself or one of the participants in the expedition whose names are given in the text as the ultimate source of information, speaks in favor of rather than against the reliability of al-Zuhrī's *isnād*. The gap in the *isnād* is all the more puzzling since the *matn* is clearly composed as a story which uses the report of one or more of the participants. There are therefore reasons to accept al-Zuhrī's statement that he heard the story from the Kaʿb b. Mālik family. The reason why the name of an original author or narrator is lacking may be that the story in the form in which al-Zuhrī received it had no identifiable author but was a condensation of the reports which the participants in the expedition had given and which were retold among the members of their tribe from generation to generation in order to praise the great deeds of their ancestors in favor of Islam. The link between the Kaʿb b. Mālik family and the assassins is obvious. The latter were all members (three of them as confederates) of the Banū Salima to whom also the descendants of Kaʿb b. Mālik belonged.[109] If this story really came from them, it had, without doubt, a long period of oral repetition and transmission behind it before it achieved its final form in which al-Zuhrī received it, which may, in addition, not have been exactly the same as that which he later transmitted.

The tradition of ʿAbd Allāh b. Unays

The version of al-Ṭabarī:

> Mūsā b. ʿAbd al-Raḥmān al-Masrūqī and ʿAbbās b. ʿAbd al-ʿAẓīm al-ʿAnbarī—Jaʿfar b. ʿAwn—Ibrāhīm b. Ismāʿīl—Ibrāhīm b. ʿAbd al-Raḥmān b. Kaʿb b. Mālik—his father—his mother, the daughter of ʿAbd Allāh b. Unays—ʿAbd Allāh b. Unays:
>
> {1} The party that the Apostle of God had sent to Ibn Abī l-Ḥuqayq, to kill him, consisted of: ʿAbd Allāh b. ʿAtīk, ʿAbd Allāh b. Unays, Abū Qatāda, an ally of theirs and a man of the Anṣār. {2} They came to Khaybar by night. {3} He [Ibn Unays] said: We went up to their doors, locking them from the outside and taking the keys, until we had locked [all] their doors upon them. {4} Then we took the keys and threw them into a well. {5} Then we came to the upper room in which Ibn Abī l-Ḥuqayq was; {6} ʿAbd Allāh b. ʿAtīk and I went up to it, while our companions sat in the garden (*fī l-ḥāʾiṭ*). {7} ʿAbd Allāh b. ʿAtīk asked to be admitted, and {8} the wife of Ibn Abī l-Ḥuqayq said: "That is the voice of ʿAbd Allāh b. ʿAtīk." {9} Ibn Abī l-Ḥuqayq said: "May your mother be deprived of you! ʿAbd Allāh b. ʿAtīk is at Yathrib. How could he be here at your house at this moment? {10}

[109] See Ibn Ḥajar, *Iṣāba,* V, 308-09 (7427); Caskel, *Ǧamhara,* I, 190.

Open the door for me! No generous person would turn away anyone from his door at this hour." {11} So she proceeded to open the door, and ʿAbd Allāh and I went in to Ibn Abī l-Ḥuqayq. {12} ʿAbd Allāh b. ʿAtīk said: "Keep an eye on [her]!" {13} So I drew my sword upon her, and I was about to strike her with it when I remembered the Apostle of God's prohibition against killing women and children, so I kept [my hand] from her. {14} ʿAbd Allāh b. ʿAtīk went in to Ibn Abī l-Ḥuqayq. He said: I could see him in the dark room because he was so white. {15} When he saw me and saw the sword, he took his pillow and fended me off with it; I tried to hit him but I could not. {16} However, I [eventually] managed to give him a minor wound with my sword. Then he came out to ʿAbd Allāh b. Unays [sic] and said: "Kill him!" He said: "Yes." {17} So ʿAbd Allāh b. Unays went in and finished him off. {18} He said: Then I came out to ʿAbd Allāh b. ʿAtīk, and we left. The woman screamed: "A night attack! A night attack!" {19} ʿAbd Allāh b. ʿAtīk fell on the stairs and said: "Oh, my foot! Oh, my foot!" {20} ʿAbd Allāh b. Unays [sic] carried him and put him down. He said: I said: "Come along! There is nothing with your foot." So we set off. We came to our companions and made off. {21} Then I remembered that I had left my bow on the stairs, so I returned for it; the people of Khaybar were milling about, saying nothing but: "Who has killed Ibn Abī l-Ḥuqayq? Who has killed Ibn Abī l-Ḥuqayq?" So whenever I caught anyone's eye, I would say: "Who has killed Ibn Abī l-Ḥuqayq?" Then I climbed the stairs, while the people were going up and down them, and took my bow from where it was. Then I left and rejoined my companions.

{22} We hid by day and travelled by night. When we hid by day, we posted a sentry to watch for us, and if he saw anything he would let us know. We proceeded until, when we were at Bayḍāʾ, I was their sentry [here al-Ṭabarī remarks: "Mūsā and ʿAbbās used different expressions" for the term sentry] and I gave the alarm. They set off at a run, and I followed them, until I caught up with them near Medina. They said: "What is it? Did you see something?" I said: "No! I knew that you were completely exhausted, and I wanted fear to carry you along."[110]

The version of al-Wāqidī:

(Abū) Ayyūb b. al-Nuʿmān—his father—ʿAṭiyya b. ʿAbd Allāh b. Unays—his father:

[110] Ṭabarī, *Taʾrīkh*, prima series, III, 1381-83. The translation is that of Mattock ("History and Fiction", 87-88) except some changes by myself. A short reference to this tradition is to be found in Bayhaqī, *Dalāʾil*, IV, 34.

{1} We left Medina and travelled until we reached Khaybar. {2} ʿAbd Allāh b. ʿAtīk's [foster-]mother,[111] a Jewess, was at Khaybar. {3} The Apostle of God had sent five of us: ʿAbd Allāh b. ʿAtīk, ʿAbd Allāh b. Unays, Abū Qatāda, al-Aswad b. Khuzāʿī and Masʿūd b. Sinān. {4} We reached Khaybar, {5} and ʿAbd Allāh sent for his foster-mother to tell her where he was; she came out to us with a bag full of choice dates and bread. We ate this, and he said to her: "Mother, it is now evening; give us lodging at your house and get us into Khaybar!" His foster-mother said: "How can you possibly enter Khaybar, when there are four thousand warriors in it? Whom are you after here?" He said: "Abū Rāfiʿ." She said: "You will not be able to get at him." He said: "By God, I will kill him or be killed in the attempt!" She said: "Then come in to me by night!" {6} So they came in to her, when[112] the people of Khaybar were asleep. {7} She had said to them: "Come in with the crowd when[113] all is quiet to make your assault [lit.: set your ambush]!". They did so and came in to her. Then she said: "The Jews do not lock their doors for security, for fear that a guest may come during the night, so that anyone arriving in the courtyard, not having been given hospitality, may find the door open and may enter and sup." When all was quiet, she said: "Go and ask to be admitted to Abū Rāfiʿ, and say: 'We have brought Abū Rāfiʿ a present', and they will open up for you." So they did this. {8} They went out, and every house-door of Khaybar that they passed they locked, until they had locked every house in the village, {9} and finally they came to a ladder at Sallām's castle.

{10} He [Ibn Unays] said: We went up, sending ʿAbd Allāh b. ʿAtīk first, because he could speak the Jewish language.[114] Then they [sic] asked to be admitted to Abū Rāfiʿ, {11} and his wife came and said: "What is your business?" {12} ʿAbd Allāh b. ʿAtīk, speaking in the Jewish language, said: "I have brought Abū Rāfiʿ a present." She opened the door for him, {13} and when she saw his weapon she made to cry out. ʿAbd Allāh b. Unays said: We crowded through the door to try to get to him first. She made to cry out, so I pointed my sword at her. I did not want my companions to beat me to him. She was silent for a while [or: immediately(?)]. Then I said to her: "Where is Abū

[111] On foster relations between Arab and Jewish clans in Medina and the correct translation of *umm* in this text, cf. M. Lecker, "ʿAmr ibn Ḥazm al-Anṣārī and Qurʾān 2,256: 'No Compulsion is There in Religion'", in *Oriens*, 35 (1996), 63-64.

[112] It seems more plausible to read *lammā* instead of *fa-lammā*.

[113] I read *idhā* instead of *fa-idhā*.

[114] The Arabic text has "*al-yahūdiyya*". W.M. Watt has equated it with "Hebrew" (*Muhammad at Medina*, 213), but Mattock's translation "Jewish", i.e. the Jewish language, is preferable, because it seems more plausible that the Jews of Medina—and Ibn Abī l-Ḥuqayq originally was one of them—spoke an Arabic mixed with Hebrew words.

Rāfiʿ? Tell me, or I will strike you with my sword!" She said: "He is there in the room." {14} We went in to him, and we could distinguish him only by his whiteness, for he looked like a cast-off Egyptian garment. We set on him with our swords; {15} his wife cried out, and one of us was on the point of going out to her but remembered that the Apostle of God had forbidden us to kill women. {16} When we reached him, we found that the ceiling was too low for us, and our swords rebounded from it.

{17} Ibn Unays said: "I was night-blind and could see only poorly at night, [but] I saw him (*taʾammaltuhu*) as though he was a moon. {18} I pressed my sword on his belly until I heard it strike the bed and I knew that he was fatally wounded [lit.: dead]. {19} The rest all kept striking him. {20} Then we descended, but Abū Qatāda forgot his bow and remembered it only after he had descended. His companions [sic] said: "Leave the bow!", but he refused and went back and retrieved it. {21} He sprained his foot, {22} and they carried him between them. {23} Abū Rāfi's wife cried out, and the people of the house took up the cry after he had been killed.

{24} The people in the houses could not release themselves until a considerable part of the night had passed. {25} The band hid themselves in one of the water-channels[115] of Khaybar. {26} [Eventually] the Jews and al-Ḥārith Abū Zaynab arrived, and Abū Rāfiʿ's wife came out to him and said: "The gang has gone now." Al-Ḥārith set out, with three thousand men, to follow us, hunting us with torches of palm-fronds. They often trod on the water-channel, but we were inside it and they were on top of it, so that they could not see us. {27} When they had completed their search and seen nothing, they returned to Abū Rāfiʿ's wife and asked her: "Did you recognise any of them?" She said: "I heard the speech of ʿAbd Allāh b. ʿAtīk among them; if he is in our country, he is with them." {28} So they started to search again, {29} and the band said to one another: "Suppose one of us went to them to see if he is dead or not?" So al-Aswad b. Khuzāʿī went out, {30} joined the crowd and mingled with them, holding in his hand a torch like theirs, until they went back to the castle again, and he went with them. He found the house full. He said: They all came up to look, to see how Abū Rāfiʿ was. {31} His wife came up with a blazing torch and leant over him to see if he was alive or dead. {32} She said: "He is dead, by the God of Moses." {33} But I was unwilling to come back without definite information, so I went in with them again, and not a vein of the man was moving. {34} The Jews came out, all keening together, and began to prepare the things for his burial. {35} I came out with them, having been rather a long time away from my compan-

[115] See note 66.

ions. I went down to them in the water-channel and gave them the news. We remained where we were for two days, until the search for us had died down. {36} Then we left, making for Medina, each of us claiming to have killed him. {37} We came to the Prophet, who was on the *minbar*. When he saw us, he said: "May you be happy!" We said: May you be happy, O Apostle of God!" He said: "Have you killed him?" We said: "Yes, {38} and each of us claims to have done it." He said: "Bring me your swords, quickly!" We brought him our swords, {39} and he said: "This one killed him. There are traces of food on the sword of ʿAbd Allāh b. Unays."

{40} Ibn Abī l-Ḥuqayq had incited Ghaṭafān and the Arab polytheists round him and he had offered them great inducements to fight the Apostle of God. So the Prophet sent these men against him.[116]

Ayyūb b. al-Nuʿmān—Khārija b. ʿAbd Allāh:

When they reached Abū Rāfiʿ, they disputed as to who should kill him, so they drew lots for him, and ʿAbd Allāh b. Unays' arrow came out. He was night-blind and he said to his companions: "Where is he?" They said: "You can/will see his whiteness, as though he were a moon." He said: "I see him." ʿAbd Allāh b. Unays went forward, while the band stood with the woman, fearing that she would cry out, having drawn their swords upon her. ʿAbd Allāh b. Unays entered and struck with his sword, but it rebounded, because the ceiling was low. So he leaned on him, he [Abū Rāfiʿ] being full of wine, until he heard the sword strike against the bed.[117]

These two versions which allegedly go back to ʿAbd Allāh b. Unays, Companion of the Prophet and participant in the expedition against Ibn Abī l-Ḥuqayq, differ in extent and content from each other much more than the variants of the other two traditions on this event did, to wit, those of Abū Isḥāq and al-Zuhrī discussed above. Despite this

[116] This unit gives the impression of an addition by another hand designed to produce a reason for the killing of Ibn Abī l-Ḥuqayq. My first conclusion was that this addition probably should be ascribed to al-Wāqidī himself, comparable to Ibn Isḥāq's procedure of adding such a reason in the introduction to his account of the event (see Ibn Hishām, *Sīra*, 714; Ṭabarī, *Ta'rīkh*, prima series, III, 1378). I had to revise my ideas, however, when I came across this fragment in later sources as part of a tradition going back to ʿUrwa b. al-Zubayr (see below, p. 222). Al-Wāqidī obviously added this fragment of ʿUrwa's tradition without naming his sources. Ibn Saʿd—following the example of Ibn Isḥāq?—put this fragment at the beginning of his summary which he gave of al-Wāqidī's version of the event (cf. Ibn Saʿd, *Ṭabaqāt*, II, 91).

[117] Al-Wāqidī, *Maghāzī*, I, 391-95. I reproduced Mattock's translation ("History and Fiction", 90-92) with some changes.

fact, even a superficial reading of both texts reveals obvious structural correspondences and many similarities in content. In order to facilitate the content-analysis and comparison of these and other versions, I broke down the texts into small units to which I assigned a number in the translation.[118] The text of al-Ṭabarī which is labelled D (daughter), contains 22 units. A comparison with that of al-Wāqidī, labelled S (son), organised in a table is as follows:

D	1	2	3	4	5	6	7	8	9	10	11
S	(3)	(6)	8	–	(9)	–	(10) 11	26	–	–	(12)

D	12	13	14	15	16	17	18	19	20	21	22
S	(13)	(15)	(14,17)	–	–	(18)	(23)	(21)	22	(20,30)	(36)

In the first line the units of content of text D are given, in the second line the equivalent units of text S. Plain numbers mean: corresponds in content; numbers in parentheses mean: the content is similar but there are differences; and the dash means: neither correspondence nor similarity is to be found. The results of the comparison are: There are 14 units similar in content, six units which have no equivalent, and four units where a clear correspondence in content is displayed. The correspondence of both texts is thus not extensive; they are, therefore, not dependent on each other. On the other hand, they do show similar features. Correspondences and similarities occur, in addition, in much the same sequence. Only four units of *matn* S appear in another sequence (units 26, 15, 23, 20), and from these four cases, only one (26) is very distant from its equivalent in *matn* D. We can conclude from this that the similarities between both texts cannot be attributed to chance. They must derive from a common source. Because of the many variations between both variants, the story related by the common source is recognizable only dimly. It can be described as follows:

Five men—among them ʿAbd Allāh b. ʿAtīk, ʿAbd Allāh b. Unays, Abū Qatāda and a confederate of theirs—were sent by the Prophet to

[118] Not all units are defined as the most elementary elements of content, for, in order to limit their number, I chose a division into only those units of contents which have parallels in the other texts for comparison's sake. Some units, therefore, are larger than others.

Ibn Abī l-Ḥuqayq who lived at Khaybar. They entered it by night and locked the doors of the houses until they arrived at the residence of Ibn Abī l-Ḥuqayq to which some of them ascended. ʿAbd Allāh b. ʿAtīk asked to be admitted. The wife of Ibn Abī l-Ḥuqayq recognized him due to his voice and let them in. One of them threatened the wife with his sword, but remembered the interdiction of the Prophet to kill any women. The attacker/s recognized Ibn Abī l-Ḥuqayq because of his white color. ʿAbd Allāh b. Unays killed him. When they had left, his wife cried out. In descending, one of them hurt his foot and was carried away by the other/s. One of them realized that he had forgotten his bow and returned to fetch it. The detachment returned to Medina.

This is only the skeleton of the story which must have been the source of the two versions, and even in this skeleton the exact place where some of the "bones" originally had their place is obscure. This is true for the detail of the wife of Ibn Abī l-Ḥuqayq recognizing the voice of Ibn ʿAtīk and of the realization of one of them that he had forgotten his bow. In addition, both texts do not correspond fully in wording. Correspondence is mostly limited to some words of general use.

The common elements apart, the two stories differ substantially in many details. Most striking are real contradictions which cannot be simply explained by assuming that they derive from either elaboration or abbreviation of the original narrative. The following five substantial differences can be given: 1) The number of persons who entered the house of Ibn Abī l-Ḥuqayq in order to kill him. According to D, there were only two: Ibn ʿAtīk and Ibn Unays; according to S, the entire group went to kill him. 2) In version D, it is Ibn Unays who, raising his sword against Ibn Abī l-Ḥuqayq's wife, remembers the prohibition of the Prophet to kill women and children; in version S, it is one of the assassins whose name is not given, but who cannot be Ibn Unays. 3) The one who hurts his foot in descending from the residence of Ibn Abī l-Ḥuqayq is Ibn ʿAtīk according to D, but Abū Qatāda according to S. 4) In D, the episode of the forgotten bow is linked to Ibn Unays, in S to Abū Qatāda and, in addition, both episodes are reported in another sequence. 5) A notable variation is also that, according to D, the wife of Ibn Abī l-Ḥuqayq recognizes the voice of Ibn ʿAtīk when he asks to be admitted into the house, whereas in S this is only mentioned when the Jews of Khaybar had heard what had happened and had started the search for the murderers. These differences, as well as the variation in the elaboration of some episodes (compare for example D 7-11 with S 10-12 and D 22 with S 36), corroborate our conclusion that both texts do not depend directly on each other.

We have established that both versions have some essential structural elements in common which they cannot possess by chance but which must derive from a common source. According to the *isnād*, the common link is Ibn Unays. Indeed, it is quite possible that the common "skeleton" of both versions derives from him or, to be more precise, the story he related, perhaps in varying forms, in the course of time. Otherwise we must postulate that the common source of both versions is the story of someone who alleged to have it from Ibn Unays but whose name has been suppressed by the transmitters of both traditions.

Despite the comparison of both versions alleged to go back to Ibn Unays and the establishment of the content of the common source from which both must derive, the issue of the common source is still not fully explored. The attentive reader of the texts of these two versions will have realized that they not only display correspondences with each other, but also with the tradition of al-Zuhrī that allegedly also goes back to members of the family of Ibn Kaʿb. The relationship of his version and also that of Abū Isḥāq to that allegedly deriving from Ibn Unays has therefore to be studied first, before a definitive answer to the issue of the source or the sources of all the versions can be given.[119]

The relationship between the different traditions

To facilitate a comparison of the two texts which are said to derive from Ibn Unays with that of al-Zuhrī, the *matn* of the latter has been cut into units of content as well (see the translation on pp. 191-92).

[119] The analysis of the different traditions on the murder of Ibn Abī l-Ḥuqayq has been limited to versions which have an *isnād*. In later sources, several other versions are found which in general derive from one of the versions which has been studied above, mostly from Ibn Isḥāq, Ibn Saʿd (al-Wāqidī) and al-Bukhārī, sometimes even mixing them together. See e.g. Ibn al-Jawzī, *Muntaẓam*, II, 342; Ibn ʿAbd al-Barr, *Durar* (see *Istidhkār*, XIV, 57-58); Ibn Kathīr, *Bidāya*, IV, 137-40; Ibn Sayyid al-Nās, *ʿUyūn*, II, 65-66; Dhahabī, *Taʾrīkh*, I, 341-45; Nuwayrī, *Nihāyat*, XVII, 197-99.

The appropriate units of the three traditions can be put alongside one another in a table. Al-Zuhrī's tradition (Z) has been taken as the reference of the other two (D = daughter of Ibn Unays, S = son of Ibn Unays). The letter "m" symbolises Maʿmar's variant of al-Zuhrī's tradition, the letter "i" Ibn Isḥāq's variant.

Z	1	2	3m = 6i	4	5	6i = 3m	7	8i	9m
D	–	–	–	(1)	–	–	2	(2)	3
S	–	–	–	3	–	–	4	–	8

Z	9i	10	11	12	13	14	15i	16	17
D	–	(5, 6)	7	–	(11)	–	–	–	(14)
S	–	(9)	(10)	11	(12)	–	–	–	14

Z	18	19i	20	21	22	23	24	25	26i
D	(13)	–	(17)	–	(19)	20	–	–	–
S	(15)	19	18	(21)	(17)	22	25	(26)	–

Z	27	28	29m	29i	30	31	32	33m	33i
D	–	–	–	–	–	–	–	–	–
S	(29)	31	–	27	32	(35)	(36)	37	38

Z	34m	34i
D	–	–
S	–	39

The comparison of the contents of al-Zuhrī's tradition with that allegedly going back to the daughter of Ibn Unays (al-Ṭabarī) leads to the following result: There are four correspondences, nine cases of similar content and 26 cases with no equivalent. The comparison with the version ascribed to Ibn Unays' son (al-Wāqidī) shows 15 correspondences, ten units of similar content and twelve cases where a relationship is lacking.

There is obviously a structural similarity between al-Zuhrī's *matn* and the two other texts, and this is further affirmed by the fact that the sequence of the units is nearly the same. In addition, a good number of cases of correspondence in content could be found. The correspondences are much more frequent between al-Zuhrī's text and S (al-Wāqidī) than D (al-Ṭabarī), even if one limits the comparison to the units 1-23 for which both S and D have an equivalent text. The relationship between Z and S is therefore closer than that between Z and D.

The relationship between al-Zuhrī's tradition and those alleged to derive from Ibn Unays becomes also evident when looking for correspondences in wording. Text S shows several close textual parallels:[120]

S	Z
– *wa-qad baʿathanā rasūl Allāh khamsat nafar: ʿAbd Allāh b. ʿAtīk wa-ʿAbd Allāh b. Unays wa-Abū Qatāda wa-l-Aswad b. Khuzāʿī wa-Masʿūd b. Sinān*	– *baʿatha rasūl Allāh* (mʿu) *khamsat nafar* (i) *ʿAbd Allāh b. ʿAtīk wa-ʿAbd Allāh b. Unays wa-Masʿūd b. Sinān al-Aswad wa-Abā Qatāda b. Ribʿī b. Baldama wa-Aswad b. Khuzāʿī ḥalīfan lahum* (mʿu)
– *thumma kharajū lā yamurrūna bi-bāb min buyūt Khaybar illā aghlaqūhu ḥattā aghlaqū buyūt al-qarya kullahā ḥattā ntahaw ilā ʿajala...fa-ṣaʿidnā*	– *fa-kharajū ḥattā jāʾū Khaybar fa-lammā dakhalū l-balad ʿamadū ilā kull bayt minhā fa-ghallaqūhu min khārijihi ʿalā ahlihi thumma asnadū ilayhi fī mashrabat lahu fī ʿajala* (m)
– *fa-mā ʿarafnāhu illā bi-bayāḍihi ka-annahu qubṭiyya mulqāt*	– *mā dallanī ʿalayhi illā bayāḍuhu ʿalā l-firāsh fī sawād al-layl ka-annahu qubṭiyya mulqāt* (m, i)
– *thumma dhakarnā anna rasūl Allāh (ṣ) nahānā ʿan qatl al-nisāʾ*	– *thumma yadhkur nahy rasūl Allāh (ṣ)...* (i) *nahā ʿan qatl al-nisāʾ wa-l-ṣibyān* (m2)
– *wa-kuntu rajulan aʿshā lā ubṣir bi-l-layl illā baṣaran ḍaʿīfan*	– *wa-kāna...rajulan sayyiʾ al-baṣar*
– *fa-attakiʾ bi-sayfī ʿalā baṭnihi ḥattā samiʿtu khashshahu fī l-firāsh*	– *taḥāmala ...ʿalayhi bi-sayfihi fī baṭnihi ḥattā anfadhahu*
– *wa-nkaffat rijluhu fa-ḥtamalūhu baynahum ...wa-khtabaʾa l-qawm fī baʿḍ manāhir Khaybar*	– *fa-wuthiʾat rijluhu wathʾan shadīdan wa-ḥtamalnāhu ḥattā naʾtī bihi manharan min ʿuyūnihim*
– *yaṭlubūnanā bi-l-nīrān fī shuʿal al-saʿaf*	– *fa-awqadū l-nīrān wa-ashʿalū fī l-saʿaf wa-jaʿalū yaltamisūn wa-yashtaddūn* (m) */wa-shtaddū fī kull wajh yaṭlubūnanā* (i)
– *samiʿtu minhum kalām ʿAbd Allāh b. ʿAtīk fa-in kāna fī bilādinā hādhihi fa-huwa maʿahum*	– *la-qad ʿaraftu ṣawt Ibn ʿAtīk thumma akdhabtu fa-qultu annā Ibn ʿAtīk bi-hādhihi l-bilād*
– *fa-qālat: fāẓa wa-lāhi Mūsā*	– *thumma qālat: fāẓa wa-lāhi yahūd*
– *qadimnā ʿalā l-nabī (ṣ) wa-huwa ʿalā l-*	– *qadimū ʿalā rasūl Allāh (ṣ) wa-huwa ʿalā*

[120] The following abbreviations shall be used for textual variants: m = Maʿmar, m2 = Maʿmar's short version, i = Ibn Isḥāq, mʿu = Mūsā b. ʿUqba, is = Ibrāhīm b. Saʿd.

	minbar, fa-lammā raʾānā qāla: aflaḥat al-wujūh! Fa-qulnā: aflaḥa wajhuka yā rasūl Allāh! Qāla: a-qataltumūhu? Qulnā: naʿam		*l-minbar* (mʿu) *fa-lammā raʾāhum* (is) *qāla: aflaḥat al-wujūh! Qālū: aflaḥa wajhuk yā rasūl Allāh. Qāla: a-qataltumūhu? Qālū: naʿam* (mʿu)
–	*wa-kullunā yaddaʿī qatlahu. Qāla: ʿajjilū ʿalayya bi-asyāfikum fa-ataynā bi-asyāfinā thumma qāla: hādhā qatalahu, hādhā athar ṭaʿām fī sayf ʿAbd Allāh b. Unays*	–	*wa-khtalafnā ʿindahu fī qatlihi wa-kullunā yaddaʿīhi fa-qāla rasūl Allāh (ṣ): hātū asyāfakum! Fa-jiʾnā bihā fa-naẓara ilayhā fa-qāla li-sayf ʿAbd Allāh b. Unays: hādhā qatalahu, arā fīhi athar al-ṭaʿām* (i)

This table shows that there are many textual correspondences between the tradition of al-Zuhrī and that ascribed to a son of Ibn Unays in al-Wāqidī's version. This could mean that al-Wāqidī or his informant may have created a new, much more elaborate narrative based on a version of al-Zuhrī's tradition without mentioning that. There are, however, indications that go against such an assumption. 1) If al-Wāqidī or his informant transmitted on the basis of al-Zuhrī's *matn*, one would have expected that they would have used one of the different versions known of it, such as that of Ibn Isḥāq or that of Maʿmar. But this is obviously not the case. al-Wāqidī's *matn* sometimes resembles that of Ibn Isḥāq, sometimes that of Maʿmar and sometimes even seems to mix them.[121] This can, perhaps, be explained by assuming that al-Wāqidī or his informant used a version of al-Zuhrī which is not preserved, or by assuming that he knew the different versions and created his own on the basis of them. Both assumptions are, to my mind, however, not satisfying. 2) The *matn* of al-Wā-

[121] J. Wellhausen, J. Horovitz and recently G. Schoeler have shown that al-Wāqidī sometimes plagiarized the text of Ibn Isḥāq without naming it as his source (G. Schoeler, *Charakter,* 134-42). This seems here, however, not to be the case. Al-Wāqidī's version corresponds with other versions of al-Zuhrī's tradition in seven places, but not with that of Ibn Isḥāq where there are only four correspondences. In two places the correspondence favors Maʿmar even in obvious contradiction to Ibn Isḥāq. The charge of plagiarism and outright fabrication of evidence raised against al-Wāqidī has been rejected by J.M. Jones, "Ibn Isḥāq and Wāqidī. The Dream of ʿĀtika and the Raid to Nakhla in Relation to the Charge of Plagiarism", in *BSOAS*, 22 (1959), 41-51 and recently again by M. Lecker in his "Wāqidī's Account" and "The Death of the Prophet Muḥammad's Father: Did Wāqidī Invent Some of the Evidence?", in *ZDMG*, 145 (1995), 9-27. It seems to me that a systematic study of al-Wāqidī's *Maghāzī* in light of all the new material available today is urgently needed before a definite judgement on al-Wāqidī can be made.

qidī displays too many substantial variations with that of al-Zuhrī's tradition to warrant dependence on it. To give some examples: In Z Ibn ʿAtīk introduces his group as Arabs seeking provisions, in S he introduces himself as a Jew bringing a present. In Z Ibn ʿAtīk had bad eyesight and therefore fell from the ladder and sprained his foot; according to S, Ibn Unays was the one who could see only poorly which, however, did not prevent him from finding his victim and killing him, and it was Ibn Qatāda who sprained his foot when trying to retrieve his bow which he had forgotten. Nothing of this is to be found in Z and it is difficult to imagine why someone would have altered al-Zuhrī's *matn* so much. 3) Al-Wāqidī produces not only a complete narrative ascribed to Ibn Unays' son ʿAṭiyya but also a variant allegedly going back to Khārija, another one of his sons, which gives a different description of the killing of Ibn Abī l-Ḥuqayq, a description which enhances the role of Ibn Unays and diminishes that of his companions. It makes no sense to assume that al-Wāqidī or his informant Ayyūb b. al-Nuʿmān invented both versions.

The structural similarities and the textual correspondences of both *matns*, that of al-Zuhrī and al-Wāqidī, cannot, therefore, be the consequence of dependence of one on the other, but must derive from one or more common sources of both. Such a conclusion is in accordance with the evidence which the *isnāds* reveal. Both versions purport to go back to different members of the Kaʿb b. Mālik family: al-Wāqidī's text to al-Nuʿmān b. ʿAbd Allāh b. Kaʿb b. Mālik, and that of al-Zuhrī to either ʿAbd al-Raḥmān b. ʿAbd Allāh b. Kaʿb b. Mālik, or his uncle ʿAbd al-Raḥmān or his father ʿAbd Allāh.

A similar conclusion is to be drawn from the comparison of al-Zuhrī's tradition and that allegedly going back via ʿAbd al-Raḥmān b. Kaʿb b. Mālik to a daughter of Ibn Unays (al-Ṭabarī). Though the relationship of the text D has more structural similarity than correspondence in content and wording, there are some striking parallels to be found.[122]

---

[122] Abbreviations: is = Ibrāhīm b. Saʿd, m = Maʿmar, i = Ibn Isḥāq, mk = Mālik b. Anas, sn = Sufyān b. ʿUyayna.

D	**Z**
– *anna l-rahṭ alladhīna baʿathahum rasūl Allāh (ṣ) ilā Ibn Abī l-Ḥuqayq li-yaqtulūhu*	– *anna l-rahṭ alladhī baʿatha rasūl Allāh (ṣ) li-qatl Ibn Abī l-Ḥuqayq* (is)
– *wa-innahum qadimū Khaybar laylan*	– *fa-kharajū ḥattā idhā qadimū Khaybar ataw dār Ibn Abī l-Ḥuqayq laylan* (i)
– *fa-ʿamadnā ilā abwābihim nughalliquhā min khārij*	– *fa-lammā dakhalū l-balad ʿamadū ilā kulli bayt minhā fa-ghallaqūhu min khārijihi ʿalā ahlihi* (m)
– *thumma jiʾnā ilā l-mashraba allatī fīhā Ibn Abī l-Ḥuqayq*	– *thumma asnadū ilayhi fī mashraba lahu* (m)
– *fa-staʾdhana ...fa-qālat imraʾat Ibn Abī l-Ḥuqayq*	– *fa-staʾdhanū fa-kharajat ilayhim imraʾatuhu fa-qālat*
– *fa-adhkur nahy rasūl Allāh (ṣ) ʿan qatl al-nisāʾ wa-l-wildān fa-akuff ʿanhā*	– *thumma yadhkur nahy rasūl Allāh (ṣ)* (i) *ʿan qatl al-nisāʾ wa-l-wildān* (mk, sn) *fa-yakuff yadahu* (i)
– *fa-saqaṭa ʿAbd Allāh b. ʿAtīk fī l-daraja*	– *fa-waqaʿa [ʿAbd Allāh b. ʿAtīk] min al-daraja* (i)

Nonetheless, the differences are such that both texts cannot depend on each other. Such differences are: According to D, only two men, Ibn ʿAtīk and Ibn Unays, entered Ibn Abī l-Ḥuqayq's house. Ibn ʿAtīk first tried to kill him but was not able to do so properly. Ibn Unays forgot his bow and returned to fetch it. The similarities and textual parallels must then derive from sources which both versions had in common.

The three versions just compared, that of al-Zuhrī and the two versions allegedly going back to Ibn Unays, seem to be derived from narratives circulating in the family of Kaʿb Mālik. These narratives vary in many details, partially in substantial ones, but display nonetheless many structural and sometimes even textual correspondences. The differences in these narratives are probably due to both different sources from which they originally derived and to a longer process of oral transmission in the course of which interferences between the different versions can have taken place. In addition, the stories could have been abbreviated or expanded (this would explain the different lengths of the versions).

Even if this history of the different versions is accepted, one may wonder why two of them have been constructed as going back to Ibn Unays, one of the participants in the expedition and, according to all versions of the Kaʿb b. Mālik family, the man who really killed Ibn Abī l-Ḥuqayq, while the other version, that of al-Zuhrī, does not specify the real author of the report. We can only speculate about the reason for this. It seems not too far-fetched to assume that every participant in the expedition narrated his own version of the events and that these versions were transmitted by their descendants and friends and became part of the "tribal memory" of the Banū Salima to whom all the participants belonged. The descendants and friends of Ibn ʿAtīk would probably have emphasized the role played by their ancestor, those of Ibn Unays would have done the same in favor of theirs. The tradition allegedly going back to al-Barāʾ may reflect the former type of origin, the version ascribed to the daughter of Ibn Unays may reflect the latter. Other transmitters may have tried to reconcile the different family biases and to concede to all of the leading participants an important role. This seems to be the case in the versions of Nuʿmān b. ʿAbd Allāh b. Kaʿb ascribed to two different sons of Ibn Unays and in al-Zuhrī's tradition from his informant, a son or grandson of Kaʿb b. Mālik.

This leaves us with the thorny question as to which of the two versions is more "original", the longer one preserved by al-Wāqidī or al-Zuhrī's shorter one? As said above, following the ideas of J. Schacht there is a tendency in Western *ḥadīth* scholarship to regard the shorter traditions as being the older ones. In my view there is no plausible reason why such a generalization should be accepted. Detailed narratives may be as old as shorter ones, and often the latter are obviously abbreviations of the former. It does not seem inconceivable to me that the version preserved by al-Wāqidī is at least as old as that which al-Zuhrī brought into wider circulation. I even tend to think that al-Zuhrī's version is more of a summary, based on at least two different, originally probably more detailed, stories. The two different versions of what happened when the detachment returned to Medina, both derived from al-Zuhrī, may serve as evidence for this hypothesis. It also seems plausible that collectors like al-Zuhrī trimmed some of the fanciful, garrulous and overly-detailed stories and harmonized obvious contradictions. An illustrative example of how collectors sometimes proceeded with long stories is Ibn Saʿd's transmission of al-Wāqidī's version of the story about the killing of Ibn Abī l-Ḥuqayq. Ibn Saʿd's cleaned-up text does not vary much from that of al-Zuhrī.[123] In the course of transmission by professional transmitters, the stories could undergo even further abbreviation, as is seen from

[123] Ibn Saʿd, *Ṭabaqāt*, II, 91-92.

the several "short stories" transmitted by or from some pupils of al-Zuhrī. The detailed *qiṣṣa* preserved by al-Wāqidī may, therefore, represent a pre-al-Zuhrī stage of development, which does not mean that all of its details must necessarily go back to the first century.[124]

If my conclusion is correct, that al-Zuhrī's version and the two traditions which are ascribed to Ibn Unays (D, S) are not dependent on each other, but derive from common older sources, then the "legal" element in which the Prophet is reported to have forbidden the killing of women and children must already belong to this pre-al-Zuhrī stage since it is part of all three of them. If it is "a hagiographical insertion", as J. Burton suggests[125]—which is far from certain—then it is a very old one.

The comparison of the versions going back to members of the Kaʿb b. Mālik family has revealed a structural similarity and several textual correspondences. This is, much less the case when they are compared with the version ascribed to al-Barāʾ b. ʿĀzib. The correspondences in content there are the following: ʿAbd Allāh b. ʿAtīk played a leading role in this expedition; he locked or opened some doors when he went at night to the house of his victim; he climbed up to him by way of a ladder and killed him, after a first unsuccessful attempt, by running a sword through his belly; when descending, the murderer missed a step and sprained his foot; the group did not leave until the death of Abū Rāfiʿ had been confirmed.

Textual correspondences are very few and might be accidental.[126] A dependence of Abū Isḥāq's *matn* on those going back to members of the Kaʿb b. Mālik family, or vice versa, can be ruled out. The com-

---

[124] As we have seen above, al-Wāqidī himself sometimes tacitly added elements from other sources. See note 116. The conclusion that this *qiṣṣa* must be old cannot be taken as proof for the thesis that most of the old traditions were the product of "professional" *quṣṣāṣ* (cf. P. Crone, *Meccan Trade and the Rise of Islam*, Princeton, 1987, 215 ff.). The contributions of persons known as such professionals are in any case not substantial in the *sīra* traditions. Cautiously, we can say that many traditions on events concerning the life of the Prophet probably had the form of narrations which were more detailed and lively than what is often preserved in the Sunnite standard collections. Cf. also M.J. Kister, "On the Papyrus of Wahb b. Munabbih", in *BSOAS*, 22 (1959), 563-64.

[125] See Mattock, "History and Fiction", 97, n. 1.

[126] To give two examples: In version S, Ibn Abī l-Ḥuqayq's house is called a *qaṣr*, as in the tradition of Abū Isḥāq, and the killing is described with the words *ḥattā samiʿtu khashshahu fī l-firāsh* which reminds one of *ḥattā samiʿtu ṣawt al-ʿaẓm* (however, only found in Yūsuf b. Isḥāq's variant of Abū Isḥāq's story).

mon elements which they display must either be due to common sources (instead of Mattock's archetype, we should talk of *archetypes*) which must be very old, older than the stories transmitted by the members of the Kaʿb b. Mālik family, or be part of the historical kernel of the stories, i.e., reflect what really happened; conceivably, both alternatives are possible at the same time as well.

The tradition of ʿUrwa

The above conclusion seems to be corroborated by a tradition on the murder of Ibn Abī l-Ḥuqayq which I have mentioned until now only in passing: the version of ʿUrwa b. al-Zubayr.[127] The most complete text of it which I have come across up to now is that preserved in al-Bayhaqī's *Dalāʾil.* It is a short version which originally may have been more detailed. The last three links of the *isnād* are Ibn Lahīʿa (d. 174/790-1)—Abū l-Aswad [Yatīm ʿUrwa] (d. 131/748-9 or later)—ʿUrwa (d. 94/712-3).[128] The text reads as follows:

> Sallām b. Abī l-Ḥuqayq had collected [forces] among the Ghaṭafān and among the polytheist Arabs in their neighborhood, inviting them to fight the Messenger of God and giving them heavy payments. The Ghaṭafān, then, conspired with them [the Jews?]. Ḥuyayy b. Akhṭab in Mecca had seduced the inhabitants of Mecca. He had told them that their tribe [Ghatafān?] frequently came to that place [Mekka?] expecting resources and money. Ghaṭafān [thus] consented with them [the

[127] Bayhaqī, *Dalāʾil,* IV, 38; fragments of it are found in al-Wāqidī, *Maghāzī,* I, 394 (without *isnād* at the end of ʿAṭiyya's report from his father), in Ibn Saʿd, *Ṭabaqāt,* II, 91 (without *isnād* and obviously taken from al-Wāqidī), Ibn Sayyid al-Nās, *ʿUyūn,* II, 66 (quoting Ibn Saʿd), Dhahabī, *Taʾrīkh,* I, 345, Ibn Ḥajar, *Fatḥ,* VII, 435 and Zurqānī, *Sharḥ,* II, 167 (according to S. Mursī al-Ṭāhir, *Bidāyat al-kitāba al-taʾrīkhiyya ʿinda l-ʿarab. Awwal sīra fī l-islām: ʿUrwa b. al-Zubayr b. al-ʿAwwām,* Beirut, 1995, 170). The just mentioned al-Ṭāhir also quotes under the heading *maqtal Ibn Abī Rāfiʿ* a fragment from Ibn Sayyid al-Nās' *ʿUyūn* with the same *isnād* (Ibn Lahīʿa—Abū l-Aswad—ʿUrwa) but with a completely different *matn* ("The Messenger of God sent ʿAbd Allāh b. ʿAtīk with 30 riders, among them ʿAbd Allāh b. Unays..."). This is, however, not a fragment which has to do with the murder of Ibn Abī l-Ḥuqayq, but belongs to the expedition against Usayr (Ibn Saʿd) or al-Yusayr b. Rizām, another Jewish leader at Khaybar. Ibn Sayyid al-Nās quotes ʿUrwa's statement in the right context and mentions also that the name ʿAbd Allāh b. ʿAtīk goes back to al-Walīd, one of Ibn Lahīʿa's pupils, whereas other transmitters from him have ʿAbd Allāh b. Rawāḥa, the man who is termed the leader of the expedition against Usayr by other reports. Cf. Ibn Sayyid al-Nās, *ʿUyūn,* II, 110.

[128] This is also the *isnād* which al-Dhahabī reproduces. Ibn Ḥajar and al-Zurqānī mention this tradition only *min ṭarīq* Abī l-Aswad [Ibn Ḥajar: al-Aswad] *ʿan* ʿUrwa.

> Meccans?][129] The Messenger of God sent ʿAbd Allāh b. ʿAtīk[130] b. Qays b. al-Aswad, Abū Qatāda al-Ribʿī and Aswad al-Khuzāʿī against Ibn Abī l-Ḥuqayq. He gave the command over them to ʿAbd Allāh b. ʿAtīk. They attacked him by night and killed him.[131]

Since there seem to be no other variants reporting this event on the authority of ʿUrwa, we have no possibility of checking the *isnād* other than looking up what biographical dictionaries provide on the transmitters. This is not very favorable, at least as far as Ibn Lahīʿa is concerned.[132] Most of the *matn* consists of an account on what causes or motives led to the expedition against Ibn Abī l-Ḥuqayq. This aspect is missing in the traditions on the event going back to the Kaʿb b. Mālik family but it is mentioned, although more briefly, in two of the variants of the tradition ascribed to al-Barāʾ.[133] The account on the expedition itself is limited to the following: a) the Prophet sent three men to Ibn Abī l-Ḥuqayq, b) these were ʿAbd Allāh b. ʿAtīk b. Qays b. al-Aswad, Abū Qatāda b. Ribʿī and Aswad al-Khuzāʿī, c) he gave the command to ʿAbd Allāh b. ʿAtīk, and d) they attacked Ibn Abī l-Ḥuqayq at night and killed him.

The three participants mentioned are also to be found in al-Zuhrī's tradition from the Kaʿb b. Mālik family but the names are not completely identical. The variants of al-Zuhrī's *matn* give neither a detailed *nasab* of Ibn ʿAtīk nor the name Aswad al-Khuzāʿī in place of Aswad b. Khuzāʿī. Most noteworthy is that there is no mention of ʿAbd Allāh b. Unays who, according to the versions of the Kaʿb b. Mālik family, was the one who killed Ibn Abī l-Ḥuqayq. These differences as well as the reduced number of participants do not speak for a direct dependence of Ibn Lahīʿa's account on that of al-Zuhrī. However, the statement "*wa-ammara ʿalayhim ʿAbd Allāh b. ʿAtīk*" does occur also in al-Zuhrī's tradition, as the variants of Ibn Isḥāq and Mūsā b. ʿUqba illustrate. This could point to a dependence on al-Zuhrī's tradition, but such a conclusion is not compelling since the same phrase is also found in the tradition of al-Barāʾ, and since nearly all traditions proceed from the fact that Ibn ʿAtīk had been the leader of the expedition. It is possible, therefore, that the version which Ibn

---

129 The text is not very clear.
130 The edition erroneously vocalizes ʿUtayk.
131 Bayhaqī, *Dalāʾil,* IV, 38.
132 See Ibn Ḥajar, *Tahdhīb,* V, 373-79.
133 See pp. 182, 189.

Lahīʿa transmitted from Abū l-Aswad is unconnected to that of al-Zuhrī and may go back to earlier sources. It cannot be excluded that one of these sources may have been an account from ʿUrwa b. al-Zubayr. We must, however, be cautious with this tradition which purports to go back to ʿUrwa. Recent studies have shown that Ibn Lahīʿa's *maghāzī* accounts with the *isnād* Abū l-Aswad *ʿan* ʿUrwa display some features which originally did not belong to ʿUrwa's *matn*.[134] We must, therefore, admit the possibility that either Ibn Lahīʿa or Abū l-Aswad used elements of al-Zuhrī's tradition which he recalled, adding other elements from unknown sources or which he invented. As long as Ibn Lahīʿa's transmissions from Abū l-Aswad have not been systematically studied and compared with other versions, and as long as variants of this alleged ʿUrwa tradition which are separate from Ibn Lahīʿa's are lacking, we should refrain from making hasty conclusions and had better not use this tradition ascribed to ʿUrwa for dating purposes.

IV. Variant Traditions

Outside the mainstream of the *maghāzī* tradition concerning the murder of Ibn Abī l-Ḥuqayq, there are other traditions about that person which differ from it in some details. These traditions are found in historical, biographical, exegetical and other compilations. The differences concern mainly the following points: 1) his names, 2) the reason why he was killed, and 3) the time of the event. Marco Schöller has collected many of these variants in his dissertation *Exegetisches Denken und Prophetenbiographie. Eine quellenkritische Analyse der Sīra-Überlieferung zu Muḥammads Konflikt mit den Juden*.[135]

As far as names and *nasab* are concerned, Schöller notes many differences in the sources.[136] In addition to a full name Abū Rāfiʿ Sallām b. Abī l-Ḥuqayq al-Aʿwar, we come across the *kunya* Abū Rāfiʿ, the *ism* Sallām or ʿAbd Allāh, and the *nasab* Ibn Abī l-Ḥu-

[134] See G. Schoeler, *Charakter*, 81-85 and the contribution of A. Görke in this volume.

[135] Wiesbaden 1998, 282-86, 336-40. The author has kindly put those parts of his book dealing with the episode at my disposal before publication.

[136] Ibid., 282-86. The texts he mentions do not, however, always have a connection to Ibn Abī l-Ḥuqayq's killing.

qayq.[137] His *nisba* is sometimes given as al-Naḍarī, sometimes as al-Quraẓī. In addition, there is a Jewish leader called Sallām b. Mishkam who is also described as collaborating with the Quraysh against the Prophet and living for a period of time at Khaybar. According to some sources, he belonged to the Banū al-Naḍīr, according to others, to the Banū Qurayẓa. In view of this "confusion" concerning the two persons mentioned, Schöller suggests that the original reports only knew one Sallām, one Ibn Abī l-Ḥuqayq and one Abū Rāfiʿ, who were actually different persons or belonged to different traditions but later became partially combined, partially individualized by putting them into new contexts and giving them different names and *nasab*s. He further assumes that the target of the expedition led by ʿAbd Allāh b. ʿAtīk was Abū Rāfiʿ, not Sallām b. Abī l-Ḥuqayq, and he states that even al-Zuhrī did not regard Sallām and Abū Rāfiʿ as one and the same person.[138] The combination of the two, then, must have taken place after al-Zuhrī.

Schöller's assumptions can be disproved, however, by the *isnād-cum-matn* analysis. If we compare the names of the murdered person which appear in the *matn*s of the variants deriving from al-Zuhrī, it becomes obvious that al-Zuhrī must already have known and transmitted the three elements of the name: Abū Rāfiʿ is transmitted by Maʿmar and Mūsā b. ʿUqba, Sallām by Maʿmar and al-Bakkāʾī *ʿan* Ibn Isḥāq, and Ibn Abī l-Ḥuqayq is used by all transmitters (but alone, i.e., without further additions, it is only used by Salama and Muḥammad b. Salama[139] *ʿan* Ibn Isḥāq, by Ibrāhīm b. Saʿd, Mālik, Sufyān b. ʿUyayna *ʿan* al-Zuhrī, and by ʿAbd Allāh b. al-Mubārak *ʿan* Maʿmar). In the study of transmission history the following rule obtains: correspondences between two or more independent variants of the same tradition most probably derive from a common source. According to this rule, al-Zuhrī must have transmitted (at least sometimes) more than one element of the name, perhaps even the complete name. As usual, most of the transmitters (and perhaps even al-

---

[137] Schöller does not mention this last possibility, which I added because it is frequent.

[138] Because he called him ʿAbd Allāh b. Abī l-Ḥuqayq, not Sallām b. Abī l-Ḥuqayq; see Schöller, *Exegetisches Denken*, 339.

[139] In his version *abī* is lacking. This is obviously a transmission error.

Zuhrī himself) preferred a short version of the name, mostly Ibn Abī l-Ḥuqayq.[140]

In the tradition complex transmitted by Abū Isḥāq al-Sabīʿī and ascribed to al-Barāʾ, almost all variants, even the late ones like those preserved by al-Bayhaqī, mention only the *kunya* Abū Rāfiʿ.[141] In the traditions alleged to go back to ʿAbd Allāh b. Unays, there is variation: the version of the daughter of ʿAbd Allāh b. Unays (al-Ṭabarī) uses Ibn Abī l-Ḥuqayq (according to al-Ḥākim's *al-Iklīl,* ʿAbd Allāh b. Abī l-Ḥuqayq)[142], while the version ascribed to Ibn Unays' son ʿAṭiyya as preserved by al-Wāqidī has Abū Rāfiʿ. The tradition allegedly going back to ʿUrwa b. al-Zubayr also shows variants concerning the name: the most detailed version (al-Bayhaqī) has Sallām b. Abī l-Ḥuqayq, the fragment contained in al-Wāqidī's *Maghāzī* has only Ibn Abī l-Ḥuqayq, and that quoted by al-Wāqidī's pupil Ibn Saʿd in his *Ṭabaqāt* has Abū Rāfiʿ b. Abī l-Ḥuqayq.[143] This comparison of the textual variants of the different tradition complexes concerned with the murder of Ibn Abī l-Ḥuqayq suggests that the different appellations used do not derive from originally different traditions which were later combined, as presumed by Schöller, but are due to the transmitters who show a tendency to abbreviate, sometimes preferring Abū Rāfiʿ, sometimes Ibn Abī l-Ḥuqayq. The complete name was already known to al-Zuhrī, perhaps even to his informants. There is no indication that the murdered man was originally only known as Abū Rāfiʿ.[144]

---

[140] For the sources, see note 22.

[141] For the sources, see note 16. Al-Rūyānī's version does not mention any name.

[142] The beginning of al-Ḥākim's version is quoted by Ibn Ḥajar (*Fatḥ,* VII, 434) without *isnād* but, according to the *matn,* it is the version of Ibn Unays' daughter which is more completely preserved by al-Ṭabarī. Schöller's claim that the name ʿAbd Allāh b. Abī l-Ḥuqayq was transmitted by al-Zuhrī seems to be based on a misunderstanding. In al-Bukhārī's *Jāmiʿ,* the earliest source to which Schöller refers, al-Zuhrī is not mentioned as a source of this name and al-Bukhārī's commentator Ibn Ḥajar clearly connects the name ʿAbd Allāh b. Abī l-Ḥuqayq with the tradition of ʿAbd Allāh b. Unays, which is not known to have been transmitted by al-Zuhrī. Seen against the evidence of the other traditions, the *ism* ʿAbd Allāh instead of Sallām is probably a transmission error made before al-Bukhārī. It may have been caused by the name ʿAbd Allāh b. ʿAtīk which follows immediately after the name Ibn Abī l-Ḥuqayq.

[143] In his introduction, however, Ibn Saʿd gives the full name: Abū Rāfiʿ Sallām b. Abī l-Ḥuqayq al-Naḍarī (*Ṭabaqāt,* II, 91)

[144] In a poem ascribed to Ḥassān b. Thābit (Ibn Hishām, *Sīra,* 716) two Jewish

The mere *ism* of Ibn Abī l-Ḥuqayq, Sallām, is not found in the earliest dateable reports of his murder. The reason may lie in the fact that this could have led to confusion with the other Jewish leader of the time, Sallām b. Mishkam, who Schöller opines is another invented character of *sīra* literature, evolved like Sallām b. Abī l-Ḥuqayq, from reports of a Jewish leader called only Sallām in order to fit into special contexts. In light of my conclusion concerning Sallām b. Abī l-Ḥuqayq, this assumption loses its plausibility. In addition, we may ask ourselves why there could not indeed have been two contemporaneous Jewish leaders with the same *ism*, both collaborating with the Quraysh against the Prophet and be killed in the course of the events. After all, both have different *kunya*s (that of Sallām b. Mishkam seems to have been Abū Ḥakam)[145] and varying *nasab*s while the correspondence between them is such that they can apply to every other leader of the Medinan Jews.

The fact, however, that both had the same *ism* may have contributed to some confusion among Muslim traditionists and scholars with regard to details of their lives. Attempts to place the reports concerning the two Jewish leaders in a chronological framework may have led to additional, sometimes contradictory details, as Schöller rightly presumes. Among those differences are the tribal affiliation (Banū l-Naḍīr or Banū Qurayẓa) and date of and reason for their being killed. These details seem to belong to a secondary stage of development. *Nisba* and date of death are lacking in all the original reports of the murder of Abū Rāfiʿ Sallām Ibn Abī l-Ḥuqayq which are examined in this article and which seem to be the earliest dateable traditions on the issue. Exact dates for the expedition against Ibn Abī l-Ḥuqayq seem to have been fixed only in the generation after al-Zuhrī, whose dating was still crude: "[His killing was] after that of Kaʿb b. al-Ashraf,"[146] which could mean shortly after or many years later.

The reason for the murder is not given in the traditions ascribed to a descendant of Kaʿb b. Mālik and to ʿAbd Allāh b. Unays and is given differently in the traditions ascribed to al-Barāʾ and to ʿUrwa b.

---

chiefs were mentioned as killed by the Muslims, Ibn al-Ashraf and Ibn Abī l-Ḥuqayq. The latter is not called Abū Rāfiʿ.

[145] Cf. Ibn Hishām, *Sīra,* 713 (in the poem by Jabal b. Jawwāl al-Thaʿlabī).

[146] Bukhārī, *Jāmiʿ,* 64:16 (heading of the *bāb*).

al-Zubayr.[147] It seems only natural to assume that in their original reports the participants in the expedition did not ponder on the reason why the Prophet may have ordered or allowed the killing, but merely recounted how they managed to do it. Reflecting on the possible reasons for the attack agrees more with the work of collectors of traditions, who tried to fit the scrambled pieces of the mosaic into a coherent picture—men such as ʿUrwa and al-Zuhrī (in whose traditions this issue actually emerges first) and later compilers.

These secondary differences should not make us jump to the conclusion that all of the other details (even variant ones) must also derive from the same effort to construct a chronologically structured and internally coherent picture of the Prophet's lifetime. We must allow for the possibility that many variant details are part of the primary stock of narrations which were recounted by different individuals. Other differences are certainly the result of the transmission process in the course of which elements may have disappeared or emerged by carelessness[148] or on purpose. Thus, I do not reject Schöller's idea that details of the *sīra* reports could be the result of "contextualization", i.e., putting reports in a new context, but I do not think that all of the variants can be explained in this manner, surely not the differences concerning the figure of Abū Rāfiʿ Sallām b. Abī l-Ḥuqayq. In the case of the latter, Schöller can only speculate whereas an *isnād-cum-matn* analysis allows us to reconstruct the transmission history with more certainty.[149]

In this context, finally, I would like to review an issue which was raised already at the beginning of this century and has been recently revived by Schöller: the question of whether the traditions on the murder of Ibn Abī l-Ḥuqayq are influenced by accounts contained in the Old Testament. P. Jensen suggested in 1922 that the traditions about the murder of Ibn Abī l-Ḥuqayq were related to the accounts of

---

[147] See p. 223.

[148] The information, for instance, that Sallām b. Abī l-Ḥuqayq was killed by an arrow fired by the Prophet can presumably be explained by a mix-up of different sons of Abū l-Ḥuqayq made by a transmitter in that, for example, only one part of the name (Sallām or Ibn Abī l-Ḥuqayq) was found in his notes, so that the real identity was not quite clear to him. The transmitter could have tried to clear up the uncertainty. In the course of this study we have come across the confusing of names several times.

[149] This must not be misunderstood to mean that by using this method speculations can be completely avoided.

the murder of Ishbaʿl (2 Samuel 4) and, in particular, to that of ʿEglōn (Judges 3). J. Horovitz accepted a possible influence of the latter story.[150] When one compares the texts, however, it becomes obvious that the correspondences are very few in number. In the narration of the murder of Ishbaʿl the only real parallel is that the man was killed when lying on his bed and sleeping. The other details are completely different. With the story of the murder of the king of Moab, ʿEglōn, the Muslim traditions have three rough parallels: a) the Israelite Ehūd killed his victim in the upper room of his palace, b) he was murdered by a dagger plunged deep into his belly, and c) Ehūd closed the doors of the room before leaving the room (by the window) so that the attack remained unnoticed for some time. Of these parallels those of the upper room and the closing of doors is found in all three traditions which tell the particulars of the expedition against Ibn Abī l-Ḥuqayq (the tradition of al-Barāʾ, Ibn Kaʿb and ʿAbd Allāh b. Unays). The closing of the doors in the house is a very prominent feature in the tradition of al-Barāʾ (but not the exit by the window). In the traditions of ʿAbd Allāh b. Unays and Ibn Kaʿb, however, the doors of the other houses were locked, not those of Ibn Abī l-Ḥuqayq's. The detail of thrusting a sword (not a dagger) deep into the belly of the victim is present in the tradition of al-Barāʾ, Ibn Kaʿb and that of ʿAṭiyya b. ʿAbd Allāh b. Unays from his father, but not in the account of the daughter of Ibn Unays.

All in all, the correspondences between the biblical accounts and the Muslim traditions are few in number and so general that a dependence of the latter on the former is not compelling. The above-mentioned details as such are not unique for an attack (which in the Bible is not described as a night attack as in the Muslim traditions) on a single person living in a fortress, and also the combination of the three features can be mere coincidence. If one wishes, nevertheless, to postulate that the Muslim traditions borrowed these details from the biblical accounts, this borrowing must have taken place in the period when the different traditions were created. Since the three tradition complexes concerning Ibn Abī l-Ḥuqayq's murder seem to be independent of each other and not traceable to a single original

---

[150] P. Jensen, "Das Leben Muhammeds und die David-Sage", in *Der Islam*, 12 (1922), 91, 95; J. Horovitz, "Biblische Nachwirkungen in der *Sīra*", in *Der Islam*, 12 (1922), 185. M. Schöller drew my attention to these two articles.

report, the authors of the different traditions must have used the biblical stories as model independently but in almost the same manner. This does not seem very probable. Alternatively, one could assume that the three traditions received their common elements which resemble the biblical stories by borrowing from a Muslim archetype[151] which must go back, then, far into the first Islamic century. For the existence of such an archetype, however, our investigation has not found any indication, and to postulate it seems superfluous because their common features most probably constitute their historical kernel.

V. Conclusion

Let us recapitulate the different steps of our investigation and their results.

Traditions concerning the murder of the Jewish leader Ibn Abī l-Ḥuqayq are found in a wide range of sources. The earliest sources are Mālik's *Muwaṭṭaʾ*, al-Wāqidī's *Maghāzī*, ʿAbd al-Razzāq's *Muṣannaf*, Ibn Hishām's *Sīra* and al-Bukhārī's *Jāmiʿ*.

On the basis of an *isnād* comparison, we have singled out four different tradition complexes: one going back to the Companion al-Barāʾ b. ʿĀzib, another to a descendant of the Companion Kaʿb b. Mālik, a third to the Companion ʿAbd Allāh b. Unays and the fourth to the Successor ʿUrwa b. al-Zubayr.

The analysis of the *isnād* bundles compiled from the variants of the four tradition complexes has produced the following results: The *isnād* bundles of the two most current traditions (al-Barāʾ and Ibn Kaʿb) show common links who died around 125/742-3 (Abū Isḥāq al-Sabīʿī, al-Zuhrī). One complex of traditions has a common link on the level of the Companions (ʿAbd Allāh b. Unays), but is only based on very few transmission lines. The fourth tradition has a common link who died in 174/790-1 (Ibn Lahīʿa).

On the basis of the *isnād* analysis, the hypothesis was made that traditions on the murder of Ibn Abī l-Ḥuqayq must be earlier than the time of the sources in which they first appear and must go back at least to Abū Isḥāq and al-Zuhrī.

[151] As postulated by J. Mattock, cf. note 14.

This hypothesis was checked by a *matn* analysis of the variants of the different traditions. As far as the traditions ascribed to al-Barāʾ and Ibn Kaʿb are concerned, the results were the following: The texts of the variants of each tradition complex seem to be independent of each other and must for that reason go back to a common source. This conclusion is supported by the *isnād* structure so that we can conclude that the common source of the *matn*s must be the common link of the *isnād*s. The text analysis has shown, however, that neither common link, Abū Isḥāq and al-Zuhrī, always told the stories in exactly the same wording.

The *matn* analysis of the versions ascribed to the companion ʿAbd Allāh b. Unays has revealed so many essential structural elements in common that they must derive from a common source as well, although the texts of the variants differ more substantially than in the case of the traditions going back to Abū Isḥāq and al-Zuhrī. We concluded from this that the common skeleton of the versions ascribed to ʿAbd Allāh b. Unays possibly goes back to him, the common link of the *isnād* bundle.

A comparison of the versions ascribed to ʿAbd Allāh b. Unays with al-Zuhrī's tradition showed structural similarities and textual correspondences as well, although a dependence of one upon the other can be ruled out. These similarities have a counterpart in the *isnād*s since all of these versions are said to have been transmitted by members of the Kaʿb b. Mālik family. This speaks in favor of the thesis that the tradition is earlier than the time of al-Zuhrī and that he most probably received the details from which he composed his tradition from the person(s) he named as his informants (descendants of Kaʿb).

Summarizing our findings we can state:

The *matn-cum-isnād* analysis of the different stories and their variants which relate the expedition against Abū Rāfiʿ b. Abī l-Ḥuqayq has revealed that these stories are much older than one would expect; this is shown by the common links which their *isnād* bundles display. We have been able to show that the different stories are not directly dependent on each other and must derive from older sources from which all of them borrowed. The two transmitters identified as common links died around 125/742-3. They certainly received their stories during the last third of the first/seventh century.[152] This is corroborated by the versions going back to ʿAbd Allāh b. Unays. Since there were several different versions already circulating in this period, it is probable that their origins are much older. In my view, it is not only possible, but probable, that their common elements reflect, at least in part, historical reality. This historical kernel is, however, rather meagre. It consists of the information that the Prophet sent a few men under the command of ʿAbd Allāh b. ʿAtīk to Abū Rāfiʿ b. Abī l-Ḥuqayq who lived outside Medina in order to kill him. The assassin (or assassins) had to ascend to his appartment and when descending he or another man missed a step and hurt his foot. They did not leave until the death of the victim had been verified. It does not make sense to assume that someone would have invented such a story at a time when many eyewitnesses of the Prophet's Medinan period were still alive.

As to the question of which of the participants really killed him, the reports vary, just as they do on many other details of the expedition. Some of the details which are given by more than one version may be historical as well, as the number and the names of the participants, the command given to Ibn ʿAtīk, or the Prophet's prohibition to kill women and children. It is, however, impossible to gain certainty on these details. We can only ask ourselves again how different people came to invent independently the same details of a story narrating the murder of Ibn Abī l-Ḥuqayq. There are no indications that the original stories about this event owe their existence to exegetical, theological or legal needs, which are often supposed to have played a role, and sometimes indeed did, in the formation of the *sīra* material. This does not mean that parts of them could not be used for such purposes. As we have seen, legal arguments were indeed derived from them as early as the time of al-Zuhrī. I have not checked whether these stories also played a role in Qurʾānic exegesis. Even if traces of them can be found in early exegesis, this will not allow us to conclude that the stories themselves were exegetical inventions until clear clues are found which substantiate such a claim.

What is the impact of our results on the study of the Prophet's biography in general? First of all, it is obvious that the biographies of

[152] This was already asserted by C. Becker, J. Horovitz, R. Sellheim and M.J. Kister for the legendary *sīra* stories. Cf. Kister, "On the Papyrus of Wahb b. Munabbih", 563-64.

the Prophet written by Western scholars do not give a historically reliable picture of his life. Their eclectic use of the sources, due to the lack of source-critical studies, prevents it. What the Western "lives of the Prophet" present as the event of the murder of Ibn Abī l-Ḥuqayq cannot pretend to be historical fact since the authors of these books did not even make an attempt to establish which of the several sources is the most reliable. M. Cook and P. Crone are perfectly right in rejecting the claim that historical reality is reconstructed in these books; they are nothing more than arbitrary summaries of the Muslim tradition on their Prophet. Cook's and Crone's conclusion from this insight, namely, that it is impossible to reconstruct historical fact on the basis of the Muslim sources, and that we are on safer ground if we rely on non-Muslim sources,[153] is not convincing, however.

In this article, I have devised and tested a source-critical method which allows us to establish which details of the different reports that the Muslim sources contain on a certain event of the Prophet's life can pretend to be very early and close to what really may have happened, and which details can not. Thus, it is possible in principle to reconstruct historical reality on the basis of the Muslim sources with no lesser certainty than in other fields of history which are dependent on traditions. Consequently, a true historical biography of the Prophet could be written if source-critical studies on all the details of his life were available. Until now there are only a few.[154] Many more, hundreds of them, are necessary before a real historical biography of the Prophet can be written.

We may wonder whether the outcome will justify the time and energy needed for such an enterprise. As we have shown, the historical facts that can be extracted from the sources relating a certain event of the Prophet's life are few. In the case of the murder of Ibn Abī l-Ḥuqayq, not even the date of the event can be established with some certainty. The historical biography which will be the outcome of

---

[153] P. Crone and M. Cook, *Hagarism. The Making of the Islamic World*, Cambridge, 1977, 3; M. Cook, *Muhammad*, Oxford, 1983, 61-76; P. Crone, *Meccan Trade*, chapter 9.

[154] In addition to the present study, G. Schoeler's studies in his *Charakter und Authentie*, A. Görke's contribution in this volume and some of M. Lecker's recent articles are instances of comprehensive source-critical studies with the aim to reconstruct the transmission history of Muslim traditions concerning an event of the Prophet's life.

all these source-critical efforts will probably be only a very small one. What we will gain, however, is more insight into the origin and development of Muslim traditions concerning the life of the Prophet. This will allow us, finally, to assess which of them are the most reliable and to detect the hidden biases of individual traditions or transmitters. Thus, the historical-critical biography of the Prophet which I have in mind will be more than a mere collection of details which constitute the historical kernel of the sources; it will also be a comprehensive study of the history of the traditions which constitute the *sīra* of the Prophet Muḥammad.

Bibliography

ʿAbd al-Razzāq b. Hammām al-Ṣanʿānī, *al-Muṣannaf*, ed. Ḥabīb al-Raḥmān al-Aʿẓamī, 11 vols., Simlak, Dabhel/Beirut, 1391/1972, ²1983.

Abū Dāwūd Sulaymān b. al-Ashʿath al-Sijistānī, *al-Sunan*, ed. Muḥammad Muḥyī l-Dīn ʿAbd al-Ḥamīd, 4 vols. in 2, n.p. [Beirut], n.d.

al-Bayhaqī, Aḥmad b. al-Ḥusayn, *al-Sunan al-kubrā*, 9 vols., Beirut, 1413/1992.

———, *Dalāʾil al-nubuwwa wa-maʿrifat aḥwāl ṣāḥib al-sharīʿa*, ed. ʿAbd al-Muʿṭī Qalʿajī, 7 vols., Beirut, 1405/1985.

Buhl, Frants, *Das Leben Muhammeds*, ²Heidelberg, 1955.

al-Bukhārī, Muḥammad b. Ismāʿīl, *al-Jāmiʿ al-ṣaḥīḥ*, publ. under the title: *Ṣaḥīḥ al-Bukhārī*, 7 vols., Beirut, 1412/1992; ed. Ḥassūna al-Nawāwī, 9 vols., Cairo, 1313/1895-6, repr. Beirut, n.d.

Burton, John, *An Introduction to the Ḥadīth*, Edinburgh, 1994.

Caskel, Werner, *Ǧamharat an-nasab. Das genealogische Werk des Hišām ibn Muḥammad al-Kalbī*, 2 vols., Leiden, 1966.

Cook, Michael, *Early Muslim Dogma*, Cambridge, 1981.

———, *Muḥammad*, Oxford, 1983.

Crone, Patricia, *Meccan Trade and the Rise of Islam*, Princeton, 1987.

——— and Michael Cook, *Hagarism. The Making of the Islamic World*, Cambridge, 1977.

Dermenghem, Emile, *The life of Mahomet*, London, 1930.

al-Dhahabī, Muḥammad b. Aḥmad, *Tadhkirat al-ḥuffāẓ*, 4 vols., Hyderabad, 1375-77/1955-58.

———, *Taʾrīkh al-islām wa-wafāyāt mashāhīr al-aʿlām. I, al-Maghāzī*, ed. ʿUmar ʿAbd al-Salām Tadmurī, Beirut, 1407/1987.

Gaudefroy-Demombynes, Maurice, *Mahomet*, ²Paris, 1969.

Grimme, Hubert, *Muḥammad. I, Das Leben*, Münster, 1892.

Guillaume, Alfred, *The Life of Muhammad. A Translation of Ibn Isḥāq's Sīrat Rasūl Allāh*, Oxford, 1955.

Horovitz, J., "Biblische Nachwirkungen in der *Sīra*", in *Der Islam*, 12 (1922), 184-89.

al-Ḥumaydī, ʿAbd Allāh b. al-Zubayr, *al-Musnad*, ed. Ḥabīb al-Raḥmān al-Aʿẓamī, 2 vols., Beirut, 1409/1988.

Ibn ʿAbd al-Barr, Yūsuf b. ʿAbd Allāh, *al-Istidhkār*, ed. ʿAbd al-Muʿṭī Amīn Qalʿajī, 30 vols., Aleppo/Damascus, 1414/1993.

Ibn Abī Shayba, Abū Bakr ʿAbd Allāh b. Muḥammad, *Kitāb al-Muṣannaf fī l-aḥādīth*

wa-l-āthār, ed. ʿAbd al-Khāliq al-Afghānī, 15 vols., Bombay, 1399-1403/1979-83.
Ibn al-Athīr, ʿAlī b. Abī l-Karam, *Usd al-ghāba fī maʿrifat al-ṣaḥāba*, 5 vols., Cairo, 1280/1863-64.
Ibn Ḥabīb, Muḥammad, *Kitāb al-Muḥabbar*, ed. Ilse Lichtenstädter, Hyderabad, 1361/1942.
Ibn Ḥajar al-ʿAsqalānī, Aḥmad b. ʿAlī, *al-Iṣāba fī maʿrifat al-ṣaḥāba*, 7 vols., Beirut, n.d.
———, *Fatḥ al-bārī bi-sharḥ Ṣaḥīḥ al-Bukhārī*, ed. ʿAbd al-ʿAzīz b. ʿAbd Allāh b. Bāz and Muḥammad Fuʾād ʿAbd al-Bāqī, 15 vols., Beirut, 1410/1989.
———, *Tahdhīb al-tahdhīb*, 12 vols., Hyderabad, 1325-27/1907-09.
Ibn Ḥibbān al-Bustī, Muḥammad, *Kitāb al-Thiqāt*, 9 vols., Hyderabad, 1393/1973.
Ibn Hishām, ʿAbd al-Mālik, *Sīrat Sayyidnā Muḥammad rasūl Allāh*, ed. Ferdinand Wüstenfeld, 2 vols., [2]Frankfurt a. M., 1961; *al-Sīra al-nabawiyya*, ed. ʿUmar ʿAbd al-Salām Tadmurī, 4 vols., Beirut, 1408/1987.
Ibn Kathīr, Ismāʿīl b. ʿUmar, *al-Bidāya wa-l-nihāya*, 14 vols., Beirut, 1966.
Ibn Saʿd, Muḥammad, *al-Ṭabaqāt al-kubrā*, ed. Iḥsān ʿAbbās, 9 vols., Beirut, n.d.
Ibn Sayyid al-Nās, Muḥammad b. ʿAbd Allāh, *al-Sīra al-nabawiyya al-musammā ʿUyūn al-athar fī funūn al-maghāzī wa-l-shamāʾil wa-l-siyar*, 2 vols., Beirut, 1406/1986.
Ibn Shabba, ʿUmar al-Numayrī, *Taʾrīkh al-Madīna al-munawwara*, ed. Ḥabīb Maḥmūd Aḥmad, 4 vols., Jidda, 1393/1973.
Jensen, P., "Das Leben Muhammeds und die David-Sage", in *Der Islam*, 12 (1922), 84-97.
Jones, J.M.B., "Ibn Isḥāq and al-Wāqidī. The Dream of ʿĀtika and the Raid to Nakhla in Relation to the Charge of Plagiarism", in *Bulletin of the School of Oriental and African Studies*, 22 (1959), 41-51.
Kister, M.J., "On the Papyrus of Wahb b. Munabbih", in *Bulletin of the School of Oriental and African Studies*, 37 (1974), 545-71.
Lammens, Henri, "Qoran et tradition. Comment fut composée la Vie de Mahomet", in *Recherches de science religieuse*, 1 (1910), 27-51.
Lecker, M., "Wāqidī's Account on the Status of the Jews of Medina: A Study of a Combined Report", in *Journal of Near Eastern Studies*, 54 (1995), 15-32.
———, "The Death of the Prophet Muḥammad's Father: Did Wāqidī Invent Some of the Evidence?", in *Zeitschrift der Deutschen Morgenländischen Gesellschaft*, 145 (1995), 9-27.
———, "ʿAmr ibn Ḥazm al-Anṣārī and Qurʾān 2,256: 'No Compulsion is There in Religion'", in *Oriens*, 35 (1996), 57-64.
MacDonald, Michael V. and William Montgomery Watt, *The Foundation of the Community*, Albany, 1987 (=*The History of al-Ṭabarī*, VII).
Majdī b. Muḥammad al-Miṣrī, *Shifāʾ al-ʿiyy bi-takhrīj wa-taḥqīq Musnad al-imām al-Shāfiʿī bi-tartīb al-ʿallāmat al-Sindī*, 2 vols., Cairo, 1416/1995-96.
Mālik b. Anas al-Aṣbaḥī, *al-Muwaṭṭaʾ* (riwāyat Yaḥyā b. Yaḥyā al-Laythī), ed. Muḥammad Fuʾād ʿAbd al-Bāqī, 2 vols., Beirut, 1406/1985.
———, *Muwaṭṭaʾ* (riwāyat Muḥammad b. al-Ḥasan al-Shaybānī), ed. ʿAbd al-Wahhāb ʿAbd al-Laṭīf, [2]Cairo, 1387/1967.
Margoliouth, David Samuel, *Muḥammad and the Rise of Islam*, New York/London, 1905.
Mattock, J.N., "History and Fiction", in *Occasional Papers of the School of Abbasid Studies*, 1 (1986), 80-97.
Motzki, H., "*Quo vadis Ḥadīṯ*-Forschung? Eine kritische Untersuchung von G.H.A. Juynboll: 'Nāfiʿ the *mawlā* of Ibn ʿUmar, and his Position in Muslim *Ḥadīth*

Literature', in *Der Islam,* 73 (1996), 40-80, 193-231.
———, "The Prophet and the Cat. On Dating Mālik's *Muwaṭṭa'* and Legal Traditions", in *Jerusalem Studies in Arabic and Islam,* 22 (1998), 18-83.
Muir, William, *The Life of Mahomet and the History of Islam to the Era of the Hegira,* 4 vols., London, 1858.
———, *The Life of Moḥammad from Original Sources,* Edinburgh, 1923.
Mūsā b. ʿUqba, *al-Maghāzī,* collected from different sources by M. Bāqshīsh Abū Mālik, Agadir, 1994.
Newby, G.D., "The *Sīrah* as a Source for Arabian Jewish History: Problems and Perspectives", in *Jerusalem Studies in Arabic and Islam,* 7 (1986), 121-38.
Rubin, Uri, *The Eye of the Beholder: The Life of Muḥammad as Viewed by The Early Muslims.* Princeton, 1995.
al-Rūyānī, Muḥammad b. Hārūn, *Musnad,* ed. Amīn ʿAlī Abū Yamānī, 3 vols., Beirut, 1416/1995.
Saʿīd b. Manṣūr al-Khurāsānī, *al-Sunan,* vol. 3/1,2, ed. Ḥabīb al-Raḥmān al-Aʿẓamī, Hyderabad, 1403/1982.
Schacht, Joseph, "A Revaluation of Islamic Traditions", in *Journal of the Royal Asiatic Society,* 49 (1949), 143-54.
———, *The Origins of Muhammad Jurisprudence,* Oxford, 1950.
———, "On Mūsā b. ʿUqba's *Kitāb al-Maghāzī*", in *Acta Orientalia,* 21 (1953), 288-300.
Schoeler, Gregor, *Charakter und Authentie der muslimischen Überlieferung über das Leben Mohammeds,* Berlin/New York, 1996.
Schöller, Marco, *Exegetisches Denken und Prophetenbiographie. Eine quellenkritische Analyse der Sīra-Überlieferung zu Muḥammads Konflikt mit den Juden,* Wiesbaden, 1998.
al-Shāfiʿī, Muḥammad b. Idrīs, *al-Umm,* ed. Muḥammad Zuhrī al-Najjār, 8 vols. in 4, Beirut, n.d.
Sprenger, Alois, *Das Leben und die Lehre des Moḥammad,* 3 vols., Berlin, 1861-65.
al-Ṭabarānī, Sulaymān b. Aḥmad, *al-Muʿjam al-kabīr,* ed. Ḥamdī ʿAbd al-Majīd al-Salafī, 25 vols., Cairo, n.d.
al-Ṭabarī, Muḥammad b. Jarīr, *Ta'rīkh al-rusul wa-l-mulūk,* ed. Michael Johan de Goeje, 15 vols., Leiden, 1879-1901.
ʿUrwa b. al-Zubayr, [*Sīra*], collected from different sources by S. Mursī al-Ṭāhir, *Bidāyat al-kitāba al-ta'rīkhiyya ʿinda l-ʿarab. Awwal sīra fī l-islām: ʿUrwa b. al-Zubayr b. al-ʿAwwām,* Beirut, 1995.
Voort, Nicolet van der, "Zoektocht naar de waarheid met behulp van het *Kitāb al-Maghāzī* in de *Muṣannaf* van ʿAbd ar-Razzāq b. Hammām aṣ-Ṣanʿānī (gest. 211/827)", unpubl. M.A.-thesis, Katholieke Universiteit Nijmegen, 1996.
Wansbrough, John, *The Sectarian Milieu. Content and Composition of Islamic Salvation History,* Oxford, 1978.
al-Wāqidī, Muḥammad b. ʿUmar, *Kitāb al-Maghāzī,* ed. Marsden Jones, 3 vols., London, 1966.
Watt, William Montgomery, *Muhammad at Medina,* Oxford, 1956.

Diagram 1

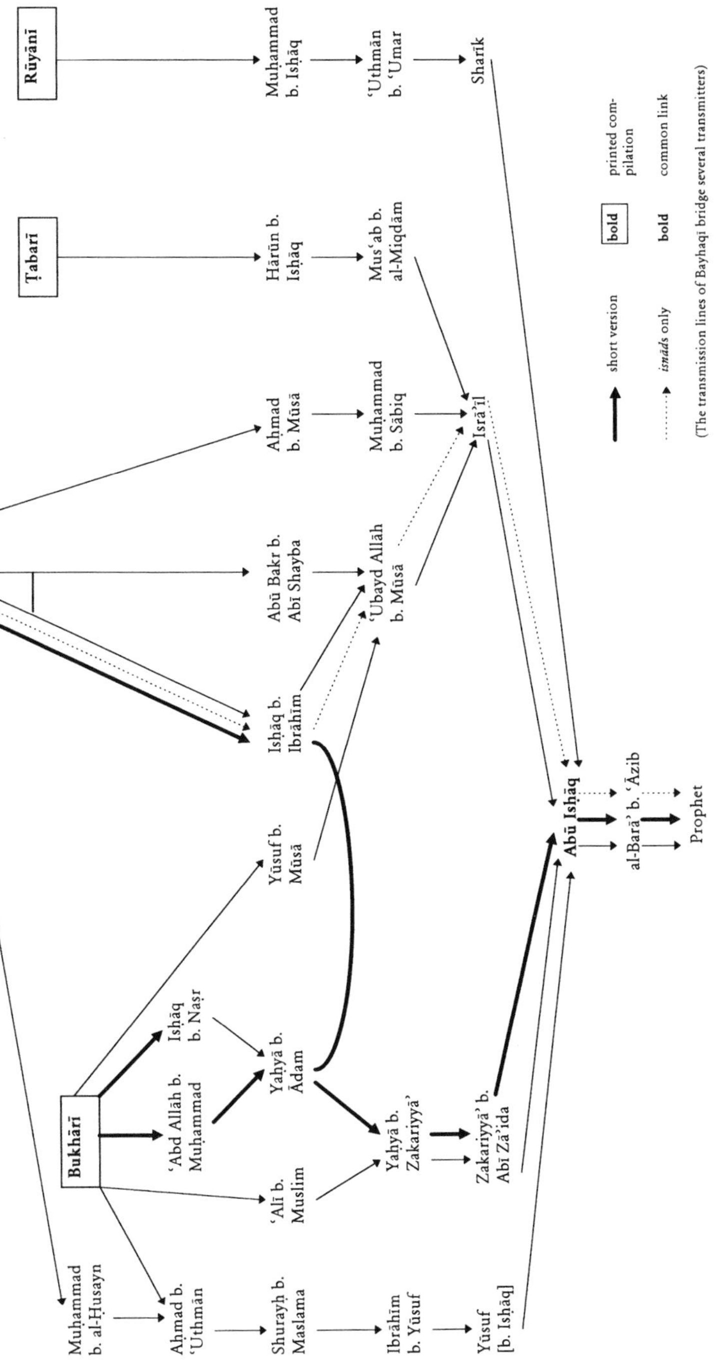
Rūyānī
Ṭabarī
Bayhaqī
Bukhārī
Muḥammad b. Isḥāq
'Uthmān b. 'Umar
Sharīk
Hārūn b. Isḥāq
Mus'ab b. al-Miqdām
Aḥmad b. Mūsā
Muḥammad b. Sābiq
Isrā'īl
Abū Bakr b. Abī Shayba
'Ubayd Allāh b. Mūsā
Isḥāq b. Ibrāhīm
Yūsuf b. Mūsā
Isḥāq b. Naṣr
'Abd Allāh b. Muḥammad
Yaḥyā b. Ādam
Yaḥyā b. Zakariyyā'
Zakariyyā' b. Abī Zā'ida
'Alī b. Muslim
Muḥammad b. al-Ḥusayn
Aḥmad b. 'Uthmān
Shurayḥ b. Maslama
Ibrāhīm b. Yūsuf
Yūsuf [b. Isḥāq]
Abū Isḥāq
al-Barā' b. 'Āzib
Prophet
short version
isnāds only
bold printed compilation
bold common link
(The transmission lines of Bayhaqī bridge several transmitters)

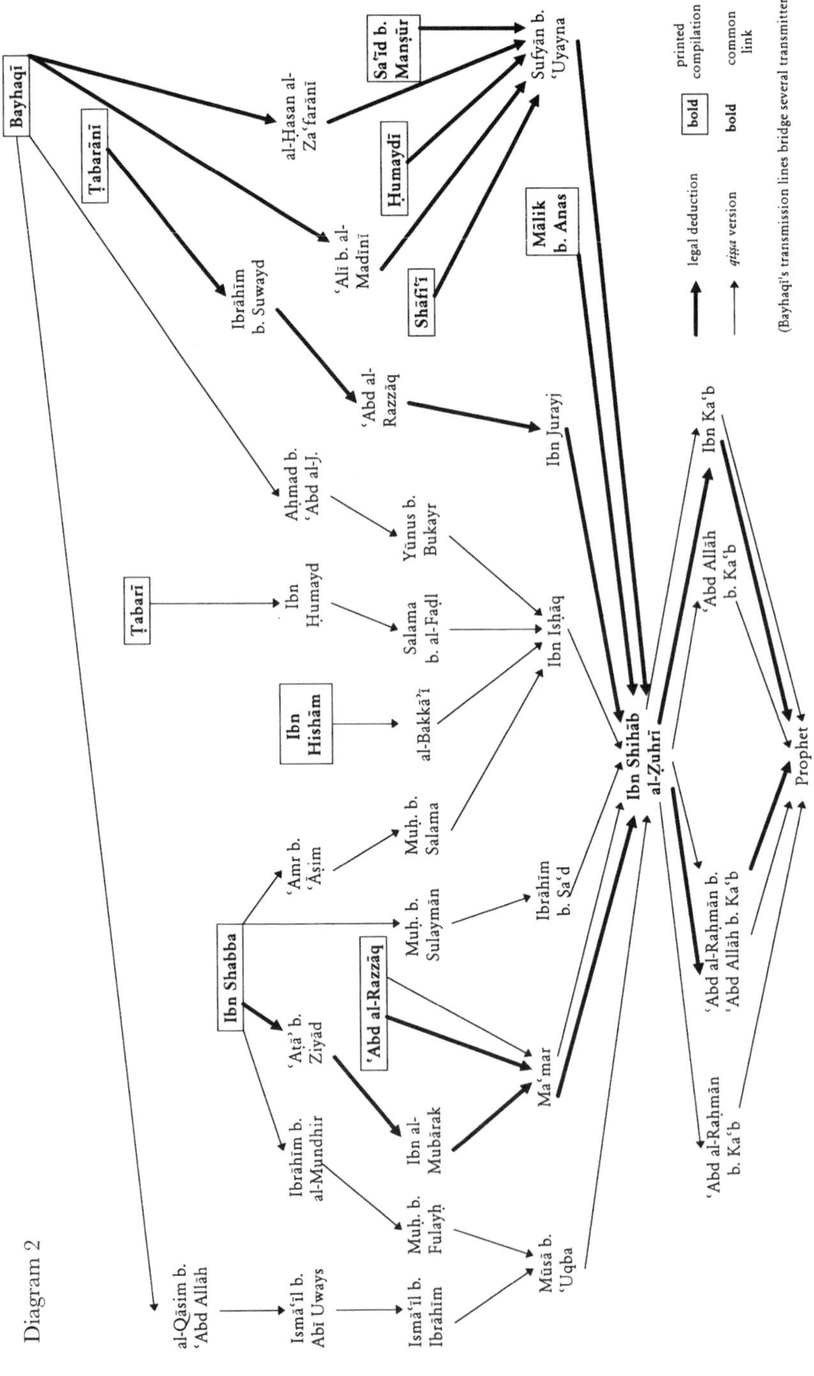
Bayhaqī
Ṭabarānī
Ṭabarī
Ibn Hishām
Ibn Shabba
al-Qāsim b. ʿAbd Allāh
Saʿīd b. Manṣūr
al-Ḥasan al-Zaʿfarānī
Ḥumaydī
ʿAlī b. al-Madīnī
Shāfiʿī
Mālik b. Anas
Sufyān b. ʿUyayna
Ibrāhīm b. Suwayd
ʿAbd al-Razzāq
Ibn Jurayj
Aḥmad b. ʿAbd al-J.
Yūnus b. Bukayr
Ibn Ḥumayd
Salama b. al-Faḍl
Ibn Isḥāq
al-Bakkāʾī
ʿAmr b. ʿĀṣim
Muḥ. b. Salama
Muḥ. b. Sulaymān
Ibrāhīm b. Saʿd
ʿAbd al-Razzāq
ʿAṭāʾ b. Ziyād
Maʿmar
Ibn al-Mubārak
Ibrāhīm b. al-Mundhir
Muḥ. b. Fulayḥ
Ismāʿīl b. Abī Uways
Ismāʿīl b. Ibrāhīm
Mūsā b. ʿUqba
Ibn Shihāb al-Zuhrī
Ibn Kaʿb
ʿAbd Allāh b. Kaʿb
ʿAbd al-Raḥmān b. ʿAbd Allāh b. Kaʿb
ʿAbd al-Raḥmān b. Kaʿb
Prophet
legal deduction
qiṣṣa version
bold printed compilation
bold common link
(Bayhaqī's transmission lines bridge several transmitters)
Diagram 2

Diagram 3

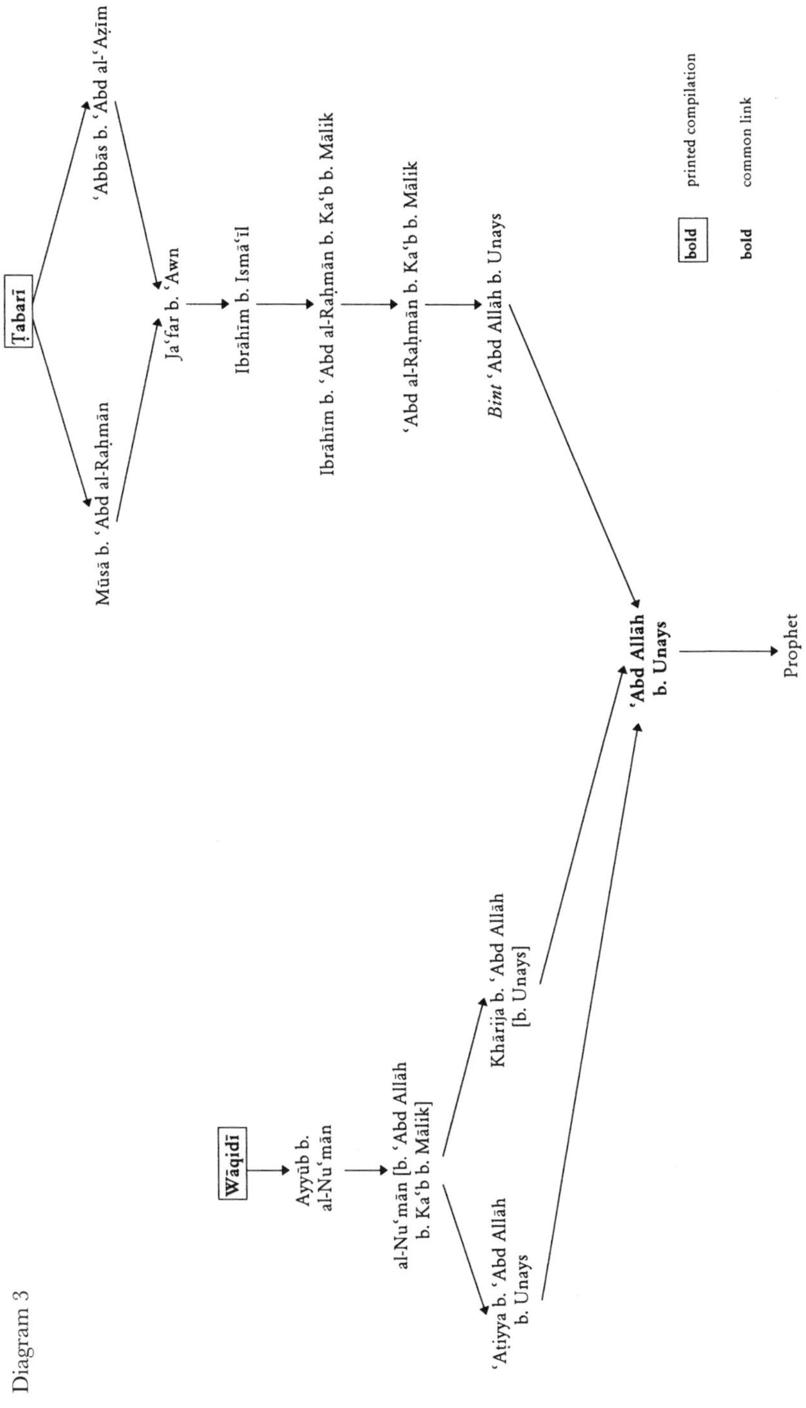
Ṭabarī
Mūsā b. ʿAbd al-Raḥmān
ʿAbbās b. ʿAbd al-ʿAẓīm
Jaʿfar b. ʿAwn
Ibrāhīm b. Ismāʿīl
Ibrāhīm b. ʿAbd al-Raḥmān b. Kaʿb b. Mālik
ʿAbd al-Raḥmān b. Kaʿb b. Mālik
Bint ʿAbd Allāh b. Unays
Wāqidī
Ayyūb b. al-Nuʿmān
al-Nuʿmān [b. ʿAbd Allāh b. Kaʿb b. Mālik]
ʿAṭiyya b. ʿAbd Allāh b. Unays
Khārija b. ʿAbd Allāh [b. Unays]
ʿAbd Allāh b. Unays
Prophet
bold printed compilation
bold common link

THE HISTORICAL TRADITION ABOUT AL-ḤUDAYBIYA
A STUDY OF ʿURWA B. AL-ZUBAYR'S ACCOUNT[1]

Andreas Görke

The events of al-Ḥudaybiya have been studied several times.[2] Some of these studies attempted to reconstruct the events by drawing on a number of sources—namely, Ibn Hishām, al-Wāqidī, Ibn Saʿd, al-Ṭabarī and the Qurʾān—to form a coherent narrative.[3] Collating these reconstructions can derive the following standard account of the events:

a) Because of a dream, Muḥammad decides to make an *ʿumra.*

b) He asks the Bedouin around Medina to accompany him, but they refuse.

c) Therefore, Muḥammad sets out for Mecca with about 700-1400 men.

d) In Dhū l-Ḥulayfa he enters the *iḥrām*, the state of ritual purity.

e) When they learn of Muḥammad's plans, the Quraysh send 200 men on horseback commanded by Khālid b. al-Walīd to Kurāʿ al-Ghamīm near ʿUsfān.

---

[1] This is an abridged and modified translation of my M.A. thesis "Die frühislamische Geschichtsüberlieferung zu Ḥudaibiya", University of Hamburg, 1996. I wish to thank Behnam Sadeghi for helping me with the English translation.

[2] E.g. F. Buhl, *Das Leben Muhammeds*, trans. by H.H. Schaeder, [2]Heidelberg, 1955, 284-92; W. M. Watt, *Muhammad at Medina*, Oxford, 1956, 46-62; C.E. Dubler and U. Quarella, "Der Vertrag von Ḥudaibiyya (März 628) als Wendepunkt in der Geschichte des frühen Islam", in *AS*, 21 (1967), 62-81; M. Alwaye, "The Truce of Hudeybiya and the Conquest of Mecca", in *Majallatu l-Azhar*, 45/9 (1973), 1-6; M. Rodinson, *Mohammed*, trans. into German by G. Meister, Luzern and Frankfurt am Main, 1975, 238-41; M. Muranyi, "Die Auslieferungsklausel des Vertrags von al-Ḥudaibiya und ihre Folgen", in *Arabica*, 23 (1976), 275-95; F.M. Donner, "Muḥammad's Political Consolidation in Arabia up to the Conquest of Mecca", in *MW*, 69 (1979), 229-47; F.B. Ali, "Al-Ḥudaybiya: An Alternative Version", in *MW*, 71 (1981), 47-62; M. Lings, *Muhammad: His Life Based on the Earliest Sources*, New York, 1983, 247-59; M. Lecker, "The Ḥudaibiyya-Treaty and the Expedition against Khaybar", in *JSAI*, 5 (1984), 1-12; G.R. Hawting, "Al-Ḥudaybiyya and the Conquest of Mecca: A Reconsideration of the Tradition about the Muslim Takeover of the Sanctuary", in *JSAI*, 8 (1986), 1-23.

[3] E.g. Watt, *Medina*, 46-62; W.M. Watt, "al-Ḥudaybiya", in *EI*[2], III, 539; Buhl, *Leben*, 284-92; Rodinson, *Mohammed*, 238-41; Lings, *Muhammad*, 247-59; Alwaye, "Truce", 1-6.

f) Muḥammad therefore decides to take a different route. At al-Ḥudaybiya his camel stops and refuses to go any further. Muḥammad orders that the camp be pitched there.
g) Water is scarce at al-Ḥudaybiya, but Muḥammad revives a dry well using an arrow.
h) Various delegates of the Quraysh come to negotiate with Muḥammad.
i) ʿUthmān is sent to Mecca for negotiations. He does not return in time and the rumor spreads that he has been killed. Muḥammad therefore summons his Companions and demands that they pledge allegiance to him. This pledge is called *bayʿat al-riḍwān* (after Q 48:18 which reads: *laqad raḍiya llāh ʿan al-muʾminīn idh yubāyiʿūnaka taḥt al-shajara*). However, the news about ʿUthmān turns out to be false.
j) The Quraysh send Suhayl b. ʿAmr to Muḥammad with instructions to make peace with him.
k) The treaty comprises the following points:
– There will be a ten-year armistice.
– The Muslims must retire this time but may enter Mecca in the following year for three days to perform the *ʿumra*.
– All tribes may decide freely to enter into an alliance with either Muḥammad or the Quraysh.
– The Muslims have to surrender any person who comes to Muḥammad without his guardian's (*walī*) permission, even if he is a Muslim. (There is no corresponding obligation for the Quraysh.)
l) After the treaty Abū Jandal, son of the afore-mentioned Suhayl, flees to Muḥammad but is handed over to the Quraysh.
m) Muḥammad calls on his Companions to shave their heads and sacrifice their animals. However, they follow him only after he sets an example.
n) On the way back to Medina, Q 48 (*al-fatḥ*) is revealed to Muḥammad.
o) Abū Baṣīr flees to Medina from Mecca but is handed over to two delegates from the Quraysh. He kills one of them and flees to the coast at al-ʿĪṣ. Seventy men join him there, among them Abū Jandal. They raid Meccan caravans until the Quraysh ask Muḥammad to let them into Medina.
p) Finally, some Muslim women come to Medina from Mecca. Q 60:10 is revealed on this occasion, a verse prohibiting their surrender to the Quraysh.

The different accounts contain some inconsistencies that have been discussed in some of the above-mentioned studies, for example, in the terms of the truce or on the question whether Khālid b. al-Walīd converted to Islam before al-Ḥudaybiya. The accounts are mostly compilations of different reports of earlier transmitters. These earlier reports can be partly reconstructed when they are supplied with *asānīd*.

This study attempts to reconstruct ʿUrwa b. al-Zubayr's report which is by far the longest early account of al-Ḥudaybiya; the other accounts comprise only a few elements. Many issues appear only in ʿUrwa's version, and his is the only one that gives a more or less complete account of the course of events. Most of the later accounts are based mainly on his report. Moreover, this version exists with numerous strands of transmission, thus making a reconstruction of his report possible. Finally, ʿUrwa is one of the most renowned scholars of the biography of the Prophet prior to Ibn Isḥāq.

I. The Reconstruction of ʿUrwa b. al-Zubayr's Tradition

ʿUrwa b. al-Zubayr was born around the year 23/643-4 and died in the year 94/712.[4] He was the son of al-Zubayr b. al-ʿAwwām, one of the first Muslims, and was one of a group of seven famous legal scholars who later became known as the seven *fuqahāʾ* of Medina, as well as a renowned expert in *ḥadīth*.[5]

I have tried to take into account as many sources as possible. I do not by any means claim exhaustiveness, however, and it is obvious that all the results and conclusions will have to be reconsidered with the emergence of new sources. Only those sources that mention ʿUrwa in the *isnād* were taken into account.

ʿUrwa b. al-Zubayr's report about al-Ḥudaybiya was transmitted by three of his students: Ibn Shihāb al-Zuhrī, Abū l-Aswad, and Hishām b. ʿUrwa. Their original versions are not extant but have to be reconstructed from later written sources. The following diagram is a simplified representation of the purported transmissions:

---

[4] A.A. Duri, *The Rise of Historical Writing Among the Arabs*, trans. by L.I. Conrad, Princeton, 1983, 77.

[5] J. Horovitz, "The Earliest Biographies of the Prophet and their Authors", I, in *Islamic Culture*, 1 (1927), 547.

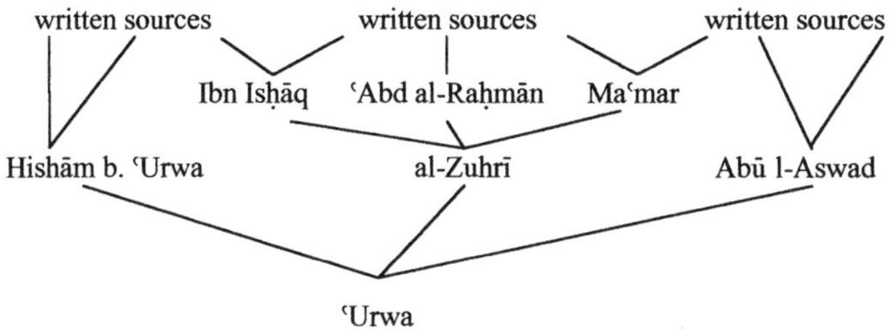

1. Zuhrī's tradition

The first strand of transmission to be discussed here is the one through al-Zuhrī (d. 124/742). Many of al-Zuhrī's students transmitted the story of al-Ḥudaybiya from him. Only six of the total of forty-five versions studied for this article do not go back to him. The traditions can be divided into long versions which give a more or less complete account of the events, and short versions which contain only a few elements. First, the traditions of Ibn Isḥāq, Maʿmar b. Rāshid and ʿAbd al-Raḥmān b. ʿAbd al-ʿAzīz will be analyzed, of which both long and short versions exist. Afterwards the other short versions going back to al-Zuhrī (which are not recorded in the diagram) will be studied.

Ibn Isḥāq's recension

Let us first consider Ibn Isḥāq's (d. 150/767) version. His work is not extant in its original form (provided there *was* a single original form, which may be doubted), but only in different variants. The most famous one is that of Ibn Hishām, but numerous other traditions going back to Ibn Isḥāq can be found in the written sources. These versions differ considerably in content, as has been shown in other studies.[6]

Ibn Isḥāq's account about al-Ḥudaybiya is based mainly on a tradition going back to al-Zuhrī—ʿUrwa b. al-Zubayr—al-Miswar b.

[6] Cf. S.M. Al-Samuk, *Die historischen Überlieferungen nach Ibn Isḥāq. Eine synoptische Untersuchung*, Frankfurt am Main, 1978, 80, 162; M. Muranyi, "Ibn Isḥāq's *K. al-Maġāzī* in der *riwāya* von Yūnus b. Bukair. Bemerkungen zur frühen Überlieferungsgeschichte", in *JSAI*, 14 (1991), 269.

Makhrama and Marwān b. al-Ḥakam. In his book, as it was transmitted by Ibn Hishām, this tradition is interspersed with many shorter traditions going back to other transmitters. It is also furnished with an introduction by Ibn Isḥāq. Since we want to reconstruct ʿUrwa's account, only the parts going back to him will be considered.

Numerous long and short versions of his account can be found in the sources (see Figure A on p. 272: The traditions going back to Ibn Isḥāq). Long versions are recorded by Ibn Hishām,[7] al-Ṭabarī,[8] Ibn Ḥanbal,[9] and al-Bayhaqī,[10] shorter versions by Ibn Abī Shayba,[11] Abū Dāwūd,[12] al-Balādhurī,[13] Abū ʿUbayd,[14] al-Wāḥidī,[15] al-Ṭabarī,[16] and al-Bayhaqī.[17] Abū Yūsuf names Ibn Isḥāq as one of his sources in addition to al-Kalbī and Hishām b. ʿUrwa. In his wording, however, he seems to follow Hishām b. ʿUrwa's version. We will therefore study his version later.

The long versions differ in form. Ibn Ḥanbal records only al-Zuhrī's tradition but not Ibn Isḥāq's additions and insertions of other traditions. Al-Ṭabarī uses different sources and does not quote the tradition of al-Zuhrī for every element. Thus only parts of the tradition can be found in his work. Similarly, al-Bayhaqī only gives parts of the tradition, mainly those dealing with the treaty itself and the events occurring after the treaty. In terms of the overall structure, Ibn Hishām's version is closest to the one Ibn Isḥāq laid down in his book. This, however, does not mean that he reproduces Ibn Isḥāq's *wording* more accurately than others.

A quick glance at the different versions shows that a single original version cannot be reconstructed, as the differences between the variants are too large. It is possible though to give an overview of the contents of the tradition. Parts that are in all versions identical in

---

7 Ibn Hishām, *Sīra*, II, 308-27.

8 Ṭabarī, *Ta'rīkh*, I, 1528 ff.

9 Ibn Ḥanbal, *Musnad*, IV, 323 ff.

10 Bayhaqī, *Sunan*, IX, 221 f., 227 f., 233 f.

11 Ibn Abī Shayba, *Muṣannaf*, XIV, 434.

12 Abū Dāwūd, *Sunan*, 15:168.2. The numbering of the *aḥādīth* from the canonical collections follows al-Mizzī's *Kashshāf* (first number = *kitāb*, number after the colon = *bāb*, number after the full stop = *ḥadīth*).

13 Balādhurī, *Ansāb*, 351 f.

14 Abū ʿUbayd, *Amwāl*, 157.

15 Wāḥidī, *Asbāb*, 285 (on Q 48), 318 (on Q 60).

16 Ṭabarī, *Tafsīr*, XXVI, 59.

17 Bayhaqī, *Sunan*, IX, 223, 228, 229.

wording can be assumed to provide Ibn Isḥāq's wording. However, they do not necessarily reflect al-Zuhrī's wording, for Ibn Isḥāq may have made additions, omissions, or other changes. This can only be verified by comparison with the other traditions going back to al-Zuhrī.

The order of the elements varies slightly in the different versions. The order given here is Ibn Hishām's. Al-Zuhrī's report as narrated by Ibn Isḥāq then comprises the following elements: Muḥammad sets out for Mecca with 700 Companions and with peaceful intentions.[18] In ʿUsfān Muḥammad learns of the opposition of the Quraysh to his plans and decides to take a different route.[19] The camel stops and refuses to go any further. Muḥammad revives the dry well.[20] Negotiations with the Quraysh are held; the Quraysh send delegates to Muḥammad, but not vice versa. In the order of their arrival the delegates are Budayl b. Warqāʾ al-Khuzāʿī,[21] Mikraz b. Ḥafṣ,[22] al-Ḥulays b. ʿAlqama,[23] and ʿUrwa b. Masʿūd al-Thaqafī.[24] Suhayl b. ʿAmr comes to conclude a treaty. ʿUmar protests against the treaty.[25] The treaty comprises the following points: a ten-year truce; a one-sided obligation for the Muslims to surrender fugitives from Mecca to the Quraysh; an agreement of mutual reconciliation and refrainment from war (*ʿayba makfūfa*),[26] and an agreement that there shall be no

---

[18] Ibn Hishām, *Sīra*, II, 306; Ṭabarī, *Taʾrīkh*, I, 1529; Ibn Ḥanbal, *Musnad*, IV, 323.

[19] Ibn Hishām, *Sīra*, II, 309; Ṭabarī, *Taʾrīkh*, I, 1530 f.; Ibn Ḥanbal, *Musnad* IV, 323. Here, one of the most important discrepancies can be observed: In the versions of Ibn Hishām and al-Ṭabarī the tradition is interrupted after the question "*man rajulun yakhruju binā ʿalā ṭarīqin ghayri ṭarīqihim allatī hum bihā*?" A different tradition by ʿAbd Allāh b. Abī Bakr is quoted which contains an answer to this question: "*anā yā rasūla llāh*." Ibn Ḥanbal does not report this passage. This question certainly is not part of al-Zuhrī's tradition, since it only makes sense in connection with the following answer. Ibn Isḥāq seems to have changed the tradition of al-Zuhrī to incorporate it into a coherent narrative. Since two of Ibn Isḥāq's students transmit this passage, it indeed does seem to go back to Ibn Isḥāq. Whether the other variant goes back to Ibn Isḥāq as well or whether Ibn Ḥanbal (or his source) eliminated this inconsistency cannot be established here.

[20] Ibn Hishām, *Sīra*, II, 310; Ṭabarī, *Taʾrīkh*, I, 1522; Ibn Ḥanbal, *Musnad*, IV, 323.

[21] Ibn Hishām, *Sīra*, II, 311 f.; Ibn Ḥanbal, *Musnad*, IV, 323.

[22] Ibn Hishām, *Sīra*, II, 312; Ibn Ḥanbal, *Musnad*, IV, 324.

[23] Ibn Hishām, *Sīra*, II, 312; Ṭabarī, *Taʾrīkh*, I, 1538; Ibn Ḥanbal, *Musnad*, IV, 324.

[24] Ibn Hishām, *Sīra*, II, 313 f.; Ibn Ḥanbal, *Musnad*, IV, 324. Another discrepancy can be observed here: Ibn Ḥanbal reports that Khirāsh b. Umayya and ʿUthmān are sent to Mecca. Ibn Hishām cites this report with a different *isnād*.

[25] Ibn Hishām, *Sīra*, II, 316 f.; Ṭabarī, *Taʾrīkh*, I, 1545 f.; Ibn Ḥanbal, *Musnad*, IV, 325; Bayhaqī, *Sunan*, IX, 221. Al-Bayhaqī does not mention the protests.

[26] See Lane, *An Arabic-English Lexicon*, London, 1863-93, s.v. *ʿ-y-b*.

raids against each other (*lā islāl wa-lā ighlāl*);[27] every tribe is free to form an alliance with either Muḥammad or the Quraysh; the Muslims have to retreat this time but may enter Mecca in the following year for three days.[28] After the signing of the treaty Abū Jandal flees to Muḥammad in chains, but is surrendered to his father Suhayl.[29] The witnesses of the treaty are named and ʿAlī is mentioned as the one who wrote down the treaty.[30] After the treaty Muḥammad performs the sacrificial rites; his Companions follow his example. On the way back to Medina the whole of Q 48 is revealed to Muḥammad.[31] The passage ends with al-Zuhrī's remark that there has been no greater victory than this in the history of Islam. In the two years between al-Ḥudaybiya and the conquest of Mecca more people converted to Islam than ever before.[32] Then follows the story of Abū Baṣīr.[33] Finally the events surrounding the women's flight to Medina are recounted. They are not surrendered because of the revelation of Q 60:10.[34] This passage is not recounted on the authority of al-Miswar and Marwān but is part of a letter of ʿUrwa b. al-Zubayr to Ibn Abī Hunayda,[35] a companion of the caliph al-Walīd b. ʿAbd al-Malik.

In addition to the four long versions, there are some ten short versions going back to Ibn Isḥāq.[36] As in the long versions, there are

[27] Lane's translation of *lā islāl wa-lā ighlāl* as "there shall be no treachery, or perfidy and no bribe or: and no stealing" does not seem to be correct. H. Motzki has pointed out to me in a private communication that both *islāl* and *ighlāl* can have the meaning "campaign", which seems to fit much better. Cf. Lane, *Lexicon*, s.v. *s-l-l*. In the following, only the Arabic terms are used.

[28] Ibn Hishām, *Sīra*, II, 317 f.; Ṭabarī, *Ta'rīkh*, I, 1546 f.; Ibn Ḥanbal, *Musnad*, IV, 325; Bayhaqī, *Sunan*, IX, 221 f., 227. In al-Ṭabarī's version the writing down of the treaty and the next two passages are reported with a different *isnād* (Burayda—Sufyān b. Farwa al-Aslamī—Muḥammad b. Kaʿb al-Quraẓī—ʿAlqama b. Qays al-Nakhaʿī—ʿAlī b. Abī Ṭālib) while in the other versions this is part of al-Zuhrī's tradition. Al-Bayhaqī gives a different order for the elements of the treaty. The freedom to form alliances is not mentioned in his version.

[29] Ibn Hishām, *Sīra*, II, 318 f.; Ṭabarī, *Ta'rīkh*, I, 1547 f.; Ibn Ḥanbal, *Musnad*, IV, 325 f.; Bayhaqī, *Sunan*, IX, 227.

[30] Ibn Hishām, *Sīra*, II, 319; Ṭabarī, *Ta'rīkh*, I, 1548.

[31] Ibn Hishām, *Sīra*, II, 319 ff.; Ibn Ḥanbal, *Musnad*, IV, 326.

[32] Ibn Hishām, *Sīra*, II, 322; Ṭabarī, *Ta'rīkh*, I, 1550 f. In this and the following passage al-Ṭabarī records the same *isnād* going back to al-Zuhrī as the other versions.

[33] Ibn Hishām, *Sīra*, II, 323 f.; Ṭabarī, *Ta'rīkh*, I, 1551 f.; Bayhaqī, *Sunan*, IX, 229.

[34] Ibn Hishām, *Sīra*, II, 326 f.

[35] Thus Ibn Hishām. Al-Wāqidī and Ibn Saʿd, who also mention this letter, have Hunayd.

[36] Ibn Abī Shayba, *Muṣannaf*, XIV, 434; Abū Dāwūd, *Sunan*, 15:168.2; Balādhurī, *Ansāb*, 351 f; Abū ʿUbayd, *Amwāl*, 157; Wāḥidī, *Asbāb*, 285 (on Q 48), 318 (on Q 60);

some differences in wording and in the names of the original narrators. Nevertheless, the short versions are close enough to the long ones to confirm that the *asānīd* are basically correct. In one of al-Bayhaqī's versions the *isnād* for the parts which in other versions only go back to al-Zuhrī or Ibn Isḥāq seems to have been extended to al-Miswar and Marwān.[37]

At first sight it may seem surprising how much the versions going back to Ibn Isḥāq differ from each other. Some parts have different *asānīd*, and the order of elements differs slightly, such as in the clauses of the treaty. Smaller differences are common: different prepositions, omission of single words, omission of parts of a name, use of religious salutations such as *ṣallā llāhu ʿalayhi wa-sallam, raḍiya llāhu ʿanhu*, etc.; in some variants whole sentences are omitted. As to the distribution of these differences, it could not be established that some versions are closer to each other than other versions. This indicates that these most probably go back to the same source (Ibn Isḥāq) independently of one another. Otherwise we would expect the versions dependent on each other to be closer to one another than to the rest.

In contrast to his predecessors, Ibn Isḥāq composed a book in the stricter meaning of the word. We might therefore expect a written transmission by him. However, the observed differences cannot be explained in terms of written transmission alone. Schoeler accounts for the discrepancies in the different *riwāyāt* by assuming that Ibn Isḥāq continued to transmit his work orally in lectures even after its written composition.[38] Under such circumstances, various causes may have led to the different versions handed down by his students: different renderings by Ibn Isḥāq at diverse *majālis*, different compositions by his students, or different transmissions from them to their students.[39] The proposed combination of written and oral transmission explains adequately the emergence of the different versions.

Maʿmar b. Rāshid's recension

The next version to be studied is that of Maʿmar b. Rāshid (d. 153/770). There are fewer variants of his version than of Ibn Isḥāq's.

Ṭabarī, *Tafsīr*, XXVI, 59; Bayhaqī, *Sunan*, IX, 223, 228, 229.

[37] Bayhaqī, *Sunan*, IX, 223.

[38] G. Schoeler, "Die Frage der schriftlichen oder mündlichen Überlieferung der Wissenschaften im frühen Islam", in *Der Islam*, 62 (1985), 212.

[39] G. Schoeler, "Weiteres zur Frage der schriftlichen oder mündlichen Überlieferung der Wissenschaften im Islam", in *Der Islam*, 66 (1989), 39.

The long versions fall into two strands: one transmitted by ʿAbd al-Razzāq (recorded by ʿAbd al-Razzāq,[40] al-Bukhārī,[41] Ibn Ḥanbal,[42] and al-Bayhaqī[43]), and the other by Muḥammad b. Thawr (recorded by Abū Dāwūd,[44] and in the *Tafsīr* of al-Ṭabarī[45]). In his *Taʾrīkh*, al-Ṭabarī names ʿAbd Allāh b. al-Mubārak as the authority in addition to Muḥammad b. Thawr[46] (see Figure B on p. 273: The traditions going back to Maʿmar).

These versions are closer to one another than those of Ibn Isḥāq. Not all of the versions are complete but the order of the elements is the same in all of them. The most complete versions are those of ʿAbd al-Razzāq, al-Ṭabarī's *Tafsīr*, Ibn Ḥanbal, and al-Bayhaqī. There are some differences (mostly different prepositions, the use of "*nabī*" instead of "*rasūlu llāh*", omission of single words), but these do not bring into question the existence of a written prototype by Maʿmar. Some of the discrepancies can be clearly identified as copying mistakes, such as *fāṣala*[47] instead of *qāḍā*[48] or *min qiṣṣatihi*[49] instead of *min qaḍīyatin*.[50] In these cases the graphemes are similar, accounting for mistakes in copying. The discrepancies occur mainly between the two strands mentioned (through ʿAbd al-Razzāq on the one hand and through Muḥammad b. Thawr on the other) and not within these strands. In any case, these variants are more homogenous than those of Ibn Isḥāq's version.

Maʿmar's account of the events of al-Ḥudaybiya differs from Ibn Isḥāq's in some points: The number of the Companions is given as several hundred. No mention is made of peaceful intentions. At Dhū l-Ḥulayfa Muḥammad and his companions enter the *iḥrām* and put collars on the necks of their sacrificial animals. Muḥammad sends a scout. At ʿUsfān this scout reports that the Quraysh have summoned their allies to prevent Muḥammad from entering the sanctuary. The Muslims discuss what to do. Abū Bakr states that they have come to

[40] ʿAbd al-Razzāq, *Muṣannaf*, V, 330 ff.
[41] Bukhārī, *Jāmiʿ*, 54:15.
[42] Ibn Ḥanbal, *Musnad*, IV, 328 ff.
[43] Bayhaqī, *Sunan*, IX, 218 ff.
[44] Abū Dāwūd, *Sunan*, 15:168.1.
[45] Ṭabarī, *Tafsīr*, XXVI, 56-58 (on Q 48:24).
[46] Ṭabarī, *Taʾrīkh*, I, 1529, 1534-38, 1539, 1549 f., 1551 f., 1553.
[47] ʿAbd al-Razzāq, *Muṣannaf*, V, 338.
[48] Ṭabarī, *Tafsīr*, XXVI, 57.
[49] Ibid., 58.
[50] ʿAbd al-Razzāq, *Muṣannaf*, V, 340.

make an *ʿumra* and not to fight.[51] Muḥammad remarks that Khālid b. al-Walīd is at Ghamīm with men on horseback from the Quraysh. He decides to take a different route. At al-Ḥudaybiya Muḥammad's camel stops and refuses to go any further, which he interprets as a divine sign. The camp is set up. Muḥammad revives the dry well. The order of the delegates of the Quraysh is slightly different from the one reported by Ibn Isḥāq. The first delegate is Budayl b. Warqāʾ (as with Ibn Isḥāq), then follows ʿUrwa b. Masʿūd (Ibn Isḥāq: fourth place), with a report similar to Ibn Isḥāq's. The next delegate is a man from Kināna; his report is similar to Ibn Isḥāq's report of al-Ḥulays. Finally comes Mikraz b. Ḥafṣ (Ibn Isḥāq: second place). Suhayl arrives to conclude the treaty. There are also some differences in the treaty compared with Ibn Isḥāq's version. The Muslims protest against the changes that Suhayl demands in the formulations. The changes are nevertheless made by order of Muḥammad. The treaty comprises only two points: the *ʿumra* which is to be held in the following year and the clause of the surrender of the fugitives (which provokes the Muslims' protest). No truce is mentioned. When Abū Jandal is surrendered, Mikraz b. Ḥafṣ agrees to protect him. ʿUmar's protest takes place only after the treaty and the surrender. No witnesses are named. It is not specified who put the treaty in writing. Muḥammad orders his Companions to perform the sacrificial rites, which they do only after Muḥammad follows the advice of Umm Salama and sets an example. While the Muslims are still at al-Ḥudaybiya, some women flee from Mecca to join them. Q 60:10 is revealed and they are not sent back. ʿUmar divorces two of his wives. The events surrounding Abū Baṣīr are recounted. After the Quraysh ask Muḥammad to allow him into Medina, Q 48:24-26 is revealed.

Several shorter versions of Maʿmar's account exist.[52] The wording is in almost all cases the same as in the corresponding passages of the long versions. In two cases the tradition is reported on the authority of a different original narrator: Ibn Ḥanbal and al-Ṭabarī each record a tradition going back to ʿAbd Allāh b. al-Mubārak—Maʿmar—al-

---

[51] ʿAbd al-Razzāq does not mention Abū Bakr in his *Muṣannaf.* However, he is mentioned in the other variants, including those going back to ʿAbd al-Razzāq. In al-Bukhārī's version this passage is missing. However, al-Bukhārī quotes this passage in a different chapter (*Jāmiʿ*, 64:36.28).

[52] Ibn Ḥanbal, *Musnad*, IV, 327 and 331; Ṭabarī, *Tafsīr*, XXVI, 58; Bayhaqī, *Sunan*, VII, 181, IX, 228, X, 109; Bukhārī, *Jāmiʿ*, 25:175.1 and 107.1; Abū Dāwūd, *Sunan*, 39:9.24; Nasāʾī, *Sunan*, 24:62; see also Mizzī, *Tuḥfa*, VIII, 372, 374, 383.

Zuhrī—al-Qāsim b. Muḥammad.[53] This tradition reports the events surrounding Abū Baṣīr and, in al-Ṭabarī's variant, also records ʿUmar's protest. The two variants are identical in wording in the corresponding passages and differ slightly from the wording of the other versions.

ʿAbd al-Raḥmān b. ʿAbd al-ʿAzīz's recension

A third long version going back to al-Zuhrī exists alongside those of Ibn Isḥāq and Maʿmar, namely, that of ʿAbd al-Raḥmān b. ʿAbd al-ʿAzīz (d. 162/778-9). Only one version of his account exists.[54] (I exclude a short version transmitted by Ibn Saʿd which has nothing in common with the long version.[55]) Therefore, the conclusions derived from this version have to be treated with caution, for the lack of parallel versions makes it impossible to determine which elements go back to which stage in the course of transmission.

On the whole the structure of his tradition resembles those of Maʿmar and Ibn Isḥāq, although there are some clear discrepancies. The wording differs remarkably from the other versions. The outline of his account is as follows: Muḥammad marches off to Mecca with 1,800 Companions. He sends a scout, a member of the Banū Khuzāʿa. At Ghadīr, at ʿUsfān, this scout reports that the Quraysh have called upon their Aḥābīsh to fight with them and that they have freed their slaves and offered them *khazīr*.[56] Muḥammad remarks that Khālid b. al-Walīd is at Ghamīm. Thus, he decides to make a detour via Baldaḥ. The camel stops and refuses to go any further, which Muḥammad interprets as a divine sign. Muḥammad revives the dry well using an arrow. The order of the delegates is the same as that reported by Maʿmar, but al-Ḥulays is mentioned by name in contrast to Maʿmar's report. The Muslims protest against the changes in the formulation. ʿUmar's protest is mentioned before the contents of the treaty (as in Ibn Isḥāq's report). He protests at first with Muḥammad, then with Abū Bakr (as in Maʿmar's report). As in Maʿmar's report, the treaty comprises only the clauses concerning the surrender of fugitives and the pilgrimage. This part displays the largest differences

[53] Ibn Ḥanbal, *Musnad*, IV, 331; Ṭabarī, *Tafsīr*, XXVI, 58.
[54] Ibn Abī Shayba, *Muṣannaf*, XIV, 444.
[55] Ibn Saʿd, *Ṭabaqāt*, VIII, 168.
[56] A dish made of meat and flour (see E. Fagnan, *Abou Yousouf Ya'koub. Le Livre de l'impot foncier* (Kitāb el-Kharādj), trans. into French and comm. E. Fagnan, Paris, 1921, 320).

with the other versions. According to ʿAbd al-Raḥmān, each side has to surrender the other side's fugitives. Both the surrender of Abū Jandal and the events surrounding Abū Baṣīr are reported at this point. Afterwards the *ʿumra* is treated, which the Quraysh insist on taking place the next year. Then follows the order to perform the sacrificial rites, which is obeyed only after Muḥammad follows Umm Salama's advice to set an example. The tradition ends with two statements of al-Zuhrī: he reports that seventy sacrificial animals were slaughtered, and that the booty of Khaybar was divided into eighteen parts, one part for each hundred men of those present at al-Ḥudaybiya.

ʿAbd al-Raḥmān's version displays certain significant differences with the versions Ibn Isḥāq and Maʿmar transmitted from al-Zuhrī. In addition to the differences concerning the clause of surrender in the treaty, there is an important variation in the position (with respect to the other elements) of the story of Abū Baṣīr and the absence of the story of the women coming to Medina. The latter might be due to this version being incomplete. On the other hand, in some parts the wording is identical to the versions of Maʿmar or Ibn Isḥāq.

Other versions

In addition to these three long versions, a number of shorter versions going back to al-Zuhrī exist (see Figure C on p. 274: The traditions going back to al-Zuhrī). Several of these short traditions go back to Sufyān (b. ʿUyayna)—al-Zuhrī.[57] All of these versions are similar in wording to the beginning of Maʿmar's version. As they consist only of a few sentences, it is impossible to draw far-reaching conclusions from them. It seems probable, however, that Maʿmar and Sufyān transmitted identical versions of al-Zuhrī. Possibly Sufyān took (at least part of) his version from Maʿmar, as is suggested in one tradition.[58]

The other short versions all deal with the revelation of Q 60:10 and the women coming to Muḥammad after the treaty was signed.[59] Parts

---

[57] Bayhaqī, *Sunan*, V, 235; Ibn Ḥanbal, *Musnad*, IV, 323, 328; Ibn Abī Shayba, *Muṣannaf*, XIV, 440; Bukhārī, *Jāmiʿ*, 64:36.10 and 36.28; Abū Dāwūd, *Sunan*, 11:15.3.

[58] In general al-Zuhrī's students transmit his traditions with different wordings (*riwāya bi-l-maʿnā*). Therefore, when two of his students give the same wording, it may be a sign that one copied the tradition from the other one. That is especially likely in this case, given Sufyān's explicit reference to the corroboration of his version by Maʿmar (*ḥafiẓtu baʿdahu wa-thabbatanī Maʿmar*; Bukhārī, *Jāmiʿ*, 64:36.28).

[59] Bukhārī, *Jāmiʿ*, 54:1 and 15, 64:36.29; Bayhaqī, *Sunan*, VII, 170 f., IX, 228.

of these versions are reported on the authority of ʿUrwa—his aunt, ʿĀʾisha. One of these traditions[60] includes a statement of ʿĀʾisha about the *bayʿa* of the women, which is interesting insofar as the *bayʿat al-nisāʾ*, which is based on Q 60:12, is usually connected with the meetings of ʿAqaba.[61] A letter by ʿUrwa in response to a question by the caliph ʿAbd al-Malik also deals with Q 60:10 and the corresponding events. Ibn Isḥāq reports part of it; longer versions are recorded by al-Wāqidī[62] and Ibn Saʿd.[63] The latter also has another version of ʿAbd al-Raḥmān going back only to al-Zuhrī.[64]

Summary: al-Zuhrī's tradition

Let us summarize the results which can be derived from the study of the versions going back to al-Zuhrī. The order of the elements in the different long versions is roughly the same: Departure (element c of the standard version), the Muslims' realization that the Quraysh intend to prevent them from entering Mecca (e), detour via al-Ḥudaybiya, the camel's refusal to go any further (f), scarceness of water (g), negotiations with the Quraysh (h), treaty (j/k), Abū Jandal (l), sacrifice and shaving (m), Abū Baṣīr (o), and the women (p). The episode of the women is sometimes mentioned before that of Abū Baṣīr; it is altogether absent from ʿAbd al-Raḥmān's version. Additionally, Ibn Isḥāq reports the revelation of Q 48 (n), and Maʿmar mentions entering the *iḥrām* (b).

While the broad outline is the same, there are differences in details. The order of the delegates is different, and ʿUmar's protest takes place at different points of time. In ʿAbd al-Raḥmān's version the episodes of Abū Jandal and Abū Baṣīr are combined. There are discrepancies in content as well. The number of Companions is several hundred in Maʿmar's version, seven hundred in Ibn Isḥāq's, and eighteen hundred in ʿAbd al-Raḥmān's. This discrepancy can be explained as follows: ʿAbd al-Raḥmān constructs a connection between the participants of al-Ḥudaybiya and the booty of Khaybar, which, according to other reports, was divided into eighteen parts and was distributed among those who took part in the campaign of al-

[60] Bukhārī, *Jāmiʿ*, 54:1; cf. Bayhaqī, *Sunan*, IX, 228.
[61] E.g. Ibn Hishām, *Sīra*, I, 431-34, especially 434.
[62] Wāqidī, *Maghāzī*, II, 631.
[63] Ibn Saʿd, *Ṭabaqāt*, VIII, 6-7.
[64] Ibid., 168.

Ḥudaybiya.[65] Ibn Isḥāq's number of seven hundred, on the other hand, appears to be an instance of the often symbolic significance of the number seven in the Islamic literature.[66] Another crucial discrepancy is the clause concerning the surrender of fugitives. ʿAbd al-Raḥmān describes it as a mutual obligation, while all the other reports describe it as a unilateral obligation of the Muslims. It seems probable that ʿAbd al-Raḥmān or his student Khālid b. Makhlad tried to make the report more favorable to the Muslims. The large number of reports with the unilateral obligation make it highly improbable that the obligation was originally mutual. Moreover, it would be difficult to explain how a forgery to the Muslims' disadvantage could become so widely acknowledged. The variants differ too much to allow a reconstruction of the wording of al-Zuhrī's report. However, the elements mentioned above, except those mentioned only by Ibn Isḥāq or Maʿmar, certainly go back to al-Zuhrī.

The study of the *asānīd* yields further conclusions. Most of al-Zuhrī's traditions go back to ʿUrwa—al-Miswar and Marwān, while some only to al-Miswar. There are indications that ʿUrwa combined different reports into a single narrative. For example, some elements subsumed in the long tradition ascribed to al-Miswar and Marwān may go back to ʿĀʾisha as the original narrator, particularly those dealing with the events connected to the revelation of Q 60:10 and the women's flight to Muḥammad after the truce. These elements also appear as independent traditions with ʿĀʾisha as the original narrator, and in some variants of the al-Miswar and Marwān tradition, ʿĀʾisha is named as the narrator of these elements. The same applies to al-Zuhrī, who probably not only used ʿUrwa's report but also used information from al-Qāsim b. Muḥammad. In some of the long versions, which are ascribed only to al-Miswar and Marwān, these reports are included. Possibly, originally independent reports were conflated in this case, leading to the loss of the various *asānīd* except for the one going back to al-Miswar and Marwān.

---

[65] E.g. Ibn Hishām, *Sīra*, II, 349 f.

[66] See L.I. Conrad, "Seven and the *Tasbīʿ*: On the Implication of Numerical Symbolism for the Study of Medieval Islamic History", in *JESHO,* 31 (1988), for example, 48: "In *ḥadīth* there are many more examples [...] that illustrate how seven-symbolism was used to indicate a large number in a general way, or to suggest the presence of divine influence in the course of human affairs." Both motives may be at work in this case.

A similar observation holds in the case of Ibn Isḥāq's traditions. In some variants parts of his tradition from al-Miswar and Marwān are transmitted with *asānīd* going back to narrators other than al-Miswar and Marwān. Most probably *asānīd* have been lost in these cases, therefore combining originally separated reports and making of them a single tradition.

Motzki observed similar phenomena in a different tradition. He observed two processes: (a) loss of *asānīd*: Two originally separate traditions are combined into one, but only one of the *asānīd* survives;[67] (b) growth of *asānīd*: A combined report is transmitted on the authority of the composer of the combined report, on the one hand, and on the authority of one of the original narrators, on the other hand.[68]

2. Hishām b. ʿUrwa's tradition

We have reconstructed the contents of al-Zuhrī's tradition, an account which was in circulation about one hundred years after the events it describes. The contents of ʿUrwa b. al-Zubayr's account, which was closer to the events by one generation, can be reconstructed as well. To that end we will study the versions going back to ʿUrwa independently from al-Zuhrī and compare them with the account of al-Zuhrī.

Let us first consider the tradition of Hishām (d. 146/763), the son of ʿUrwa (see Figure D on p. 275: The traditions going back to ʿUrwa b. al-Zubayr). His report is recorded by Ibn Abī Shayba[69] and by Abū Yūsuf.[70] Ibn Abī Shayba's version is incomplete, amounting to approximately two-thirds of Abū Yūsuf's version. Since the two versions are to a large degree identical in wording, we can conclude that Hishām had a written version. Abū Yūsuf names Ibn Isḥāq and al-Kalbī as his sources in addition to Hishām b. ʿUrwa.[71] However, the wording mostly follows that of Hishām as recorded by Ibn Abī Shayba.

There are some considerable discrepancies with al-Zuhrī's version. Hishām dates the events in Shawwāl, whereas in the later Islamic

---

[67] H. Motzki, "Der Fiqh des -Zuhrī: die Quellenproblematik", in *Der Islam*, 68 (1991), 39.

[68] Ibid., 34-38.

[69] Ibn Abī Shayba, *Muṣannaf*, XXIV, 429.

[70] Abū Yūsuf, *Kharāj*, 128-30.

[71] Ibid., 128.

historical tradition Dhū l-Qaʿda is generally accepted as the date for the events. Hishām does not mention the number of Companions taking part in the campaign. At ʿUsfān, some men[72] of the Banū Kaʿb report that the Quraysh have assembled their Aḥābīsh and offered them *khazīr* with the intention of hindering Muḥammad from reaching Mecca. After leaving ʿUsfān, the Muslims encounter Khālid b. al-Walīd and therefore make a detour via Ghamīm. They discuss whether to march towards Mecca or to attack the Aḥābīsh. Abū Bakr convinces Muḥammad to march directly towards Mecca. Al-Miqdād remarks that, in contrast to the Jews, the Muslims would not have their Prophet fight alone. At the boundary of the *ḥaram* the camel stops and refuses to go any further, which Muḥammad interprets as a divine sign. Another detour is made via Dhāt al-Ḥanẓal to al-Ḥudaybiya. Muḥammad revives the dry well using an arrow. The order of the delegates differs significantly from the traditions of al-Zuhrī, and some names are different. While in al-Zuhrī's traditions one of the delegates is named Ḥulays, in this tradition it is a man from the Banū Ḥulays (or Banū Ḥils). Budayl b. Warqāʾ is not mentioned at all. The first delegate is the above-mentioned man from the Banū Ḥulays/Ḥils. Then follows ʿUrwa b. Masʿūd. Mikraz b. Ḥafṣ and Suhayl together negotiate with Muḥammad to conclude a treaty. The treaty comprises more issues than Maʿmar's version, among others the clauses *lā islāl wa-lā ighlāl* and *ʿayba makfūfa*,[73] but no truce is mentioned. As in Ibn Isḥāq's version, no protests by the Muslims against the changing of the formulations are recorded. As in Maʿmar's version, Mikraz b. Ḥafṣ agrees to protect Abū Jandal. The remaining passages are recorded by Abū Yūsuf only, therefore we cannot establish whether they go back to Hishām, to al-Kalbī, or to Ibn Isḥāq. What follows are the episodes of sacrificing and shaving, of Abū Baṣīr, who in this version flees to Dhū l-Ḥulayfa after Muḥammad refuses to allow him into Medina, and of the women in connection with the revelation of Q 60:10. Abū Yūsuf's account continues with the conquest of Mecca after mentioning that the treaty was observed until the Banū Bakr violated it.

[72] According to Ibn Abī Shayba only one.
[73] On these terms, see note 26.

3. Abū l-Aswad's tradition

In addition to Hishām b. ʿUrwa's version, there is another tradition that goes back to ʿUrwa independently of al-Zuhrī: That of Abū l-Aswad (d. 131/748). It is recorded by Abū ʿUbayd,[74] al-Balādhurī,[75] Ibn Kathīr,[76] and above all by Ibn Ḥajar al-ʿAsqalānī, who gives by far the longest variant.[77] Al-Balādhurī has an abridged version of the traditions by Abū ʿUbayd. These versions, as well as that of Ibn Kathīr, have an *isnād* going back to Ibn Lahīʿa—Abū l-Aswad, while Ibn Ḥajar does not give an *isnād*. All versions are reported on the authority of ʿUrwa as the original narrator. Only fragments of Abū l-Aswad's account are extant; these show considerable differences with all the other versions studied. By combining all the fragments, we arrive at the following account:

The events are dated to Dhū l-Qaʿda of the year 6/628.[78] After it is reported that the road is blocked by the Quraysh, Muḥammad asks if anybody knows a road to the coast, eliciting one man's affirmative response.[79] The Muslims reach al-Ḥudaybiya in the hot weather. There they have access to only one well.[80] Muḥammad rinses his mouth, pours the water into the well and stirs with an arrow, whereupon the well overflows with water.[81] Two of the associates of the first delegate, Budayl b. Warqāʾ, are named: Khārija b. Karz and Yazīd b. Umayya.[82] ʿUthmān is sent to Mecca to tell the Muslims there that their freedom (*faraj*) is near.[83] Al-Mughīra b. Shuʿba tries to hide from one of the delegates, ʿUrwa b. Masʿūd.[84] While negotiations take place between Suhayl and Muḥammad, someone from one of the parties throws a stone at the other party. The parties clash due to this incident. The Quraysh take ʿUthmān and his associates hostage, as do the Muslims Suhayl and his associates. At this point the *bayʿa* takes

[74] Abū ʿUbayd, *Amwāl*, 156.
[75] Balādhurī, *Ansāb*, 351.
[76] Ibn Kathīr, *al-Bidāya wa-l-nihāya*, IV, 164.
[77] Ibn Ḥajar, *Fatḥ al-bārī*, VI, 258 ff. Aʿẓamī in his compilation of the *maghāzī* of ʿUrwa b. al-Zubayr (in the *riwāya* of Abū l-Aswad) does not include this tradition of Ibn Ḥajar but has a different tradition of his. See ʿUrwa b. al-Zubayr, *Maghāzī*, 192 f.
[78] Ibn Kathīr, *al-Bidāya wa-l-nihāya*, IV, 164.
[79] Ibn Ḥajar, *Fatḥ al-bārī*, VI, 259 f.
[80] Ibid., 261.
[81] Ibid., 262.
[82] Ibid.
[83] Ibid., 264.
[84] Ibid., 266.

place under a tree; the Muslims pledge not to flee. The Quraysh learn about this and are frightened by God (*arʿabahum Allāh*). Thereupon the treaty is concluded. Q 48:24 is revealed on this occasion.[85] The treaty comprises a truce for four years, the clause of the surrender of fugitives and the phrase *lā islāl wa-lā ighlāl*. In addition, it is agreed that Muslims coming to Mecca for a *ḥajj* or *ʿumra* or on the way south shall be safe, as shall be the Quraysh passing by Medina on the way to Syria or the east (*mashriq*). The Banū Kaʿb enter into an alliance with Muḥammad, as do the Banū Kināna with the Quraysh.[86] Abū Jandal flees to Muḥammad,[87] but is handed over to the Quraysh. Mikraz b. Ḥafṣ promises to protect him and accompanies him to a tent.[88] Muḥammad orders that the animals be sacrificed. The Muslims attempt to drive them to the *ḥaram* but are prevented from doing so by the Quraysh. Therefore, Muḥammad orders that they be sacrificed outside the *ḥaram*.[89] Abū Baṣīr is surrendered to two delegates from the Quraysh, but kills one of them and escapes.[90] Abū Jandal flees from Mecca with seventy Muslim men on horseback to join Abū Baṣīr. They camp near Dhū l-Marwa and raid caravans of the Quraysh that pass by. They avoid going to Medina in order not to be handed over to the Quraysh. The Quraysh send Abū Sufyān to Muḥammad to make him take them in. The clause of the surrender of fugitives is nullified (*wa-man kharaja minnā ilayka fa-huwa laka ḥalālun ghayru ḥarajin*). Muḥammad takes in the rebels.[91]

This version is in large parts incompatible with the other traditions going back to ʿUrwa. While some elements do occur in the other versions, there are many elements that are unique in this tradition. We do not know the path of transmission for most parts of the tradition. In the short parts which are supplied with *asānīd*, the name of Ibn Lahīʿa, a weak traditionist according to *rijāl* critics, stands out.[92]

---

[85] Ibid., 271; cf. ʿUrwa b. al-Zubayr, *Maghāzī*, 192 f. Abū ʿUbayd only records the *bayʿa* and the revelation. See Abū ʿUbayd, *Amwāl*, 156. In al-Balādhurī's version, this part of Abū ʿUbayd's tradition is missing altogether.

[86] Abū ʿUbayd, *Amwāl*, 156.

[87] Ibn Ḥajar, *Fatḥ al-bārī*, VI, 271.

[88] Ibid., 272.

[89] Ibid., 274 f.

[90] Ibid., 278.

[91] Ibid., 279.

[92] G. Schoeler, *Charakter und Authentie der muslimischen Überlieferung über das Leben Mohammeds*, Berlin, New York, 1996, 85; see also G.H.A. Juynboll, *Muslim Tradition: Studies in Chronology, Provenance and Authorship of early Ḥadīth*, Cambridge, 1983, 110 and 155.

Possibly he is responsible for this version. There are several indications that Abū l-Aswad's traditions do not go back to ʿUrwa b. al-Zubayr or, at least, include material from other sources as well. Firstly, these additional elements are never reported on the authority of ʿUrwa in any other tradition. They do occur in accounts about al-Ḥudaybiya, but not in those going back to ʿUrwa. Parallels to other accounts can be shown. For instance, the motif of the scarceness of water at al-Ḥudaybiya displays many similarities with al-Wāqidī's account.[93] Both al-Wāqidī and Abū l-Aswad[94] mention the intense heat (*ḥarr shadīd*) at al-Ḥudaybiya. The Quraysh occupy all but one well (al-Wāqidī: *innamā hiya biʾr wāḥida, wa-qad sabaqa l-mushrikūn (...) ʿalā miyāhihā;* Abū l-Aswad: *wa-sabaqat Quraysh ilā l-māʾ (...) wa-laysa bihā illā biʾr wāḥida*); Muḥammad rinses his mouth (*maḍmaḍa*) and pours the water into the well (*ṣabbahu fī l-biʾr*) before stirring with an arrow, as is familiar from the other versions. In these cases the versions of Abū l-Aswad and al-Wāqidī closely correspond to each other in both content and wording. It is therefore probable that they are not unconnected to each other. None of the major *ḥadīth* collections records Abū l-Aswad's version, nor do the important historiographical works, apart from Ibn Kathīr's citation of the date (Dhū l-Qaʿda) on Abū l-Aswad's authority. It is not the only case in which a tradition of Abū l-Aswad does not match the other versions: Schoeler observed a similar problem in a different tradition. In that case, too, a variant going back to Ibn Lahīʿa—Abū l-Aswad shows considerable discrepancies with the other versions.[95] Parts of Abū l-Aswad's tradition display embellishments, which might signify that the tradition is late.

Considering these facts, it seems probable that this tradition does not go back to ʿUrwa. While it may include elements from ʿUrwa's account, these cannot be separated from elements imported from other traditions.

4. ʿUrwa b. al-Zubayr's tradition: results

To reconstruct the contents of ʿUrwa's account, we therefore have two versions at our disposal: Those of Hishām b. ʿUrwa and al-Zuhrī. As these versions have been shown to be independent of each other,

[93] Wāqidī, *Maghāzī*, II, 577.
[94] Ibn Ḥajar, *Fatḥ al-bārī*, VI, 261 f.
[95] Schoeler, *Charakter und Authentie*, 81-85.

elements that occur in both most probably go back to ʿUrwa. These elements are: departure (c); information about Khālid b. al-Walīd (e); detour via al-Ḥudaybiya where the camel stops and refuses to go any further (f); initial scarceness and subsequent replenishment of water (g); different delegates of the Quraysh (h); conclusion of the treaty with Suhayl (j); as elements of the treaty: the clause of the surrender of fugitives, probably the agreement on an *ʿumra* in the following year, possibly the agreement on freedom of forming alliances (parts of k); Abū Jandal (l); sacrifice and shaving (m); Abū Baṣīr (o) and the revelation of Q 60:10 in connection with the women fleeing to Muḥammad (p). In all likelihood, some other elements go back to ʿUrwa, since they can be found in some traditions of both al-Zuhrī and Hishām, for example, Mikraz's protection of Abū Jandal and the phrases *lā islāl wa-lā ighlāl* and *ʿayba makfūfa.*

ʿUrwa is the most famous of the early scholars dealing with *maghāzī.* Therefore, we may presume that his account reflects what was in circulation about al-Ḥudaybiya in the second half of the first century AH. His account, however, need not necessarily be a description of what really happened. Changes may have occurred in the process of transmission from the eyewitnesses to ʿUrwa.[96]

ʿUrwa's account is not homogenous but is composed of several shorter reports. This is indicated by the fact that some elements were transmitted separately, in some cases with different *asānīd,* and that the order of elements differs in the different variants. In the long versions these separate accounts have been concatenated, using formulae such as *thumma* (then) to connect the reports. At least some of these concatenations are due to ʿUrwa himself, as al-Zuhrī and Hishām record the same elements mostly in the same order. It is impossible to say whether the different elements originally belonged together.[97] Since we do not have any other reports that draw on ʿUrwa's sources, it is impossible to determine what redactional changes ʿUrwa made when composing his account, whether he made abridgments or harmonized contradictory accounts. Thus, it is diffi-

[96] Cf. S. Leder, "The Literary Use of the *Khabar*: A Basic Form of Historical Writing", in A. Cameron and L.I. Conrad, eds., *The Byzantine and Early Islamic Near East, I: Problems in the Literary Source Material,* Princeton, 1992, 278 f.

[97] Cf. A. Noth, *The Early Arabic Historical Tradition: A Source-Critical Study,* Princeton, 1994, 176.

cult to delve any farther back into the half century or so that separates ʿUrwa from the events.

A study of ʿUrwa's material raises considerable doubts about whether his account describes what really happened. The Prophet's image is already transfigured. He miraculously revives the well. Miracles in connection with water are a common motif in the legendary literature about Muḥammad and are encountered in various instances.[98] ʿUrwa b. Masʿūd is quoted as not having seen any ruler whose men honor him as Muḥammad's Companions honor Muḥammad. This is further embellished in Ibn Isḥāq's version.[99] These glorifications and transfigurations can be observed in the earliest versions, making it difficult to determine what really happened.

Besides, signs of formalization call into question the historicity of the events. Geminations and triplications occur in all the versions, making it probable that ʿUrwa's account already showed some formalization. For example, ʿUmar's protest consists of three questions posed twice, the Muslims are ordered three times to perform the sacrificial rites before they obey, and the delegates of the Quraysh are addressed with the same formulae every time.

The *dramatis personae* on the Muslim side are the later caliphs Abū Bakr and ʿUmar, and al-Mughīra b. Shuʿba, which could signify a later construction. In Ibn Isḥāq's version ʿAlī is given a major role, a late development due probably to Ibn Isḥāq himself. Here, at least three influences may have shaped the tradition. The "rightly guided" caliphs were regarded as models by subsequent generations.[100] Therefore, in the understanding of these generations, they must have played major roles in almost every incident. The mention of ʿAlī might be a politically motivated attempt to legitimize and bolster his claim to the caliphate. Finally, it was common to use well-known names to enhance the credibility of traditions.[101]

---

[98] Cf. Ibn Hishām, *Sīra*, II, 527; cf. T. Andrae, *Die Person Muhammeds in Lehre und Glauben seiner Gemeinde*, Stockholm, 1918, 47 f.; J. Horovitz, "Zur Muḥammadlegende", in *Der Islam*, 5 (1914), 47.

[99] Ibn Hishām, *Sīra*, II, 314. In the traditions that go back to al-Zuhrī more legendary material can be found than in Hishām b. ʿUrwa's version.

[100] Cf. Noth, *The Early ... Tradition*, 80, also 138-42.

[101] See Noth, *The Early ... Tradition*, 111-29, especially 128; see also R. Paret, *Die legendäre Maghāzī-Literatur: Arabische Dichtungen über die muslimischen Kriegszüge zu Mohammeds Zeit*, Tübingen, 1930, 190-211, especially 202.

In previous studies, parallels between some elements of the al-Ḥudaybiya tradition and biblical or other stories have been shown.[102] Certain other elements seem to be topoi, i.e., they recur frequently in Muslim traditions. We have observed this already in the case of the water miracle. Ibn Isḥāq mentions that the Quraysh sent two hundred men on horseback to Kurāʿ al-Ghamīm near ʿUsfān. On a different occasion, the Muslims are said to have gone to ʿUsfān with two hundred men on horseback and to have sent two scouts to Kurāʿ al-Ghamīm.[103] Among the participants in the campaign against Khaybar, again, two hundred men on horseback are said to have been present.[104] It seems that part of the al-Ḥudaybiya account was composed by adjoining motifs that are more or less independent of (and not in the first instance connected to) al-Ḥudaybiya.

Having seen how the tradition was influenced by later redactions and opinions, the question remains as to what factual historical events, if any, can be extracted from it. Here we have to take into account that this study focuses on the tradition of ʿUrwa b. al-Zubayr, which is part of what has become the "canonical" tradition. Possibly other reports existed which just failed to make it into the collections. Thus, trying to reconstruct historical facts from ʿUrwa's version alone might yield misleading results. Nevertheless, I would hold that certain elements are in all probability based on historical events, especially those presenting the Muslims in an unfavorable manner or in a way that is contrary to usual patterns. Thus, we can quite safely assume that there was a treaty which comprised at least the clause of the surrender of fugitives, since there is no apparent motive which would account for its fabrication. It seems that extraditions actually did take place. The place name may be historical as well, especially as it has no specific meaning. However, the special location of the place[105] could signify a fabrication. Several of the other elements might have a historical core which, however, cannot be determined. The problem is that, as we have seen above, ʿUrwa's account is a composite of different reports. Therefore some of the elements which seem to be historical (due to the absence of apparent motives for their fabrica-

[102] Dubler/Quarella, "Ḥudaibiyya", 74, 76; R. Sellheim, "Prophet, Chalif und Geschichte. Die Muhammed-Biographie des Ibn Isḥāq", in *Oriens*, 18-19 (1967), 64.
[103] Ibn Hishām, *Sīra*, II, 280.
[104] Ibid., 350.
[105] At the border of the *ḥaram*. Cf. Dubler/Quarella, "Ḥudaibiyya", 77.

tion) possibly do not belong to the original tradition about al-Ḥudaybiya. They may be later accretions or authentic reports about events other than al-Ḥudaybiya.

II. ʿUrwa and the Development of the Standard Account

The standard account outlined at the beginning of this article is based largely on ʿUrwa's report. Several elements can be found only in his tradition. The standard account, however, comprises some elements which do not go back to ʿUrwa. The origin of these motifs will be studied in the following. The study will shed some light on the development of the al-Ḥudaybiya tradition and hence on the development of the early historical tradition in general. As will be seen, the tradition was influenced by above all the Qurʾān and, to a lesser degree, the *ḥadīth*. The name al-Ḥudaybiya is not mentioned in the Qurʾān, but Q 48 is generally believed to have been revealed on that occasion.[106] In this *sūra* all the elements of the standard account missing in ʿUrwa's tradition can be found, namely, the *bayʿat al-riḍwān*, the Bedouin, and the dream Muḥammad has. The verses remain too vague, however, to allow a reconstruction of the events from the Qurʾān alone.

Verses 11, 12, 15, and 16 deal with the Bedouin. The information which can be derived from these verses is all we know about this element; there is no additional information in the Islamic historical tradition. Ibn Isḥāq mentions the Bedouin in his introduction to the events of al-Ḥudaybiya, but they do not figure in any of the traditions he gives. Al-Wāqidī, too, mentions them without any *isnād*. Therefore, we do not know from where he got his information. Al-Ṭabarī only quotes Ibn Isḥāq. There are no traditions in the *ḥadīth*-collections that mention the Bedouin. Therefore, it seems that this element was not originally included in the tradition, otherwise we would expect other traces of it in the Islamic historical tradition. The element, however, is not detectable in the al-Ḥudaybiya traditions before Ibn Isḥāq and al-Wāqidī. The same is true of the dream, alluded to in Q 48:27, which Muḥammad is said to have had before the campaign. ʿUrwa does not mention it. It is mentioned in some traditions given by Ibn Isḥāq, but

[106] Ali, "al-Ḥudaybiya", 54.

not in his introduction. Al-Wāqidī mentions it without giving an *isnād*. Al-Ṭabarī has only the tradition of Ibn Isḥāq. Here, again, the Qurʾān seems to be the only source for this event. The verse does not even fit into the tradition well, since it states that the dream was already fulfilled.[107]

Q 48:18-19 deals with the *bayʿa*, which is said to be connected to al-Ḥudaybiya. There are numerous traditions about the *bayʿa*. Thus, it seems strange that ʿUrwa does not mention it. It is unlikely that these elements were originally included in ʿUrwa's tradition and yet failed to make it to any of the extant variants. In none of the traditions of Hishām b. ʿUrwa and al-Zuhrī is the *bayʿa* mentioned. Nor is it, to my knowledge, ever reported on the authority of ʿUrwa in any *ḥadīth*-collection, historical work, or Qurʾānic commentary, barring the dubious ascription to ʿUrwa by Abū l-Aswad.[108]

Did ʿUrwa fail to notice these elements? That is highly improbable, since the *bayʿa* forms an integral part of the story in the later historical tradition. Numerous traditions show the outstanding importance of the *bayʿa*, whose participants shall not enter Hell[109] and regard the *bayʿa* as the first *fatḥ* (before the conquest of Mecca).[110] It is hard to believe that ʿUrwa's informants did not mention this event.

More likely the above-mentioned verses of Q 48 did not originally refer to the events reported by ʿUrwa but were applied to them only later. It cannot be established whether they refer to another event at al-Ḥudaybiya, or why they were applied to the events of ʿUrwa's report. The connection seems to have taken place in Ibn Isḥāq's generation, or possibly already in al-Zuhrī's time. In Maʿmar's tradition from al-Zuhrī, at least one verse of the *sūra* is cited. The only Qurʾānic allusions that definitely go back to ʿUrwa are those to Q 60:10.

Some other facts corroborate the proposed dissociation of the events described in Q 48—traditionally believed to refer to al-Ḥudaybiya—and the events reported by ʿUrwa: In the sources surveyed practically no tradition combines the motifs of ʿUrwa's account, such

---

[107] See ibid., 54 f.

[108] See above on Abū l-Aswad's tradition.

[109] See for example Tirmidhī, *Jāmiʿ*, 46:132, 133.3,4 (in this case the difference between al-Mizzī's numbering and that of the edition used is considerable. In the latter the traditions are recorded under 46:58 and 59.3,4); Ibn Māja, *Sunan*, 37:33.9; Ibn Ḥanbal, *Musnad*, III, 349, 350, 396.

[110] Cf. Bukhārī, *Jāmiʿ*, 64:36.4; Ṭabarī, *Tafsīr*, XXVI, 40; Bayhaqī, *Sunan*, IX, 223; Abū Zurʿa, *Taʾrīkh*, I, 166.

as the treaty, with any of the Qur'ānic elements. Al-Yaʿqūbī does not mention the *bayʿa* in his account of al-Ḥudaybiya.[111] There is a tradition which states that the Byzantines defeated the Persians on the day of al-Ḥudaybiya, and that its news reached the Prophet on the day of *bayʿat al-riḍwān*.[112] This would entail at least a two-week interval between the two days. Paret holds that at least Q 48:1 alludes to Badr and not to al-Ḥudaybiya.[113] Rubin mentions traditions dealing with events that occur after the *fatḥ* but while the Quraysh are still *mushrikūn*.[114] Thus, he proposes identifying "*fatḥ*" with the conquest of Khaybar, which took place shortly after the treaty of al-Ḥudaybiya. But the "*fatḥ*" might also be identified with the *bayʿa* if it is dissociated from the treaty. It is clear from the context that the treaty was already concluded, making an identification of "*fatḥ*" with the treaty impossible.

At this point it is worthwhile reconsidering a thesis that Hawting has proposed.[115] He observed that material dealing with the opening of the Kaʿba is scarce in the accounts of the conquest of Mecca but does occur in other contexts. He concluded that this material was not originally part of the tradition of the conquest but was attached to it later. He also emphasized the importance of the term "*fatḥ*" in connection with the campaign of al-Ḥudaybiya. Considering the findings of the present study, one might postulate three separate events that were later conflated into two reports: (i) the expedition to al-Ḥudaybiya and the treaty, (ii) the *bayʿa* and the opening of the Kaʿba, possibly connected with the revelation of Q 48, and (iii) the conquest of Mecca. In the later transmission some elements would have been included into the report about al-Ḥudaybiya, namely, the *bayʿa*, the dream of the opening of the Kaʿba, and the term "*fatḥ*" via Q 48, while the term "*fatḥ*" (used for the conquest) and the reports of the opening of the Kaʿba were included into the tradition about the conquest of Mecca.

---

[111] Yaʿqūbī, *Ta'rīkh*, II, 54 f.

[112] Lecker, "The Ḥudaybiyya-treaty", 9. This tradition implies that the *bayʿa* took place after the day of al-Ḥudaybiya (which most probably is the day on which the treaty was concluded), while usually the *bayʿa* is mentioned before the treaty. However, this tradition should not be overemphasized, as numerous traditions give the usual order.

[113] R. Paret, *Der Koran. Kommentar und Konkordanz*, [4]Stuttgart, 1989, 451.

[114] U. Rubin, "Muḥammad's Curse of Muḍar and the Blockade of Mecca", in *JESHO*, 31 (1988), 256.

[115] See Hawting, "al-Ḥudaybiyya".

This disjunction of the three events is speculative, but it would help explain some of the anomalies in the reports about al-Ḥudaybiya, in particular the questions of how the *bayʿa* (and thus the treaty) came to be considered a great victory, and whether Khālid b. al-Walīd converted to Islām before al-Ḥudaybiya.[116] Anyhow, the separation of the events of al-Ḥudaybiya as reported by ʿUrwa from those alluded to in Q 48 is likely.

The Qurʾānic elements seem to have been inserted into the historical tradition only at a later stage. It is irrelevant to this study whether verses from the Qurʾān were adduced in corroboration of existing traditions, as Rubin argues,[117] or whether some events (such as the *bayʿat al-riḍwān*) owe their existence only to the interpretation of Qurʾānic verses, as Crone maintains.[118] Q 48 may allude to a historical event, but probably not to the one in ʿUrwa's tradition.

As to the *ḥadīth*, there are certain other traditions about al-Ḥudaybiya, but none of them comes close to ʿUrwa's in terms of length and the number of elements treated. They mostly consist of short passages dealing with single aspects of alleged events at al-Ḥudaybiya. The main themes are in some respects relevant to law or other *ḥadīth* genres (such as *faḍāʾil*). Zaman's statement about al-Bukhārī applies to all the *ḥadīth* collections:

> Al-Bukhari does seem to presuppose a narrative (or narratives) of Hudaybiyya; but his traditions do not themselves constitute one. [...] they are not *about* Hudaybiyya: Hudaybiyya is relevant to them (or they to it) solely because it was on that occasion that certain significant doctrinal and juristic matters were enunciated or precedents established.[119]

Ḥadīth collections deal with the following topics apropos of al-Ḥudaybiya: the *bayʿa*, the sacrificial rites, proper conduct during the state of *iḥrām*, the miraculous revival of the well, and the contents of the treaty. The historicity of these elements shall not be discussed here in detail. Nevertheless, some considerations that cast doubt on their his-

---

[116] See for example Ṭabarī, *Taʾrīkh*, I, 1531. Ibn Hishām reports that Khālid's conversion took place shortly before the *fatḥ* (*qubayla l-fatḥ*), but the corresponding passage is mentioned before al-Ḥudaybiya. See Ibn Hishām, *Sīra*, II, 276 ff.

[117] U. Rubin, *The Eye of the Beholder: The Life of Muḥammad as Viewed by the Early Muslims*, Princeton, 1995, 227.

[118] P. Crone, *Meccan Trade and the Rise of Islam*, Princeton, 1987, 215.

[119] M.Q. Zaman, "*Maghāzī* and the *Muḥaddithūn*": Reconsidering the Treatment of 'Historical' Materials in Early Collections of *Ḥadith*", in *IJMES*, 28 (1996), 10.

toricity shall be mentioned. Part of this material consists of embellishments of individual elements, for example in the case of the miracle of the well, which is not yet a miracle in the traditions of al-Zuhrī and Hishām. Another part consists of events that are mentioned in other contexts as well. For example, the sacrifice of Abū Jahl's camel is mentioned in connection with both al-Ḥudaybiya[120] and the farewell pilgrimage,[121] and the question of shaving the hair versus shortening it slightly is mentioned in connection with al-Ḥudaybiya,[122] the *ʿumrat al-qaḍāʾ*,[123] and without historical context.[124] It seems that in these cases a setting was required in order to make the tradition sound more credible.[125] Many circumstances met this requirement, leading to the appearance of the same element in reports of different events.

This material from the *ḥadīth* cannot be found in ʿUrwa's tradition. Ibn Isḥāq, too, only mentions a few of these elements, such as the sacrifice of Abū Jahl's camel and the issue of shaving versus shortening one's hair. Al-Wāqidī, however, mentions numerous such elements. In addition to those of Ibn Isḥāq, he treats: proper conduct during the state of *iḥrām*, Muḥammad's refusal of gifts from heathens, additional sacrifices to be made when one shaves before the completion of the *ʿumra*, and Muḥammad's decision to immediately slaughter an animal that collapsed rather than sacrifice it at the end of the *ʿumra*. These can safely be presumed to have been added later to the historical tradition for various purposes. On the one hand, these decisions relevant to law cannot be found in the early al-Ḥudaybiya traditions going back to ʿUrwa. ʿUrwa b. al-Zubayr was an important *faqīh*, and he would have probably mentioned such rulings by Muḥammad in his account. On the other hand, some of the rulings indicate an advanced state in the development of jurisprudence. An example is the expiatory rites in the case of shaving prematurely which consist of sacrificing a sheep, fasting for three days, or giving alms of two units of barley to six needy persons.[126] This ruling presumes the previous appearance of various problems, such as what

---

[120] Ibn Ḥanbal, *Musnad*, I, 314 f.; Abū Dāwūd, *Sunan*, 11:13; Ibn Hishām, *Sīra*, II, 320.

[121] Tirmidhī, *Jāmiʿ*, 7:6.1.

[122] Wāqidī, *Maghāzī*, II, 615; Ibn Hishām, *Sīra*, II, 319.

[123] Wāqidī, *Maghāzī*, III, 1109.

[124] Abū Dāwūd, *Sunan*, 11:79.1; Tirmidhī, *Jāmiʿ*, 7:74.1.

[125] See E. Stetter, *Topoi und Schemata im Ḥadīṯ*, Tübingen, 1965, 4-8.

[126] Wāqidī, *Maghāzī*, II, 578.

is to be done when no sheep are available. It does not seem to be a ruling made by Muḥammad during a specific situation.

III. Conclusion

The portrayal of al-Ḥudaybiya conveyed to us by the earliest extant sources is the result of a long process of transmission and redaction. Some phases of this process were studied in this article. We may summarize the development of the tradition as follows:

The earliest version that can be reconstructed is that of ʿUrwa b. al-Zubayr. He most probably had several eyewitness reports at his disposal dealing with al-Ḥudaybiya and events possibly connected with al-Ḥudaybiya. In the first stage of redaction he formed a single narrative from these reports. It cannot be established whether all the elements he combined in his account belonged originally to the same historical event. The salient components of his account are the treaty with the clause of the surrender of fugitives, and the subsequent extradition of some people. These elements can be regarded as the historical core of the tradition. Some legendary material can already be observed. Allusions to the Qurʾān, however, are still marginal.

The transmission of the report to ʿUrwa's students al-Zuhrī and Hishām b. ʿUrwa most probably took place orally, presumably in lectures. At any rate, their reports include the same elements in more or less the same order, but are completely different in terms of wording.

While Hishām seems to have written down his version—the variants are largely similar in wording—, al-Zuhrī presumably transmitted his version in lectures, since the versions going back to him are alike in content but not in wording. Written composition in this case began a generation later with Maʿmar b. Rāshid, Ibn Isḥāq, and ʿAbd al-Raḥmān b. ʿAbd al-ʿAzīz.

Al-Zuhrī's tradition is best suited for studying redactional changes in the generation following ʿUrwa due to its wide distribution. *Asānīd* going back farther than ʿUrwa to al-Miswar b. Makhrama and Marwān b. al-Ḥakam and to ʿĀʾisha only occur in al-Zuhrī's version. These authorities may be responsible for parts of the tradition, but this cannot be established beyond doubt. Al-Zuhrī makes an allusion to a Qurʾānic verse (48:24 f.), but does not mention the other themes of Q 48. He may be responsible for some of the legendary elements.

In the next stage of transmission and redaction (al-Zuhrī to Ibn Isḥāq, Maʿmar, ʿAbd al-Raḥmān and others), significant changes take place. The most important one is the inclusion of the whole Q 48 into the tradition by Ibn Isḥāq. Three of the motifs of the *sūra*—the dream as the cause for the campaign, the Bedouin who refuse to accompany Muḥammad, and the *bayʿat al-riḍwān*—are incorporated into the account at this stage[127] while the other elements occur only in the statement that the whole Q 48 was revealed on this occasion.

The report according to ʿĀʾisha, presumably still separated in al-Zuhrī's version, is included into the tradition ascribed to al-Miswar and Marwān. More changes can be found in Ibn Isḥāq's version. He modifies al-Zuhrī's report to combine it with other reports into a single tradition. A loss of *isnād* can be observed in his case due to the incorporation of a presumably independent tradition going back to a different original narrator into al-Zuhrī's tradition.

While Maʿmar's version seems to have been passed on mostly by written transmission, Ibn Isḥāq presumably continued to transmit his work in lectures even after it was written down, which could account for the differences in the versions going back to him. No statements about ʿAbd al-Raḥmān's work can be made here, since it only exists in a single version.

Two generations later, numerous themes specific to the *ḥadīth* literature are incorporated into the al-Ḥudaybiya tradition, as can be observed in al-Wāqidī's work. Some of these elements show an advanced state of jurisprudence, while others occur in different contexts. They certainly have nothing to do with the actual events of al-Ḥudaybiya.

The very problematic tradition of Abū l-Aswad seems to indicate a stage of development between those of Ibn Isḥāq and al-Wāqidī, or possibly even later. The connection with the *bayʿa* is already made, and there are parallels to al-Wāqidī's wording. This version definitely does not go back to ʿUrwa, although ʿUrwa's tradition may have served as its basis.

---

[127] In Ibn Isḥāq's version the dream is not yet a separate element, but is alluded to in one tradition. Therefore, we may conclude that the connection prevailed at Ibn Isḥāq's time.

Bibliography

ʿAbd al-Razzāq b. Hammām al-Ṣanʿānī, *al-Muṣannaf*, ed. Ḥabīb al-Raḥmān al-Aʿẓamī, 11 vols., Beirut, 1970-72.

Abū Dāwūd, Sulaymān b. al-Ashʿath al-Sijistānī, *Sunan Abī Dāwʾūd*, ed. Muḥammad Muḥyī al-Dīn ʿAbd al-Ḥamīd, 4 vols., Beirut, n.d.

Abū ʿUbayd al-Qāsim b. Sallām, *Kitāb al-Amwāl*, ed. M.Kh. Harrās, [3]Cairo, 1401/1981.

Abū Yūsuf Yaʿqūb b. Ibrāhīm al-Anṣārī, *Kitāb al-Kharāj*, Cairo, 1302 AH.

Abū Zurʿa al-Dimashqī, *Taʾrīkh*, ed. Shukr Allāh al-Qawjānī, 2 vols., Damascus, 1400/1980.

Ali, F.B., "Al-Ḥudaybiya: An Alternative Version", in *The Muslim World*, 71 (1981), 47-62.

Alwaye, M., "The Truce of Hudeybiya and the Conquest of Mecca", in *Majallatu l-Azhar*, 45/9 (1973), 1-6.

Andrae, Tor, *Die Person Muhammeds in Lehre und Glauben seiner Gemeinde*, Stockholm, 1918.

al-Balādhurī, Abū l-ʿAbbās Aḥmad b. Yaḥyā, *Ansāb al-ashrāf*, vol. 1, ed. M. Ḥamīd Allāh, Cairo, n.d.

al-Bayhaqī, Abū Bakr Aḥmad b. al-Ḥusayn, *al-Sunan al-kubrā*, 10 vols., Hyderabad, 1344-55 AH.

Buhl, Frants, *Das Leben Muhammeds*, trans. H.H. Schaeder, [2]Heidelberg, 1955.

al-Bukhārī, Muḥammad b. Ismāʿīl, *Ṣaḥīḥ al-Bukhārī*, ed. Muḥammad Tawfīq ʿUwayḍa, 9 vols., Cairo, 1386-1411/1966-91.

Conrad, L.I., "Seven and the *Tasbīʿ*: On the Implications of Numerical Symbolism for the Study of Medieval Islamic History", in *Journal of the Economic and Social History of the Orient*, 31 (1988), 42-73.

Cook, Michael, *Early Muslim Dogma. A Source-Critical Study*, Cambridge, 1981.

Crone, Patricia, *Meccan Trade and the Rise of Islam*, Princeton, 1987.

Donner, F.M., "Muḥammad's Political Consolidation in Arabia up to the Conquest of Mecca", in *The Muslim World*, 69 (1979), 229-47.

Dubler, C.E./Quarella, U., "Der Vertrag von Ḥudaybiyya (März 628) als Wendepunkt in der Geschichte des frühen Islam", in *Asiatische Studien*, 21 (1967), 62-81.

al-Durī, ʿAbd al-ʿAzīz, *The Rise of Historical Writing among the Arabs*, trans. L.I. Conrad, Princeton, 1983.

Fagnan, Edmond, *Abou Yousouf Ya'koub. Le Livre de l'impot foncier* (Kitab el-Kharādj), trans. and comm. E. Fagnan, Paris, 1921.

Guillaume, Alfred, *The Life of Muhammad. A Translation of [Ibn] Isḥāq's Sīrat Rasūl Allāh. With Introduction and Notes*, Oxford, 1955.

Hawting, G.R., "Al-Ḥudaybiyya and the Conquest of Mecca: A Reconsideration of the Tradition about the Muslim Takeover of the Sanctuary", in *Jerusalem Studies in Arabic and Islam*, 8 (1986), 1-23.

Horovitz, J., "The Earliest Biographies of the Prophet and Their Authors", I-IV, in *Islamic Culture*, 1 (1927), 535-59, 2 (1928), 22-50, 164-82, 495-526.

——, "Zur Muḥammadlegende", in *Der Islam*, 5 (1914), 41-53.

Ibn Abī Shayba, ʿAbd Allāh b. Muḥammad, *al-Kitāb al-Muṣannaf fī l-aḥādīth wa-l-āthār*, ed. ʿAbd al-Khāliq al-Afghānī, 15 vols., Bombay, 1399-1403/1979-83.

Ibn Ḥajar al-ʿAsqalānī, *Fatḥ al-bārī bi-sharḥ [ṣaḥīḥ] al-Bukhārī*, 17 vols., Cairo, 1378/1959.

Ibn Ḥanbal, Ahmad b. Muḥammad, *al-Musnad*, 6 vols., Cairo, 1313 AH.

Ibn Hishām, ʿAbd al-Malik, *al-Sīra al-nabawiyya*, ed. Muṣṭafā al-Saqqā et al., 2 vols., ²Cairo, 1375/1955.
Ibn Kathīr, Abū l-Fidāʾ al-Ḥāfiẓ, *al-Bidāya wa-l-nihāya*, 14 parts in 7 vols., Beirut, 1966.
Ibn Māja, Abū ʿAbd Allāh Muḥammad b. Yazīd al-Qazwīnī, *Sunan Ibn Māja*, ed. Muḥammad Fuʾād ʿAbd al-Bāqī, 2 vols., repr., Beirut, 1373/1954.
Ibn Saʿd, Abū ʿAbdallāh Muḥammad, *Kitāb al-Ṭabaqāt al-kabīr*, ed. Eduard Sachau et al., 9 vols., Leiden, 1904-40.
Juynboll, Gautier H.A., *Muslim Tradition: Studies in Chronology, Provenance and Authorship of Early Ḥadīth*, Cambridge, 1983.
Lane, Edward William, *An Arabic-English Lexicon*, London, 1863-93.
Lecker, M., "The Ḥudaybiyya-Treaty and the Expedition Against Khaybar", in *Jerusalem Studies in Arabic and Islam*, 5 (1984), 1-12.
Leder, S., "The Literary Use of the *Khabar*: A Basic Form of Historical Writing", in Averil Cameron and Lawrence I. Conrad, eds., *The Byzantine and Early Islamic Near East, I: Problems in the Literary Source Material*, Princeton, 1992, 277-315.
Lings, Martin, *Muhammad: His Life Based on the Earliest Sources*, New York, 1983.
al-Mizzī, Jamāl al-Dīn Abū l-Ḥajjāj, *Tuḥfat al-ashrāf bi-maʿrifat al-aṭrāf*, 13 vols., Bombay, 1384-1403/1965-82.
——, *al-Kashshāf ʿan abwāb marājiʿ tuḥfat al-ashrāf bi-maʿrifat al-aṭrāf*, Bombay, 1386/1966.
Motzki, H., "Der Fiqh des -Zuhrī: die Quellenproblematik", in *Der Islam*, 68 (1991), 1-44.
Muranyi, M., "Die Auslieferungsklausel des Vertrags von al-Ḥudaibiya und ihre Folgen", in *Arabica*, 23 (1976), 275-95.
——, "Ibn Isḥāq's *K. al-Maġāzī* in der *riwāya* von Yūnus b. Bukair. Bemerkungen zur frühen Überlieferungsgeschichte", in *Jerusalem Studies in Arabic and Islam*, 14 (1991), 214-75.
al-Nasāʾī, Abū ʿAbd al-Raḥmān Aḥmad b. Shuʿayb, *Sunan al-Nasāʾī bi-sharḥ al-ḥāfiẓ Jalāl al-Dīn al-Suyūṭī*, 8 parts in 4 vols., Beirut, n.d.
Noth, Albrecht, *The Early Arabic Historical Tradition: A Source-Critical Study*, 2nd ed. in collaboration with Lawrence I. Conrad, trans. M. Bonner, Princeton, 1994.
Paret, Rudi, *Die legendäre Maghāzi-Literatur. Arabische Dichtungen über die muslimischen Kriegszüge zu Mohammeds Zeit*, Tübingen, 1930.
——, *Der Koran. Kommentar und Konkordanz*, ⁴Stuttgart, 1989.
Rodinson, Maxime, *Mohammed*, trans. into German G. Meister, Luzern and Frankfurt am Main, 1975.
Rubin, Uri, "Muḥammad's Curse of Muḍar and the Blockade of Mecca", in *Journal of the Economic and Social History of the Orient*, 31 (1988), 249-64.
——, *The Eye of the Beholder: The Life of Muḥammad As Viewed by the Early Muslims*, Princeton, 1995.
al-Samuk, Sadun Mahmud, *Die historischen Überlieferungen nach Ibn Isḥāq. Eine synoptische Untersuchung*, Frankfurt am Main, 1978.
Schoeler, Gregor, "Die Frage der schriftlichen oder mündlichen Überlieferung der Wissenschaften im frühen Islam", in *Der Islam*, 62 (1985), 201-30.
——, "Weiteres zur Frage der schriftlichen oder mündlichen Überlieferung der Wissenschaften im Islam", in *Der Islam*, 66 (1989), 38-67.
——, *Charakter und Authentie der muslimischen Überlieferung über das Leben Mohammeds*, Berlin and New York, 1996.
Sellheim, R., "Prophet, Chalif und Geschichte. Die Muhammed-Biographie des Ibn Isḥāq", in *Oriens*, 18-19 (1967), 33-91.

Stetter, Eckart, *Topoi und Schemata im Ḥadīṯ*, Ph.D. thesis, Tübingen, 1965.
al-Ṭabarī, Muḥammad b. Jarīr, *Taʾrīkh al-rusul wa-l-mulūk*, ed. Michael Johan de Goeje et al., 15 vols., Leiden, 1879-1901.
——, *Jāmiʿ al-bayān fī tafsīr al-Qurʾān*, 30 parts in 11 vols., Cairo, 1321/1903 f.
al-Tirmidhī, Abū ʿĪsā Muḥammad b. ʿĪsā, *al-Jāmiʿ al-ṣaḥīḥ wa-huwa sunan al-Tirmidhī*, 5 vols., n.p., 1387-96/1962-78.
ʿUrwa b. al-Zubayr, *Maghāzī rasūl Allāh bi-riwāyat Abū l-Aswad ʿanhu*, ed. M.M. al-Aʿẓamī, Riyad, 1981.
al-Wāḥidī, ʿAlī b. Aḥmad, *Asbāb al-nusūl*, repr. of the Cairo ed. 1316/1898, Beirut, n.d.
al-Wāqidī, Muḥammad b. ʿUmar, *Kitāb al-Maghāzī*, ed. Marsden Jones, 3 vols., London, 1966.
Watt, William Montgomery, *Muhammad at Medina*, Oxford, 1956.
——, "al-Ḥudaybiya", *Encyclopaedia of Islam*, new edition, III, 539.
al-Yaʿqūbī, Aḥmad b. Abī Yaʿqūb, *Taʾrīkh al-Yaʿqūbī*, 2 vols., Beirut, 1379/1960.
Zaman, M.Q., "*Maghāzī* and the *Muḥaddithūn*: Reconsidering the Treatment of "Historical" Materials in Early Collections of *Ḥadīth*", in *International Journal of Middle East Studies*, 28 (1996), 1-18.

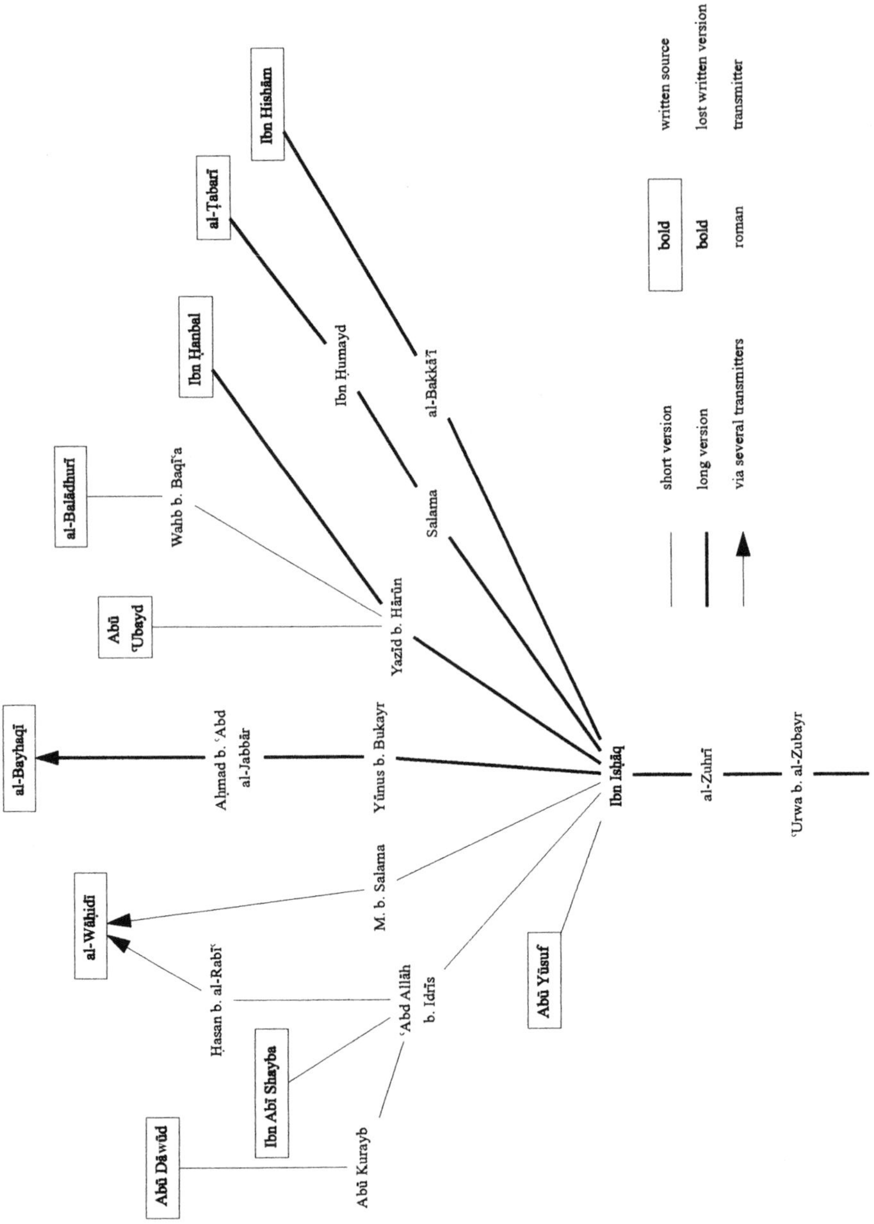

Figure A: The traditions going back to Ibn Isḥāq

Figure B: The traditions going back to Maʿmar

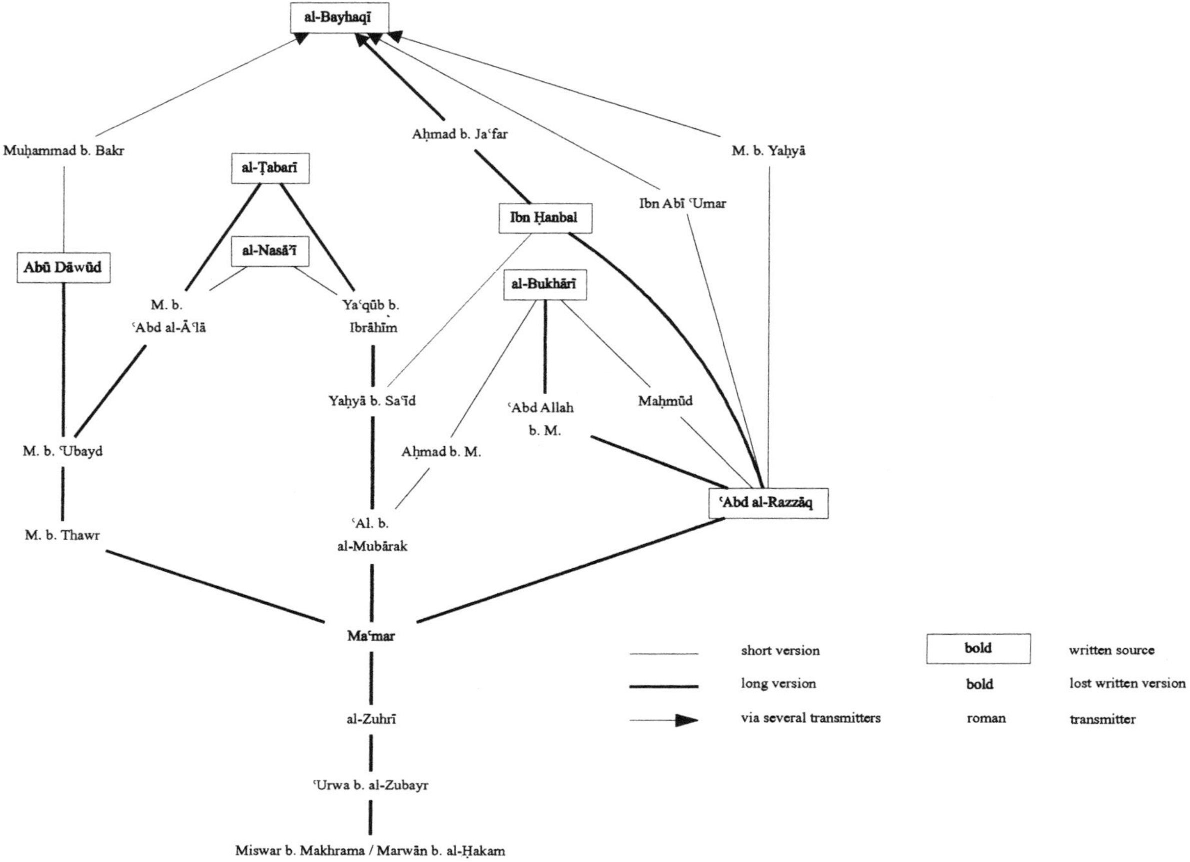

Figure C: The traditions going back to al-Zuhrī

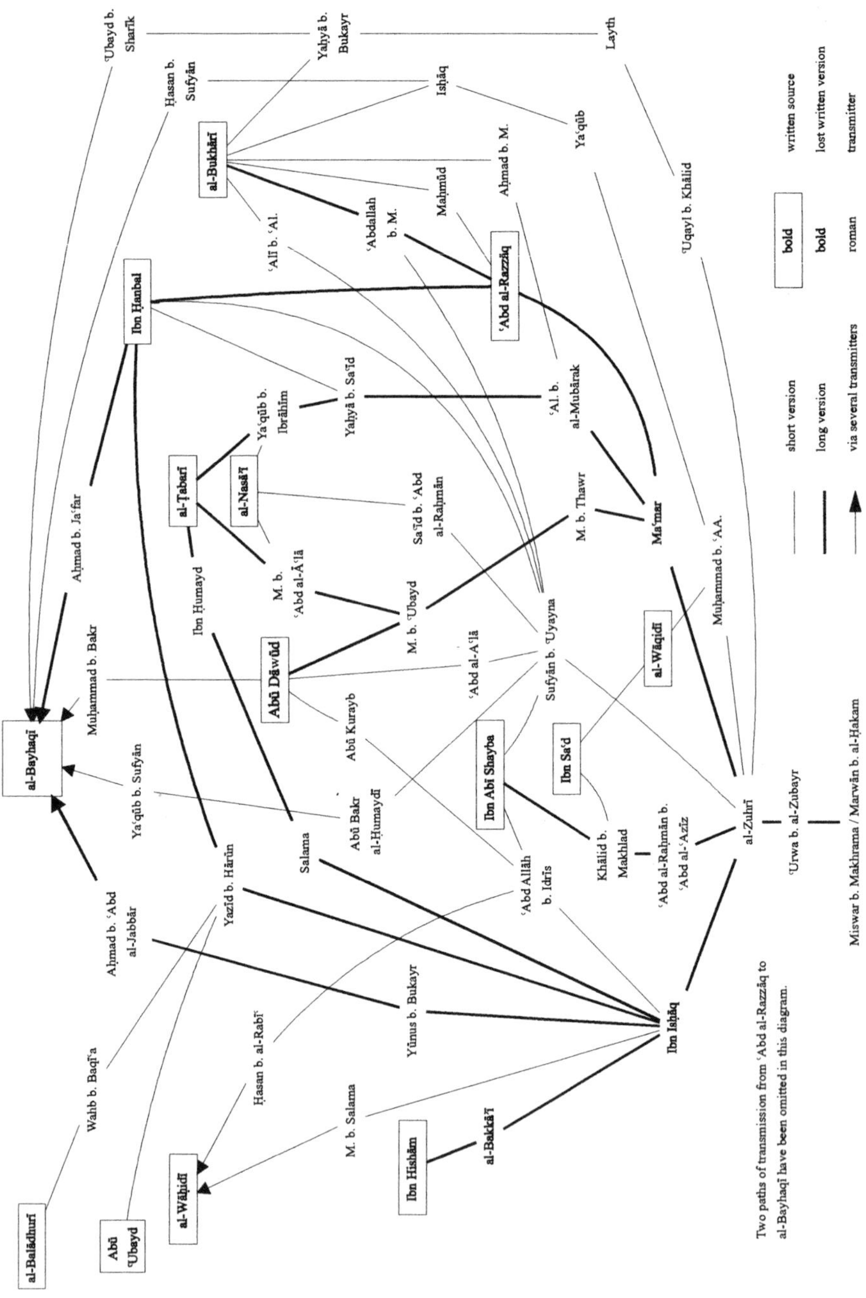

Two paths of transmission from ʿAbd al-Razzāq to al-Bayhaqī have been omitted in this diagram.

Figure D: The traditions going back to 'Urwa b. al-Zubayr

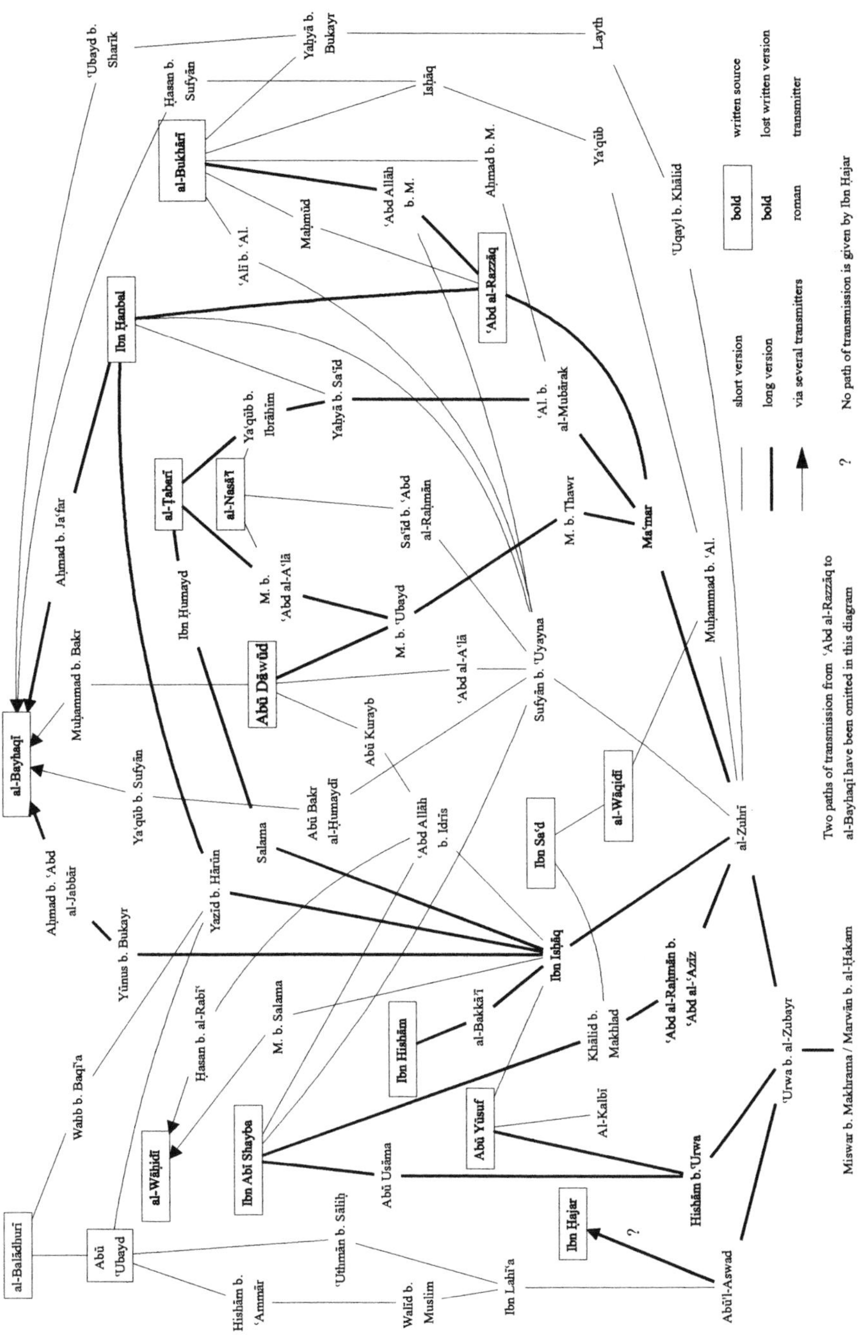

THE EARLIEST CHRISTIAN WRITINGS ON MUḤAMMAD: AN APPRAISAL[1]

Robert G. Hoyland

I. Introduction

When Blaise Pascal (1623-62) wrote that since Muḥammad "worked no miracles and was not foretold" he could not be a true prophet, he was simply echoing the judgment of John of Damascus (wr. ca. 730) passed more-than 900 years earlier.[2] Similarly, the explanation of Muḥammad's revelation as the result of epileptic fits, found in numerous thirteenth-century and later texts, was already given by the Byzantine monk and chronicler Theophanes the Confessor (d. 818).[3] The same is true for various other attributes, deeds and doctrines of Muḥammad, which recur for centuries in European polemical tracts and all of which have their roots in the very earliest Eastern Christian writings about the Prophet. That makes these earliest accounts of interest, since, as well as revealing to us what were the initial reactions of the inhabitants of the Near East to Islam and its founder, they can in addition help to elucidate the provenance of medieval and even contemporary Western (mis)conceptions.

But is this the limit of their worth? Can such writings not tell us anything about what the Muslims themselves said and did, rather than just how such sayings and actions were regarded? In his "Note

---

[1] All the Christian sources used in this article were first used in a systematic way for Islamic history by P. Crone and M. Cook, *Hagarism: The Making of the Islamic World*, Cambridge, 1977. All receive full discussion in my *Seeing Islam as Others Saw It. A Survey and Evaluation of Christian, Jewish and Zoroastrian Writings on Early Islam*, Studies in Late Antiquity and Early Islam 13, Princeton, 1997, from which I draw in this article.

[2] John of Damascus, *De haeresibus*, in *PG*, XCIV, 765C, 768A, and in a "Refutation against the Saracens" transmitted *dia phōnēs Iōannou Damaskēnou* by Theodore Abū Qurra (d. ca. 825), *PG*, XCIV, 1596-97; B. Pascal, *Oeuvres*, ed. L. Brunschvig, Paris, 1921, XIV, 37-38. John of Damascus was particularly important as a source for Byzantine and Western Christian views of Muḥammad, being the first to speak of Muḥammad's revelation and legislation, portrayal of Christ, carnal vision of Paradise, his many wives and his instruction by a monk.

[3] Norman Daniel, *Islam and the West. The Making of an Image*, Edinburgh, 1966, 27-28, citing, amongst others, Vincent of Beauvais, Alexandre du Pont and Ricoldo da Monte Cruce, all of the second half of the thirteenth century; Theophanes, *Chronographia*, 334.

sur l'accueil des chrétiens d'Orient à l'islam", written three decades ago, Claude Cahen posed the question whether "la première réaction proprement religieuse des chrétiens", evoked before conversion to Islam had put the Church on the defensive and before Byzantium had begun to use words as well as weapons in its war against the Muslims, might not differ from "la littérature polémique ultérieure". Might it not be free of "le besoin de mettre en place une argumentation antimusulmane" and so be able to inform us about Islam in its formative phase?[4] Patricia Crone and Michael Cook in their book *Hagarism* took up this point and used only sources external to the Muslim tradition to sketch an alternative account of early Islam.[5] Their methodology and conclusions attracted much criticism, but little was said about the material they had gone to such great trouble to unearth. This article will reexamine a small body of this material, namely, the earliest Christian portrayals of Muḥammad, those dating from the first two centuries of Islam (1-200/622-815), and then try to assess their value for the historian.

II. The Texts

Muḥammad the Initiator of the Conquests

The earliest clear Christian reference to the Prophet is to be found in the Syriac chronicle of Thomas the Presbyter, a resident of northern Mesopotamia.[6] Since he states that his brother Simon was killed in 636 during an Arab raid upon Ṭūr ʿAbdīn and does not mention the death of the emperor Heraclius (610-41), we may assume that Thomas was writing ca. 640. In his chronicle he relates that:

---

[4] Claude Cahen, "Note sur l'accueil des chrétiens d'Orient à l'islam", in *Revue de l'histoire des religions,* 166 (1964), 51-52, 56-58.

[5] Crone and Cook, *Hagarism,* esp. 3-34.

[6] There are two possibly earlier references. A Greek anti-Jewish tract entitled *Doctrina Jacobi,* purportedly composed in Africa in July 634, mentions a "prophet who has appeared with the Saracens" and who condones "the shedding of men's blood", but he is not named (see Crone and Cook, *Hagarism,* 3-4, and Hoyland, *Seeing Islam,* 55-61, for references and discussion). A few lines about the Arab conquests which appear on the front fly-leaf of a sixth-century Syriac Gospel manuscript are stated by E.W. Brooks to contain a mention of Muḥammad, but Sebastian Brock finds the reading "very uncertain" (in Andrew Palmer, *The Seventh Century in the West-Syrian Chronicles,* Translated Texts for Historians 15, Liverpool, 1993, 2, note 70).

> In the year 945, indiction 7, on Friday 4 February (634) at the ninth hour, there was a battle between the Romans and the Arabs of Muḥammad (*ṭayyāyē d-Mḥmṭ*).[7]

The implication here is that Muḥammad was a military leader of some kind. This is also intimated by another Syriac chronicler, most likely writing in Khūzistān ca. 660, who conveys the following information amid his account of the reign of Yazdigird III (632-52):

> Then God brought the Ishmaelites against them like sand on the sea shore; their leader (*mdabbrānā*) was Muḥammad (*Mḥmd*), and neither walls nor gates, armor or shield, withstood them: they gained control over the entire land of the Persians.[8]

An anonymous history of Armenia, which concludes with the victory of Muʿāwiya in the first Arab civil war (656-61) and is usually attributed to a bishop Sebeos, has Muḥammad preach to the Arabs, saying:

> You are the sons of Abraham, and God will realize in you the promise made to Abraham and his posterity. Only love the God of Abraham, and go and take possession of your country which God gave to your father Abraham, and none will be able to resist you in battle, for God is with you.[9]

Four later texts are more explicit. The first is by a certain George, "the archdeacon and companion of the father and patriarch Abba Simon, patriarch of Alexandria (692-700)", who "informed us what occurred in the time of the arch-unbeliever Marcian and what troubles came upon our fathers and what came after them up to the time of Sulaymān b. ʿAbd al-Malik, king of the Muslims (715-17)".[10]

---

[7] *Chronica minora II*, 148.

[8] *Chronica minora I*, 30. The Khūzistānī provenance is suggested by the chronicler's preoccupation with that region as regards the latest events; the date of composition follows from the fact that the title declares the finishing point to be "the end of the Persian kingdom" and from the lack of a clear reference to an event later than 652. The chronicle is also known as the *Anonymous Guidi* after the name of its first editor.

[9] Sebeos, XXX (trans. Macler, 95-96). Various indications in the text suggest that Sebeos was contemporary with the events he relates (see Hoyland, *Seeing Islam*, 125). I use the name Sebeos here simply as a shorthand for the text of the anonymous history and for its original compiler.

[10] *History of the Alexandrian Patriarchs*, in *PO*, V, 90-91. This text comprises the biographies of the leaders of the Coptic church beginning with St. Mark; George was responsible for *Lives*, 27-42, covering the period from Chalcedon to the early eighth century. The first attempt to compile all the material and translate it into Arabic was made by Mawhūb b. Manṣūr b. Mufarrij (d. ca. 1100). That the comments of earlier authors often survive suggests that the editing was not heavy-handed, but the

About Muḥammad George says that "he took possession of Damascus and Syria, crossed the Jordan and...".[11] The second text is by a mid-eighth-century Spanish writer, who preserves in Latin translation a chronicle ultimately of Syrian provenance and who notes:

> When a most numerous multitude of Saracens had gathered together, they invaded the provinces of Syria, Arabia and Mesopotamia. Above them, holding the leadership, was one Muḥammad (*Mahmet*) by name.[12]

The next two are again Syriac chronicles, both of which are anonymous and halt at the year 775. The one known as the *Chronicle of Zuqnin*, because it was composed by a resident of the monastery of that name in Mesopotamia, simply says that "they (the Arabs) had conquered the Romans in battle under his (Muḥammad's) direction".[13] The other, entitled "an account of how the generations and races and years were from Adam until today", makes the declaration that:

> In 930 of Alexander (618-19), Heraclius and the Romans entered Constantinople, and Muḥammad (*Mḥmṭ*) and the Arabs went forth from the south and entered the land and subdued it.[14]

The idea that Muḥammad initiated the Arab conquests comes through very clearly in these sources. And this idea is further spelled out in the account of Theophilus of Edessa (d. 785), astrologer to the

---

corruption evident in parts of the notice on Muḥammad (see next note) shows that translation from Coptic and subsequent copying took its toll.

[11] *History of the Alexandrian Patriarchs*, in *PO*, I, 492. The last word is *sādamahu* ("damned its waters"?); cf. *History of the Alexandrian Patriarchs (Hamburg)*, 99: "This Muḥammad and his companions took possession of Damascus and Syria, crossed the Jordan and...(*sbādāmyh*?)."

[12] *Continuatio Byzantia Arabica*, §13 (so-called because it is a continuation of John of Biclar's chronicle with an obvious Arab focus). The Syrian provenance of this text is evident from the fact that the Umayyad caliphs are each described in a relatively positive vein, all reference to ʿAlī is omitted, Muʿāwiya II is presented as a legitimate and uncontested ruler, and the rebel Yazīd b. al-Muhallab is labeled "a font of wickedness".

[13] *Chronicle of Zuqnin*, 149. This chronicle is also known as the "pseudo-Dionysius", since it was once thought to be by the patriarch Dionysius of Tellmahre. Note that the author explicitly states when he is writing: "...the present year, which is the year 1086 of Alexander and the year 158 (775) of the Muslims" (ibid., 145).

[14] *Chronica minora III*, 348. The date should perhaps be read 940 (628-29), though this reference to AG 930 is not isolated; for example, Jacob of Edessa (d. 708) has Muḥammad travel to Syria three years before "the beginning of the kingdom of the Arabs" (in AG 933), so again in AG 930 (*Chronica minora III*, 326), and an inscription on the wall of a church at Ehnesh in northern Syria notes that "in the year 930 the Arabs came to the land" (Palmer, *West-Syrian Chronicles*, 71).

caliph al-Mahdī, which survives to a greater or lesser degree in the chronicle, begun before 805,[15] of the Jacobite patriarch Dionysius of Tellmahre (818-45):[16]

> This Muḥammad, while in the age and stature of youth, began to go up and down from his town of Yathrib to Palestine for the business of buying and selling. While so engaged in the country, he saw the belief in one God and it was pleasing to his eyes.[17] When he went back down to his tribesmen, he set this belief before them, and he convinced a few and they became his followers. In addition, he would extol the bountifulness of this land of Palestine, saying: "Because of the belief in one God, the like of this good and fertile land was given to them." And he would add: "If you listen to me, God will give to you, too, a land flowing with milk and honey." To corroborate his word, he led a band of them who were obedient to him and began to go up to the land of Palestine, plundering, enslaving and pillaging. He returned laden [with booty] and unharmed, and thus he had not fallen short of his promise to them.
>
> Since love of possessions impels an act towards a habit, they began going back and forth on raids. When those who had not as yet joined him saw those who had submitted to him acquiring great riches, they were drawn without compulsion into his service. And when, after these [expeditions], his followers had become many men and a great force, he would allow them to raid while he sat in honor at his seat in Yathrib, his city.[18] Once dispatched, it was not enough for them to frequent Palestine alone, but they ranged far and wide, killing openly, enslaving, ravaging and plundering. Even this was not enough for them, but they

---

[15] When describing an event of the Sixth Ecumenical Council of 680-81, Dionysius says: "And is it not still so today, 125 years after this wicked synod?" (preserved in Michael the Syrian, *Chronique*, IV, 435/II, 453).

[16] Itself preserved in Michael the Syrian, *Chronique*, IV, 405-07/II, 403-05, and the *Chronicle of 1234*, 227-29. The wording of the account is identical or very similar in these works, but Michael makes a few emendations of a polemical nature, more likely added than omitted, so I translate from the *Chronicle of 1234*. For the dependence of the *Chronicle of 1234* and of Michael upon Dionysius and of Dionysius upon Theophilus, see Hoyland, *Seeing Islam*, 400-09, 416-19.

[17] Michael has: "While engaged with the Jews, he learnt from them the belief in one God, and seeing that his tribesmen worshipped stones and wood and every created thing, he adhered to the belief of the Jews, which pleased him."

[18] The *Chronicle of 1234* has "did *not* allow", but cf. Michael: "When many had submitted to him, he no longer went up in person as leader of those going up to raid, rather he would send others at the head of his forces while he would sit in honor at his city." This is repeated by the tenth-century Nestorian *Chronicle of Siirt* (in *PO*, XIII, 601), evidently ultimately reliant upon the same source: "When Islam became strong, he refrained from going out in person to war and began to dispatch his companions." Michael adds: "Whoever did not accept the teaching of his doctrine, no longer by persuasion but by the sword did he subject them; those who refused, he killed."

> would make them pay tribute and enslave them. Thus, gradually, they grew strong and spread abroad. And they grew so powerful that they subjected almost all the land of the Romans and also the kingdom of the Persians under their sway.[19]

Muḥammad the Trader

The first comment that the Armenian chronicler Sebeos (wr. 660s) makes about Muḥammad is that he was a "merchant" (*t'ankangar*).[20] This fact is also known to the scholar Jacob of Edessa (d. 708), who announces in his chronicle that "Muḥammad went down for trade to the lands of Palestine, Arabia and Syrian Phoenicia".[21] Possibly it is Jacob's notice which underlies the explanation given by Theophilus of Edessa of how Muḥammad came to acquire knowledge about monotheism:

> This Muḥammad, while in the age and stature of youth, began to go up and down from his town of Yathrib to Palestine for the business of buying and selling. While so engaged in the country, he saw the belief in one God and it was pleasing to his eyes...[22]

---

[19] This last sentence is not in Michael. Besides Dionysius, two other chroniclers make heavy use of Theophilus for early Islamic history, namely, Theophanes the Confessor (d. 818) and Agapius, bishop of Manbij (d. ca. 950). For their notices on Muḥammad, however, they diverge considerably from Theophilus. As regards Muḥammad's role in the conquests, Theophanes just says his "heresy prevailed in the region of Ethribos, in the last resort by war: at first secretly for ten years, and by war another ten, and openly nine"; and Agapius, 457: "He waged war against whomsoever refused and resisted him, and he killed chiefs among the Arabs, from his own tribe and others, and he conquered many towns of neighbouring peoples."

[20] Sebeos, XXX (trans. Macler, 95). G. Abgaryan, in his edition (Erevan, 1979), corrects the manuscripts to *t'angar* on the basis of Thomas of Artsruni's account. In either case this is a usual term to have used; it derives from the Syriac *taggārā* and perhaps reflects that Sebeos has his information on Muḥammad and the Arab conquests from fugitives "who had been eyewitnesses thereof", as he himself states.

[21] *Chronica minora III*, 326.

[22] Cited in full above from Dionysius of Tellmahre. The chronicler Theophanes (d. 818), who in general also makes heavy use of Theophilus' chronicle, simply says: "Whenever he came to Palestine, he consorted with Christians and Jews and sought from them certain scriptural matters" (Theophanes, 334). Though this is too brief to be sure that it is from the same source as that used by Dionysius, one might note that they both make the same polemical point, that Muḥammad had his knowledge of monotheism from Christians and Jews.

Muḥammad the King

A Maronite chronicle, which contains firsthand information relevant to the 650s, makes the comment that Muʿāwiya "placed his throne in Damascus and refused to go to Muḥammad's throne".[23] The implication is that Muḥammad was a ruler like Muʿāwiya, and indeed this is how he is most often described in Christian sources. In his chronicle, which halts in 692, Jacob of Edessa refers to "Muḥammad, the first king (*malkā*) of the Arabs", and this is echoed by the *Chronicle of Zuqnin* ("the first king was a man from among them by the name of Muḥammad").[24] Moreover, numerous texts speak about the "reign" of Muḥammad: a Syriac "report giving information about the kingdom of the Arabs and how many kings they produced" concluding with the accession of Walīd I "in AG 1017 (705), at the beginning of October" ("he reigned for seven years"),[25] the mid-eighth-century Spanish chronicler ("he fulfilled ten years of his rule"),[26] an anonymous Greek chronographical compilation of 818 ("In the year 6131 of the world and the thirteenth year of Heraclius there began the rule of the Saracens: Mouameth, 9 years; ..."),[27] and so on. This manner of description also crops up in disputation texts, as, for example, that recording the dialogue between the monk Abraham of Tiberias and an Arab emir, allegedly held in Jerusalem ca. 820, where the former maintains that Muḥammad is "a king approved by God, in whom and by whom God has fulfilled His promise to Abraham regarding Ishmael".[28]

---

[23] *Chronica minora II*, 71.

[24] *Chronica minora III*, 326; *Chronicle of Zuqnin*, 149.

[25] Translated by Palmer, *West-Syrian Chronicles*, 43.

[26] *Continuatio Byzantia Arabica*, §17.

[27] Edited in A. Schoene, *Eusebi chronicorum libri duo*, Berlin, 1875, vol. I, Appendix IV, 97. The text contains a number of chronological lists, one of Arab rulers, which ends: "Aarōn...(Hārūn al-Rashīd), 20 years; anarchy and war among the latter's sons for 7 years until the present 11th indiction. Presently God will curtail the years of their rule and will raise the horn of the Christian empire against them." Hārūn died in 809 and so seven years of civil war would take us to 816; the nearest 11th indiction to this is 818.

[28] Abraham of Tiberias, *Dialogue*, §110; a reference to Genesis 17:20; 21:13.

Muḥammad the Monotheist Revivalist

The Armenian chronicler Sebeos, writing ca. 660, seems to envisage Muḥammad as having turned the Arabs away from idolatry and having led them to take up once more their ancestral religion, the core of which was Abrahamic monotheism:

> At this time there was an Ishmaelite called Mahmet, a merchant; he presented himself to them as though at God's command, as a preacher, as the way of truth, and taught them to know the God of Abraham, for he was very well informed and very well acquainted with the story of Moses. Since the command came from on high, they all came together, at a single order, in unity of religion, and, abandoning vain cults, returned to the living God who had revealed himself to their father Abraham.[29]

The chronicler of Khūzistān, also writing ca. 660, likewise remarks upon this ancestral Abrahamic connection:

> Regarding the dome of Abraham, we have been unable to discover what it is except that, because the blessed Abraham grew rich in property and wanted to get away from the envy of the Canaanites, he chose to live in the distant and spacious parts of the desert. Since he lived in tents, he built that place for the worship of God and for the offering of sacrifices. It took its present name from what it had been,[30] since the memory of the place was preserved with the generations of their race. Indeed it was no new thing for the Arabs to worship there, but goes back to antiquity, to their early days, in that they show honor to the father of the head of their people.[31]

And, in general, it is very common for Muḥammad to be portrayed as having brought his people back into line with the dictates of monotheism: "As a result of this man's guidance they held to the worship of the one God in accordance with the customs of ancient law" (John bar Penkaye); "he returned the worshippers of idols to the knowledge of the one God" (*History of the Alexandrian Patriarchs*); "he had turned them away from cults of all kinds and taught them that there was one God, Maker of Creation" (*Chronicle of Ẓuqnin*); "he enjoined them to belief in the one God, Who has no companion, and to reject idolatry"

---

[29] Sebeos, XXX (trans. Macler, 94-95).

[30] One wonders whether the chronicler had heard of the term Kaʿba—note that Jacob of Edessa (d. 708), *Letters*, fol. 124a, writes it *Kʿbtā*—and thought that it derived from the dome (*Qūbtā*) of Abraham.

[31] *Chronica minora I*, 38.

(Agapius); "he summoned the Arabs to the worship of God Almighty" (*Chronicle of Siirt*).

Muḥammad the Lawgiver

John bar Penkaye, a monk of northern Mesopotamia who states that he is writing "in the year 67 of the rule of the Arabs" (686-87), calls Muḥammad a "guide" (*mhaddyānā*) and "instructor" (*tarʿā*), and observes of the Arabs that:

> They kept to the tradition of Muḥammad...to such an extent that they inflicted the death penalty on anyone who was seen to act brazenly against his laws (*nāmōsawh*).[32]

This image of Muḥammad as a lawgiver is very common. The archdeacon George, responsible for the portion of the *History of the Alexandrian Patriarchs* relating to the seventh century, mentions that Muḥammad gave to the Arabs a "covenant" (*ʿahd*) "which they call the law" (*al-nāmūs*).[33] A plausibly late Umayyad Christian-Muslim disputation between a monk of Beth Hale monastery and an Arab notable has the Christian interlocutor defend veneration of the cross, though it is not stipulated in the Gospel, by saying:

> I think that for you, too, not all your laws and commandments are in the Qur'ān which Muḥammad taught you; rather there are some which he taught you from the Qur'ān, and some are in Sūrat al-Baqara and in the Gospel and in the Torah.[34]

And the *Chronicle of Zuqnin* asserts that "he laid down laws for them (the Arabs)" and refers to him as "their guide and legislator" (*mhaddyānhōn w-sāʾem nāmōsayhōn*).[35] Other Christian authors are even able to

---

[32] John bar Penkaye, 146-47/175. The Arab "kingdom" (*malkūtā*) is dealt with in the last book of John's "Book of Salient Points" (*Ktābā d-rīsh mellē*), which is characterized in the heading as "a chronicle of the world" extending from Creation to "the severe chastisement of today", treating "the salient points" of history "in a brief fashion".

[33] *History of the Alexandrian Patriarchs*, in *PO*, I, 494.

[34] Ms. Diyarbakir 95, fol. 6a. The text begins: "With God's help we shall write down the debate that took place between a man of the Arabs and a certain monk of the monastery of Beth Hale." Nothing is known about its transmission before its appearance in two manuscripts, one from Diyarbakir of the early eighteenth century, the other at Mardin copied in 1890. The text continues by saying that "this Arab man...was one of the chief men before the emir Maslama", whose mention, if we identify him with Maslama ibn ʿAbd al-Malik, gives a *terminus post quem* of 710, when he was appointed governor of Mesopotamia. See Crone and Cook, *Hagarism*, 163, note 23; Hoyland, *Seeing Islam*, 465-72.

[35] *Chronicle of Zuqnin*, 149, 299.

give examples of some of the laws which Muḥammad enacted for his followers. Thus Sebeos tells us:

> He legislated (*awrinadre*) for them not to eat carrion, not to drink wine, not to speak falsely and not to commit fornication.[36]

And John of Damascus (wr. ca. 730), last of the fathers of the Greek Orthodox church, remarks, in a rather polemical vein:

> He prescribed that they be circumcised, women as well, and he commanded neither to observe the Sabbath nor to be baptized, to eat those things forbidden in the Law and to abstain from others. Drinking of wine he forbade absolutely.[37]

Muḥammad the Prophet/False Prophet

In its entry upon the rise of Islam the *Chronicle of Zuqnin* makes the following statement:

> Since he (Muḥammad) had shown them the one God, and they had conquered the Romans in battle under his direction, and he had appointed laws for them according to their desire, they called him prophet (*nbīyā*) and messenger (*rasūlā*) of God.[38]

This fact, that the Muslims regarded Muḥammad as a prophet and messenger of God, was known to Christians from at least the late seventh century. In his section of the *History of the Alexandrian Patriarchs* the archdeacon George (wr. ca. 720) records that during the time of the patriarch Isaac of Rakoti (689-92) the governor ʿAbd al-ʿAzīz b. Marwān "wrote a number of notices and placed them on the doors of the churches in Miṣr and the Delta, saying in them: Muḥammad is the great messenger (*al-rasūl al-kabīr*) who is God's".[39] A Syriac king list, which concludes with the death of Yazīd II (105/724), begins: "A notice of the life of Muḥammad the messenger (*rasūlā*) of God."[40] And the mid-eighth-century Spanish chronicler recounts:

> It is he whom they (the Saracens) to this day hold in such great honor and reverence that they affirm him to be the apostle and prophet of God in all their oaths and writings.[41]

---

[36] Sebeos, XXX (trans. Macler, 95).
[37] John of Damascus, *De haeresibus*, in *PG,* XCIV, 773A.
[38] *Chronicle of Zuqnin*, 149.
[39] *History of the Alexandrian Patriarchs*, in *PO,* V, 25.
[40] *Chronica minora II*, 155.
[41] *Continuatio Byzantia Arabica*, § 17.

However, just because the Christians knew Muḥammad was deemed a prophet by his own people does not mean that they themselves accepted him as such. In general, of course, they did not. Christians living in Muslim-ruled lands were at least content to say that Muḥammad "walked in the way of the prophets" in that he brought his people to knowledge of the one true God and recognition of virtue,[42] but Byzantine authors designated him rather as "the forerunner of the Antichrist" (*prodromos tou antichristou*) and "a false prophet" (*pseudoprophētēs*).[43]

III. Christian Polemic Against Muḥammad

In their provision of a response to the situation facing them, namely, that a new religio-political entity had unexpectedly arisen, achieved dazzling military successes and promoted itself as favored by God and in possession of His latest dispensation, only very rarely did the conquered peoples evince an interest in the motives and actions of the Muslims themselves. Their chief concern was rather to minimize the damage done to their own former status and self-image, to play down the gains won by their new masters and to extend some hope that they would themselves rise to the fore once again.

Thus, for example, much of the reason for the presentation by Christian writers of Muḥammad as a reviver of an original or Abrahamic religion was to emphasize that his religion was nothing new, indeed that it was primitive, not having benefited from any of Jesus' modernizations. The Arabs are seen as having ascended to the first rung of the monotheist ladder, but as being still a long way off from the more lofty heights of Christianity. And Muḥammad is depicted as a revivalist who reacquainted the Arabs with the one God, from whose service they had lapsed. Muḥammad himself had, we are told, knowledge of Christian doctrines, but it was not possible for him to teach them to the Arabs since their minds were as yet too immature. This is carefully explained by a monk of Beth Hale monastery to

---

[42] As is, for example, stated by the catholicos Timothy I (780-823) to the caliph al-Mahdī (Timothy I, *Apology*, §§159-62).

[43] The earliest recorded application of these terms to Muḥammad is by John of Damascus in his *De haeresibus* (*PG*, XCIV, 764A, 764B), and thereafter they are commonly used by Byzantine writers (e.g. Theophanes, *Chronographia*, 333).

his Muslim antagonist in the plausibly late Umayyad disputation text mentioned above:

> Arab: "Tell me the truth, how is Muḥammad our prophet considered in your eyes?"
> Monk: "As a wise and God-fearing man who freed you from idolatry and brought you to know the one true God."
> Arab: "Why, if he was wise, did he not teach us from the beginning about the mystery of the Trinity as you profess [it]?"
> Monk: "You know, of course, that a child, when it is born, because it does not possess the full faculties for receiving solid food, is nourished with milk for two years, and [only] then do they feed it with meat. Thus also Muḥammad, because he saw your simpleness and the deficiency of your understanding, he first taught you of the one true God..., for you were children in terms of your understanding."[44]

This same tack is pursued in the story of the monk Baḥīra, where Muḥammad is given a simplified version of Christianity to take to the Arabs. Even then he has often to remind his instructor, Baḥīra, that "my comrades are uncouth desert Arabs who are not accustomed to fasting and prayer, nor to anything which causes them trouble or bother". And in the end he has to request something more in accord with their capacities: "I taught what you described to me and they did not understand it, so give them something succinct enough that their minds can accept it."[45]

Similarly, the discussion of Muḥammad's prophethood by Christians was conducted chiefly with the aim of discrediting his credentials. Two trump cards were played by the Christians. The most common, that Muḥammad was not announced in the scriptures and had worked no miracles, was first put forward by John of Damascus, and remained in play for centuries thereafter,[46] even though the Muslims came up with numerous examples of biblical prophecies about Muḥammad and of signs worked by him.[47] The second, that Muḥammad

[44] Ms. Diyarbakir, fol. 5a; cf. 1 Corinthians 3:2: "I have fed you with milk and not with meat, for hitherto you were not able to bear it, nor yet now are you able."

[45] R. Gottheil, "A Christian Bahira Legend", in *Zeitschrift für Assyrologie,* 15 (1900), 64, 73. This story of how the monk Baḥīra fashioned for Muḥammad and his people a book and a new religion that was a simplified version of Christianity seems already to have circulated by the late eighth century, but to have been added to for centuries thereafter and to have passed from its original Syriac to Christian Arabic, Armenian, Hebrew and Latin (see Hoyland, *Seeing Islam*, 476-79).

[46] See the first sentence of this paper and the note thereto.

[47] See Sarah Stroumsa, "The Signs of Prophecy: The Emergence and Early Development of a Theme in Arabic Theological Literature", in *Harvard Theological*

had won adherents with physical incentives rather than spiritual riches, first appears in a disputation that allegedly took place between the caliph ʿAbd al-Malik and a monk of Mar Sabas named Michael.[48] The former opens with the question: "Did not Muḥammad convert the Persians and the Arabs and smash their idols to pieces?", to which Michael replies that Muḥammad had relied on physical inducements and force of arms whereas Paul came in peace:

> Paul possessed neither swords nor treasures. He was toiling with his hands and he was being provided for by means of that, and he was conducting himself in accordance with all [the laws]; he was commanding fasting and holiness, not abominable fornication. Nor was he making promises of eternal eating or marriage, but rather of [an eternal] kingdom.[49]

This idea became further developed by later apologetes as a way of testing the veracity of a religion. If it could be shown that its success derived from mundane circumstances (*asbāb al-dunyā, asbāb al-arḍ*), then that religion was evidently not from God, but a religion of men. The Jacobite theologian Abū Rāʾiṭa (d. 830s) proposed six categories of unworthy motives for adoption of a religion: worldly desire, ambition, fear, license, personal whim and partisanship, and these are found with only minor variations in a host of other polemical works.[50] Inevitably Islam was found guilty on all counts, and so discounted as a divinely inspired religion and labeled "a religion established by the sword and not a faith confirmed by miracles".[51]

Review, 78 (1985), 16-42.

[48] Even if not explicitly articulated, the same argument does, of course, appear in other genres; compare, for example, the words of Dionysius of Tellmahre cited above: "(Muḥammad) would add: 'If you listen to me, God will give to you, too, a land flowing with milk and honey.' To corroborate his word, he led a band of them... to go up to the land of Palestine plundering, enslaving and pillaging...."

[49] Translated by Monica J. Blanchard, "The Georgian Version of the Martyrdom of Saint Michael, Monk of Mar Sabas Monastery", in *Aram*, 6 (1994), §8. The text was most likely composed in the late eighth or early ninth century.

[50] Abū Rāʾiṭa, *Rasāʾil VIII* (*Fī ithbāt al-dīn al-naṣrāniyya*), 131-32. Other examples and further discussion are given by Sidney H. Griffith, "Comparative Religion in the Apologetics of the First Christian Arabic Theologians", in *Proceedings of the Patristic, Medieval and Renaissance Conference, Villanova, Pennsylvania*, 4 (1979), 63-86.

[51] As the catholicos Hnanishoʿ (686-93) declared to ʿAbd al-Malik (Bar Hebraeus, *Chron. eccles.*, II, 136). Much of the purpose of this polemic by Christians and Jews was to discourage conversion to Islam amongst their own people.

IV. Christian Knowledge of Muḥammad?

In the various reviews of Crone and Cook's *Hagarism* one criticism that recurs again and again is: how could external observers know better than initiates? To use the words of Josef van Ess:

> We cannot demand that an observer from outside, who could even less evaluate the radical novelty of the event, should have had a clearer concept of what was really happening. We should rather expect that he tried to describe the phenomenon with his own categories.[52]

This is hardly to be denied. Of course, Christians presented their information about Islam and its adherents on their own terms, which inevitably entailed a greater or lesser degree of distortion, but the point to note is that this information either had its basis in personal observation or else ultimately derived from the Muslims themselves. When the Gallic bishop Arculf, on pilgrimage in the Near East ca. 670, says that in Damascus "a kind of church" (*quaedam ecclesia*) has been built for "the unbelieving Saracens",[53] he is, of course, using Christian vocabulary, and with a dose of polemic, but surely we can still infer from this that there was some sort of Muslim place of worship in the city. And when Anastasius of Sinai says that during his stay in Jerusalem ca. 660 he was woken up in the morning by Egyptian laborers clearing the Temple Mount, one might doubt his accompanying comment that demons collaborated in this task, but surely not the undertaking of the work itself.[54]

The excursus of the aforementioned chronicler of Khūzistān (wr.

---

[52] J. van Ess, "The Making of Islam" (review art.), in *The Times Literary Supplement*, Sept. 8 (1978), 998. Cf. Norman Daniel in *JSS*, 24 (1979), 298: "It is easier to believe that Muslims are better witnesses to Islam than Christian or Jewish writers who may more naturally be supposed to have known very little about it"; R.B. Serjeant in *JRAS*, 1978, 78: "Why should the Syriac sources,...with their hostility to Islam, be considered more trustworthy than the Arabic histories?"; J. Wansbrough in *BSOAS*, 41 (1978), 156: "My reservations...turn upon what I take to be the authors' methodological assumptions, of which the principal must be that a vocabulary of motives can be freely extrapolated from a discrete collection of literary stereotypes composed by alien and mostly hostile observers...."

[53] Adomnan, *De locis sanctis*, II, XXVIII, 220 (Arculf dictated his experiences to Adomnan, abbot of Iona, on his return). Note that the church of St. John the Baptist is mentioned separately from the Muslim "church".

[54] Anastasius of Sinai, *Narrationes*, C3. The incident occurred, says Anastasius, "before these thirty years", and he relates it "because of those who think and say that it is the Temple of God (*naos theou*) being built now in Jerusalem", a reference to the Dome of the Rock completed in 691.

ca. 660) upon the Arabs' "dome of Abraham" is a concoction of elements from the Book of Genesis,[55] but the impetus to blend them at all must have come from outside. The chronicler can only be using biblical antecedents to make sense of the report, albeit rather vague, that has reached him regarding the Muslim sanctuary.[56] Likewise, the presentation of Muḥammad as the instigator of the Arab conquests, detailed above, may be confused in its chronology[57] and may be embellished to emphasize his un-prophetlike behavior, but the essence of it is already encountered in the very foundation document of the Muslim community, the so-called *Constitution of Medina*, which unites believers under the "protection of God" to fight on his behalf and to "help one another against whomsoever fights the signatories of this document".[58] The narrative of Theophilus of Edessa, quoted above, seems more directly to rely upon Muslim tradition, where, too, Muḥammad initially heads most raids, but as time goes by increasingly stays behind at Medina and appoints commanders in his stead.[59]

---

[55] Compare with the chronicler's account cited above: Genesis 12:9, 20:1 (Abraham makes frequent wanderings southwards); 12:6, 13:7 (he displays a certain apprehensiveness regarding the Canaanites); 13:2 (he is "very rich in cattle, in silver and in gold"); 12:8 ("he pitches his tent...and there built an altar to the Lord and called upon the name of the Lord"); 12:2, 17:20 (God promises both to Abraham and to Ishmael to make of them "a great nation").

[56] From Qur'ān 2:125-28 one can infer that Abraham, the fount of the Arab people, built a sanctuary which is still used as such by his ancestors. And in the conflict that occurred during the second Arab civil war (683-92) over the layout of the Meccan sanctuary, the point of contention was the status of the *ḥijr*, a place generally associated in some way with Ishmael; Ibn al-Zubayr sought to include it within the sanctuary, wishing to reinstate "the foundation of Abraham" (see Gerald R. Hawting, "The Origins of the Muslim Sanctuary at Mecca", in G.H.A. Juynboll (ed.), *Studies on the First Century of Islamic Society*, Carbondale and Edwardsville, 1982, 33-34, 42-43).

[57] Though Crone and Cook, *Hagarism*, 4 and 24, argue that it is the Muslim sources which are misleading: "The Prophet was disengaged from the original Palestinian venture by a chronological revision whereby he died two years before the invasion began."

[58] R.B. Serjeant, "The *Sunnah Jāmiʿah*: Analysis and Translation of the Documents Comprised in the So-Called 'Constitution of Medina'", in *BSOAS*, 41 (1978), esp. 17, 19, 33. Its authenticity has been accepted by most scholars, most recently by Patricia Crone, *Slaves on Horses*, Cambridge, 1980, 7.

[59] In the "Lists of Expeditions and Dates" given in W. Montgomery Watt, *Muhammad at Medina*, Oxford 1956, 339-43, Muḥammad is cited as the leader of nineteen raids in the first five years of the Hijra, but of only eight in the second five years (excluding two pilgrimages and the division of the spoil of Hawāzin at Jiʿrāna), none of which occurred in the last two years of his life. Note that our extant sources usually distinguish between *ghazawāt*, raids led by the Prophet, and *sarāyā*, raids led by his commanders; of the former there are usually said to have been about twenty-seven, in nine of which the Prophet actually fought, and of the latter as few as eighteen or as

What then, one may ask, is the value of Christian sources if all they do is give a distorted version of Muslim accounts? The answer is two-fold. In the first place, they are often precisely dateable, which for the first two centuries of Islam cannot normally be said to be true of Muslim writings. Since the Muslim perception of Muḥammad underwent major change during this period, this means that Christian sources can sometimes provide evidence for this change where Muslim sources are silent. It is instructive, for instance, to compare the comment of John bar Penkaye (wr. 687), cited above, that the Arabs "kept to the tradition (*mashlmānūtā*) of Muḥammad...to such an extent that they inflicted the death penalty on anyone who was seen to act brazenly against his laws" with the following remark of the chronicler of Zuqnin (wr. 775), writing in the same region but nearly a century later:

> They are a very covetous and carnal people, and any law, whether prescribed by Muḥammad or another God-fearing person, that is not set in accord with their desire, they neglect and abandon. But what is in accord with their will and complements their desires, though it be instituted by one contemptible among them, they hold to it saying: "This was appointed by the Prophet and Messenger of God, and moreover it was charged to him thus by God."[60]

The expression "the tradition of Muḥammad" used by John bar Penkaye suggests something handed down, but one doubts that a defined corpus of rulings is meant. Most likely John is simply passing on the message given out by the Muslims themselves, that they adhere to and enforce the example of their Prophet. Since he writes at a time when there still survived a few Companions of the Prophet, this example would most likely have been living and only orally conveyed rather than fixed and written down. The situation was evidently very different by the time of the chronicler of Zuqnin. Despite the highly polemical tone of his notice, it is patent that this author is writing at a time when Prophetic *ḥadīth* had already gained currency, when a practice might receive sanction by saying: "This was appointed by the Prophet...."

In the second place, Christian sources often preserve information which the Muslims passed over, whether because it was no longer

---

many as sixty. Though Muḥammad himself never transgresses the confines of Arabia, his commanders get as far as central Jordan and southern Palestine.

[60] *Chronicle of Zuqnin*, 149-50.

congruent with their received view of things or just for lack of interest.[61] For example, Christian authors reveal to us how numerous were the prisoners-of-war taken by the Muslims and how extensively this affected non-Muslim society, both physically and mentally. They illustrate how preoccupied the Muslims were with matters of security and how suspicious they were that Christians might be conspiring with the Byzantines against them. They record a number of caliphal decrees that are not found in Muslim sources, such as that ʿAbd al-Malik ordered a slaughter of pigs in Syria and Mesopotamia, that al-Walīd required magicians to be tried by ordeal, that ʿUmar II forbade consumption of wine and the testimony of a Christian against a Muslim, that Yazīd II banned the display of images, and that al-Mahdī prescribed the death penalty for converts to Islam who subsequently apostatized. They also bear witness to Muslim hostility to the cross at a very early stage and to a number of cultic practices performed by Muslims.[62] With regard to Muḥammad, Christian writings divulge nothing much new about his biography,[63] but they can tell us something about how and when his people first set about demonstrating the truth of his prophethood. There are no extant treatises by Muslims on this subject before the mid-ninth century;[64] Christian apologetic texts can help to fill this gap, in particular showing the extent to which Muslim theologians, from a very early date, ransacked the Bible for allusions to their Prophet.[65]

---

[61] In general, Muslim writings exhibit little interest in the Late Antique civilization which Islam slowly replaced or in the inhabitants whom the Muslims conquered and employed to run their empire. This means that Christian sources are essential for helping us to understand the setting and gain the right perspective for various events and developments that took place in Muslim-ruled lands.

[62] References to these instances and further discussion are given in Hoyland, *Seeing Islam*, 591-98.

[63] There do exist a few unusual reports as, for example, that Muḥammad appointed sacrifices for the Arabs: "He made the first sacrifice and had the Arabs eat them against their custom" (*Chronicle of 819*, prefixed to *Chronicle of 1234*, 11); "The misguided Jews thought he was the Messiah...and they remained with him until his [first] sacrifice" (Theophanes, 333).

[64] The earliest Muslim apologetes are ʿAlī b. Rabban al-Ṭabarī (d. 855), Qāsim b. Ibrāhīm (d. ca. 860), Abū ʿĪsā al-Warrāq (d. 861) and Abū ʿUthmān al-Jāḥiẓ (d. 869). There is also an alleged letter of the caliph Hārūn al-Rashīd (786-809) to the Byzantine emperor Constantine VI (780-97), calling him to Islam and pointing out to him its advantages, but this is likely to be attributed (edition, translation and commentary by Hadi Eid, *Lettre du calife Hārūn al-Rašīd à l'empereur Constantin VI*, Paris, 1992).

[65] Camilla Adang, *Muslim Writers on Judaism and the Hebrew Bible*, Leiden, 1996, 141-43.

In conclusion I would like to emphasize the danger of interpreting historical patterns and events in the early medieval Near East in terms of simplistic dichotomies, in this case Christian/Muslim. To quote a colleague:

> It is of course true that groups and categories with some meaningful identity may quite legitimately be identified and viewed in relation to other groups and categories, but when the labels thus generated are taken beyond their descriptive function, assigned determinative values of their own, and juxtaposed to one another as vehicles for interpretation, the risk of oversimplification quickly becomes acute.[66]

Christians living in the Byzantine realm were to a large degree insulated from contact with Muslims, but for those living under the latter's rule it was a different story. The claim of the Mesopotamian monk John bar Penkaye that "there was no distinction between pagan and Christian, the believer was not known from a Jew" may be exaggerated,[67] but is nevertheless instructive. The initial indifference of the Muslims to divisions among the peoples whom they conquered, when compounded with the flight and enslavement of an appreciable proportion of the population and with the elimination of internal borders across a huge area extending from northwest Africa to India, meant that there was considerable human interaction across social, ethnic and religious lines.[68] This was especially true for those who sought employment in the bustling cosmopolitan garrison cities of the new rulers, where one was exposed to contact with men of very diverse origin, creed and status. In addition, there were the widespread phenomena of conversion and apostasy, of inter-confessional marriage and festival attendance, of commercial contacts and public debate, all of which served to break down confessional barriers.

An excellent illustration of this point is provided by the life, sadly little studied, of the aforementioned Theophilus bar Thomas of Edessa.[69] If we can believe an anecdote that relates how he died within a

---

[66] Lawrence I. Conrad, "Muḥammad and the Faith of Islam in Eastern Christian Historiography under the Early Abbasids", Paper given at the Seventh International Colloquium: From Jahiliyya to Islam, July-August 1996, 4-5.

[67] John bar Penkaye, 151/179.

[68] Compare again John bar Penkaye, 147/175: "Their robber bands went annually to distant parts and to the islands, bringing back captives from all the peoples under the heavens." Anastasius of Sinai, *Narrationes*, C5, gives us an example of Jewish and Christian prisoners-of-war performing forced labor together at Clysma in Sinai.

[69] The following information on Theophilus is drawn from my *Seeing Islam*, 400-09.

few days of the caliph al-Mahdī (775-85) at the age of ninety, then he was born in 695 and, as his name suggests, at the city of Edessa in northern Syria. We first hear of him in the late 750s when he was accompanying al-Mahdī on a campaign in the east, presumably acting as the future caliph's astrological adviser.[70] Thereafter he remained in the service of al-Mahdī, becoming chief astrologer during his reign and taking up residence in Baghdad. Very popular among his scientific writings was his *Peri katarchōn polemikōn* (On Military Forecasts), which was cited by later Muslim astrologers and chapters of which made their way to Byzantium to become incorporated in a mid-ninth century collection of astrological writings. In addition, Theophilus translated into Syriac Galen's *On the Method of Maintaining Good Health*, Homer's *Iliad*, and possibly Aristotle's *Sophistici*.[71] Finally, he penned a "fine work of history", which seems to have been an attempt at continuing the genre of secular classicizing history and which describes at length the reign of Marwān II, the last Umayyad caliph, and the ʿAbbāsid revolution. Theophilus cannot, therefore, be viewed as simply a Christian who writes under Muslim rule; he is evidently a highly educated man, still influenced by the traditions of Antiquity as well as cognizant with the culture of his employers.

None of this is to say that religious affiliation did not count for a great deal; it obviously did so. But it did not exert, in some predictable fashion, an all-encompassing power to direct patterns of social relations in such a way as to prevent external influence or positive response to that influence. Religious leaders of the various confessions in the Near East might well have wished that that were the case, but

[70] *CCAG,* V, 1, 234; Theophilus addresses his son Deukalion: "I was urged, as you know, by those holding power to undertake these things (i.e., write a treatise on military forecasts) at the time when we made the expedition with them to the east in the province of *Marganēs*" (i.e., Margiana, the Merw oasis). A second edition of this work contains a chapter *De stellis fixis* which gives a planetary conjunction correct for 768 (*CCAG* V, 1, 212). The campaign must, therefore, be before 768 and very likely refers to al-Mahdī's activities in 141/758-59 in Khurāsān, quelling the revolt of its governor ʿAbd al-Jabbār with the help of Khāzim b. Khuzayma, and in Ṭabāristān (Ṭabarī, III, 134-37).

[71] In his *Fihrist* Ibn al-Nadīm says that Yaḥyā b. ʿAdī (d. 974) translated the version of Theophilus [of Aristotle's *Sophistici*] into Arabic. F.E. Peters, *Aristoteles arabus*, Leiden, 1968, 25, takes this to refer to Theophilus of Edessa, saying that "his translation of the *Sophistici elenchi* is frequently cited in the notes to ʿĪsā b. Zurʿah's version". These notes, however, only ever refer to *Thāwufīlā*; as with Ibn al-Nadīm's remark, the reference could well be to Theophilus of Edessa, but not necessarily so.

the region was and remained too diverse in terms of culture, ethnicity, history, language and so on for that ever to happen.

Bibliography

Abraham of Tiberias, *Dialogue* = Giacinto Bulus Marcuzzo (ed./trans.), *Le dialogue d'Abraham de Tibériade avec ʿAbd al-Raḥmān al-Hāšimī à Jérusalem vers 820*, Rome, 1986.

Abū Rā'iṭa, *Rasā'il* = Georg Graf (ed./trans.), *Die Schriften des Jacobiten Ḥabīb ibn Hidma Abū Rā'iṭa*, in *CSCO*, 130-31, *scr. arabici* 14-15, Louvain, 1951.

Adang, Camilla, *Muslim Writers on Judaism and the Hebrew Bible*, Leiden, 1996.

Adomnan, *De locis sanctis* = Ludwig Bieler (ed.), *Itinera et alia geographica, in Corpus Christianorum Series Latina*, 175 (1965), 177-234.

Agapius = Alexandre Vasiliev (ed./trans.), "Kitab al-ʿUnvan, histoire universelle écrite par Agapius (Mahboub) de Menbidj", Part 2.2, in *PO*, 8 (1912), 399-547 (covers the years 380-761).

Anastasius of Sinai, *Narrationes*, C1-18 = ms. Vaticanus gr. 2592, fols. 123-35.

Bar Hebraeus, *Chronicon ecclesiasticum*, ed. Johannes Babtista Abbeloos and Thomas Josephus Lamy, Paris and Louvain, 1872-77.

Blanchard, M.J., "The Georgian Version of the Martyrdom of Saint Michael, Monk of Mar Sabas Monastery", in *Aram*, 6 (1994), 149-63.

Cahen, Cl., "Note sur l'accueil des chrétiens d'Orient à l'islam", in *Revue de l'Histoire des Religions*, 166 (1964), 51-58.

CCAG = *Catalogus codicum astrologorum graecorum*, ed. Franz Cumont et al., Brussels, 1898-1936.

Chronica minora I-III, (ed./trans.) I. Guidi, E.W. Brooks and J.B. Chabot, in *CSCO*, 1-6, Paris 1903-05.

Chronicle of 1234 = J.B. Chabot (ed./trans.), *Chronicon ad annum Christi 1234 pertinens*, vol. 1, in *CSCO*, 81/109, *scr. syri* 36/56, Paris, 1916/1937.

Chronicle of Siirt = Addai Scher (ed./trans.), "Histoire nestorienne. Chronique de Séert", in *PO*, 4 (1908), 215-312; 5 (1910), 221-334; 7 (1911), 99-201; 13 (1919), 437-636.

Chronicle of Zuqnin = J.B. Chabot (ed.), *Incerti auctoris chronicon anonymum pseudo-Dionysianum vulgo dictum*, vol. 2, in *CSCO*, 104, *scr. syri* 53, Paris, 1933; French translation with same title by Robert Hespel, in *CSCO*, 507, *scr. syri* 213, Louvain, 1989.

Conrad, L.I. "Muḥammad and the Faith of Islam in Eastern Christian Historiography under the Early Abbasids", Paper given at the Seventh International Colloquium: From Jahiliyya to Islam, July-August 1996, 1-78, unpubl.

Continuatio Byzantia Arabica, ed. Theodor Mommsen, in *Monumenta Germaniae Historica, auctores antiquissimi*, XI.2, Berlin, 1894, 334-59. There is an English translation in my *Seeing Islam*, 611-27.

Crone, Patricia, and Michael Cook, *Hagarism: The Making of the Islamic World*, Cambridge, 1977.

Crone, Patricia, *Slaves on Horses*, Cambridge, 1980.

CSCO = *Corpus Scriptorum Christianorum Orientalium*.

Daniel, Norman, *Islam and the West. The Making of an Image*, Edinburgh, 1966.

Eid, Hadi, *Lettre du calife Hārūn al-Rašīd à l'empereur Constantin VI*, Paris, 1992.

Ess, J. van, "The Making of Islam" (review art.), in *The Times Literary Supplement*, Sept. 8 (1978), 997-98.
Gottheil, R., "A Christian Bahira Legend", in *Zeitschrift für Assyrologie*, 13 (1898), 189-242; 14 (1899), 203-68; 15 (1900), 56-102; 17 (1903), 125-66.
Griffith, S.H., "Comparative Religion in the Apologetics of the First Christian Arabic Theologians", in *Proceedings of the Patristic, Medieval and Renaissance Conference*, Villanova, Pennsylvania, 4 (1979), 63-86.
Hawting, G.R., "The Origins of the Muslim Sanctuary at Mecca", in G.H.A. Juynboll (ed.), *Studies on the First Century of Islamic Society*, Carbondale and Edwardsville, 1982, 23-47.
History of the Alexandrian Patriarchs = B. Evetts (ed./trans.), "History of the Patriarchs of the Coptic Church of Alexandria", in *PO*, 1 (1907), 105-214, 383-518; 5 (1910), 3-215; 10 (1915), 359-547. This edition is based on the "Vulgate" recension in the fifteenth-century ms. Paris arab 301-302.
History of the Alexandrian Patriarchs (Hamburg) = Christian Friedrich Seybold (ed.), *Severus ibn al-Muqaffaʿ. Alexandrinische Patriarchengeschichte von S. Marcus bis Michael I (61-767)*, Hamburg, 1912. This edition is based on the earliest dated manuscript, ms. Hamburg arab 304, dated 1260.
Hoyland, Robert G., *Seeing Islam as Others Saw It. A Survey and Evaluation of Christian, Jewish and Zoroastrian Writings on Early Islam*, Princeton, 1997.
Jacob of Edessa, *Letters*, ms. British Library Add. 12,172, fols. 65-135 (preserves 27 letters).
John bar Penkaye (wrote *Ktābā d-rīsh mellē* in 15 books) = A. Mingana (ed./trans.), *Sources syriaques*, Leipzig, 1907, Part 2, 1-171/172-97. The last book is translated by Sebastian Brock, "North Mesopotamia in the Late Seventh Century: Book XV of Bar Penkaye's *Rīš Mellē*", in *Jerusalem Studies in Arabic and Islam*, 9 (1987), 51-75.
John of Damascus, *De haeresibus* = *PG*, XCIV, 677-780. The chapter on Islam has been edited and translated by Daniel J. Sahas, *John of Damascus on Islam*, Leiden, 1972, 132-41; R. le Coz, *Jean Damascène. Ecrits sur l'Islam*, Paris, 1992, 210-27; R. Glei and A.T. Khoury, *Johannes Damaskenos und Theodor Abū Qurra. Schriften zum Islam*, Würzburg and Altenberge, 1995, 74-83.
Michael the Syrian, *Chronique*, ed./trans. J.B. Chabot, IV, 405-07/II, 403-05.
Ms. Diyarbakir 95, fols. 1-8: contains the dispute between an Arab notable and a monk of the monastery of Beth Hale.
Pascal, Blaise, *Oeuvres*, ed. L. Brunschvig, Paris, 1921.
Palmer, Andrew, *The Seventh Century in the West-Syrian Chronicles*, Liverpool, 1993.
Peters, Francis Edward, *Aristoteles arabus*, Leiden, 1968.
PG = Jacques-Paul Migne, *Patrologiae cursus completus : Series Graeca*, Paris, 1857-66.
PO = René Graffin/F. Nau (eds.), *Patrologia Orientalis*, Paris, 1903 ff.
Schoene, Alfred, *Eusebi chronicorum libri duo*, Berlin, 1875.
Sebeos = K. Patkanian (ed.), *Patmut'iwn Sebeosi*, St. Petersburg, 1879; F. Macler (trans.), *Histoire d'Héraclius par l'évêque Sebēos*, Paris, 1904.
Serjeant, R.B., "The *Sunnah Jāmiʿah*: Analysis and Translation of the Documents Comprised in the So-Called 'Constitution of Medina'", in *Bulletin of the School of Oriental and African Studies*, 41 (1978), 1-42.
Stroumsa, S., "The Signs of Prophecy: The Emergence and Early Development of a Theme in Arabic Theological Literature", in *Harvard Theological Review*, 78 (1985), 16-42.
al-Ṭabarī, Muḥammad b. Jarīr, *Taʾrīkh al-rusul wa-l-mulūk/Annales*, ed. Michael Johan de Goeje et al., Leiden, 1879-1901.

Theophanes, *Chronographia*, ed. Carl de Boor, Leipzig, 1883; full translation by Cyril Mango and Roger Scott, *The Chronicle of Theophanes Confessor*, Oxford, 1997.
Timothy I, *Apology* = Hans Putman (ed./trans.), *L'église et l'Islam sous Timothée I*, Beirut, 1975, 1-51 (back)/213-77. This is the Arabic version; for the Syriac version see A. Mingana, "The Apology of Timothy the Patriarch before the Caliph Mahdi", in *Woodbroke Studies*, 2 (1928), 1-162.
Watt, William Montgomery, *Muhammad at Medina*, Oxford, 1956.

MUḤAMMAD IN THE QUR'ĀN: READING SCRIPTURE IN THE 21ST CENTURY

Andrew Rippin

I

> On the extent of the reliability of the *Sīra* and *Ḥadīth* accounts, I am not yet prepared to render a final judgement. I can, however, speak with some confidence about the Qur'ān as our primary historical source for the life of the Prophet and the origins of the Muslim community and Islamic faith and practice. I am confident that the contents, although not the final arrangement, of the Qur'ān date from the time of Muḥammad, and that the Qur'ān is utterly reliable as a historical source, if it is properly interpreted.[1]

Thus wrote Alford Welch in 1983; from this starting point he was able to proceed to write almost 40 pages about "Muḥammad's understanding of himself" based upon the Qur'ān. Of course, Welch recognizes that "The Qur'ān is an unusual historical source" in that "it contains no historical narrative or description, and it does not have as its purpose the recording of history or biography."[2] Still, Welch finds the person of Muḥammad fully imbedded in the text.

Welch is, of course, far from alone in taking this position; it is a stance which is held in common with the earliest Muslim exegesis of the Qur'ān (and underlies the entire theory of the *sunna*) and with the majority of scholarship ever since (for a recent example, see N.A. Newman, *Muḥammad, the Qur'an and Islam*,[3] who speaks of the Qur'ān as an "inherent witness" to the life of Muḥammad and the rise of Islam). Even a more careful and considered work, Neal Robinson's *Discovering the Qur'an*[4] which subtitles itself *A Contemporary Approach to a Veiled Text*, does not see any other possibility when it comes to interpreting the Qur'ān. Starting from observations of a character in Margaret Drabble's novel *Natural Curiosity*, Robinson highlights the idea that the reader of the Qur'ān is "put off to discover that the orig-

---

[1] A.T. Welch, "Muḥammad's Understanding of Himself: The Qur'ānic Data", in R.G. Hovannisian and S. Vryonis, Jr. (eds.), *Islam's Understanding of Itself*, Malibu, 1983, 15.

[2] Ibid., 15-6.

[3] Hatfield, 1996.

[4] London, 1996.

inal editors of the sacred text had arranged the chapters not in chronological order but in order of decreasing length" (p. 1). Clearly Robinson agrees that chronology—that is, the integration of the text into contemporary history—is the key to understanding the text, for he spends the first four chapters of his book discussing the issue. But, as I said, Robinson is more careful than Welch, and he admits that a cautious correlation between Qur'ān and *sīra* can still only provide the barest of chronological outlines.

Within the framework suggested by such authors, history and Muḥammad are the "obvious" ways of interpreting the Qur'ān. To take a well-worn example of what is meant here, the example of *sūra* 93 is sufficient:[5]

> By the white forenoon
> and the brooding light!
> Thy Lord has neither forsaken thee nor hates thee
> and the Last shall be better for thee than the First.
> Thy Lord shall give thee, and thou shall be satisfied.
> Did He not find thee an orphan, and shelter thee?
> Did He not find thee erring, and guide thee?
> Did He not find thee needy, and suffice thee?
> As for the orphan, do not oppress him,
> and as for the beggar, scold him not;
> and as for thy Lord's blessing, declare it.

The details are well known. Here we have reference to Muḥammad's youth (an orphan, needy and in error) as well as insights into the social conditions of the time (orphans, beggars). To many—probably most—scholars, this is the "natural", if not the only, "logical" interpretation of the verses. What other possible referent could there be?

I do not wish to belabor the methodological point here. I would merely state that there is nothing absolutely compelling about interpreting the above passage in light of the life or the lifetime of Muḥammad. The "thee" of this passage does not *have* to be Muḥammad. It certainly could be, but it does not have to be. (I might also point out that Arberry's translation also suggests the necessity of "he" as God [i.e., "He"] which is also not necessarily compelling.) All the elements in the verses are motifs of religious literature (and, indeed, themes of the Qur'ān) and they need not be taken to reflect historical "reality"

---

[5] All Qur'ān translations are from A.J. Arberry, *The Koran Interpreted*, London, 1955.

as such, but, rather, could well be understood as the foundational material of monotheist religious preaching.

Muḥammad is, of course, actually named in the Qurʾān. The data are well known, but it is worth reviewing them once again.

> Q 3:144:
> Muḥammad is naught but a Messenger; Messengers have passed away before him.
>
> Q 33:40:
> Muḥammad is not the father of any one of your men, but the Messenger of God, and the Seal of the Prophets; God has knowledge of everything.
>
> Q 47:2:
> Those who believe and do righteous deeds and believe in what is sent down to Muḥammad—and it is the truth from their Lord—He will acquit them of their evil deeds, and dispose their minds aright.
>
> Q 48:29:
> Muḥammad is the Messenger of God and those who are with him are hard against the unbelievers, merciful one to another.

It is interesting to note that in none of these passages is Muḥammad himself addressed: he is referred to, but not addressed directly. One might consider adding the Aḥmad passage here (Q 61:6: "And when Jesus son of Mary said, 'Children of Israel, I am indeed the Messenger of God to you, confirming the Torah that is before me, and giving good tidings of a Messenger who shall come after me, whose name shall be Aḥmad'") although in biographical terms, there is little to be gained by doing so. In addition, one can point to a number of references in the Qurʾān which attest to persons or events of a "historical" nature. Michael Cook has provided a convenient summary of the material:

> Taken on its own, the Koran tells us very little about the events of Muhammad's career. It does not narrate these events, but merely refers to them; and in doing so, it has a tendency not to name names. Some do occur in contemporary contexts: four religious communities are named (Jews, Christians, Magians, and the mysterious Sabians), as are three Arabian deities (all female), three humans (of whom Muhammad is one), two ethnic groups (Quraysh and the Romans), and nine places. Of the places, four are mentioned in military connections (Badr, Mecca, Hunayn, Yathrib), and four are connected with the sanctuary.... The final place is Mount Sinai, which seems to be associated with the growing of olives.... Identifying what the Koran is talking

> about in a contemporary context is therefore usually impossible without interpretation....[6]

Now, one might argue on the basis of all these passages put together that we do have, in fact, good grounds for interpreting the Qurʾān in light of Muḥammad and his historical context. Muḥammad is explicitly the messenger and Muḥammad is explicitly the recipient of revelation, according to specific passages of the Qurʾān. One could therefore extrapolate and suggest that Muḥammad, the person, his time and his place, may be taken as being the reference point of all the text that could reasonably be assumed to refer to him and his time.

It is here, I think, that we confront a basic issue in our reading of texts as individuals living at the very end of the 20th century and, in a sense, we make a choice as to our reading strategy. It seems to me that many of us have become more aware of our ability to impose consistency upon texts (and our propensity to do so), stemming from our desire to "make sense" of things. We have become aware of this as a result of many factors, some of which include the intentional play with narrative in the literary work of authors such as Borges and the films of directors such as Fellini. We have come to realize that no longer can the "apparent" narrator be trusted, that "point of view" is a deceptive and manipulated structure, and that the "pleasure of the text" precisely emerges from those moments in which our struggles with the text have to be re-evaluated.

A quote from a book on contemporary discussions surrounding the Bible may be of assistance here:

> By embracing scientific method as the key in the search for historical truth, modern biblical scholarship has kept faith with the Enlightenment's desire to do away with ambivalence and uncertainty once and for all by effectively isolating the text and its criticism from the reader's cultural context, values, and interests. The pervasive modern emphasis on the objective recovery of the ancient context in which biblical texts were produced has the double effect of obscuring the significance of the Bible in contemporary Western culture and of turning the Bible into an historical relic, an antiquarian artifact. It has also produced a modern biblical scholarship that, for many, has become a curatorial science in which the text is fetishized, its readings routinized, its readers bureaucratized. Moreover, historical criticism has implicitly veiled the histori-

---

[6] M. Cook, *Muhammad*, Oxford, 1983, 69-70.

> cal character of biblical scholarship's entanglements with modernity and has therefore left unexamined its own critical and theoretical assumptions as well as the cultural conditions that produced, sustained, and validated them.[7]

I find the last sentence of that quotation particularly provocative and one which, in my opinion, strikes right to the heart of the issue.

But where does that leave us with the Qur'ān? This is not the place (nor am I the person) to pursue a theoretical discourse on theories of interpretation. Better, it seems to me, is for scholars who choose a different view of texts to illustrate how their readings might be able to construct a stance which is in opposition to the existing and seemingly "natural" picture which is now generally accepted. The construction of the counter-model is precisely what will "deconstruct" the existing model. It seems that, for many people, the inability to be able to conceive *how* things could possibly be thought of differently is precisely the limiting factor in these discussions. But too, it does seem to me that the burden of proof falls upon those who wish to suggest a different view, so it is also necessary first to point out precisely what the dimensions of the issues and its problems are.

II

Some of the "difficulties" which still exist in the text of the Qur'ān and with which exegesis has had to struggle have been inventoried by Nöldeke,[8] whose work still provides a useful basis for many discussions. Most relevant to the question of the biographical element is the idea of the "addressee" of the text, a topic only touched upon in passing by Nöldeke. In brief, a detailed study of the addressee of the Qur'ān reveals a less cohesive picture—or, at least, a less clear picture—than most Muslim exegesis and later scholarship have imposed upon the text.

A coherent picture of Muḥammad is frequently thought to emerge from the Qur'ān (in an article such as Welch's) when the assumed

---

[7] The Bible and Culture Collective, *The Postmodern Bible*, New Haven, 1995, 1-2.

[8] Th. Nöldeke, "Zur Sprache des Korāns II: Stilistische und syntaktische Eigentümlichkeiten der Sprache des Korāns", in his *Neue Beiträge zur semitischen Sprachwissenschaft*, Strasbourg, 1910, 12-13.

reader/reciter—that is, the addressee—of the text is seen to be the Prophet. Certainly the person of the "prophet" or "messenger" who is involved in this message has a role within the text. I do not think that one could argue that the Qurʾān assumes the reader/reciter of the entire text to *always* be the community or the individual believer, for example. There are occasions upon which one is "listening in" upon conversations between God and the Messenger, certainly. The extent to which this is so, however, and whether consistency can be created even within those specific passages are at least open to question, especially if we contemplate the nature, form and language of the prophetic idiom in which the Qur'ān is couched. The commonality of the experience of the Messenger with all other prophets is certainly one of the themes of the Qurʾān and, therefore, to assume that a single historical, reconstructable personality lies behind such didactic passages seems misguided.

The addressee of the text may be analyzed into four basic categories, if we ignore the (majority of the) text in which the addressee is ambiguous (i.e., it could be any of the first three below and, frequently, only reading such a passage within a larger context will allow any statement to be made about the addressee).

1) singular "you" (in Arberry, "thou", "thee" or "thy"), for example as a pronominal object or in a singular imperative; on many occasions this person is understood to be Muḥammad. Obvious examples are in the Qur'ānic idiom of "Say!" prefaced to words which might otherwise be taken as non-divine speech, where it is understood that Muḥammad is to recite these verses, or in the stock phrase, "They will question thee concerning ..." in which Muḥammad is understood to be receiving a response to a problem in the community. One final example may be provided in the following (Q 2:6): "As for the unbelievers, alike it is to them whether thou hast warned them or thou hast not warned them, they do not believe", in which the person of Muḥammad is understood to be the actor addressed. Overall, the singular "you" as the addressee of the text is frequently assumed to be Muḥammad unless there is good reason to suggest otherwise. It is possible to read the singular "you", however, as an address to the reader or reciter of the text in general. That, of course, might be said to include Muḥammad—and indeed much Muslim exegesis has taken the text that way—but not limited to him. In Robinson's felicitous

phrase, this category is "the implied privileged addressee"[9] but the identity of that addressee is not always clear.

2) the dual "you" is used very seldom as an addressee, but it is found in *sūra* 55. Few people seem to have difficulty understanding this as prophetic idiom, although it is notable that at least some exegetes[10] want to identify the "two" as "people and the *jinn*" and thus treat it as a plural addressee.

3) plural "you", for example as a pronominal object or in a plural imperative; this is generally understood to be the community (including Muḥammad). It is difficult to provide an accurate sense of the proportion of the text which is addressed to a plural audience as compared to the singular. Until a fully morphologically analyzed text of the Qurʾān is available on computer disk, the job will remain tedious in the extreme. A sense of it may be derived from analysis of the Arberry English translation: the words "you", "your" and "yours" are used 3966 times, whereas "thou", "thee" and "thy" are used 1878 times. These numbers are misleading perhaps, although proportionally they may represent a fair estimate of the text in terms of addressee. What is not represented in these figures are most imperatives, and what is included are narrative passages which use the second person but which have no relevance to the addressee of the text. A quick survey of 200 uses of the imperatives which start with an *alif* (i.e., those of the first and fourth verbal conjugations, such forms being the easiest to isolate via a quick search of the Arabic text of the Qurʾān) indicates that less than 10 percent are addressed to Muḥammad specifically (or so it may be presumed), 65 percent are directed to other people, and the rest are in the mouths of other prophets in narrative passages addressed to a variety of people.

4) disruptions. There are occasions in the Qurʾān in which we might have thought that a singular would have been more appropriate if Muḥammad were to be seen as the addressee of the text but yet the plural is used. This also happens the other way around, when a plural might be more appropriate yet a singular is used. One might also point to some of the passages which are disruptions within the "point of view" or "speaker" of the text, for example, *sūra* 1 in which the speaker is the community (or, at least, not God, unlike most of the

[9] *Discovering the Qur'an*, 240.
[10] See, for example, Muqātil b. Sulaymān, *Tafsīr*, Cairo, 1988, IV, 196.

rest of the Qur'ān) and the addressee is God. Given the exegetical attention to such passages, however, the more subtle examples of "disruptions" in addressee are perhaps worthy of greater attention for our purposes here.

Robinson has isolated four passages ("at least" four such passages exist, he says) in which "the second person singular is employed for an addressee other than Muḥammad".[11] Q 82:6-8 and 84:6 both start *yā-ayyuhā l-insān* and then use the singular "you" afterwards, but given the general treatment of *al-insān* as a singular this does not seem odd. Q 17:24 and 29:8 are both instances in which the singular addressee is spoken of in terms inappropriate for Muḥammad, according to Robinson. In the first instance, the reference is to parents who raised the person being addressed and, in the second instance, parents are spoken of "striving with thee to make thee associate with Me that whereof thou hast no knowledge". Robinson says, "In view of the fact that Muḥammad was an orphan (94:6) [sic: read 93:6], the addressee cannot be him, but must rather be the typical believer."[12] The grounds for this conclusion are startling, and I would argue that these verses are no different than many other of the "implied privileged addressee" passages which may be read in general terms also. In fact, these verses are precisely the ones which urge consideration of a more radical view of the text.

Other passages provide more interesting examples of true disruptions because they suggest that a reading of the text biographically creates some serious problems that argue against such an assumption. Q 2:155-6 is one such case: "Surely We will try you (*kum*) with something of fear and hunger, and diminution of goods and lives and fruits; yet give thou (*bashshir*, singular imperative) good tidings unto the patient who, when they are visited by an affliction, say, 'Surely we belong to God, and to Him we return'." The switch from plural to singular makes this verse complex. One (masculine) person seems to be isolated from among his fellows as having a role to play. Could this be addressed to the individual believer or must it be historicized? This is especially problematic in passages which the consensus wishes to read as personal messages to Muḥammad but which, in fact, are frequently seen to have an "additional sense" of general applicability.

---

[11] *Discovering the Qur'an*, 241.
[12] Ibid., 242.

Q 58:8 states: "Hast thou not regarded those who were forbidden to converse secretly together, then they return to that they were forbidden, and they converse secretly together in sin and enmity, and in disobedience to the Messenger?" To be logically (although perhaps not rhetorically) consistent, the last "Messenger" should simply be "thou"; as it stands, the "thou" must be somebody different than the "Messenger" (if one reads this without any assistance of grammatical/exegetical resolution whereby it might be suggested that we have a type of inversion here).

The variation between *a-raʾayta* and *a-raʾaytum*, and between *a-lam tarā* and *a-lam taraw*, provide other interesting examples. *A-lam tarā*, "Has thou not regarded", is used frequently in this singular form and is clearly rhetorical; it takes little imagination to read such questions as addressed to the reader/reciter (which could, of course, include Muḥammad) rather than Muḥammad alone: it is used at least 30 times, whereas the plural is used only twice. (The use of "Have they not seen...", used about 10 times, is ambiguous as to addressee until it is read in a specific context.) Both are used in the context of the signs of God: "Hast thou not seen (*a-lam tarā*) that God created the heavens?" (Q 14:19) versus "Have you not regarded (*a-lam taraw*) how God created seven heavens?" (Q 71:15; also see 31:20)

Q 2:75 is an example of where some of the Muslim exegetical tradition[13] has taken a plural "you" as a reference to the singular Muḥammad: "Are you then so eager that they should believe you (*yuʾminū lakum*), seeing there is a party of them that heard God's word, and then tampered with it, and that after they had comprehended it, wittingly?"

Some of the difficulties in the Qurʾān with the matter of the addressee are such that exegesis cannot really solve the problem except through an obvious ignoring of the issues. In fact, one of the passages that Robinson cites as not being addressed to Muḥammad is far more complex and disruptive than he allows. Q 17:23-5 states: "Thy (*sing.*) Lord has decreed that you (*plur.*) shall not serve any but Him, and to be good to parents, whether one or both of them attains old age with thee (*sing.*); say (*sing.*) not to them, 'fie', neither chide them, but speak unto them words respectful, ... Your (*plur.*) Lord

[13] E.g. *Tafsīr Ibn ʿAbbās, ad loc.*

knows very well what is in your (*plur.*) hearts if you (*plur.*) are righteous, for He is All-forgiving to those who are penitent."

Robinson has also analyzed the question of the shifts in addressee such as occurs in this latter passage. He argues for a change in emphasis as the point of all these "disruptions". He thus summarizes the use of such shifts as "characteristic of the Qur'ānic discourse".[14] Once again, this is an interesting case of two different ways of reading the evidence. Others, myself included, read such shifts as characteristic of rushed composition, compilation and editing of the text. Shifts have, of course, *become* "characteristic of Qur'ānic discourse", but that is just to say that people have characterized Qur'ānic discourse that way and it is of no significance in my view.

III

It would seem excessive to argue that the Qur'ān provides no evidence of the life of Muḥammad and that therefore it is pointless to refer to it in discussions about the sources for the life of Muḥammad. I do not wish to make such a claim. I would make the claim, however, that the close correlation between the *sīra* and the Qur'ān can be taken to be more indicative of exegetical and narrative development within the Islamic community rather than evidence for thinking that one source witnesses the veracity of another.

To me, it does seem that in no sense can the Qur'ān be assumed to be a primary document in constructing the life of Muḥammad. The text is far too opaque when it comes to history; its shifting referents leave the text in a conceptual muddle for historical purposes. This is the point of my quick look at the evidence of the "addressee" of the text; the way in which the shifts occur renders it problematic to make any assumption about the addressee and his (or her) historical situation. If one wishes to read the Qur'ān in a historical manner, then it can only be interpreted in light of other material. But the question remains of how it came to be read in this manner and how we could understand it if we choose to approach it differently. Brief responses to those questions must suffice in the present context. Obviously, this

---

[14] *Discovering the Qur'an*, 254.

is a topic which requires extensive research and consideration in order to reach any firm conclusions.

The genius of Muslim interpretational strategies in dealing with the Qur'ān, probably starting with the redaction of the text itself, has been to provide a consistent and coherent picture of Muḥammad as a background to the text. Through this process, an opaque text was rendered intelligible and (legally and religiously) relevant to the living Muslim community. This was likely done by both creating a *sīra* based upon imaginative readings of the Qur'ān and grafting a pre-existent and emerging *sīra* onto the Qur'ān. The process also created a unified text of the Qur'ān: the implications of that, however, take us outside the concern with Muḥammad and into the field of the origins of the Qur'ān. Interestingly, the strategy also produced problems for the community. The jurists, for example, found it necessary to expand the application of the law from the specific—Muḥammad—to the general—the community—on many occasions. Had the text not initially been read in light of Muḥammad, then the problem would not have existed. (It can also be seen that, on occasion, reading the text in light of Muḥammad was a way of rendering the text innocuous legally; so the perspective was double-edged, certainly.) The Ṣūfīs were the most adventurous when appreciating the universal and timeless qualities of the text of the Qur'ān; the mystical reading of the text (frequently encoded in the word *ta'wīl*) demanded that the historical dimension of the text be, at best, only one of many meanings.

What then does the Qur'ān mean? To what does it refer? The answer must be found in the element common to the Near Eastern monotheistic religious milieu rather than the specific historical period within Arabia. Other studies illustrate the point more directly than I am able to do here. In a recent article about the "commercial-theological" terminology of the Qur'ān, I have argued that these terms were, in fact, not necessarily reflective of a lived reality but of an eschatological vision of the perfect society using imagery common to the Near Eastern religious milieu.[15] G.R. Hawting's work—for example, a recent paper he read on the identification of the *mushrikūn* not as Arab polytheists but rather as monotheists who fall short of the mark,

---

[15] A. Rippin, "The Commerce of Eschatology", in S. Wild (ed.), *The Qur'an as Text*, Leiden, 1996, 125-35.

a standard "monotheist" preaching polemic which became historicized in the transformation into the Arab idolaters—provides yet another example. As more investigations of this type are concluded, it may be easier to determine the true place of the Qur'ān within the religious milieu of the time.

Bibliography

Arberry, Arthur J., *The Koran Interpreted*, London, 1955.

Bible and Culture Collective, The, *The Postmodern Bible*, New Haven, 1995.

Cook, Michael, *Muhammad*, Oxford, 1983.

Muqātil b. Sulaymān, *Tafsīr*, ed. ʿAbd Allāh Maḥmūd Shiḥāta, Cairo, 1980-87.

Newman, N.A., *Muḥammad, the Qur'an and Islam*, Hatfield, 1996.

Nöldeke, Theodor, "Zur Sprache des Korāns II: Stilistische und syntaktische Eigentümlichkeiten der Sprache des Korāns", in ibid., *Neue Beiträge zur semitischen Sprachwissenschaft*, Strasbourg, 1910.

Rippin, A., "The Commerce of Eschatology", in Stefan Wild (ed.), *The Qur'an as Text*, Leiden, 1996.

Robinson, Neil, *Discovering the Qur'an: A Contemporary Approach to a Veiled Text*, London, 1996.

Welch, A.T., "Muḥammad's Understanding of Himself: The Qur'ānic Data", in Richard G. Hovannisian and Speros Vryonis, jr. (eds.), *Islam's Understanding of Itself*, Malibu, 1983.

CONTRIBUTORS

ANDREAS GÖRKE has received his M.A. in Islamic Studies from the University of Hamburg. At present he is preparing a Ph.D. thesis on Abū ʿUbayd's *K. al-Amwāl.* His major research interest concerns the early Islamic period. He has published "Die frühislamische Geschichtsüberlieferung zu Ḥudaybiya", in *Der Islam* 74 (1997).

ROBERT HOYLAND studied at Pembroke College Oxford, Princeton and Groningen and received his Ph.D. in 1994 from Pembroke College. Until 1998 he was Juniour Research Fellow, and he is now British Academy Research Fellow at St. John's College, Oxford. His fields of interests are the inter-confessional interaction and the transmission of knowledge in early Islam, settlement patterns in late Antiquity and early Islam, early Arabic inscriptions and the work of al-Jāḥiẓ. He published as co-author (together with Andrew Palmer and Sebastian Brock *The Seventh Century in West-Syrian Chronicles* (Liverpool, 1993) and wrote *Seeing Islam as Others Saw It. A Survey and Evaluation of Christian, Jewish and Zoroastrian Writings on Early Islam* (Princeton, 1997).

MAHER JARRAR was educated at the American University of Beirut and the University of Tubingen from where he received his Ph.D. At present he is Associate Professor of the American University of Beirut. He published *Die Prophetenbiographie im islamischen Spanien. Ein Beitrag zur Überlieferungs- und Redaktionsgeschichte* (Frankfurt and Bern, 1989) and several articles on early Islamic tradition and on modern Arabic novels. His research interests include the development of the *sīra* literature, early Shīʿī religious literature, and narratology.

MICHAEL LECKER is Associate Professor of Arabic Language and Literature at the Hebrew University of Jerusalem. He studied at the Universities of Tel Aviv and the Hebrew University of Jerusalem. His Ph.D. thesis with the title "On the Prophet Muḥammad's Activity in Medina" written under the supervision of Prof. M.J. Kister was completed in 1983. His research interests are Islamic history and literature. He published *Muslims, Jews and pagans: Studies on early Islamic Medina* (Leiden, 1995) and a collection of articles written by him has appeared under the title *Jews and Arabs in pre- and early Islamic Arabia* (Aldershot, 1998).

ADRIEN LEITES received his undergraduate training at the University of Paris III. He earned a Ph.D. from Princeton University in June 1997. He is now Assistant Professor of Arabic at the University of Paris IV-Sorbonne, and teaches in that capacity at the Institut Français d'Etudes Arabes de Damas (IFEAD). His general area of interest is religious thought as articulated in Islamic tradition. An article of his on conceptions of time in *sīra* literature will be published in *Studia Islamica*. He is now working on ethical conceptions in Muslim exegetical literature.

HARALD MOTZKI is Associate Professor of Islamic Studies at the Catholic University of Nijmegen. He received his academic formation at Bonn University (Ph.D. in 1978) and was between 1983 and 1991 Lecturer and Research fellow at the University of Hamburg from where he received his Habilitation. His research focuses on social history of Islam, *ḥadīth*, early Islamic jurisprudence and the transmission of knowledge in early Islam. His major publications are *Dimma und Egalité. Die nichtmuslimischen Minderheiten Ägyptens in der zweiten Hälfte des 18. Jahrhunderts und die Expedition Bonapartes (1798-1801)* (Bonn and Wiesbaden, 1979) and *Die Anfänge der islamischen Jurisprudenz. Ihre Entwicklung in Mekka bis zur Mitte des 2./8. Jahrhunderts* (Stuttgart, 1991).

ANDREW RIPPIN studied at the University of Toronto and received his Ph.D. from McGill University. Since 1981 he has taught at the University of Calgary and is currently Professor of Religious Studies and Associate Dean (Student Affairs) of the Faculty of Humanities. His major research interest is Qur'ān and *tafsīr*. He published *Muslims, their religious beliefs and practices*, 2 volumes (London, 1990, 1993).

URI RUBIN (Ph.D. from the Tel Aviv University) is Professor of Arabic and Islamic Studies in the Tel Aviv University and specializes in the study of the Qur'ān and the early Islamic tradition. He is interested mainly in exegetical and historiographical traditions as a key to the evolution of the Islamic historical perception during the first Islamic era. Prof. Rubin has recently published a study of the traditions describing the life of the Prophet Muḥammad (*The Eye of the*

Beholder, Princeton, 1995), and is preparing a book about the position of the Children of Israel in Islamic tradition (*Between Bible and Qur'ān*).

GREGOR SCHOELER is Professor of Islamic Studies at the University of Basel. He studied at the universities of Marburg, Giessen and Frankfort and earned his Ph.D. and Habilitation from the University of Giessen. He is working in the field of Arabic and Persian literature, especially poetry and belles lettres, *ḥadīth*, *sīra*, transmission of sciences in early Islam, the legacy of antiquity in Islam and Arabic manuscripts. Among his publications are *Der Dīwān des Abū Nuwās. Teil IV [al-ghazal]* (Wiesbaden, 1982), *Arabische Handschriften, Teil II* (Stuttgart, 1990) and *Charakter und Authentie der muslimischen Überlieferung über das Leben Mohammeds* (Berlin and New York, 1996).

MARCO SCHÖLLER studied Islamic studies, philosophy and political science at the universities of Erlangen, Aleppo and St. Andrews (Ph.D. 1997 from the University of Erlangen). Since 1998 he has been Assistant Lecturer and Research Fellow at the Institute for Oriental and Islamic Studies, University of Cologne. His research focuses on classical Islamic thought and religion, the history of ideas (Geistes- und Ideengeschichte) as well as the sociological, cultural and epistemological framework of pre-modern scholarship and academic discourse. Apart from various articles, he has published *Exegetisches Denken und Prophetenbiographie* (Wiesbaden, 1998).

INDEX

References to the Qur'ān

ISLAMIC HISTORY AND CIVILIZATION

STUDIES AND TEXTS

1. Lev, Y. *State and Society in Fatimid Egypt.* 1991. ISBN 90 04 09344 3.
2. Crecelius, D. and ʿAbd al-Wahhab Bakr, trans. *Al-Damurdashi's Chronicle of Egypt, 1688-1755.* Al-Durra al Musana fi Akhbar al-Kinana. 1991. ISBN 90 04 09408 3
3. Donzel, E. van (ed.). *An Arabian Princess Between Two Worlds.* Memoirs, Letters Home, Sequels to the Memoirs, Syrian Customs and Usages, by Sayyida Salme/Emily Ruete. 1993. ISBN 90 04 09615 9
4. Shatzmiller, M. *Labour in the Medieval Islamic World.* 1994. ISBN 90 04 09896 8
5. Morray, D. *An Ayyubid Notable and His World.* Ibn al-ʿAdīm and Aleppo as Portrayed in His Biographical Dictionary of People Associated with the City. 1994. ISBN 90 04 09956 5
6. Heidemann, S. *Das Aleppiner Kalifat (A.D. 1261).* Vom Ende des Kalifates in Bagdad über Aleppo zu den Restaurationen in Kairo. 1994. ISBN 90 04 10031 8
7. Behrens-Abouseif, D. *Egypt's Adjustment to Ottoman Rule.* Institutions, Waqf and Architecture in Cairo (16th and 17th Centuries). 1994. ISBN 90 04 09927 1
8. Elad, A. *Medieval Jerusalem and Islamic Worship.* Holy Places, Ceremonies, Pilgrimage. 1995. ISBN 90 04 10010 5
9. Clayer, N. *Mystiques, État et Société.* Les Halvetis dans l'aire balkanique de la fin du XVe siècle à nos jours. ISBN 90 04 10090 3
10. Levanoni, A. *A Turning Point in Mamluk History.* The Third Reign of al-Nāsīr Muḥammad ibn Qalāwūn (1310-1341). 1995. ISBN 90 04 10182 9
11. Essid, Y. *A Critique of the Origins of Islamic Economic Thought.* 1995. ISBN 90 04 10079 2
12. Holt, P.M. *Early Mamluk Diplomacy (1260-1290).* Treaties of Baybars and Qalāwūn with Christian Rulers. 1995. ISBN 90 04 10246 9
13. Lecker, M. *Muslims, Jews and Pagans.* Studies on Early Islamic Medina. 1995. ISBN 90 04 10247 7
14. Rabbat, N.O. *The Citadel of Cairo.* A New Interpretation of Royal Mamluk Architecture. 1995. ISBN 90 04 10124 1
15. Lee, J.L. *The 'Ancient Supremacy'.* Bukhara, Afghanistan and the Battle for Balkh, 1731-1901. 1996. ISBN 90 04 10399 6
16. Zaman, M.Q. *Religion and Politics under the Early ʿAbbasids.* The Emergence of the Proto-Sunnī Elite. 1997. ISBN 90 04 10678 2
17. Sato, T. *State and Rural Society in Medieval Islam.* Sultans, Muqtaʿs and Fallahun. 1997. ISBN 90 04 10649 9
18. Dadoyan, S.B. *The Fatimid Armenians.* Cultural and Political Interaction in the Near East. 1997. ISBN 90 04 10816 5
19. Malik, J. *Islamische Gelehrtenkultur in Nordindien.* Entwicklungsgeschichte und Tendenzen am Beispiel von Lucknow. 1997. ISBN 90 04 10703 7
20. Mélikoff, I. *Hadji Bektach: un mythe et ses avatars.* Genèse et évolution du soufisme populaire en Turquie. 1998. ISBN 90 04 10954 4
21. Guo, L. *Early Mamluk Syrian Historiography.* Al-Yūnīnī's Dhayl Mir'āt al-zamān. 2 vols. 1998. ISBN *(set)* 90 04 10818 1
22. Taylor, C.S. *In the Vicinity of the Righteous. Ziyāra* and the Veneration of Muslim Saints in Late Medieval Egypt. 1999. ISBN 90 04 11046 1
23. Madelung, W. and P.E. Walker. *An Ismaili Heresiography.* The "Bāb al-shayṭān" from Abu Tammām's *Kitāb al-shajara.* 1998. ISBN 90 04 11072 0
24. Amitai-Preiss, R. and D.O. Morgan (eds.). *The Mongol Empire and its Legacy.* 1999. ISBN 90 04 11048 8
25. Giladi, A. *Infants, Parents and Wet Nurses.* Medieval Islamic Views on Breastfeeding and Their Social Implications. 1999. ISBN 90 04 11223 5

26. Holt, P.M. *The Sudan of the Three Niles.* The Funj Chronicle 910-1288/ 1504-1871. 1999. ISBN 90 04 11256 1
27. Hunwick, J. *Timbuktu and the Songhay Empire.* Al-Saʿdi's Taʾrīkh al-sūdān down to 1613 and other Contemporary Documents. 1999. ISBN 90 04 11207 3
28. Munis, S.M.M. and M.R.M. Agahi. *Firdaws al-iqbāl.* History of Khorezm. Translated from Chagatay and annotated by Y. Bregel. 1999. ISBN 90 04 011365 7
29. Jong, F. de and B. Radtke. *Islamic Mysticism Contested.* Thirteen centuries of controversies and polemics. 1999. ISBN 90 04 11300 2
30. Meier, F. *Essays on Islamic Piety and Mysticism.* Translated by J. O'Kane, with editorial assistance of B. Radtke. 1999. ISBN 90 04 10865 3
31. B. Radtke, J.O'Kane, K.S. Vikør & R.S. O'Fahey. *The Exoteric Aḥmad Ibn Idrīs.* A Sufi's Critique of the Madhāhib and the Wahhābīs. 2000. ISBN 90 04 11375 4
32. H. Motzki (ed.). *The Biography of Muḥammad.* The Issue of the Sources. 2000. ISBN 90 04 11513 7